Negotiations

A Reader

for Writers

Negotiations

A Reader

for Writers

Judith Summerfield

*Queens College–City University
of New York*

McGraw-Hill, Inc.

*New York   St. Louis   San Francisco   Auckland
Bogotá   Caracas   Lisbon   London   Madrid
Mexico   Milan   Montreal   New Delhi   Paris
San Juan   Singapore   Sydney   Tokyo   Toronto*

This book was developed by STEVEN PENSINGER, Inc.

Negotiations: A Reader for Writers

Acknowledgments appear on pages 561–566, and on this page by reference.

1 2 3 4 5 6 7 8 9 0 DOC DOC 9 0 9 8 7 6 5 4 3 2 1

ISBN 0-07-062574-3

This book was set in Times Roman by Ruttle, Shaw & Wetherill, Inc.
The editors were Steve Pensinger and David A. Damstra;
the designer was Robin Hoffmann;
the production supervisor was Kathryn Porzio.
R. R. Donnelley & Sons Company was printer and binder.

Library of Congress Cataloging-in-Publication Data

Summerfield, Judith, (date).
    Negotiations: a reader for writers / Judith Summerfield.
        p.   cm.
    ISBN 0-07-062574-3
    1. College readers.   2. English language—Rhetoric. ˇ I. Title.
PE1417.S854   1992
808'.0427—dc20   91-28775

For

Geoffrey Summerfield

Contents

*   Short story

*   Short story

Preface

For the past several months, as I've been writing and rewriting this book, I've been considering my own developing life as a reader and writer. I realize that, somewhere way back when, I used to consider the text to be a sacred object and the reader as one in pursuit of its mysteries: if only the reader turned the page to the right angle or held it to the proper light, then the text would reveal its secrets and mysteries, and, presto, the reader would "get it."

Much has happened in literary studies in the past few years to rectify those narrow views of reading, the reader, and the text. These days teachers and scholars consider the reader as well as the text, and recognize that how we read depends largely upon who we are and what we ourselves bring to the text—our personal, textual, and cultural knowledge. *Hamlet* is not the same for us as it was for theatergoers of the seventeenth century or for nineteenth-century readers (see Laura Bohannan's "Shakespeare in the Bush," p. 293). There are no universal readings: *Hamlet* speaks to us in our own age, and we speak back to *Hamlet* out of our own era. And there are many ways to read *Hamlet*. As readers, we negotiate with every text we read: we submit and/or resist and/or compromise. Our own experiences, our values, and our culture are all implicated in our reading, whether we realize it or not. Reading is a social act, a social interaction between reader and text.

Negotiations is divided into two parts: Part 1 sets out to explore possibilities of reading within the college course in composition. Each of the first six chapters offers a different angle on reading: Chapter 1 looks to the kinds of knowledge—personal, textual, and cultural—that the reader brings to the text and raises the question of how readers respond to a text, particularly within the constraints of schooling, culture, and gender.

Chapter 2 introduces the notion of performance—that to read a text, we must hear it and that one of the best ways to hear is to listen to the ways in which ordinary language is used in ordinary situations, to listen to the spoken and the unspoken, and to consider how to exercise our expectations, our observations, and our inferences, in life and in text.

Chapters 3, 4, and 5 explore ways of writing on writing. Chapter 3 looks to fragmentary writings—notes, journals, diaries—as well as to ways of capturing impressions, associations, and expectations, our own responses to what we read. Chapter 4 considers intertextuality, how texts are implicated in other texts through versions, transformations, gaps, and other kinds of textual influences. Chapter 5 takes up the matter of textual conventions, as it focuses on differences and similarities between stories and essays, and as it looks to questions of misreading.

Chapter 6 zeroes in more particularly on the reader-writer as a negotiator of values—a critic, particularly within the elastic forms of the essay, where as writers, we have ample opportunity to "try" ourselves before any subject we choose, to consider the limits and opportunities of open and closed texts; to enter various frames of mind, as participants or as spectators; and to use our own writing for acts of resistance.

Part 2 offers a selection of texts to read, essays and short fiction, so that the readers can play the conventions of one form off against the other, to experience the structuralist principle: meanings reside in differences. Here students and instructor can make their own course, intersecting with the suggestions for reading offered in Part 1. (Alternatively, instructors may wish to begin with Part 2, and pick up sections of Part 1 as they choose.)

The selections in Part 2, arranged alphabetically, offer a variety of texts: short, informal, personal reflections as well as long, demanding, challenging analyses, explication, and argument in various genres: autobiographical and biographical sketches, journalism, history, folklore, literary criticism, semiotic analysis. They range from old chestnuts such as George Orwell's "The Hanging" to new chestnuts such as Richard Selzer's "The Masked Marvel's Last Toe-Hold." They range from selections by such well-known writers as Orwell, Virginia Woolf, E. B. White, Russell Baker, and James Baldwin to "unknowns"—ordinary citizens who are provoked to write, particularly for the op-ed page of the daily newspaper or for a Sunday supplement or magazine. One piece, "Thoreau, Cinderella, and Buttercream Roses," written by Janice Gordon, a former student of mine at Queens College, the City University of New York, was subsequently published in *The New York Times*. (The writer, in fact, was paid a small fee for her efforts.) The selections range from light to the heavy, from the witty musings of Dave Barry and Steve Brody to the critical analyses of Roland Barthes and John Berger.

Various themes are carried throughout the entire book and can be arranged in thematic clusters: for example, Ernest Hemingway's short story "Hills Like White Elephants," introduced in Chapter 1, is followed through Chapter 2 (on performance and Hemingway's own writings on writing) and into Chapter 3 (on influences); and into Part 2, with a text by Frank O'Connor on Hemingway (writing on writing), and with a text on abortion (an issue raised in the story) by Sallie Tisdale. Myths, fairy tales, and folklore are introduced in Chapter 4 as we briefly consider the fairy tale "Cinderella" in two versions and several transformations; in Part 2, Toni Morrison, Janice Gordon, W. H. Auden, and Robert Darnton play on the effects of the Cinderella myth in personal and cultural reflections and analyses. Civil rights, gender issues, AIDS, the death penalty, fashion, sports, schooling and education, the uses and abuses of language, and the act of reading—both texts and the world—these are some of the issues, questions, and considerations of Part 2.

Although *Negotiations* is divided between theory and practice (Parts 1 and 2), theory is always implicated in practice and practice in theory, and the play, the interaction, between the two is always a matter for negotiation.

ACKNOWLEDGMENTS

This book, I am convinced, has a life and mind of its own, intersecting with my own life and that of the profession when it made up its mind to do so. It began as another book in another decade with another publisher: through a number of disruptions and upheavals in the world of college textbook publishing, it managed to hang on, until, at the critical moment, my reliable, imaginative editor Steve Pensinger rescued it, negotiated for it, and set it afloat. When, suddenly, it emerged in this totally revised version, as *Negotiations,* he said, "Yes," and cheered it on.

The old book stands as it did: this new one surfaced in a negotiation with one sentence of the old book, and before I could hold it back, it had become something else: a transformation, a new shape, new voice, new book.

It stands to reason: any textbook that emerges out of the heat of the classroom cannot stay still. Negotiations happen every semester, every course, every new set of minds, and every new set of student writings; and all that takes place inside the classroom happens within the larger context of culture and history. In February 1991, when I drafted the first version of this preface, in the context of my teaching in the diverse and challenging multiculturalism of Queens College, in the City University of New York, students, themselves, could not sit still: the war in the Persian Gulf pressed in through the walls, so that the classroom turned and moved on the pressures, complexities, and tensions of that moment, in the hope that our talk and our writing could somehow make some difference. The war is now officially over, but other wars, the little wars in our own lives and the big wars in the world outside the classroom, infiltrate, modify, challenge, and change what happens in the classroom.

The textbook, itself, enlarges those conversations: it is my hope that you will negotiate with this book—use and abuse it, misuse it, throw it against the wall, stand it on its head, submit to it and resist—as part of that extended conversation among us students and teachers. That's what the reviewers Bette Ann Moskowitz, Queens College–CUNY; Lucille Schultz, University of Cincinnati; James Seitz, Long Island University; Sally Taylor, Brigham Young University; and Michael Vivion, University of Missouri–Kansas City did with it: in some cases, they will see I submitted; in others, I went ahead anyway. Bette Moskowitz negotiates with me daily, with her unrelenting provocation, nudge, insistency, and belief. She keeps me on my toes. Michael Vivion gave this text a tough, resistant reading and asked why we couldn't offer something "different" with an instructor's manual. Jim Seitz, simultaneously, suggested an instructor's manual that would speak to students as well as instructors, to "deprivatize" the manual. He did so in an innovative "reading" of *Negotiations,* where he plays many roles: colleague, teacher, writer, literary critic, composition theorist, student, performer, as he, finally, made the book his own: the ultimate negotiation. I am grateful for this invigorating collaboration.

I am pleased to acknowledge, once again, my daughter Lauren Fishman for her steady, intelligent, and perceptive advice; my daughter Sharon for her wit and good humor; and my friend Sylvia Moss for taking a steely pen to a final draft.

To my students, particularly to Michael Sherry, Eric Schram, Liz Fonseca, Janice Gordon, Uri Ottensoser, Leslie Horowitz, Judy Katz, Leah Simon, Jennifer Tax, Laura Di Serio, George Williams, Joe Maldonado, and George Pina, I am grateful for their conversation and their writing.

Thanks to the team at McGraw-Hill: to David Damstra, an expert manager, and to Sylvia Warren, whose capable hands did more than copy edit; she helped me steady this final version.

This little book has lived, too, through the death of my husband, colleague, friend, and first critic, Geoffrey Summerfield. I dedicate this book to him.

Judith Summerfield

Negotiations

A Reader

for Writers

PART I

Theory:

Ways of

Reading

The Door
Miroslav Holub

Go and open the door.
  Maybe outside there's
  a tree, or a wood,
  a garden,
  or a magic city.

Go and open the door.
  Maybe a dog's rummaging,
  Maybe you'll see a face,
or an eye,
or the picture
                of a picture.

Go and open the door.
  If there's a fog
  it will clear.

Go and open the door.
  Even if there's only
  the darkness ticking,
  even if there's only
  the hollow wind,
  even if
          nothing
                    is there,
  go and open the door.
At least
there'll be
a draught.

Source: Translated from the Czech poem by Ian Milner.

CHAPTER 1

Opening

Doors

A DEEPER AND BROADER
AND TALLER UNDERSTANDING

Why not begin by reading? Here's an essay by Dave Barry entitled "Historians We're Not."

Historians We're Not
Dave Barry

Tragically, many Americans know very little about the history of their own country. We constantly see surveys that reveal this ignorance, especially among our high-school students, 78 percent of whom, in a recent nationwide multiple-choice test, identified Abraham Lincoln as "a kind of lobster." That's right: More than *three quarters* of our nation's youth could not identify the man who invented the telephone.

What is the cause of this alarming situation? Partly, of course, it is that our young people are stupid. Young people have *always* been stupid, dating back to when you were a young person (1971–1973) and you drank an entire quart of Midnight Surprise Fruit Wine and Dessert Topping and threw up in your best friend's father's elaborate saltwater aquarium containing $6,500 worth of rare and, as it turned out, extremely delicate fish. (You thought we didn't know about that? We know *everything*. We are historians.)

But another major part of the problem is the system used to teach history in our schools, a system known technically, among professional educators, as the Boring Method.

You were probably taught via this method, which features textbooks that drone on eternally as follows:

EARLY EXPLORATIONS

The region was first explored by the Spanish explorer Juan Ponce de Rigueur (1534–1579), who in 1541 was commissioned by King Charles "Chuck" IV of England (1512–1583), under the terms of the Treaty of Weems (1544) as authorized by Pope Bilious XIV (1511–1598), to end the Nine-Years-Three-Months-and-the-Better-Part-of-a-Week War (May 4, 1534–August 8, 1543, at about 1:30 P.M.), under which France (1243–present) would cede an area "north of the seventeenth parallel, west of the one-hundred-and-sixty-third longitude, and convenient to shopping" to England in exchange for those lands originally conquered by Denmark during the Reign of Large Unattractive Featured Hats (1387–1396) and subsequently granted to Italy under the Treaty of . . .

And so on. Little wonder that our young people choose to ignore their nation's history and instead focus their intellectual energies on procuring designer clothing. Not that you, the reader, should feel superior. You are probably not such a history whiz yourself. In fact, we are willing to bet that you cannot even name the man who served as Gerald Ford's running mate in 1976.* Which is why it is a darned good thing for all concerned that you are reading this.

To sum up, we hope that someday you will gain a deeper and broader and taller understanding of how We, the People, through the sweat of our armpits, created this great nation, a nation of which it can truly be stated, in the words of the famous folksinger Woody Guthrie:

This land is your land,
This land is my land,
Looks like one of us
Has a forged deed to this land.

Now write down some quick responses to these questions:

1. How does Barry's text "sound" to you?

2. How do you sound out that first word, *tragically*?

3. How would you characterize his tone? Serious? Playful? Ironic? Humorous? Irreverent? Solemn? Mock-serious? Didactic? Silly? Joking? Frivolous? Matter-of-fact?

4. Where in the text do you first realize that he might be kidding around?

5. Do you think he's raising some serious issues? If so, what are they?

6. Does he "speak" directly to your own experiences with history textbooks? How so?

---

* It doesn't matter.

7. How do you read that fourth paragraph on early explorations? Is this a real example, from an actual textbook? If not, what is Barry doing here? Do you know the word *parody?**

8. What do you need to *know* in order to enjoy this text?

9. Do you know anything about Dave Barry? If so, how did your knowledge affect your reading of the text?

10. Where in the text do you find him playing games with words? With sentences? With facts?

11. Do you think his primary purpose is to give us a laugh? To convey information? To give us something to think about?

12. Compare your responses with those of other readers.

THE LADY OR THE TIGER?

How long did it take you to realize that Dave Barry was *not* going to lead you to a "tragedy," in the conventional sense of the word? He's considering issues, ideas, questions which matter, but which do not necessarily involve tragedy. Do you agree? Did Barry mislead you by that first word, *tragically*, raising your expectations that he would lead you in one direction but having you end up somewhere else? Those readers who know Barry as a daily syndicated columnist—a humorist—were prepared for such word games, but if you were an unsuspecting reader, he probably disarmed you. Reading can do that: you enter one place and end up somewhere else.

Reading can be downright dangerous. You open a book, entering in slowly at first, then quietly, mysteriously, becoming so totally engrossed that you "lose yourself." You forget the time of day. You leave the kettle boiling on the stove. You let the phone ring and ring and ring. And even after you close the book, the words keep talking to you: you feel nagged, overtaken, distracted. You laugh out loud. The spaces in your head are full.

Writing can be just as dangerous: you find yourself off in space, on another planet, trying to tackle words that float in and out of your mind. You try to hold them still, get them down on the page, only you can't write that fast or that furiously, and they keep eluding you, playing hide and seek. You find yourself walking into walls, driving off the road: even when you're not writing, you go on writing .

"Where are you?" You *look* as if you're here. But your roommate talks to you, and you don't answer. She shouts your name. "Wake up!" "What are you doing?" Daydreaming? Off in space? Spaced out? Obsessed? Preoccupied? Kidnapped? The acts of both reading and writing are often so elusive, complex, and mysterious because we find ourselves in what the psychologist D. W. Winnicott called "transitional space." We're in limbo—in a liminal space, neither "here" nor "there." Oh, we're physically present all right, but we're off somewhere else. In our own minds? No, not quite there, somewhere else. Somebody else's words are taking over the spaces of our mind. We're captivated. Captured. Yet we know where we are in space, don't we? Our feet are on the ground. We're "safe." Or are we?

---

*   *Parody:* a humorous or satirical imitation of a serious piece of literature or music.

When we read, we can open doors into thousands of rooms—those that are satisfyingly familiar and safe, and those that are unfamiliar and dangerous; those where everything settles down and is neatly tied up, and those where we're left hanging, with lots of loose ends, with the unresolved. We open the doors of a book to all kinds of experience—to find pleasure and delight, thrills and terror, challenge and provocation, knowledge and ideas.

A book on accounting takes us into the world of accounting, as we puzzle over columns of numbers, graphs, and tables. A book on geography takes us to representations of actual places, of rivers, mountains, the oceans, continents. We can come to "know" the world through the written word, as we explore the cosmos—the earth and stars, the rocks and planets. Medicine, biology, history, anthropology—we open doors to these worlds through words. And often our ways of reading are functional and pragmatic: we need information or instruction. We know exactly what we want, and go after it.

But what about mysteries? Horror stories? What kinds of doors do we open then? Do we want to be truly frightened or horrified? Or is it vicarious terror we're after—the pleasure of entering into a dangerous place at the very same time that we're sitting in our own kitchens, safe? What kinds of doors do we open—what kinds of spaces do we enter— when we read romances? Science fiction? Realistic novels and short stories? Poetry? Do we invite ourselves into different kinds of explorations, different kinds of experiments?

Sometimes we know exactly the places a door will open on to. When we pick up a *kind* of book we particularly enjoy, or an author we know well, we feel as if we're visiting old friends. This kind of reading is like plopping down in our favorite chair and settling in. We know what to expect. At other times we'll find ourselves in unfamiliar spaces, unfamiliar rooms. Everything is strange and unexpected, topsy-turvy. One room leads into another— upstairs and downstairs, we find ourselves opening doors leading to long, dark corridors, ending up in musty old attics and cavernous basements. We feel unsettled. Ill at ease. Uncomfortable. We're filled with unanswered questions. We may shut the door, but the questions won't stop nagging: it's as if we've left the door open and still feel the draft.

• • •

How long do you want to go on reading, reading, and reading about reading here without *doing* anything? Don't you sometimes feel the need to *do* something when you read: shut the door or the book? Take a walk? Stretch your legs? Make a phone call? Eat something? Drink a cup of coffee? In *Negotiations*, I'll break in from time to time in the first six chapters, to invite you to enter the text—particularly when you meet the conventions I've set up: *Consider this* or *Try this.*

For now, consider this:

In one sense, we're always doing something when we read. In fact, when we go through doors as readers, we inescapably become writers: we are inevitably anticipating and predicting what will come next. We're always reading ahead and filling in the.

You won't let me get away with that sentence, will you? The conventions of the sentence will not let us end a sentence with *the*. Even though the sentence is unfinished (left "open") on the page, you probably closed it yourself by filling in the blank. With what word or words?

When we read, we inevitably read ahead, anticipating and filling in the next word. We feel disconcerted, perplexed, unnerved by the unclosed:

Once upon a _____.

The mailman delivered a _____.

He dived into the _____.

The cat chased a _____.

Although I love you _____.

We expect a conventional closing; don't we?

Once upon a *time*, . . .

That's what we've come to expect through our exposure to fairy tales. We don't even think about it; it goes without saying. When we meet the following, what happens?

Once upon a mattress.

The mailman delivered a bottle of milk.

He dived into the cereal box.

The cat chased an elephant.

Although I love you, I will, nevertheless, marry your cousin.

Surprise? Delight? Satisfaction? Confusion?

Even a single word—Dave Barry's *tragically*—sets up certain expectations. All literature, says the writer Frank Kermode, "is the arousal of expectations that are either satisfied or denied." That may be true for all kinds of writing: we are always anticipating, filling in gaps, hearing "voices" in our heads, as we make sense out of the page. We fill in the next word, we finish the sentence, and we anticipate the ending. What's going to happen? Will the prince marry the princess? As in the once well-known story, "The Lady or the Tiger" (it used to be a standard in American high school anthologies), we can open doors that lead to danger or delight. Very often, the writer leaves gaps for the reader to fill in. In this case, the writer Frank Richard Stockton leaves us right smack in the middle of a crisis, with the hero's fate undecided. The hero literally has two doors to choose between. Here is the Stockton ending:

> He could open either door he pleased. . . . If he opened the one, there came out of it a hungry tiger, the fiercest and most cruel that could be procured, which immediately sprang upon him, and tore him to pieces, as a punishment for his guilt. . . . But if the accused person opened the other door, there came forth from it a lady, the most suitable to his years and station that his Majesty could select among his fair subjects. . . . So I leave it with all of you: Which came out of the opened door—the lady or the tiger?

Stockton's ending leaves the reader in a spot just like that of his hero: we have to make the next move. There's no *closure* here. Events have not been ended or wrapped up for the characters in the story. The reader is left in the middle of the crisis—without a fairy-tale ending, without *any* ending.

Many who have read "The Lady or the Tiger" remember the unended ending—and, many years later, can recall the tensions left by this unresolved, open text. Recently, when I mentioned "The Lady or the Tiger" in one of my classes, a student remembered this devilishly ambiguous ending that she herself had written in the fourth grade:

> She quickly came out and caressed his body as she tore his heart from his soul!

Our different reactions to Stockton's ending help characterize the ways readers "write" when they read. The ending dramatizes the demands that writers make of us readers, by leaving some doors closed for us to open and others open for us to close—leaving us, as readers, to do the work.

Consider this:

Describe the best kinds of reading experiences you've had. Have any been dangerous? What kinds of doors do you open when you read a newspaper? A weekly news magazine? Books or magazines on your preoccupations: music, computers, sports, cars, fashion, history, politics, science fiction? A short story or an essay? A college textbook? Which ones take over the spaces in your mind? Now describe the ways you read.

PERSONAL KNOWLEDGE

Inescapably, as readers we are brought *into* the page, and inescapably, we bring ourselves *to* the page. In one sense, then, no matter which door we open, we always meet ourselves. Think for a moment about a page in a book—this page, for example. Imagine that you've never seen a book before—that you're looking at a page for the very first time. What do you see? Black squiggles? Weird heiroglyphs? White spaces?

A book is silent without a reader. Like a song unsung. Or a song you hear but don't listen to. You, the reader, bring it into your life, the life inside your head. And you bring *to* the book your own life: your ability to read—to hear and to listen; your history as a reader—your preferences and your prejudices; your history of the day—your fatigue or energy, your interest or impatience. You bring your expectations and predictions and values—and your willingness to open doors.

Ways of reading vary and change, grow and develop over time. When you reread a favorite book—one that you particularly enjoyed as a child—your experience cannot be the same as that first, innocent reading. Each time you read it, you'll make it new. Many readers, unfortunately, believe that there is only one right way to read, that somehow the book calls all the shots, and that they are meant to crack open the "theme" of the book or "get the meaning," as if it were a message in a bottle. That simply isn't so, for reading is a personal act—an interaction between you and the page. You bring to the page who you are. What you focus on, what strikes you, what you remember, what you "get" from a book will be inescapably different from what I "get." (And it will also be similar—as we'll see below.)

If you think for a moment about all of this, you'll see that the idea is a commonplace one and that it doesn't simply relate to reading a book. It is one of the most fundamental facts of our everyday existence: what appeals to you, what you notice, what you remember is particular to you. If you're seated on a crowded bus, what you see will be different from what I see, sitting right next to you. I notice the people: a tall woman in a navy business suit wearing running shoes; an old woman riffling through her handbag; a strange man wearing a beret. You notice the advertisements: you read them, absorbed in the various displays of shampoo and beer and city services. You *see* the other passengers, but don't *look at* them. I hardly see the ads.

If you and I were to compare notes after our ride, we could confirm for each other that, yes, there were, in fact, people on the bus and that there were advertisements—but our interests took us on different rides. You didn't notice the woman's star-spangled finger-nails, and I didn't see the prizewinning student poster showing a cowboy-hatted skeleton riding into "Cancer Country" with a cigarette dangling from his mouth. By comparing notes we can enrich our very different rides: we can learn from each other.

Just as some readers think there is only one way for everyone to read, others believe that whatever *they* get out of a text is all there is. If an essay on fireflies reminds them of their childhood summers in Pennsylvania, then that is what the text is "about." But that simply isn't so. When we read, associations swarm in on us, sometimes overtaking what's in the book, and we go off in our own world—that can be one of the inexhaustible pleasures of reading. Memories, fantasies, anticipations, all pop into mind, unbidden. A story about fireflies *may* suddenly and powerfully evoke memories of my childhood in the hills of Pennsylvania, but that is *not* what the essay is about—it's about fireflies. And just as we can verify what we actually saw on the bus, we can verify what is actually in the book. We may quibble about *interpretations,* but we must agree on the words that we actually see before us there on the page. You might say, then, that reading is always a *negotiation* between what we *actually* see on the page and how we *interpret* what the words offer. Remember that the word *negotiation* derives from the Latin *negotiare: neg* means "not"; *otiare* means "ease," "quiet." (That's another thing we can do when we read. We can check the dictionary to find the *etymology* of a word—that is, the roots of the word: where it came from and what it meant in that context. By so doing, we can often understand the word in a new light. Many English words, in fact, derive from the Latin. See Rita Mae Brown's discussion of Latin and Anglo-Saxon words, page 305.) To enter into negotiations with a text, then, means to reckon with the unease or disquiet or unsettling thoughts that arise from *your* reading.

Try this:

1. Jot down whatever comes to mind when you see the following words:
   snow
   ocean
   trainride
   shoe

2. Do the same with the following newspaper fillers.

In Transit

She got on the 14th Street bus, a nattily dressed woman in her tailored suit, scarlet blouse and matching high-heeled scarlet pumps. She sat down and took out of her shopping bag a pair of running shoes and a pair of pink socks, which she proceeded to put on.

Then, to the astonishment of her fellow passengers, she took her scarlet pumps – first one and then the other – and flung them out the open bus window.

Woman's Will Snubs Family

By the Associated Press

An elderly Manhattan millionaire left "best wishes" to family members in her will and left her fortune to friends and casual acquaintances. Essaye Buchter, 85 years old, who inherited her estate from her husband, Morris, died Jan. 20 and left an estimated $2 million. Her will, written last December, was filed in Manhattan Surrogate Court on Friday. "I leave my best wishes to members of my family, including Morris' family and want them to get whatever they gave me – nothing," the will said.

TEXTUAL KNOWLEDGE

You give yourself to the text, and the text gives itself back to you, in all kinds of ways that you probably are not aware of. Whether you realize it or not, you know a great deal about a great many kinds of texts. That knowledge, though, is *tacit,* that is, unspoken. (The word *tacit* derives from the Latin *tacitus,* which means "silent.") It's knowledge that's understood without your needing to explain to yourself or to anyone else what you know, simply because you've come to take it for granted.

Try this:

Take a quick glance at the following textual forms, without attempting to read the words— they don't matter—and see if you can identify the kinds of texts you're "seeing."

used in the formation of compound words: *rhodolite.* Also, *esp. before a vowel,* rhod-. [< Gk, comb. form of *rhódon*]
rho·do·chro·site (rō'də krō'sīt), *n.* a mineral, manganese carbonate, MnCO₃, usually rose-red in color: a minor ore of manganese; manganese spar. [< Gk *rhodóchrōs* rose-colored (*rhódo*(n) RHODO- + *chrōs* color) + -ITE¹]
rho·do·den·dron (rō'də den'drən), *n.* any evergreen or deciduous, ericaceous shrub or tree of the genus *Rhododendron,* having showy, pink, purple, or white flowers. [< L < Gk *rhodódendron* (*rhódo*(n) RHODO- + *déndron* tree)]
rho·do·lite (rōd'līt), *n.* a rose or reddish-violet garnet used as a gem.
rho·do·nite (rōd'ənīt), *n.* a rose-red mineral, manganese silicate, MnSiO₃; manganese spar. [< G *Rhodonit* < Gk *rhódon* rose + G -it -ITE¹]
Rhod·o·pe (rod'ə pē, ro dō'-), *n.* a mountain range in SW Bulgaria. Highest peak, Musala, 9597 ft.
rho·dop·sin (rō dop'sin), *n.* Biochem. a bright-red photo-sensitive pigment found in the rod-shaped cells of the retina of certain fishes and most higher vertebrates. Also called **visual purple.** [RHOD- + OPSIN]
rho·do·ra (rō dôr'ə, -dōr'ə, rə-), *n.* a low, ericaceous shrub, *Rhododendron canadensis,* of North America, having rose-colored flowers which appear before the leaves. [< L *hodōrā* name of a plant]
Rho·dos (rô'thôs), *n.* Greek name of Rhodes (defs. 2, 3).
rhoea, var. of **-rrhea.**
rhomb (rom, romb), *n.* rhombus. [< L *rhomb*(us); cf. F *rombe*]
rhom·ben·ceph·a·lon (rom'ben sef'ə lon'), *n., pl.* **-lons, -la).** *Anat.* the hindbrain.
rhom·bic (rom'bik), *adj.* 1. having the form of a rhombus. 2. having a rhombus as base or cross section. 3. bounded by rhombuses, as a solid. 4. *Crystall.* orthorhombic. Also, **rhom'bi·cal.**
rhom·bo·he·dron (rom'bə hē'drən), *n., pl.* **-drons, -dra** (-drə). a solid bounded by six rhombic planes. [< Gk *rhómbo*(s) RHOMBUS + -HEDRON] —**rhom'bo·he'dral,** *adj.*
rhom·boid (rom'boid), *n.* 1. an oblique-angled parallelogram with only the opposite sides equal. —*adj.* 2. Also, having a form like or similar to that of a rhombus; shaped like a rhomboid. [< LL *rhomboid*(es) < Gk *rhomboeidés* (*schéma*) rhomboid (form, shape). See RHOMBUS, -OID] —**rhom·boi'dal·ly,** *adv.*
rhom·bus (rom'bəs), *n., pl.* **-bus·es, -bi** (-bī). 1. an oblique-angled equilateral parallelogram. 2. a rhombohedron. [< L < Gk *rhómbos* anything that may be spun around < *rhémbein* to revolve]
rhon·chus (rong'kəs), *n., pl.* **-chi** (-kī). a coarse rattling noise in the bronchial tubes, caused by an accumulation of mucus or other material; rale. [< L: a snoring, croaking < Gk *rhónchos,* var. of *rhénchos*] —**rhon·chi·al** (rong'kē əl), **rhon·chal** (rong'kal), *adj.*
Rhon·dda (ron'də), *n.* a city in S Wales. 86,400.
Rh... , *n.* 1. a river flowing from the Alps in S Switz...igh the Lake of Geneva and SE France into the ...n. 504 mi. long. 2. a wine-growing region in

[illustration labels:] Rhomboid · Rhombus

Barbara B. Love Becomes a Bride

Barbara Biddeford Love, t... daughter of Mr. and Mrs. Dean... Wilford Love of Sarasota, Fla., wa... married yesterday to Johnston Hamlin... Smith, a son of Mrs. Smith of Bedford... Hills, N.Y., and the late Mr. Smith. The Rev. Dr. Thomas S. Eliot performed the ceremony at St. Mary's Episcopal Church in Bedford Hills.

Mrs. Smith, 29 years old, is the marketing director for the Charleston (W.V.) arts festival. Her father retired as chief financial officer of the Manufacturer's Hanover Trust Company in New York. The bridegroom, 33, a Columbia College graduate, is president of Smith and James, Auctioneers, specializing in Shaker and 18th century American furniture. His father was a lawyer and secretary of the New York Bar Association.

Building Strike Settled

Nobody Happy

Workers Return Tomorrow

Wild Nights – Wild Nights!
Were I with thee
Wild Nights should be
Our luxury!

Futile – the Winds –
To a Heart in port –
Done with the Compass –
Done with the Chart!

Rowing in Eden –
Ah, the Sea!
Might I but moor – Tonight –
In Thee!

THE FAX OF LIFE

In one sense, you "read" the forms shown, just as you "read" things all the time. You read people, places, and situations, as well as texts. You read the faces of your friend for changes of mood, the sky for signs of rain, the intersection before you cross it, the flow of traffic as you negotiate the highway. You know all kinds of conventions—daily rules for negotiating. You know what's expected of you at the dinner table, the movies, sports events, weddings.

It's the same with texts. You don't pick up a poem when you need instructions for fixing your broken washing machine. When a fire breaks out in the kitchen and you dash for the fire extinguisher in the hall closet, you want the words to give you what you need—immediately, without fail:

TO OPERATE

1. Swing horn up. Pull pin.
2. Squeeze lever.
3. Direct discharge at base of flame.

You're not at all interested in pondering these words, in feeling the rhythm of the short phrases, in hearing the "tone," or in experiencing pleasure as you read. The last thing you need is ambiguity or humor or irony. You don't need Dave Barry's word play. You read just as when you read instructions for installing your VCR or completing a job application or filing your income tax return—so you'll know what to *do*. But what of other kinds of reading—all the other texts you encounter in your lives: love letters and comic strips, textbooks and poetry, autobiography and popular fiction? What kinds of knowledge do you need to read such a range of texts?

Francis Bacon, the seventeenth-century scientist and philosopher, said that some books are for tasting quickly and others for chewing slowly and digesting. Some books are like custard or frozen yogurt—they slide down without much effort at all. Others are like a cheap cut of meat—it's not easy to get your teeth going. So much, of course, has to do with your tastes and interests and needs. What's custard for you might be another person's shoe leather steak.

Some readers want story. They need a narrative fix. They devour romances or mysteries or science fiction or fantasy; they get vicarious pleasure from finding out what happens next, in rooms other than their own. They read what they have to for work or for school, but their reading pleasures are derived primarily from fiction.

Other readers are addicted to a different kind of story. For their work or research or preoccupations or hobbies they follow the news on the changing political landscape of Eastern Europe or on global warming or on computer software or on their favorite rock group or sports figure. They also need to know what happens next, but they read to keep up with ongoing narratives in the "real" world, in the field of psychoanalysis or in the playing field. What's Darrell Strawberry doing now? What's his record? This week? This month? This season? What's going to happen next?

Sometimes the same readers read quickly, at other times slowly: their textual knowledge enables them to *negotiate* with the texts—to read slowly, painstakingly, to stop and consider, to reread. When we read a complex, demanding essay in philosophy or political science or anthropology, we may plod along, stopping to take notes or underline, scratching questions in the margin or outlining a whole chapter, looking up a word in the dictionary or getting some *context*, some history in the encyclopedia, until we feel satisfied that we've begun to make some sense of the text. We may engage in a dialogue with the text—arguing, denying, questioning, composing *alternative* ways of looking at the issues.

Try this:

Look again at Dave Barry's "Historians We're Not" and then do the following:

1. Look up the word *tragic* in the dictionary. Then consider how the definition of the word may affect your reconsideration of Barry's use of the word. When do you typically use the word?
2. Take on the role of a high school history teacher. Write a letter to Barry, agreeing or disagreeing with his perspective on our knowledge of American history.

Just as we know that different kinds of friends make different demands of us and give us different satisfactions, so it is with different kinds of reading. Some friends we enjoy for intimate talk, others for listening to music or going dancing or going to football games or mountain climbing. Rarely do we find someone who shares all of our needs and enthusiasms—when we introduce one friend to another, we sometimes find ourselves embarrassed at their inability to talk to each other, and we wonder why we tried to bring them together at all. We realize that at times we actually feel as if we're different people when we're with one friend or another. So it is with reading. You might say that we enter different roles as readers. At times, we're the seeker of information, trying to get what we need to know in order to act in the world. Other times, we're the pleasure seeker, wanting an escape from our ordinary life, wanting to escape into the past or "back to the future," through the creative imagination of the artist who makes things happen in a fictive world. Now we're after facts and statistics, wanting to piece together the puzzle of the social world we live in. Now we're reading for the latest gossip on our favorite celebrity. Now we're reading the codes on our computer screen, to send a rocket to the moon. Now we're reading to pass the time, to take in the print on everything around us, from cereal boxes to soap wrappers. But we always have the option of becoming as adventurous as we dare. The more knowledge we have about what texts can give us, the more versatile and acrobatic—the more *athletic*—we can become.

Readers who believe that there is only one way to read assume somehow that the words will automatically *impress* themselves on their minds, that they need only sit back passively, as if they were watching images on a screen. They imagine that good readers all read quickly: they feel handicapped if they, themselves, read ploddingly. Accomplished readers, however, can read quickly—and they can read slowly—if they so *choose*. Some readers go after the whole—they want to see where a piece begins and where it ends. They skim. They scan. They take in large chunks. Then, perhaps, they go back to pick up details. They reread, knowing that each time they read they will discover something else. Others read slowly, focusing on detail, imagining scenes and character. They observe how a piece is built, working their way from its beginning to its end.

Consider this:

If you find reading to be sheer drudgery, then you might consider why that is so—and take the time to reflect on the attitudes you've developed toward reading. Did you *ever* enjoy reading? Were you read to as a child? Do you read aloud? What are your attitudes toward the text? What do you think you're supposed to get out of a text? What are you supposed to put in? Do you think that texts are "right" simply because they are in print? How many roles do you play as a reader?

Try this:

You know more than you think you do about reading. You know a great deal about textual conventions—for example, the different ways in which words can be laid out on a page—and these provide clues to the demands a text will make on you, even before you read a word. The look of a page can alert you to whether you should read seriously and carefully or quickly, for information or pleasure, or for both information and pleasure.

Write down quickly whatever comes to mind about the ways you think you "should" read the following kinds of texts:

a short story

a poem

a newspaper editorial page

this textbook

a history textbook

an essay

NEGOTIATING WITH TEXTS

In "Writing the Australian Crawl," the poet William Stafford talks about being responsive as a reader, being open, ready and willing to negotiate with a text. He encourages readers to trust their own personal responses to what they read. Reading, he says, "is not all your own ideas, and not all the other person's ideas. You toss back and forth against a live backboard. And, particularly, if it is a congenial poem—or friend—you are reading or hearing, you furnish a good half of the life. The travel circuit of an idea or impression is a sequence of reboundings between you and the page."

How can a reader be responsive, ready, willing, and open to interact with the page? In *Negotiations*, we'll consider various ways of reading, some of which, perhaps, you've never thought of before. Often, we'll need to stop to consider a word, a phrase, or an idea. We'll do that here by distinguishing between two words: *observation* and *inference*. We *observe* when we pay close attention to what is there. What we observe must be visible and verifiable: you and I must agree that something is there. We *infer*, on the other hand, when we bring to our observations various acts of mind: predicting, anticipating, guessing, theorizing, making assumptions, intuiting, questioning, comparing, speculating, wondering, interpreting, evaluating, judging.

We do the same, of course, in our social lives in the world. We are continually observing and inferring, as we interpret our worlds and try to make sense of our lives. When we're on familiar ground, we take things for granted, but when we're plunged into the new or strange, or when familiar ground is disrupted, then the processes of observation and inference may assume extraordinary importance. At the moment of my writing these words, the entire nation is gripped by a series of horrific murders on a college campus in Florida. It is the start of the semester; students, who had planned to settle into their dorms and courses, are unsettled, terrified. Undoubtedly, they are walking through their campus looking at everything anew. The familiar landscape, people's faces—both familiar and unfamiliar—are reframed, observed in a new, a different light, as the students negotiate this charged and dangerous situation.

In the realm of routine observation, we may disagree on the observable *(Was that a car or a van in front of the house? Was it blue or black? A Toyota or a Honda?)*, but we will agree that *some* vehicle was parked in front of the house. In the realm of inference, we can expect to disagree; we can even expect dispute. So and so brought you a gift—an observable fact. But why? Now that's the question: what was he trying to "say" by giving the gift? You wonder. You try to read his motives, his character, his meaning. Does he want something?

The word *infer* comes from the Latin *inferre*, which means to "carry in," "to bring in." When we infer, we carry to the world and to texts our own experiences, assumptions, and values. We can't get through a day without observing and inferring, but we usually do so *habitually*, without consciously considering our acts of mind. You look out the window and observe that someone is carrying an umbrella rolled up. "Good," you say to yourself, "it's not raining yet." You know it's supposed to rain because you've listened to the day's weather forecast (in fact, you've brought your umbrella to work). You assume that it's not raining "yet" because you know about rain and umbrellas: people don't usually walk around with unopened umbrellas when it's raining.

Your observation-inference isn't neutral at all: you're not simply recording information. It's encased in an affective value judgment, an *evaluation*. The fact that it is not raining *affects* you: you're pleased that it isn't raining, it's "good" that it isn't raining. You'll see in our work on evaluation, particularly in reading William James's essay, "On a Certain Blindness in Human Beings" (p. 204), that our observations and inferences and evaluations can lead us into misreadings, because we can get stuck behind closed doors, in our own habits of mind.

All the time we are playing the role of detective: testing our hypotheses—what Frank Smith calls our *theories of the world*—against what we observe. As he says,

> What we have in our heads is a *theory* of what the world is like, a theory that is the basis of all our perceptions and understanding of the world, the root of all learning, the source of all hopes and fears, motives and expectancies, reasoning and creativity. And this theory is all we have. If we can make sense of the world at all, it is by interpreting our interactions with the world in light of our theory. The theory is our shield against bewilderment.

Some of our "detective work" is almost instantaneous. We read the clues—the hot stove, red light, icy sidewalk—so quickly that we don't stop to think about how much we take in, how much we observe, and how quickly we size things up. The detective is a master of observation: *everything* can be a clue. (The word *clue* can be traced to the Old English *cliewen*, meaning "mass" or "ball" [of yarn]. The thread [from the ball of yarn], or clue, can lead one through a maze or a difficult investigation.) In the following dialogue, the detective Sherlock Holmes (a fictive character invented by the physician-writer Sir Arthur Conan Doyle) speaks with a new client, Helen Stone, and "threads" his way. The narrator here is Holmes's associate, Dr. Watson:

> "You have come in by train this morning, I see."
> "You know me, then?"
> "No, but I observe the second half of a return ticket in the palm of your left glove. You must have started early, and yet you had a good drive in a dog-cart, along heavy roads, before you reached the station."
> The lady gave a violent start, and stared in bewilderment at my companion.
> "There is no mystery, my dear madam," he said, smiling. "The left arm of your jacket is spattered with mud in no less than seven places. The marks are perfectly fresh. There is no vehicle save a dog-cart which throws up mud that way, and then only when you sit on the left-hand side of the driver."
>
> "The Speckled Band"

The woman is startled because Holmes almost simultaneously observes, infers, and concludes. He notices details—the ticket in her hand, the mud on her jacket. His inferences are supported by his empirical knowledge of the world around him. They are not frivolous or irrational; they are not wild hunches. And from what he sees, he draws conclusions and then tests them by calling for verification. She confirms his deductions. Holmes repeatedly tells his sidekick, Dr. Watson, "Sharpen your powers of observation." Watson admires Holmes, whose powers of observation, he says, are "rapid deductions, as swift as intuitions, and yet always founded on a logical basis."

What are *rapid deductions?*

Watson says that they're "as swift as intuitions." It's worth making the distinction. We might say that intuition is based more on feeling than on fact, more on a "sense of things" than on reasoning things out. You look at a couple, say, at their wedding and you simply *know* that things won't work out for them—and they don't! Later, you try to put the puzzle together, trying to figure out how you *knew*. Your powers of mind work so quickly that you can't sort them out. Two moves of mind, however, are useful to distinguish:

Induction is rooted in the observable. From the known, the facts right in front of you, you draw inferences. The process looks like this:

Observation ⟶ Inference ⟶ Conclusion
[Familiar or new phenomenon]   [Provisional or final]

Sometimes, on the other hand, you begin with a provisional theory, a hypothesis, which is based on general principles, and then test your hypothesis by going back to make observations, to examine the evidence. This process is known as *deduction*:

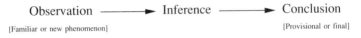

Hypothesis ⟶ Observation ⟶ Inference and Conclusion

Usually, we move between the two, *negotiating* our worlds and our texts by coming to provisional conclusions, testing our observations, and *renegotiating*. There is a two-way street between observation and inference.

$$\text{Observing} \rightleftharpoons \text{Inferring}$$

Although you read differently for different occasions—at times reading for sheer pleasure, escapism, absorption (at least, I hope so), at times for knowledge, and at times for both pleasure and knowledge—you are continually interacting with the words on the page, moving between observation and inference and bringing to the page *who* you are, the person that is you.

Try this:

Here is a Sherlock Holmes exercise.* From the clues offered below, size up the character you are about to meet:

> Reginald Peacock awakened to his wife's shout. As was his habit, while the bath water was running, he tried out his voice and looked out of the window. It was raining and foggy again. In front of the mirror, he began to do his breathing exercises, and then he dressed in his morning coat, dark grey trousers and grey socks. He studied himself in the mirror, first his hair, and then his dress: it would do. Everyone else was already downstairs. He walked into the dining room and sat down before a pile of letters, a copy of the morning paper, a little covered dish, and a pot of tea.

Now answer these questions:

1. Where does Reginald Peacock live?
2. How old is he?
3. What does he do for a living?
4. What is in the little covered dish?
5. What period in history have we entered? Now? Before World War I? Between the Wars? After World War II?
6. Who's written him a letter?
7. How would you describe his relationship with his wife?
8. How would you describe Reginald Peacock's character?

Compare your answers with your classmates. Which are similar? Which are not?

---

* The idea for this exercise came from a colleague, Mitchell Leaska, at New York University.

• • •

I have played the Reginald Peacock game with many readers over the past few years, and most of them come up with surprisingly similar responses, no matter what their own various backgrounds.

Or is that not so surprising?

Most students agree that Reginald Peacock is an older (over 40!) man living in London or some place in England. Most students agree that he *is* English. Did you? Why? What details did you observe? What inferences did you draw from the details? What knowledge did you bring to the text?

What clues decided you on England? The morning coat? Maybe. Although you may not be sure what a morning coat is. Is it a robe? You're not sure. People don't call their robes morning coats today (but then you wonder: maybe a morning coat isn't a robe). Now you're beginning to think that the story may be set in an earlier epoch. When? You're not sure. You might imagine a rather formal coat with tails: you've seen them in old movies when the man of the house comes down to have his breakfast. And that brings you to the pot of tea. The English and tea are like the sea and sand. They go together. And the rain—and, yes, the fog. Isn't it always rainy and foggy in London? (You remember the song: "A Foggy Day in London Town.")

And what about the name? Reginald might be English—like Thackeray or Oliver or Hattie. (Then you remember Reggie Jackson!) And what about Peacock? It could be English, but it sounds as if it's *invented,* doesn't it? Maybe the writer meant to *influence* us by choosing the name Peacock? What comes to mind when you think of a peacock? Glorious feathers? Mating rituals? Astonishing cries? Pride? You might recall the phrase, "proud as a peacock." That might bring you to that line about Reginald studying himself in the mirror: What's he looking for? Is he simply vain? Does any of this—or all of it—influence the way you read Reginald's character?

The "facts" about Reginald Peacock are these: I adapted the opening paragraph for this exercise from a short story, "Mr. Reginald Peacock's Day," by the New Zealand writer Katherine Mansfield. In her story, Reginald Peacock *is* an Englishman, a stuffy, middle-aged, self-centered music teacher (an aspiring *artiste* who has not "made it") who is dreadfully concerned about the way he looks, who is always preening himself and always on the look-out for an impressionable, unattached young woman to admire his feathers. Is he married? Yes, and that's his problem: he'd rather be free to roam. (And the letter? It's an adoring letter from one of his young women students.)

CULTURAL KNOWLEDGE

Where does the knowledge that you brought to Reginald Peacock come from? Was it similar to that of your classmates? Why might that be so?

We've already talked about the personal knowledge that you bring to a text and the textual knowledge you already have. Now we need to recognize what we can call *cultural knowledge*—that knowledge that we share with others of our own culture and which affects just about everything that we do or think. Like personal and textual knowledge, cultural knowledge is also tacit, and unless we stop to consider it very carefully, we tend to accept it as the way things simply "are." It affects all of our choices—what we eat and wear, how we spend our time, the work we do, our choice of friends, and even who we marry. It affects the choices we make in music, television programs, sports, and books. It affects the ways we have been raised and the ways we raise our children, how we treat them as girls or boys. It determines what we believe, value, and respect, whether we want to go to college, what we major in, and what we do with our lives. It shapes our prejudices and stereotypes, our religious and political views: it influences the ways we see others who we consider different from ourselves.

Consider this:

How do you value love? Is it important to seek? What about happiness? (Where do your views on love and happiness come from?) What about success? (Which people do you consider successful?) Money? (Is it to be saved or spent?) Travel? (Are you a stay-at-home or an adventurer?) Nature? (Do you value flat or hilly land? Trees or water?)

What might you name your children (if you decide to have any)? What might influence your choice of a name? Might these choices be different from those that your parents or grandparents made?

Our choices of and responses to big matters and small, to the big decisions we make and to daily habits that involve food, rituals, holidays, music, sports, leisure, and so forth are largely culturally determined. Of course, the phrase "culturally determined" is problematic. In the United States, so much of our cultural heritage is multifaceted that what is often referred to as the dominant, or mainstream, culture is actually a rich amalgam of elements from "other" cultures.

Some critics of American culture believe that every "literate" American must know certain facts and concepts and be able to use such basic knowledge to function in contemporary society. Other critics question the very notion of "basic" knowledge and call for a "relevant" knowledge, what matters only here and now. What should we, as Americans living in the 1900s, know? The question is being hotly debated in schools throughout the country and brings to mind the very notion of "mainstream" as a metaphor.

Consider this:

If the mainstream ("main stream") is the main part of a river, then, presumably, there are creeks and smaller streams, all flowing into it and continuing on in various ways: these smaller waterways would be tributaries. What do you consider to be the "main stream" of your cultural knowledge and beliefs? Where does it come from? Where is it going? And what are the tributaries, the little streams, that flow into it? Do they come from a "subculture," different from the mainstream? In what ways? Would you say that your values differ from those of your family, or from what you consider to be the mainstream culture?

• • •

So the simple act of "reading" Reginald Peacock brings into play a complex and rich range of observations coupled with private and public associations, assumptions, attitudes, prejudices, and values—what the American philosopher John Dewey called *funding*: you might say, then, that we are all richly endowed with personal, private, and social fundings, all the stuff of experience that comes from living—and reading.

Try this:

Listed below are words that you may or may not recognize. Read them quickly, and almost just as quickly, write down what you know about them. Which do you consider part of the mainstream, and which from the tributaries?

Berlin Wall	Madonna
Big Mac	Malcolm X
Challenger	Marlboro
Cinderella	Martin Luther King
Confucius	Michael Jackson
Desert Storm	Mickey Mouse
Dungeons and Dragons	Nat Turner
Eric Clapton	Pele
Four score and seven years ago	Pizza
George Washington	Roseanne Barr
Hallmark	1776
Harriet Tubman	Schwarzkopf
Ice T	Simon Bolívar
Ivory Snow	Shakespeare
Jamaica Kincaid	Stephen King
jazz	Super Bowl
John Lennon	Young and Restless
Lao-Tzu	Woody Allen
Life, liberty, and	
the pursuit of happiness	

Try this:

Get together with a group of classmates and make up a list that you know your parents' generation would not understand at all.

Try this:

What do you need to know? Texts intersect with each other in all kinds of ways, calling up or alluding to, or playing on, other texts. What cultural funding do you need to "read" the following cartoon, so as to understand, appreciate, and enjoy the rich play of meanings— to "get the joke"?

"Look, honey, the glass slipper still fits."

Suppose you didn't know that the cartoon plays on the Cinderella tale. Look closely at the drawing—the figures, their clothing, their facial expressions, as well as the words. How might you read the scene if you didn't know the story of Cinderella? How might you *frame* your perceptions of the characters and their circumstances, their dress, their mood?

Your knowing Cinderella takes the scene into another dimension, doesn't it? The version of the tale that most of us are familiar with stops with the conventional fairy-tale ending: "and they lived happily ever after." Here, in this rendition of the tale, we skip past the years of the happy couple's enchantment and youth, into the "middle years," with the once-happy prince now a balding, overweight, disgruntled husband. And Cinderella? All, presumably, that remains of her former shape and beauty is the size of her foot!

But press further. Move from physical change over time to the quality of the relationship. The Cinderella story has become one of the myths of our culture—the tacit, unwritten belief in youth and romance, discovery, and transformation. Here, the joke hinges on a reversal: Cinderella and her prince, still in their fancy dress, strike us as any old ordinary married couple, the wife trying to recapture a bit of the old sparks of the days of enchantment. There's an incongruity here: their dress and their behavior are inharmonious, discordant, off-key.

How else do you read the joke?

And what kinds of knowledge do you need to read the following cartoons?

"Your husband went back to his first wife and is already on board."

"This is impossible. Let's take the next boat."

• • •

Garrison Keillor, who made his reputation as the radio broadcaster for the show "Prairie Home Companion," invented the fictive world of Lake Wobegon, which many Midwesterners claim is nothing less than "true to life." (Other Midwesterners we know accuse Keillor of idealizing his own past.) In this selection from his book *Lake Wobegon Days,* Keillor shows us how it was in school, where the cultural influences included not only George Washington and Abraham Lincoln but also learning what was not specifically taught (learning between the lines).

School
Garrison Keillor

School started the day after Labor Day, Tuesday, the Tuesday when my grandfather went, and in 1918 my father, and in 1948 me. It was the same day, in the same brick schoolhouse, the former New Albion Academy, now named Nelson School. The same misty painting of George Washington looked down on us all from above the blackboard, next to his closest friend, Abraham Lincoln. Lincoln was kind and patient and we looked to him for sympathy. Washington looked as if he had a headache. His mouth was set in a prim, pained expression of disapproval. Maybe people made fun of him for his long, frizzy hair, which resembled our teacher's, Mrs. Meiers', and that had soured his disposition. She said he had bad teeth—a good lesson for us to remember: to brush after every meal, up and down, thirty times. The great men held the room in their gaze, even the back corner by the windows. I bent over my desk, trying to make fat vowels sit on the line like fruit, the tails of consonants hang below, and colored the maps of English and French empires, and memorized arithmetic tables and state capitals and major exports of many lands, and when I was stumped, looked up to see George Washington's sour look and Lincoln's of pity and friendship, an old married couple on the wall. School, their old home, smelled of powerful floor wax and disinfectant, the smell of patriotism.

Mine was a vintage desk with iron scrollwork on the sides, an empty inkwell on top, a shelf below, lumps of petrified gum on the underside of it and some ancient inscriptions, one from '94 ("Lew P.") that made me think how old I'd be in '94 (fifty-two) and wonder who would have my place. I thought of leaving that child a message. A slip of paper stuck in a crack: "Hello. September 9, 1952. I'm in the 5th grade. It's sunny today. We had wieners for lunch and we played pom-pom-pullaway at recess. We are studying England. I hope you are well and enjoy school. If you find this, let me know. I'm 52 years old."

But Bill the janitor would find it and throw it away, so I only scratched my name and the date next to Sylvester Krueger's ('31), a distinguished person whose name also appeared on a brass plaque by the library, "In Memoriam. Greater love hath no man than that he lay down his life for his friends."

It was an honor to have Sylvester's desk, a boy who probably sat and whiled away the hours with similar thoughts about Washington and Lincoln, cars, peckers, foreign lands, lunch. School was eternity, a quiet pool of imagination where we sat together and dreamed, interrupted by teaching, and thought of the boy Lindbergh (from Little Falls, a little east of us), the boy Lincoln, Wilbur and Orville, Lou Gehrig, all heroes, and most of all, I imagined Sylvester who left the room and died in France where his body was buried. Strange to think of him there, French guys mowing the grass over him and speaking French; easy to think of him here, working fractions under George Washington's gaze.

His mother came to school one day. Maybe it was Arbor Day, I remember we planted a tree in the memory of those who died for freedom, and I wasn't one of the children chosen to shovel the dirt in. Bill the janitor dug the hole, and the filling honors went to the six children who were tops in school citizenship, which didn't include me. They were lunchroom and hall monitors, flag-raisers, school patrol, and I was a skinny kid with wire-rim glasses who had to do what they said. Mrs. Krueger was a plump lady in a blue dress who put on her specs to read a few remarks off a card. I studied her carefully on account of my special relationship with her son, Sylvester. She was nervous. She licked her lips and read fast. It was hot. Some kids were fooling around and had to be shushed. "I know Sylvester would be very proud of you and glad that you remember him," she said. The little sliver of tree was so frail; it didn't last the spring. Bill had dug the hole in left field and the tree got stomped in a kittenball game at the All-School Picnic. Mrs. Krueger looked like a person who was lost. Mrs. Meiers walked her to the corner, where she would take McKinley Street home. I tagged along behind, studying. Mrs. Krueger seemed to have very sore feet. At the corner, she thanked Mrs. Meiers for the very nice ceremony. She said, "A person never forgets it when they lose a son, you know. To me, it's like it was yesterday."*

The same day we planted the tree, our all-school picture was taken by a man with a sliver of a mustache who crouched behind his tripod and put a cloth over his head. Jim told me we could be in the picture twice—at both ends of the group—by running around back while he shot it, but I left the right end too soon and got to the left end too late, and so appeared as two slight blurs. I looked at the print and thought of Sylvester and me.

School gave us marks every nine weeks, three marks for each subject: work, effort, and conduct. Effort was the important one, according to my mother, because that mark showed if you had gumption and stick-to-itiveness, and effort was my poorest showing. I was high in conduct except when dared to do wrong by other boys, and then I was glad to show what I could do. Pee on the school during recess? You don't think I would? Open the library door, yell "Boogers!" and run? Well, I showed them. I was not the one who put a big gob on the classroom doorknob during lunch though, the one that Darla Ingqvist discovered by putting her hand on it. Of all the people you'd want to see touch a giant gob, Darla was No. 1. She yanked her hand back just as Brian said, "Snot on you!" but she already knew. She couldn't wipe it off on her dress because she wore such nice dresses so she burst into tears and tore off to the girls' lavatory. Mrs. Meiers blamed me because I laughed. Brian, who did it, said, "That was a mean thing to do, shame on you" and I sat down on the hall floor and laughed myself silly. It was so *right* for Darla to be the one who

---

* Once a bat got loose in Mrs. Krueger's house and swooped from room to room and scared her silly. She lay on the floor, then crawled to the phone and called Gary and LeRoy to come and kill it, meanwhile her big cat Paul, named for her late husband, sat on the highboy studying the bat's flight and in one well-timed leap knocked it to the floor where Gary and LeRoy found it. They offered to look around the house for more bats. They took their time about it, never having seen her house before. Upstairs, although she lived alone, they found five single beds each neatly made and the covers turned down, and the kitchen table was set for two. The radio was on, playing one Glenn Miller tune after another. Out in the squad car, they searched the radio for Glenn Miller and couldn't find any. LeRoy went back in, thinking he might have left his glove or something, and her radio was still playing Glenn Miller, "Tuxedo Junction."

got a gob in her hand. She was a jumpy, chatty little girl who liked to bring money to school and show it to everyone. Once a five-dollar bill—we never had a five-dollar bill, so all the kids crowded around to see it. That was what she wanted. She made us stand in line. It was dumb. All those dumb girls took turns holding it and saying what they would do if they had one, and then Darla said she had $400 in her savings account. "Liar, liar, pants on fire," Brian said, but we all knew she probably did have $400. Later Brian said, "I wish I had her five dollars and she had a feather in her butt, and we'd both be tickled," which made me feel a little better, but putting the gob on the knob, knowing that Darla was monitor and had the privilege of opening the door, *that* was a stroke of genius. I almost didn't mind Mrs. Meiers making me sit in the cloakroom for an hour. I put white paste on slips of paper and put them in the pockets of Darla's coat, hoping she'd think it was more of the same.

It was Booger Day. When Mrs. Meiers turned her back to write her loopy letters on the board, John Potvin whispered, "Bunny boogers. Turkey tits. Panda poop," to Paul who was unprepared for it and laughed out loud. Mrs. Meiers snatched him out of his seat and made him stand in front, facing the class, a terrible humiliation. Everyone except Darla felt embarrassment for poor Paul; only Darla looked at him and gloated; so when Paul pretended to pull a long one out of his nose, only Darla laughed, and then she stood up in front and he sat down. Nobody looked at her, because she was crying.

On the way home, we sang with special enthusiasm,

> On top of old Smoky, two thousand feet tall,
> I shot my old teacher with a big booger ball.
> I shot her with glory, I shot her with pride.
> How could I miss her? She's thirty feet wide.

I liked Mrs. Meiers a lot, though, She was a plump lady with bags of fat on her arms that danced when she wrote on the board: we named them Hoppy and Bob. That gave her a good mark for friendliness in my book, whereas Miss Conway of fourth grade struck me as suspiciously thin. What was her problem? Nerves, I suppose. She bit her lips and squinted and snaked her skinny hand into her dress to shore up a strap, and she was easily startled by loud noises. Two or three times a day, Paul or Jim or Lance would let go with a book, dropping it flat for maximum whack, and yell, "Sorry, Miss Conway!" as the poor woman jerked like a fish on the line. It could be done by slamming a door or dropping the window, too, or even scraping a chair, and once a loud slam made *her* drop a stack of books, which gave us a double jerk. It worked better if we were very quiet before the noise. Often, the class would be so quiet, our little heads bent over our work, that she would look up and congratulate us on our excellent behavior, and when she looked back down at her book, *wham!* and she did the best jerk we had ever seen. There were five classes of spasms: The Jerk, The Jump, The High Jump, The Pants Jump, and The Loopdeloop, and we knew when she was prime for a big one. It was after we had put her through a hard morning workout, including several good jumps, and a noisy lunch period, and she had lectured us in her thin weepy voice, then we knew she was all wound up for the Loopdeloop. All it required was an extra effort: *throwing* a dictionary flat at the floor or dropping the globe, which sounded like a car crash.

We thought about possibly driving Miss Conway to a nervous breakdown, an event we were curious about because our mothers spoke of it often. "You're driving me to a nervous breakdown!" they'd yell, but then, to prevent one, they'd grab us and shake us silly. Miss Conway seemed a better candidate. We speculated about what a breakdown might include—some good jumps for sure, maybe a couple hundred, and talking gibberish with spit running down her chin.

Miss Conway's nervous breakdown was prevented by Mrs. Meiers, who got wind of it from one of the girls—Darla, I think. Mrs. Meiers sat us boys down after lunch period and said that if she heard any more loud noises from Room 4, she would keep us after school for a half hour. "Why not the girls?" Lance asked. "Because I know that you boys can accept responsibility," Mrs. Meiers said. And that was the end of the jumps, except for one accidental jump when a leg gave way under the table that held Mr. Bugs the rabbit in his big cage. Miss Conway screamed and left the room, Mrs. Meiers stalked in, and we boys sat in Room 3 from 3:00 to 3:45 with our hands folded on our desks, and remembered that last Loopdeloop, how satisfying it was, and also how sad it was, being the last. Miss Conway had made some great jumps.

QUESTIONS FOR CLASS DISCUSSION

1. Can you name other American Presidents whose pictures make you feel uneasy?
2. If you wrote a message to the child who will have your desk in thirty years, what would you write?
3. Do you think the author should have worked harder in school?

Consider this: Incongruities

Keillor's "Questions for Class Discussion" are a parody of textbook conventions. There's an incongruity here in that Keillor is *not* writing a textbook. He breaks out of the conventions of narrating an experience and into another textual frame, one that isn't ordinarily found together with a narrative. Rather than resting comfortably, then, at the end of his story, we're confronted by a bit of discourse that "belongs" somewhere else. We don't expect the shift. Does he catch your attention? Do you generally read "Questions for Class Discussion" in textbooks—or skip them?

Consider this: Juxtapositions

In the following excerpt from her well-known book *The Second Sex*, Simone de Beauvoir raises questions of gender—of what little boys and little girls are taught in books and in life. Consider how de Beauvoir might negotiate with Keillor's representation of his schooling. What might she say to him about the portraits on the wall in his classroom? What might he say to her about the title of her book, *The Second Sex*. How do you make sense out of the title of her book?

Do titles matter?

When we *juxtapose* two objects, ideas, texts, etc., we position them beside each other. (The root *juxta* is from the Latin meaning "beside" or "near.") In this case, we're negotiating our readings of two texts by placing one next to the other, and considering how they relate to each other, where they are similar, where they differ, and where they allow us to reframe or extend or question one of them in light of the other.

The Second Sex
Simone de Beauvoir

Everything helps to confirm [a] hierarchy in the eyes of the little girl. The historical and literary culture to which she belongs, the songs and legends with which she is lulled to sleep, are one long exaltation of man. It was men who built up Greece, the Roman Empire, France, and all other nations, who have explored the world and invented the tools for its exploitation, who have governed it, who have filled it with sculptures, paintings, works of literature. Children's books, mythology, stories, tales, all reflect the myths born of the pride and the desires of men; thus it is that through the eyes of men the little girl discovers the world and reads therein her destiny.

The superiority of the male is, indeed, overwhelming: Perseus, Hercules, David, Achilles, Lancelot, the old French warriors Du Guesclin and Bayard, Napoleon—so many men for one Joan of Arc; and behind her one descries the great male figure of the archangel Michael! Nothing could be more tiresome than the biographies of famous women: they are but pallid figures compared with great men; and most of them bask in the glory of some masculine hero. Eve was not created for her own sake but as a companion for Adam, and she was made from his rib. There are few women in the Bible of really high renown: Ruth did no more than find herself a husband. Esther obtained favor for the Jews by kneeling before Ahasuerus, but she was only a docile tool in the hands of Mordecai; Judith was more audacious, but she was subservient to the priests, and her exploit, of dubious aftertaste, is by no means to be compared with the clean, brilliant triumph of young David. The goddesses of pagan mythology are frivolous or capricious, and they all tremble before Jupiter. While Prometheus magnificently steals fire from the sun, Pandora opens her box of evils upon the world.

There are in legend and story, to be sure, witches and hags who wield fearful powers. Among others, the figure of the Mother of the Winds in Andersen's *Garden of Paradise* recalls the primitive Great Goddess: her four gigantic sons obey her in fear and trembling, she beats them and shuts them up in sacks when they misbehave. But these are not attractive personages. More pleasing are the fairies, sirens, and undines, and these are outside male domination; but their existence is dubious, hardly individualized; they intervene in human affairs but have no destiny of their own: from the day when Andersen's little siren becomes a woman, she knows the yoke of love, and suffering becomes her lot.

In modern tales as in ancient legends man is the privileged hero. Mme de Ségur's books are a curious exception: they describe a matriarchal society where the husband, when he is not absent, plays a ridiculous part; but commonly the figure of the father, as in the real world, is haloed with glory. The feminine dramas of *Little Women* unfold under the aegis of a father deified by absence. In novels of adventure it is the boys who take a trip around the world, who travel as sailors on ships, who live in the jungle on breadfruit. All important events take place through the agency of men. Reality confirms what these novels and legends say. If the young girl reads the papers, if she listens to the conversation of grown-ups, she learns that today, as always, men run the world. The political leaders, generals, explorers, musicians, and painters whom she admires are men; certainly it is men who arouse enthusiasm in her heart.

Consider this:

De Beauvoir considers the question of gender, of how being female affects our negotiations with a male-dominated culture. In the next passage, the Indian writer R. K. Narayan describes the ways he, as a child learning to read in his native India, negotiated with the English culture of the schools.

English in India
R. K. Narayan

When I was five years old I was initiated into the mysteries of letters with the appropriate religious ceremonies. I was taught to shape the first two letters of the alphabet with corn spread out on a tray, both in Sanskrit and Tamil. Sanskrit, because it was the classical language of India, Tamil because it was the language of the province in which I was born and my mother tongue. But in the classroom neither of these two languages was given any importance; they were assigned to the most helpless among the teachers, the *pandits* who were treated as a joke by the boys, since they taught only the 'second language', the first being English as ordained by Lord Macaulay when he introduced English education in India. English was taught by the best teacher in the school, if not by the ruling star of the institution, the headmaster himself. The English Primer itself looked differently styled from the other books in the school-bag with its strong binding and coloured illustrations, for those were days when educational material was imported and no one could dream of producing a school-book in India. The first lesson in the glossy Primer began 'A was an Apple Pie' (or was it just Apple, I don't remember); and went on to explain, 'B bit it' and 'C cut it'. The activities of B and C were understandable, but the opening line itself was mystifying. What was an Apple Pie? From B 's and C's zestful application, we could guess that it had to do with some ordinary business of mankind, such as eating. But what was it that was being eaten? Among fruits we were familiar with the mango, banana, guava, pomegranate and grape, but not the apple (in our part of the country) much less an Apple Pie. To our eager questioning, the omniscient one, our English teacher, would just state, 'It must be some stuff similar to our *idli,* but prepared with apple.' This information was inadequate and one popped up to ask, 'What would it taste like? Sweet or sour?' The teacher's patience now being at an end, he would say, 'Don't be a nuisance, read your lessons,' a peremptory order which we obeyed by reciting like a litany 'A was an Apple Pie'. We were left free to guess, each according to his capacity, at the quality, shape, and details of the civilization portrayed in our class-books. Other subjects were also taught in English. We brooded over arithmetical problems in which John did a piece of work in half the time that Sam took . . . if they labored jointly, when would the work be completed? We also wrestled with bushels of oats and wages paid in pounds, shillings and pence, although the characters around us in actual life called themselves Rama and Krishna and handled rupees and annas rather than half-crowns and farthings. Thus we got used to getting along splendidly with unknown quantities in our studies. At a later stage, we read and enjoyed the best of English prose, overlooking detail in the process of enjoying literature. Chaucer and Ben Jonson, Pope and Dryden, Boswell and Goldsmith and a hundred others became almost our next door neighbours. Through books alone we learnt to love the London of

English literature. I have a friend, an engineer, who happening to visit West Germany on a technical mission, took off a fortnight in order to go to England and see the literary landmarks. His literary map included not only Keats's house at Hampstead, but also the amphibian world of the Thames bargemen described in the stories of W.W. Jacobs; he tried to follow the trails of Oliver Twist and David Copperfield, and also obtain, if possible, a glimpse of the comfortable world of Soames Forsyte, nor could he overlook the Drones Club mentioned by P.G. Wodehouse. He rounded off the trip with a visit to Stratford-on-Avon and the Lake District, and returned home feeling profoundly happy. Sometime ago a more scholarly work appeared entitled *My English Pilgrimage by* Professor Sadhan Kumar Ghose wherein one could find a methodical account of a devoted scholar's travels in search of Literary England past and present.

In our home my father's library was crammed with Carlyle, Ruskin, Walter Pater, and double-column editions of Wordsworth, Byron, Browning and Shakespeare. My father enjoyed reading Carlyle and Ruskin, and persuaded me not to miss them. For his sake I read thirty pages of *The French Revolution, Sartor Resartus;* and *Miscellaneous Essays;* twenty-five pages of *Marius the Epicurean;* a hundred pages of Fielding and Thackeray, and skipped through a dozen novels of Sir Walter Scott. We also read many European and Greek classics in English translation. We relied on *The Times Literary Supplement, Bookman, London Mercury, Life and Letters,* and the book pages of the weekly journals, for our knowledge of 'contemporary' literature. We enjoyed the literary gossip generated in a society dominated by Shaw, Wells, and Chesterton. We were aware of not only what they wrote or were about to write at any given time, but also what they thought of each other and how much they earned in royalties.

For an Indian classical training begins early in life. Epics, mythology and *Vedic* poetry (of Sanskrit origin and of tremendous antiquity) are narrated to everyone in childhood by the mother or the grandmother in a cosy corner of the house when the day's tasks are done and the lamps are lit. Later one reads them all through one's life with a fresh understanding at each stage. Our minds are trained to accept without surprise characters of godly or demoniac proportions with actions and reactions set in limitless worlds and progressing through an incalculable time-scale.

With the impact of modern literature we began to look at the gods, demons, sages, and kings of our mythology and epics, not as some remote concoctions but as types and symbols, possessing psychological validity even when seen against the contemporary background. When writing we attempted to compress the range of our observation and subject the particle to an intense scrutiny. Passing, inevitably, through phases of symbolic, didactic, or over-dramatic, writing, one arrived at the stage of valuing realism, psychological explorations, and technical virtuosity. The effort was interesting, but one had to differ from one's models in various ways. In an English novel, for instance, the theme of romance is based on a totally different conception of the man-woman relationship from ours. We believe that marriages are made in heaven and a bride and groom meet, not by accident or design, but by the decree of fate, the fitness for a match not to be gauged by letting them go through a period of courtship but by a study of their horoscopes; boy and girl meet and love after marriage rather than before. The Eternal Triangle, a standby for a western writer, is worthless as a theme for an Indian, our social circumstances not providing adequate facilities for the Eternal Triangle. We, however, seek excitement in our system of living known as the Joint Family, in which several members of a family live under the same roof.

The strains and stresses of this kind of living on the individual, the general structure of a society emerging from it, and the complexities of the caste system, are inexhaustible subjects for us. And the hold of religion and the conception of the gods ingrained in us must necessarily find a place in any accurate portrayal of life. Nor can we overlook the rural life and its problems, eighty-five out of a hundred Indians being village folk.

English has proved that if a language has flexibility any experience can be communicated through it, even if it has to be paraphrased rather than conveyed, and even if the factual detail, as in the case of the Apple Pie, is only partially understood. In order not to lose the excellence of this medium a few writers in India took to writing in English, and produced a literature that was perhaps not first-rate; often the writing seemed imitative, halting, inept or an awkward translation of a vernacular rhetoric, mode, or idiom; but occasionally it was brilliant. We are still experimentalists. I may straightaway explain what we do not attempt to do. We are not attempting to write Anglo-Saxon English. The English language, through sheer resilience and mobility, is now undergoing a process of Indianization in the same manner as it adopted US citizenship over a century ago, with the difference that it is the major language there but here one of the fifteen. I cannot say whether this process of transmutation is to be viewed as an enrichment of the English language or a debasement of it. All that I am able to confirm, after nearly thirty years of writing, is that it has served my purpose admirably, of conveying unambiguously the thoughts and acts of a set of personalities, who flourish in a small town named Malgudi supposed to be located in a corner of South India.

English has been with us for over a century, but it has remained the language of the intelligentsia, less than ten per cent of the population understanding it. In view of this limitation our constitution provides for the changing over of the official language to Hindi in due course. Interestingly, side by side, special institutes are established where English teachers are trained, and the subject occupies a high place in all universities. I feel, however, that it must reach the market-place and the village green if it is to send down roots. In order to achieve this, the language must be taught in a simpler manner, through a basic vocabulary, simplified spelling, and explained and interpreted through the many spoken languages of India. When such a technique of propagation is perfected, we shall see English, whatever its official status, assimilated in the soil of India and growing again from it.

Try this:

How were you first introduced to the world of print? What incongruities or mismatches did you encounter? Did your gender or native language or culture clash with what was offered as "mainstream," via the textbooks used?

WHAT DO YOU THINK?
INSTANTANEOUS RESPONSE

Consider this scene: You've just finished reading Keillor's piece, and since I've already read it and can't wait to talk about it with you, I jump right in:

"Are you finished?" I ask.

"Hmmmmmm," you say.

"Well, what do you think?" I ask.

"What?" you say.

"What do you think?"

"I don't *think anything* right now," you say. "Maybe later."

Maybe later. One of the problems with reading in schools is that readers are usually expected to make *immediate* responses—without time for reflection.

"Any comments?"

"Any questions?"

"What do you feel?"

You're not ready. It's as if you haven't had a chance to taste the food and the cook asks, "Well, how is it?" Or you've just walked out of a riveting movie, and your companion says, "What'd you think?" and you're simply not ready to say a word. You still want to be *in* the movie. You're in that space inside your own head—in that transitional space—and you're not ready to close the door on your inner experience. But now you're being yanked out of that place, asked to shift roles—to come *out*.

When asked to comment in the classroom, it's even worse: whoever speaks first in class often determines the way the discussion will move, and you may find yourself being diverted from what you think important. You may find yourself listening, perhaps a bit frustrated. Those of us (myself included) who are "delayed" respondents often don't know what we want to say (if anything) until later (if then), until we've had time for reflection. Sometimes we have to "let it sink in," or "sleep on it," or even dream about it. Sometimes we don't know what we think for months, and then as we're reacting to one situation, we discover, to our surprise, that we're reminded of another. And yet we often feel pressured—to come up with a comment, to say what we like or don't like, or to try to get to some "deeper" meaning in the text, even to show off our abilities to articulate an adequate or appropriate response. Some people seem to know what they think about things immediately, on the spot. Many of us, on the other hand, find ourselves in a whirlpool of opinions and comments, wondering why we didn't have something to say. Sometimes it feels as if what we wanted to say has been "stolen" by someone else.

Sometimes, though, being thrown into "crisis," being put on the spot, makes you come up with reactions that surprise you: you had no idea you'd come out with what you did, and now that you've said or written it, you feel a strong sense of satisfaction.

For now I want to encourage silence. I want to encourage you to let things sink in—and to do what the writer James Britton often does after he reads a story or essay or poem to a group of students: *nothing*.

• • •

Here is a short story, "Hills Like White Elephants," written by the American writer Ernest Hemingway. Read it and don't feel obliged to do anything else.

Hills Like White Elephants
Ernest Hemingway

The hills across the valley of the Ebro were long and white. On this side there was no shade and no trees and the station was between two lines of rails in the sun. Close against the side of the station there was the warm shadow of the building and a curtain, made of strings of bamboo beads, hung across the open door into the bar, to keep out flies. The American and the girl with him sat at a table in the shade, outside the building. It was very hot and the express from Barcelona would come in forty minutes. It stopped at this junction for two minutes and went on to Madrid.

"What should we drink?" the girl asked. She had taken off her hat and put it on the table.

"It's pretty hot," the man said.

"Let's drink beer."

"Dos cervezas," the man said into the curtain.

"Big ones?" a woman asked from the doorway.

"Yes. Two big ones."

The woman brought two glasses of beer and two felt pads. She put the felt pads and the beer glasses on the table and looked at the man and the girl. The girl was looking off at the line of hills. They were white in the sun and the country was brown and dry.

"They look like white elephants," she said.

"I've never seen one," the man drank his beer.

"No, you wouldn't have."

"I might have," the man said. "Just because you say I wouldn't have doesn't prove anything."

The girl looked at the bead curtain. "They've painted something on it," she said. "What does it say?"

"Anis del Toro. It's a drink."

"Could we try it?"

The man called "Listen" through the curtain. The woman came out from the bar.

"Four reales."

"We want two Anis del Toro."

"With water?"

"Do you want it with water?"

"I don't know," the girl said. "Is it good with water?"

"It's all right."

"You want them with water?" asked the woman.

"Yes, with water."

"It tastes like licorice," the girl said and put the glass down.

"That's the way with everything."

"Yes," said the girl. "Everything tastes of licorice. Especially all the things you've waited so long for, like absinthe."

"Oh, cut it out."

"You started it," the girl said. "I was being amused. I was having a fine time."

"Well, let's try and have a fine time."

"All right. I was trying. I said the mountains looked like white elephants. Wasn't that bright?"

"That was bright."

"I wanted to try this new drink. That's all we do, isn't it—look at things and try new drinks?"

"I guess so."

The girl looked across at the hills.

"They're lovely hills," she said. "They don't really look like white elephants. I just meant the coloring of their skin through the trees."

"Should we have another drink?"

"All right."

The warm wind blew the bead curtain against the table.

"The beer's nice and cool," the man said.

"It's lovely," the girl said.

"It's really an awfully simple operation, Jig," the man said. "It's not really an operation at all."

The girl looked at the ground the table legs rested on.

"I know you wouldn't mind it, Jig. It's really not anything. It's just to let the air in."

The girl did not say anything.

"I'll go with you and I'll stay with you all the time. They just let the air in and then it's all perfectly natural."

"Then what will we do afterward?"

"We'll be fine afterward. Just like we were before."

"What makes you think so?"

"That's the only thing that bothers us. It's the only thing that's made us unhappy."

The girl looked at the bead curtain, put her hand out and took hold of two of the strings of beads.

"And you think then we'll be all right and be happy."

"I know we will. You don't have to be afraid. I've known lots of people that have done it."

"So have I," said the girl. "And afterward they were all so happy."

"Well," the man said, "if you don't want to you don't have to. I wouldn't have you do it if you didn't want to. But I know it's perfectly simple."

"And you really want to?"

"I think it's the best thing to do. But I don't want you to do it if you don't really want to."

"And if I do it you'll be happy and things will be like they were and you'll love me?"

"I love you now. You know I love you."

"I know. But if I do it, then it will be nice again if I say things are like white elephants, and you'll like it?"

"I'll love it. I love it now but I just can't think about it. You know how I get when I worry."

"If I do it you won't ever worry?"

"I won't worry about that because it's perfectly simple."

"Then I'll do it. Because I don't care about me."

"What do you mean?"

"I don't care about me."

"Well, I care about you."

"Oh, yes. But I don't care about me. And I'll do it and then everything will be fine."

"I don't want you to do it if you feel that way."

The girl stood up and walked to the end of the station. Across, on the other side, were fields of grain and trees along the banks of the Ebro. Far away, beyond the river, were mountains. The shadow of a cloud moved across the field of grain and she saw the river through the trees.

"And we could have all this," she said. "And we could have everything and every day we make it more impossible."

"What did you say?"

"I said we could have everything."

"We can have everything."

"No, we can't."

"We can have the whole world."

"No, we can't."

"We can go everywhere."

"No, we can't. It isn't ours any more."

"It's ours."

"No, it isn't. And once they take it away, you never get it back."

"But they haven't taken it away."

"We'll wait and see."

"Come on back in the shade," he said. "You mustn't feel that way."

"I don't feel any way," the girl said. "I just know things."

"I don't want you to do anything that you don't want to do——"

"Nor that isn't good for me," she said. "I know. Could we have another beer?"

"All right. But you've got to realize——"

"I realize," the girl said. "Can't we maybe stop talking?"

They sat down at the table and the girl looked across at the hills on the dry side of the valley and the man looked at her and at the table.

"You've got to realize," he said, "that I don't want you to do it if you don't want to. I'm perfectly willing to go through with it if it means anything to you."

"Doesn't it mean anything to you? We could get along."

"Of course it does. But I don't want anybody but you. I don't want anyone else. And I know it's perfectly simple."

"Yes, you know it's perfectly simple."

"It's all right for you to say that, but I do know it."

"Would you do something for me now?"

"I'd do anything for you."

"Would you please please please please please please please stop talking?"

He did not say anything but looked at the bags against the wall of the station. There were labels on them from all the hotels where they had spent nights.

"But I don't want you to," he said, "I don't care anything about it."

"I'll scream," the girl said.

The woman came out through the curtains with two glasses of beer and put them down on the damp felt pads. "The train comes in five minutes," she said.

"What did she say?" asked the girl.

"That the train is coming in five minutes."

The girl smiled brightly at the woman, to thank her.

"I'd better take the bags over to the other side of the station," the man said. She smiled at him.

"All right. Then come back and we'll finish the beer."

He picked up the two heavy bags and carried them around the station to the other tracks. He looked up the tracks but could not see the train. Coming back, he walked through the barroom, where people waiting for the train were drinking. He drank an Anis at the bar and looked at the people. They were all waiting reasonably for the train. He went out through the bead curtain. She was sitting at the table and smiled at him.

"Do you feel better?" he asked.

"I feel fine," she said. "There's nothing wrong with me. I feel fine."

CHAPTER 2

Performing

a Text

EAVESDROPPING

Try this: Eavesdropping I

Plant yourself in an inconspicuous spot in a public place, such as a bus or train, a bus stop, an airport, a restaurant, or a laundromat, where you can sit and look as if you're minding your own business, but are in reality eavesdropping, listening in on a conversation between strangers. Discreetly, jot down the dialogue. The actual words they use. Make as many *observations* as you are able. Take in the scene.

How important is the context of the conversation—what you might call the who, where, what, when, and why of the situation? Who's talking to whom? Where and when is the conversation taking place? What are they talking about? Why do they appear to be talking to each other?

How do they "sound"? How would you characterize their tones of voice? Cheerful? Despondent? Animated? Cool? Angry? Agitated? Thoughtful? Provocative? Teasing? Diffident? How do you capture the "uh's," "um's," and "you know's"? How do you capture the pauses and the silences? Are they looking at each other? What are they doing with their hands?

Now make *inferences:* what do you infer about the facts of the relationship: are they parent and child, husband and wife, or what? Do you suppose that the conversation might be different if the speakers were in a private setting such as their own homes? What clues have you used to "read" the people you're listening to?

From your notes, write a representation of the dialogue you've overheard. Write it in the form of a *script* to be performed.

From these same notes, *tell* a friend (or a classmate) what you overheard, and how the strangers struck you. Did you favor one over the other? If they were arguing, did you think one was "in the right" and the other "in the wrong"?

Finally, reflect upon the differences between (1) *the overheard conversation and* your written representation, and (2) *the overheard conversation and* your oral representation.

ETHNOGRAPHY

Do you often find yourself irresistibly drawn to eavesdropping on strangers' conversations: in doctors' waiting rooms, in movie lines, in supermarkets or restaurants? Sometimes, perhaps, you can't help yourself. There you are sitting quietly, reading a newspaper or daydreaming, not bothering a soul, and suddenly, your attention shifts: other voices invade your inner space and you find yourself now only pretending to read, as you strain to hear every word. At other times, because you notice someone who *looks* interesting—strange or theatrical, flamboyant or extravagant—you position yourself to overhear. You set yourself up to *spy*.

Ethnographers are social scientists who try to capture what people say and do in the contexts in which the people themselves live and work and carry out the activities of their lives. If they want to study the development of children's language, for example, they'll take themselves into homes and schools and playgrounds. They'll listen to children talking while playing in the sandbox. They often use camcorders so as to capture gestures, intonations, pauses, and silences, in addition to words.

In transcribing dialogue, ethnographers often use line breaks to try to represent the pauses and silences, but they all attest to the almost insurmountable difficulties of the task. "How do you make up for the loss?" they ask. The spoken voice is divested of inflection and tonality and rhythm when it is transcribed into *text*.

Ordinary language is rich with all the complexities and nuances of great literature— and of soap opera. Writers walk around with open ears and notebooks "capturing" the language they hear all around them. Like ethnographers, they may try to be true to the facts, to get them right, to be accurate; or, if they are writers of fiction, they may use overheard conversations as grist for their creative mills. You might be surprised to discover that many people are actually paid to eavesdrop.

You may not consider yourself an ethnographer or a writer, but I suspect that you are interested in listening in on conversations, simply because people are interested in other people, because they want and need to find out how other human beings get on with their lives, how they negotiate with each other—in love and in war. You may often find yourself the unwitting observer of little human dramas acted out right before your eyes. When you walk into a conversation between members of your family or friends, you're entering an ongoing conversation. You don't need to be put in the picture: you know the *context*. You would understand, without being told, this kind of talk:

> If I told Harry once, I've told him a thousand times not to mention Lucille's name
> to Sam.

But when you observe strangers and overhear their conversations, you are walking into an ongoing conversation where you need more information than you have to understand who Harry, Lucille, and Sam are and how they relate to each other, and why Sam doesn't want to hear about Lucille!

Try this: Eavesdropping II

Record a brief conversation between people you *know* so well that you may not even need to listen to the words to know what they're saying!

From your notes, write a transcription of their conversation in the form of a script to be performed. Allow space in the transcription for pauses, particularly at the end of lines, where you want to gain emphasis. For example:

> *Sara:* I know you want me to finish school,
> but,   well,   how can I
> do anything   now?
> You know what I mean.

Now give your script to classmates to read aloud. After they're finished, compare their reading with what you know of the "original." How far off or how close were they in capturing the feel of the original situation?

Ask them to jot down the kinds of *inferring* they had to do about the people and the context from the language of your script they've observed.

In Eavesdropping I (page 36), you were asked to overhear a conversation between strangers, and in Eavesdropping II, you observed people you know. How would you characterize the similarities and differences of the two acts for you, the eavesdropper?

READING BY EAR

The drama of the written word can be "performed" only by the reader—either by reading silently or by trying the words aloud. Mostly, we read silently and hear the words—where? In our eyes? Our forehead? Or in the same spaces in our minds where we daydream or "talk" to ourselves? Where do you "hear" the words you read? Or don't you hear them at all? Do you only *see* them?

One of the most effective ways of reading—of trying out various possibilities of interpreting a text—is to read aloud, to read with the ear as well as the eye. That's what I mean here by performing a text. We'll never get inside the mind of the writer who has written a text. And even if we could ask about a writer's intentions, ask Hemingway, say, about his intentions in "Hills Like White Elephants," how could we know that he still "knows" what he intended when he wrote a piece in the past. Much of what we intend is often hidden even from ourselves.

We can become aware, though, that texts can be performed variously—that our readings are shaped and determined by the personal, textual, and cultural knowledge that we bring to a text.

Let's go back now to Hemingway's story, to "perform" it. Perhaps your instructor will enable you to perform it in class, once or twice, so that you can "hear the voices" of the drama. If you are watching your classmates perform the text—or if you are reading the whole aloud to yourself—imagine that you are "actually" eavesdropping on a conversation while you're waiting for a train. And while you observe, begin to make inferences.

Consider, too, how this second reading of the story differs from your first, silent reading.

Now, consider this:

How do you "read" the American and the girl? What are they saying? What aren't they saying? If you were to fill in the lines where you *know* that words are *not* being said, where you "feel the gaps," what would those words be? Where in the text do you "hear" voices changing note or key? How does the narrator (the storytelling voice) *sound* in the beginning paragraph?

> The hills across the valley of the Ebro were long and white. On this side there was no shade and no trees and the station was between two lines of rails in the sun. Close against the side of the station there was the warm shadow of the building and a curtain, made of strings of bamboo beads, hung across the open door into the bar, to keep out flies. The American and the girl with him sat at a table in the shade, outside the building. It was very hot and the express from Barcelona would come in forty minutes. It stopped at this junction for two minutes and went on to Madrid.

Read aloud these opening lines by yourself or in class. Then ask someone else to read the same lines. Do they sound different? How? Where?

Where are your emphases? What words do you stress? For example, I stress the word *this* in the first line: "On *this* side. . . . " I slightly emphasize the negatives: " . . . there was *no* shade and *no* trees." I emphasize the word *outside* in line 5. And I keep hearing the repetition of the word *and;* it slows the pace of my reading. How does your reading compare with mine?

In Chapter 1, we looked at the notion of personal knowledge, the fundings you bring to a text. When you perform a text—hear it with the ear as well as read with the eye—you perform with *your* own "voices." You perform in your own particular ways: the ways *you* speak—your tone, emphasis, stress, inflections, and rhythms; the ways you hear pauses and silences; the ways you "feel" the text and the force of the words. Think about a group of actors all trying out for the same part: each one will translate as she "hears" the text. We can imagine, in fact, how the playwright who hears his words "*mis*performed," "*mis*read," will cry out, "No, no, that isn't the way. Stop! Do it my way. Do it as I have it in my own head." But that, of course, is an impossibility. For every translation from the "voice" inside the writer's head—to the written text, to the ways the actor hears the voice inside her head, to her performance on the stage, to the ways the audience then hears the voice in their heads—there will be a different version of the inner text. The playwright has no control over the actor or over you. Once the words are down on the page, they, in effect, become *yours*.

You may have felt the difficulties of trying to "capture" and then transcribe the aural into writing when you were trying to represent the conversation you overheard. That goes for the *re*presentation of the written as it is taken by the reader—when reading silently, with the eyes alone, and when reading by ear. For there will be as many different *versions* of a text as there are different readers. You might want to experiment with two, three, or four readings of the same text and then consider this question: How are *written* texts different from the oral? How are they similar?

THE NARRATOR

How would you characterize the narrator's voice in "Hills Like White Elephants"? Cheerful? Sad? Pessimistic? Optimistic? Matter-of-fact? Enthusiastic? Good-tempered? Puzzled? Impartial? Detached?

Follow the voice of the narrator throughout the entire story. How does he sound to you? What kinds of details does he *observe?* Does he offer any judgments of the characters?

Do you notice any adverbs (usually *-ly* words) in his telling? What would be the difference between his saying *"the girl said"* and *"the girl said sadly"?*

Now, what do you make of the narrator's voice on the last page, in the paragraph beginning "He picked up the two heavy bags . . . " and ending with "She was sitting at the table and smiled at him"? Think again of the way you transcribed the conversation you overheard between two strangers in a public place. *Did you use any words to describe the ways you heard the words?*

Consider the effects of adverbs:

He said.

He said longingly.

He said angrily.

He said despairingly.

He said expectantly.

He said wisely.

He said lovingly.

He said menacingly.

By now, you probably realize that Hemingway doesn't often use adverbs in this story. (Nor does he use many adjectives. See page 69.) His dialogue is written very much like that in a play, where the characters speak their lines, and we, the audience, are tempted to read between the lines as we did in "real" life when listening in on strangers. If, then, "Hills . . . " had been written like a play, it would probably have looked like this:

The girl:	"What should we drink?"
The American:	"It's pretty hot."
The girl:	"Let's drink beer."
The American:	"Dos cervezas."

Now go back once more to the Hemingway story. Think of yourself in the role of the narrator, and begin to read the "unspoken," to read between the lines. Are there places in the story where the narrator seems to be *for* the American? *For* the girl? Against the American? Against the girl? Is he impartial—simply reporting? Neutral? What kind of "knowledge" does he have? How well does he know these characters? Does he know, for example, about their past lives? Where in the text does he reveal any knowledge about what they've done *before* this scene? Does he appear to know what they'll do next?

The text is a short story—it is fiction. What does that mean to you? Would you read the text differently if you knew it was nonfiction, part of a reported observation of actual people?

Every text, whether it is fiction or nonfiction, is "told" by someone: the narrator. The narrator is the voice that *tells,* whether the text is a short story, a novel, a biography, a newspaper article or editorial, an essay, or a textbook. You might say, then, that behind every text is the overhearer—in the same role you were in when you listened in on a conversation. Sometimes the narrator is part of the action—a *participant.* At other times, the narrator is a watcher, an observer, a listener, a viewer—a *spectator.* (We will return to these terms in Chapter 6.)

THE SAID AND THE UNSAID

For now, let's look closely at the notion of reading the lines and reading between the lines. The Russian psychologist Lev Vygotsky (1896–1934) investigated relationships between thought, speech, and writing. He looked at the ways people actually use language in their lives; he studied the language we use to "talk to ourselves"—what he called "inner speech"; and he studied the ways that writers use language to represent people using language. He compared everyday, actual speech patterns with what he found in novels and plays. He was convinced that every bit of language "creates a connection, fulfills a function, solves a problem." In the following excerpt from his book *Thought and Language,* Vygotsky considers the work of Russian theater director Konstantin Stanislavsky and the method he used to enable actors to read between the lines.

Inner Speech
Lev Vygotsky

As we have said, every thought creates a connection, fulfills a function, solves a problem. The flow of thought is not accompanied by a simultaneous unfolding of speech. The two processes are not identical, and there is no rigid correspondence between the units of thought and speech. This is especially obvious when a thought process miscarries—when, as Dostoevski put it, a thought "will not enter words." Thought has its own structure, and the transition from it to speech is no easy matter. The theatre faced the problem of the thought behind the words before psychology did. In teaching his system of acting, Stanislavsky required the actors to uncover the "subtext" of their lines in a play. In Griboedov's comedy *Woe from Wit,* the hero, Chatsky, says to the heroine, who maintains that she has never stopped thinking of him, "Thrice blessed who believes. Believing warms the heart." Stanislavsky interpreted this as "Let us stop this talk"; but it could just as well be interpreted as "I do not believe you. You say it to comfort me," or as "Don't you see how you torment me? I wish I could believe you. That would be bliss." Every sentence that we say in real life has some kind of subtext, a thought hidden behind it. In the examples we gave earlier of the lack of coincidence between grammatical and psychological subject and predicate, we did not pursue our analysis to the end. Just as one sentence may express different thoughts, one thought may be expressed in different sentences. For instance, "The clock fell," in answer to the question "Why did the clock stop?" could mean: "It is not my fault that the clock is out of order; it fell." The same thought, self-justification, could take the form of "It is not my habit to touch other people's things. I was just dusting here," or a number of others.

Thought, unlike speech, does not consist of separate units. When I wish to communicate the thought that today I saw a barefoot boy in a blue shirt running down the street, I do not see every item separately: the boy, the shirt, its blue color, his running, the absence of shoes. I conceive of all this in one thought, but I put it into separate words. A speaker often takes several minutes to disclose one thought. In his mind the whole thought is present at once, but in speech it has to be developed successively. A thought may be compared to a cloud shedding a shower of words. Precisely because thought does not have its automatic counterpart in words, the transition from thought to word leads through meaning. In our speech, there is always the hidden thought, the subtext. Because a direct transition from thought to word is impossible, there have always been laments about the inexpressibility of thought:

> How shall the heart express itself?
> How shall another understand?
> [F. Tjutchev]

   Direct communication between minds is impossible, not only physically but psychologically. Communication can be achieved only in a roundabout way. Thought must pass first through meanings and then through words.

   We come now to the last step in our analysis of verbal thought. Thought itself is engendered by motivation, i.e., by our desires and needs, our interests and emotions. Behind every thought there is an affective-volitional tendency, which holds the answer to the last "why" in the analysis of thinking. A true and full understanding of another's thought is possible only when we understand its affective-volitional basis. We shall illustrate this by an example already used: the interpretation of parts in a play. Stanislavsky, in his instructions to actors, listed the motives behind the words of their parts. For example:

Text of the Play	Parallel Motives
Sophya: O, Chatsky, but I am glad you've come.	Tries to hide her confusion
Chatsky: You are glad, that's very nice; But gladness such as yours not easily one tells. It rather seems to me, all told, That making man and horse catch cold I've pleased myself and no one else.	Tries to make her feel guilty by teasing her. Aren't you ashamed of yourself! Tries to force her to be frank.
Liza: There, sir, and if you'd stood on the same landing here Five minutes, no, not five ago You'd heard your name clear as clear. You say, Miss! Tell him it was so.	Tries to calm him. Tries to help Sophya in a difficult situation.
Sophya: And always so, no less, no more. No, as to that, I'm sure you can't reproach me.	Tries to reassure Chatsky. I am not guilty of anything!
Chatsky: Well, let's suppose it's so. Thrice blessed who believes. Believing warms the heart. [A. Griboedov, *Woe from Wit,* Act I]	Let us stop this conversation; etc.

   To understand another's speech, it is not sufficient to understand his words—we must understand his thought. But even that is not enough—we must also know its motivation. No psychological analysis of an utterance is complete until that plane is reached.

Consider this: Rereading a difficult passage

Does reading the Vygotsky text come to you as easily as reading the Hemingway short story? Or is it more demanding? With each successive reading, more and more can come to light. Reread the Vygotsky passage, keeping in mind that we have here an excerpt from a much longer work as well as a translation into English of a Russian text written some years ago, and that Vygotsky is attempting to represent the elusive, inaccessible relationship between thought and language. How does he do it? Note the ways he makes connections. Note the language he uses to talk about language, the metaphors he relies on. Thoughts "hide behind the words." Thoughts are under the words: "subtexts." Thoughts are like "clouds shedding a shower of words." Finally, he says, to understand words, we must reach the "plane" of motivation. Throughout, Vygotsky struggles to make observable that which is, ultimately, inferential.

"Every sentence that we say in real life has some kind of subtext, a thought hidden behind it."

How do Vygotsky's words strike you? Do you agree with him that understanding words is not enough—that we must also try to understand thoughts and purposes, and what he calls the "*affective-volitional*" basis of our words—the desires, needs, interests, and wishes that drive the words? Would you agree that every sentence we utter, then, has its affective-volitional interior, that every sentence we write has its subtext? That in reading as in speaking, we try to understand text and subtext, the said and the unsaid?

A Stanislavsky exercise

Take this short passage from Eugene O'Neill's play *Long Day's Journey Into Night*. This is the opening scene of the play, with the husband, Tyrone, speaking to his wife, Mary. On a sheet of paper, write down what you guess to be the parallel motives of their speech—even though you have only this brief scene to consider:

Tyrone: You're a fine armful now, Mary, with those twenty pounds you've gained.

Mary: I've gotten too fat, you mean, dear. I really ought to reduce.

Tyrone: None of that, my lady! You're just right. We'll have no talk of reducing. Is that why you ate so little breakfast?

Mary: So little? I thought I ate a lot.

Tyrone: You didn't. Not as much as I'd like to see, anyway.

Mary: Oh you! You expect everyone to eat the enormous breakfast you do. No one else in the world could without dying of indigestion.

Tyrone: I hope I'm not as big a glutton as that sounds. But thank God, I've kept my appetite and I've the digestion of a young man of twenty, if I am sixty-five.

Mary: You surely have, James. No one could deny that.

Now consider this: How would you read the same dialogue if you had one of the following behind-the-scene pieces of information:

1. The wife is sincere, the husband is not.
2. The husband is sincere, the wife is not.
3. They are both being sarcastic.
4. The play is a parody of a soap opera.
5. The husband intends to murder the wife.

Do you think O'Neill had a sharp ear for the way people talk? (Consider your own eavesdropping activities.) The text of a play is not an actual transcript of the ways in which people actually talk in real life; even so, it is the task of the playwright and of the actors to convince an audience that the dialogue is lifelike. Do you think O'Neill's text actually helps actors to sound like real people?

Words convey only so much. Sometimes the match between the said and the unsaid is close. You say, "I'm thirsty," and you mean that you want a glass of water. You've just come in from a hard day at work and you are, literally, thirsty for some H_2O. Sometimes the match between the said and the unsaid or intended is much more complicated: A simple "I'm thirsty" could mean that you are thirsty for "life" or that you are a wife or husband waiting to be served by your spouse! "I'm thirsty, dear," the wife says as she slides into an easy chair after a hard day at work, and what she intends is that her husband, who has spent the day at home minding the children, should get her a cocktail. She wants the drink . . . and his attention. Children are using words in a similar way when they open the refrigerator door, stand before it, and mumble, "I'm thirsty," or "I'm hungry," hoping that Mom will produce a ready-made sandwich for them. Actual meanings rely on situations, on contexts, on the moment of utterance, on who's talking to whom, on negotiations between people, and on the often elusive and mysterious motives behind our behaviors.

In reading texts, then, where all you have is the page before you, the demands being made of you, the reader, are often weighty. Every text—from newspaper reporting to Shakespeare's plays—invites interpretation and negotiations of meaning, as you interact with the page.

Try this:

Go back now to Dave Barry's essay "Historians We're Not" on page 3. Read the first paragraph aloud in at least two different ways: first seriously and then mock seriously, or first matter-of-factly and then overdramatically, etc. How would you characterize the parallel motives of Barry's text? Which of your performances best represents your understanding of those motives? How so?

EXERCISES IN EXPECTATIONS

Try this:

1. Read the following texts, which are all beginnings of selections you will find in *Negotiations*. Read aloud, first, without feeling an obligation to "do" anything *with* or *to* these passages except to perform them, so as to "hear" the sounds of the

text. See if you can find a partner, who will offer at least one other performance, and then compare notes.

Remember: the "tone" of a text is your rendition of the text. It doesn't "sound" except through the tone of your own voice.

2. After you have heard the texts, write down quickly in your notebooks your expectations of what you anticipate will follow in each case. What *kinds* of texts do you expect—fiction, nonfiction, newspaper article, essay, etc., and what do you expect the texts to be about.

3. Now reread. Which words in each *triggered* your expectations—one way or another? Which words are charged positively or negatively? For example, look again at selection 8:

It was in Burma, a sodden morning of the rains. A sickly light, like yellow tinfoil, was slanting over the high walls into the jail yard.

Here is one reader's reaction:

The big trigger word for me comes right at the end: *jail yard*. On rereading everything now gravitates toward that—sodden, rains, sickly, high wall. All are charged negatively. Burma is an alien place for me—rains and floods and heat. Key word is "it"—what's it? Not very pleasant at all. Suffocation. I don't know if this is fiction or nonfiction. I do know that something is going to happen. This is the setting for something bad to happen. Something, probably, to a prisoner in the jail yard. Everything closed in—tight, no escape. Things building up.

Beginnings:

1. Many deplorable features of modern life, irrationalism, nationalism, idolization of mass-feeling and mass-opinion may be traced back to the Romantic reaction against the Enlightenment and its Polite learning. . . .

2. Knowing that Mrs. Mallard was afflicted with a heart trouble, great care was taken to break to her as gently as possible the news of her husband's death.

3. When I'm in New York but feeling lonely for Wyoming I look for the Marlboro ads in the subway. What I'm aching to see is horseflesh, the glint of a spur, a line of distant mountains, brimming creeks, and a reminder of the ranchers and cowboys I've ridden with for the last eight years.

4. That night our mother went to the shop and she didn't come back. Ever. What happened? I don't know. My father also had gone away one day and never come back; but he was fighting in the war. We were in the war, too, but we were children, we were like our grandmother and grandfather, we didn't have guns.

5. If you go to Antigua as a tourist, this is what you will see. If you come by aeroplane, you will land at the V.C. Bird International Airport. Vere Cornwall (V.C.) Bird is the Prime Minister of Antigua. You may be the sort of tourist who would wonder why a Prime Minister would want an airport named after him—why not a school, why not a hospital, why not a great public monument?

6. The scrub grass glistened in the sun; swirls of dust on the mound blew into the pitcher's eye and the manager came out of the dugout with a Kleenex. Time was called, and the catcher took advantage of it to take his allergy medicine. The left fielder left the field to deliver a handful of dandelions to his mother in the stands, and the chunky third baseman looked wistfully toward the hot dog truck in foul territory.

7. "Women's language" is that pleasant (dainty?), euphemistic, never-aggressive way of talking we learned as little girls. Cultural bias was built into the language we were allowed to speak, the subjects we were allowed to speak about, and the ways we were spoken of. Having learned our linguistic lesson well, we go out in the world, only to discover that we are communicative cripples—damned if we do and damned if we don't.

8. It was in Burma, a sodden morning of the rains. A sickly light, like yellow tinfoil, was slanting over the high walls into the jail yard.

9. I stand here ironing, and what you asked me moves tormented back and forth with the iron.

"I wish you would manage the time to come in and talk with me about your daughter. I'm sure you can help me understand her. She's a youngster who needs help and whom I'm deeply interested in helping."

VOICES

Try this:

Read, silently, the following poem by Gwendolyn Brooks. Now read the poem aloud as "bravado," with the voices sounding "cool." Then read the poem as "tragedy," with the voices sounding doomed.

We Real Cool
Gwendolyn Brooks

The Pool Players.
Seven at the Golden Shovel.

We real cool. We
Left school. We

Lurk late. We
Strike straight. We

Sing sin. We
Thin gin. We

Jazz June. We
Die soon.

The Welsh-American poet Denise Levertov experimented with line-end pauses; the stops at the ends of her lines represent what she claims was felt in her inner voice. Here is how she defines *inner voice*:

> What [inner voice] means to me is that a poet, a verbal kind of person, is constantly talking to himself, inside of himself, constantly approximating and evaluating and trying to grasp his experience in words. And the "sound" inside his head, of that voice is not necessarily identical with his literal speaking voice, nor is his inner vocabulary identical with that which he uses in conversation. At their best sound and words are song, not speech. The written poem is then a record of that inner song.
>
> "The Poet in the World"
> *New Directions,* 1960

Levertov breaks her lines, she says, "where the silences fall." Read her poem "O Taste and See" twice, first without stopping at the end of the lines, so that you run one line into the next, and then stopping fully at the end of each line. How would you characterize the differences?

Then read "We Real Cool" again, stopping completely at the end of each line. What happens to your reading?

O Taste and See
Denise Levertov

The world is
not with us enough.
O taste and see

the subway Bible poster said,
meaning **The Lord**, meaning
if anything all that lives
to the imagination's tongue,

grief, mercy, language,
tangerine, weather, to
breathe them, bite,
savor, chew, swallow, transform

into our flesh our
deaths, crossing the street, plum, quince,
living in the orchard and being

hungry, and plucking
the fruit.

ETHNOGRAPHERS AT WORK

Here, to end this chapter, are two readings: the first is a short story, "Anxiety," by Grace Paley. The second, "Joseph Patsah's Agenda," is a work of nonfiction by the anthropologist Hugh Brody, the opening chapter of his book *Maps and Dreams.* In each, we find instances of people observing people. Consider the two texts in light of the work of Chapter 2 on observing people, overhearing conversations, drawing inferences, considering the said and the unsaid, and on performing texts, particularly on the arousal and satisfaction of expectations. Paley, the writer of fiction, allows her narrator to "read" the conversations she overhears—and to enter into the conversations. Brody, the writer of nonfiction, enables us to consider some of the problems he considers as he begins gathering research in order to map the lands and ways of life of a small group of Beaver Indians who live in the direct path of a proposed oil pipeline in northeastern British Columbia. In both situations, we observe an observer observing strangers. What other similarities do you see between the two texts?

You might want to perform at least the opening of the Paley story in two or more ways, so as to hear possibilities for reading that you might miss when you read silently. Try reading the opening of Brody's text aloud, too. How would you characterize the voice of the narrator in this text? Is he a neutral observer?

Anxiety
Grace Paley

The young fathers are waiting outside the school. What curly heads! Such graceful brown mustaches. They're sitting on their haunches eating pizza and exchanging information. They're waiting for the 3 p.m. bell. It's springtime, the season of first looking out the window. I have a window box of greenhouse marigolds. The young fathers can be seen through the ferny leaves.

The bell rings. The children fall out of school, tumbling through the open door. One of the fathers sees his child. A small girl. Is she Chinese? A little. Up u-u-p, he says, and hoists her to his shoulders. U-u-p, says the second father, and hoists his little boy. The little boy sits on top of his father's head for a couple of seconds before sliding to his shoulders. Very funny, says the father.

They start off down the street, right under and past my window. The two children are still laughing. They try to whisper a secret. The fathers haven't finished their conversation. The frailer father is uncomfortable; his little girl wiggles too much.

Stop it this minute, he says.

Oink, oink, says the little girl.

What'd you say?

Oink, oink, she says.

The young father says What! three times. Then he seizes the child, raises her high above his head, and sets her hard on her feet.

What'd I do so bad, she says, rubbing her ankle.

Just hold my hand, screams the frail and angry father.

I lean far out the window. Stop! Stop! I cry.

The young father turns, shading his eyes, but sees. What? he says. His friend says, Hey? Who's that? He probably thinks I'm a family friend, a teacher maybe.

Who're you? he says.

I move the pots of marigold aside. Then I'm able to lean on my elbow way out into unshadowed visibility. Once, not too long ago, the tenements were speckled with women like me in every third window up to the fifth story, calling the children from play to receive orders and instruction. This memory enables me to say strictly, Young man, I am an older person who feels free because of that to ask questions and give advice.

Oh? he says, laughs with a little embarrassment, says to his friend, Shoot if you will that old gray head. But he's joking, I know, because he has established himself, legs apart, hands behind his back, his neck arched to see and hear me out.

How old are you? I call. About thirty or so?

Thirty-three.

First I want to say you're about a generation ahead of your father in your attitude and behavior toward your child.

Really? Well? Anything else, ma'am.

Son, I said, leaning another two, three dangerous inches toward him. Son, I must tell you that madmen intend to destroy this beautifully made planet. That the murder of our children by these men has got to become a terror and a sorrow to you, and starting now, it had better interfere with any daily pleasure.

Speech speech, he called.

I waited a minute, but he continued to look up. So, I said, I can tell by your general appearance and loping walk that you agree with me.

I do, he said, winking at his friend; but turning a serious face to mine, he said again, Yes, yes, I do.

Well then, why did you become so angry at that little girl whose future is like a film which suddenly cuts to white. Why did you nearly slam this little doomed person to the ground in your uncontrollable anger.

Let's not go too far, said the young father. She *was* jumping around on my poor back and hollering oink oink.

When were you angriest—when she wiggled and jumped or when she said oink?

He scratched his wonderful head of dark well-cut hair. I guess when she said oink.

Have you ever said oink oink? Think carefully. Years ago, perhaps?

No. Well maybe. Maybe.

Whom did you refer to in this way?

He laughed. He called to his friend, Hey Ken, this old person's got something. The cops. In a demonstration. Oink oink, he said, remembering, laughing.

The little girl smiled and said, Oink oink.

Shut up, he said.

What do you deduce from this?

That I was angry at Rosie because she was dealing with me as though I was a figure of authority, and it's not my thing, never has been, never will be.

I could see his happiness, his nice grin, as he remembered this.

So, I continued, since those children are such lovely examples of what may well be the last generation of humankind, why don't you start all over again, right from the school door, as though none of this had ever happened.

Thank you, said the young father. Thank you. It would be nice to be a horse, he said, grabbing little Rosie's hand. Come on Rosie, let's go. I don't have all day.

U-up, says the first father. U-up, says the second.

Giddap, shout the children, and the fathers yell neigh neigh, as horses do. The children kick their fathers' horsechests, screaming giddap giddap, and they gallop wildly westward.

I lean way out to cry once more, Be careful! Stop! But they've gone too far. Oh, anyone would love to be a fierce fast horse carrying a beloved beautiful rider, but they are galloping toward one of the most dangerous street corners in the world. And they may live beyond that trisection across other dangerous avenues.

So I must shut the window after patting the April-cooled marigolds with their rusty smell of summer. Then I sit in the nice light and wonder how to make sure that they gallop safely home through the airy scary dreams of scientists and the bulky dreams of automakers. I wish I could see just how they sit down at their kitchen tables for a healthy snack (orange juice or milk and cookies) before going out into the new spring afternoon to play.

Joseph Patsah's Agenda
Hugh Brody

The oldest man at the Reserve is Joseph Patsah. He lights a fire in the woods with all the precision and attention to detail that is the untroubled self-consciousness of those who, with age, are resolved that what they represent be respected. He selects each piece of wood, pauses before placing it in the flame; pauses to look at it, frozen for an instant in some thought about its suitability or texture or species. It is easy to feel impatient with this pace and attentiveness to detail, with its touches of zeal, even fanaticism. Easy to be impatient, that is, until you remember what fire signifies to hunters of the sub-Arctic forest: fires and walking are the two ways to keep warm—clothes are light—and the old cannot always walk long enough or fast enough to keep out the cold. Excellence with fires is essential. Joseph Patsah does not flaunt his skill.

No one could fail to notice Joseph's standing in his community. Dealings with him (as with the elderly in many societies) are marked by a jocular respect, a celebration of an old man's importance and authority. To tease the elderly is to show that you are on terms of happy intimacy with your own heritage. It shows that you are glad to be a part of your society. Everyone, except his own children, calls Joseph by his nickname "Callan." And from time to time the young men call on his authority: Is this as far as the fence rails should extend? Is this the line along which to cut a horse's hooves? Do you ever find lynx on such and such a hillside?

I first met Joseph Patsah at his home on the Reserve. It was a cool but sunny day in late summer. The Reserve is sited in a wide valley, and the houses have been built on flat lands that abut a wide and fast-flowing river. In the far distance I could see the Rocky Mountains.

Thick stands of mixed woodland covered a succession of ridges that rose above the houses and shaped the wide river valley below. The poverty and violence so widely associated with northern Indian reserves were, at this first impression at least, eclipsed by the beauty of the setting.

Brian Akattah, the young man whom the Reserve had chosen as their local research worker and mapmaker, insisted that we should go and talk to Joseph. Everyone who comes here with any questions, with any concerns that are taken seriously, is soon taken to see Joseph Patsah. So we went to his home as the starting point of our work.

His house stands at the far end of the Reserve, near two other houses and a tiny dilapidated cabin. It is about a quarter of a mile from the main cluster of homes often referred to as "the village," or—with a sardonic grin—as "downtown." Joseph's place is a prefabricated, three-bedroom standard-issue government house. It sits a short distance from the edge of a small bluff, whose face is eroded by trails. The regular scurries of children on their way from home to the wide, scrubby bank of the river keep pebbles and small earth slides loose and shifting on it. Below the bluff the children hunt birds and rabbits with slingshots and borrowed .22 rifles and, in summer and early fall, pick basketfuls of berries. The slopes and bank are also marked by horses that roam towards the river and must be herded home when they are needed. The firmer trails on the bluff have side paths. Some lead nowhere in particular, others to springs that now spurt out of two- or three-inch pipes jammed into fissures where water once seeped out of the ground. None of the houses has running water. Trips to the piped springs are a recurrent task, mainly for women and children.

Beside Joseph's house is all the paraphernalia of an encampment, so much so that the house itself is diminished, and becomes a far less dismaying sight than if it were a home as such, a place to which domestic life is restricted. The appearance of poverty has its place in a more complicated system of life; Joseph's Reserve home is one of several camps, cabins, and accumulations of equipment that together are far more important than the condition, size, or furniture of the house we were now visiting.

As Brian Akattah and I approached, it was impossible not to be both apprehensive and impressed. A welcome from the Patsahs would amount to a welcome from most, if not all, of the community. We also knew that maps drawn by Joseph and his household members would represent the most significant account of the whole region's hunting and trapping patterns. Contact with him was going to be a test of the validity of the work. If Joseph thought it was a good idea to represent the needs and claims of the people as land-use maps, then the whole project would be endorsed.

The approach to the household is impressive because of the curious mixture of pleasure, surprise, and familiarity that flickers through the mind when suddenly you see evidence of ways of life that are supposedly survivals from ancient times, that resemble old photographs or ethnographic films. You think immediately of the word "traditional," which so quickly and easily blinds the eye with mythical images that prevent your seeing gun scabbards hung ready for use by the door, the sharpness of the axes, the bags of dried meat, a box of new beaver traps—the means of satisfying present-day cultural and economic needs. To look for and find the traditional at Joseph Patsah's home is to imply that it is an intriguing relic that does not serve real life—and that is far from the truth.

Joseph was sitting with two middle-aged men in the partial shelter of a tarpaulin stretched over a tent frame. At one side were the barely smoking ashes of a fire, and around the fireplace were spruce boughs on which people could sit or lie, warm and dry on the ground. No more than twenty yards from this sheltered area was a teepee, about ten feet high, with its irregular upside-down funnel of frame poles rising out of a covering of overlapped pieces of canvas and plastic. To the left of the shelter blazed a large fire over which was set a very simple frame for drying and smoking meat. This fire had been laid in such a way as to heat a large drum of water, behind which were three women using the hot water to wash clothes. These (I learned later) were Joseph's wife Liza, her mother Reza, and her daughter Shirley. On the boughs in front of the fire lay a middle-aged man, stretched on his back, his head resting on his cupped hands, his elbows slightly raised from the ground. Beyond the fire, in a small oval corral fenced with long, thin wooden rails, were several horses, squat, barrel-chested, and powerful looking: three browns, two greys, and a sandy-coloured colt.

Between the front of Joseph's house and the fire was a wide area littered with odds and ends of equipment and supplies. An amazing profusion: a pile of green poplar firewood felled in late summer when it is wet with sap, then cut into large blocks and left to dry; three or four upturned saddles, their horns to the ground and stirrups flopped sideways; blankets and canvas casually draped over pieces of gear as protection against weather; more saddles on a rail fixed between two trees; pails; axes; a pile of clothing ready for the wash; coils of rope; long ends of fraying string; empty oat sacks, which hunters hang across their shoulders or tie behind a saddle to make a lightweight pack; a shovel, interesting for its large homemade handle. Almost merged with the grass lay another level of less obvious and identifiable items, bits and ends and things. Initially, these were noticeable only in a cumulative way as a kind of texture or fuzz, part of an overall appearance. On closer to the ground inspection, it was possible to discern slivers of wood shaped to some purpose, fragments of metal or plastic, jettisoned close by but later to be found and used again, and scraps or strips of leather that can be turned into thongs to fix bridle lines and stirrups. It is this blur of stuff, this texture, that causes visitors to see dirt and untidiness where there is often in reality a minor store of all manner of spare parts. A combination of these odds and ends with the larger equipment, with the complex of shelters and buildings, with the fires, with the frames and spruce boughs—all these create the extraordinary and indefinable qualities of a camp, the combination of permanence and transience, the reconciled contradiction with which hunting, trapping, and fishing peoples confront and confound us.

In the centre of all this sat Joseph. As we approached, the man lying by the washing-water fire raised his head and turned with the least of movements to look at us. His face was wide and deeply lined. Even from a distance the lines were remarkable—great bands of parallel creases that ran from temple to jawbone. His expression was watchful but not unwelcoming. As we came closer, he rolled into a half-kneeling position, then, with a decisive precision, got up and walked towards Joseph as if to warn or consult or find some shelter—at least to be prepared for our intrusion. This was Atsin, one of Liza's older brothers.

Joseph himself seemed hardly to notice our arrival. Even when we were within a few yards he no more than glanced at us, then turned to rekindle the fire. Brian spoke about the maps he had undertaken to draw for his people. Joseph seemed not to hear. His face was impassive, almost rigid; his occasional looks hardly more than quick, sharp glances. Had it not been for these movements I might have thought him deaf or merely indifferent to our presence.

Suddenly, he jumped up and hurried from the shelter to the house. It seemed that Joseph Patsah had rejected our visit. But Brian sat down by the fire, as at ease as could be, either impervious to rejection or content that all was well. Atsin meanwhile took up the axe that Joseph had been using and began to split firewood, first into narrow pieces and then along about four inches of their length, until every piece bore a splayed fringe that would burn with all the quick heat of so many matchsticks. The speed and precision with which he could wield a large axe to such intricate effect was spellbinding. As Atsin used the fringed kindling to blaze the fire, Joseph reappeared with a table. They had turned the shelter into a work place, and I was told to unroll the maps we carried with us and to lay them out on the table. Large topographical map sheets are cumbersome and difficult to align. With their maze of contour lines and streams, they are also hard to decipher. As I arranged and rearranged the sheets, Brian and I explained the work and the maps as best we could. I was uncertain about both Joseph's and Atsin's reactions to us, and wished to be as reassuring and clear as possible.

But there was little need for explanations. Joseph had his own agenda and his own explanations to give. He stood by the table, looked at the map, and located himself by identifying the streams and trails that he used. Periodically he returned to the map as a subject in its own right, intrigued by the pattern of contours, symbols, and colours and perhaps also by his recognition of the work that had brought us to his home. But if the map had any real importance for him, it seemed to be through its evocation of other times and other places. He looked at it with an intent silence, as if poised with a weapon to strike some prey.

Joseph's eyes, softly opaque with age, were startlingly attentive. He had not only the expertise but also the authority of his eighty-some years. But his composure and eloquence were not those of an old man; they expressed the completeness and distinctiveness of a culture. Joseph Patsah has always lived by hunting, trapping, and fishing, and has always depended upon the demanding conventions of an oral tradition. He had many things to say about his way of life, his society's needs, and he said them with graceful and cautious circumlocutions. His presence and manner caused the map to fade into the background.

It is difficult, perhaps impossible, to render Joseph's speech into written English. It is so firmly rooted in oral and Athapaskan modes as to defy a written version. As if this were not a source of enough difficulty, he also likes to speak to outsiders in English—an English that comes with a richness of unexpected rhythms, an ungrammatical shape, and with hesitancies and gestures that wonderfully overcome limitations of vocabulary. It is difficult, therefore, to do even remote justice to all he said as he looked at the map, while we sat on the spruce boughs by the fire, drinking mugs of tea.

He spoke first of all about his Daddy—the incongruity of the word made extreme by the unselfconscious and strong emphasis Joseph gave to it. "Daddy, he first came here nineteen-twelve. First comes to this place, way down Ospika. Nineteen-twelve up this river, pretty hard that time. I bet you not many people then. Sometime Daddy work like white man, panning gold. I learn all that, pan gold. . . ." The reminiscence thus spoken, and accompanied by an occasional search on the map for Ospika, the creeks tributary to the Midden River, or perhaps the mountains through which the family had travelled, slowly established his way of life. Since such poor justice to the power of the spoken word is done by the writing of it, especially verbatim, I give here only the main outline of Joseph's narrative.

For twenty or thirty years, around the turn of the century, moose populations in northwestern Canada were low. Moose, like caribou and many other herbivorous mammals, experience a long-term population cycle that is little understood. In years when other resources were not readily available, the scarcity of moose used to bring extreme hardship to many Indian hunting bands. (The buffalo, whose northern range once brought them into lands hunted by the Patsah family, had by the 1880s been more or less exterminated.) After several years of struggle and near starvation, Joseph's family moved north and west, higher into the foothills of the Rockies. Patsah's people had long regarded these higher foothills as a sort of meat bank on which they could draw when the usual game resources or hunting patterns failed. Now they hoped that moose, along with sheep, mountain goats, and caribou, would provide a more substantial and perhaps a permanent subsistence base.

So Joseph—then about fourteen years old—went with his family up the Midden River, then along the creeks and streams that cut routes through the edges of the mountains. They moved with their horses, hunting and fishing as they travelled, until they came to the Bluestone River. Here they camped with as much sense of permanence, as clear an idea of having arrived, and with as complete a feeling of change as are consistent with a way of life that depends on a perpetual readiness to move. They had arrived, they felt, because here they imagined they would be able once again to establish the whole year's round of camps and trading journeys in a new hunting territory. The family looked at the Bluestone and adjacent creeks, the Midden valley, the sharp and thinly wooded foothills not far beyond with confidence, hope, and determination. Within these valleys, forests, and uplands, surely there must be moose and mule deer. Higher still, within a day's walk or ride, there would be caribou, sheep, marmots—to say nothing of the rainbow trout, Dolly Varden, grayling, and Rocky Mountain whitefish (Joseph likes to recite names in lists) to be caught in many of the eddying elbows and pools of all those creeks. This area and its resources were new, but not entirely unknown. The Patsahs were still at the edge of the family's old hunting territory, their fallback, their bank vaults. They had moved from a centre to a periphery; but what was for them a periphery was for other Beaver Indian families the centre. They would now share resources, because they already shared a system that made it possible to move without fear of conflicts.

Yet Joseph's Daddy, along with the others, sought a confirmation of the new area's potential. This was done by means of dream prophecy and the erection of a medicine cross. They stripped a tall straight pine of its bark and affixed a crosspiece about four-fifths of the way along its length, then attached smaller crosses to the crosspiece—one at each end. They nailed a panel, also in cross formation, close to the base of the pole. Even when its base was sunk into the ground, this cross, or set of crosses, was twice the height of a tall man. When it was in place, Patsah and others hung skin clothing and medicine bundles from the main crosspiece, and on the panel near the base they inscribed "all kinds of fancy"—drawings of animals that had figured in the people's dreams, animals of the place that would make themselves available for the hunt.

The night the cross was completed, an augury came to one of the elders in a dream. A young cow moose, moving to the Patsah camp from the Bluestone Creek area, circled the base of the cross, then went off in the direction from which she had come. Two days after this dream, hunters discovered the tracks of a young cow moose, and, following these, recognized them to be the tracks of the dream animal. The tracks led to the cross, circled it, then returned to the Bluestone. The dream prediction had been auspiciously fulfilled. The new area would provide abundantly.

Despite this sign, after a while Joseph's father decided to return to the old heartland of his hunting area, and he moved once again towards the Ospika River. Joseph, along with some others, was opposed to the return and remained for the rest of his life in the lands where the cross had been set. However, Bluestone Creek and the location of the cross itself—a low, level stretch of woodland between the Bluestone and the Midden—did not come to be the most productive and evocative of the several locales that comprised this new territory. About ten miles northwest of the cross is another tributary of the Midden—the Sechin River. Sechin is a Beaver word, and means "to make a kill when hunting." This small, beautiful stream flows out of the very edge of the Rockies in a succession of bends and rapids. Both the Indians and local Whites know it by an English name—Quarry—a name that spills over to include the land around it. This area is a source of plenty and strength. To Joseph, his family, and many others of the Reserve, Quarry means home.

As Joseph Patsah told his story, he searched the map until he found a particular bend in a river. Here a hunter, standing on a steep bank, can look out onto open flats and easily spot moose and beaver, and sometimes, with a long shot from above, can even make a kill. He sought the exact place where, in September or October, it is easy to catch fat rainbow trout. He traced the length of a trail that each year he and others used to travel from a spring beaver-hunting camp to the trading post at Hudson's Hope. He satisfied himself that we understood the exact distance between the Reserve (a spot where he used to camp for part of each summer) and the best of his winter cabins. And at times, as he talked, Joseph made use of the map in the most general, even abstract way: with no more than a slight flutter of a gesture he established Quarry as his. At different times he said, "This land, all this my country"; "I bet you every place this country my country"; "No white man this place."

It was often not clear, perhaps not even intended to be clear, whether or not his words floated back to some former time or were addressed to the realities of Quarry now. It was too soon to understand the subtleties of Joseph Patsah's sense of time. But at least, in this first conversation, centered on his own arrival and his claim to the place, he had introduced us to Quarry. He had brought us as far as the cross.

Every now and then, Joseph broke into his story and, by way of a parenthesis seemingly at odds with the story's place in the past, remarked that we should go to Quarry. With a gesture towards the northwest he said, "Sometime we go up Quarry. Maybe tomorrow. Someday." Such a statement was an invitation and a recognition that the place, with all its importance and meaning, is still there. Joseph emphasized this in one of his asides by adding, "It's no good in these flats. Better go up Quarry. Live up there, die up there. No damn good here. Home is that place."

He had established Quarry and had located the whole Quarry area on a map. Mapping as such was now completed, and Joseph made this clear by a decisive movement. He stood up, pushed back his shoulders a couple of times, as though to say that it was time to break out of this cramped business. So he stretched, at the same time looking into an out-of-focus distance. The meeting was over, but his thought continued: he seemed to contemplate in his mind's eye the place he had established on the map. Just as we were packing up, helping to move the table back into the house, removing, insofar as possible, at least the physical disruption this mapping business had caused, Joseph turned to me and said, "We'll go to Quarry. I'll show you the cross. Good country. You'll see."

Joseph is an old man. However compelling his words, however ageless his manner, as soon as we had left his encampment-home, some of the magic evaporated. I kept thinking that perhaps he had missed the point. In the course of talking, and prompted by Brian, Joseph had shown his hunting, trapping, and fishing areas on the map; had marked, with coloured felt pens, all the places he had lived during a long life. Yet he had drawn circles and lines in an absent-minded way. As an elder, he had spoken beyond us, addressing the richness of another culture, another spiritual domain, even another time altogether. Perhaps he had not sought to understand the work. He did not question its purpose, still less its technique. When he marked the map he did so with a seeming indifference. At the times he sought precision, it was usually to locate some exact spot in order to digress even further from the job I thought that we had come to do. If he focussed our attention on Quarry, with all its historic meaning to him, this might nonetheless be tangential to present realities. Maybe his concerns were locked in memories, with few links to the importance of the land or its resources for people of today. These thoughts eroded the confidence that Joseph had inspired in me as he talked. A remark by Brian Akattah then added to my unease: "Old man, Joseph. Old-timer." There is ambiguity in the use of these terms. Old-timers are sources of wisdom—but old men? Who knows? Perhaps Brian hoped to explain away Joseph's manner as understandable but senile.

Brian did not, however, seem discouraged. Joseph's welcome and words had given him enough confidence to go directly to another house. And even my pessimistic thoughts lasted only as long as it took to walk from the shelter to the tiny cabin that stands no more than a hundred yards from Joseph's, perched tight on the edge of the bluff. This turned out to be Atsin's place. He had gone home midway through the talk with Joseph and somehow must have known he would be visited next. By the time we came in, he had already cleared the floor space, which is to say the whole space, and had made a surface for the maps—a sheet of old cardboard.

There, in the darkness of a cabin lit only by the bit of light that shone through a tiny frame window, with three people crowded shoulder to shoulder on the floor, Atsin began to explain how he had lived. Stories. And a periodic, almost eruptive reference to the impossibility of such explanation: "Crazy white man. He never understands. Too many, too many." By which Atsin meant that he could never, even in a hundred interviews, mark down all the places he had hunted and travelled. Yet he tried, for he was in fact eager to show how comprehensively he knew his land. He was proud, also, of the immense work and of the achievement such detailed and extensive knowledge represents.

Soon after Atsin had begun his explanation, Joseph and three other men appeared at the cabin doorway. All except Joseph joined Atsin on the floor and watched as he drew his hunting areas. But Joseph just stood at the doorway, listening. Then, taking a few steps inside, and standing just behind Atsin's crouched and kneeling body, Joseph began to speak. This time he did not address the map, or his past, or make reference to specific places. Nor did he speak to any one person. Instead he addressed the room, his people, the issue. In a mixture of Beaver and English, in broken, almost staccato phrases, with all the pauses and gestures that are essential to anyone who speaks in a language not his own, he affirmed the importance of the maps and the mapping. It was political discourse, and had touches of exhortation.

There is no longer time to wait, he said. There is no more room for the white man's intrusions. Now the people have to stand up and defend what has always been theirs. There must be no fooling around, no bullshit. There must be no failure to take advantage of whatever opportunities may now be offered. If Indians are going to continue to be Indians in this place, in these places, in this whole region, then their presence must be made known to everyone, everywhere. This, as he understood it, is the point of messing around with maps; this, he insisted, is the reason for speaking at length and with great truthfulness. Perhaps young people do not understand, perhaps some people of all ages do not want to understand. He knew, however, that the time had come for the Beaver Indians, for all Indians, to insist on the land, a right to its use, and on their right to protect it. The land, using the land in the proper way, is inseparable from the people who live there.

It was clear, finally and unequivocally, from the way that everyone in that dark and ragged cabin listened, from the respectful stillness, from their occasional grunted agreements, that Joseph spoke as an old-timer and elder, not as an old man. He finished what he had to say, once again, by insisting that he would take us to Quarry. A directive seemed to have gone out, at least to the few people there, and perhaps through them to other homes and reserves, that everyone should use the map-making in whatever way he could, to show his own Quarry River. Whatever mapping and researching might be carried out, Joseph Patsah had drawn up his own agenda.

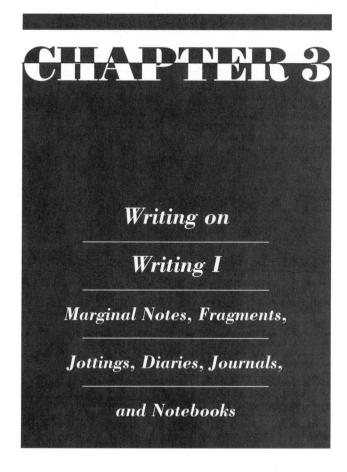

CHAPTER 3

Writing on

Writing I

Marginal Notes, Fragments,

Jottings, Diaries, Journals,

and Notebooks

NOTES IN THE MARGINS

Silence is one way of interacting with a text. So is performance. So is conversation—with friends, with other students in your class, and with yourself. You can also react to texts as *writers,* exploring various ways of considering and reflecting upon the texts you read. These next three chapters will offer suggestions for writing on writing, for intervening in texts, *negotiating* with what is there on the page—submitting, resisting, compromising— coming into dialogue with the text, and exploring differences. Saying *yes and no. Either . . . or. Yes, but . . . . Maybe.*

   Buy yourself a notebook that you can carry with you, preferably a hardback one so that you won't feel tempted to tear out the pages. This can be a notebook for you to use for writing on writing—trying to capture your reactions as you read; for writing on whatever else you choose; and for keeping a diary or journal of your personal doings and thinking, if you so choose. There are no formulas here, no rules to follow when you write on writing. You can experiment and play; you can try to do what other writers do—imitating, "stealing," playing one text off against another. You can "talk back" to the texts you read.

   You can also write in the margins, jot ideas down on note cards, write on your word processor. I once knew a man who papered an entire study with his note cards on the readings he was doing in order to write a book of his own. There came a point where he'd papered over the windows, too, and blocked out the sunlight. His writings on writing took over his life.

Here's a page of my marginal notes and underlinings on the first page of Virginia Woolf's short story "Moments of Being." It's a story that still puzzles me. I keep changing my mind about it; it's still an open door. Fairly soon, I'll have to find a clean copy, because my notes, made at various times over the years, are beginning to obscure Woolf's words!

MOMENTS OF BEING

"SLATER'S pins have no points—don't you always find that?" said Miss Craye, turning round as the rose fell out of Fanny Wilmot's dress, and Fanny stooped, with her ears full of the music, to look for the pin on the floor.

The words gave her an extraordinary shock, as Miss Craye struck the last chord of the Bach fugue. Did Miss Craye actually go to Slater's and buy pins then, Fanny Wilmot asked herself, transfixed for a moment. Did she stand at the counter waiting like anybody else, and was she given a bill with coppers wrapped in it, and did she slip them into her purse and then, an hour later, stand by her dressing table and take out the pins? What need had she of pins? For she was not so much dressed as cased like a beetle compactly in its sheath, blue in winter, green in summer. What need had she of pins—Julia Craye—who lived, it seemed, in the cool glassy world of Bach fugues, playing to herself what she liked, and only consenting to take one or two pupils at the Archer Street College of Music (so the Principal, Miss Kingston, said) as a special favour to herself, who had "the greatest admiration for her in every way." Miss Craye was left badly off, Miss Kingston was afraid, at her brother's death. Oh, they used to have such lovely things, when they lived at Salisbury, and her brother Julius was, of course, a very well-known

103

[Handwritten marginal notes surround the text, including: "Beginning of Miss Craye's words.", "Fanny doesn't answer—she's transfixed.", "why???", "what did Craye say ???", "= a perfectly ordinary passing—the time of day comment such as 'how are you' or 'how's the weather?'", "What's going on?", "Interesting metaphor: how does it apply to a beetle? Specimen beetles are cased in cardboard", "Such English words: greatest admiration... such lovely things... coppers.", "Why all the fuss about pins! She's talking about straight pins, I guess."]

INNER STREAMS OF LANGUAGE

It's often said that we don't know what we think until we have said it aloud or written it down: Then we can "handle" it, try to hold it down. But often, as you know, even if we write, there's no guarantee that things will be finally settled. Say you write a "difficult" letter—something you've wanted to say to someone for a long time, something you *need* to say, but haven't been able to. You get "it" down on the page. *It* feels right one minute, you think you've got *it,* said *it,* you think you'll send *it,* get *it* off your chest, out of your mind. Then you read *it* over and you are aghast. *It* doesn't do *it* at all. How could you ever . . . ? The tone is all wrong: *it* sounded one way in your head and now when you read *it* to yourself, you hear *it* differently. You tear *it* up and start all over. But you still haven't realized at all what's in your mind. You're still far away. The *it* still eludes you! (Have you ever considered how often we rely on the elusive *it?*) You put the letter in your "unsent letter" drawer and are relieved that you didn't mail it. Maybe another time. Maybe someday. The problems remain unresolved. Open. Sometimes our own writings are like that. They persist—they remain open, unresolved—but because they're written down, we may have the illusion that they are finished, over.

Other texts, of course, are finished, resolved, complete, for both writer and reader. Once we get the words down, we feel the problems solved, the questions answered. We feel as if we have matters under control. In both situations, as writers, we're *negotiating* with the stuff in our minds, trying to realize it through words.

Consider this:

Have you experienced any real-life situations or read any texts or seen any movies that are still "open," that nag you because you haven't closed the door on them—texts with an unresolved ending, such as "The Lady and the Tiger," or texts with unresolved ideas that you are wondering about, questioning, reconsidering? Make a note of them in your notebook, and consider what it is that keeps *irritating* you. Keep track of *irritations.*

Try this:

Write a "forbidden" letter—one that attempts to say the unsaid, what you've been grappling with for a long time, one that you don't necessarily want to send but want to use to get things off your chest, to try to capture the *it* that's been an irritant for some time. It may be to a parent or a boss or a friend or to a public figure.

Don't edit. Let the words come.

After you've finished, let it settle for a while. And then reread it. Does it do?

Do you want to send it?

Consider now Vygotsky's comments on what he calls "inner speech":

Inner speech is not the interior aspect of external speech—it is a function in itself. It still remains speech, i.e., thought connected with words. But while in external speech thought is embodied in words, in inner speech words die as they bring forth thought. Inner speech is to a large extent thinking in pure meanings. It is a dynamic, shifting, unstable thing, fluttering between word and thought, the two more or less stable, more or less firmly delineated components of verbal thought. . . .

Thought and Language

Whatever we attend to—whether we're just sitting quietly and reading, listening to music, working or taking a walk, or talking to others—we're moving in and out of the dynamic, shifting, unstable "flutterings" of our own minds. Even if we're saying things out loud, inside there remains much that is *unsaid,* either because we can't get hold of it or because we think it's totally irrelevant (to what we think is going on) or because it sounds like silly babble inside our heads or because it's dangerous. Maybe if we said what was really going on inside our heads, we'd find ourselves in deep trouble. We've learned how to edit out what's inside, and to speak what we feel to be appropriate. We cut things off, stop them in our tracks, close the door on what we know will irritate or hurt or startle.

Try this:

Try now to hold your mind perfectly and absolutely "still," for two minutes. Concentrate on only one topic or issue or question or word or image or person. Hold it still . . . steady . . . make it stable. Concentrate.

What happens? Can you do it?

Compare notes with a friend.

Try this:

For two minutes, *don't* think of white cats.

In Chapter 1, we looked at how we bring ourselves to what we read: our fundings, our memories and associations, our predictions for the future, our wishes and desires. Our minds are continually reacting to what happens around us and inside of us, to what William James called "the buzzing, booming mass of sensations" that explode around us and in us a million miles a minute. We're always monitoring two things at once, always living both outside and inside.

Sometimes the two match. At other times, they clash, and we have to hold the inner stuff in, close the door on it. Vygotsky was convinced that the greatest production of language occurs inside rather than outside. Tapping into the mind's fluttering, to that continuous inner stream, then, enables us to "see" some of what's going on in the "unsaid" of our own minds. Sigmund Freud used as evidence for his theories of the unconscious the "leakages" from this inner stream of language—our dreams, nightmares, and slips of the tongue. And the writer James Joyce, among others, tried to represent the constant flow of inner speech through what has come to be known, in William James's words, as "stream of consciousness."

Try this:

Keep your notebook and pen ready by your bed. Upon waking, try to represent a dream you have just awakened from. Try to "capture" the images, voices, narrative, actions fluttering in your mind. Don't worry about writing in whole sentences. Just get the stuff down on the page.

• • •

In my classes, I often ask students to tap into their streams of inner speech by *writing* very quickly in all kinds of ways, to experiment with language, and particularly, with writing on writing.

I ask students to write on the spot, often about a text they've had time to read before the class, but sometimes I put the pressure on and ask them to write about a text they've *just* read or heard in class. Then we use their writing for our talk. There's no doubt that there's tension in such situations: the clock ticks; the pens scratch; you look at your neighbor. She has written more than you have! But, through practice, you'll be surprised at how much you can get down on the page in such moments of quiet, when you can be "alone" in the classroom.

Here are some sentences students wrote in class after they'd had a chance to put on a performance of "Hills Like White Elephants":

- I still don't understand what's going on. What operation?
- I'm furious. Hemingway is a chauvinist. He hates women. And this is just another blatant example.
- The American is a creep.
- That's the way people really talk.
- That reminds me of a friend of mine and how her boyfriend didn't understand why she was so upset.
- If that were me, I would have socked him in the nose.
- She should just leave him.
- That reminds me of a bad relationship I had. We kept talking to cover over the cracks.
- The waitress should have hit him over the head.
- I hate men who treat women that way.
- The girl is really a whiner. She would drive me crazy.
- Why doesn't she say what she means?
- I was in Spain last summer, and it was really hot like that.
- I am still confused.
- Why is life always so complicated?
- I hate endings like that, where you don't know what's going to happen next. "She just smiled at him"; what the heck does that mean?
- I think this is a story about the failure of relationships because of the failure of communication.
- So what about the title—what's this about "Hills Like White Elephants"?
- I like that line where she says, "We could have the whole world." Sometimes I feel like that.
- I like it when she tells him to please please please please please please stop talking.

- There's a lot that they're not saying. They keep saying that everything's fine, but I don't think it's fine at all.
- That waitress really saw a lot, didn't she? But could she understand English?
- There's no ending.
- I wonder where they'd been—they had lots of labels on their suitcases. Maybe he had a wife somewhere and was running away from her and didn't really want to get involved.
- The girl seemed really young, and the American seemed older. Maybe he was her father.
- There's no moral to this story.

Try this:

Look again at the responses above: how do you "read" the readings?
How would you classify these comments? How many "piles" would you make? Let's divide them into two groups:

Autobiographical responses: Here the focus is on the reader and her reaction to the text. (That reminds me . . . . If that were me . . . . Sometimes I feel like that . . . . I am still confused . . . .)

Textual responses: Here the focus is on the text. (There's no moral. . . . This is a story about . . . . What operation?)

In some cases, a particular *part* of the text evoked the autobiographical response. ("I like that line where she says, 'We could have the whole world.' Sometimes I feel like that.")

Try this:

1. Reread Paley's short (short) story, "Anxiety," on page 49. Write quickly your reactions to it. Give yourself time (about ten minutes) to get things down on the page. Don't edit or strain.

2. Now consider these questions: Did the narrator actually break into the conversation? Did she imagine such a break-in? Find evidence in the text to support both positions.

3. Create a situation where a narrator overhears a conversation and then breaks in. You might want to use one of the conversations you overheard—where you were only a spectator and not a participant. Or you might want to borrow Paley's situation of an adult mishandling a child. (We've all been witness to such scenes, haven't we—where we want to rush in and do better than we perceive the parent to be doing?)

KEEPING A NOTEBOOK

We can keep notebooks for all kinds of reasons. To write secrets. Make promises. Try to organize our lives, by seeing how things look on paper. Remember the big events of our lives, the extraordinary happenings, the once-in-a-lifetime moments: births, deaths, graduations, trips, loves. Remember the dailiness, the ordinary ways we live our lives: the music we listen to, the books we read, the movies we see, the work we do, the people we meet. To keep track, then, of the ordinary and the extraordinary. And to do so in a "safe place," where we can try out the many voices within ourselves without getting caught, without taking risks with others.

I've been a notebook keeper for twenty years or so. I began sometime in college when I didn't think that anyone understood how I was feeling about life. I was unhappy in love at that moment and needed to bare my soul to "someone." The safest, least dangerous place was the blank page. Those pages have long disappeared, but in the years since then, I've kept thirty or so notebooks—not in any orderly, scheduled ways. I made up the rules. I decided not to be a slave to the notebook, that I would be in control—that I'd write in my notebook only when I was moved to do so. There have been times that I have written nearly every day. And there have been times when months have slipped by without my writing a word. Recently, I sat down to reread my notebooks. And as I leafed through the hefty pile of various shaped and sized and colored tablets, spirals, looseleafs, and hardbound books I'd kept over the years, I realized that I use my notebooks for all manner of things:

Saying what I want to say but feel I can't

Rehearsing what I'm determined to say to others

Secrets

Promises

Lists

Jokes

Words I want to relish

Books I want to read

Dreams

Interpretations of dreams

Nightmares

Other people's words I want to remember (these are taken from books and from actual conversations)

Sentences that I like and my imitations of them

Observations of my children growing up: their conversations, our conversations, their odd, curious, surprising sayings, their discoveries

Reflections on reading

Ruminations on the state of the world, on history, politics, the news

Plots of stories I want to write

Images for poems I want to write

Plans for changing the world

Recipes

Journeys (I often write in cars, planes, trains, and in airports)

Vacations

Facts

First lines I might do something with one day

Questions

Answers

Memories

Keeping the notebooks, for me, is like keeping a messy drawer—an "anything drawer," where I can throw in screws and bolts, thumbtacks and envelopes, packets of seeds and spare keys. It's only when I reread that I find *patterns,* repetitions. Then I'm able to sort things out if I want to—to recognize cycles, preoccupations, rhythms, the things that keep recurring time after time, in some cases, year after year. In writing fast and carelessly, you can throw in anything you want. Later, you can reread and reflect on what you've written. The two acts are very different. As William Carlos Williams says, "Write carelessly, so that nothing that is not green will survive."

I recommend that you, yourself, keep a notebook—for you, the individual, and for you, the writer-reader in this course—and that as you read, you *also write:* all manner of things. For now, look again at the informal responses to "Hills Like White Elephants." "Read the patterns" to see what *kinds* of autobiographical and textual responses students have made to the story. Here are some possibilities for beginning to write your own reactions to what you read:

That reminds me . . .

If that were me . . .

She shouldn't have . . .

I don't understand . . .

What????

I wonder . . .

The story is about . . .

The title is . . .

What's happening between the lines . . .

HEMINGWAY'S WRITING ON WRITING

Hemingway was not, to my knowledge, a keeper of notebooks. Nor did he like to write or talk much about his own writing. But in letters to friends, and particularly to his publisher; in interviews; in his autobiographical sketches; and even in his fiction, he talked about his craft. Here are some bits and pieces from a collection of his writings on writing, *Ernest Hemingway on Writing,* edited by Larry W. Phillips:

> There's no rule on how it is to write. Sometimes it comes easily and perfectly. Sometimes it is like drilling rock and then blasting it out with charges.
>
>

To Charles Poore, 1953
Selected Letters

> I love to write. But it has never gotten any easier to do and you can't expect it to if you keep trying for something better than you can do.
>
>

To L. H. Brague, Jr., 1959
Selected Letters

> The hardest thing in the world to do is to write straight honest prose on human beings. First you have to know the subject; then you have to know how to write. Both take a lifetime to learn . . . .
>
>

By-Line, 1933

> All my life I've looked at words as though I were seeing them for the first time . . . .
>
>

to Mary Welsh, 1945
Selected Letters

> The most essential gift for a good writer is a built-in, shockproof, shitproof shit detector. This is the writer's radar and all great writers have it.
>
>

from George Plimpton,
"An Interview with Ernest Hemingway"
The Paris Review Spring 1958

> A writer without a sense of justice and of injustice would be better off editing the year book of a school for exceptional children than writing novels.
>
>

Ibid.

> I've seen the marlin mate and know about that. So I leave that out. I've seen a school (or pod) of more than fifty sperm whales in that same stretch of water and harpooned one nearly sixty feet in length and lost him. So I left that out. All the stories I know from the fishing village I leave out. But the knowledge is what makes the underwater part of the iceberg.
>
>

Ibid.

I sat in a corner with the afternoon light coming in over my shoulder and wrote in the notebook. The waiter brought me a *cafe creme* and I drank half of it when it cooled and left it on the table while I wrote. When I stopped writing I did not want to leave the river where I could see the trout in the pool, its surface pushing and swelling smooth against the resistance of the log-driven piles of the bridge. The story ["Big Two-Hearted River"] was about coming back from the war but there was no mention of the war in it.

A Moveable Feast, 1964

It was a very simple story called 'Out of Season' and I had omitted the real end of it which was that the old man hanged himself. This was omitted on my new theory that you could omit anything if you knew that you omitted and the omitted part would strengthen the story and make people feel something more than they understood.

Ibid.

. . . [S]ometimes when I was starting a new story and I could not get it going, I would sit in front of the fire and squeeze the peel of the little oranges into the edge of the flame and watch the sputter of value that they made. I would stand and look out over the roofs of Paris and think, "Do not worry. You have always written before and you will write now. All you have to do is write one true sentence. Write the truest sentence that you know." So finally I would write one true sentence, and then go on from there. It was easy because there was always one true sentence that I knew or had seen or had heard someone say. If I started to write elaborately, or like someone introducing or presenting something, I found that I could cut that scrollwork or ornament out and throw it away and start with the first true simple declarative sentence I had written.

Ibid.

I think you should learn about writing from everybody who has ever written that has anything to teach you.

to F. Scott Fitzgerald, 1925
Selected Letters

My attitude toward punctuation is that it ought to be as conventional as *possible.* The game of golf would lose a good deal if croquet mallets and billiard cues were allowed on the putting green. You ought to be able to show that you can do it a good deal better than anyone else with the regular tools before you have a license to bring in your own improvements.

to Horace Liveright, 1925
Selected Letters

Consider this:

I have not come across Hemingway commenting on the power of the adverb, but he has this to say about adjectives.

[Ezra Pound * was] . . . the man who had taught me to distrust adjectives as I would later learn to distrust certain people in certain situations.

A Moveable Feast

* Pound, an American poet living in Paris in the twenties, influenced Hemingway's writing and his thinking about writing.

• • •

Why do you suppose that Hemingway "distrusted" adjectives? What's there to distrust about adjectives? How would we read "Hills" had Hemingway inserted a few adjectives:

the (selfish) American and his (innocent) girlfriend

the (selfless) American and his (conniving) girlfriend

the (wonderful) American and his (beautiful) girlfriend

Consider this: Metaphors we live by

Hemingway's comments on what he knows and what he chooses to leave out have become a golden rule for countless young writers learning the craft. In one sense, he could be talking about the importance of *funding*—about knowing the world, and then, as a writer, selecting details that *don't* give the reader all that you know. That leaves work for the reader to do. Underneath the surface or between the lines, the "knowledge" is still there, though, lurking, like the "underwater part of the iceberg."

His iceberg metaphor intrigues me. With icebergs, there's more there than meets the eye. What is above the surface is relatively safe, but beneath the surface, the unsaid, the unseen, the hidden, the mysterious—that's another matter. Icebergs can be treacherous, fatal. How do you "read" the iceberg metaphor?

Here we have another water metaphor (see page 19), and another example of how metaphors work. Metaphors are not simply "poetic language" but ways of thinking. George Lakoff, a linguist, and Mark Johnson, a philosopher, in their book *Metaphors We Live By* argue that metaphors shape the ways we perceive, think, and act. Metaphors, they insist, are a good index to cultural values and beliefs.

How, for example, do you characterize love? Or time? Or life, itself? So often these abstract, elusive concepts are conceptualized through metaphor:

You're *wasting* my time.

My life is a *journey*.

Your life is a *quest*.

I could feel the *electricity* between us.

There were *sparks*.

So much of what is tacit, then, is metaphor: Lakoff and Johnson claim that one of the controlling metaphors of our lives is that argument is like war, to be won or lost. Read the first chapter from their book in Part II, page 419. In the meantime, try this:

Try this:

Jot down all the "argument is war" metaphors you can think of, and the water metaphors, too. I hope that your mind is now *streaming* with ideas!

Consider this:

Hemingway knew what he was leaving out—the "unsaid." Can we get to his "unsaid," to what he left out? Is that an impossibility?

Surely, it is. He's dead and gone, and even if he were here right next to us, we would still have difficulties with some of what he's saying, as well as with what he's not saying. Remember: as readers, the text becomes "ours"; we're the ones who realize and perform it into sense.

In some of his comments, Hemingway "sounds like" a moralist, standing on the top of the hill, and passing judgment: "A writer without a sense of justice and of injustice would be better off editing the year book of a school for exceptional children than writing novels." How else does Hemingway "sound" to you in his comments on writing? Do any of them speak to you about your own thinking on writing?

READING OTHERS' NOTEBOOKS AND DIARIES

Who keeps notebooks or diaries? Writers. Philosophers. Scientists. Artists. Ordinary people, like you and me. They write out of the ordinariness and the extraordinariness of their lives, out of cozy, safe tranquility, and out of the extreme situations: illness, war, imprisonment. Anne Frank, given a diary for her thirteenth birthday, saw it, as many teenagers do, as a "true friend" to whom she could tell everything. She addressed her imaginary friend, "Dear Kitty." "I hope," she says, "I shall to able to confide in you completely as I have never been able to do in anyone before, and I hope that you will be a great support and comfort to me." Her diary is one of the most extraordinary documents we have of human courage and growth during one of the most extreme periods of human suffering in history.

Often those who are confined—through illness or through imprisonment—hold on to a sense of the *normal* through paper and pen.

Queen Victoria kept a diary, so did Lee Harvey Oswald, the presumed assassin of John F. Kennedy. Charles Darwin kept an account of his voyage on *The Beagle.* Christa McAuliffe had planned to keep an account of her six-day journey aboard the ill-fated space shuttle *Challenger.* Samuel Pepys, famous for his diary, wrote 3,000 pages on the years 1660 to 1669. Pepys's account puts us in touch with the man and his times as no later historian could. He was there: he was a participant. Had he planned to have his diaries published? Probably not: he actually tried to conceal some of his more revealing entries by writing in a secret code.

Gwendolyn Fairfax in Oscar Wilde's play *The Importance of Being Earnest* has this to say about her diary: "I never travel without my diary. One should always have something sensational to read on the train." Her diary enabled her to reread herself! Cecily Cardew, another character in Wilde's play, kept a diary to keep track of "the wonderful secrets in my life. If I didn't write them down I should probably forget about them."

Secrets. Confidences. Making rules. Here is what Leo Tolstoy promises to his diary:

> I wrote down a lot of rules all of a sudden and wanted to follow them all, but I wasn't strong enough to do so. But now I want to set myself one rule only, and to add another one to it

only when I've got used to following that one. The first rule which I prescribe is as follows. No. 1. Carry out everything you have resolved must be carried out. *I haven't carried out this rule.*

April 18, 1847
Tolstoy's Diaries

Keeping a diary or journal or notebook is, for writers, often a way of limbering up, practicing, becoming fluent. Here is Anthony Trollope, the nineteenth-century English novelist, commenting on his early journal keeping:

> Early in life, at the age of fifteen, I had commenced the dangerous habit of keeping a journal, and this I maintained for ten years. The volumes remained in my possession, unregarded—never looked at—till 1870, when I examined them, and, with many blushes, destroyed them. They convinced me of folly, ignorance, indiscretion, idleness, extravagance, and conceit. But they habituated me to the rapid use of pen and ink, and taught me to express myself with facility.
>
> *An Autobiography*

Unlike Trollope, who gave up journal writing in his twenties, Virginia Woolf, whose published diaries now run to several volumes, kept a journal throughout her life, convinced of its benefits:

> As I think, this diary has greatly helped my style; loosened the ligatures.
> November 1, 1924

Of her diaries, W. H. Auden wrote: "I have never read any book that more truthfully conveyed what a writer's life is like . . . ."

F. Scott Fitzgerald used his notebooks for work—for "exercising," for making notes, sketching, planning, recording bits of overheard conversation, stashing ideas for stories, observing the stuff around him—much as a painter would use a sketchbook.

Why read other people's notebooks, journals, diaries? Perhaps some of us are addicted to reading others' diaries and journals for the same reasons we read scandal newspapers or watch soap operas or read biography: we're interested in getting the inside story, in finding out what people do in their private lives. We love others' secrets. We feel as if we're eavesdropping. One answer then: we read diaries to satisfy our insatiable curiosity about other people. We want to find out what they're "really" like. People are, after all, inexhaustibly interesting. We read the lines, and we infer the "whole" person from between the lines.

Another answer: as writers, we like to find out what other writers do with words.

Here is a selection, taken from the diaries of a number of diarists, all mixed together, so that *you* can read patterns, repetitions, recurring themes, for your own pleasure.

> . . . Within a week I have had made a pair of corduroy pants, which cost when done $1.60. They are of that peculiar clay color, reflecting the light from portions of their surface. They have this advantage, that, beside being very strong, they will look about as well three months hence as now—or as ill, some would say. Most of my friends are disturbed by my

wearing them. I can get four or five pairs for what one ordinary pair would cost in Boston, and each of the former will last two or three times as long under the same circumstances. The tailor said that the stuff was not made in this country; that it was worn by the Irish at home, and now they would not look at it, but others would not wear it, durable and cheap as it is, because it is worn by the Irish. Moreover, I like the color on other accounts. Anything but black clothes.

Henry David Thoreau
May 8, 1857

A good day—a bad day—so it goes on. Few people can be so tortured by writing as I am. Only Flaubert I think. Yet I see it now, as a whole. I think I can bring it off, if I only have courage and patience: take each scene quietly: compose: I think it may be a good book. And then—oh when it's finished!

Not so clear today, because I went to dentist and then shopped. My brain is like a scale: one grain pulls it down. Yesterday it balanced: today dips.

Virginia Woolf
June 23, 1936

Always, as I walk through the Underground stations, sickened by the advertisements, the silly staring faces and strident colours, the general frantic struggle to induce people to waste labour and material by consuming useless luxuries or harmful drugs. How much rubbish this war will sweep away, if only we can hang on throughout the summer. War is simply a reversal of civilised life; its motto is "Evil be thou my good", and so much of the good of modern life is actually evil that it is questionable whether on balance war does harm.

George Orwell
June 14, 1940

I haven't written for a few days, because I wanted first of all to think about my diary. It's an odd idea for someone like me to keep a diary; not only because I have never done so before, but because it seems to me that neither I—nor for that matter anyone else—will be interested in the unbosomings of a thirteen-year-old schoolgirl. Still, what does that matter? I want to write, but more than that, I want to bring out all kinds of things that lie buried deep in my heart.

There is a saying that "paper is more patient than man"; it came back to me on one of my slightly melancholy days, while I sat chin in hand, feeling too bored and limp even to make up my mind whether to go out or stay at home. Yes, there is no doubt that paper is patient and as I don't intend to show this cardboard-covered notebook, bearing the proud name of "diary," to anyone, unless I find a real friend, boy or girl, probably nobody cares. And now I come to the root of the matter, the reason for my starting a diary: it is that I have no such real friend.

Anne Frank
June 20, 1942

Finished *Jane Eyre,* which is really a wonderful book very peculiar in parts, but so powerfully and admirably written, such a fine tone in it, such fine religious feeling, and such beautiful writing. The description of the mysterious maniac's nightly appearances awfully thrilling, Mr Rochester's character a very remarkable one, and Jane Eyre's herself a beautiful one. The end is very touching, when Jane Eyre returns to him and finds him blind, with one hand gone from injuries during the fire in his house, which was caused by his mad wife.

Queen Victoria
November 23, 1880

Chekhov made a mistake in thinking that if he had had more time he would have written more fully, described the rain, and the midwife and the doctor having tea. The truth is one can get only *so much* into a story; there is always a sacrifice. One has to leave out what one knows and longs to use. Why? I haven't any idea, but there it is. It's always a kind of race to get in as much as one can before it *disappears*.

But time is not really in it. Yet wait. I do not understand even now. I am pursued by time myself. The only occasion when I ever felt at leisure was while writing *The Daughters of the Late Colonel.* And then at the end I was so terribly unhappy that I wrote as fast as possible for fear of dying before the story was sent. I should like to prove this, to work at *real leisure.* Only thus can it be done.

Katherine Mansfield
January 17, 1922

A beautiful still sunshiny morning. We rose very late. I put the rag-boxes into order. We walked out while the goose was roasting—we walked to the top of the hill. M. and I followed Wm.—he was walking upon the turf between John's Grove and the lane. It was a most sweet noon. We did not go into John's Grove, but we walked among the rocks and there we sate. Mr Oliff passed Mary and me upon the road—Wm. still among the rocks. The lake beautiful from the orchard. Wm. and I walked out before tea—The crescent moon—we sate in the slate quarry—I sate there a long time alone. Wm. reached home before me—I found them at tea. There were a thousand stars in the sky.

Dorothy Wordsworth
November 12, 1801

- But perhaps the universe is suspended on the tooth of some monster.
- How pleasant it is to respect people! When I see books, I am not concerned with how authors loved or played cards; I see only their marvelous works.
- The so-called pure childlike joy of life is animal joy.
- I cannot bear the crying of children, but when my child cries, I don't hear.
- And I dreamt that, as it were, what I considered reality was a dream, and the dream was reality.
- I observed that after marriage people cease to be curious.
- It usually takes as much time to feel happy as to wind up one's watch.

Anton Chekhov
(from *The Notebooks*)

I will learn shorthand, typing, and write and read and write and read, and talk to myself about attitudes, see the Aldriches and neighbors, and be nice and friendly and outgoing, and forget my damn ego-centered self in trying to learn and understand about what makes life rich and what is most important.

Sylvia Plath
July 19, 1953

- "Call me Mickey Mouse," she said suddenly.
  "Why?"
  "I don't know—it was fun when you called me Mickey Mouse."

- "She's really radiant," she said, "really radiunt."
- "Remember you're physically repulsive to me."
- "I like writers. If you speak to a writer you often get an answer."
- "He wants to make a goddess out of me and I want to be Mickey Mouse."
- "You look to me like a very ordinary three piece suit."

F. Scott Fitzgerald
(from *The Notebooks:* "Conversation and Things Overheard")

My recent reading of Morike's autobiography to my sisters began well enough but improved as I went on, and finally, my fingertips together, it conquered inner obstacles with my voice's unceasing calm, provided a constantly expanding panorama for my voice, and finally the whole room round about me dared admit nothing but my voice. Until my parents, returning from business, rang.

Franz Kafka
December 3, 1911

REREADING OURSELVES

Many inexperienced writers dread rereading their own work. They believe in the "muse," in the myth that writing must come to you out of the blue, that the writer is struck by lightning—and that if they reread their own writing, the magic will evaporate. They hand in their written work—to their teachers or employers—and pray for the best. But when they learn to reread their own words, to realize that they can renegotiate with their own texts, to see patterns, repetitions, recurring metaphors, telling adverbs, they begin to realize that they have opportunities for wordplay that they never imagined. They open new doors for themselves as writers. They realize that they have preferences—they enjoy using adjectives (as Hemingway did not), or they try out various ways of using punctuation (as Woolf did). Keeping a notebook can give you a way to sketch and doodle and change or keep words. Rereading your own notebooks can give you material—words to cut and seam and redesign, words to handle and use. Once it's written down, it can be added to, changed, erased.

   Joan Didion, novelist, journalist, Hollywood scriptwriter, has written an essay on keeping a notebook. In writing the essay, she rereads herself by repositioning herself in relation to her own past writings, her notebooks. She says that she began keeping a notebook as a child when her mother gave her a Big Five tablet "with the sensible suggestion that I stop whining." In fact, I find that she's never stopped whining—that her intense, sometimes anguished consciousness is irritating! But I read her, nevertheless, because her style of writing and her ideas provoke me. Read on and see what you think.

On Keeping a Notebook
Joan Didion

"'That woman Estelle,'" the note reads, "'is partly the reason why George Sharp and I are separated today.' *Dirty crepe-de-Chine wrapper, hotel bar, Wilmington RR, 9:45 a.m. August Monday morning.*"

Since the note is in my notebook, it presumably has some meaning to me. I study it for a long while. At first I have only the most general notion of what I was doing on an August Monday morning in the bar of the hotel across from the Pennsylvania Railroad station in Wilmington, Delaware (waiting for a train? missing one? 1960? 1961? why Wilmington?), but I do remember being there. The woman in the dirty crepe-de-Chine wrapper had come down from her room for a beer, and the bartender had heard before the reason why George Sharp and she were separated today. "Sure," he said, and went on mopping the floor. "You told me." At the other end of the bar is a girl. She is talking, pointedly, not to the man beside her but to a cat lying in the triangle of sunlight cast through the open door. She is wearing a plaid silk dress from Peck & Peck, and the hem is coming down.

Here is what it is: the girl has been on the Eastern Shore, and now she is going back to the city, leaving the man beside her, and all she can see ahead are the viscous summer sidewalks and the 3 a.m. long-distance calls that will make her lie awake and then sleep drugged through all the steaming mornings left in August (1960? 1961?). Because she must go directly from the train to lunch in New York, she wishes that she had a safety pin for the hem of the plaid silk dress, and she also wishes that she could forget about the hem and the lunch and stay in the cool bar that smells of disinfectant and malt and make friends with the woman in the crepe-de-Chine wrapper. She is afflicted by a little self-pity, and she wants to compare Estelles. That is what that was all about.

Why did I write it down? In order to remember, of course, but exactly what was it I wanted to remember? How much of it actually happened? Did any of it? Why do I keep a notebook at all? It is easy to deceive oneself on all those scores. The impulse to write things down is a peculiarly compulsive one, inexplicable to those who do not share it, useful only accidentally, only secondarily, in the way that any compulsion tries to justify itself. I suppose that it begins or does not begin in the cradle. Although I have felt compelled to write things down since I was five years old, I doubt that my daughter ever will, for she is a singularly blessed and accepting child, delighted with life exactly as life presents itself to her, unafraid to go to sleep and unafraid to wake up. Keepers of private notebooks are a different breed altogether, lonely and resistant rearrangers of things, anxious malcontents, children afflicted apparently at birth with some presentiment of loss.

My first notebook was a Big Five tablet, given to me by my mother with the sensible suggestion that I stop whining and learn to amuse myself by writing down my thoughts. She returned the tablet to me a few years ago; the first entry is an account of a woman who believed herself freezing to death in the Arctic night, only to find, when day broke, that she had stumbled onto the Sahara Desert, where she would die of the heat before lunch. I have no idea what turn of a five-year-old's mind could have prompted so insistently "ironic" and exotic a story, but it does reveal a certain predilection for the extreme which has dogged me into adult life; perhaps if I were analytically inclined I would find it a truer story than any I might have told about Donald Johnson's birthday party or the day my cousin Brenda put Kitty Litter in the aquarium.

So the point of my keeping a notebook has never been, nor is it now, to have an accurate factual record of what I have been doing or thinking. That would be a different impulse entirely, an instinct for reality which I sometimes envy but do not possess. At no point have I ever been able successfully to keep a diary; my approach to daily life ranges from the grossly negligent to the merely absent, and on those few occasions when I have tried dutifully to record a day's events, boredom has so overcome me that the results are mysterious at best. What is this business about "shopping, typing piece, dinner with E, depressed"? Shopping for what? Typing what piece? Who is E? Was this "E" depressed, or was I depressed? Who cares?

In fact I have abandoned altogether that kind of pointless entry; instead I tell what some would call lies. "That's simply not true," the members of my family frequently tell me when they come up against my memory of a shared event. "The party was *not* for you, the spider was *not* a black widow, *it wasn't that way at all.*" Very likely they are right, for not only have I always had trouble distinguishing between what happened and what merely might have happened, but I remain unconvinced that the distinction, for my purposes, matters. The cracked crab that I recall having for lunch the day my father came home from Detroit in 1945 must certainly be embroidery, worked into the day's pattern to lend verisimilitude; I was ten years old and would not now remember the cracked crab. The day's events did not turn on cracked crab. And yet it is precisely that fictitious crab that makes me see the afternoon all over again, a home movie run all too often, the father bearing gifts, the child weeping, an exercise in family love and guilt. Or that is what it was to me. Similarly, perhaps it never did snow that August in Vermont; perhaps there never were flurries in the night wind, and maybe no one else felt the ground hardening and summer already dead even as we pretended to bask in it, but that was how it felt to me, and it might as well have snowed, could have snowed, did snow.

How it felt to me: that is getting closer to the truth about a notebook. I sometimes delude myself about why I keep a notebook, imagine that some thrifty virtue derives from preserving everything observed. See enough and write it down, I tell myself, and then some morning when the world seems drained of wonder, some day when I am only going through the motions of doing what I am supposed to do, which is write—on that bankrupt morning I will simply open my notebook and there it will be, a forgotten account with accumulated interest, paid passage back to the world out there: dialogue overheard in hotels and elevators and at the hat-check counter in Pavillon (one middle-aged man shows his hat check to another and says, "That's my old football number"); impressions of Bettina Aptheker and Benjamin Sonnenberg and Teddy ("Mr. Acapulco") Stauffer; careful *aperçus* about tennis bums and failed fashion models and Greek shipping heiresses, one of whom taught me a significant lesson (a lesson I could have learned from F. Scott Fitzgerald, but perhaps we all must meet the very rich for ourselves) by asking, when I arrived to interview her in her orchid-filled sitting room on the second day of a paralyzing New York blizzard, whether it was snowing outside.

I imagine, in other words, that the notebook is about other people. But of course it is not. I have no real business with what one stranger said to another at the hat-check counter in Pavillon; in fact I suspect that the line "That's my old football number" touched not my own imagination at all, but merely some memory of something once read, probably "The Eighty-Yard Run." Nor is my concern with a woman in a dirty crepe-de-Chine wrapper in a Wilmington bar. My stake is always, of course, in the unmentioned girl in the plaid silk dress. *Remember what it was to be me:* that is always the point.

It is a difficult point to admit. We are brought up in the ethic that others, any others, all others, are by definition more interesting than ourselves; taught to be diffident, just this side of self-effacing. ("You're the least important person in the room and don't forget it,"

Jessica Mitford's governess would hiss in her ear on the advent of any social occasion; I copied that into my notebook because it is only recently that I have been able to enter a room without hearing some such phrase in my inner ear.) Only the very young and the very old may recount their dreams at breakfast, dwell upon self, interrupt with memories of beach picnics and favorite Liberty lawn dresses and the rainbow trout in a creek near Colorado Springs. The rest of us are expected, rightly, to affect absorption in other people's favorite dresses, other people's trout.

And so we do. But our notebooks give us away, for however dutifully we record what we see around us, the common denominator of all we see is always, transparently, shamelessly, the implacable "I." We are not talking here about the kind of notebook that is patently for public consumption, a structural conceit for binding together a series of graceful *pensées;* we are talking about something private, about bits of the mind's string too short to use, an indiscriminate and erratic assemblage with meaning only for its maker.

And sometimes even the maker has difficulty with the meaning. There does not seem to be, for example, any point in my knowing for the rest of my life that, during 1964, 720 tons of soot fell on every square mile of New York City, yet there it is in my notebook, labeled "FACT." Nor do I really need to remember that Ambrose Bierce liked to spell Leland Standford's name "£eland $tanford" or that "smart women almost always wear black in Cuba," a fashion hint without much potential for practical application. And does not the relevance of these notes seem marginal at best?

> In the basement museum of the Inyo County Courthouse in Independence, California, sign pinned to a mandarin coat: "This MANDARIN COAT was often worn by Mrs. Minnie S. Brooks when giving lectures on her TEAPOT COLLECTION."

> Redhead getting out of car in front of Beverly Wilshire Hotel, chinchilla stole, Vuitton bags with tags reading:
> MRS LOU FOX
> HOTEL SAHARA
> VEGAS

Well, perhaps not entirely marginal. As a matter of fact, Mrs. Minnie S. Brooks and her MANDARIN COAT pull me back into my own childhood, for although I never knew Mrs. Brooks and did not visit Inyo county until I was thirty, I grew up in just such a world, in houses cluttered with Indian relics and bits of gold ore and ambergris and the souvenirs my Aunt Mercy Farnsworth brought back from the Orient. It is a long way from that world to Mrs. Lou Fox's world, where we all live now, and is it not just as well to remember that? Might not Mrs. Minnie S. Brooks help me to remember what I am? Might not Mrs. Lou Fox help me to remember what I am not?

But sometimes the point is harder to discern. What exactly did I have in mind when I noted down that it cost the father of someone I know $650 a month to light the place on the Hudson in which he lived before the Crash? What use was I planning to make of this line by Jimmy Hoffa: "I may have my faults, but being wrong ain't one of them"? And although I think it interesting to know where the girls who travel with the Syndicate have their hair done when they find themselves on the West Coast, will I ever make suitable use of it? Might I not be better off just passing it on to John O'Hara? What is a recipe for sauerkraut doing in my notebook? What kind of magpie keeps this notebook? *"He was born the night the* Titanic *went down."* That seems a nice enough line, and I even recall who said it, but is it not really a better line in life than it could ever be in fiction?

But of course that is exactly it: not that I should ever use the line, but that I should remember the woman who said it and the afternoon I heard it. We were on her terrace by the sea, and we were finishing the wine left from lunch, trying to get what sun there was, a California winter sun. The woman whose husband was born the night the *Titanic* went down wanted to rent her house, wanted to go back to her children in Paris. I remember wishing that I could afford the house, which cost $1,000 a month. "Someday you will," she said lazily. "Someday it all comes." There in the sun on her terrace it seemed easy to believe in someday, but later I had a low-grade afternoon hangover and ran over a black snake on the way to the supermarket and was flooded with inexplicable fear when I heard the checkout clerk explaining to the man ahead of me why she was finally divorcing her husband. "He left me no choice," she said over and over as she punched the register. "He has a little seven-month-old baby by her, he left me no choice." I would like to believe that my dread then was for the human condition, but of course it was for me, because I wanted a baby and did not then have one and because I wanted to own the house that cost $1,000 a month to rent and because I had a hangover.

It all comes back. Perhaps it is difficult to see the value in having one's self back in that kind of mood, but I do see it; I think we are well advised to keep on nodding terms with the people we used to be, whether we find them attractive company or not. Otherwise they turn up unannounced and surprise us, come hammering on the mind's door at 4 a.m. of a bad night and demand to know who deserted them, who betrayed them, who is going to make amends. We forget all too soon the things we thought we could never forget. We forget the loves and the betrayals alike, forget what we whispered and what we screamed, forget who we were. I have already lost touch with a couple of people I used to be; one of them, a seventeen-year-old, presents little threat, although it would be of some interest to me to know again what it feels like to sit on a river levee drinking vodka-and-orange juice and listening to Les Paul and Mary Ford and their echoes sing "How High the Moon" on the car radio. (You see I still have the scenes, but I no longer perceive myself among those present, no longer could even improvise the dialogue.) The other one, a twenty-three-year-old, bothers me more. She was always a good deal of trouble, and I suspect she will reappear when I least want to see her, skirts too long, shy to the point of aggravation, always the injured party, full of recriminations and little hurts and stories I do not want to hear again, at once saddening me and angering me with her vulnerability and ignorance, an apparition all the more insistent for being so long banished.

It is a good idea, then, to keep in touch, and I suppose that keeping in touch is what notebooks are all about. And we are all on our own when it comes to keeping those lines open to ourselves: Your notebook will never help me, nor mine you. *"So what's new in the whiskey business?"* What could that possibly mean to you? To me it means a blonde in a Pucci bathing suit sitting with a couple of fat men by the pool at the Beverly Hills Hotel. Another man approaches, and they all regard one another in silence for a while. "So what's new in the whiskey business?" one of the fat men finally says by way of welcome, and the blonde stands up, arches one foot and dips it in the pool, looking all the while at the cabana where Baby Pignatari is talking on the telephone. That is all there is to that, except that several years later I saw the blonde coming out of Saks Fifth Avenue in New York with her California complexion and a voluminous mink coat. In the harsh wind that day she looked old and irrevocably tired to me, and even the skins in the mink coat were not worked the way they were doing them that year, not the way she would have wanted them done, and there is the point of the story. For a while after that I did not like to look in the mirror, and my eyes would skim the newspapers and pick out only the deaths, the cancer victims, the premature coronaries, the suicides, and I stopped riding the Lexington Avenue IRT because I noticed for the first time that all the strangers I had seen for years—the man with the seeing-eye dog, the spinster who read the classified pages every day, the fat girl who always got off with me at Grand Central—looked older than they once had.

It all comes back. Even that recipe for sauerkraut: even that brings it back. I was on Fire Island when I first made that sauerkraut, and it was raining, and we drank a lot of bourbon and ate the sauerkraut and went to bed at ten, and I listened to the rain and the Atlantic and felt safe. I made the sauerkraut again last night and it did not make me feel any safer, but that is, as they say, another story.

REPOSITIONINGS

"My brain is like a scale," says Virginia Woolf, "one grain pulls it down. Yesterday it balanced: today dips." Chekhov gives us a different balancing act: the universe suspended on the tooth of some monster. When we reread, we can reposition texts: we can disorder the order; we can pull out recurrent themes; we can place Woolf next to Chekhov. We can enter in ourselves, conjuring up our own metaphors of our minds at work: How would you characterize the workings of your "brain"? A scale? A computer? How would you characterize your speculations on the nature of the universe. Our negotiations through our new repositionings enable us to *juxtapose* themes, ideas, issues, metaphors, to see and make new relationships.

Reread the journal entries on pages 72 to 74. What relationships do you see when you put Thoreau next to Orwell, Mansfield next to Plath, etc.?

One way to reposition an idea or theme or perspective is through parody, through a humorous or satirical imitation of a serious work. Dave Barry's text in Chapter 1 can be seen as a parody of the typical report on the dire state of education in the country. We expect them at least once a year: SAT scores are going down; students are learning less (in this case, less history) and watching television more. Barry is not dismissing the problem, but he's repositioning himself in relation to it—taking another angle, turning things upside down, and, in the end, turning our attention to the ways history is presented in textbooks.

In this following excerpt, "The Wordsmiths at Gorsemere," we see another parody. To appreciate it, you'll need this cultural funding: Dorothy Wordsworth, whose journal entry you saw on page 73, was the sister of the English poet William Wordsworth, who is one of the most celebrated literary figures in the English-speaking world. For some years she kept a journal, which tells of their lives together in nineteenth-century rural England, in the village of Grasmere, in what is known as the Lake District. Dorothy kept house for her brother before and after he married; she cooked and cleaned (and "put the rag-boxes in order," see page 73) and minded her nieces and nephews. She kept a garden, took long walks (it was nothing for her to walk 10 miles a day), enjoyed the world of nature, entertained company, fed the homeless, and copied William's poems to send to publishers. Above all, she tried to make it possible for William to have peace and quiet to write. Her devotion to him was boundless. In fact, it was for William, she says, that she began her Grasmere Journal on May 14, 1800. With him gone off to Yorkshire, she "resolved to write a journal of the time till W. and J. [her brother John] return, and I set about keeping my resolve, because I will not quarrel with myself, and because I shall give Wm. pleasure by it when he comes home again."

   Sue Limb has written a parody of Dorothy's journal, in what she calls *The Wordsmiths at Gorsemere*. Note the play on words! In this, Sue Limb's rendering of Dorothy's journal, we find the poet's sister hard at work, making sure that he can be a poet.

March 14th 1799

Day. of V.V. Great Joy.!! For today we removed to Vole Cottage, in Cumberland. A _dear_ place! Not quite _in_ the village (of Gorsemere), & not quite out! But nestling under the majestic peaks, of Flabbergoat Fell! So fatigued can scarce hold my pen. Worn out with carrying cupboards, etc up the steep bank to the house.

   Wm asleep on the sopha. I have placed a bunch of Toadflax by his head. So v. weary can scar—

Toad-Flax (quite rampant) by the Sod-Wall!)

March 18th   So fatigued last night, fell asleep at my journal! And this ——→ dozing stream of ink, is the result. Wm says, it looks like the course of the River Pudden, a local torrent. The darling-! (Wm, I mean) This shows so clearly, the penetrating power of his Fancy! A line of ink, transfigured into a mountain Beck! It reminds me, that when I have leisure, I intend to dangle my toes in the Pudden! Unpacked, etc. No sign of the teapot. Am obliged to make tea, in an-other Vessel, ~~and am not sure if it is altogether~~ Rained, incessantly.

CHAPTER 4

Writing on

Writing II

Intertextuality:

Versions, Transformations,

Gaps, and Influences

INTERTEXTUALITY

Poems, stories, essays, plays, film and television scripts, songs don't come out of the blue. They are written by writers who have their own personal fundings, their own knowledge about the world and about texts, through their immersion in poems, stories, scripts, poems, and other texts. You might believe that writers, through some creative "magic," construct their works out of nothing, that the minds of creative geniuses are the mental equivalents of desert islands. Not so. Writers know how to "steal": they take Hemingway's advice about reading everyone, and they're often not embarrassed to admit their influences.

Texts, therefore, interact, interconnect, and intersect with other texts in all kinds of surprising, strange, delightful, and provocative ways. This is what is meant by *intertextuality*. Texts can take on lives of their own, popping up like jack-in-the-boxes, haunting or even taking over other texts. It happens in other media and in our lives. One movie, we realize, reminds us of another for all kinds of reasons: the plot, the characters, setting, theme, background music—there are echoes of one in another.

So when you write, don't be stuck in what has come to be known as the "cult of originality." Realize instead that the ghosts of other texts inevitably appear in your own writing. In fact, the more you read, the more you may welcome the ways that one text collides with or plays upon another in your mind—and in your own texts, particularly, as you try another version of a familiar story, or transform one sliver of an idea into another, or fill in a missing piece of one story by writing another. Consider how the past interacts with the present in our own lives. We "read" what happens *now* in the light of *then*—and realize the intertextuality of all of our experience.

VERSIONS

Consider this:

Imagine yourself back in childhood for a moment: Who did you dream of "becoming"? What fairy-tale or fantasy figure—from books, comic books, television, or the movies—caught your fancy?

• • •

If you are anything like the students in my classes, you'll have come up with responses such as these: Peter Pan, Batman, Robin Hood, G.I. Joe, Dick Tracy, Rambo, Cinderella, Wonder Woman, Snow White, the Cookie Monster, or Miss Piggy on Sesame Street!

How do you think your gender affected your choice?

Try this:

Here's an exercise for your notebook: Write down whatever associations come to mind about the fairy-tale figure Cinderella.

Now consider this:

What do you know about Cinderella? And how do you know? Where have you encountered her? In a storybook? The movies? Songs? Where? And when?

What's the ending of the story?

• • •

Now read these two versions of the Cinderella story, first Charles Perrault's and then Grimm's.

Cinderella, or the Little Glass Slipper
Charles Perrault

Once there was a gentleman who married, for his second wife, the proudest and most haughty woman that was ever seen. She had, by a former husband, two daughters of her own humor, who were, indeed, exactly like her in all things. He had likewise, by another wife, a young daughter, but of unparalleled goodness and sweetness of temper, which she took from her mother, who had been the best creature in the world.

No sooner were the ceremonies of the wedding over than the stepmother began to show herself in her true colors. She could not bear the good qualities of this pretty girl, and the less because they made her own daughters appear the more odious. She employed her in the meanest work of the house: she scoured the dishes, tables, etc., and scrubbed madam's chamber, and those of the misses, her daughters. She lay up in a sorry garret, upon a wretched straw bed, while her sisters lay in fine rooms, with floors all inlaid, upon beds of the newest fashion, and where they had looking glasses so large that they might see themselves at their full length from head to foot.

The poor girl bore all patiently, and dared not tell her father, who would have rattled her off; for his wife governed him entirely. When she had done her work, she used to go into the chimney corner, and sit down among cinders and ashes, which made her commonly be called *Cinderwench;* but the youngest, who was not so rude and uncivil as the eldest, called her Cinderella. However, Cinderella, notwithstanding her mean apparel, was a hundred times handsomer than her sisters, though they were always dressed very richly.

It happened that the King's son gave a ball, and invited all persons of fashion to it. Our young misses were also invited, for they cut a very grand figure among the quality. They were mightily delighted at this invitation, and wonderfully busy in choosing out such gowns, petticoats, and headclothes as might become them. This was a new trouble to Cinderella; for it was she who ironed her sisters' linen, and plaited their ruffles; they talked all day long of nothing but how they should be dressed.

"For my part," said the eldest, "I will wear my red velvet suit with French trimming."

"And I," said the youngest, "shall have my usual petticoat; but then, to make amends for that, I will put on my gold-flowered manteau, and my diamond stomacher, which is far from being the most ordinary one in the world."

They sent for the best tirewoman they could get to make up their headdresses and adjust their double pinners, and they had their red brushes and patches from Mademoiselle de la Poche.

Cinderella was likewise called up to them to be consulted in all these matters, for she had excellent notions, and advised them always for the best, nay, and offered her services to dress their heads, which they were very willing she should do. As she was doing this, they said to her:

"Cinderella, would you not be glad to go to the ball?"

"Alas!" she said, "you only jeer me; it is not for such as I am to go thither."

"Thou art in the right of it," replied they. "It would make the people laugh to see a cinderwench at a ball."

Anyone but Cinderella would have dressed their heads awry, but she was very good, and dressed them perfectly well. They were almost two days without eating, so much were they transported with joy. They broke more than a dozen laces in trying to be laced up close, that they might have a fine slender shape, and they were continually at their looking glass. At last the happy day came; they went to court, and Cinderella followed them with her eyes as long as she could, and when she had lost sight of them, she fell a-crying.

Her godmother, who saw her all in tears, asked her what was the matter.

"I wish I could—I wish I could——"; she was not able to speak the rest, being interrupted by her tears and sobbing.

This godmother of hers, who was a fairy, said to her, "Thou wishest thou couldst go to the ball; is it not so?"

"Y-es," cried Cinderella, with a great sigh.

"Well," said her godmother, "be but a good girl, and I will contrive that thou shalt go." Then she took her into her chamber, and said to her, "Run into the garden, and bring me a pumpkin."

Cinderella went immediately to gather the finest she could get, and brought it to her godmother, not being able to imagine how this pumpkin could make her go to the ball. Her godmother scooped out all the inside of it, having left nothing but the rind; which done, she struck it with her wand, and the pumpkin was instantly turned into a fine coach, gilded all over with gold.

She then went to look into her mousetrap, where she found six mice, all alive, and ordered Cinderella to lift up a little the trap door, when, giving each mouse, as it went out, a little tap with her wand, the mouse was that moment turned into a fine horse, which altogether made a very fine set of six horses of a beautiful mouse-colored dapple gray. Being at a loss for a coachman:

"I will go and see," says Cinderella, "if there is not a rat in the rattrap—we may make a coachman of him."

"Thou art in the right," replied her godmother. "Go and look."

Cinderella brought the trap to her, and in it there were three huge rats. The fairy made choice of one of the three which had the largest beard, and, having been touched with her wand, he was turned into a fat, jolly coachman, who had the smartest whiskers eyes ever beheld. After that, she said to her:

"Go again into the garden, and you will find six lizards behind the watering pot. Bring them to me."

She had no sooner done so but her godmother turned them into six footmen, who skipped immediately behind the coach, with their liveries all bedaubed with gold and silver, and clung as close behind each other as if they had done nothing else their whole lives. The fairy then said to Cinderella:

"Well, you see here an equipage fit to go to the ball with; are you not pleased with it?"

"Oh, yes!" cried she. "But must I go thither as I am, in these nasty rags?"

Her godmother only just touched her with her wand, and, at the same instant, her clothes were turned into cloth of gold and silver, all beset with jewels. This done, she gave her a pair of glass slippers, the prettiest in the whole world. Being thus decked out, she got up into her coach; but her godmother, above all things, commanded her not to stay till after midnight, telling her, at the same time, that if she stayed one moment longer, the coach would be a pumpkin again, her horses mice, her coachman a rat, her footmen lizards, and her clothes become just as they were before.

She promised her godmother she would not fail to leave the ball before midnight; and then away she drives, scarce able to contain herself for joy. The King's son, who was told that a great princess, whom nobody knew, was come, ran out to receive her; he gave her his hand as she alighted from the coach, and led her into the hall, among all the company. There was immediately a profound silence. The people stopped dancing, and the violins ceased to play, so attentive was everyone to contemplate the singular beauties of the unknown newcomer. Nothing was then heard but a confused noise of:

"Ha! how handsome she is! Ha! how handsome she is!"

The King himself, old as he was, could not help watching her, and telling the Queen softly that it was a long time since he had seen so beautiful and lovely a creature.

All the ladies were busied in considering her clothes and headdress, that they might have some made next day after the same pattern, provided they could meet with such fine material and as able hands to make them.

The King's son conducted her to the most honorable seat, and afterward took her out to dance with him; she danced so very gracefully that they all more and more admired her. A fine collation was served up, whereof the younger prince ate not a morsel, so intently was he busied in gazing on her.

She went and sat down by her sisters, showing them a thousand civilities, giving them part of the oranges and citrons which the Prince had presented her with, which very much surprised them, for they did not know her. While Cinderella was thus amusing her sisters, she heard the clock strike eleven and three quarters, whereupon she immediately made a courtesy to the company and hasted away as fast as she could.

When she got home she ran to seek out her godmother, and, after having thanked her, she said she could not but heartily wish she might go next day to the ball, because the King's son had desired her.

As she was eagerly telling her godmother whatever had passed at the ball, her two sisters knocked at the door, which Cinderella ran and opened.

"How long you have stayed!" cried she, gaping, rubbing her eyes and stretching herself as if she had been just waked out of her sleep; she had not, however, any manner of inclination to sleep since they went from home.

"If thou hadst been at the ball," said one of her sisters, "thou wouldst not have been tired with it. There came thither the finest princess, the most beautiful ever was seen with mortal eyes; she showed us a thousand civilities, and gave us oranges and citrons."

Cinderella seemed very indifferent in the matter; indeed, she asked them the name of that princess. But they told her they did not know it, and the King's son was very uneasy on her account and would give all the world to know who she was. At this Cinderella, smiling, replied:

"She must, then, by very beautiful indeed; how happy you have been! Could not I see her? Ah! dear Miss Charlotte, do lend me your yellow suit of clothes which you wear every day."

"Ay, to be sure!" cried Miss Charlotte. "Lend my clothes to such a dirty cinderwench as thou art! I should be a fool."

Cinderella, indeed, expected well such answer, and was very glad of the refusal; for she would have been sadly put to it if her sister had lent her what she asked for jestingly.

The next day the two sisters were at the ball, and so was Cinderella, but dressed more magnificently than ever before. The King's son was always by her, and never ceased his compliments and kind speeches to her; to whom all this was so far from being tiresome that she quite forgot what her godmother had recommended to her; so that she, at last, counted the clock striking twelve when she took it to be no more than eleven; she then rose up and fled, as nimble as a deer. The Prince followed, but could not overtake her. She left behind one of her glass slippers, which the Prince took up most carefully. She got home, but quite out of breath, and in her nasty old clothes, having nothing left of all her finery but one of the little slippers, fellow to that she dropped. The guards at the palace gate were asked if they had not seen a princess go out.

Who said: They had seen nobody go out but a young girl, very meanly dressed, and who had more the air of a poor country wench than a gentlewoman.

When the two sisters returned from the ball Cinderella asked them if they had been well diverted, and if the fine lady had been there.

They told her: Yes, but that she hurried away immediately when it struck twelve, and with so much haste that she dropped one of her little glass slippers, the prettiest in the world, which the King's son had taken up; that he had done nothing but look at her all the time at the ball, and that most certainly he was very much in love with the beautiful person who owned the glass slipper.

What they said was very true; for a few days after, the King's son caused it to be proclaimed, by sound of trumpet, that he would marry her whose foot the slipper would just fit. They whom he employed began to try it upon the princesses, then the duchesses and all the court, but in vain; it was brought to the two sisters, who did all they possibly could to thrust their foot into the slipper, but they could not effect it. Cinderella, who saw all this, and knew her slipper, said to them, laughing:

"Let me see if it will not fit me."

Her sisters burst out a-laughing, and began to banter her. The gentleman who was sent to try the slipper looked earnestly at Cinderella, and, finding her very handsome, said it was but just that she should try, and that he had orders to let everyone make trial.

He obliged Cinderella to sit down, and, putting the slipper to her foot, he found it went on very easily, and fitted her as if it had been made of wax. The astonishment her two sisters were in was excessively great, but still abundantly greater when Cinderella pulled out of her pocket the other slipper, and put it on her foot. Thereupon, in came her godmother, who, having touched with her wand Cinderella's clothes, made them richer and more magnificent than any of those she had before.

And now her sisters found her to be that fine, beautiful lady whom they had seen at the ball. They threw themselves at her feet to beg pardon for all the ill-treatment they had made her undergo. Cinderella took them up, and, as she embraced them, cried that she forgave them with all her heart, and desired them always to love her.

She was conducted to the young Prince, dressed as she was; he thought her more charming than ever, and, a few days after, married her. Cinderella, who was no less good than beautiful, gave her two sisters lodgings in the palace, and that very same day matched them with two great lords of the court.

Ash Girl (Aschenputtel)
Jacob and Wilhelm Grimm

A rich man's wife fell ill and, feeling that her end was approaching, called her only daughter to her bedside and said, "Dear child, remain devout and good; then dear God will ever be with you, and I'll look down on you from Heaven and be near you." Then she closed her eyes and passed away. Every day the girl used to go out to her mother's grave and weep and remained devout and good. When winter came, the snow laid a white blanket on the grave, and when in the spring the sun had taken it off again, the man married a second wife.

The wife brought two daughters of her own into the home; they were pretty and fair of face but ugly and black in their hearts. Then evil days began for the poor stepchild. "Is the stupid goose to sit with us in the living room?" they'd say. "Whoever wants to eat bread must earn it—out with the scullery maid!" They took away her fine clothes, dressed her in an old gray smock and wooden shoes. "Just look at the proud princess! See how dressed up she is!" they'd cry and, laughing, lead her into the kitchen. There she had to do heavy work from morning till night, get up before dawn, carry water, light the fire, cook, and wash. On top of it all her sisters played all sorts of mean tricks on her, mocked her, and used to pour peas and lentils into the ashes so that she'd have to sit and pick them out again. In the evening when she was tired from work, there was no bed for her; she just had to lie down in the ashes beside the hearth. And since for this reason she always looked dusty and dirty, they called her Ash Girl.

Now it so happened that her father was once going to a fair and asked his two stepdaughters what to bring them. "Fine clothes," said one. "Pearls and jewels," said the other. "And you, Ash Girl," he said, "what do you want?" "Father, bring me the first twig that brushes against your hat on the way home. Break if off for me." So he bought fine clothes, pearls and jewels for the two stepsisters. As he was riding home through a green thicket, a hazel twig brushed against him and knocked off his hat; then he broke off the twig and brought it along. When he got home, he gave his stepdaughters what they'd asked for and gave Ash Girl the hazel twig. She thanked him, went to her mother's grave, planted the twig, and wept so bitterly that her tears fell on it and watered it. It grew and became a fine tree. Three times a day Ash Girl would go down there, weep and pray, and every time a little white bird would light on the tree, and every time she uttered a wish, the bird would throw down to her what she had wished.

Now, in order that his son might choose a bride, the king proclaimed a festival which was to last three days and to which all the pretty girls in the land were invited. When the two stepdaughters heard that they, too, were to appear, they were in high spirits and, calling Ash Girl, said, "Comb our hair! brush our shoes! and fasten our buckles! We're going to the festival at the king's palace." Ash Girl obeyed them, but she wept, for she would have liked to go along to the ball, and begged her stepmother to let her. "You, Ash Girl!" she said, "you're covered with dust and dirt, and you want to go to the festival? You've got no clothes and no shoes and you want to dance?" But when she kept on begging, the stepmother finally said, "I emptied a dish of lentils in the ashes; if you pick out the lentils within two hours, you may come along." The girl went out the back door into the garden and cried out, "You tame pigeons, you turtledoves, and all you birds under heaven, come and help me pick them out,

the good lentils into the pot,
the bad lentils into your crop."

Then two pigeons came in through the kitchen window and after them the turtledoves, and finally all the birds under heaven whirred and flocked in and settled down around the ashes. And the pigeons bobbed their heads and began "peck, peck" and then the others began "peck, peck" and they pecked all the good lentils into the dish. It was hardly an hour before they were finished and all flew out again. Then the girl joyfully brought the dish to her stepmother and thought that she might now be allowed to go to the festival, but the stepmother said, "No, Ash Girl, you've got no clothes and don't know how to dance; you'll only be laughed at." When she wept, her stepmother said, "If you can pick two dishes of lentils from the ashes in one hour, you may come along," thinking, "she'll never be able to do this." When she'd emptied the two dishes of lentils into the ashes, the girl went out the back door into the garden and cried, "You tame pigeons, you turtledoves, all you birds under heaven, come and help me pick them out,

> the good lentils into the pot,
> the bad into your crop."

The two white pigeons came in through the kitchen window and after them the turtledoves, and finally all the birds under heaven whirred and flocked in and settled down around the ashes. And the pigeons bobbed their heads and began "peck, peck—peck, peck" and then the others began "peck, peck—peck, peck" and they pecked all the good lentils into the dishes. And it was hardly half an hour before they finished and all flew out again. Then the girl brought the dishes to her stepmother and was glad, because she thought that she might now go along to the festival. But the latter said, "It'll do you no good. You're not coming along, for you've got no clothes and don't know how to dance. We'd only be ashamed of you." Then she turned her back on her and hurried off with her two haughty daughters.

When everyone had gone, Ash Girl went to her mother's grave under the hazel bush and cried,

> "Little tree, jiggle yourself and shake yourself;
> Scatter gold and silver over me."

Then the bird threw her down a gold and silver dress and silk slippers embroidered with silver. She put the dress on in a hurry and went to the festival. Her sisters, however, and her stepmother didn't recognize her and thought she must be some foreign princess, so beautiful did she look in her gold dress. They didn't so much as think of Ash Girl, who they thought was sitting at home in the dirt, picking lentils out of the ashes. The king's son went up to her, took her by the hand, danced with her, and wouldn't dance with anyone else. He never let go her hand, and when anyone else came to ask her to dance, he'd say, "She's my partner."

She danced till evening and then wanted to go home, but the king's son said, "I'll go with you and escort you," for he wanted to see whose daughter the beautiful girl was. She slipped away from him, however, and jumped into the dovecote. The king's son waited till her father came and told him that the foreign girl had jumped into the dovecote. The old man thought, "Can it be Ash Girl?" They had to fetch him an ax and a pick to break down the dovecote, but there was no one inside. And when they got home, there was Ash Girl in her dirty clothes lying in the ashes, and a dim oil lamp was burning in the fireplace. For Ash Girl had jumped down quickly out the back of the dovecote and had run to the hazel bush.

There she'd taken off her fine clothes and laid them on the grave, and the bird had taken them away again, and then she'd sat down in her gray smock in the ashes in the kitchen.

Next day when the festival was resumed, and her parents and stepsisters had gone, Ash Girl again went to the hazel bush and said,

> "Little tree, jiggle yourself and shake yourself;
> Scatter gold and silver over me."

Then the bird threw down an even finer dress than the day before, and when she appeared at the festival in this dress, everyone was amazed at her beauty. The king's son had, however, waited for her coming, at once took her by the hand, and danced only with her. When others came and asked her for a dance, he'd say, "She's my partner." When evening came, she wanted to go, and the king's son followed her to see into which house she went, but she ran away from him and into the garden behind the house. A fine big tree stood there, full of the most magnificent pears. She climbed among the branches like a squirrel, and the king's son didn't know where she'd got to. But he waited till her father came and said to him, "The stranger slipped away from me, and I think she climbed the pear tree." The father thought, "Can it be Ash Girl?" He had an ax fetched and cut down the tree, but there was no one in it. And when they got to the kitchen, there was Ash Girl lying in the ashes as usual, for she'd jumped down on the other side of the tree, had returned her fine clothes to the bird in the hazel bush, and put on her gray smock.

On the third day, when her parents and sisters had gone, Ash Girl again went to her mother's grave and said to the tree,

> "Little tree, jiggle yourself and shake yourself;
> Scatter gold and silver over me."

Then the bird threw down a dress more magnificent and more splendid than anybody had ever had, and the slippers were of solid gold. When she arrived at the festival in this dress, no one from amazement knew what to say. The king's son danced only with her, and when anybody else asked her for a dance, he'd say, "She's my partner."

When it was evening, Ash Girl wanted to leave, and the king's son wanted to escort her, but she got away from him so fast that he couldn't follow her. He had, however, resorted to a trick and had coated the stairs with pitch, so when she ran down stairs, the girl's left slipper stuck there. The king's son picked it up, and it was tiny and dainty and of solid gold. The next morning he went with it to the man and said to him, "Nobody else shall be my wife but the girl whose foot this shoe fits." Then the two sisters rejoiced, for they had pretty feet. The eldest took the shoe to her room and was going to try it on, and her mother was standing beside her, but she couldn't get her big toe in, for the shoe was too small for her. Then her mother handed her a knife saying, "Cut the toe off; once you're queen, you won't have to walk any more." The girl cut off her toe, forced her foot into the shoe, and, suppressing her pain, went out to the king's son. He took her on his horse as his bride and rode off with her. But they had to pass the grave, and there the two pigeons were sitting on the hazel bush and cried out,

"Look, look!
There's blood in the shoe!
The shoe's too small.
The right bride's still at home!"

Then he looked at her foot and saw the blood oozing out. He turned his horse about and brought the false bride home again. He said she wasn't the right bride and that the other sister should try on the shoe. So the latter went into her room and managed to get her toes in, but her heel was too large. Then her mother handed her a knife, saying, "Cut a piece off your heel; once you're queen, you won't have to walk any more." The girl cut off a piece of her heel, forced her foot into the shoe, and, suppressing her pain, went out to the king's son. He took her on his horse as his bride and rode off with her. As they were passing the hazel bush, the two pigeons were sitting there and cried out,

"Look, look!
There's blood in the shoe!
The shoe's too small.
The right bride's still back home."

He looked down at her foot and saw the blood oozing out of the shoe, dyeing her white stockings red. Then he turned his horse about and brought the false bride back home. "She isn't the right bride either," he said, "Haven't you any other daughter?" "No," said the man, "there's only a little misshapen Ash Girl, daughter by my late wife, but she can't possibly be the bride." The king's son told him to send her up, but her mother replied, "Oh no, she's much too dirty and mustn't be seen." But he insisted on it, and Ash Girl had to be called. She first washed her face and hands and then went and made a deep curtsy before the king's son, who handed her the gold shoe. Then she sat down on a stool, drew her foot out of the heavy wooden shoe and put it in the slipper, which fitted her perfectly. When she stood up and the king looked into her face, he recognized her as the beautiful girl with whom he'd danced and cried, "That's the right bride!" The stepmother and the two sisters were frightened and turned pale with vexation, but he took Ash Girl on his horse and rode off with her. As they passed the hazel bush, the two white pigeons cried,

"Look, look!
No blood in the shoe!
The shoe's not too small
He's bringing the right bride home."

And when they'd called out thus, they both came flying down and perched on Ash Girl's shoulders, one on the right, the other on the left, and stayed there.

When her wedding with the king's son was to be celebrated, the two false sisters came and wanted to ingratiate themselves and have a share in her good fortune. As the bridal couple was going to church, the elder sister walked on the right, the younger on the left. Then the pigeons pecked out one of each of their eyes. Later, when they came out of the church, the elder was on the left and the younger on the right. Then the pigeons pecked out the other of their two eyes. Thus for their malice and treachery they were punished with blindness for the rest of their lives.

How would you characterize the *effects* of the two different endings on you? Which version have you known? How do you account for the variations in the tales?

Folklorists tell us that approximately 700 different versions of the Cinderella folktale have been recorded, from all over the world, including China, Africa, and India. The story varies from place to place, but most tell how a stepchild (usually a female, but sometimes a male) is cruelly treated by a wicked stepmother and/or stepsisters. Through magic, she is transformed into a raving beauty, who mesmerizes a handsome prince who, at the end of the story, makes her his bride. In some a fairy godmother (the good mother) appears; in others, a bird or an animal brings about the transformation. In the Walt Disney version, squeaky little mice help the fairy godmother turn Cinderella into a dazzling creature, replete with a pumpkin-coach, and, of course, the glass slipper.

CINDERELLA;

OR, THE

LITTLE GLASS SLIPPER.

LONDON c. 1828

   The Perrault version, which you read above, is undoubtedly the most popular of all the retellings of the Cinderella tale. Charles Perrault (1628–1703) was a French lawyer and architect who, apparently with his son, collected, recorded, and then published popular European folktales which until that time had been part of the oral tradition, that is, passed on from generation to generation by word of mouth. The tale printed here is taken from Andrew Lang's nineteenth-century English translation in his collection called *The Blue Fairy Book*. The tale you just read, then, has a long history: from oral tellings to Perrault's written representation in the seventeenth century to the English translation in the nineteenth century. (A manuscript version of Perrault's tales, discovered a few years ago, includes descriptions of gestures used by the storytellers as they told the tales to Perrault.)

The Grimm version comes to us from the German: the Grimm brothers, Jacob (1785–1863) and Wilhelm (1786–1859) transformed the oral into their particular adaptation of the folktales they collected. According to folklorist Alan Dundes, "no two individuals did more to stimulate the study of folklore than the Grimm brothers." The publication of the first volume of their tales in 1812 and the second in 1814 "burst like a literary bombshell on the European scene." Although they claimed that they were presenting tales directly from the "folk," it turns out that they combined versions of different tales, borrowed from this tale or that, and rewrote what they chose. Their written versions do not, therefore, represent "pure" tales from the oral traditions, but Dundes says that we shouldn't "judge them too harshly. . . . Rewriting folktales was the accepted practice in the nineteenth century and before."*

Which ending of Cinderella do you prefer and why? Which one would you read to children? Why?

TRANSFORMATIONS

We find modern-day versions of Cinderella in Prokofiev's famous opera, *Cinderella* (1944), and in Walt Disney's even more famous movie, *Cinderella*, released in 1950. The Cinderella story—the rise from rags to riches—has been transformed into many shapes and sizes. It is one of the most powerful *myths* of our culture. It has crept into our everyday lives—our literature, songs, movies, television shows, advertisements, and, most importantly, our sense of what is possible in our own lives, and of what we can expect within our roles as men and women. From Jane Austen's *Pride and Prejudice* to Alice Walker's *The Color Purple;* from Marilyn Monroe in *The Prince and the Showgirl* to Melanie Griffith in *Working Girl*, we meet transformations of the Cinderella story. The particular culture in which a transformation is produced modifies the story to suit its particular circumstances and values: Melanie Griffith, in the movie *Working Girl*, from her provincial world of Staten Island, dreams of "making it" in the high-tech, hard-driving competitive world of Wall Street—across the ferry. Her wicked stepsister—her boss—wants to steal the poor working girl's ideas, but, fortunately, a prince charming (in the guise of Harrison Ford) saves the day. Her reward is not a glittering castle—but her very own executive office and her very own secretary *and* the man she loves! And both, of course, live happily ever after. (See Daphne Merkin's "Prince Charming," page 121.)

Do you know the song from Disney's movie: "Some Day My Prince Will Come"? Or the words to the song "Young at Heart"?

> Fairy tales will come true
> They will happen to you
> If you're young at heart. . . .

---

*   Alan Dundes, *Cinderella: A Casebook*, Madison, Wisconsin, University of Wisconsin Press, 1982.

Do you see the original Cinderella as a "heroine"? What does she "do" to attract the prince? How do you read her character? Do you think her story appeals to boys as well as to girls?

Here's a fantasy about a different kind of transformation, taken from Joseph Conrad's novel, *Lord Jim,* where the young boy Jim dreams of becoming a hero:

> He saw himself saving people from sinking ships, cutting away masts in a hurricane, swimming through a surf with a line; or as a lonely castaway, barefooted and half-naked, walking on uncovered reefs in search of shellfish to stave off starvation. He confronted savages on tropical shores, quelled mutinies on the high seas, and in a small boat upon the ocean kept up the hearts of despairing men—always an example of devotion to duty, and as unflinching as a hero in a book.

When we read "Cinderella," or Jim's fantasy, we can tease out cultural messages (the "unsaid," the tacit assumptions) about the writer's view of our place in the world, our expectations, our values, and our sense of "power" (who holds the power? who are the powerless?) and of the possible (who are the rescuers? who are the rescued?). Robert Darnton, a historian, situates fairy tales in a peasant culture, where the most powerless— the peasants—envisage ways of escaping out of poverty, disease, and squalor, and, in some cases, taking revenge on the upper, ruling classes. (See excerpts from his *The Great Cat-Massacre* on page 316.)

In "Cinderella," we see the possibility of transformation; the magical overnight "Hey presto!" of the rags-to-riches story. (Would the prince have fallen in love with a Cinderella dressed in rags? Or did the clothes make the woman? See Janice Gordon's reflections on these questions on page 359.) We meet here, too, the hope of *discovery,* the belief that all one has to do is *be there—and, of course, be beautiful*—for the prince (or princess!) to come along and find out who you "really" are. And, of course, we all know the ending—the reward of "living happily ever after." In Jim, we see the adventurer—the courageous hero braving storms and wars and disasters. What battles and storms do modern heroes fight? Who are the enemies of the Mutant Ninja Turtles? Aliens? Spies? Drug dealers? What constitutes the "bad guy" in the media today? What effect has the end of the Cold War had on the characterization of heroes and villains?

How do you "read" the assumptions—between the lines—in the stories of such popular heroes as Robin Hood, Superman, Lois Lane, Peter Pan, Batman, Wonder Woman, Dick Tracy, and G.I. Joe? How many of these are heroes (or heroines) today? And what about cartoon figures such as Mickey Mouse, Donald Duck, Popeye, and Roger Rabbit? Or the Sesame Street Muppets? Miss Piggy? Big Bird? Kermit? (Is Miss Piggy a transformation of Cinderella?) Why are there so few female figures on the list? Can you add any others?

What other fantasy figures do children "believe in"? Barbie? Ken? Cabbage-Patch Dolls? What toys do they play with? What cultural messages do you read "between the lines" in these figures? (See Dave Barry's essay on his son and dinosaurs, page 264, and Roland Barthes's "Toys," page 267.)

A culture's fantasy heroes are, of course, influences—for "types" of potential, for possible roles for men and women. They are the basis of much of children's cultural knowledge—their *funding.*

Try this:

Try one or all of these suggestions for your own transformations of the Cinderella story:

1. Write a modern Cinderella tale: set a contemporary stage for your princess (or prince!), using, if you wish, the plot of either Perrault's or Grimm's version.

2. Let the father in the Perrault version "speak," then do the same for the Grimm version: where "was" he while his own daughter was being mistreated? Create his "inner character."

3. Let the stepmother "speak" in one of the two versions you've read: tell the story from her point of view. What does she have to do to get the reader to see things "her" way?

And now look at three variations of Cinderella, a poem, a drawing, and a short story.

. . . And Then the Prince Knelt Down and Tried to Put the Glass Slipper on Cinderella's Foot
Judith Viorst

I really didn't notice that he had a funny nose.
And he certainly looked better all dressed up in fancy clothes.
He's not nearly as attractive as he seemed the other night.
So I think I'll just pretend that this glass slipper feels too tight.

Try this:

What must you do to negotiate this drawing?

Here is one of the most famous stories in all of Western literature, "The Diamond Necklace," by the French writer Guy de Maupassant (1850–1893). Perhaps you've read it already. Reread it now, keeping the Cinderella myth in mind. What happens to the Cinderella story in this transformation? Which version—the Perrault or the Grimm—do you find to be the greater influence on "The Diamond Necklace"?

The Diamond Necklace
Guy de Maupassant

She was one of those pretty, charming young ladies, born, as if through an error of destiny, into a family of clerks. She had no dowry, no hopes, no means of becoming known, appreciated, loved, and married by a man either rich or distinguished; and she allowed herself to marry a petty clerk in the office of the Board of Education.

She was simple, not being able to adorn herself; but she was unhappy, as one out of her class; for women belong to no caste, no race; their grace, their beauty, and their charm serving them in the place of birth and family. Their inborn finesse, their instinctive elegance, their suppleness of wit are their only aristocracy, making some daughters of the people the equal of great ladies.

She suffered incessantly, feeling herself born for all delicacies and luxuries. She suffered from the poverty of her apartment, the shabby walls, the worn chairs, and the faded stuffs. All these things, which another woman of her station would not have noticed, tortured and angered her. The sight of the little Breton, who made this humble home, awoke in her sad regrets and desperate dreams. She thought of quiet antechambers, with their Oriental hangings, lighted by high, bronze torches, and of the two great footmen in short trousers who sleep in the large armchairs, made sleepy by the heavy air from the heating apparatus. She thought of large drawing-rooms, hung in old silks, of graceful pieces of furniture carrying bric-à-brac of inestimable value, and of the little perfumed coquettish apartments, made for five o'clock chats with most intimate friends, men known and sought after, whose attention all women envied and desired.

When she seated herself for dinner, before the round table where the tablecloth had been used three days, opposite her husband who uncovered the tureen with a delighted air, saying: "Oh! the good potpie! I know nothing better than that—" she would think of the elegant dinners, of the shining silver, of the tapestries peopling the walls with ancient personages and rare birds in the midst of fairy forests; she thought of the exquisite food served on marvelous dishes, of the whispered gallantries, listened to with the smile of the sphinx, while eating the rose-colored flesh of the trout or a chicken's wing.

She had neither frocks nor jewels, nothing. And she loved only those things. She felt that she was made for them. She had such a desire to please, to be sought after, to be clever, and courted.

She had a rich friend, a schoolmate at the convent, whom she did not like to visit, she suffered so much when she returned. And she wept for whole days from chagrin, from regret, from despair, and disappointment.

One evening her husband returned elated bearing in his hand a large envelope.

"Here," he said, "here is something for you."

She quickly tore open the wrapper and drew out a printed card on which were inscribed these words:

The Minister of Public Instruction and Madame George Ramponneau ask the honor of Mr. and Mrs. Loisel's company Monday evening, January 18, at the Minister's residence.

Instead of being delighted, as her husband had hoped, she threw the invitation spitefully upon the table murmuring:

"What do you suppose I want with that?"

"But, my dearie, I thought it would make you happy. You never go out, and this is an occasion, and a fine one! I had a great deal of trouble to get it. Everybody wishes one, and it is very select; not many are given to employees. You will see the whole official world there."

She looked at him with an irritated eye and declared impatiently:

"What do you suppose I have to wear to such a thing as that?"

He had not thought of that; he stammered:

"Why, the dress you wear when we go to the theater. It seems very pretty to me—"

He was silent, stupefied, in dismay, at the sight of his wife weeping. Two great tears fell slowly from the corners of his eyes toward the corners of his mouth; he stammered:

"What is the matter? What is the matter?"

By a violent effort, she had controlled her vexation and responded in a calm voice, wiping her moist cheeks:

"Nothing. Only I have no dress and consequently I cannot go to this affair. Give your card to some colleague whose wife is better fitted out than I."

He was grieved, but answered:

"Let us see, Matilda. How much would a suitable costume cost, something that would serve for other occasions, something very simple?"

She reflected for some seconds, making estimates and thinking of a sum that she could ask for without bringing with it an immediate refusal and a frightened exclamation from the economical clerk.

Finally she said, in a hesitating voice:

"I cannot tell exactly, but it seems to me that four hundred francs ought to cover it."

He turned a little pale, for he had saved just this sum to buy a gun that he might be able to join some hunting parties the next summer, on the plains of Nanterre, with some friends who went to shoot larks up there on Sunday. Nevertheless, he answered:

"Very well. I will give you four hundred francs. But try to have a pretty dress."

The day of the ball approached and Mme. Loisel seemed sad, disturbed, anxious. Nevertheless, her dress was nearly ready. Her husband said to her one evening:

"What is the matter with you? You have acted strangely for two or three days."

And she responded: "I am vexed not to have a jewel, not one stone, nothing to adorn myself with. I shall have such a poverty-laden look. I would prefer not to go to this party."

He replied: "You can wear some natural flowers. At this season they look very *chic.* For ten francs you can have two or three magnificent roses."

She was not convinced. "No," she replied, "there is nothing more humiliating than to have a shabby air in the midst of rich women."

Then her husband cried out: "How stupid we are! Go and find your friend Mrs. Forestier and ask her to lend you her jewels. You are well enough acquainted with her to do this."

She uttered a cry of joy: "It is true!" she said. "I had not thought of that."

The next day she took herself to her friend's house and related her story of distress. Mrs. Forestier went to her closet with the glass doors, took out a large jewel-case, brought it, opened it, and said: "Choose, my dear."

She saw at first some bracelets, then a collar of pearls, then a Venetian cross of gold and jewels and of admirable workmanship. She tried the jewels before the glass, hesitated, but could neither decide to take them nor leave them. Then she asked:

"Have you nothing more?"

"Why, yes. Look for yourself. I do not know what will please you."

Suddenly she discovered, in a black satin box, a superb necklace of diamonds, and her heart beat fast with an immoderate desire. Her hands trembled as she took them up. She placed them about her throat against her dress, and remained in ecstasy before them. Then she asked, in a hesitating voice, full of anxiety:

"Could you lend me this? Only this?"

"Why, yes, certainly."

She fell upon the neck of her friend, embraced her with passion, then went away with her treasure.

The day of the ball arrived. Mme. Loisel was a great success. She was the prettiest of all, elegant, gracious, smiling, and full of joy. All the men noticed her, asked her name, and wanted to be presented. All the members of the Cabinet wished to waltz with her. The Minister of Education paid her some attention.

She danced with enthusiasm, with passion, intoxicated with pleasure, thinking of nothing, in the triumph of her beauty, in the glory of her success, in a kind of cloud of happiness that came of all this homage, and all this admiration, of all these awakened desires, and this victory so complete and sweet to the heart of woman.

She went home toward four o'clock in the morning. Her husband had been half asleep in one of the little salons since midnight, with three other gentlemen whose wives were enjoying themselves very much.

He threw around her shoulders the wraps they had carried for the coming home, modest garments of everyday wear, whose poverty clashed with the elegance of the ball costume. She felt this and wished to hurry away in order not to be noticed by the other women who were wrapping themselves in rich furs.

Loisel retained her: "Wait," said he. "You will catch cold out there. I am going to call a cab."

But she would not listen and descended the steps rapidly. When they were in the street, they found no carriage; and they began to seek for one, hailing the coachmen whom they saw at a distance.

They walked along toward the Seine, hopeless and shivering. Finally they found on the dock one of these old, noctural *coupés* that one sees in Paris after nightfall, as if they were ashamed of their misery by day.

It took them as far as their door in Martyr street, and they went wearily up to their apartment. It was all over for her. And on his part, he remembered that he would have to be at the office by ten o'clock.

She removed the wraps from her shoulders before the glass, for a final view of herself in her glory. Suddenly she uttered a cry. Her necklace was not around her neck.

Her husband, already half undressed, asked: "What is the matter?" She turned toward him excitedly:

"I have—I have—I no longer have Mrs. Forestier's necklace." He arose in dismay: "What! How is that? It is not possible."

And they looked in the folds of the dress, in the folds of the mantle, in the pockets, everywhere. They could not find it.

He asked: "You are sure you still had it when we left the house?"

"Yes, I felt it in the vestibule as we came out."

"But if you had lost it in the street, we should have heard it fall. It must be in the cab."

"Yes. It is probable. Did you take the number?"

"No. And you, did you notice what it was?"

"No."

They looked at each other utterly cast down. Finally, Loisel dressed himself again.

"I am going," said he, "over the track where we went on foot, to see if I can find it."

And he went. She remained in her evening gown, not having the force to go to bed, stretched upon a chair, without ambition or thoughts.

Toward seven o'clock her husband returned. He had found nothing.

He went to the police and to the cab offices, and put an advertisement in the newspapers, offering a reward; he did everything that afforded them a suspicion of hope.

She waited all day in a state of bewilderment before this frightful disaster. Loisel returned at evening with his face harrowed and pale; and had discovered nothing.

"It will be necessary," said he, "to write to your friend that you have broken the clasp of the necklace and that you will have it repaired. That will give us time to turn around."

She wrote as he dictated.

At the end of a week, they had lost all hope. And Loisel, older by five years, declared:

"We must take measures to replace this jewel."

The next day they took the box which had inclosed it, to the jeweler whose name was on the inside. He consulted his books:

"It is not I, Madame," said he, "who sold this necklace; I only furnished the casket."

Then they went from jeweler to jeweler seeking a necklace like the other one, consulting their memories, and ill, both of them, with chagrin and anxiety.

In a shop of the Palais-Royal, they found a chaplet of diamonds which seemed to them exactly like the one they had lost. It was valued at forty thousand francs. They could get it for thirty-six thousand.

They begged the jeweler not to sell it for three days. And they made an arrangement by which they might return it for thirty-four thousand francs if they found the other one before the end of February.

Loisel possessed eighteen thousand francs which his father had left him. He borrowed the rest.

He borrowed it, asking for a thousand francs of one, five hundred of another, five louis of this one, and three louis of that one. He gave notes, made ruinous promises, took money of usurers and the whole race of lenders. He compromised his whole existence in fact, risked his signature, without even knowing whether he could make it good or not, and, harassed by anxiety for the future, by the black misery which surrounded him, and by the prospect of all physical privations and moral torture, he went to get the new necklace, depositing on the merchant's counter thirty-six thousand francs.

When Mrs. Loisel took back the jewels to Mrs. Forestier, the latter said to her in a frigid tone:

"You should have returned them to me sooner, for I might have needed them."

She did open the jewel-box as her friend feared she would. If she should perceive the substitution, what would she think? What should she say? Would she take her for a robber?

Mrs. Loisel now knew the horrible life of necessity. She did her part, however, completely heroically. It was necessary to pay this frightful debt. She would pay it. They sent away the maid; they changed their lodgings; they rented some rooms under a mansard roof.

She learned the heavy cares of a household, the odious work of a kitchen. She washed the dishes, using her rosy nails upon the greasy pots and the bottoms of the stewpans. She washed the soiled linen, the chemises and dishcloths, which she hung on the line to dry; she took down the refuse to the street each morning and brought up the water, stopping at each landing to breathe. And, clothed like a woman of the people she went to the grocer's, the butcher's and the fruiterer's, with her basket on her arm, shopping, haggling to the last sou her miserable money.

Every month it was necessary to renew some notes, thus obtaining time, and to pay others.

The husband worked evenings, putting the books of some merchants in order, and nights he often did copying at five sous a page.

And this life lasted for ten years.

At the end of ten years, they had restored all, all, with interest of the usurer, and accumulated interest besides.

Mrs. Loisel seemed old now. She had become a strong, hard woman, the crude woman of the poor husband. Her hair badly dressed, her skirts awry, her hands red, she spoke in a loud tone, and washed the floors with large pails of water. But sometimes, when her husband was at the office, she would seat herself before the window and think of that evening party of former times, of that ball where she was so beautiful and so flattered.

How would it have been if she had not lost that necklace? Who knows? Who knows? How singular is life, and how full of changes! How small a thing will ruin or save one!

One Sunday, as she was taking a walk in the Champs-Elysées to rid herself of the cares of the week, she suddenly perceived a woman walking with a child. It was Mrs. Forestier, still young, still pretty, still attractive. Mrs. Loisel was affected. Should she speak to her? Yes, certainly. And now that she had paid, she would tell her all. Why not?

She approached her. "Good morning, Jeanne."

Her friend did not recognize her and was astonished to be so familiarly addressed by this common personage. She stammered:

"But, Madame—I do not know—You must be mistaken—"

"No, I am Matilda Loisel."

Her friend uttered a cry of astonishment: "Oh! my poor Matilda! How you have changed—"

"Yes, I have had some hard days since I saw you; and some miserable ones—and all because of you—"

"Because of me? How is that?"

"You recall the diamond necklace that you loaned me to wear to the Commissioner's ball?"

"Yes, very well."

"Well, I lost it."

"How is that, since you returned it to me?"

"I returned another to you exactly like it. And it has taken us ten years to pay for it. You can understand that it was not easy for us who have nothing. But it is finished and I am decently content."

Madame Forestier stopped short. She said:

"You say that you bought a diamond necklace to replace mine?"

"Yes. You did not perceive it then? They were just alike."

And she smiled with a proud and simple joy. Madame Forestier was touched and took both her hands as she replied:

"Oh! my poor Matilda! Mine were false. They were not worth over five hundred francs!"

And, finally, a modern-day fairy tale, "The Moon Ribbon," by Jane Yolen. I found this story in a witty collection of feminist fairy tales, entitled *Don't Bet on the Prince,* edited by Jack Zipes.

The Moon Ribbon
Jane Yolen

There was once a plain but good-hearted girl named Sylva whose sole possession was a ribbon her mother had left her. It was a strange ribbon, the color of moonlight, for it had been woven from the gray hairs of her mother and her mother's mother and her mother's mother's mother before her.

Sylva lived with her widowed father in a great house by the forest's edge. Once the great house had belonged to her mother, but when she died, it became Sylva's father's house to do with as he willed. And what he willed was to live simply and happily with his daughter without thinking of the day to come.

But one day, when there was little enough to live on, and only the great house to recommend him, Sylva's father married again, a beautiful widow who had two beautiful daughters of her own.

It was a disastrous choice, for no sooner were they wed when it was apparent the woman was mean in spirit and meaner in tongue. She dismissed most of the servants and gave their chores over to Sylva, who followed her orders without complaint. For simply living in her mother's house with her loving father seemed enough for the girl.

After a bit, however, the old man died in order to have some peace, and the house passed on to the stepmother. Scarcely two days had passed, or maybe three, when the stepmother left off mourning the old man and turned on Sylva. She dismissed the last of the servants without their pay.

'Girl,' she called out, for she never used Sylva's name, 'you will sleep in the kitchen and do the charring.' And from that time on it was so.

Sylva swept the floor and washed and mended the family's clothing. She sowed and hoed and tended the fields. She ground the wheat and kneaded the bread, and she waited on the others as though she were a servant. But she did not complain.

Yet late at night, when the stepmother and her own two daughters were asleep, Sylva would weep bitterly into her pillow, which was nothing more than an old broom laid in front of the hearth.

One day, when she was cleaning out an old desk, Sylva came upon a hidden drawer she had never seen before. Trembling, she opened the drawer. It was empty except for a silver ribbon with a label attached to it. *For Sylva* read the card. *The Moon Ribbon of Her Mother's Hair.* She took it out and stared at it. And all that she had lost was borne in upon her. She felt the tears start in her eyes, and, so as not to cry, she took the tag off and began to stroke the ribbon with her hand. It was rough and smooth at once, and shone like the rays of the moon.

At that moment her stepsisters came into the room.

'What is that?' asked one. 'It is nice? It is mine.'

'I want it. I saw it first,' cried the other.

The noise brought the stepmother to them. 'Show it to me,' she said.

Obediently, Sylva came over and held the ribbon out to her. But when the stepmother picked it up, it looked like no more than strands of gray hair woven together unevenly. It was prickly to touch.

'Disgusting,' said the stepmother dropping it back into Sylva's hand. 'Throw it out at once.'

'Burn it,' cried one stepsister.

'Bury it,' cried the other.

'Oh, please. It was my mother's. She left it for me. Please let me keep it,' begged Sylva.

The stepmother looked again at the gray strand. 'Very well,' she said with a grim smile. 'It suits you.' And she strode out of the room, her daughters behind her.

Now that she had the silver ribbon, Sylva thought her life would be better. But instead it became worse. As if to punish her for speaking out for the ribbon, her sisters were at her to wait on them both day and night. And whereas before she had to sleep by the hearth, she now had to sleep outside with the animals. Yet she did not complain or run away, for she was tied by her memories to her mother's house.

One night, when the frost was on the grass turning each blade into a silver spear, Sylva threw herself to the ground in tears. And the silver ribbon, which she had loosely about her hair, slipped off and lay on the ground before her. She had never seen it in the moonlight. It glittered and shone and seemed to ripple.

Sylva bent over to touch it and her tears fell upon it. Suddenly the ribbon began to grow and change, and as it changed the air was filled with a woman's soft voice speaking these words:

Silver ribbon, silver hair,
Carry Sylva with great care,
Bring my daughter home.

And there at Sylva's feet was a silver river that glittered and shone and rippled in the moonlight.

There was neither boat nor bridge, but Sylva did not care. She thought the river would wash away her sorrows. And without a single word, she threw herself in.

But she did not sink. Instead, she floated like a swan and the river bore her on, on past houses and hills, past high places and low. And strange to say, she was not wet at all.

At last she was carried around a great bend in the river and deposited gently on a grassy slope that came right down to the water's edge. Sylva scrambled up onto the bank and looked about. There was a great meadow of grass so green and still it might have been painted on. At the meadow's rim, near a dark forest, sat a house that was like and yet not like the one in which Sylva lived.

'Surely someone will be there who can tell me where I am and why I have been brought here,' she thought. So she made her way across the meadow, and only where she stepped down did the grass move. When she moved beyond, the grass sprang back and was the same as before. And though she passed larkspur and meadowsweet, clover and rye, they did not seem like real flowers, for they had no smell at all.

'Am I dreaming?' she wondered, 'or am I dead?' But she did not say it out loud, for she was afraid to speak into the silence.

Sylva walked up to the house and hesitated at the door. She feared to knock and yet feared equally not to. As she was deciding, the door opened of itself and she walked in.

She found herself in a large, long, dark hall with a single crystal door at the end that emitted a strange glow the color of moonlight. As she walked down the hall, her shoes made no clatter on the polished wood floor. And when she reached the door, she tried to peer through into the room beyond, but the crystal panes merely gave back her own reflection twelve times.

Sylva reached for the doorknob and pulled sharply. The glowing crystal knob came off in her hand. She would have wept then, but anger stayed her; she beat her fist against the door and it suddenly gave way.

Inside was a small room lit only by a fireplace and a round white globe that hung from the ceiling like a pale, wan moon. Before the fireplace stood a tall woman dressed all in white. Her silver-white hair was unbound and cascaded to her knees. Around her neck was a silver ribbon.

'Welcome, my daughter,' she said.

'Are you my mother?' asked Sylva wonderingly, for what little she remembered of her mother, she remembered no one as grand as this.

'I am if you make me so,' came the reply.

'And how do I do that?' asked Sylva.

'Give me your hand.'

As the woman spoke, she seemed to move away, yet she moved not at all. Instead the floor between them moved and cracked apart. Soon they were separated by a great chasm which was so black it seemed to have no bottom.

'I cannot reach,' said Sylva.

'You must try,' the woman replied.

So Sylva clutched the crystal knob to her breast and leaped, but it was too far. As she fell, she heard a woman's voice speaking from behind her and before her and all about her, warm with praise.

'Well done, my daughter. You are halfway home.'

Sylva landed gently on the meadow grass, but a moment's walk from her house. In her hand she still held the knob, shrunk now to the size of a jewel. The river shimmered once before her and was gone, and where it had been was the silver ribbon, lying limp and damp in the morning frost.

The door to the house stood open. She drew a deep breath and went in.

'What is that?' cried one of the stepsisters when she saw the crystalline jewel in Sylva's hand.

'I want it,' cried the other, grabbing it from her.

'I will take it,' said the stepmother, snatching it from them all. She held it up to the light and examined it. 'It will fetch a good price and repay me for my care of you. Where did you get it?' she asked Sylva. Sylva tried to tell them of the ribbon and the river, the tall woman and the black crevasse. But they laughed at her and did not believe her. Yet they could not explain away the jewel. So they left her then and went off to the city to sell it. When they returned, it was late. They thrust Sylva outside to sleep and went themselves to their comfortable beds to dream of their new riches.

Sylva sat on the cold ground and thought about what had happened. She reached up and took down the ribbon from her hair. She stroked it, and it felt smooth and soft and yet hard, too. Carefully she placed it on the ground.

In the moonlight, the ribbon glittered and shone. Sylva recalled the song she had heard, so she sang it to herself:

Silver ribbon, silver hair,
Carry Sylva with great care,
Bring my daughter home.

Suddenly the ribbon began to grow and change, and there at her feet was a silver highway that glittered and glistened in the moonlight.

Without a moment's hesitation, Sylva got up and stepped out onto the road and waited for it to bring her to the magical house.

But the road did not move.

'Strange,' she said to herself. 'Why does it not carry me as the river did?'

Sylva stood on the road and waited a moment more, then tentatively set one foot in front of the other. As soon as she had set off on her own, the road set off, too, and they moved together past fields and forests, faster and faster, till the scenery seemed to fly by and blur into a moon-bleached rainbow of yellows, grays, and black.

The road took a great turning and then quite suddenly stopped, but Sylva did not. She scrambled up the bank where the road ended and found herself again in the meadow. At the far rim of the grass, where the forest began, was the house she had seen before.

Sylva strode purposefully through the grass, and this time the meadow was filled with the song of birds, the meadowlark and the bunting and the sweet jug-jug-jug of the nightingale. She could smell fresh-mown hay and the pungent pine.

The door of the house stood wide open, so Sylva went right in. The long hall was no longer dark but filled with the strange moonglow. And when she reached the crystal door at the end, and gazed at her reflection twelve times in the glass, she saw her own face set with strange gray eyes and long gray hair. She put up her hand to her mouth to stop herself from crying out. But the sound came through, and the door opened of itself.

Inside was the tall woman all in white, and the globe above her was as bright as a harvest moon.

'Welcome, my sister,' the woman said.

'I have no sister,' said Sylva, 'but the two stepsisters I left at home. And you are none of those.'

'I am if you make me so.'

'How do I do that?'

'Give me back my heart which you took from me yesterday.'

'I did not take your heart. I took nothing but a crystal jewel.'

The woman smiled. 'It was my heart.'

Sylva looked stricken. 'But I cannot give it back. My stepmother took it from me.'

'No one can take unless you give.'

'I had no choice.'

'There is always a choice,' the woman said.

Sylva would have cried then, but a sudden thought struck her. 'Then it must have been your choice to give me your heart.'

The woman smiled again, nodded gently, and held out her hand.

Sylva placed her hand in the woman's and there glowed for a moment on the woman's breast a silvery jewel that melted and disappeared.

'Now will you give me your heart?'

'I have done that already,' said Sylva, and as she said it, she knew it to be true.

The woman reached over and touched Sylva on her breast, and her heart sprang out onto the woman's hand and turned into two fiery red jewels. 'Once given, twice gained,' said the woman. She handed one of the jewels back to Sylva. 'Only take care that you give each jewel with love.'

Sylva felt the jewel warm and glowing in her hand, and at its touch felt such comfort as she had not had in many days. She closed her eyes and a smile came on her face. And when she opened her eyes again, she was standing on the meadow grass not two steps from her own door. It was morning, and by her feet lay the silver ribbon, limp and damp from the frost.

The door to her house stood open.

Sylva drew in her breath, picked up the ribbon, and went in.

'What has happened to your hair?' asked one stepsister.

'What has happened to your eyes?' asked the other.

For indeed Sylva's hair and eyes had turned as silver as the moon.

But the stepmother saw only the fiery red jewel in Sylva's hand. 'Give it to me,' she said, pointing to the gem.

At first Sylva held out her hand, but then quickly drew it back. 'I *can* not,' she said.

The stepmother's eyes became hard. 'Girl, give it here.'

'I *will* not,' said Sylva.

The stepmother's eyes narrowed. 'Then you shall tell me where you got it.'

'That I shall, and gladly,' said Sylva. She told them of the silver ribbon and the silver road, of the house with the crystal door. But strange to say, she left out the woman and her words.

The stepmother closed her eyes and thought. At last she said, 'Let me see this wondrous silver ribbon, that I may believe what you say.'

Sylva handed her the ribbon, but she was not fooled by her stepmother's tone.

The moment the silver ribbon lay prickly and limp in the stepmother's hand, she looked up triumphantly at Sylva. Her face broke into a wolfish grin. 'Fool,' she said, 'the magic is herein. With this ribbon there are jewels for the taking.' She marched out of the door, and the stepsisters hurried behind her.

Sylva walked after them, but slowly, stopping in the open door.

The stepmother flung the ribbon down. In the early morning sun it glowed as if with a cold flame.

'Say the words, girl,' the stepmother commanded.

From the doorway Sylva whispered:

Silver ribbon, silver hair,
Lead the ladies with great care,
Lead them to their home.

The silver ribbon wriggled and withered in the sunlight, and as they watched, it turned into a silver-red stair that went down into the ground.

'Wait,' called Sylva. 'Do not go.' But it was too late.

With a great shout, the stepmother gathered up her skirts and ran down the steps, her daughters fast behind her. And before Sylva could move, the ground had closed up after them and the meadow was as before.

On the grass lay the silver ribbon, limp and dull, Sylva went over and picked it up. As she did so, the jewel melted in her hand and she felt a burning in her breast. She put her hand up to it, and she felt her heart beating strongly beneath. Sylva smiled, put the silver ribbon in her pocket, and went back into her house.

After a time, Sylva's hair returned to its own color, except for seven silver strands, but her eyes never changed back. And when she was married and had a child of her own, Sylva plucked the silver strands from her own hair and wove them into the silver ribbon, which she kept in a wooden box. When Sylva's child was old enough to understand, the box with the ribbon was put into her safekeeping, and she has kept them for her own daughter to this very day.

```
    I remember well my sensation as we first entered
the house. I knew instantly that something was
very wrong. I realized that my father's chair had
been sat in, as well as my mother's and my own.
The porridge we had left on the table to cool had
been partially eaten. None of this, however, pre-
pared me for what we were about to discover up-
stairs. . . .
```

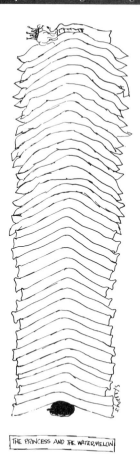

THE PRINCESS AND THE WATERMELON

FILLING THE GAPS

Some texts are closed, finished; all the threads are sewn together with invisible seams. Mysteries are often like this: we expect them to be "finished," with no loose ends. But many stories—those we meet both in texts and in life—are "open"; that is, even after we have "finished" a short story or a novel or an intriguing biography or autobiography, or have heard (or seen or read) a particularly unsettling news story, or have read or heard of bizarre or strange happenings to a friend (or experienced them ourselves), we find that the story keeps "talking" to us. It's unfinished, unsettled; it "leaks." There are gaps to be filled. We keep finishing the story. Or we want to make changes: to go back to the "beginning" and start all over again, or transform the villain and make the good win out over the bad, or turn someone back to what they were, or wave a magic wand and heal the dying hero.

At the end of "The Diamond Necklace" De Maupassant leaves us hanging, standing on the street with "poor Matilda" as she hears the news that all her and her poor husband's efforts were in vain: the diamond necklace was fake! What does she say? What happens next? We can't, of course, extract any other ending from De Maupassant. (John Fowles was so moved by readers protesting the ending of one of his novels, *The Magus,* that he obliged them by writing another!) We can take pen in hand, though, and take over the text, if we so choose. Why not?

Try this:

Take over De Maupassant's "The Diamond Necklace" and "continue the ending." What happens next? Put words into Matilda's mouth, and take her home to her husband. What does she tell him? And what is his reaction?

What other gaps can you fill? Where are the holes for you in the story?

· · ·

We return, now, to Hemingway's "Hills Like White Elephants," this time for a different reading, a different purpose—to fill in some of his gaps.

In his now-famous comments on "the underwater part of the iceberg," Hemingway actually talks about deliberately making gaps in his stories, leaving holes. Reading "Hills Like White Elephants" is like meeting an iceberg, isn't it? We know that we're only getting the visible, above-the-water part of the iceberg. We overheard a bit of conversation, a "strip" of human interaction: we know that this is *not* the whole story, and yet this *is* all the text we have. So we're left wondering: what's the American *really* thinking? What's the girl *really* thinking? What does the waitress think? The waitress, after all, is in very much the position that we are in—we, like her, are overhearers. In fact, the man calls to "the woman" through the curtain:

> The man called "Listen" through the curtain.
> The woman came out from the bar.

What are they going to do when the train comes? Will "the girl" get on with the American? Or will she stay? Hemingway leaves us waiting for that train!

Try this:

One way of *reading* the text is to let our imaginations loose and to fill in some of the gaps. Try it now, before you read on. Choose one or all of these exercises:

1. Choose a moment or two in the story where you sense a gap—the underwater part of the iceberg—and allow the American to "speak his mind." Represent his inner speech, that is, the inner stream of language going on in his mind.
2. Do the same for the girl, Jig.

3. Allow the waitress to speak—either to herself, or to another person. What does she see, and how does she interpret what she sees and hears?

4. Continue on with the ending. What happens next? Try to imitate what you see as Hemingway's style.

• • •

Now read the following reactions, from three of my students: here are their versions of the American, the girl, and the waitress.

1. The American

"I'd better take the bags over to the other side of the station," the man said. She smiled at him.

"All right. Then come back and we'll finish the beer."

He picked up the two heavy bags and carried them around the station to the other tracks. He looked up the tracks but could not see the train.

What in the hell am I doing here? he thought to himself. I need to get away. How did I ever get involved with this brainless winning child? I swear I should have my head examined. Have I lost my senses? Traveling clear across the country, dragging that child from hotel to hotel—I need a break. White Elephants—just like before—what was it we actually had before? Nothing. I at last know that much—no, nothing—heartache—more than I need. . . . it's not worth it. Worth what? I don't need any ties. I don't need anyone slowing me down. I don't need a full time bedwarmer. I don't need these problems. If things were just different . . . I don't know, maybe if this hadn't happened, things would be better—who knows? Things would be the same. They weren't so bad. . . . huh, we had some pretty good times back then—aw, who knows? I'll stay with her, straighten out this mess, and at least I'll know better for the next time. She needs me, what would she do without me? I can't just leave her alone. No, I'll stay, for now anyway, who knows, maybe things'll work out for the best. Heck, they don't make guys like me anymore. I'm too soft. . . .

Coming back, he walked through the barroom, where people waiting for the train were drinking. He drank an Anis at the bar and looked at the people. They were all waiting reasonably for the train. He went out through the bead curtain. She was sitting at the table and smiled at him.

"Do you feel better?" he asked.

"I feel fine," she said. "There's nothing wrong with me. I feel fine."

Mark Rothenberg

2. The waitress

The waitress put the felt pads and the beer glasses on the table and looked at the man and the girl and she started thinking about them.

"This is a very pretty girl and he is a handsome man; it's a nice couple. But I don't think that they are married to each other because both of them look very young; they must be between eighteen and twenty years old.

It seems to me that they have a problem. They don't seem happy; maybe something is bothering them.

Look at the girl. She is looking at the hills, but her eyes look worried. She said something about the hills, but she is very serious and pensive. The man is looking at her, and he is trying to tell her something.

I think the man is calling me now. They want another drink.

But what are they talking about? Did I hear well? The man said something about an operation. But what kind of operation? Is the girl sick? He said that it's a very simple operation and he is not worried. "I love you." "I won't worry." "It's perfectly simple," he keeps telling her. I think he is trying to convince the girl to do this operation, but the girl doesn't want to. "But I don't want anybody but you. I don't want anyone else. And I know it's perfectly simple," the man said.

Yes I think I know what they are talking about. The girl must be pregnant, and the man doesn't want the baby.

I don't understand these men. First, they like one girl, they go with her and then when the girl becomes pregnant, they don't want to keep the baby. Men."

Pareskevi Loizou

3. A New Ending

"You look worried, but there is nothing to worry about, you know," said the man.

The girl was silent, but she got up from her seat near the table and walked towards the track.

"They are lovely hills," she said, "so white and. . . ." She spotted the train; it was coming from behind the hills. "It will arrive any minute now," she said. Then, she turned to the man.

"Where are my bags?" she asked. "I will go alone; it will be better this way. You will wait for me here until I return, when I will be ready."

"What? You are going alone?" asked the man. "I told you I would do anything for you. I will come with you and I will be with you. Then we will come back here and everything will be fine and we will be happy and. . . . Are you sure you want to go by yourself?"

The girl wasn't listening. She looked at the hills and watched the train getting closer to the station. She turned to the man and looked at him with vivid eyes and then she picked up her bags.

Liora Tziyon

Edgar Allan Poe in a moment of writer's block

INFLUENCES

Consider this:

Look at how Gary Larson's "new" takes on the "old":

What's the joke?

Probably most of you recognize the play on Edgar Allan Poe's short story, "The Tell-Tale Heart." The recognition comes from your cultural *funding*. And if you do make the connection, recognize the source (the "literary allusion"), then you feel a part of a particular club—the same as when you get an "inside joke." You're privy to the unwritten rules of a cultural game.

What if you don't get the joke? It's useful to recognize that *we'll never get every joke*—no matter how "funded" we are—but that the more we learn about all kinds of things, the more we will find one kind of knowledge intersecting with another.

What "inside information" do you need to "get" the following jokes? Are all the allusions literary? If not, where do ghosts come from?

On a clear day, Eugene rose and looked around him and, regrettably, saw who he was.

"Why, thank you. ... Thank you very much!"

"Hold it! There's a car across the street — you sure
you weren't followed, Mary?"

RAPUNZEL AT THE HOP

"No, he's not busy. . . . In fact, that whole thing is
just a myth."

What about this one? What do you need to know to get the joke?

"But can they save themselves?"

Consider this:

Ghostly interlocutors may serve as nagging reminders of the promises and failures of the past. Martin Luther King's powerful speech, "I Have a Dream" (1968), marking the struggles of the Civil Rights Movement, harkens back to Abraham Lincoln's promises and hopes for the war-torn nation of the Civil War, articulated in his "Gettysburg Address" (1865).

Read Lincoln's words first, and then King's. How and where do you, specifically, hear Lincoln in King?

The Gettysburg Address
Abraham Lincoln

Four score and seven years ago our fathers brought forth on this continent, a new nation, conceived in Liberty, and dedicated to the proposition that all men are created equal.

Now we are engaged in a great civil war, testing whether that nation, or any nation so conceived and so dedicated, can long endure. We are met on a great battle-field of that war. We have come to dedicate a portion of that field, as a final resting place for those who here gave their lives that that nation might live. It is altogether fitting and proper that we should do this.

But, in a larger sense, we can not dedicate—we can not consecrate—we can not hallow—this ground. The brave men, living and dead, who struggled here, have consecrated it, far above our poor power to add or detract. The world will little note, nor long remember what we say here, but it can never forget what they did here. It is for us the living, rather, to be dedicated here to the unfinished work which they who fought here have thus far so nobly advanced. It is rather for us to be here dedicated to the great task remaining before us—that from these honored dead we take increased devotion to that cause for which they gave the last full measure of devotion—that we here highly resolve that these dead shall not have died in vain—that this nation, under God, shall have a new birth of freedom—and that government of the people, by the people, for the people, shall not perish from the earth.

I Have a Dream
Martin Luther King, Jr.

Five score years ago, a great American, in whose symbolic shadow we stand, signed the Emancipation Proclamation. This momentous decree came as a great beacon light of hope to millions of Negro slaves who had been seared in the flames of withering injustice. It came as a joyous daybreak to end the long night of captivity.

But one hundred years later, we must face the tragic fact that the Negro is still not free. One hundred years later, the life of the Negro is still sadly crippled by the manacles of segregation and the chains of discrimination. One hundred years later, the Negro lives on a lonely island of poverty in the midst of a vast ocean of material prosperity. One hundred years later, the Negro is still languishing in the corners of American society and finds himself an exile in his own land. So we have come here today to dramatize an appalling condition.

In a sense we have come to our nation's Capitol to cash a check. When the architects of our republic wrote the magnificent words of the Constitution and the Declaration of Independence, they were signing a promissory note to which every American was to fall heir. This note was a promise that all men would be guaranteed the unalienable rights of life, liberty, and the pursuit of happiness.

It is obvious today that America has defaulted on this promissory note insofar as her citizens of color are concerned. Instead of honoring this sacred obligation, America has given the Negro people a bad check; a check which has come back marked "insufficient funds." But we refuse to believe that the bank of justice is bankrupt. We refuse to believe that there are insufficient funds in the great vaults of opportunity of this nation. So we have come to cash this check—a check that will give us upon demand the riches of freedom and the security of justice. We have also come to this hallowed spot to remind America of the fierce urgency of *now*. This is no time to engage in the luxury of cooling off or to take the tranquilizing drug of gradualism. *Now* is the time to make real the promises of Democracy. *Now* is the time to rise from the dark and desolate valley of segregation to the sunlit path of racial justice. *Now* is the time to open the doors of opportunity to all of God's children. *Now* is the time to lift our nation from the quicksands of racial injustice to the solid rock of brotherhood.

It would be fatal for the nation to overlook the urgency of the moment and to underestimate the determination of the Negro. This sweltering summer of the Negro's legitimate discontent will not pass until there is an invigorating autumn of freedom and equality. 1963 is not an end, but a beginning. Those who hope that the Negro needed to blow off steam and will now be content will have a rude awakening if the nation returns to business as usual. There will be neither rest nor tranquility in America until the Negro is granted his citizenship rights. The whirlwinds of revolt will continue to shake the foundations of our nation until the bright day of justice emerges.

But there is something I must say to my people who stand on the warm threshold which leads into the palace of justice. In the process of gaining our rightful place we must not be guilty of wrongful deeds. Let us not seek to satisfy our thirst for freedom by drinking from the cup of bitterness and hatred. We must forever conduct our struggle on the high plane of dignity and discipline. We must not allow our creative protest to degenerate into physical violence. Again and again we must rise to the majestic heights of meeting physical force with soul force. The marvelous new militancy which has engulfed the Negro community must not lead us to a distrust of all white people, for many of our white brothers, as evidenced by their presence here today, have come to realize that their destiny is tied up with our destiny and their freedom is inextricably bound to our freedom. We cannot walk alone.

And as we walk, we must make the pledge that we shall march ahead. We cannot turn back. There are those who are asking the devotees of civil rights, "When will you be satisfied?" We can never be satisfied as long as the Negro is the victim of the unspeakable horrors of police brutality. We can never be satisfied as long as our bodies, heavy with the fatigue of travel, cannot gain lodging in the motels of the highways and the hotels of the cities. We cannot be satisfied as long as the Negro's basic mobility is from a smaller ghetto to a larger one. We can never be satisfied as long as a Negro in Mississippi cannot vote and a Negro in New York believes he has nothing for which to vote. No, no, we are not satisfied, and we will not be satisfied until justice rolls down like waters and righteousness like a mighty stream.

I am not unmindful that some of you have come here out of great trials and tribulations. Some of you have come fresh from narrow jail cells. Some of you have come from areas where your quest for freedom left you battered by the storms of persecution and staggered by the winds of police brutality. You have been the veterans of creative suffering. Continue to work with the faith that unearned suffering is redemptive.

Go back to Mississippi, go back to Alabama, go back to South Carolina, go back to Georgia, go back to Louisiana, go back to the slums and ghettoes of our northern cities, knowing that somehow this situation can and will be changed. Let us not wallow in the valley of despair.

I say to you today, my friends, that in spite of the difficulties and frustrations of the moment I still have a dream. It is a dream deeply rooted in the American dream.

I have a dream that one day this nation will rise up and live out the true meaning of its creed: "We hold these truths to be self-evident; that all men are created equal."

I have a dream that one day on the red hills of Georgia the sons of former slaves and the sons of former slave-owners will be able to sit down together at the table of brotherhood.

I have a dream that the state of Mississippi, a desert state sweltering with the heat of injustice and oppression, will be transformed into an oasis of freedom and justice.

I have a dream that my four little children will one day live in a nation where they will not be judged by the color of their skin but by the content of their character.

I have a dream today.

I have a dream that the state of Alabama, whose governor's lips are presently dripping with the words of interposition and nullification, will be transformed into a situation where little black boys and black girls will be able to join hands with little white boys and white girls and walk together as sisters and brothers.

I have a dream today.

I have a dream that one day every valley shall be exalted, every hill and mountain shall be made low, the rough places will be made plain, and the crooked places will be made straight, and the glory of the Lord shall be revealed, and all flesh shall see it together.

This is our hope. This is the faith with which I return to the South. With this faith we will be able to hew out of the mountain of despair a stone of hope. With this faith we will be able to transform the jangling discords of our nation into a beautiful symphony of brotherhood. With this faith we will be able to work together, to pray together, to struggle together, to go to jail together, to stand up for freedom together, knowing that we will be free one day.

This will be the day when all of God's children will be able to sing with new meaning:

My country, 'tis of thee
Sweet land of liberty
   Of thee I sing:
Land where my fathers died,
Land of the pilgrims' pride,
From every mountainside
   Let freedom ring.

And if America is to be a great nation this must become true. So let freedom ring from the prodigious hilltops of New Hampshire. Let freedom ring from the heightening Alleghenies of Pennsylvania!

Let freedom ring from the snowcapped Rockies of Colorado!

Let freedom ring from the curvaceous peaks of California!

But not only that; let freedom ring from Stone Mountain of Georgia!

Let freedom ring from every hill and molehill of Mississippi. From every mountainside, let freedom ring.

When we let freedom ring, when we let it ring from every village and every hamlet, from every state and every city, we will be able to speed up that day when all of God's children, black men and white men, Jews and Gentiles, Protestants and Catholics, will be able to join hands and sing in the words of the old Negro spiritual, "Free at last! free at last! thank God almighty, we are free at last!"

Finally, look at how Daphne Merkin in her essay, "Prince Charming Comes Back," considers the Cinderella myth in her discussion of the film, *Pretty Woman*. Do you need to have seen the film to make sense of her argument about our transformation of the fairy tale? Is the film even around at this moment when you're reading her review? What current films might apply to Merkin's critical frame of reference—that "we still need our myths, our amatory fictions" because "they help us endure."

MIMI POND

Prince Charming Comes Back

Prince Charming Comes Back
Daphne Merkin

Just the other day it happened again: I was sifting through a rack of charming but inflationary baby clothes together with my friend Susan when she said, sotto voce: "I talked to my cousin yesterday. She saw 'Pretty Woman.' She said she loved it, too." Although I doubt Susan's cousin loves the movie as much as Susan does (she's seen it three times), the list of suspects keeps growing. My friend Willa is up to four viewings. I myself have gone twice so far and have devoted several phone conversations to rapt discussions of the movie—one of which concerned the motivation of the Richard Gere character, at the sort of arcane level of discourse more usually to be found in a graduate seminar on "Middlemarch."

It's a small but noteworthy phenomenon, this illicit affection for a glossy cinematic fairy tale about a prostitute and a high-rolling businessman that's gripped the hearts and minds of a surprising number of the women I know. Independent-minded women all, ranging from 20-year-olds to a friend's 83-year-old aunt, most of them admit to their fondness abashedly, as though they've been caught indulging a taste for something unworthy or sickly sweet. There are those who have confessed only under duress, in the line of direct questioning; I have found this to be particularly true for women in their early 20's. Inheritors of the feminist mystique, they are peers of the women who felt compelled to protest the choice of Barbara Bush as a commencement speaker.

For self-aware young women such as these, owning up to the pleasures of a retro, gender-structured movie like "Pretty Woman" verges on the "politically incorrect"—and thus is even more of a statement, a sign that you dare think for yourself. "Not only did I enjoy the movie," says a 22-year-old writer, "I don't like the people who don't. They disturb me. I think they lack humor and perspective."

Others, like my friend Deborah, a decade older and more bemused, have less personally at stake but still concede the issue with a foreordained defensiveness: "I liked it," she says, "I liked it completely."

Another voice: "It's been a long time since I've thought about a movie so much, wishing for the sequel to come soon." So speaks Sara, a skeptical-to-the-bone woman, divorced, a family therapist, relatively immune to the myth of The Redemptive Male—the right man will provide you with the right life—that women have historically lived by. Or is she? Are, indeed, any of us, with or without husbands or lovers? Judging by the response to this brightly shellacked and cannily updated Pygmalion story, the answer is no. If it weren't already a movie, it could be a book, one of those best-selling syndrome books purporting to explain the inexplicable behavior of the female of the species: "Pretty Woman: Why Smart Women Still Long for the Knight on the White Horse."

It would be foolish to suggest that the popularity of the film disproves any of feminism's claims or offsets criticism of it, including the fact that the movie glamorizes prostitution. Still, it does point to certain gaps—fissures, I should say—in that movement's re-envisioning of the world, as well as in its perception of the female imagination. For one thing, it seems to me that feminism has never paid enough attention to the intractable nature of fantasy life, its pervasive hold on our more adult selves. Along with that oversight, in focusing on the hostile or infantile tone of so many of the patriarchal images of women, it fails to take note of the fact that fantasies—however primitive and unenlightened—aren't exclusively the domain of men.

This is especially true of romance, where the rational and the prescriptive don't hold nearly as much sway as we'd like. For every man who dreams of the hooker with a heart of gold, there must be a woman who dreams of the lost little boy inside the ruthless tycoon. Just as certain prototypical male fantasies—of sexual domination and emotional submission—seem to linger on no matter how disapproving the culture, so, too, do certain crude female scenarios—of sexual submission and emotional domination—continue to flourish.

Would "Pretty Woman" have been possible—i.e., would it have been the box-office hit it has become—in the 70's or even the early 80's? Somehow, I doubt it. As the conceits of our society—those notions it deems valuable versus those it deems antiquated or, worse, inimical—change, it is to be supposed our attitudes toward those conceits get revised, too.

Not too long ago, about the time of Paul Mazursky's then-hip "An Unmarried Woman" (winter '78, to be exact), we seemed to want our romantic horizons contracted, brought closer to the ground—as reflected in a new stringency about the sexes. So we warmed (albeit a tad incredulously) to Jill Clayburgh sniffling red-nosedly into a handkerchief, choosing the succor of self-definition over the succor of Alan Bates. I suppose one fantasy is as valid as another, although in that era of newly raised consciousness, we were probably in real danger of mistaking the image of the uncoupled, unencumbered woman for the reality. Enough water has passed over the dam since then, however, for us not only to be able to reconsider some hitherto rejected fantasies—the knight in shining Armani who rescues the damsel in distressed jeans—but to recognize their enduring appeal.

"Pretty Woman" is about a fetching prostitute who, in the course of teaching a driven corporate raider how to feel, earns not only a whole new wardrobe culled from Rodeo Drive, but also his love. From what I can tell, the movie is far more popular with women than it is with men; it seems only to bewilder or anger the latter. And small wonder: as far as fairy tales go, this one not only has Prince Charming, but it also has an audacious, instinctive, principled heroine who reforms the Prince—getting him to take off his shoes and walk barefoot in the park—before she will have him. In other words, the only one who has to do any real self-examination is the man! The hooker may learn to dress up and to distinguish one fork from another, but it is the corporate raider who learns to look at life differently and is humanized in the process. What we have is the myth of the redemptive male, but with a shrewd fillip, Hollywood's bow to the New Cinderella, who has the movie's last line: "She rescues him right back."

Of course, so glossy a piece of movie making as this works at least as much on its charm as its subliminal message. Set in Los Angeles at its glitziest, half the fun of the film is getting to watch beautiful people wear beautiful clothes as they move around beautiful settings—the race track, the opera and a baronial hotel suite—saying beautiful things, such as "strawberries help the taste of champagne." Yes, the premises of "Pretty Woman" are improbable from the get-go: it's hard to believe, in these AIDS-ridden times, that any successful businessman, even so insouciant a one as Richard Gere, would hazard sex with a hooker who works the Strip, even so soft-mouthed a one as Julia Roberts. (The movie gets around this with the briefest of acknowledgments—a visual gag involving a rainbow-colored assortment of condoms.)

And yes, there is something unsettling about its glib appropriation of old and new themes, as well as its fudged sense of morality. But it appears that in the post-modernist, post-feminist, closing decade of the 20th century, we still need our myths, our amatory fictions; they help us endure. We are ready again for the mad, implausible embrace.

Syntax

The ways in which words are arranged to make sentences—in all languages—is called *syntax.* Our funding—our tacit knowledge about the workings of our native language—compels us to arrange sentences in conventional patterns. In English, verbs generally follow subjects to form the basic sentence patterns (the verbs are in italics):

Dogs *bark.*

Dogs *are* animals.

Dogs *chase* cats.

These three patterns, in fact, are the building blocks of the entire language: out of them we shape sentences that are as short or long, simple or complex as we choose. As we saw briefly in Chapter 1, the conventions of the sentence are such that we are always reading ahead, anticipating and filling in the blanks. Our grammatical funding is so firmly set that we know word order inside out. We know what *form* of word to expect:

> The cat chased a _____ .

We'd be surprised to meet a verb in the slot:

> The cat chased a to be.
> The cat chased a give.

Or an adjective:

> The cat chased a beautiful.

Or an adverb:

> The cat chased a carefully.

And we even know what *kind* of noun generally fills the slot. That's why we're surprised when we meet:

> The cat chased a cloud.
>
> > *or*
>
> The cat chased a whale.

We know, too, how to combine the patterns:

> The cat chased a cloud and then he chased a whale.
>
> > *or*
>
> After the cat chased a cloud, he then chased a whale.

By the time we're seven or eight, most of us know how to make various combinations of the basic patterns, even though nobody actually taught us to. We can produce these kinds of combinations:

> I fed the dog because it looked hungry.
>
> I don't like him, but I can't tell you why.
>
> I met her when I was coming home from the movie.

Without paying *conscious* attention to the act of making connections such as *because, but,* or *when,* we do this almost every time we speak. Similarly, when we speak, we rarely compose the sentences we are going to speak. They simply are available.

The situations in which we talk are usually very different from those in which we write. One difference is that the person we're addressing is usually absent. We have no feedback—until they write back or phone (or give us a grade on a paper!). When we write a loving letter to cheer a friend, we can't know how our words are "taken." We can't see her smiling. We don't even know if she *is* smiling.

But when we write, we have far more control over our words than we generally have when we are talking. We can write notes and outlines and rough drafts, revise the beginning, change the ending, and rewrite sentences. We can monitor the language we're producing. We generally have time to consider our words. We can do things in writing that we don't usually try when we're talking. Most of our talk takes the form of *parataxis;* in writing, we can produce all the variations of *hypotaxis.*

Parataxis

Parataxis is derived from the Greek word *paratassein,* which means *"to arrange side by side."* Series, sequences, lists, parallel constructions are usually paratactic.

I love apples, oranges, grapes, watermelon, and you.

I love to ski, hike, swim, jog, and win.

I love it when it rains and when it snows.

There's no end to the lists or series we can make—in speech and in writing. We can achieve in language a sense of the ways thoughts "hit" us, giving the reader a "feel" of inner speech, of the spontaneous formation of thought. We can also leave the connections for the reader to make:

I came, I saw, I conquered.
Julius Caesar

We rely on one conjunction over and over again: *and.*

And God said let there be light, *and* there was light.
Genesis

The gaps in the above declarations are gargantuan: the reader is expected to leap from one to the other, making necessary connections: Caesar came and then he saw and then he conquered! And what force the *and* has in " And God said . . . , and there was light." God's *words* caused there to be light. It is taken for granted that readers know how to "read" these kinds of syntactic structures—as well as how to read the particular world view behind them: that's why writers can surprise us when they play with and juggle the same kinds of syntactic units:

I awakened this morning and brushed my teeth and drank some coffee and read my newspaper and shot my dog and drove to work and had a good day.

What surprises in the sentence? And how does the surprise work? What is it in the structure of the sentence that makes "and shot my dog" disconcerting?

Try this:

Using only the word *and* as a connector, write a surprising or disconcerting fifty-word sentence that begins with "I left school this morning . . . ."

• • •

Hemingway experimented with parataxis—setting one action next to another and letting the reader make causal or temporal or logical connections. His sentences are spare and lean. Let's look closely at some of the ways in which he arranges sentences. Look again at some of the opening sentences of "Hills Like White Elephants":

> The hills across the valley of the Ebro were long and white.
>
> On this side there was no shade and no trees and the station was between two lines of rails in the sun. . . .
>
> It was very hot and the express from Barcelona would come in forty minutes.
>
> It stopped at this junction for two minutes and went on to Madrid.

Hypotaxis

What happens when you try to connect the sentences in other ways, using conjunctions such as *but* or *although* or *since* or *when?*

How does this sound to you:

> Although the hills across the valley were long and white, on this side there was no shade and no trees. The station was between two lines of rails in the sun.

How would you characterize the differences?

How would you describe the effects Hemingway's writing has on you? Do you like it?

Try this:

Write a Hemingway-like description of a scene, preparing your reader for a conversation between two people. You might, in fact, go back once more to the conversation *you* overheard, and set the stage for the dialogue.

• • •

Hypotaxis (from the Greek *hypotassein,* "to arrange under") refers to a syntactical arrangement in which some parts are *structurally* dependent on others. Here, conjunctions such as *although, because, whenever, while,* and *if* enable us to foreground one sentence part and background another.

Although I love you, I can't afford to marry you.

Because I love you, I'll make every effort to save money so that we can get married.

Consider this:

Imagine these sentences being spoken by one person (X) to another (Y) for the very first time in their relationships. What does Y feel as X's voice reaches the place marked by the comma?

Now, imagine the second sentence *inverted:* I'll make every effort to save money so that we can get married because I love you. What has been lost in terms of the dramatic representation of this moment in the relationship?

Dependent syntactical structures arouse our expectations. If they aren't completed, the listener—or reader—is left hanging in midair:

Because I love you. . . .

Although I love you. . . .

Then what? The word *although* sets up a particular kind of expectation—that what follows may not be what is hoped for:

Although I love you, I can't stand your dog.

The possibilities for wordplay here are various: the one word, *although,* takes center stage, and we wait for completion. What's coming next? We want to know. We can keep our readers hanging—and delay closure:

Although I love you and all that you believe in and stand for and although I appreciate the ways you treat other people, particularly small living creatures and plants, and although you make enough money for both of us to live comfortably, and although the glass slipper does fit perfectly, I will not be anyone's Cinderella.

You've probably realized that parataxis will take you only so far, that going on and on with simple sentences joined by *and, or,* and *then* achieves certain effects but can be disjointed and monotonous. If you use only parataxis, you don't allow yourself, as a writer, the varieties of emphasis that can be achieved by a variety of structures and rhythms. The two modes—parataxis and hypotaxis—work together for us as writers and readers, giving us elasticity and variety. As writers, we can arrange and combine sentence parts, to play with readers' expectations and interest, to keep them guessing, to keep them awake. As readers, when we begin to catch on to the ways writers rely upon various uses of syntax, then our negotiations with their texts become easier. We become used to Hemingway's parataxis and realize the effects of his style, just as we realize that particular kinds of texts rely on specific textual conventions.

Consider this:

Look again at Liora Tziyon's text on page 112, particularly at her ending,

> "I told you I would do anything. I will come with you and I will be with you. Then we will come back here and everything will be fine and we will be happy and. . . . Are you sure you want to go by yourself?"
>
> The girl wasn't listening. She looked at the hills and watched the train getting closer to the station. She turned to the man and looked at him with vivid eyes and then she picked up her bags.

How would you characterize these sentences? What effect do they have on you? Do they sound like people talking? How are the sentences connected? Liora was trying to imitate Hemingway's style of writing. Do you think she succeeded? How does the adjective "vivid" in the final sentence work for you? What effect do you think she might have been working for?

Try this:

Read the lead article in today's newspaper. Look at the ways the sentences are put together. Are they primarily hypotactic or paratactic? Look for the conjunctions for textual clues: *and, because, when, although, if, but.*

Try this:

Write a hypotactic sentence where you begin with one (or all) of these openings, and then delay the completion by at least fifty words:

Whenever I look into your eyes. . . .

Because I must finish my college education. . . .

If only you'd give me the keys to the car. . . .

If I had a million dollars. . . .

• • •

You by now realize that Hemingway was a master of parataxis. In fact, his influence, particularly on American writers, has been considerable. He forged a very distinctive way of writing stories, where, as he says, what's missing is just as crucial as what is stated or given, and where he relied on the simple sentence, the conjunction *and,* few adjectives, and the occasional telling adverb. Hemingway, of course, had *his* influences. Frank O'Connor, in his critical reading of Hemingway (Part 2, page 449), says that James Joyce, Sherwood Anderson, Gertrude Stein, and the Russian writer Turgenev all had a powerful influence on the young Hemingway.

• • •

Would you believe that writing Hemingway-like sentences could win you a free trip to Italy? It can. Every year since 1977 there has been a write-like-Hemingway contest called Harry's Bar and American Grill International Imitation Hemingway Competition.

Gene and Melle Washington, who live in Logan, Utah, have entered the contest several times, and have written a *parody* of the Hemingway style. Here, you can read their local newspaper account of their latest attempt—as you'll see, they reached the finals.

You can read, too, their entry, which begins with the first sentence of—what else?—"Hills Like White Elephants." The Washingtons claim it as "their favorite short story of them all."

Gene and Melle Washington
Michelle Parkinson

Gene and Melle Washington admit they really don't like some of the works of Ernest Hemingway at all.

But one short story and a chance to win a trip to Florence, Italy, was enough reason to study and imitate the works of Hemingway and enter the 11th Annual Harry's Bar and American Grill International Imitation Hemingway Competition.

And although they didn't win, the Washingtons' entry was one of 21 from among the 2,432 entries received from all over the world which made the final competition. This was the third time they have entered the event.

"We thought of entering the competition when a friend clipped a story about it in the newspaper and gave it to us," said Melle. "We noticed a trip to Florence was the prize and have entered ever since—because we will do anything to get a free trip to Italy; it is our favorite country to visit."

So how does a person win an Imitation Hemingway Competition?

"All you have to do is write a very good page of bad Hemingway," Gene said jokingly.

Gene and Melle entered a 233-word story titled, "The Next Sentence," based on one of Hemingway's short stories, "Hills Like White Elephants," their favorite short story of them all, said Gene.

The story is about a man and a woman talking about an abortion; the characters are named Jig and the American, said Gene.

Gene and Melle's story begins with the sentence Hemingway started with in "Hills Like White Elephants." And their story, like his, has characters named Jig and the American.

Gene, an associate professor in the Utah State University department of English, specializes in satire and 18th century literature. Melle is the past director of the University Press.

"Melle and I write the stories together; we have a lot of fun doing them," said Gene. It took them about two weeks to write "The Next Sentence."

What does it take for Gene and Melle to "write a very good page of bad Hemingway"?

"You have to get close to his (Hemingway's) style, with puns and a surprise ending; and mention the name "Harry's Bar and American Grill"—that's part of the rules," said Melle.

"It is just the basic character, conflict, and spoof on a male-female relationship story," she said.

Gene and Melle laughed about all of the "Hemingway-imitation" puns they have thought of.

"The first story we entered was the best of all of them, and it didn't even get an honorable mention," said Melle. But both previous entries were published in a journal in Michigan.

"We plan on adding to this one—maybe five or six pages—and maybe it will be published also," said Gene.

The Washingtons say they enter the contest not to win, but to have some fun.

"It is a challenge to write something that sounds like Hemingway, but isn't," Gene said.

Is Hemingway a favorite?

"I don't like his novels at all, but I do think some of his short stories are the best in world literature," said Gene. "The first two pages of Hemingway's "Farewell to Arms" is exquisite, but he couldn't maintain the quality all through the novel; that is why he is the best at short stories," he said.

Imitating Hemingway is not the only thing the Washingtons enjoy.

"We love to travel, especially to Italy," said Melle. "We have gone to Italy three times and always want to return for another trip—which we are planning on in two years for Gene's sabbatical.

"We love Italy because it is an incredibly old and sophisticated civilization; it is very subtle," said Melle.

Gene and Melle also spend time gardening, cross-country skiing, hiking, and "all the other things you do in Logan," said Gene.

So do the Washingtons plan on entering next year?

"There is always the next sentence," replies Gene in a Hemingway fashion.

THE NEXT SENTENCE

The American wrote, "The hills across the valley of the Ebro were long and white."

"It needs a lot of work," Jig said.

"Work?"

"It has too many words in it."

She was probably right. Or at least words with too many letters. Later he would go back and change 'white' to 'brown,' his favorite color. But now he had to go on to the next sentence. He wanted to stop for another beer. But it was getting late and the last mail train this year was due in 10 minutes.

He tried, "On this side there was no shade and the station was between two lines of rails in the sun."

"It's hard to read. Put a comma after 'shade,' and 'station' and a semi-colon after 'trees,'" Jig said.

He knew all the big punctuation marks. But he refused to use them. He had seen what it had done to his friends in London, Rome, and New York. Sentences you would never punctuate that way unless you were tired of war, women and beer.

He thought about the next sentence. It had to be right. Something with 'and,' 'said' and 'you' in it.

"You need a footnote," Jig said.

"A footnote?"

"To tell the judges at Harry's Bar and American Grill how hard it was."

"Hard?"

"The next sentence and no time for another beer."

Gene and Melle Washington

CHAPTER 5

Writing on

Writing III

Stories and Essays:

"Experiments with the Dangers

and Difficulties of Words"

EXPERIMENTS WITH WORDS

Perhaps the quickest way to understand the elements of what a novelist is doing is not to read, but to write: to make your own experiment with the dangers and difficulties of words. . . . Recall, then, some event that has left a distinct impression on you—how at the corner of the street, perhaps, you passed two people talking. A tree shook; an electric light danced; the tone of the talk was comic, but also tragic; a whole vision, an entire conception, seemed contained in that moment.

Virginia Woolf
"How Should One Read a Book?"

Try it. Recall some experience that left a deep but not necessarily clear impression. We've all had them—split seconds in our lives when something happened "inside" of us that altered our day or our lives: the effects may be short-lived or lasting. (Woolf, elsewhere, called this a "moment of being." James Joyce used the word "epiphany" to characterize such moments, and William Wordsworth used the phrase "spot of time.")

Begin to begin. As Woolf suggests, try to express the "whole vision," the "entire conception," the sense of significance, that you registered then, in the past. Write a few

132

lines, and then stop and consider this. As you attempt such a representation of a past moment, you may call up familiar experiences of writing. You may begin this way:

I had the most extraordinary experience the other day. . . .

or this way:

The most amazing thing happened to me the other day. . . .

or this way:

I remember that strange day. . . .

Then you stop. "Boring!" you say to yourself, "boring." If anything destroys the mystery, that's it, to begin with the "result," the "effects," the end. You're telling your reader what happened before you even begin. There's no buildup. You don't give your reader a chance to go through anything: you're already there, at the end.

On the other hand, you think, starting at the end may whet your reader's appetite: maybe the reader wonders *what* was extraordinary or amazing or strange and reads on to find out. You'll have given her a sneak preview.

You wonder.

But to begin that way sounds like an essay, you say—doing the *conventional* English assignment: "what I did last summer" or a "turning point" or "memorable experience" in your life. You've done all this before, you think. You know how to write an "essay": state the main idea or the thesis sentence at the beginning of the essay and then tell what happened as support.

That is the formula. But then you start thinking: Woolf's talking here about a novel. You don't have time to write a whole novel, but you could try a story—a short story. A short story is fiction, and that's what she's talking about. How then would you begin?

Well, you could begin with things as you *actually* experienced them. That's what she suggests: *"Recall, then, some event that has left a distinct impression on you."* You try again.

I was walking down the street that day. . . .

That's better. But then, you think, you've already arrived close to the moment of insight and haven't given yourself much room to maneuver. Maybe you want some more "buildup," or need to establish the suspense, get the reader interested, arouse her expectations, start with something gripping. Maybe you should "back up a bit" in time:

From the moment I woke up that very day, I knew I was headed for trouble.

There, you suddenly realize that you have decisions to make about *time*. You don't have to start *at* the "moment of being"; you can begin earlier. Maybe you could even begin with the day you were born!

My whole life, as I look back, seemed to point to that day.

Wait, wait, you say, now that sounds like autobiography, and not fiction. But never mind, for the moment you've suddenly realized you have interesting options: you can control time. What else? You wonder. Well, what would happen if you disguised yourself a bit? You try another approach, entirely:

> *She* walked down the street.

Not bad, you think: the options are somehow different here, just with the simple change from "I" to "she." You go on:

> She walked down the street, slowly, without looking back. No, once she left, she really left. And what was ahead, she didn't know, but she kept walking.

Now you're into something—you know it's fiction: you *feel* it, just as you knew when you were into an essay or into autobiography. You've enough textual knowledge to know the differences. But what makes it fiction? And what makes it nonfiction?

Consider this:

Let's look at several beginnings from stories and essays—fiction and nonfiction, all taken from selections in Part 2. Can you tell from these opening lines which is which?

> Mabel had her first serious suspicion that something was wrong as she took her cloak off. . . .
>
> She sat at the window watching the evening invade the avenue.
>
> My mother and I sat up almost all night once when I was 9.
>
> True!—nervous—very, very dreadfully nervous I had been and am; but why *will* you say that I am mad?
>
> I saw my ex-husband in the street. I was sitting on the steps of the new library.
>
> It was in Burma, a sodden morning of the rains.
>
> I would like particularly to talk about the need to develop a new style of aging in our own society.
>
> Her doctor had told Julian's mother that she must lose twenty pounds on account of her blood pressure, so on Wednesday nights Julian had to take her downtown on the bus for a reducing class at the Y.
>
> A boy and girl are taking a shower together in the bathroom.
>
> Morning rounds. On the fifth floor of the hospital, in the west wing, I know that a man is sitting up in his bed, waiting for me.

Here are two versions of the "same" event, as represented by a student trying out Woolf's experiment. The first she calls nonfiction; the second, fiction:

> 1. Sometimes I believe in a sixth sense, in a kind of knowing that has no name. What was it that drew me to the window that night when I caught a burglar red-handed? What aroused me from my sleep?

2. Night brings silences that stir memories. She sat by the window, musing. It was another sleepness night. The moon was full: the city street glistened from the rain. A figure suddenly emerged out of the darkness.

How would you characterize the differences between the two beginnings. If you hadn't been told that the first was nonfiction and the second fiction, would you know?

BEFORE READING

As we considered in Chapter 1, before we even begin to read, our responses are being shaped by our textual knowledge. If the text we are going to read is a work of fiction, we carry in very specific, but, most likely, *tacit* expectations, assumptions, predictions—about fiction. If it's nonfiction, then we expect a different kind of reading experience. As the writer Wayne Booth says, "We simply read differently when we believe that a story claims to be true than we do when we take it as 'made up.' "*

Consider this:

What are the differences for you? Take a few moments to jot them down in your notebook. What do you expect from fiction? From nonfiction? From a short story? From an essay?

Try this:

Let's carry on now with Woolf's exercise but with a slight variation: represent a moment of being in two distinctly different ways:

1. As fiction—the beginnings of a short story
2. As nonfiction—the beginnings of an essay

When you've finished, reflect on the differences between the two texts.

Consider this:

What did you want to *do* to your reader in the short story? In the essay? Did you have different purposes? How did your purposes affect the choices you made in each version?

CONVENTIONS OF READING

The word *convention* comes from the Latin *conventionem,* which means "to come together." When you say that someone is conventional, you generally mean that person "comes together" with or abides by the largely unwritten or tacit rules that govern daily life: what one wears; what one eats; what one does for a living; who one marries; what one

---

* Wayne C. Booth, *The Company We Keep: An Ethics of Fiction,* Berkeley, California, University of California Press, 1988.

says; what one writes. We are all bound by conventions—although we probably don't stop to think about them very often.

> Eggs, toast, oatmeal, orange juice, waffles, pancakes for breakfast? Conventional.
>
> The same for dinner? Unconventional.
>
> Spaghetti for breakfast? Unconventional
>
> Sneakers with a tuxedo? Unconventional.
>
> Taking your own lunch to eat at a fancy restaurant? Unconventional.
>
> Sending a Christmas card on Valentine's day? Unconventional.
>
> Wearing a bathing suit to your job at the bank: Unconventional.
>
> Smoking in public places? Getting to be unconventional. Rules for "conduct"— that is, for conducting ourselves in public—change.
>
> Kissing in public? (You tell me!)

Our cultural knowledge—our funding—carries with it an enormous amount of information about the *dos* and *don'ts* of a culture: what to do and when; when to speak and to whom (don't speak to strangers); what kind of language to use (don't swear!) Acculturation is the process whereby we learn the rules—or else! When we step out of line, we usually know it.

Our cultural knowledge also teaches us a great deal about the conventions of reading and, particularly, of reading *genres*—that is, types or kinds or categories of writings—so that before we even read a text, we already know what to expect. We don't expect to read a biology textbook in the form of poetry or a love letter in the form of a lab report; we don't expect a news report to be fiction.

What are the conventions of writing that shape our reading?

The largest cut we often make in talking about writing is to separate fiction from nonfiction.

FICTION   NONFICTION

Within fiction, we distinguish the short story, the novella, and the novel; within nonfiction, we distinguish history, biography, autobiography, letters, newspapers, magazines, textbooks, how-to manuals, etc. Why do we read fiction? Nonfiction? Which do you prefer? How would you characterize your "desert island" books? What does fiction give to you that nonfiction doesn't, and vice versa?

These are hotly debated issues in some academic circles. Some critics say that fiction (and poetry, too) is *generally* written for *aesthetic* or *artistic* purposes. They agree with W. H. Auden, who says that literature "doesn't make anything happen." Nonfiction, on the other hand, can make things happen, for it is, *generally,* written for *pragmatic, functional* purposes—to carry on business in the world. What do you think on these matters?

The essay—as you will see in the next chapter—can live in a world of aesthetics, in a world of pragmatics, or in both at once, depending upon the ways writers and readers "read" the text.

For now, read the beginnings of two different kinds of texts on the "same" subject: strangers meeting on some form of public transportation, in one, a train, and in the other, a bus. One is fiction, the other nonfiction. Which is which ?

TEXT 1

My first assertion . . . is that everyone . . . is a judge of character. Indeed it would be impossible to live for a year without disaster unless one practised character-reading and had some skill in the art. Our marriages, our friendships depend on it, our business largely depends on it; every day questions arise which can only be solved by its help. . . . So, if you will allow me, instead of analyzing and abstracting, I will tell you a simple story which, however pointless, has the merit of being true, of a journey from Richmond to Waterloo, in the hope that I may show you what I mean by character itself; that you may realize the different aspects it can wear; and the hideous perils that beset you directly you try to describe it in words.

TEXT 2

Her doctor had told Julian's mother that she must lose twenty pounds on account of her blood pressure, so on Wednesday nights Julian had to take her downtown on the bus for a reducing class at the Y. The reducing class was designed for working girls over fifty, who weighed from 165 to 200 pounds. His mother was one of the slimmer ones, but she said ladies did not tell their age or weight. She would not ride the buses by herself at night since they had been integrated, and because the reducing class was one of her few pleasures, necessary for her health, and *free,* she said Julian could at least put himself out to take her, considering all she did for him. Julian did not like to consider all she did for him, but every Wednesday night he braced himself and took her.

Text 1 is nonfiction, taken from Virginia Woolf's essay "Mr. Bennett and Mrs. Brown." Text 2 is fiction, taken from Flannery O'Connor's short story "Everything That Rises Must Converge."

Now look again at the two texts and see if you can establish ways of distinguishing between the nonfiction and the fiction.

Consider the following textual features:

1. Pronouns:

    first person (I, we)

    second person (you)

    third person (he, she, it, they)

2. Nouns referring to people:

    common (a man, a woman)

    proper—first name only (John)

    proper—first and last names (John Smith)

3. Nouns referring to place:

    common (town, city)

    proper—London, New York

4. Articles:

    indefinite: *a* town; *a* man

    definite: *the* man; the bus

Compare the Woolf and the O'Connor. How do they use names? How do they refer to place? What does their choice of an article (*a* or *the*) assume on the part of the reader? (I'm taking *a* bus to town. I'm taking *the* bus to town.)

What changes might you make to transform O'Connor's first sentence so that it sounds like the beginning of an essay? Perhaps:

> Julian Smith's mother had been told by her doctor that she must lose twenty pounds on account of her blood pressure, so on Wednesday nights Julian had to take her downtown on the bus for a reducing class at the Y.

A pronoun or an article or a last name can make all the difference in our identifying the conventions of genre: the writer of fiction, working within the largely unwritten conventions of fiction, takes liberties with the reader, assuming familiarity, even an intimacy, with the reader. Julian is simply Julian. O'Connor doesn't have to tell us "who" Julian is, his full name, age, or occupation—we know, from the conventions, that Julian is invented for the purpose of the fiction. We don't need to know what town he lives in or what bus he's taking.

The reader of nonfiction, *conventionally,* expects to be given such information, to be put in the picture more clearly: when people are named, we are to know who they are and why they're being written about:

> Julian Smith, a young man living in Atlanta, Georgia, with his sixty-five-year-old mother. . . .

The critical word here is *context,* both the specific, particular details that we, as readers, are given so that we can "find our feet," understanding the *what, who, where, how, and why* of what we're reading, as well as the larger context of genre, which prepares us to conduct our reading in particular ways. *In fiction, we expect and tolerate a withholding of context. In nonfiction, we expect context to be up front.* These are two tacit "rules" of fiction and nonfiction, generally unwritten, but known by writers and expected by readers. *Genre* is one of the most fundamental bridges between readers and writers. Without the writer spelling things out, we know when we pick up a lab report what to expect—once, of course, we have become used to reading the likes of lab reports. Imagine writing or reading a love letter in the form of a lab report! Or a lab report in the form of a poem!

Of course, rules of genre, and other "rules" as well, are sometimes "broken" by writers who are deliberately playing with conventions so as to surprise or shock or unsettle their readers!

Here, now, are several panels from the unconventional *Fungus the Bogeyman* by Raymond Briggs. Briggs has virtually turned the whole world upside down to create the land of Bogeydom, where bogeymen and bogeywomen revel in a way of life that the "civilized" residents of the typical family comic strip would gag on: dirt, dark, dampness, and smelly armpits! Fungus, our hero (or antihero), lives with his "drear" wife below the ground in crud, crust, and crumb. They love it.

Read on.

MISREADINGS

Virginia Woolf's essay, "Mr. Bennett and Mrs. Brown," excerpted above, describes the writer's encounter with two strangers on a train. Nothing happened between Woolf and the strangers. There *was* no encounter. Woolf merely eavesdropped, much as you were invited to do in Chapter 2, and out of that small incident came an essay on the work of the novelist, and on literature in England at the turn of the century. Here is the rest of Woolf's "story" about Mrs. Brown, the stranger on the train. The Mr. Bennett she refers to is Arnold Bennett, an English novelist and contemporary of Woolf's. Bennett insisted that for the novel to be convincing, the characters must be "real," but Woolf insists that one writer's "reality" may not necessarily be another's. "What is reality?" she asks, "And who are the judges of reality?" Mr. Bennett would attend to the world *outside* the character, what Mrs. Brown sees *outside* the window of the train she is riding. Woolf, as you will see, attends to other matters entirely, in order to capture "reality."

Mr. Bennett and Mrs. Brown
Virginia Woolf

I have said that people have to acquire a good deal of skill in character-reading if they are to live a single year of life without disaster. But it is the art of the young. In middle age and in old age the art is practised mostly for its uses, and friendships and other adventures and experiments in the art of reading character are seldom made. But novelists differ from the rest of the world because they do not cease to be interested in character when they have learnt enough about it for practical purposes. They go a step further, they feel that there is something permanently interesting in character in itself. When all the practical business of life has been discharged, there is something about people which continues to seem to them of overwhelming importance, in spite of the fact that it has no bearing whatever upon their happiness, comfort, or income. The study of character becomes to them an absorbing pursuit; to impart character an obsession. And this I find it very difficult to explain: what novelists mean when they talk about character, what the impulse is that urges them so powerfully every now and then to embody their view in writing.

So, if you will allow me, instead of analysing and abstracting, I will tell you a simple story which, however pointless, has the merit of being true, of a journey from Richmond to Waterloo, in the hope that I may show you what I mean by character in itself; that you may realize the different aspects it can wear; and the hideous perils that beset you directly you try to describe it in words.

One night some weeks ago, I was late for the train and jumped into the first carriage I came to. As I sat down I had the strange and uncomfortable feeling that I was interrupting a conversation between two people who were already sitting there. Not that they were young or happy. Far from it. They were both elderly, the woman over sixty, the man well over forty. They were sitting opposite each other, and the man, who had been leaning over and talking emphatically to judge by his attitude and the flush on his face, sat back and became silent. I had disturbed him, and he was annoyed. The elderly lady, however, whom I will call Mrs. Brown, seemed rather relieved. She was one of those clean, threadbare old ladies whose extreme tidiness—everything buttoned, fastened, tied together, mended and brushed up—suggests more extreme poverty than rags and dirt. There was something pinched about her—a look of suffering, of apprehension, and, in addition, she was extremely small. Her feet, in their clean little boots, scarcely touched the floor. I felt that she had nobody to support her; that she had to make up her mind for herself; that, having been deserted, or left a widow, years ago, she had led an anxious, harried life, bringing up an only son, perhaps, who, as likely as not, was by this time beginning to go to the bad. All this shot through my mind as I sat down, being uncomfortable, like most people, at travelling with fellow passengers unless I have somehow or other accounted for them. Then I looked at the man. He was no relation of Mrs. Brown's I felt sure; he was of a bigger, burlier, less refined type. He was a man of business I imagined, very likely a respectable corn-chandler from the North, dressed in good blue serge with a pocket-knife and a silk handkerchief, and a stout leather bag. Obviously, however, he had an unpleasant business to settle with Mrs. Brown; a secret, perhaps sinister business, which they did not intend to discuss in my presence.

"Yes, the Crofts have had very bad luck with their servants," Mr. Smith (as I will call him) said in a considering way, going back to some earlier topic, with a view to keeping up appearances.

"Ah, poor people," said Mrs. Brown, a trifle condescendingly. "My grandmother had a maid who came when she was fifteen and stayed till she was eighty" (this was said with a kind of hurt and aggressive pride to impress us both perhaps).

"One doesn't often come across that sort of thing nowadays," said Mr. Smith in conciliatory tones.

Then they were silent.

"It's odd they don't start a golf club there—I should have thought one of the young fellows would," said Mr. Smith, for the silence obviously made him uneasy.

Mrs. Brown hardly took the trouble to answer.

"What changes they're making in this part of the world," said Mr. Smith, looking out of the window, and looking furtively at me as he did so.

It was plain, from Mrs. Brown's silence, from the uneasy affability with which Mr. Smith spoke, that he had some power over her which he was exerting disagreeably. It might have been her son's downfall, or some painful episode in her past life, or her daughter's. Perhaps she was going to London to sign some document to make over some property. Obviously against her will she was in Mr. Smith's hands. I was beginning to feel a great deal of pity for her, when she said, suddenly and inconsequently:

"Can you tell me if an oak-tree dies when the leaves have been eaten for two years in succession by caterpillars?"

She spoke quite brightly, and rather precisely, in a cultivated, inquisitive voice.

Mr. Smith was startled, but relieved to have a safe topic of conversation given him. He told her a great deal very quickly about plagues of insects. He told her that he had a brother who kept a fruit farm in Kent. He told her what fruit farmers do every year in Kent, and so on, and so on. While he talked a very odd thing happened. Mrs. Brown took out her little white handkerchief and began to dab her eyes. She was crying. But she went on listening quite composedly to what he was saying, and he went on talking, a little louder, a little angrily, as if he had seen her cry often before; as if it were a painful habit. At last it got on his nerves. He stopped abruptly, looked out of the window, then leant towards her as he had been doing when I got in, and said in a bullying, menacing way, as if he would not stand any more nonsense:

"So about that matter we were discussing. It'll be all right? George will be there on Tuesday?"

"We shan't be late," said Mrs. Brown, gathering herself together with superb dignity.

Mr. Smith said nothing. He got up, buttoned his coat, reached his bag down, and jumped out of the train before it had stopped at Clapham Junction. He had got what he wanted, but he was ashamed of himself; he was glad to get out of the old lady's sight.

Mrs. Brown and I were left alone together. She sat in her corner opposite, very clean, very small, rather queer, and suffering intensely. The impression she made was overwhelming. It came pouring out like a draught, like a smell of burning. What was it composed of—that overwhelming and peculiar impression? Myriads of irrelevant and incongruous ideas crowd into one's head on such occasions; one sees the person, one sees Mrs. Brown, in the centre of all sorts of different scenes. I thought of her in a seaside house, among queer ornaments: sea-urchins, models of ships in glass cases. Her husband's medals were on the mantelpiece. She popped in and out of the room, perching on the edges of chairs, picking meals out of saucers, indulging in long, silent stares. The caterpillars and the oak-trees seemed to imply all that. And then, into this fantastic and secluded life, in broke Mr. Smith. I saw him blowing in, so to speak, on a windy day. He banged, he slammed. His dripping umbrella made a pool in the hall. They sat closeted together.

And then Mrs. Brown faced the dreadful revelation. She took her heroic decision. Early, before dawn, she packed her bag and carried it herself to the station. She would not let Smith touch it. She was wounded in her pride, unmoored from her anchorage; she came of gentlefolks who kept servants—but details could wait. The important thing was to realize her character, to steep oneself in her atmosphere. I had no time to explain why I felt it somewhat tragic, heroic, yet with a dash of the flighty and fantastic, before the train stopped, and I watched her disappear, carrying her bag, into the vast blazing station. She looked very small, very tenacious; at once very frail and very heroic. And I have never seen her again, and I shall never know what became of her.

The story ends without any point to it. But I have not told you this anecdote to illustrate either my own ingenuity or the pleasure of travelling from Richmond to Waterloo. What I want you to see in it is this. Here is a character imposing itself upon another person. Here is Mrs. Brown making someone begin almost automatically to write a novel about her. I believe that all novels begin with an old lady in the corner opposite. I believe that all novels, that is to say, deal with character, and that it is to express character—not to preach doctrines, sing songs, or celebrate the glories of the British Empire, that the form of the novels, so clumsy, verbose, and undramatic, so rich, elastic, and alive, has been evolved. To express character I have said; but you will at once reflect that the very widest interpretation can be put upon those words. For example, old Mrs. Brown's character will strike you very differently according to the age and country in which you happen to be born. It would be easy enough to write three different versions of that incident in the train, an English, a French, and a Russian. The English writer would make the old lady into a "character"; he would bring out her oddities and mannerisms; her buttons and wrinkles; her ribbons and warts. Her personality would dominate the book. A French writer would rub out all that; he would sacrifice the individual Mrs. Brown to give a more general view of human nature; to make a more abstract, proportioned, and harmonious whole. The Russian would pierce through the flesh; would reveal the soul—the soul alone, wandering out into the Waterloo Road, asking of life some tremendous question which would sound on and on in our ears after the book was finished. And then besides age and country there is the writer's temperament to be considered. You see one thing in character, and I another. You say it means this, and I that. And when it comes to writing each makes a further selection on principles of his own. Thus Mrs. Brown can be treated in an infinite variety of ways, according to the age, country, and temperament of the writer.

Mrs. Brown becomes "material" for Woolf, the essayist. Mrs. Brown, a total stranger, is the stuff of everyday, ordinary life that feeds her writerly imagination. In her essay, she uses the event to make a point about novel writing. In a novel, Mrs. Brown, of course, would be turned into *character*. (See Ian Hacking's essay, "Making Up People," page 363. Hacking believes that all of us "read" character in the ways that Woolf appropriates for the novelist.)

In writing the essay, Woolf has allowed her inferential powers free rein, so that they become imaginings, fantasies, and speculations. But though Woolf's imaginings are firmly rooted in what she perceived to be the *character* of Mrs. Brown, she never steps over the line from her role of observer to the role of participant, never actually *speaks* to "Mrs. Brown" (whose very name is, after all, made up by Woolf). She never steps into someone else's story, as Grace Paley's narrator did in "Anxiety," nor does she play Sherlock Holmes, demonstrating her deductive infallibility.

And in fact our inferences can be wrong. We size up a person, a situation, a conversation—we jump to conclusions, and sometimes we're totally off base. Recently, I drove my car with a broken exhaust pipe up my driveway, the exhaust fumes billowing after me. My next-door neighbor, looking out the window at that exact moment, saw my house enveloped *by smoke*. Within two minutes, my house was surrounded by three fire engines and four police cars!

All the signs had pointed to a house on fire—to my neighbor's eyes.

Sherlock Holmes was not always right. And part of the enjoyment of reading Holmes and other mysteries is for us, as readers, to use our own inferential powers, alongside the detective—to see if we can outguess him. Julian's mother in Flannery O'Connor's story, "Everything That Rises Must Converge," misjudges the character of a stranger on a bus. Look at what happens to her.

Everything That Rises Must Converge
Flannery O'Connor

Her doctor had told Julian's mother that she must lose twenty pounds on account of her blood pressure, so on Wednesday nights Julian had to take her downtown on the bus for a reducing class at the Y. The reducing class was designed for working girls over fifty, who weighed from 165 to 200 pounds. His mother was one of the slimmer ones, but she said ladies did not tell their age or weight. She would not ride the buses by herself at night since they had been integrated, and because the reducing class was one of her few pleasures, necessary for her health, and *free,* she said Julian could at least put himself out to take her, considering all she did for him. Julian did not like to consider all she did for him, but every Wednesday night he braced himself and took her.

She was almost ready to go, standing before the hall mirror, putting on her hat, while he, his hands behind him, appeared pinned to the door frame, waiting like Saint Sebastian for the arrows to begin piercing him. The hat was new and had cost her seven dollars and a half. She kept saying. "Maybe I shouldn't have paid that for it. No, I shouldn't have. I'll take it off and return it tomorrow. I shouldn't have bought it."

Julian raised his eyes to heaven. "Yes, you should have bought it," he said. "Put it on and let's go." It was a hideous hat. A purple velvet flap came down on one side of it and stood up on the other; the rest of it was green and looked like a cushion with the stuffing out. He decided it was less comical than jaunty and pathetic. Everything that gave her pleasure was small and depressed him.

She lifted the hat one more time and set it down slowly on top of her head. Two wings of gray hair protruded on either side of her florid face, but her eyes, sky-blue, were as innocent and untouched by experience as they must have been when she was ten. Were it not that she was a widow who had struggled fiercely to feed and clothe and put him through school and who was supporting him still, "until he got on his feet," she might have been a little girl that he had to take to town.

"It's all right, it's all right," he said. "Let's go." He opened the door himself and started down the walk to get her going. The sky was a dying violet and the houses stood out darkly against it, bulbous liver-colored monstrosities of a uniform ugliness though no two were alike. Since this had been a fashionable neighborhood forty years ago, his mother persisted in thinking they did well to have an apartment in it. Each house had a narrow collar of dirt around it in which sat, usually, a grubby child. Julian walked with his hands in his pockets, his head down and thrust forward and his eyes glazed with the determination to make himself completely numb during the time he would be sacrificed to her pleasure.

The door closed and he turned to find the dumpy figure, surmounted by the atrocious hat, coming toward him. "Well," she said, "you only live once and paying a little more for it, I at least won't meet myself coming and going."

"Some day I'll start making money," Julian said gloomily—he knew he never would—"and you can have one of those jokes whenever you take the fit." But first they would move. He visualized a place where the nearest neighbors would be three miles away on either side.

"I think you're doing fine," she said, drawing on her gloves. "You've only been out of school a year. Rome wasn't built in a day."

She was one of the few members of the Y reducing class who arrived in hat and gloves and who had a son who had been to college. "It takes time," she said, "and the world is in such a mess. This hat looked better on me than any of the others, though when she brought it out I said, 'Take that thing back. I wouldn't have it on my head,' and she said, 'Now wait till you see it on,' and then she put it on me, I said, 'We-ull,' and she said, 'If you ask me, that hat does something for you and you do something for the hat, and besides,' she said, 'with that hat, you won't meet yourself coming and going.'"

Julian thought he could have stood his lot better if she had been selfish, if she had been an old hag who drank and screamed at him. He walked along, saturated in depression, as if in the midst of his martyrdom he had lost his faith. Catching sight of his long, hopeless, irritated face, she stopped suddenly with a grief-stricken look, and pulled back on his arm. "Wait on me," she said. "I'm going to the house and take this thing off and tomorrow I'm going to return it. I was out of my head. I can pay the gas bill with that seven-fifty."

He caught her arm in a vicious grip. "You are not going to take it back," he said. "I like it."

"Well," she said, "I don't think I ought . . ."

"Shut up and enjoy it," he muttered, more depressed than ever.

"With the world in the mess it's in," she said, "it's a wonder we can enjoy anything. I tell you, the bottom rail is on the top."

Julian sighed.

"Of course," she said, "if you know who you are, you can go anywhere." She said this every time he took her to the reducing class. "Most of them in it are not our kind of people," she said, "but I can be gracious to anybody. I know who I am."

"They don't give a damn for your graciousness," Julian said savagely. "Knowing who you are is good for one generation only. You haven't the foggiest idea where you stand now or who you are."

She stopped and allowed her eyes to flash at him. "I most certainly do know who I am," she said, "and if you don't know who you are, I'm ashamed of you."

"Oh hell," Julian said.

"Your great-grandfather was a former governor of this state," she said. "Your grandfather was a prosperous landowner. Your grandmother was a Godhigh."

"Will you look around you," he said tensely, "and see where you are now?" and he swept his arm jerkily out to indicate the neighborhood, which the growing darkness at least made less dingy.

"You remain what you are," she said. "Your great-grandfather had a plantation and two hundred slaves."

"There are no more slaves," he said irritably.

"They were better off when they were," she said. He groaned to see that she was off on that topic. She rolled onto it every few days like a train on an open track. He knew every stop, every junction, every swamp along the way, and knew the exact point at which her conclusion would roll majestically into the station: "It's ridiculous. It's simply not realistic. They should rise, yes, but on their own side of the fence."

"Let's skip it," Julian said.

"The ones I feel sorry for," she said, "are the ones that are half white. They're tragic."

"Will you skip it?"

"Suppose we were half white. We would certainly have mixed feelings."

"I have mixed feelings now," he groaned.

"Well let's talk about something pleasant," she said. "I remember going to Grandpa's when I was a little girl. Then the house had double stairways that went up to what was really the second floor—all the cooking was done on the first. I used to like to stay down in the kitchen on account of the way the walls smelled. I would sit with my nose pressed against the plaster and take deep breaths. Actually the place belonged to the Godhighs but your grandfather Chestny paid the mortgage and saved it for them. They were in reduced circumstances," she said, "but reduced or not, they never forgot who they were."

"Doubtless that decayed mansion reminded them," Julian muttered. He never spoke of it without contempt or thought of it without longing. He had seen it once when he was a child before it had been sold. The double stairways had rotted and been torn down. Negroes were living in it. But it remained in his mind as his mother had known it. It appeared in his dreams regularly. He would stand on the wide porch, listening to the rustle of oak leaves, then wander through the high-ceilinged hall into the parlor that opened onto it and gaze at the worn rugs and faded draperies. It occurred to him that it was he, not she, who could have appreciated it. He preferred its threadbare elegance to anything he could name and it was because of it that all the neighborhoods they had lived in had been a torment to him—whereas she had hardly known the difference. She called her insensitivity "being adjust-able."

"And I remember the old darky who was my nurse, Caroline. There was no better person in the world. I've always had a great respect for my colored friends," she said. "I'd do anything in the world for them and they'd . . ."

"Will you for God's sake get off that subject?" Julian said. When he got on a bus by himself, he made it a point to sit down beside a Negro, in reparation as it were for his mother's sins.

"You're mighty touchy tonight," she said. "Do you feel all right?"

"Yes I feel all right," he said. "Now lay off."

She pursed her lips. "Well, you certainly are in a vile humor," she observed. "I just won't speak to you at all."

They had reached the bus stop. There was no bus in sight and Julian, his hands still jammed in his pockets and his head thrust forward, scowled down the empty street. The frustration of having to wait on the bus as well as ride on it began to creep up his neck like a hot hand. The presence of his mother was borne in upon him as she gave a pained sigh. He looked at her bleakly. She was holding herself very erect under the preposterous hat, wearing it like a banner of her imaginary dignity. There was in him an evil urge to break her spirit. He suddenly unloosened his tie and pulled it off and put it in his pocket.

She stiffened. "Why must you look like *that* when you take me to town?" she said. "Why must you deliberately embarrass me?"

"If you'll never learn where you are," he said, "you can at least learn where I am."

"You look like a—thug," she said.

"Then I must be one," he murmured.

"I'll just go home," she said. "I will not bother you. If you can't do a little thing like that for me . . ."

Rolling his eyes upward, he put his tie back on. "Restored to my class," he muttered. He thrust his face toward her and hissed, "True culture is in the mind, the *mind*," he said, and tapped his head, "the mind."

"It's in the heart," she said, "and in how you do things and how you do things is because of who you *are*."

"Nobody in the damn bus cares who you are."

"I care who I am," she said icily.

The lighted bus appeared on top of the next hill and as it approached, they moved out into the street to meet it. He put his hand under her elbow and hoisted her up on the creaking step. She entered with a little smile, as if she were going into a drawing room where everyone had been waiting for her. While he put in the tokens, she sat down on one of the broad front seats for three which faced the aisle. A thin woman with protruding teeth and long yellow hair was sitting on the end of it. His mother moved up beside her and left room for Julian beside herself. He sat down and looked at the floor across the aisle where a pair of thin feet in red and white canvas sandals were planted.

His mother immediately began a general conversation meant to attract anyone who felt like talking. "Can it get any hotter?" she said and removed from her purse a folding fan, black with a Japanese scene on it, which she began to flutter before her.

"I reckon it might could," the woman with the protruding teeth said, "but I know for a fact my apartment couldn't get no hotter."

"It must get the afternoon sun," his mother said. She sat forward and looked up and down the bus. It was half filled. Everybody was white. "I see we have the bus to ourselves," she said. Julian cringed.

"For a change," said the woman across the aisle, the owner of the red and white canvas sandals. "I come on one the other day and they were thick as fleas—up front and all through."

"The world is in a mess everywhere," his mother said. "I don't know how we've let it get in this fix."

"What gets my goat is all those boys from good families stealing automobile tires," the woman with the protruding teeth said. "I told my boy, I said you may not be rich but you been raised right and if I ever catch you in any such mess, they can send you on to the reformatory. Be exactly where you belong."

"Training tells," his mother said. "Is your boy in high school?"

"Ninth grade," the woman said.

"My son just finished college last year. He wants to write but he's selling typewriters until he gets started," his mother said.

The woman leaned forward and peered at Julian. He threw her such a malevolent look that she subsided against the seat. On the floor across the aisle there was an abandoned newspaper. He got up and got it and opened it out in front of him. His mother discreetly continued the conversation in a lower tone but the woman across the aisle said in a loud voice, "Well that's nice. Selling typewriters is close to writing. He can go right from one to the other."

"I tell him," his mother said, "that Rome wasn't built in a day."

Behind the newspaper Julian was withdrawing into the inner compartment of his mind where he spent most of his time. This was a kind of mental bubble in which he established himself when he could not bear to be a part of what was going on around him. From it he could see out and judge but in it he was safe from any kind of penetration from without. It was the only place where he felt free of the general idiocy of his fellows. His mother had never entered it but from it he could see her with absolute clarity.

The old lady was clever enough and he thought that if she had started from any of the right premises, more might have been expected of her. She lived according to the law of her own fantasy world, outside of which he had never seen her set foot. The law of it was to sacrifice herself for him after she had first created the necessity to do so by making a mess of things. If he had permitted her sacrifices, it was only because her lack of foresight had made them necessary. All her life had been a struggle to act like a Chestny without the

Chestny goods, and to give him everything she thought a Chestny ought to have; but since, said she, it was fun to struggle, why complain? And when you had won, as she had won, what fun to look back on the hard times! He could not forgive her that she had enjoyed the struggle and that she thought *she* had won.

What she meant when she said she had won was that she had brought him up successfully and had sent him to college and that he had turned out so well—good looking (her teeth had gone unfilled so that his could be straightened), intelligent (he realized he was too intelligent to be a success), and with a future ahead of him (there was of course no future ahead of him). She excused his gloominess on the grounds that he was still growing up and his radical ideas on his lack of practical experience. She said he didn't yet know a thing about "life," that he hadn't even entered the real world—when already he was as disenchanted with it as a man of fifty.

The further irony of all this was that in spite of her, he had turned out so well. In spite of going to only a third-rate college, he had, on his own initiative, come out with a first-rate education; in spite of growing up dominated by a small mind, he had ended up with a large one; in spite of all her foolish views, he was free of prejudice and unafraid to face facts. Most miraculous of all, instead of being blinded by love for her as she was for him, he had cut himself emotionally free of her and could see her with complete objectivity. He was not dominated by his mother.

The bus stopped with a sudden jerk and shook him from his meditation. A woman from the back lurched forward with little steps and barely escaped falling in his newspaper as she righted herself. She got off and a large Negro got on. Julian kept his paper lowered to watch. It gave him a certain satisfaction to see injustice in daily operation. It confirmed his view that with a few exceptions there was no one worth knowing within a radius of three hundred miles. The Negro was well dressed and carried a briefcase. He looked around and then sat down on the other end of the seat where the woman with the red and white canvas sandals was sitting. He immediately unfolded a newspaper and obscured himself behind it. Julian's mother's elbow at once prodded insistently into his ribs. "Now you see why I won't ride on these buses by myself," she whispered.

The woman with the red and white canvas sandals had risen at the same time the Negro sat down and had gone further back in the bus and taken the seat of the woman who had got off. His mother leaned forward and cast her an approving look.

Julian rose, crossed the aisle, and sat down in the place of the woman with the canvas sandals. From this position, he looked serenely across at his mother. Her face had turned an angry red. He stared at her, making his eyes the eyes of a stranger. He felt his tension suddenly lift as if he had openly declared war on her.

He would have liked to get in conversation with the Negro and to talk with him about art or politics or any subject that would be above the comprehension of those around them, but the man remained entrenched behind his paper. He was either ignoring the change of seating or had never noticed it. There was no way for Julian to convey his sympathy.

His mother kept her eyes reproachfully on his face. The woman with the protruding teeth was looking at him avidly as if he were a type of monster new to her.

"Do you have a light?" he asked the Negro.

Without looking away from his paper, the man reached in his pocket and handed him a packet of matches.

"Thanks," Julian said. For a moment he held the matches foolishly. A No SMOKING sign looked down upon him from over the door. This alone would not have deterred him; he had no cigarettes. He had quit smoking some months before because he could not afford it. "Sorry," he muttered and handed back the matches. The Negro lowered the paper and gave him an annoyed look. He took the matches and raised the paper again.

His mother continued to gaze at him but she did not take advantage of his momentary discomfort. Her eyes retained their battered look. Her face seemed to be unnaturally red, as if her blood pressure had risen. Julian allowed no glimmer of sympathy to show on his face. Having got the advantage, he wanted desperately to keep it and carry it through. He would have liked to teach her a lesson that would last her a while, but there seemed no way to continue the point. The Negro refused to come out from behind the paper.

Julian folded his arms and looked stolidly before him, facing her but as if he did not see her, as if he had ceased to recognize her existence. He visualized a scene in which, the bus having reached their stop, he would remain in his seat and when she said, "Aren't you going to get off," he would look at her as at a stranger who had rashly addressed him. The corner they got off on was usually deserted, but it was well lighted and it would not hurt her to walk by herself the four blocks to the Y. He decided to wait until the time came and then decide whether or not he would let her get off herself. He would have to be at the Y at ten to bring her back, but he could leave her wondering if he was going to show up. There was no reason for her to think she could always depend on him.

He retired again into the high-ceilinged room sparsely settled with large pieces of antique furniture. His soul expanded momentarily but then he became aware of his mother across from him and the vision shriveled. He studied her coldly. Her feet in little pumps dangled like a child's and did not quite reach the floor. She was training on him an exaggerated look of reproach. He felt completely detached from her. At that moment he could with pleasure have slapped her as he would have slapped a particularly obnoxious child in his charge.

He began to imagine various unlikely ways by which he could teach her a lesson. He might make friends with some distinguished Negro professor or lawyer and bring him home to spend the evening. He would be entirely justified but her blood pressure would rise to 300. He could not push her to the extent of making her have a stroke, and moreover, he had never been successful at making any Negro friends. He had tried to strike up an acquaintance on the bus with some of the better types, with ones that looked like professors or ministers or lawyers. One morning he had sat down next to a distinguished-looking dark brown man who had answered his questions with a sonorous solemnity but who had turned out to be an undertaker. Another day he had sat down beside a cigar-smoking Negro with a diamond ring on his finger, but after a few stilted pleasantries, the Negro had rung the buzzer and risen, slipping two lottery tickets into Julian's hand as he climbed over him to leave.

He imagined his mother lying desperately ill and his being able to secure only a Negro doctor for her. He toyed with that idea for a few minutes and then dropped it for a momentary vision of himself participating as a sympathizer in a sit-in demonstration. This was possible but he did not linger with it. Instead, he approached the ultimate horror. He brought home a beautiful suspiciously Negroid woman. Prepare yourself, he said. There is nothing you can do about it. This is the woman I've chosen. She's intelligent, dignified, even good, and she's suffered and she hasn't thought it *fun*. Now persecute us, go ahead and persecute us. Drive her out of here, but remember, you're driving me too. His eyes were narrowed and through the indignation he had generated, he saw his mother across the aisle, purple-faced, shrunken to the dwarf-like proportions of her moral nature, sitting like a mummy beneath the ridiculous banner of her hat.

He was tilted out of his fantasy again as the bus stopped. The door opened with a sucking hiss and out of the dark a large, gaily dressed, sullen-looking colored woman got on with a little boy. The child, who might have been four, had on a short plaid suit and Tyrolean hat with a blue feather in it. Julian hoped that he would sit down beside him and that the woman would push in beside his mother. He could think of no better arrangement.

As she waited for her tokens, the woman was surveying the seating possibilities—he hoped with the idea of sitting where she was least wanted. There was something familiar-looking about her but Julian could not place what it was. She was a giant of a woman. Her face was set not only to meet opposition but to seek it out. The downward tilt of her large lower lip was like a warning sign: DON'T TAMPER WITH ME. Her bulging figure was encased in a green crepe dress and her feet overflowed in red shoes. She had on a hideous hat. A purple velvet flap came down on one side of it and stood up on the other; the rest of it was green and looked like a cushion with the stuffing out. She carried a mammoth red pocketbook that bulged throughout as if it were stuffed with rocks.

To Julian's disappointment, the little boy climbed up on the empty seat beside his mother. His mother lumped all children, black and white, in the common category, "cute," and she thought little Negroes were on the whole cuter than little white children. She smiled at the little boy as he climbed on the seat.

Meanwhile the woman was bearing down upon the empty seat beside Julian. To his annoyance, she squeezed herself into it. He saw his mother's face change as the woman settled herself next to him and he realized with satisfaction that this was more objectionable to her than it was to him. Her face seemed almost gray and there was a look of dull recognition in her eyes, as if suddenly she had sickened at some awful confrontation. Julian saw that it was because she and the woman had, in a sense, swapped sons. Though his mother would not realize the symbolic significance of this, she would feel it. His amusement showed plainly on his face.

The woman next to him muttered something unintelligible to herself. He was conscious of a kind of bristling next to him, a muted growling like that of an angry cat. He could not see anything but the red pocketbook upright on the bulging green thighs. He visualized the woman as she had stood waiting for her tokens—the ponderous figure, rising from the red shoes upward over the solid hips, the mammoth bosom, the haughty face, to the green and purple hat.

He eyes widened.

The vision of the two hats, identical, broke upon him with the radiance of a brilliant sunrise. His face was suddenly lit with joy. He could not believe that Fate had thrust upon his mother such a lesson. He gave a loud chuckle so that she would look at him and see that he saw. She turned her eyes on him slowly. The blue in them seemed to have turned a bruised purple. For a moment he had an uncomfortable sense of her innocence, but it lasted only a second before principle rescued him. Justice entitled him to laugh. His grin hardened until it said to her as plainly as if he were saying aloud: Your punishment exactly fits your pettiness. This should teach you a permanent lesson.

Her eyes shifted to the woman. She seemed unable to bear looking at him and to find the woman preferable. He became conscious again of the bristling presence at his side. The woman was rumbling like a volcano about to become active. His mother's mouth began to twitch slightly at one corner. With a sinking heart, he saw incipient signs of recovery on her face and realized that this was going to strike her suddenly as funny and was going to be no lesson at all. She kept her eyes on the woman and an amused smile came over her face as if the woman were a monkey that had stolen her hat. The little Negro was looking up at her with large fascinated eyes. He had been trying to attract her attention for some time.

"Carver!" the woman said suddenly. "Come heah!"

When he saw that the spotlight was on him at last, Carver drew his feet up and turned himself toward Julian's mother and giggled.

"Carver!" the woman said. "You heah me? Come heah!"

Carver slid down from the seat but remained squatting with his back against the base of it, his head turned slyly around toward Julian's mother, who was smiling at him. The woman reached a hand across the aisle and snatched him to her. He righted himself and hung backwards on her knees, grinning at Julian's mother. "Isn't he cute?" Julian's mother said to the woman with the protruding teeth.

"I reckon he is," the woman said without conviction.

The Negress yanked him upright but he eased out of her grip and shot across the aisle and scrambled, giggling wildly, onto the seat beside his love.

"I think he likes me," Julian's mother said, and smiled at the woman. It was the smile she used when she was being particularly gracious to an inferior. Julian saw everything lost. The lesson had rolled off her like rain on a roof.

The woman stood up and yanked the little boy off the seat as if she were snatching him from contagion. Julian could feel the rage in her at having no weapon like his mother's smile. She gave the child a sharp slap across the leg. He howled once and then thrust his head into her stomach and kicked his feet against her shins. "Behave," she said vehemently.

The bus stopped and the Negro who had been reading the newspaper got off. The woman moved over and set the little boy down with a thump between herself and Julian. She held him firmly by the knee. In a moment he put his hands in front of his face and peeped at Julian's mother through his fingers.

"I see yooooooooo!" she said and put her hand in front of her face and peeped at him.

The woman slapped his hand down. "Quit yo' foolishness," she said, "before I knock the living Jesus out of you!"

Julian was thankful that the next stop was theirs. He reached up and pulled the cord. The woman reached up and pulled it at the same time. Oh my God, he thought. He had the terrible intuition that when they got off the bus together, his mother would open her purse and give the little boy a nickel. The gesture would be as natural to her as breathing. The bus stopped and the woman got up and lunged to the front, dragging the child who wished to stay on, after her. Julian and his mother got up and followed. As they neared the door, Julian tried to relieve her of her pocketbook.

"No," she murmured, "I want to give the little boy a nickel."

"No!" Julian hissed. "No!"

She smiled down at the child and opened her bag. The bus door opened and the woman picked him up by the arm and descended with him, hanging at her hip. Once in the street she set him down and shook him.

Julian's mother had to close her purse while she got down the bus step but as soon as her feet were on the ground, she opened it again and began to rummage inside. "I can't find but a penny," she whispered, "but it looks like a new one."

"Don't do it!" Julian said fiercely between his teeth. There was a streetlight on the corner and she hurried to get under it so that she could better see into her pocketbook. The woman was heading off rapidly down the street with the child hanging backward on her hand.

"Oh little boy!" Julian's mother called and took a few quick steps and caught up with them just beyond the lamppost. "Here's a bright new penny for you," and she held out the coin, which shone bronze in the dim light.

The huge woman turned and for a moment stood, her shoulders lifted and her face frozen with frustrated rage, and started at Julian's mother. Then all at once she seemed to explode like a piece of machinery that had been given one ounce of pressure too much. Julian saw the black fist swing out with the red pocketbook. He shut his eyes and cringed as he heard the woman shout, "He don't take nobody's pennies!" When he opened his eyes, the woman was disappearing down the street with the little boy staring wide-eyed over her shoulder. Julian's mother was sitting on the sidewalk.

"I told you not to do that," Julian said angrily. "I told you not to do that!"

He stood over her for a minute, gritting his teeth. Her legs were stretched out in front of her and her hat was on her lap. He squatted down and looked her in the face. It was totally expressionless. "You got exactly what you deserved," he said. "Now get up."

He picked up her pocketbook and put what had fallen out back in it. He picked the hat up off her lap. The penny caught his eye on the sidewalk and he picked that up and let it drop before her eyes into the purse. Then he stood up and leaned over and held his hands out to pull her up. She remained immobile. He sighed. Rising above them on either side were black apartment buildings, marked with irregular rectangles of light. At the end of the block a man came out of a door and walked off in the opposite direction. "All right," he said, "suppose somebody happens by and wants to know why you're sitting on the sidewalk?"

She took the hand and, breathing hard, pulled heavily up on it and then stood for a moment, swaying slightly as if the spots of light in the darkness were circling around her. Her eyes, shadowed and confused, finally settled on his face. He did not try to conceal his irritation. "I hope this teaches you a lesson," he said. She leaned forward and her eyes raked his face. She seemed trying to determine his identity. Then, as if she found nothing familiar about him, she started off with a headlong movement in the wrong direction.

"Aren't you going on to the Y?" he asked.

"Home," she muttered.

"Well, are we walking?"

For answer she kept going. Julian followed along, his hands behind him. He saw no reason to let the lesson she had had go without backing it up with an explanation of its meaning. She might as well be made to understand what had happened to her. "Don't think that was just an uppity Negro woman," he said. "That was the whole colored race which will no longer take your condescending pennies. That was your black double. She can wear the same hat as you, and to be sure," he added gratuitously (because he thought it was funny), "it looked better on her than it did on you. What all this means," he said, "is that the old world is gone. The old manners are obsolete and your graciousness is not worth a damn." He thought bitterly of the house that had been lost for him. "You aren't who you think you are," he said.

She continued to plow ahead, paying no attention to him. Her hair had come undone on one side. She dropped her pocketbook and took no notice. He stooped and picked it up and handed it to her but she did not take it.

"You needn't act as if the world had come to an end," he said, "because it hasn't. From now on you've got to live in a new world and face a few realities for a change. Buck up," he said, "it won't kill you."

She was breathing fast.

"Let's wait on the bus," he said.

"Home," she said thickly.

"I hate to see you behave like this," he said. "Just like a child. I should be able to expect more of you." He decided to stop where he was and make her stop and wait for a bus. "I'm not going any farther," he said, stopping. "We're going on the bus."

She continued to go on as if she had not heard him. He took a few steps and caught her arm and stopped her. He looked into her face and caught his breath. He was looking into a face he had never seen before. "Tell Grandpa to come get me," she said.

He stared, stricken.

"Tell Caroline to come get me," she said.

Stunned, he let her go and she lurched forward again, walking as if one leg were shorter than the other. A tide of darkness seemed to be sweeping her from him. "Mother!" he cried. "Darling, sweetheart, wait!" Crumpling, she fell to the pavement. He dashed forward and fell at her side, crying, "Mamma, Mamma!" He turned her over. Her face was fiercely distorted. One eye, large and staring, moved slightly to the left as if it had become unmoored. The other remained fixed on him, racked his face again, found nothing and closed.

"Wait here, wait here!" he cried and jumped up and began to run for help toward a cluster of lights he saw in the distance ahead of him. "Help, help!" he shouted, but his voice was thin, scarcely a thread of sound. The lights drifted farther away the faster he ran and his feet moved numbly as if they carried him nowhere. The tide of darkness seemed to sweep him back to her, postponing from moment to moment his entry into the world of guilt and sorrow.

Julian's mother "misreads" character. She relies upon what she regards as immutable social conventions; she assumes that things will simply stay the same, that "some people" will always know their place, even though some of those conventions have been challenged. But we are warned: we see in the very first paragraph of the story that Julian's mother "would not ride the buses by herself at night since they had been *integrated*." Here, for Julian's mother, conventions are stereotypes: she expects African Americans to abide by the "rules," but the rules have been irrevocably changed. Both for Julian and his mother one moment turns their entire world upside down.

Conventions—whether in the worlds in which we live or in the texts we read and write—are not etched in stone. They are open for question, debate, alteration, opposition, and eradication. But perceptions may be slow to change; and it may be that it is only after the "new" has been firmly established that the change of perception is registered—and, then, as a shock. Woolf talks about conventions in writing and in manners:

> You may well complain of the vagueness of my language. What is a convention, a tool, you may ask. . . . The question is difficult: I will attempt a short cut. A convention in writing is not much different from a convention in manners. Both in life and in literature it is necessary to have some means of bridging the gulf between the hostess and her unknown guest on the one hand, the writer and his unknown reader on the other. The hostess bethinks her of the weather, for generations of hostesses have established the fact that this is a subject of universal interest in which we all believe. She begins by saying that we are having a wretched May, and, having thus got into touch with her unknown guest, proceeds to matters of greater interest. So it is in literature. The writer must get into touch with his reader by putting before him something which he recognizes, which therefore stimulates his imagination, and makes him willing to co-operate in the far more difficult business of intimacy. And it is of the highest importance that this common meeting-place should be reached easily, almost instinctively, in the dark, with one's eyes shut. . . .
>
> "Mr. Bennett and Mrs. Brown," pages 110–111

Woolf concludes by insisting that conventions *change,* that each age and generation decides on its own literature and its own manners. Reading, then, means to become aware of what you know with your eyes *shut*—to open your eyes and realize that writers rely upon various and complex conventions as they write and that they depend upon your tacit understanding and acceptance of their tools. As you will see, however, in the next chapter, readers can resist—and discover that the "meeting place" of the text is the locus for negotiations.

Consider this:

Woolf wrote "Mr. Bennett and Mrs. Brown" for a lecture she gave in 1924. What signs do you find in the essay that the text was written to be read aloud to a group?

Woolf is an English writer. What "Englishisms" do you find in the text? What conventions does she use that now sound dated?

O'Connor's story was published in 1961. Where in the story do you find outmoded social conventions?

Try this:

Here is a "filler" that you first met in Chapter 1. Reread it now, with Woolf's invitation in mind: turn this snippet into the beginnings of a short story.

Then turn the same material to nonfiction: an essay.

In Transit

She got on the 14th Street bus, a nattily
dressed woman in her tailored suit, scarlet
blouse and matching high-heeled scarlet
pumps. She sat down and took out of her
shopping bag a pair of running shoes and
a pair of pink socks, which she proceeded
to put on.

Then, to the astonishment of her fellow
passengers, she took her scarlet pumps –
first one and then the other – and flung
them out the open bus window.

• • •

Now, for your enjoyment, read Russell Baker's "Muddle in a Puddle," to see the tables
turned: Baker is the one who is being "read" by his fellow travelers:

A Muddle in a Puddle
Russell Baker

At Penn Station in New York I sat in a puddle of beer.

I had not intended to sit in a puddle of beer. My family will swear to that. I can imagine
any of them in the witness chair:

"Puddle of beer? Nyah, the old man didn't say nothing about going to Penn Station to
sit in a puddle of beer. He said he was just going there to catch the train to Washington."

Furthermore, I do not like to sit in puddles of beer and had never done so before, since
I had always suspected that sitting in a puddle of beer would make the seat of my best slacks
give off an odor that would attract bar rags.

Imagine my amazement then to discover myself in the Penn Station waiting room
sitting in a puddle of beer. This particular puddle of beer had been poured into the contour
depression of a waiting-room chair seat, by whom or why I could only guess. Nor did I
think of guessing at first.

My first thoughts came in the following sequence:

1. I am sitting in a puddle of liquid.

2. This being New York, the nature of the puddle now penetrating my best slacks
   and soaking my underwear could be truly unspeakable.

3. Now I understand why, though every other seat around me is occupied, and
   hundreds of other people are standing around me desperate with fatigue, this seat
   alone was not taken until I sat down.

4. The fumes rising around me are very similar to fumes that used to fill the barracks early on Sunday mornings in 1943, which means that the puddle I'm sitting in is almost certainly a puddle of beer.

5. This being New York, and this being the Penn Station waiting room, I ought to be thankful that the puddle is merely a puddle of beer.

All these thoughts were thought in a fraction of an instant, but as my brain cooled I dealt swiftly and calmly with the main policy problem confronting a man who has just sat in a puddle of beer in the presence of a large audience.

Problem: Should that man leap up screaming curses?

Of course not. The hundreds of people pointedly not looking at me had doubtless watched intently (without looking) while I sat in the puddle of beer. Obviously, every one of them knew the puddle of beer was there, and any one could have spoken out as one human might speak to another.

"Wouldn't sit there if I was you, mister, 'cause there's a puddle of beer there, y'see."

Not one had said that, yet surely, even in New York, not all could be poor dumb wordless beasts utterly indifferent to a fellow traveler wearing his best slacks. Only two possibilities could explain their apparent brutality:

One, the person who had poured the puddle of beer was heavily armed and had announced that anyone who tried to prevent me from sitting in it would be instantly rubbed out.

Two, the puddle-of-beer pourer was an entertainer hired by the railroad to amuse passengers waiting for trains that were far behind schedule. This clown, after pouring the puddle of beer, had promised everybody a big laugh when, discovering that my best slacks had been ruined, I leaped up screaming curses.

Contingency One meant there was an armed maniacal beer-puddle pourer, possibly with his finger on the trigger. Any abrupt movement, such as leaping, might be fatal.

Contingency Two, though less dangerous, meant that hundreds of waiting passengers were now waiting not for their trains, but for me to leap up cursing, so they could collapse in laughter.

It is a terrible confession to make, but I hated my fellow passengers then, loathed them for their eagerness to laugh at my ruined pants, detested them for despicable sheep who hadn't enough character even to warn a good, decent, kind man against sitting in a puddle of beer. I would never, never satisfy their craving for a good laugh.

And so I sat there, as though I sat in puddles of beer three times every day and all night long while watching television.

The expression on my face, I hoped, said, "Ah, how nice to find a good comfy puddle of beer in the depot waiting room."

When osmosis had lifted the puddle of beer through my nether garments and up into the woof and warp of my best jacket, I rose with the calmly dripping dignity befitting a traveler to Washington. And when I arrived there the cab driver said, "Ah, you're from New York, I smell."

Exercises in misreading

Try this:

Imagine yourself watching Baker taking and sitting in that one remaining wet seat in the train station. What inferences might you make about why he keeps sitting and sitting and sitting?

• • •

We go through our lives reading people and situations, hypothesizing and then testing our hypothesis, if we can. Sometimes we get it right, sometimes not. We judge a book by its cover—as Julian's mother did—and we pay the price. We size up someone's face or their dress—and we're dead wrong. We misread.

Try this:

Represent a time when you sized up a person or a situation wrongly. Certain clues led you to certain conclusions, but then something happened to make you realize that you'd misread and you had to revise that first reading.

• • •

Sometimes a misreading arises out of our lack of experience: we've simply not been there before, in that situation or that place. We find ourselves in a strange land. We've opened new doors. We don't have the cultural knowledge we need to get the joke. The joke hinges on one word and we don't get it. Much writing, in fact, is about misreading: politicians misread their constituents; parents, their children; teachers, their students; husbands, their wives; etc. Sometimes the consequence is a good laugh. Sometimes the misreading takes you to a dead end. (I misfollowed road signs once in Ireland and almost drove into the sea!) Moving from one culture to another, we can expect to be misread or to misread. In the following excerpt, Clifford Geertz, a well-known anthropologist, describes the ways in which he sees and is seen in a new culture: one moment is all it takes for perceptions to change.

Deep Play: Notes on the Balinese Cockfight
Clifford Geertz

The Raid

Early in April of 1958, my wife and I arrived, malarial and diffident, in a Balinese village we intended, as anthropologists, to study. A small place, about five hundred people, and relatively remote, it was its own world. We were intruders, professional ones, and the villagers dealt with us as Balinese seem always to deal with people not part of their life who yet press themselves upon them: as though we were not there. For them, and to a degree for ourselves, we were nonpersons, specters, invisible men.

We moved into an extended family compound (that had been arranged before through the provincial government) belonging to one of the four major factions in village life. But except for our landlord and the village chief, whose cousin and brother-in-law he was, everyone ignored us in a way only a Balinese can do. As we wandered around, uncertain, wistful, eager to please, people seemed to look right through us with a gaze focused several yards behind us on some more actual stone or tree. Almost nobody greeted us; but nobody scowled or said anything unpleasant to us either, which would have been almost as satisfactory. If we ventured to approach someone (something one is powerfully inhibited from doing in such an atmosphere), he moved, negligently but definitively, away. If, seated or leaning against a wall, we had him trapped, he said nothing at all, or mumbled what for the Balinese is the ultimate nonword—"yes." The indifference, of course, was studied; the villagers were watching every move we made and they had an enormous amount of quite accurate information about who we were and what we were going to be doing. But they acted as if we simply did not exist, which, in fact, as this behavior was designed to inform us, we did not, or anyway not yet.

This is, as I say, general in Bali. Everywhere else I have been in Indonesia, and more latterly in Morocco, when I have gone into a new village people have poured out from all sides to take a very close look at me, and, often, an all-too-probing feel as well. In Balinese villages, at least those away from the tourist circuit, nothing happens at all. People go on pounding, chatting, making offerings, staring into space, carrying baskets about while one drifts around feeling vaguely disembodied. And the same thing is true on the individual level. When you first meet a Balinese, he seems virtually not to relate to you at all; he is, in the term Gregory Bateson and Margaret Mead made famous, "away." Then—in a day, a week, a month (with some people the magic moment never comes)—he decides, for reasons I have never been quite able to fathom, that you *are* real, and then he becomes a warm, gay, sensitive, sympathetic, though, being Balinese, always precisely controlled person. You have crossed, somehow, some moral or metaphysical shadow line. Though you are not exactly taken as a Balinese (one has to be born to that), you are at least regarded as a human being rather than a cloud or a gust of wind. The whole complexion of your relationship dramatically changes to, in the majority of cases, a gentle, almost affectionate one—a low-keyed, rather playful, rather mannered, rather bemused geniality.

My wife and I were still very much in the gust of wind stage, a most frustrating, and even, as you soon begin to doubt whether you are really real after all, unnerving one, when, ten days or so after our arrival, a large cockfight was held in the public square to raise money for a new school.

Now, a few special occasions aside, cockfights are illegal in Bali under the Republic (as, for not altogether unrelated reasons, they were under the Dutch), largely as a result of the pretensions to puritanism radical nationalism tends to bring with it. The elite, which is not itself so very puritan, worries about the poor, ignorant peasant gambling all his money away, about what foreigners will think, about the waste of time better devoted to building up the country. It sees cockfighting as "primitive," "backward," "unprogressive," and generally unbecoming an ambitious nation. And, as with those other embarrassments— opium smoking, begging, or uncovered breasts—it seeks, rather unsystematically, to put a stop to it.

Of course, like drinking during prohibition or, today, smoking marihuana, cockfights, being a part of "The Balinese Way of Life," nonetheless go on happening, and with extraordinary frequency. And, like prohibition or marihuana, from time to time the police (who, in 1958 at least, were almost all not Balinese but Javanese) feel called upon to make a raid, confiscate the cocks and spurs, fine a few people, and even now and then expose some of them in the tropical sun for a day as object lessons which never, somehow, get learned, even though occasionally, quite occasionally, the object dies.

As a result, the fights are usually held in a secluded corner of a village in semisecrecy, a fact which tends to slow the action a little—not very much, but the Balinese do not care to have it slowed at all. In this case, however, perhaps because they were raising money for a school that the government was unable to give them, perhaps because raids had been few recently, perhaps, as I gathered from subsequent discussion, there was a notion that the necessary bribes had been paid, they thought they could take a chance on the central square and draw a larger and more enthusiastic crowd without attracting the attention of the law.

They were wrong. In the midst of the third match, with hundreds of people, including, still transparent, myself and my wife, fused into a single body around the ring, a superorganism in the literal sense, a truck full of policemen armed with machine guns roared up. Amid great screeching cries of "pulisi! pulisi!" from the crowd, the policemen jumped out, and springing into the center of the ring, began to swing their guns around like gangsters in a motion picture, though not going so far as actually to fire them. The superorganism came instantly apart as its components scattered in all directions. People raced down the road, disappeared head first over walls, scrambled under platforms, folded themselves behind wicker screens, scuttled up coconut trees. Cocks armed with steel spurs sharp enough to cut off a finger or run a hole through a foot were running wildly around. Everything was dust and panic.

On the established anthropological principle, When in Rome, my wife and I decided, only slightly less instantaneously than everyone else, that the thing to do was run too. We ran down the main village street, northward, away from where we were living, for we were on that side of the ring. About half-way down another fugitive ducked suddenly into a compound—his own, it turned out—and we, seeing nothing ahead of us but rice fields, open country, and a very high volcano, followed him. As the three of us came tumbling into the courtyard, his wife, who had apparently been through this sort of thing before, whipped out a table, a tablecloth, three chairs, and three cups of tea, and we all, without any explicit communication whatsoever, sat down, commenced to sip tea, and sought to compose ourselves.

A few moments later, one of the policemen marched importantly into the yard, looking for the village chief. (The chief had not only been at the fight, he had arranged it. When the truck drove up he ran to the river, stripped off his sarong, and plunged in so he could say, when at length they found him sitting there pouring water over his head, that he had been away bathing when the whole affair had occurred and was ignorant of it. They did not believe him and fined him three hundred rupiah, which the village raised collectively.) Seeing my wife and I, "White Men," there in the yard, the policeman performed a classic double take. When he found his voice again he asked, approximately, what in the devil did we think we were doing there. Our host of five minutes leaped instantly to our defense, producing an impassioned description of who and what we were, so detailed and so accurate that it was my turn, having barely communicated with a living human being save my landlord and the village chief for more than a week, to be astonished. We had a perfect right to be there, he said, looking the Javanese upstart in the eye. We were American professors; the government had cleared us; we were there to study culture; we were going to write a book to tell Americans about Bali. And we had all been there drinking tea and talking about cultural matters all afternoon and did not know anything about any cockfight. Moreover, we had not seen the village chief all day, he must have gone to town. The policeman retreated in rather total disarray. And, after a decent interval, bewildered but relieved to have survived and stayed out of jail, so did we.

The next morning the village was a completely different world for us. Not only were we no longer invisible, we were suddenly the center of all attention, the object of a great outpouring of warmth, interest, and, most especially, amusement. Everyone in the village knew we had fled like everyone else. They asked us about it again and again (I must have told the story, small detail by small detail, fifty times by the end of the day), gently, affectionately, but quite insistently teasing us: "Why didn't you just stand there and tell the police who you were?" "Why didn't you just say you were only watching and not betting?" "Were you really afraid of those little guns?" As always, kinesthetically minded and, even when fleeing for their lives (or, as happened eight years later, surrendering them), the world's most poised people, they gleefully mimicked, also over and over again, our graceless style of running and what they claimed were our panic-stricken facial expressions. But above all, everyone was extremely pleased and even more surprised that we had not simply "pulled out our papers" (they knew about those too) and asserted our Distinguished Visitor status, but had instead demonstrated our solidarity with what were now our covillagers. (What we had actually demonstrated was our cowardice, but there is fellowship in that too.) Even the Brahmana priest, an old, grave, half-way-to-Heaven type who because of its associations with the underworld would never be involved, even distantly, in a cockfight, and was difficult to approach even to other Balinese, had us called into his courtyard to ask us about what had happened, chuckling happily at the sheer extraordinariness of it all.

In Bali, to be teased is to be accepted. It was the turning point so far as our relationship to the community was concerned, and we were quite literally "in." The whole village opened up to us, probably more than it ever would have otherwise (I might actually never have gotten to that priest, and our accidental host became one of my best informants), and certainly very much faster. Getting caught, or almost caught, in a vice raid is perhaps not a very generalizable recipe for achieving that mysterious necessity of anthropological field work, rapport, but for me it worked very well. It led to a sudden and unusually complete acceptance into a society extremely difficult for outsiders to penetrate. It gave me the kind of immediate, inside-view grasp of an aspect of "peasant mentality" that anthropologists not fortunate enough to flee headlong with their subjects from armed authorities normally do not get. And, perhaps most important of all, for the other things might have come in other ways, it put me very quickly on to a combination emotional explosion, status war, and philosophical drama of central significance to the society whose inner nature I desired to understand. By the time I left I had spent about as much time looking into cockfights as into witchcraft, irrigation, caste, or marriage.

Try this:

Represent a time when you misread or were misread in an unfamiliar or new or foreign situation: perhaps you were traveling in a foreign country; perhaps you had emigrated to the United States, without English. What signals did you misread? How did you find your way?

In the following two texts, we read of two important experiences. In the first, Leo Rosten introduces us to H*Y*M*A*N K*A*P*L*A*N, a fictional character, who is attending a night class for new immigrants. The scene is presented not from Kaplan's point of view but from his teacher's, who has more difficulty with Kaplan's misreadings than Kaplan seems to have. The second text is nonfiction, an excerpt from Eva Hoffman's autobiographical *Lost in Translation: A Life in a New Language.* Hoffman emigrated at the age of thirteen from Poland to Vancouver, where she found herself in exile, in an alien land and among people speaking an alien language. What is lost in translation from one language to another? What is lost in translation from one culture to another? These are the questions she raises.

The Rather Difficult Case of Mr. K*A*P*L*A*N
Leo Rosten

In the third week of the new term, Mr. Parkhill was forced to the conclusion that Mr. Kaplan's case was rather difficult. Mr. Kaplan first came to his special attention, out of the thirty-odd adults in the beginners' grade of the American Night Preparatory School for Adults ("English—Americanization—Civics—Preparation for Naturalization"), through an exercise the class had submitted. The exercise was entitled "Fifteen Common Nouns and Their Plural Forms." Mr. Parkhill came to one paper which included the following:

house . . . . makes . . . . . . houses

dog . . . . " . . . . dogies

library . . . . " . . . . Public library

cat . . . . " . . . . Katz

Mr. Parkhill read this over several times, very thoughtfully. He decided that here was a student who might, unchecked, develop into a "problem case." It was clearly a case that called for special attention. He turned the page over and read the name. It was printed in large, firm letters with red crayon. Each letter was outlined in blue. Between every two letters was a star, carefully drawn, in green. The multi-colored whole spelled, unmistakably, H∗Y∗M∗A∗N K∗A∗P∗L∗A∗N.

This Mr. Kaplan was in his forties, a plump, red-faced gentleman, with wavy blond hair, *two* fountain pens in his outer pocket, and a perpetual smile. It was a strange smile, Mr. Parkhill remarked: vague, bland, and consistent in its monotony. The thing that emphasized it for Mr. Parkhill was that it never seemed to leave the face of Mr. Kaplan, even during Recitation and Speech period. This disturbed Mr. Parkhill considerably, because Mr. Kaplan was particularly bad in Recitation and Speech.

Mr. Parkhill decided he had not applied himself as conscientiously as he might to Mr. Kaplan's case. That very night he called on Mr. Kaplan first.

"Won't *you* take advantage of Recitation and Speech practice, Mr. Kaplan?" he asked, with an encouraging smile.

Mr. Kaplan smiled back and answered promptly, "Vell, I'll tell abot Prazidents United States. Fife Prazidents United States is Abram Lincohen, he vas freeink de neegers; Hodding, Coolitch, Judge Vashington, an' Banjamin Frenklin."

Further encouragement revealed that in Mr. Kaplan's literary Valhalla the "most famous tree American wriders" were Jeck Laundon, Valt Viterman, and the author of "Hawk L. Barry-Feen," one Mocktvain. Mr. Kaplan took pains to point out that he did not mention Relfvaldo Amerson because "He is a poyet, an' I'm talkink abot wriders."

Mr. Parkhill diagnosed the case as one of "inability to distinguish between 'a' and 'e.'" He concluded that Mr. Kaplan *would* need special attention. He was, frankly, a little disturbed.

Mr. Kaplan's English showed no improvement during the next hard weeks. The originality of his spelling and pronunciation, however, flourished—like a sturdy flower in the good, rich earth. A man to whom "Katz" is the plural of "cat" soon soars into higher and more ambitious endeavor. As a one-paragraph "Exercise in Composition," Mr. Kaplan submitted:

> When people is meating on the boulvard, on going away one is saying, "I am glad I mat you," and the other is giving answer, "Mutual."

Mr. Parkhill felt that perhaps Mr. Kaplan had overreached himself, and should be confined to the simpler exercises.

Mr. Kaplan was an earnest student. He worked hard, knit his brows regularly (albeit with that smile), did all his homework, and never missed a class. Only once did Mr. Parkhill feel that Mr. Kaplan might, perhaps, be a little more *serious* about his work. That was when he asked Mr. Kaplan to "give a noun."

"Door," said Mr. Kaplan, smiling.

It seemed to Mr. Parkhill that "door" had been given only a moment earlier, by Miss Mitnick.

"Y-es," said Mr. Parkhill. "Er—and another noun?"

"Another door," Mr. Kaplan replied promptly.

Mr. Parkhill put him down as a doubtful "C." Everything pointed to the fact that Mr. Kaplan might have to be kept on an extra three months before he was ready for promotion to Composition, Grammar, and Civics, with Miss Higby.

One night Mrs. Moskowitz read a sentence, from "English for Beginners," in which "the vast deserts of America" were referred to. Mr. Parkhill soon discovered that poor Mrs. Moskowitz did not know the meaning of "vast." "Who can tell us the meaning of 'vast'?" asked Mr. Parkhill lightly.

Mr. Kaplan's hand shot up, volunteering wisdom. He was all proud grins. Mr. Parkhill, in the rashness of the moment, nodded to him.

Mr. Kaplan rose, radiant with joy. "'Vast!' It's commink fromm *diraction.* Ve have four diractions: de naut, de sot, de heast, and de vast."

Mr. Parkhill shook his head. "Er—that is 'west,' Mr. Kaplan." He wrote "VAST" and "WEST" on the blackboard. To the class he added, tolerantly, that Mr. Kaplan was apparently thinking of "west," whereas it was "vast" which was under discussion.

This seemed to bring a great light into Mr. Kaplan's inner world. "So is 'vast' vat you eskink?"

Mr. Parkhill admitted that it was "vast" for which he was asking.

"Aha!" cried Mr. Kaplan. "You minn '*vast*,' not"—with scorn—"'vast.'"

"Yes," said Mr. Parkhill, faintly.

"Hau Kay!" said Mr. Kaplan, essaying the vernacular. "Ven I'm buyink a suit clothes, I'm gattink de cawt, de pents, an' de vast!"

Stunned, Mr. Parkhill shook his head, very sadly. "I'm afraid that you've used still another word, Mr. Kaplan."

Oddly enough, this seemed to give Mr. Kaplan great pleasure.

Several nights later Mr. Kaplan took advantage of Open Questions period. This ten-minute period was Mr. Parkhill's special innovation in the American Night Preparatory School for Adults. It was devoted to answering any questions which the students might care to raise about any difficulties which they might have encountered during the course of their adventures with the language. Mr. Parkhill enjoyed Open Questions. He liked to clear up *practical* problems. He felt he was being ever so much more constructive that way. Miss Higby had once told him that he was a born Open Questions teacher.

"Plizz, Mr. Pockheel," asked Mr. Kaplan as soon as the period opened. "Vat's de minnink fromm—" It sounded, in Mr. Kaplan's rendition, like "a big department."

"'A big department,' Mr. Kaplan?" asked Mr. Parkhill, to make sure.

"Yassir!" Mr. Kaplan's smile was beauteous to behold. "In de stritt, ven I'm valkink, I'm hearink like 'I big de pottment.'"

It was definitely a pedagogical opportunity.

"Well, class," Mr. Parkhill began. "I'm sure that you have all—"

He told them that they had all probably done some shopping in the large department stores. (Mr. Kaplan nodded.) In these large stores, he said, if they wanted to buy a pair of shoes, for example, they went to a special *part* of the store, where only shoes were sold—a *shoe* department. (Mr. Kaplan nodded.) If they wanted a table, they went to a different *part* of the store, where *tables* were sold. (Mr. Kaplan nodded.) If they wanted to buy, say, a goldfish, they went to still another part of the store, where goldfish . . . (Mr. Kaplan frowned; it was clear that Mr. Kaplan had never bought a goldfish.)

"Well, then," Mr. Parkhill summed up hastily, "each article is sold in a different *place*. These different and special places are called *departments*." He printed "D-E-P-A-R-T-M-E-N-T" on the board in large, clear capitals. "And a *big* department, Mr. Kaplan, is merely such a department which is large—*big!*"

He put the chalk down and wiped his fingers.

"Is that clear now, class?" he asked, with a little smile. (It was rather an ingenious explanation, he thought; it might be worth repeating to Miss Higby during the recess.)

It *was* clear. There were thirty nods of approval. But Mr. Kaplan looked uncertain. It was obvious that Mr. Kaplan, a man who would not compromise with truth, did *not* find it clear.

"Isn't that clear *now*, Mr. Kaplan?" asked Mr. Parkhill anxiously.

Mr. Kaplan pursed his lips in thought. "It's a *fine* haxplination, Titcher," he said generously, "but I don' unnistand vy I'm hearink de voids de vay I do. Simms to me it's used in annodder minnink."

"There's really only one meaning for 'a big department.'" Mr. Parkhill was definitely worried by this time. "*If* that's the phrase you mean."

Mr. Kaplan nodded gravely. "Oh, dat's de phrase—ufcawss! It sonds like dat—or maybe a leetle more like '*I* big de pottment.'"

Mr. Parkhill took up the chalk. ("*I* big department" was obviously a case of Mr. Kaplan's own curious audition.) He repeated the explanation carefully, this time embellishing the illustrations with a shirt department, a victrola section, and "a separate part of the store where, for example, you buy canaries, or other birds."

Mr. Kaplan sat entranced. He followed it all politely, even the part about "canaries, or other birds." He smiled throughout with consummate reassurance.

Mr. Parkhill was relieved, assuming, in his folly, that Mr. Kaplan's smiles were a testimony to his exposition. But when he had finished, Mr. Kaplan shook his head once more, this time with a new and superior firmness.

"Is the explanation *still* not clear?" Mr. Parkhill was genuinely concerned by this time.

"Is de haxplination clear!" cried Mr. Kaplan with enthusiasm. "Ha! I should live so! Soitinly! Clear like *gold!* So clear! An' netcheral too! But Mr. Pockheel—"

"Go on, Mr. Kaplan," said Mr. Parkhill, studying the white dust on his fingers. There was, after all, nothing more to be done.

"Vell! I think it's more like '*I* big de pottment.'"

"Go on, Mr. Kaplan, go on." (*Domine, dirige nos.*)

Mr. Kaplan rose. His smile was broad, luminous, transcendent; his manner was regal.

"I'm hearink it in de stritt. Sometimes I'm stendink in de stritt, talkink to a frand, or mine vife, mine brodder—or maybe only stendink. An' somvun is pessink arond me. An' by hexident he's givink me a bump, you know, a *poosh!* Vel, he says, 'Axcuse me!' no? But somtimes, an' *dis* is vat I minn, he's sayink, '*I big de pottment!*'"

Mr. Parkhill studied the picture of "Abram Lincohen" on the back wall, as if reluctant to face reality. He wondered whether he could reconcile it with his conscience if he were to promote Mr. Kaplan to Composition, Grammar, and Civics—at once. Another three months of Recitation and Speech might, after all, be nothing but a waste of Mr. Kaplan's valuable time.

Exile
Eva Hoffman

We are in Montreal, in an echoing, dark train station, and we are huddled on a bench waiting for someone to give us some guidance. Timidly, I walk a few steps away from my parents to explore this terra incognita, and I come back with snippets of amazing news. There is this young girl, maybe my age, in high-heeled shoes and lipstick! She looks so vulgar, I complain. Or maybe this is just some sort of costume? There is also a black man at whom I stare for a while; he's as handsome as Harry Belafonte, the only black man whose face I know from pictures in Polish magazines, except here he is, big as life. Are all black men this handsome, I wonder?

Eventually, a man speaking broken Polish approaches us, takes us to the ticket window, and then helps us board our train. And so begins yet another segment of this longest journey—all the longer because we don't exactly know when it will end, when we'll reach our destination. We only know that Vancouver is very far away.

The people on the train look at us askance, and avoid sitting close to us. This may be because we've brought suitcases full of dried cake, canned sardines, and sausages, which would keep during the long transatlantic journey. We don't know about dining cars, and when we discover that this train has such a thing, we can hardly afford to go there once a day on the few dollars that my father has brought with him. Two dollars could buy a bicycle, or several pairs of shoes in Poland. It seems like a great deal to pay for four bowls of soup.

The train cuts through endless expanses of terrain, most of it flat and monotonous, and it seems to me that the relentless rhythm of the wheels is like scissors cutting a three-thousand-mile rip through my life. From now on, my life will be divided into two parts, with the line drawn by that train. After a while, I subside into a silent indifference, and I don't want to look at the landscape anymore; these are not the friendly fields, the farmyards of Polish countryside; this is vast, dull, and formless. By the time we reach the Rockies, my parents try to pull me out of my stupor and make me look at the spectacular landscapes we're passing by. But I don't want to. These peaks and ravines, these mountain streams and enormous boulders hurt my eyes—they hurt my soul. They're too big, too forbidding, and I can't imagine feeling that I'm part of them, that I'm in them. I recede into sleep; I sleep through the day and the night, and my parents can't shake me out of it. My sister, perhaps recoiling even more deeply from all this strangeness, is in a state of feverish illness and can hardly raise her head.

On the second day, we briefly meet a passenger who speaks Yiddish. My father enters into an animated conversation with him and learns some thrilling tales. For example, there's the story of a Polish Jew who came to Canada and made a fortune—he's now a millionaire!—on producing Polish pickles. Pickles! If one can make a fortune on that, well—it shouldn't be hard to get rich in this country. My father is energized, excited by this story, but I subside into an even more determined sullenness. "Millionaire" is one of those fairy-tale words that has no meaning to me whatsoever—a word like "emigration" or "Canada." In spite of my parents' protestations, I go back to sleep, and I miss some of the most prized sights on the North American continent.

By the time we've reached Vancouver, there are very few people left on the train. My mother has dressed my sister and me in our best outfits—identical navy blue dresses with sailor collars and gray coats handmade of good gabardine. My parents' faces reflect anticipation and anxiety. "Get off the train on the right foot," my mother tells us. "For luck in the new life."

I look out of the train window with a heavy heart. Where have I been brought to? As the train approaches the station, I see what is indeed a bit of nowhere. It's a drizzly day, and the platform is nearly empty. Everything is the color of slate. From this bleakness, two figures approach us—a nondescript middle-aged man and woman—and after making sure that we are the right people, the arrivals from the other side of the world, they hug us; but I don't feel much warmth in their half-embarrassed embrace. "You should kneel down and kiss the ground," the man tells my parents. "You're lucky to be here." My parents' faces fill with a kind of naïve hope. Perhaps everything will be well after all. They need signs, portents, at this hour.

Then we all get into an enormous car—yes, this is America—and drive into the city that is to be our home.

The Rosenbergs' house is a matter of utter bafflement to me. This one-story structure surrounded by a large garden surely doesn't belong in a city—but neither can it be imagined in the country. The garden itself is of such pruned and trimmed neatness that I'm half afraid to walk in it. Its lawn is improbably smooth and velvety (Ah, the time and worry spent on the shaving of these lawns! But I will only learn of that later), and the rows of marigolds, the circles of geraniums seem almost artificial in their perfect symmetries, in their subordination to orderliness.

Still, I much prefer sitting out here in the sun to being inside. The house is larger than any apartment I have seen in Poland, with enormous "picture" windows, a separate room for every member of the family and soft pastel-colored rugs covering all the floors. These are all features that, I know, are intended to signify good taste and wealth—but there's an incongruity between the message I'm supposed to get and my secret perceptions of these surroundings. To me, these interiors seem oddly flat, devoid of imagination, ingenuous. The spaces are so plain, low-ceilinged, obvious; there are no curves, niches, odd angles, nooks or crannies—nothing that gathers a house into itself, giving it a sense of privacy, or of depth—of interiority. There's no solid wood here, no accretion either of age or dust. There is only the open sincerity of the simple spaces, open right out to the street. (No peering out the window here, to catch glimpses of exchanges on the street; the picture windows are designed to give everyone full view of everyone else, to declare there's no mystery, nothing to hide. Not true, of course, but that's the statement.) There is also the disingenuousness of the furniture, all of it whitish with gold trimming. The whole thing is too revealing of an aspiration to good taste, but the unintended effect is thin and insubstantial—as if it was planned and put up just yesterday, and could just as well be dismantled tomorrow. The only rooms that really impress me are the bathroom and the kitchen—both of them so shiny, polished, and full of unfamiliar, fabulously functional appliances that they remind me of interiors which we occasionally glimpsed in French or American movies, and which, in our bedraggled Poland, we couldn't distinguish from fantasy. "Do you think people really live like this?" we would ask after one of these films, neglecting all the drama of the plot for the interest of these incidental features. Here is something worth describing to my friends in Cracow, down to such mind-boggling details as a shaggy rug in the bathroom and toilet paper that comes in different colors.

For the few days we stay at the Rosenbergs', we are relegated to the basement, where there's an extra apartment usually rented out to lodgers. My father looks up to Mr. Rosenberg with the respect, even a touch of awe due to someone who is a certified millionaire. Mr. Rosenberg is a big man in the small Duddy Kravitz community of Polish Jews, most of whom came to Canada shortly after the war, and most of whom have made good in junk peddling and real estate—but none as good as he. Mr. Rosenberg, who is now almost seventy, had the combined chutzpah and good luck to ride on Vancouver's real-estate boom—and now he's the richest of them all. This hardly makes him the most popular, but it automatically makes him the wisest. People from the community come to him for business advice, which he dispenses, in Yiddish, as if it were precious currency given away for free only through his grandiose generosity.

In the uncompromising vehemence of adolescence and injured pride, I began to see Mr. Rosenberg not as our benefactor but as a Dickensian figure of personal tyranny, and my feeling toward him quickly rises to something that can only be called hate. He has made stinginess into principle; I feel it as a nonhuman hardness, a conversion of flesh and feeling into stone. His face never lights up with humor or affection or wit. But then, he takes himself very seriously; to him too his wealth is the proof of his righteousness. In accordance with his principles, he demands money for our train tickets from Montreal as soon as we arrive. I never forgive him. We've brought gifts we thought handsome, but in addition, my father gives him all the dollars he accumulated in Poland—something that would start us off in Canada, we thought, but is now all gone. We'll have to scratch out our living somehow, starting from zero; my father begins to pinch the flesh of his arms nervously.

Mrs. Rosenberg, a worn-faced, nearly inarticulate, diffident woman, would probably show us more generosity were she not so intimidated by her husband. As it is, she and her daughter, Diane, feed us white bread with sliced cheese and bologna for lunch, and laugh at our incredulity at the mushy textures, the plastic wrapping, the presliced convenience of the various items. Privately, we comment that this is not real food: it has no taste, it smells of plastic. The two women also give us clothing they can no longer use. I can't imagine a state of affairs in which one would want to discard the delicate, transparent bathrobes and the angora sweaters they pass on to us, but luscious though these items seem—beyond anything I ever hoped to own—the show of gratitude required from me on receiving them sours the pleasure of new ownership. "Say thank you," my mother prompts me in preparation for receiving a batch of clothing. "People like to be appreciated." I coo and murmur ingratiatingly; I'm beginning to master the trick of saying thank you with just the right turn of the head, just the right balance between modesty and obsequiousness. In the next few years, this is a skill I'll have to use often. But in my heart I feel no real gratitude at being the recipient of so much mercy.

On about the third night at the Rosenbergs' house, I have a nightmare in which I'm drowning in the ocean while my mother and father swim farther and farther away from me. I know, in this dream, what it is to be cast adrift in incomprehensible space; I know what it is to lose one's mooring. I wake up in the middle of a prolonged scream. The fear is stronger than anything I've ever known. My parents wake up and hush me up quickly; they don't want the Rosenbergs to hear this disturbing sound. I try to calm myself and go back to sleep, but I feel as though I've stepped through a door into a dark place. Psychoanalysts talk about "mutative insights," through which the patient gains an entirely new perspective and discards some part of a cherished neurosis. The primal scream of my birth into the New World is a mutative insight of a negative kind—and I know that I can never lose the knowledge it brings me. The black, bituminous terror of the dream solders itself to the chemical base of my being—and from then on, fragments of the fear lodge themselves in my consciousness, thorns and pinpricks of anxiety, loose electricity floating in a psyche that has been forcibly pried from its structures. Eventually, I become accustomed to it; I know that it comes, and that it also goes; but when it hits with full force, in its pure form, I call it the Big Fear.

After about a week of lodging us in his home, Mr. Rosenberg decides that he has done enough for us, and, using some acquired American wisdom, explains that it isn't good for us to be dependent on his charity: there is of course no question of kindness. There is no question, either, of Mrs. Rosenberg intervening on our behalf, as she might like to do. We have no place to go, no way to pay for a meal. And so we begin.

"Shut up, shuddup," the children around us are shouting, and it's the first word in English that I understand from its dramatic context. My sister and I stand in the schoolyard clutching each other, while kids all around us are running about, pummeling each other, and screaming like whirling dervishes. Both the boys and the girls look sharp and aggressive to me—the girls all have bright lipstick on, their hair sticks up and out like witches' fury, and their skirts are held up and out by stiff, wiry crinolines. I can't imagine wanting to talk their harsh-sounding language.

We've been brought to this school by Mr. Rosenberg, who, two days after our arrival, tells us he'll take us to classes that are provided by the government to teach English to newcomers. This morning, in the rinky-dink wooden barracks where the classes are held, we've acquired new names. All it takes is a brief conference between Mr. Rosenberg and the teacher, a kindly looking woman who tries to give us reassuring glances, but who has seen too many people come and go to get sentimental about a name. Mine—"Ewa"—is easy to change into its near equivalent in English, "Eva." My sister's name—"Alina"— poses more of a problem, but after a moment's thought, Mr. Rosenberg and the teacher decide that "Elaine" is close enough. My sister and I hang our heads wordlessly under this careless baptism. The teacher then introduces us to the class, mispronouncing our last name—"Wydra"—in a way we've never heard before. We make our way to a bench at the back of the room; nothing much has happened, except a small, seismic mental shift. The twist in our names takes them a tiny distance from us—but it's a gap into which the infinite hobgoblin of abstraction enters. Our Polish names didn't refer to us; they were as surely us as our eyes or hands. These new appellations, which we ourselves can't yet pronounce, are not us. They are identification tags, disembodied signs pointing to objects that happen to be my sister and myself. We walk to our seats, into a roomful of unknown faces, with names that make us strangers to ourselves.

When the school day is over, the teacher hands us a file card on which she has written, "I'm a newcomer. I'm lost. I live at 1785 Granville Street. Will you kindly show me how to get there? Thank you." We wander the streets for several hours, zigzagging back and forth through seemingly identical suburban avenues, showing this deaf-mute sign to the few people we see, until we eventually recognize the Rosenbergs' house. We're greeted by our quietly hysterical mother and Mrs. Rosenberg, who, in a ritual she has probably learned from television, puts out two glasses of milk on her red Formica counter. The milk, homogenized, and too cold from the fridge, bears little resemblance to the liquid we used to drink called by the same name.

Every day I learn new words, new expressions. I pick them up from school exercises, from conversations, from the books I take out of Vancouver's well-lit, cheerful public library. There are some turns of phrase to which I develop strange allergies. "You're welcome," for example, strikes me as a gaucherie, and I can hardly bring myself to say it—I suppose because it implies that there's something to be thanked for, which in Polish would be impolite. The very places where language is at its most conventional, where it should be most taken for granted, are the places where I feel the prick of artifice.

Then there are words to which I take an equally irrational liking, for their sound, or just because I'm pleased to have deduced their meaning. Mainly they're words I learn from books, like "enigmatic" or "insolent"—words that have only a literary value, that exist only as signs on the page.

But mostly, the problem is that the signifier has become severed from the signified. The words I learn now don't stand for things in the same unquestioned way they did in my native tongue. "River" in Polish was a vital sound, energized with the essence of riverhood, of my rivers, of my being immersed in rivers. "River" in English is cold—a word without an aura. It has no accumulated associations for me, and it does not give off the radiating haze of connotation. It does not evoke.

The process, alas, works in reverse as well. When I see a river now, it is not shaped, assimilated by the word that accommodates it to the psyche—a word that makes a body of water a river rather than an uncontained element. The river before me remains a thing, absolutely other, absolutely unbending to the grasp of my mind.

When my friend Penny tells me that she's envious, or happy, or disappointed, I try laboriously to translate not from English to Polish but from the word back to its source, to the feeling from which it springs. Already, in that moment of strain, spontaneity of response is lost. And anyway, the translation doesn't work. I don't know how Penny feels when she talks about envy. The word hangs in a Platonic stratosphere, a vague prototype of all envy, so large, so all-encompassing that it might crush me—as might disappointment or happiness.

I am becoming a living avatar of structuralist wisdom; I cannot help knowing that words are just themselves. But it's a terrible knowledge, without any of the consolations that wisdom usually brings. It does not mean that I'm free to play with words at my wont; anyway, words in their naked state are surely among the least satisfactory play objects. No, this radical disjoining between word and thing is a desiccating alchemy, draining the world not only of significance but of its colors, striations, nuances—its very existence. It is the loss of a living connection.

The worst losses come at night. As I lie down in a strange bed in a strange house—my mother is a sort of housekeeper here, to the aging Jewish man who has taken us in in return for her services—I wait for that spontaneous flow of inner language which used to be my nighttime talk with myself, my way of informing the ego where the id had been. Nothing comes. Polish, in a short time, has atrophied, shriveled from sheer uselessness. Its words don't apply to my new experiences; they're not coeval with any of the objects, or faces, or the very air I breathe in the daytime. In English, words have not penetrated to those layers of my psyche from which a private conversation could proceed. This interval before sleep used to be the time when my mind became both receptive and alert, when images and words rose up to consciousness, reiterating what had happened during the day, adding the day's experiences to those already stored there, spinning out the thread of my personal story.

Now, this picture-and-word show is gone; the thread has been snapped. I have no interior language, and without it, interior images—those images through which we assimilate the external world, through which we take it in, love it, make it our own—become blurred too. My mother and I met a Canadian family who live down the block today. They were working in their garden and engaged us in a conversation of the "Nice weather we're having, isn't it?" variety, which culminated in their inviting us into their house. They sat stiffly on their couch, smiled in the long pauses between the conversation, and seemed at a loss for what to ask. Now my mind gropes for some description of them, but nothing fits. They're a different species from anyone I've met in Poland, and Polish words slip off of them without sticking. English words don't hook on to anything. I try, deliberately, to come up with a few. Are these people pleasant or dull? Kindly or silly? The words float in an uncertain space. They come up from a part of my brain in which labels may be manufactured but which has no connection to my instincts, quick reactions, knowledge. Even the simplest adjectives sow confusion in my mind; English kindliness has a whole system of morality behind it, a system that makes "kindness" an entirely positive virtue. Polish kindness has the tiniest element of irony. Besides, I'm beginning to feel the tug of prohibition, in English, against uncharitable words. In Polish, you can call someone an idiot without particularly harsh feelings and with the zest of a strong judgment. Yes, in Polish these people might tend toward "silly" and "dull"—but I force myself toward "kindly" and "pleasant." The cultural unconscious is beginning to exercise its subliminal influence.

The verbal blur covers these people's faces, their gestures with a sort of fog. I can't translate them into my mind's eye. The small event, instead of being added to the mosaic of consciousness and memory, falls through some black hole, and I fall into it. What has happened to me in this new world? I don't know. I don't see what I've seen, don't comprehend what's in front of me. I'm not filled with language anymore, and I have only a memory of fullness to anguish me with the knowledge that, in this dark and empty state, I don't really exist.

Mrs. Lieberman, in the bathroom of her house, is shaving my armpits. She has taken me there at the end of her dinner party, and now, with a kind decisiveness, she lifts my arms and performs this foreign ablution on the tufts of hair that have never been objectionable to anyone before. She hasn't asked me whether I would like her to do it; she has simply taken it upon herself to teach me how things are done here.

Mrs. Lieberman is among several Polish ladies who have been in Canada long enough to consider themselves well versed in native ways, and who seem to find me deficient in some quite fundamental respects. Since in Poland I was considered a pretty young girl, this requires a basic revision of my self-image. But there's no doubt about it; after the passage across the Atlantic, I've emerged as less attractive, less graceful, less desirable. In fact, I can see in these women's eyes that I'm a somewhat pitiful specimen—pale, with thick eyebrows, and without any bounce in my hair, dressed in clothes that have nothing to do with the current fashion. And so they energetically set out to rectify these flaws. One of them spends a day with me, plucking my eyebrows and trying various shades of lipstick on my face. "If you were my daughter, you'd soon look like a princess," she says, thus implying an added deficiency in my mother. Another counselor takes me into her house for an evening, to initiate me into the mysteries of using shampoos and hair lotions, and putting my hair up in curlers; yet another outfits me with a crinoline and tells me that actually, I have a perfectly good figure—I just need to bring it out in the right ways. And several of them look at my breasts meaningfully, suggesting to my mother in an undertone that really, it's time I started wearing a bra. My mother obeys.

I obey too, passively, mulishly, but I feel less agile and self-confident with every transformation. I hold my head rigidly, so that my precarious bouffant doesn't fall down, and I smile often, the way I see other girls do, though I'm careful not to open my lips too wide or bite them, so my lipstick won't get smudged. I don't know how to move easily in the high-heeled shoes somebody gave me.

Inside its elaborate packaging, my body is stiff, sulky, wary. When I'm with my peers, who come by crinolines, lipstick, cars, and self-confidence naturally, my gestures show that I'm here provisionally, by their grace, that I don't rightfully belong. My shoulders stoop, I nod frantically to indicate my agreement with others, I smile sweetly at people to show I mean well, and my chest recedes inward so that I don't take up too much space— mannerisms of a marginal, off-centered person who wants both to be taken in and to fend off the threatening others.

About a year after our arrival in Vancouver, someone takes a photograph of my family in their backyard, and looking at it, I reject the image it gives of myself categorically. This clumsy looking creature, with legs oddly turned in their high-heeled pumps, shoulders bent with the strain of resentment and ingratiation, is not myself. Alienation is beginning to be inscribed in my flesh and face.

The final selection in this chapter, Sonia Sanchez's "Traveling on an Amtrak Train Could Humanize You," takes us, again, to a train ride, with the narrator overhearing two fellow passengers engaged in a conversation that bridges two cultures—or does it?

Traveling on an Amtrak Train
Could Humanize You
Sonia Sanchez

I saw him enter the train. His walk announced a hipster for all seasons; his clothing said doorways, hunger and brawls. A lifetime of insults.

I immediately put my large brown bag on the seat next to mine, lowered my eyes, turned my head to peer out at the figures rushing to catch the train to NYC. From Newark to NYC in one short easy ride.

He looked at me, nodded, walked to the seat behind me. I heard the seat collapse with his weight, heard the tight intake of breath from the businessman who pulled himself up straight as white lace.

His voice was loud but strangely soft as he said, "Let me see your hands, man. They're smooth as ice. You ain't never worked a hard day in your life, have you man? Where you go to school? Harvard? You make big money, I bet. Don'tcha? I have a high school diploma. Are you in hiring? My name's Herbert. What's yours?"

The stillness caressed the red-cushioned car crashing against the chatter of Thursday afternoon commuters, students and shoppers.

He continued. "I ain't drunk or crazy. I just like talking to people, successful people like you. I like to know what you about. What it feels like to have made it. What kind of job you got? You in a big corporation or something, ain't ya?"

The businessman stirred in his seat. He cleared his throat of all tentative sounds and then words darted from his tongue so fast I heard centuries passing through his voice.

"I'm a securities analyst for a firm in New York, and I make enough (nervous laugh) to take care of my family. No, I'm not hiring at all. My name is John Glantz, though. Glad to meet you, ahem, Herbert. Very glad to meet you."

I heard the shaking of hands, their voices momentarily silenced by their hands shaking in tune to color and noise. Questions and answers.

"Told you your hands were soft."

Herbert's short laugh bounced from his lips with ease. "My hands," he continued, "are certified razors. Go on, touch them. Feel them. They won't bite 'less I say sic'em. Go on, feel them, man. They so rough they might cut you in two."

And again the sound of a voice, higher and clearer than before. A voice moving across years like freshly polished silver. A voice circling new terrain.

"Yes. They are quite rough, but strong. A man's hands." The businessman's voice struggled with forced words.

"My ole lady used to feel my hands, you know, and she said keep them hard things offa me, man, they too rough for my body, always laying in ambush for me. She wanted me to have smooth hands like yours. My hands always embarrassed her, calloused by the rhythm of work. She called them alligator hands, she did."

The train charged ahead full tilt, tilting memories. As it leaped and settled inside the tunnel, the light flickered out. Men and words fused into one slow-moving silence. The silence of darkness. The silence of tension peeling from the windows.

The lights returned.

"Thought you wuz a goner for a moment, didn't ya? Ha! Ha! Naw, man. It ain't that way a-tall. Hey! You ever see Hurricane Carter fight? I used to spar with him some years ago. He was a tough dude, bad in the ring. He could take care of some business. Did you see him fight his last fight?"

"Yes, I did. He was a good fighter. I think I liked Muhammad Ali better, though. My boys always liked Ali. We used to watch him fight together. They don't watch boxing anymore. They think it's crude and violent. Imagine that. All they play is soccer now."

"You have just the two boys?"

"Yes, just two sons. They're 15 and 14. I don't see them often. They're away at school now."

"I have one son, 14 years old, too. He's a smart young dude. That school ain't teaching him nothing, though. I gotta keep him smart too. Can't have him traveling from Newark to New York everyday for a quick hustle. Anyway, your ass gits worn out ya know from all this traveling everyday. You know what I mean?"

Their laughter traveled down the long carpeted car, bouncing off ears closed by sleep and habit. Their laughter resounded against years of locked doors and minds. Their male laughter came like sea birds tasting new foam.

"Seriously, though. What do you do in New York everyday, Herbert? You have a good head on your shoulders. Why aren't you working?"

"Ain't had a real job in fourteen years, not since I hurt my back 14 years ago. Can't work the way I used to. Harvard. You don't know what it means not to work. I was a man, a father, a husband cocked before the world; now my body sweats in retirement. And they talkin' about taking away my disability payments. How we gonna make it, man? How I'm gonna be a man?"

Silence. Pauses of yellow silence walking barefoot on the train. Voices of people getting ready to disembark, searching the train for traces of themselves.

Here we are, people, I wanted to cry out. Here we are in NYC without the slightest idea of why and who when we ignore the men and women keloiding before us with pain.

Time to reassess before leaving.

I was in my seat watching the train run from Philly to Newark to New York;
There were trains going in opposite directions;
I was alone, but I saw people, hermetically sealed with their own styles of breathing;
I was on a train, and I heard tongues swell and grow;

But I was not alone;
I had come from Graterford, where all the men are immortal;
They never die;
They merely depart or disintegrate down crowded cells;
I had come from Graterford, where they do pilgrimage each day in their cells without
incense.

I followed the two men up the stairs to Eighth Avenue. They parted. Herbert walked on an Eighth Avenue tide of dancing taxis and flesh. I turned eastward toward the river, toward the U.N. where a geography of men and women gargle with surplus words.

Traveling on an Amtrak train could humanize you.

CHAPTER 6

Reading and

Writing Essays:

Negotiations and

Renegotiations

NEGOTIATING VALUES

Conventions in writing are like conventions in manners, says Virginia Woolf. Both involve bridging gulfs between people. Writing, no matter what form it takes, is an attempt at conversation, at "speaking" to others. It is an attempt to affect them, to arouse their memories about their own experiences, to arouse their curiosity, wonderment, pity, and terror—their anger or frustration—about their worlds. Writers want to move readers—to laughter, tears, reflection, and action. Writers may also want to move readers to write, themselves—to pick up their pens and write in protest or complaint, in support or encouragement. They may want readers to write "on" their writing, in the hopes of effecting changes, or making things happen. They may want to *change* readers—to get them to accept their values, their ways of reading the world.

In conversation, every time we speak with an actual listener, we're always involved, implicitly or explicitly, in an exchange of our beliefs, values, convictions—of what we think matters. It is the same in writing, which is also a "conversation," but one in which the writer is absent, and the listener silent. At the heart of the exchange is a question of values, of *evaluation*.

Consider this: I tell you a story: it's about my cat running into the middle of the road and getting killed. I'm feeling miserable. I want your sympathy, and you give it. You tell me about your cat who also ran into the middle of the road and got killed by a car. You share my values. I'm still missing my cat, but I certainly feel a lot better. I've spoken with someone who understands and identifies with my plight.

Then I tell X the same story: it's about my cat running into the middle of the road and getting killed. I'm feeling miserable. I want X to sympathize, but, instead, she laughs! She says that I'm silly to waste my time worrying over little furry creatures when there are so many problems in the world. I wanted her to commiserate, to understand, but she ridiculed me. *Our values clashed.* I wanted her to see things my way, but she refused. I probably won't tell her any more stories about cats. Maybe I won't tell her any more stories at all. (See John Berger's views on humans and animals on page 269.)

When we speak and when we write, we often take risks; we risk that our listeners or readers will laugh when we want them to cry, or shrug, sigh, or yawn when we want them to laugh. In conversation, we meet our listeners face to face. We can make amends, change our minds, apologize, plead: we're involved in the give and take of dialogue. We can resist others' values, refuse them altogether, submit to some of them, agree to all of them. We can *negotiate*. We might diagram the process of negotiation like this:

When we write, we give ourselves over to our readers. We have no control over how they ultimately "read" us. As Roland Barthes says, "To write is to offer others, from the start, the last word." In a sense, our readers *write* us: Once we turn the page over to them, they "perform" our texts: they hear how we "sound"; they fill in the gaps; they kidnap our ideas. (See Montaigne on "borrowing" from books he has read, page 181.) They misread. They laugh in the "wrong" spots, find us boring, out of touch, ridiculous: those are the chances we take. Whatever we do—in life and on the page—we're inevitably involved in exchanges of values between listener and speaker, reader and writer.

William Labov, a sociolinguist, has studied the way people tell stories and has distinguished two chief features of the story:

1. Every story must have a "narrative," a representation of a happening, signaled by the notion of *and then.*

   A happened *and then* B happened.

   The cat ran into the street and then got run over.

2. Every story must contain an expression of values, an *evaluation.* "Evaluation," says Labov, is "perhaps the most important element in addition to the basic narrative clause." It is:

   . . . the means used by the narrator to indicate the point of the narrative; its *raison d' etre:* why it was told and what the narrator was getting at. . . . There are many ways to tell the same story to make different points. Pointless stories are met (in English) with the withering rejoinder, "So what?" Every good narrator is continually warding off this question; when his narrative is over, it should be unthinkable for a bystander to say, "So what?" Instead, the appropriate remark would be "He did?" or similar means of registering the reportable character of the events of the narrative. . . . Evaluative devices say to us: this was terrifying, dangerous, weird, wild, crazy; or amusing, hilarious, and wonderful; more generally, that it was strange, uncommon, or unusual—that is, worth reporting.

Language in the Inner City, page 366

Consider, again, our brief narrative:

The cat ran into the street and then got run over.

So what? What's the point? Labov says that we have no story unless we have an evaluation. Think for a moment of a friend telling you a very, very long story or joke: he goes on and on and on and on. You begin to twitch and squirm. "So what?" "What's the point?" You wonder. Why's he telling this story? Won't it ever end?

Teenagers often tell what appear to adults to be pointless stories: "Like, he goes . . . ," and "then, I go . . . ," and "like, he goes." They're caught in a stream of *and then and then and then,* with no letup and no perceivable point—to those who don't share their values.

Labov insists that the very best storytellers are always verbal *performers:* they are keenly aware of their audience, anticipating the question *so what?* They're on the alert, taking their listener's pulse, knowing what to emphasize, what to omit, how to keep their listener listening. They know when to give and when to withhold—how to get their messages across explicitly or implicitly.

Storytellers use explicit evaluative devices, words which tell us specifically where they stand on things, what they think, where their sympathies lie, what their judgments are.

1. The cat ran out into the street and got killed. Poor cat.
2. The cat ran out into the street and got killed. I should have made sure that darned door was closed.
3. The cat ran out into the street and got killed. I hope that cab driver has nightmares.
4. The cat ran out into the street and got killed. Domestic animals should be kept in the house at all times.

You can begin to see how "the point" *frames* and *focuses* the minimal narrative, and how each "point" then *reframes* and *refocuses* the story in a different way—with a different emphasis. In sentence 1, the focus is on the cat. In 2, the focus is on the narrator. In 3, on the driver, and in 4, on the larger subject of domestic animals. In each case, the points are *explicitly* stated.

Storytellers use implicit evaluative devices, words which do not openly state how they judge the event represented; the "unsaid" lurks underneath, and we may not be certain how we are to "hear" the words actually written.

5. The cat ran out into the street and got killed. My little brother had to miss school the next day.

6. The cat ran out into the street and got killed. My neighbor saw the whole thing; she said he didn't know what hit him.

7. The cat ran out into the street and, unfortunately, got killed.

8. The cat ran out into the street and, fortunately, got killed.

With explicit evaluation, we, as readers, are *given* a point and a position: it *appears* as if we know what we're supposed to know—that is, why the story was told. The text appears to be closed, wrapped up. There are few gaps to be filled.

With examples 5 to 8, we have more work to do as readers: we are invited to read between the lines, to infer, make connections, fill in the gaps—for example, between the death of the cat and the brother's staying home from school. Presumably the brother stayed home because he was upset about the cat. That's what we probably infer, isn't it?

In 5, 6, and 7 above, we know fairly well what the narrator's stance is, but in 8, we confront a more "open" text—with a curious gap to fill. We're left wondering about the word *fortunately*. Is the narrator an animal hater? A loather of this particular cat? Or is the narrator joking? Playing with words—being sarcastic? Or ironic? That one word unsettles and energizes the whole narrative. We don't know what to expect.

The unsaid in 8 might be:

> The cat ran out in the street and, fortunately, got killed. (I say fortunately because I think that all pets are a waste of time and money—they are pure middle-class self-indulgence. Look at all the people starving throughout the world. Imagine how much money is wasted on pet food.)

If all this had been stated, there would be no doubt about why the little story had been told: we would get the point, all right. We would have no questions—or would we?

Evaluation involves an exchange of values. Even the slightest story is an expression of values, and the evaluation may be contained in an explicit, clearly articulated statement, or it may take form as the implicit, the unsaid, the barely hinted at. It is often the location for debate, for dialogue, for negotiation. Your friend, after fifteen minutes, finally gets to the point of his long-winded story—but you simply don't care! You find the subject uninteresting, or you find the point he's making about the subject not worth the time of day, or you think that he's wrong in his way of looking at things—in fact, you're surprised that he's taken this particular point of view. You're like the listener who *devalues* the story about the cat: you think the story is not even worth telling—in your view, it's not *tellable*. This is one of the worst receptions to a story, isn't it?—when your listener understands but devalues your representations of your experiences.

As you have probably realized, we can also use this notion of evaluation to talk about the essay as well as the story: in fact, we can use evaluation to talk about all forms of language, *because we are, inescapably and continually, evaluating our own and others' experiences.* Reading texts focuses our attention on two fundamental ways in which we habitually react to both explicit and implicit evaluations: getting the point and evaluating the point.

Getting the point

Sometimes "the point" will hit you over the head: it's explicit. ("That was the strangest/ saddest/most bizarre/most wonderful/most terrifying/most extraordinary thing that ever happened to me.") We see most of the iceberg.

Other times the point will be more subtle, more implicit. You'll have to read between the lines, to understand what's tacit, what's below the surface. To borrow Hemingway's metaphor: much of the iceberg lies beneath the water.

Sometimes, what the point is *said* to be is not what *you* see as the point at all. You see an entirely different "point." What the writer or speaker says is the iceberg is, for you, not the iceberg at all.

"Getting the point," then, is not simply finding a message in the bottle; it's also a matter of reading, interpretation, negotiations—between you and the oral or written text.

Evaluating the point

Your own values come into play: you resist or submit or compromise. You bridge the gulf of values, weighing and measuring, reflecting, considering, questioning. You accept or refute, argue and debate, are impartial or indifferent or confused. You may finally refuse to accept the point at all. Or you may need time to make up your mind, to reflect upon the issues. Negotiation is the key.

All of these acts of mind come into play whether you are reading or writing, listening or speaking.

Your reading turns you into a *critic*. That is, you don't simply accept the words, but evaluate the situation and the evaluation. You agree, disagree, compromise, negotiate, renegotiate—and, finally, *judge,* relying upon your own moral sense of what is right and wrong. (The word *critic* comes from the Latin *criticus* and the Greek *krites,* which mean "judge.")

Try this:

In your notebook, represent a single event in two different ways:

1. In which the point is explicitly stated: "That was a bizarre experience." "It was a strange event." "Boy, was I scared."
2. In which the point is "hidden" in the text.

Identify the evaluative devices you used to get the point across in version 2.

Try this:

Write down two or three anecdotes that you overhear in an eavesdropping situation. Then isolate and list the value-laden parts of the exchange. Are they implicit or explicit? Which do you find to be most effective?

EXERCISES IN EVALUATION

Try this:

Here are more reframings of the cat narrative mentioned above. How do they reframe and refocus the narrative for you? Which are explicit? Which are implicit?

The cat ran into the street and got run over.

1. And of all the rotten luck, it happened near my car.
2. It was the worst thing that could have ever happened to me or the cat. I was supposed to be caring for the poor creature while my aunt was away. She loved the mangy little thing—she'll never forgive me.
3. It was a horrible scene. All its blood was splattered in the street.
4. I guess he'll stop killing birds now.
5. I can't get the picture out of my mind.
6. It was the first time I had ever seen anything die. I had nightmares for weeks.
7. After five years of coming down in the morning, to feed that silly dumb cat at my door. I fed it every day. Every day. Silly dumb cat.
8. Finally, I get to throw out all of that smelly cat food that's been stinking up the closet.
9. Given his promiscuous behavior, he really did end up as my father predicted.
10. And it was a good thing it died that way because it was already dying of cancer and this way it died so much quicker.
11. The driver didn't even turn to see what happened to the poor cat.
12. A little girl came flying out of a nearby house and shouted, "Mom, our cat is dead, now I want a puppy."
13. Cab drivers would run over everything and everyone in their way.
14. And the dog stopped chasing her.
15. Now who will listen to my problems?
16. The dog barked victoriously.

CONVENTIONS OF ESSAYS

What is an essay? What are the conventions of the essay?

The word *essay* derives from the French *essayer,* which means "to attempt," "to try." The term was first used by Michel de Montaigne (1533–1595), a French lawyer who wrote a very peculiar autobiography: rather than writing a chronicle of his life from birth, he wrote short, autobiographical commentaries on a range of subjects—education, books, friendship, travel, conversation, experience, relationships. He was not a scholar: in fact, he dipped into books as he chose, used them as he wished. Here are several excerpts from Montaigne's *essai* "On Books"; you may find his views on reading rather unconventional.

I have no doubt that I often speak of things which are better treated by the masters of the craft, and with more truth. This is simply a *trial* of my natural faculties, and not of my acquired ones. If anyone catches me in ignorance, he will score no triumph over me, since I can hardly be answerable to another for my reasonings, when I am not answerable for them to myself, and am never satisfied with them. Let the man who is in search of knowledge fish for it where it lies; there is nothing that I lay less claim to. These are my fancies, in which I make no attempt to convey information about things, only about myself. I may have some objective knowledge one day, or may perhaps have had it in the past when I happened to light on passages that explained things. But I have forgotten it all; for though I am a man of some reading, I am one who retains nothing.

So I can offer nothing certain except to recount the extent of my knowledge at the present moment. No attention should be paid to the matter, only to the shape that I give it. Let it be judged from what I borrow [from books] whether I have chosen the right means of exalting my theme. For I make others say what I cannot say so well myself, sometimes from poverty to expression, sometimes from lack of understanding. I do not count my borrowings, I weigh them; had I wished them to be valued by their number, I could have loaded myself with twice as many. . . .

If I get myself into a muddle, if there is something empty and faulty in my reasoning that I am unable to perceive for myself, or incapable of seeing when it is pointed out to me, then for this I may be held to account. Mistakes often escape our eyes, but it is the sign of a poor judgement if we are unable to see them when shown to us by another. Knowledge and truth may dwell in us without judgement, and judgement also without them; indeed to recognize one's ignorance is one of the best and surest signs of judgement that I know. I have no other drill-sergeant than chance to put order into my writings. As my thoughts come into my head, so I pile them up; sometimes they press on in crowds, sometimes they come dragging in single file. . . .

In books I only look for the pleasure of honest entertainment; or if I study, the only learning I look for is that which tells me how to know myself, and teaches me how to die well and to live well.

When I meet with difficulties in my reading, I do not bite my nails over them; after making one or two attempts I give them up. If I were to sit down to them, I should be wasting myself and my time; my mind works at the first leap. What I do not see immediately, I see even less by persisting. Without lightness I achieve nothing; application and over-serious effort confuse, depress, and weary my brain. My vision becomes blurred and confused. I must look away, and then repeatedly look back; just as in judging the brilliance of a scarlet cloth, we are told to pass the eye lightly over it, glancing at it several times in rapid succession. If one book bores me, I take up another; and I turn to reading only at such times as I begin to be tired of doing nothing. . . .

Try this:

What do you think of Montaigne's attitudes toward reading and toward books? In your notebook, negotiate with his views:

1. Resist them, from the role of a twelfth-grade English teacher, who is trying to persuade him to labor over books so that he can get a high score on his SATs!

2. Now read quickly John Holt's essay, page 394, and respond to Montaigne's comments from Holt's point of view. Does Holt support Montaigne's views on reading?

3. Where do you stand on these matters?

4. Write an essay using your own experiences of reading, Montaigne's representations of his experiences, and Holt's perspectives on the teaching of reading.

Montaigne, as you can infer from the above passage, brought himself to each subject as if he were on *trial:* his task was to test himself, to uncover and express his beliefs. In a sense, he was an "armchair philosopher," using his pen to explore whatever struck his fancy and to leave a portrait of himself for his relatives and friends, so that they "may recover some features of my character and disposition, and thus keep the memory they have of me more completely and vividly alive." In a sense, his essays are like a scrapbook of verbal photographs. He was wealthy enough to live off his lands, and to have the leisure to reflect upon the state of the world. He used the writing of essays as an occasion to *judge* the world and to judge himself.

He began a new literary form, the essay, which has come to mean any short, nonfiction writing on any subject in the world. It is one of the most fluid, elastic, experimental forms of writing: it borrows from the techniques of storytellers, poets, historians, statisticians, novelists, journalists, etc. It questions, explores, considers, analyzes, and judges, using whatever it needs: history, example, cases, anecdotes, descriptions, definitions, comparisons, interviews, and quotations. It can be retrospective and prospective at the same time: *reviewing the past and previewing the future.*

Where is it found? Everywhere—newspapers, magazines, scholarly journals, college textbooks, and television. You may not think of, say, Andy Rooney on the CBS program *60 Minutes* as an essayist, but he is: at the end of the hour, there he is, sitting at his desk, commenting on the state of paper clips, packaging, or muffler repair shops, or on the state of political debate in Washington, D.C. He is wry, witty, droll, irreverent, and humorous. He follows a long tradition of commentators in print, on stage, and on the screen who are watchdogs—judges, moralists, *evaluators* of ethics, habits, and customs—who keep us on our toes. He can be the one who says what we might want to say, but, for various reasons, can't. Sometimes he provokes, antagonizes, and teases his viewers: sometimes he offends, and they protest. Recently, the CBS network chastised him for going too far and (briefly) took him off the air.

In the syndicated columns of our newspapers, we find the likes of him in Art Buchwald, Russell Baker, Dave Barry, Lewis Gizzard, Anna Quindlen, Ellen Goodman, Ellen Willis, Fran Leibowitz, and Erma Bombeck. Sometimes the scope is domestic, as they consider what happens in the home between husbands and wives, parents and children; they may reflect on clothes, school, games, pastimes, shopping, and toys. Sometimes the scope is larger, as they consider problems of national or international importance—serious social and political issues, the environment, the economy, war and peace, natural or human disasters, civil rights, education. The concerns are almost always *timely.* Many essays arise out of crisis or tension: something happens that arouses, heightens, and intensifies the essayist's feelings about an event that engages his or her value system, and the essayist reacts. Others are more lighthearted: they engage our attention but make us laugh at the same time. The most compelling essays will spout not simply opinion—but rather conviction.

Consider this:

What do you see as the differences between *opinion* and *conviction?* Check the dictionary for definitions.

OPEN AND CLOSED TEXTS

How do you read essays? What are you reading *for?* What do you expect? And how does such reading enable you to write essays in college?

Here are two ways for you to approach the essay:

1. *Closed texts.* In some courses and some disciplines, you may be asked to write within very specific boundaries and conventions, producing what we might call a *closed text.* These are some expectations of this kind of text:

   • Write with clarity, above all else.

   • Take no detours, digressions, or side roads. Take a position; make a point and stick to it. (Here the evaluation would be explicit.)

   • In your introduction, state the point explicitly in the form of a "thesis sentence." The movement here will most likely be deductive, beginning with a hypothesis and following with "support."

   • The "body" of your text will offer support for the point, and the conclusion will, most likely, rephrase it. (In some situations, you may be asked to write a five-paragraph text: paragraph 1, introduction; paragraphs 2 to 4, body; paragraph 5, conclusion. This five-paragraph essay form is popularly known as the "sandwich.")

   • (Know, however, that what you, the writer, consider "closed" will be given over to the reader, who will, undoubtedly, find openings!)

2. *Open texts.* In other situations, you may be asked to write within much looser conventions. Here, like Montaigne, you would be foregrounding your "trials"— weighing and measuring your own values, beliefs, opinions, and convictions. This kind of exploration, where you do not offer your reader conclusions but rather speculations—various ways of considering an issue or a problem or an event—is what we might call an *open text:*

   • Speculation, conjecture, and various perspectives are invited.

   • Digressions and meanderings are perfectly acceptable.

   • The "point" or "points" may be left unstated—so that the reader will be engaged in debate, in a dialectic that involves playing off *a* against *b, b* against *c.* The evaluation will be implicit.

- The movement may be inductive: beginning with observations and leading to inferences.
- The conclusion may be inconclusive.

As with any piece of writing, these categories and distinctions will make no sense unless you try them out—unless you use them, and not see them as mutually exclusive. *They represent two extremes, between which you as a writer can negotiate.* If you are writing on a subject where there is absolutely no doubt about what you want to do to your readers, where your purpose is pragmatic, where you want them to stand up and take notice, and to do something, then, as with instructions on a fire extinguisher, your path to the reader must be unimpeded. You tell them how to put out the fire, without fail. Without impediments—no stumbling blocks, no detours. You get right to the point and stay there.

On the other hand, you may want to take your reader on a very different journey, to give your reader an entirely different reading experience. You may want to offer food for thought, an invitation for speculation, reflection, consideration, thoughtfulness, on any number of subjects—yourself or other people, issues, problems, or crises. The ways you choose may be very different. Know for yourselves as writers in this course, and as potential writers outside the course and outside of college, that the essay as a short, prose piece offers you many options and possibilities for affecting your readers in any number of ways.

Closed and tight: Taking a position

The following texts I see as "closed" because they state specific, explicit positions and then offer support for those positions. They are not closed or finished, however, in terms of the arguments they present: they can be prised open by the reader who takes an opposing position, who resists the text.

Read, first, this brief editorial, "Women Stereotyping Women," where the position taken (about women stereotyping women) is clearly stated at the end of paragraph two in the *if. . . then* sentence.

Women Stereotyping Women: The Risky Business of Gender Politics
Joyce Purnick

Molly Yard, president of the National Organization for Women, predicts "the feminization of power" as more women win public office. Women politicians talk enthusiastically about the "decade of the woman." Dianne Feinstein, the Democratic nominee for governor of California, says that a woman official can protect abortion rights more reliably than a man.

These developments, many women argue, are good for the future of women in America. But are they? What does the feminization of power mean? If Ms. Yard is suggesting that a woman in office is, by definition, superior to a man in office, then all it means is more stereotyping.

That's precisely the kind of bias that women have fought against for years. Some women are better qualified for public office than men. Some are not. But such obvious truths disappear as many women seem determined to prove themselves as capable of narrowness and prejudice as narrow and prejudiced men.

There's little new or surprising about appeals to ethnic, racial or religious loyalties. They have always figured prominently in politics. Gender politics is the latest variation on an old theme, a welcome sign that women have come into their political own. But there's something troubling about the way some women candidates are campaigning these days. By telling women she can better represent them on the sensitive issue of abortion, Dianne Feinstein insults men and women.

Imagine the outcry if Gov. Mario Cuomo of New York promised Italian-American voters that they would benefit from his election because he is of Italian descent. Or if Mayor Tom Bradley of Los Angeles pledged the equivalent to African-Americans. Yet Ms. Feinstein, who has been running against pro-choice men, argues that "it's correct for women to believe they are best protected by a woman who is governor."

Why should that be so? A woman who has had to choose whether to have an abortion might well understand the issue better than most men. But better than a woman who hasn't faced that choice? Or better than a man who, as the partner of a pregnant woman, has struggled with the same decision?

Men are as capable of empathy as women, and women are as capable of insensitivity as men. Experience and character are what matter on so profound an issue, not gender. To argue otherwise is offensive and sexist. It implies that women think alike. In fact, American women have struggled hard to erase stereotypes and have earned the right to disagree with one another.

In effect, Ms. Feinstein and other candidates who trade on their gender, race or ethnicity are appealing to prejudice. If, in their pursuit of equality, women have won the right to be just as mediocre as the next guy, they have also won the chance to be wiser.

In the next text, Robin Lakoff, a linguist at the University of California, Berkeley, also takes a position and makes a point about the ways "women's language" affects their "go[ing] out in the world." At the end of the first paragraph, you'll find her point. Note that in both texts, the point is made after a brief introduction: one of the conventions of essay writing is for the point to appear early on in the text. We expect to know the writer's stance toward her subject fairly quickly. Read Lakoff's essay quickly, noting, as you do, the kinds of examples she offers for support.

You Are What You Say
Robin Lakoff

"Women's language" is that pleasant (dainty?), euphemistic, never-aggressive way of talking we learned as little girls. Cultural bias was built into the language we were allowed to speak, the subjects we were allowed to speak about, and the ways we were spoken of.

Having learned our linguistic lesson well, we go out in the world, only to discover that we are communicative cripples—damned if we do, and damned if we don't.

If we refuse to talk "like a lady," we are ridiculed and criticized for being unfeminine. ("She thinks like a man" is, at best, a left-handed compliment.) If we do learn all the fuzzy-headed, unassertive language of our sex, we are ridiculed for being unable to think clearly, unable to take part in a serious discussion, and therefore unfit to hold a position of power.

It doesn't take much of this for a woman to begin feeling she deserves such treatment because of inadequacies in her own intelligence and education.

"Women's language" shows up in all levels of English. For example, women are encouraged and allowed to make far more precise discriminations in naming colors than men do. Words like *mauve, beige, ecru, aquamarine, lavender,* and so on, are unremarkable in a woman's active vocabulary, but largely absent from that of most men. I know of no evidence suggesting that women actually see a wider range of colors than men do. It is simply that fine discriminations of this sort are relevant to women's vocabularies, but not to men's; to men, who control most of the interesting affairs of the world, such distinctions are trivial—irrelevant.

In the area of syntax, we find similar gender-related peculiarities of speech. There is one construction, in particular, that women use conversationally far more than men: the tag-question. A tag is midway between an outright statement and a yes-no question; it is less assertive than the former, but more confident than the latter.

A *flat statement* indicates confidence in the speaker's knowledge and is fairly certain to be believed; a question indicates a lack of knowledge on some point and implies that the gap in the speaker's knowledge can and will be remedied by an answer. For example, if, at a Little League game, I have had my glasses off, I can legitimately ask someone else: "Was the player out at third?" A *tag question,* being intermediate between statement and question, is used when the speaker is stating a claim, but lacks full confidence in the truth of that claim. So if I say, "Is Joan here?" I will probably not be surprised if my respondent answers "no"; but if I say, "Joan is here, isn't she?" instead, chances are I am already biased in favor of a positive answer, wanting only confirmation. I still want a response, but I have enough knowledge (or think I have) to predict that response. A tag question, then, might be thought of as a statement that doesn't demand to be believed by anyone but the speaker, a way of giving leeway, of not forcing the addressee to go along with the views of the speaker.

Another common use of the tag-question is in small talk when the speaker is trying to elicit conversation: "Sure is hot here, isn't it?"

But in discussing personal feelings or opinions, only the speaker normally has any way of knowing the correct answer. Sentences such as "I have a headache, don't I" are clearly ridiculous. But there are other examples where it is the speaker's opinions, rather than perceptions, for which corroboration is sought, as in "The situation in Southeast Asia is terrible, isn't it?"

While there are, of course, other possible interpretations of a sentence like this, one possibility is that the speaker has a particular answer in mind—"yes" or "no"—but is reluctant to state it baldly. This sort of tag question is much more apt to be used by women than by men in conversation. Why is this the case?

The tag question allows a speaker to avoid commitment, and thereby avoid conflict with the addressee. The problem is that, by so doing, speakers may also give the impression of not really being sure of themselves, or looking to the addressee for confirmation of their views. This uncertainty is reinforced in more subliminal ways, too. There is a peculiar sentence intonation-pattern, used almost exclusively by women, as far as I know, which changes a declarative answer into a question. The effect of using the rising inflection typical of a yes-no question is to imply that the speaker is seeking confirmation, even though the speaker is clearly the only one who has the requisite information, which is why the question was put to her in the first place:

(Q) When will dinner be ready?

(A) Oh . . . around six o'clock . . . ?

It is as though the second speaker were saying, "Six o'clock—if that's okay with you, if you agree." The person being addressed is put in the position of having to provide confirmation. One likely consequence of this sort of speech-pattern in a woman is that, often unbeknownst to herself, the speaker builds a reputation of tentativeness, and others will refrain from taking her seriously or trusting her with any real responsibilities since she "can't make up her mind," and "isn't sure of herself."

Such idiosyncrasies may explain why women's language sounds much more "polite" than men's. It is polite to leave a decision open, not impose your mind, or views, or claims, on anyone else. So a tag-question is a kind of polite statement, in that it does not force agreement or belief on the addressee. In the same way a request is a polite command, in that it does not force obedience on the addressee, but rather suggests something to be done as a favor to the speaker. A clearly stated order implies a threat of certain consequences if it is not followed, and—even more impolite—implies that the speaker is in a superior position and able to enforce the order. By couching wishes in the form of a request, on the other hand, a speaker implies that if the request is not carried out, only the speaker will suffer; noncompliance cannot harm the addressee. So the decision is really up to the addressee. The distinction becomes clear in these examples:

Close the door.

Please close the door.

Will you close the door?

Will you please close the door?

Won't you close the door?

In the same ways as words and speech patterns used *by* women undermine her image, those used to *describe* women make matters even worse. Often a word may be used of both men and women (and perhaps of things as well); but when it is applied to women, it assumes a special meaning that, by implication rather than outright assertion, is derogatory to women as a group.

The use of euphemisms has this effect. A euphemism is a substitute for a word that has acquired a bad connotation by association with something unpleasant or embarrassing. But almost as soon as the new word comes into common usage, it takes on the same old bad connotations, since feelings about the things or people referred to are not altered by a change of name: thus new euphemisms must be constantly found.

There is one euphemism for *woman* still very much alive. The word, of course, is *lady*. *Lady* has a masculine counterpart, namely *gentleman,* occasionally shortened to *gent*. But for some reason *lady* is very much commoner than *gent(leman)*. The decision to use *lady* rather than *woman,* or vice versa, may considerably alter the sense of a sentence, as the following examples show:

(a) A woman (lady) I know is a dean at Berkeley.

(b) A woman (lady) I know makes amazing things out of shoelaces and old boxes.

The use of *lady* in (a) imparts a frivolous, or nonserious, tone to the sentence: the matter under discussion is not one of great moment. Similarly, in (b), using *lady* here would suggest that the speaker considered the "amazing things" not to be serious art, but merely a hobby or an aberration. If *woman* is used, she might be a serious sculptor. To say *lady doctor* is very condescending, since no one ever says *gentleman doctor* or even *man doctor*. For example, mention in the San Francisco *Chronicle* of January 31, 1972, of Madalyn Murray O'Hair as the *lady atheist* reduces her position to that of scatterbrained eccentric. Even *woman atheist* is scarcely defensible: sex is irrelevant to her philosophical position.

Many women argue that, on the other hand, *lady* carries with it overtones recalling the age of chivalry: conferring exalted stature on the person so referred to. This makes the term seem polite at first, but we must also remember that these implications are perilous: they suggest that a "lady" is helpless, and cannot do things by herself.

Lady can also be used to imply frivolousness, as in titles of organizations. Those that have a serious purpose (not merely that of enabling "the ladies" to spend time with one another) cannot use the word *lady* in their titles, but less serious ones may. Compare the *Ladies' Auxiliary* of a men's group, or the *Thursday Evening Ladies' Browning and Garden Society* with *Ladies' Liberation* or *Ladies' Strike for Peace*. What is curious about this split is that *lady* is in origin a euphemism—a substitute that puts a better face on something people find uncomfortable—for *woman*. What kind of euphemism is it that subtly denigrates the people to whom it refers? Perhaps *lady* functions as a euphemism for *woman* because it does not contain the sexual implications present in *woman;* it is not "embarrassing" in that way. If this is so, we may expect that, in the future, *lady* will replace woman as the primary word for the human female, since *woman* will have become too blatantly sexual. That this distinction is already made in some contexts at least is shown in the following examples, where you can try replacing *woman* with *lady*.

(a) She's only twelve, but she's already a woman.

(b) After ten years in jail, Harry wanted to find a woman.

(c) She's my woman, see, so don't mess around with her.

Another common substitute for *woman* is *girl*. One seldom hears a man past the age of adolescence referred to as a boy, save in expressions like "going out with the boys," which are meant to suggest an air of adolescent frivolity and irresponsibility. But women of all ages are "girls": one can have a man—not a boy—Friday, but only a girl—never a woman or even a lady—Friday; women have girlfriends, but men do not—in a nonsexual sense— have boyfriends. It may be that this use of *girl* is euphemistic in the same way the use of *lady* is; in stressing the idea of immaturity, it removes the sexual connotations lurking in *woman*. *Girl* brings to mind irresponsibility; you don't send a girl to do a woman's errand (or even, for that matter, a boy's errand). She is a person who is both too immature and too far from real life to be entrusted with responsibilities or with decisions of any serious or important nature.

Now let's take a pair of words which, in terms of the possible relationships in an earlier society, were simple male-female equivalents, analogous to *bull:cow*. Suppose we find that, for independent reasons, society has changed in such a way that the original meanings now are irrelevant. Yet the words have not been discarded, but have acquired new meanings, metaphorically related to their original senses. But suppose these new meta- phorical uses are no longer parallel to each other. By seeing where the parallelism breaks down, we discover something about the different roles played by men and women in this culture. One good example of such a divergence through time is found in the pair, *master: mistress*. Once used with reference to one's power over servants, these words have become unusable today in their original master-servant sense as the relationship has become less prevalent in our society. But the words are still common.

Unless used with reference to animals, *master* now generally refers to a man who has acquired consummate ability in some field, normally nonsexual. But its feminine counter- part cannot be used this way. It is practically restricted to its sexual sense of "paramour." We start out with two terms, both roughly paraphrasable as "one who has power over another." But the masculine form, once one person is no longer able to have absolute power over another, becomes usable metaphorically in the sense of "having power over *some- thing*." *Master* requires as its object only the name of some activity, something inanimate and abstract. But *mistress* requires a masculine noun in the possessive to precede it. One cannot say: "Rhonda is a mistress." One must be *someone's* mistress. A man is defined by what he does, a woman by her sexuality, that is, in terms of one particular aspect of her relationship to men. It is one thing to be an *old master* like Hans Holbein, and another to be an *old mistress*. The same is true of the words *spinster* and *bachelor*—gender words for "one who is not married." The resemblance ends with the definition. While *bachelor* is a neuter term often used as a compliment, *spinster* normally is used pejoratively, with connotations of prissiness, fussiness, and so on. To be a bachelor implies that one has the choice of marrying or not, and this is what makes the idea of a bachelor existence attractive, in the popular literature. He has been pursued and has successfully eluded his pursuers. But a spinster is one who has not been pursued, or at least not seriously. She is old, unwanted goods. The metaphorical connotations of *bachelor* generally suggest sexual freedom; of *spinster*, puritanism or celibacy.

These examples could be multiplied. It is generally considered a *faux pas*, in society, to congratulate a woman on her engagement, while it is correct to congratulate her fiancé. Why is this? The reason seems to be that it is impolite to remind people of things that may be uncomfortable to them. To congratulate a woman on her engagement is really to say, "Thank goodness! You had a close call!" For the man, on the other hand, there was no such danger. His choosing to marry is viewed as a good thing, but not something essential.

The linguistic double standard holds throughout the life of the relationship. After marriage, bachelor and spinster become man and wife, not man and woman. The woman whose husband dies remains "John's widow"; John, however, is never "Mary's widower."

Finally, why is it that salesclerks and others are so quick to call women customers "dear," "honey," and other terms of endearment they really have no business using? A male customer would never put up with it. But women, like children, are supposed to enjoy these endearments, rather than being offended by them.

In more ways than one, it's time to speak up.

Try this:

Lakoff's primary interest is in the ways people (in this case, women) use words. You might imagine that she does a good bit of eavesdropping, listening in on women's conversations, observing them in stores and restaurants, homes, and places of work. How else might she collect her data?

Suppose that you were a linguist devoted to the study of men's language or children's language (perhaps distinguishing between boys and girls). How would you go about collecting data? Try an ethnographic study, where you collect samples of men's talk or children's talk (distinguishing gender). Write a sharply focused essay—where you take a position and make a point about your data.

Try this:

Resist one of Lakoff's arguments. You might disagree that "women's language" works against them, or you might dispute the very existence of "women's language."

Leaky texts: Opening doors

What follows now are two pieces by the writer Michelle Cliff. The first, "A Journey into Speech," is a rather straightforward essay explaining why Cliff has chosen to write unconventional fragmentary texts. Her cultural funding had prepared her to write what was expected of her in academia. It was only after she had completed a dissertation that she was driven to explore other textual possibilities. Closed, resolved, orderly texts no longer worked for her. She needed the language on the page to try to capture the warring tensions within her, particularly the tensions of her two languages, English and the patois of her native Jamaica.

The second text, "If I Could Write This in Fire, I Would Write This in Fire," is just such an attempt: it is "strung together [of] myth, dream, historical detail, observation," her patois and English. Cliff defies closure, insisting at the end of her piece that her ending is not an ending at all because "there is no ending to the piece of writing."

How does her writing work for you? Without conventional textual markers (clearly marked beginnings, conventional paragraph structure, etc.), how do you find your way among the fragments? Do her fragments add up to a whole for you? Is her "no ending," nevertheless, an ending?

A Journey into Speech
Michelle Cliff

The first piece of writing I produced, beyond a dissertation on intellectual game-playing in the Italian Renaissance, was entitled "Notes on Speechlessness," published in *Sinister Wisdom,* no. 5. In it I talked about my identification with Victor, the wild boy of Aveyron, who, after his rescue from the forest and wildness by a well-meaning doctor of Enlightenment Europe, became "civilized," but never came to speech. I felt, with Victor, that my wildness had been tamed—that which I had been taught was my wildness.

My dissertation was produced at the Warburg Institute, University of London, and was responsible for giving me an intellectual belief in myself that I had not had before, while at the same time distancing me from who I am, almost rendering me speechless about who I am. At least I believed in the young woman who wrote the dissertation—still, I wondered who she was and where she had come from.

I could speak fluently, but I could not reveal. I immersed myself in the social circles and academies of Siena, Florence, Urbino, as well as Venice, creating a place for myself there, and describing this ideal world in eloquent linear prose.

When I began, finally, partly through participation in the feminist movement, to approach myself as a subject, my writing was jagged, nonlinear, almost shorthand. The "Notes on Speechlessness" were indeed notes, written in snatches on a nine-to-five job. I did not choose the note form consciously; a combination of things drew me to it. An urgency for one thing. I also felt incompetent to construct an essay in which I would describe the intimacies, fears, and lies I wrote of in "Speechlessness." I felt my thoughts, things I had held within for a lifetime, traversed so wide a terrain, had so many stops and starts, apparent non sequiturs, that an essay—with its cold-blooded dependence on logical construction, which I had mastered practically against my will—could not work. My subject could not respond to that form, which would have contradicted the idea of speechlessness. This tender approach to myself within the confines and interruptions of a forty-hour-a-week job and against a history of forced fluency was the beginning of a journey into speech.

To describe this journey further, I must begin at the very beginning, with origins, and the significance of these origins. How they have made me the writer I am.

I originate in the Caribbean, specifically on the island of Jamaica, and although I have lived in the United States and in England, I travel as a Jamaican. It is Jamaica that forms my writing for the most part, and which has formed for the most part, myself. Even though I often feel what Derek Walcott expresses in his poem "The Schooner *Flight*": "I had no nation now but the imagination." It is a complicated business.

Jamaica is a place halfway between Africa and England, to put it simply, although historically one culture (guess which one) has been esteemed and the other denigrated (both are understatements)—at least among those who control the culture and politics of the island—the Afro-Saxons. As a child among these people, indeed of these people, as one of them, I received the message of anglocentrism, of white supremacy, and I internalized it. As a writer, as a human being, I have had to accept that reality and deal with its effect on me, as well as finding what has been lost to me from the darker side, and what may be hidden, to be dredged from memory and dream. And it *is* there to be dredged. As my writing delved longer and deeper into this part of myself, I began to dream and imagine. I was able to clearly envision Nanny, the leader of a group of guerrilla fighters known as the Windward Maroons, as she is described: an old Black woman naked except for a necklace made from the teeth of white men. I began to love her.

It is a long way from the court of Urbino to Nanny the Coromantyn warrior. (Coromantyn, or Coromantee, was used by the British in Jamaica to describe slaves from the Gold Coast of Africa, especially slaves who spoke Akan.)

One of the effects of assimilation, indoctrination, passing into the anglocentrism of British West Indian culture is that you believe absolutely in the hegemony of the King's English and in the form in which it is meant to be expressed. Or else your writing is not literature; it is folklore, and folklore can never be art. Read some poetry by West Indian writers—some, not all—and you will see what I mean. You have to dissect stanza after extraordinary anglican stanza for Afro-Caribbean truth; you may never find the latter. But this has been our education. The anglican ideal—Milton, Wordsworth, Keats—was held before us with an assurance that we were unable, and would never be enabled, to compose a work of similar correctness. No reggae spoken here.

To write as a complete Caribbean woman, or man for that matter, demands of us retracing the African part of ourselves, reclaiming as our own, and as our subject, a history sunk under the sea, or scattered as potash in the canefields, or gone to bush, or trapped in a class system notable for its rigidity and absolute dependence on color stratification. On a past bleached from our minds. It means finding the art forms of these of our ancestors and speaking in the *patois* forbidden us. It means realizing our knowledge will always be wanting. It means also, I think, mixing in the forms taught us by the oppressor, undermining his language and co-opting his style, and turning it to our purpose. In my current work-in-progress, a novel, I alternate the King's English with *patois,* not only to show the class background of characters, but to show how Jamaicans operate within a split consciousness. It would be as dishonest to write the novel entirely in *patois* as to write entirely in the King's English. Neither is the novel a linear construction; its subject is the political upheavals of the past twenty years. Therefore, I have mixed time and incident and space and character and also form to try to mirror the historical turbulence.

For another example, I wrote a long poem, actually half-poem, half-prose, in which I imagine the visit of Botha of South Africa to the heads of western Europe in the summer of 1984. I wrote this as a parody of Gilbert and Sullivan because their work epitomizes salient aspects of the British Empire which remain vibrant. And because as a child I was sick to death of hearing "I am the very model of a modern major general." I enjoyed writing this, playing with rhyme and language—it was like spitting into their cultural soup.

We are a fragmented people. My experience as a writer coming from a culture of colonialism, a culture of Black people riven from each other, my struggle to get wholeness from fragmentation while working within fragmentation, producing work which may find its strength in its depiction of fragmentation, through form as well as content, is similar to the experience of other writers whose origins are in countries defined by colonialism.

Ama Ata Aidoo, the Ghanaian writer, in her extraordinary book, *Our Sister Killjoy or Reflections from a Black-Eyed Squint* (NOK Publishers, Lagos and New York, 1979), plots this fragmentation, and shows how both the demand and solace of the so-called mother country can claim us, while we long for our homeland and are shamed for it and ourselves at the same time. The form Aidoo uses to depict this dilemma of colonial peoples—part prose, fictional and epistolary, part poetry—illustrates the fragmentation of the heroine and grasps the fury of the heroine, living in Europe but drawn back to Ghana, knowing she can never be European. She will only be a been-to; that is, one who has been to the mother country. *Our Sister Killjoy* affected me directly, not just because like Aidoo's heroine I was a been-to. I was especially drawn by the way in which Aidoo expresses rage against colonialism—crystallized for her by the white man she calls the "Christian Doctor" throughout, excising Black African hearts to salvage white South African lives. In her expression of the rage she feels her prose breaks apart sharply into a staccato poetry— direct, short, brilliantly bitter—as if measured prose would disintegrate under her fury.

I wanted that kind of directness in my writing, as I came into closer contact with my rage, and a realization that rage could fuel and shape my work. As a light-skinned colonial girlchild, both in Jamaica and in the Jamaican milieu of my family abroad, rage was the last thing expected of me.

After reading Aidoo I knew I wanted to tell exactly how things were, what had been done, to us and by us, without muddying the issue with conventional beauty, avoiding becoming trapped in the grace of language for its own sake, which is always seductive.

In *Claiming an Identity They Taught Me to Despise,* a piece published before I read Aidoo, halfway between poetry and prose, as I am halfway between Africa and England, patriot and expatriate, white and Black, I felt my use of language and imagery had sometimes masked what I wanted to convey. It seemed sometimes that the reader was able to ignore what I was saying while admiring the way in which it was said.

And yet, *Claiming* is an honest self-portrait of who I was at the time. Someone who was unable, for the most part, to recapture the native language of Jamaica, and who relied on the King's English and European allusions, but who wrote from a feminist conscious-ness and a rapidly evolving consciousness of colonialism, and a knowledge of self-hatred. Someone who also dreamed in Latin—as I did and as I recorded in the title section, included here. *Claiming*'s strengths, I think, are in the more intimate, private places of the piece, which I constructed much as the "Notes on Speechlessness" are constructed. Shorthand—almost—as memory and dream emerge; fast, at once keen, at once incom-plete. I was also, in those sections, laboring under the ancient taboos of the assimilated: don't tell outsiders anything real about yourself. Don't reveal *our* secrets to *them*. Don't make us seem foolish, or oppressed. Write it quickly before someone catches you. Before you catch yourself.

After reading *Our Sister Killjoy,* something was set loose in me, I directed rage outward rather than inward, and I was able to write a piece called "If I Could Write This in Fire I Would Write This in Fire." In it I let myself go, any thought of approval for my words vanished; I strung together myth, dream, historical detail, observation, as I had done before, but I added native language, tore into the indoctrination of the colonizer, surprised myself with the violence of my words.

That piece of writing led to other pieces in which I try to depict personal fragmentation and describe political reality, according to the peculiar lens of the colonized.

If I Could Write This in Fire, I Would Write This in Fire
Michelle Cliff

I

We were standing under the waterfall at the top of Orange River. Our chests were just beginning to mound—slight hills on either side. In the center of each were our nipples, which were losing their sideways look and rounding into perceptible buttons of dark flesh. Too fast it seemed. We touched each other, then, quickly and almost simultaneously, raised our arms to examine the hairs growing underneath. Another sign. Mine was wispy and light-brown. My friend Zoe had dark hair curled up tight. In each little patch the riverwater caught the sun so we glistened.

The waterfall had come about when my uncles dammed up the river to bring power to the sugar mill. Usually, when I say "sugar mill" to anyone not familiar with the Jamaican countryside or for that matter my family, I can tell their minds cast an image of tall smokestacks, enormous copper cauldrons, a man in a broad-brimmed hat with a whip, and several dozens of slaves—that is, if they have any idea of how large sugar mills once operated. It's a grandiose expression—like plantation, verandah, out-building. (Try substituting farm, porch, outside toilet.) To some people it even sounds romantic.

Our sugar mill was little more than a round-roofed shed, which contained a wheel and woodfire. We paid an old man to run it, tend the fire, and then either bartered or gave the sugar away, after my grandmother had taken what she needed. Our canefield was about two acres of flat land next to the river. My grandmother had six acres in all—one donkey, a mule, two cows, some chickens, a few pigs, and stray dogs and cats who had taken up residence in the yard.

Her house had four rooms, no electricity, no running water. The kitchen was a shed in the back with a small pot-bellied stove. Across from the stove was a mahogany counter, which had a white enamel basin set into it. The only light source was a window, a small space covered partly by a wooden shutter. We washed our faces and hands in enamel bowls with cold water carried in kerosene tins from the river and poured from enamel pitchers. Our chamber pots were enamel also, and in the morning we carefully placed them on the steps at the side of the house where my grandmother collected them and disposed of their contents. The outhouse was about thirty yards from the back door—a "closet" as we called it—infested with lizards capable of changing color. When the door was shut it was totally dark, and the lizards made their presence known by the noise of their scurrying through the torn newspaper, or the soft shudder when they dropped from the walls. I remember most clearly the stench of the toilet, which seemed to hang in the air in that climate.

But because every little piece of reality exists in relation to another little piece, our situation was not that simple. It was to our yard that people came with news first. It was in my grandmother's parlor that the Disciples of Christ held their meetings. Zoe lived with her mother and sister on borrowed ground in a place called Breezy Hill. She and I saw each other almost every day on our school vacations over a period of three years. Each morning early—as I sat on the cement porch with my coffee cut with condensed milk—she appeared: in her straw hat, school tunic faded from blue to gray, white blouse, sneakers hanging around her neck. We had coffee together, and a piece of hard-dough bread with butter and cheese, waited a bit and headed for the river. At first we were shy with each other. We did not start from the same place.

There was land. My grandparents' farm. And there was color.

(My family was called *red*. A term which signified a degree of whiteness. "We's just a flock of red people," a cousin of mine said once.) In the hierarchy of shades I was considered among the lightest. The countrywomen who visited my grandmother commented on my "tall" hair—meaning long. Wavy, not curly.

I had spent the years from three to ten in New York and spoke—at first—like an American. I wore American clothes: shorts, slacks, bathing suit. Because of my American past I was looked upon as the creator of games. Cowboys and Indians. Cops and Robbers. Peter Pan.

(While the primary colonial identification for Jamaicans was English, American colonialism was a strong force in my childhood—and of course continues today. We were sent American movies and American music. American aluminum companies had already discovered bauxite on the island and were shipping the ore to their mainland. United Fruit bought our bananas. White Americans came to Montego Bay, Ocho Rios, and Kingston for their vacations and their cruise ships docked in Port Antonio and other places. In some ways America was seen as a better place than England by many Jamaicans. The farm laborers sent to work in American agribusiness came home with dollars and gifts and new clothes; there were few who mentioned American racism. Many of the middle class who emigrated to Brooklyn or Staten Island or Manhattan were able to pass into the white American world—saving their blackness for other Jamaicans or for trips home; in some cases, forgetting it altogether. Those middle-class Jamaicans who could not pass for white managed differently—not unlike the Bajans in Paule Marshall's *Brown Girl, Brownstones*—saving, working, investing, buying property. Completely separate in most cases from Black Americans.)

I was someone who had experience with the place that sent us triple features of B-grade westerns and gangster movies. And I had tall hair and light skin. And I was the granddaughter of my grandmother. So I had power. I was the cowboy, Zoe was my sidekick, the boys we knew were Indians. I was the detective, Zoe was my "girl," the boys were the robbers.

I was Peter Pan, Zoe was Wendy Darling, the boys were the lost boys. And the terrain around the river—jungled and dark green—was Tombstone, or Chicago, or Never-Never Land.

This place and my friendship with Zoe never touched my life in Kingston. We did not correspond with each other when I left my grandmother's home.

I never visited Zoe's home the entire time I knew her. It was a given: never suggested, never raised.

Zoe went to a state school held in a country church in Red Hills. It had been my mother's school. I went to a private all-girls school where I was taught by white Englishwomen and pale Jamaicans. In her school the students were caned as punishment. In mine the hardest punishment I remember was being sent to sit under the *lignum vitae* to "commune with nature." Some of the girls were out-and-out white (English and American), the rest of us were colored—only a few were dark. Our uniforms were blood-red gabardine, heavy and hot. Classes were held in buildings meant to recreate England: damp with stone floors, facing onto a cloister, or quad as they called it. We began each day with the headmistress leading us in English hymns. The entire school stood for an hour in the zinc-roofed gymnasium.

Occasionally a girl fainted, or threw up. Once, a girl had a grand mal seizure. To any such disturbance the response was always "keep singing." While she flailed on the stone floor, I wondered what the mistresses would do. We sang "Faith of Our Fathers," and watched our classmate as her eyes rolled back in her head. I thought of people swallowing their tongues. This student was dark—here on a scholarship—and the only woman who came forward to help her was the gamesmistress, the only dark teacher. She kneeled beside the girl and slid the white web belt from her tennis shorts, clamping it between the girl's teeth. When the seizure was over, she carried the girl to a tumbling mat in a corner of the gym and covered her so she wouldn't get chilled.

Were the other women unable to touch this girl because of her darkness? I think that now. Her darkness and her scholarship. She lived on Windward Road with her grandmother; her mother was a maid. But darkness is usually enough for women like those to hold back. Then, we usually excused that kind of behavior by saying they were "ladies." (We were constantly being told we should be ladies also. One teacher went so far as to tell us many people thought Jamaicans lived in trees and we had to show these people they were mistaken.) In short, we felt insufficient to judge the behavior of these women. The English ones (who had the corner on power in the school) had come all this way to teach us. Shouldn't we treat them as the missionaries they were certain they were? The creole Jamaicans had a different role: they were passing on to those of us who were light-skinned the creole heritage of collaboration, assimilation, loyalty to our betters. We were expected to be willing subjects in this outpost of civilization.

The girl left school that day and never returned.

After prayers we filed into our classrooms. After classes we had games: tennis, field hockey, rounders (what the English call baseball), netball (what the English call basketball.) For games we were divided into "houses"—groups named for Joan of Arc, Edith Cavell, Florence Nightingale, Jane Austen. Four white heroines. Two martyrs. One saint. Two nurses. (None of us knew then that there were Black women with Nightingale at Scutari.) One novelist. Three involved in white men's wars. Two dead in white men's wars. *Pride and Prejudice.*

Those of us in Cavell wore red badges and carried her last words before a firing squad in W. W. I: "Patriotism is not enough. I must have no hatred or bitterness toward anyone."

Sorry to say I grew up to have exactly that.

Looking back: To try and see when the background changed places with the foreground. To try and locate the vanishing point: where the lines of perspective converge and disappear. Lines of color and class. Lines of history and social context. Lines of denial and rejection. When did *we* (the light-skinned middle-class Jamaicans) take over for *them* as oppressors? I need to see when and how this happened. When what should have been reality was overtaken by what was surely unreality. When the house nigger became master.

"What's the matter with you? You think you're white or something?"
"Child, what you want to know 'bout Garvey for? The man was nothing but a damn fool."
"They not our kind of people."
Why did we wear wide-brimmed hats and try to get into Oxford? Why did we not return?

Great Expectations: a novel about origins and denial. about the futility and tragedy of that denial. about attempting assimilation. We learned this novel from a light-skinned Jamaican woman—she concentrated on what she called the "love affair" between Pip and Estella.

Looking back: Through the last page of *Sula.* "And the loss pressed down on her chest and came up into her throat. 'We was girls together,' she said as though explaining something." It was Zoe, and Zoe alone, I thought of. She snapped into my mind and I remembered no one else. Through the greens and blues of the riverbank. The flame of red hibiscus in front of my grandmother's house. The cracked grave of a former landowner. The fruit of the ackee which poisons those who don't know how to prepare it.

"What is to become of us?"
We borrowed a baby from a woman and used her as our dolly. Dressed and undressed her. Dipped her in the riverwater. Fed her with the milk her mother had left with us: and giggled because we knew where the milk had come from.

A letter: "I am desperate. I need to get away. I beg you one fifty-dollar."

I send the money because this is what she asks for. I visit her on a trip back home. Her front teeth are gone. Her husband beats her and she suffers blackouts. I sit on her chair. She is given birth control pills which aggravate her "condition." We boil up sorrel and ginger. She is being taught by Peace Corps volunteers to embroider linen mats with little lambs on them and gives me one as a keepsake. We cool off the sorrel with a block of ice brought from the shop nearby. The shopkeeper immediately recognizes me as my grandmother's grand-daughter and refuses to sell me cigarettes. (I am twenty-seven.) We sit in the doorway of her house, pushing back the colored plastic strands which form a curtain, and talk about Babylon and Dred. About Manley and what he's doing for Jamaica. About how hard it is. We walk along the railway tracks—no longer used—to Crooked River and the post office. Her little daughter walks beside us and we recite a poem for her: "Mornin' buddy/Me no buddy fe wunna/Who den, de 1 I saw?" and on and on.

I can come and go. And I leave. To complete my education in London.

II

Their goddam kings and their goddam queens. Grandmother Victoria spreading herself thin across the globe. Elizabeth II on our TV screens. We stop what we are doing. We quiet down. We pay our respects.

1981: In Massachusetts I get up at 5 a.m. to watch the royal wedding. I tell myself maybe the IRA will intervene. It's got to be better than starving themselves to death. Better to be a kamikaze in St. Paul's Cathedral than a hostage in Ulster. And last week Black and white people smashed storefronts all over the United Kingdom. But I really don't believe we'll see royal blood on TV. I watch because they once ruled us. In the back of the cathedral a Maori woman sings an aria from Handel, and I notice that she is surrounded by the colored subjects.

To those of us in the commonwealth the royal family was the perfect symbol of hegemony. To those of us who were dark in the dark nations, the prime minister, the parliament barely existed. We believed in royalty—we were convinced in this belief. Maybe it played on some ancestral memories of West Africa—where other kings and queens had been. Altars and castles and magic.

The faces of our new rulers were everywhere in my childhood. Calendars, newsreels, magazines. Their presences were often among us. Attending test matches between the West Indians and South Africans. They were our landlords. Not always absentee. And no matter what Black leader we might elect—were we to choose independence—we would be losing something almost holy in our impudence.

WE ARE HERE BECAUSE YOU WERE THERE
BLACK PEOPLE AGAINST STATE BRUTALITY
BLACK WOMEN WILL NOT BE INTIMIDATED
WECOME TO BRITAIN . . . WELCOME TO SECOND-CLASS CITIZENSHIP
(slogans of the Black movement in Britain)

Indian women cleaning the toilets in Heathrow airport. This is the first thing I notice. Dark women in saris trudging buckets back and forth as other dark women in saris—some covered by loosefitting winter coats—form a line to have their passports stamped.

The triangle trade: molasses/rum/slaves. Robinson Crusoe was on a slave-trading journey. Robert Browning was a mulatto. Holding pens. Jamaica was a seasoning station. Split tongues. Sliced ears. Whipped bodies. The constant pretense of civility against rape. Still. Iron collars. Tinplate masks. The latter a precaution: to stop the slaves from eating the sugar cane.

A pregnant woman is to be whipped—they dig a hole to accommodate her belly and place her face down on the ground. Many of us became light-skinned very fast. Traced ourselves through bastard lines to reach the duke of Devonshire. The earl of Cornwall. The lord of this and the lord of that. Our mothers' rapes were the things unspoken.

You say: But Britain freed her slaves in 1833. Yes.

Tea plantations in India and Ceylon. Mines in Africa. The Cape-to-Cairo Railroad. Rhodes scholars. Suez crisis. The white man's bloody burden. Boer War. Bantustans. Sitting in a theatre in London in the seventies. A play called *West of Suez*. A lousy play about British colonials. The finale comes when several well-known white actors are machine-gunned by several lesser-known Black actors. (As Nina Simone says: "This is a show tune but the show hasn't been written for it yet.")

The red empire of geography classes. "The sun never sets on the British empire and you can't trust it in the dark." Or with the dark peoples. "Because of the Industrial Revolution European countries went in search of markets and raw materials." Another geography (or was it a history) lesson.

Their bloody kings and their bloody queens. Their bloody peers. Their bloody generals. Admirals. Explorers. Livingstone. Hillary. Kitchener. All the bwanas. And all their beaters, porters, sherpas. Who found the source of the Nile. Victoria Falls. The tops of mountains. Their so-called discoveries reek of untruth. How many dark people died so they could misname the physical features in their blasted gazetteer. A statistic we shall never know. Dr. Livingstone, I presume you are here to rape our land and enslave our people.

There are statues of these dead white men all over London.

An interesting fact: The swear word "bloody" is a contraction of "by my lady"—a reference to the Virgin Mary. They do tend to use their ladies. Name ages for them. Places for them. Use them as screens, inspirations, symbols. And many of the ladies comply. While the national martyr Edith Cavell was being executed by the Germans in 1915 in Belgium (called "poor little Belgium" by the allies in the war), the Belgians were engaged in the exploitation of the land and peoples of the Congo.

And will we ever know how many dark peoples were "imported" to fight in white men's wars. Probably not. Just as we will never know how many hearts were cut from African people so that the Christian doctor might be a success—i.e., extend a white man's life. Our Sister Killjoy observes this from her black-eyed squint.

Dr. Schweitzer—humanitarian, authority on Bach, winner of the Nobel Peace Prize—on the people of Africa: "The Negro is a child, and with children nothing can be done without the use of authority. We must, therefore, so arrange the circumstances of our daily life that my authority can find expression. With regard to Negroes, then, I have coined the formula: 'I am your brother, it is true, but your elder brother.'" (*On the Edge of the Primeval Forest,* 1961)

They like to pretend we didn't fight back. We did: with obeah, poison, revolution. It simply was not enough.

"Colonies . . . these places where 'niggers' are cheap and the earth is rich." (W.E.B. DuBois, "The Souls of White Folk"). . . .

III

My grandmother: "Let us thank God for a fruitful place."
My grandfather: "Let us rescue the perishing world."

This evening on the road in western Massachusetts there are pockets of fog. Then clear spaces. Across from a pond a dog staggers in front of my headlights. I look closer and see that his mouth is foaming. He stumbles to the side of the road—I go to call the police.

I drive back to the house, radio playing "difficult" piano pieces. And I think about how I need to say all this. This is who I am. I am not what you allow me to be. Whatever you decide me to be. In a bookstore in London I show the woman at the counter my book and she stares at me for a minute, then says: "You're a Jamaican." "Yes." "You're not at all like our Jamaicans."

Encountering the void is nothing more nor less than understanding invisibility. Of being fogbound.

    Then: It was never a question of passing. It was a question of hiding. Behind Black and white perceptions of who we were—who they thought we were. Tropics. Plantations. Calypso. Cricket. We were the people with the musical voices and the coronation mugs on our parlor tables. I would be whatever figure these foreign imaginations care for me to be. It would be so simple to let others fill in for me. So easy to startle them with a flash of anger when their visions got out of hand—but never to sustain the anger for myself.

It could become a life lived within myself. A life cut off. I know who I am but you will never know who I am. I may in fact lose touch with who I am.

I hid from my real sources. But my real sources were also hidden from me.

    Now: It is not a question of relinquishing privilege. It is a question of grasping more of myself. I have found that in the real sources are concealed my survival. My speech. My voice. To be colonized is to be rendered insensitive. To have those parts necessary to sustain life numbed. And this is in some cases—in my case—perceived as privilege. The test of a colonized person is to walk through a shantytown in Kingston and not bat an eye. This I cannot do. Because part of me lives there—and as I grasp more of this part I realize what needs to be done with the rest of my life.

Sometimes I used to think we were like the Marranos—the Sephardic Jews forced to pretend they were Christians. The name was given to them by the Christians, and meant "pigs." But once out of Spain and Portugal, they became Jews openly again. Some settled in Jamaica. They knew who the enemy was and acted for their own survival. But they remained Jews always.

We also knew who the enemy was—I remember jokes about the English. Saying they stank. saying they were stingy. that they drank too much and couldn't hold their liquor. that they had bad teeth. were dirty and dishonest. were limey bastards. and horse-faced bitches. We said the men only wanted to sleep with Jamaican women. And that the women made pigs of themselves with Jamaican men.

But of course this was seen by us—the light-skinned middle class—with a double vision. We learned to cherish that part of us that was them—and to deny the part that was not. Believing in some cases that the latter part had ceased to exist.

None of this is as simple as it may sound. We were colorists and we aspired to oppressor status. (Of course, almost any aspiration instilled by Western civilization is to oppressor status: success, for example.) Color was the symbol of our potential: color taking in hair "quality," skin tone, freckles, nose-width, eyes. We did not see that color symbolism was a method of keeping us apart: in the society, in the family, between friends. Those of us who were light-skinned, straight-haired, etc., were given to believe that we could actually attain whiteness—or at least those qualities of the colonizer which made him superior. We were convinced of white supremacy. If we failed, we were not really responsible for our failures: we had all the advantages—but it was that one persistent drop of blood, that single rogue gene that made us unable to conceptualize abstract ideas, made us love darkness rather than despise it, which was to be blamed for our failure. Our dark part had taken over: an inherited imbalance in which the doom of the creole was sealed.

I am trying to write this as clearly as possible, but as I write I realize that what I say may sound fabulous, or even mythic. It is. It is insane.

Under this system of colorism—the system which prevailed in my childhood in Jamaica, and which has carried over to the present—rarely will dark and light people co-mingle. Rarely will they achieve between themselves an intimacy informed with identity. (I should say here that I am using the categories light and dark both literally and symbolically. There are dark Jamaicans who have achieved lightness and the "advantages" which go with it by their successful pursuit of oppressor status.)

Under this system light and dark people will meet in those ways in which the light-skinned person imitates the oppressor. But imitation goes only so far: the light-skinned person becomes an oppressor in fact. He/she will have a dark chauffeur, a dark nanny, a dark maid, and a dark gardener. These employees will be paid badly. Because of the slave past, because of their dark skin, the servants of the middle class have been used according to the traditions of the slavocracy. They are not seen as workers for their own sake, but for the sake of the family who has employed them. It was not until Michael Manley became prime minister that a minimum wage for houseworkers was enacted—and the indignation of the middle class was profound.

During Manley's leadership the middle class began to abandon the island in droves. Toronto. Miami. New York. Leaving their houses and businesses behind and sewing cash into the tops of suitcases. Today—with a new regime—they are returning: "Come back to the way things used to be" the tourist advertisement on American TV says. "Make it Jamaica again. Make it your own."

But let me return to the situation of houseservants as I remember it: They will be paid badly, but they will be "given" room and board. However, the key to the larder will be kept by the mistress in her dresser drawer. They will spend Christmas with the family of their employers and be given a length of English wool for trousers or a few yards of cotton for dresses. They will see their children on their days off: their extended family will care for the children the rest of the time. When the employers visit their relations in the country, the servants may be asked along—oftentimes the servants of the middle class come from the same part of the countryside their employers have come from. But they will be expected to work while they are there. Back in town, there are parts of the house they are allowed to move freely around; other parts they are not allowed to enter. When the family watches the TV the servant is allowed to watch also, but only while standing in a doorway. The servant may have a radio in his/her room, also a dresser and a cot. Perhaps a mirror. There will usually be one ceiling light. And one small square louvered window.

A true story: One middle-class Jamaican woman ordered a Persian rug from Harrod's in London. The day it arrived so did her new maid. She was going downtown to have her hair touched up, and told the maid to vacuum the rug. She told the maid she would find the vacuum cleaner in the same shed as the power mower. And when she returned she found that the fine nap of her new rug had been removed.

The reaction of the mistress was to tell her friends that the "girl" was backward. She did not fire her until she found that the maid had scrubbed the teflon from her new set of pots, saying she thought they were coated with "nastiness."

The houseworker/mistress relationship in which one Black woman is the oppressor of another Black woman is a cornerstone of the experience of many Jamaican women.

I remember another true story: In a middle-class family's home one Christmas, a relation was visiting from New York. This woman had brought gifts for everybody, including the housemaid. The maid had been released from a mental institution recently, where they had "treated" her for depression. This visiting light-skinned woman had brought the dark woman a bright red rayon blouse and presented it to her in the garden one afternoon, while the family was having tea. The maid thanked her softly, and the other woman moved toward her as if to embrace her. Then she stopped, her face suddenly covered with tears, and ran into the house, saying, "My God, I can't, I can't."

We are women who come from a place almost incredible in its beauty. It is a beauty which can mask a great deal and which has been used in that way. But that the beauty is there is a fact. I remember what I thought the freedom of my childhood, in which the fruitful place was something I took for granted. Just as I took for granted Zoe's appearance every morning on my school vacations—in the sense that I knew she would be there. That she would always be the one to visit me. The perishing world of my grandfather's graces at the table, if I ever seriously thought about it, was somewhere else.

Our souls were affected by the beauty of Jamaica, as much as they were affected by our fears of darkness.

There is no ending to this piece of writing. There is no way to end it. As I read back over it, I see that we/they/I may become confused in the mind of the reader: but these pronouns have always co-existed in my mind. The Rastas talk of the "I and I"—a pronoun in which they combine themselves with Jah. Jah is a contraction of Jahweh and Jehova, but to me always sounds like the beginning of Jamaica. I and Jamaica is who I am. No matter how far I travel—how deep the ambivalence I feel about ever returning. And Jamaica is a place in which we/they/I connect and disconnect—change place.

Try this:

Try a fragmentary, unresolved, autobiographical text, such as Cliff's second essay, where the short passages you include add up to a whole "statement" about your life, interests, beliefs, and values. Go back to Cliff's text for ideas for material—dreams, history, myth, family legend, conversations, etc.

PARTICIPANT OR SPECTATOR?

Following Virginia Woolf's suggestions, one of the best ways to read essays is to write essays—to experiment with the dangers and difficulties of words. As you have seen, essayists range far and wide: they can be lighthearted and playful commentators or profoundly serious moralists.

They may be so concerned, provoked, aroused about their subject that they leave no room for the reader to wonder where they stand: they *tell* you right out, in explicit statements of evaluation. They hit you over the head with their "message," closing up as many gaps as they anticipate, so that you will have little doubt what they think. Or they may want to leave you wondering, with unanswered questions, unfilled gaps.

Whatever their motives, whether they choose to please or instruct, to condemn, judge, ridicule, or lecture, they will take on the role of "participant" or "spectator." In the following selection from his essay, "On a Certain Blindness in Human Beings," the American psychologist and philosopher William James gives us his views on what it means to be a spectator—on the outside, looking in.

On a Certain Blindness in Human Beings
William James

Our judgments concerning the worth of things, big or little, depend on the *feelings* the things arouse in us. Where we judge a thing to be precious in consequence of the *idea* we frame of it, this is only because the idea is itself associated already with a feeling. If we were radically feelingless, and if ideas were the only things our mind could entertain, we should lose all our likes and dislikes at a stroke, and be unable to point to any one situation or experience in life more valuable or significant than any other.

Now the blindness in human beings, of which this discourse will treat, is the blindness with which we all are afflicted in regard to the feelings of creatures and people different from ourselves.

We are practical beings, each of us with limited functions and duties to perform. Each is bound to feel intensely the importance of his own duties and the significance of the situations that call these forth. But this feeling is in each of us a *vital secret,* for sympathy with which we vainly look to others. The others are too much absorbed in their own vital secrets to take an interest in ours. Hence the stupidity and injustice of our opinions, so far as they deal with the significance of alien lives. Hence the falsity of our judgments, so far as they presume to decide in an absolute way on the value of other persons' conditions or ideals.

Take our dogs and ourselves, connected as we are by a tie more intimate than most ties in this world; and yet, outside of that tie of friendly fondness, how insensible, each of us, to all that makes life significant for the other!—we to the rapture of bones under hedges, or smells of trees and lamp-posts, they to the delights of literature and art. As you sit reading the most moving romance you ever fell upon, what sort of a judge is your fox-terrier of your behavior? With all his good will toward you, the nature of your conduct is absolutely excluded from his comprehension. To sit there like a senseless statue, when you might be taking him to walk and throwing sticks for him to catch! What queer disease is this that comes over you every day, of holding things and staring at them like that for hours together, paralyzed of motion and vacant of all conscious life? The African savages came nearer the truth; but they, too, missed it, when they gathered wonderingly round one of our American travellers who, in the interior, had just come into possession of a stray copy of the New York *Commercial Advertiser,* and was devouring it column by column. When he got through, they offered him a high price for the mysterious object; and, being asked for what they wanted it, they said: "For an eye medicine,"—that being the only reason they could conceive of for the protracted bath which he had given his eyes upon its surface.

The spectator's judgment is sure to miss the root of the matter, and to possess no truth. The subject judged knows a part of the world of reality which the judging spectator fails to see, knows more while the spectator knows less; and, wherever there is conflict of opinion and difference of vision, we are bound to believe that the truer side is the side that feels the more, and not the side that feels the less.

Let me take a personal example of the kind that befalls each one of us daily:—

Some years ago, while journeying in the mountains of North Carolina, I passed by a large number of 'coves,' as they call them there, or heads of small valleys between the hills, which had been newly cleared and planted. The impression on my mind was one of unmitigated squalor. The settler had in every case cut down the more manageable trees, and left their charred stumps standing. The larger trees he had girdled and killed, in order that their foliage should not cast a shade. He had then built a log cabin, plastering its chinks with clay, and had set up a tall zigzag rail fence around the scene of his havoc, to keep the pigs and cattle out. Finally, he had irregularly planted the intervals between the stumps and trees with Indian corn, which grew among the chips; and there he dwelt with his wife and babes—an axe, a gun, a few utensils, and some pigs and chickens feeding in the woods, being the sum total of his possessions.

The forest had been destroyed; and what had 'improved' it out of existence was hideous, a sort of ulcer, without a single element of artificial grace to make up for the loss of Nature's beauty. Ugly, indeed, seemed the life of the squatter, scudding, as the sailors say, under bare poles, beginning again away back where our first ancestors started, and by hardly a single item the better off for all the achievements of the intervening generations.

Talk about going back to nature! I said to myself, oppressed by the dreariness, as I drove by. Talk of a country life for one's old age and for one's children! Never thus, with nothing but the bare ground and one's bare hands to fight the battle! Never, without the best spoils of culture woven in! The beauties and commodities gained by the centuries are sacred. They are our heritage and birthright. No modern person ought to be willing to live a day in such a state of rudimentariness and denudation.

Then I said to the mountaineer who was driving me, "What sort of people are they who have to make these new clearings?" "All of us," he replied. "Why, we ain't happy here, unless we are getting one of these coves under cultivation." I instantly felt that I had been losing the whole inward significance of the situation. Because to me the clearings spoke of naught but denudation, I thought that to those whose sturdy arms and obedient axes had made them they could tell no other story. But, when *they* looked on the hideous stumps, what they thought of was personal victory. The chips, the girdled trees, and the vile split rails spoke of honest sweat, persistent toil and final reward. The cabin was a warrant of safety for self and wife and babes. In short, the clearing, which to me was a mere ugly picture on the retina, was to them a symbol redolent with moral memories and sang a very pæan of duty, struggle, and success.

I had been as blind to the peculiar ideality of their conditions as they certainly would also have been to the ideality of mine, had they had a peep at my strange indoor academic ways of life at Cambridge.

Consider this:

James distinguishes between two frames of mind, two roles: the participant and the spectator: for him, "the spectator's judgment is sure to miss the root of the matter, and to possess no truth." Do you agree?

Try this:

In your notebook, write representations of two situations:

1. A situation where you, as a spectator, believe that you knew the "truth" and the participant didn't.
2. A situation where you believe that the participant knew one kind of truth, and the spectator, another. How were the differences negotiated?

• • •

James uses a story against himself to make his point, and he does so explicitly: he condemns himself for being so narrow-minded as to "read" the world through his own peculiar cultural eyes, failing to recognize others' perspectives. The event becomes food for thought, a powerful lesson for him and for his readers. The essay becomes an occasion for him to represent a change of mind.

Try this:

Imagine now the "participants"—those "settlers" whom James views: how do they "read" him? Take on the role of the participants representing this city dweller looking at them. Are they participants now or spectators?

James tells us that he saw only the tip of the iceberg: his first reading resulted in misreading. New information, a new slant on the situation, demanded a second reading. Appearances can be misleading, he concluded. He saw only with the eyes of an onlooker, a spectator—cool, detached, reflective—but, fortunately, *willing* to reread.

We might now usefully construct a model for reading the narrator of any text, whether in fiction or nonfiction. Consider the narrator—the storyteller or the essay teller—as the "voice that tells," the voice that *shapes* the tellings. We might then ask of *any text* whether the narrator *is a participant, a spectator, or a combination of the two.*

The *participant* is *in* the event as it is unfolding. The participant is "doing," involved *in* happenings.

The *spectator* is *outside,* an onlooker, *watching* participants involved in events as they are unfolding—as you were when you eavesdropped on a conversation between strangers, as you are, say, when you watch a basketball game or a fire or an argument between others.

The spectator is also a commentator, an evaluator, a critic, a judge, reflecting on events that they themselves or others have participated in. The spectator is thinking about what has been done, what has happened. But the spectator is removed in time from things that have happened—by a few moments, a few days, months, years, or centuries. You can reflect on your own immediate past or on what happened in the twelfth century.

The two roles should be seen as two hypothetical ends of a spectrum: the participant observes and infers and evaluates close up. The spectator observes and infers and evaluates from a distance—in space and in time. Later on in his essay, James characterizes the participant as one who "flies" and the spectator as one who "perches":

Participant 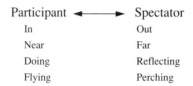 Spectator

Participant	Spectator
In	Out
Near	Far
Doing	Reflecting
Flying	Perching

Through time and distance, participants turn into spectators. Participants are in the thick of it, not yet able to make sense of things. Spectators have time for reflecting, for putting things together.

As participants, we can often hear only what is actually being said. It is as spectators that we have a better chance of considering the unsaid, seeing the part of the iceberg that is beneath the water, and making wiser, more considered judgments.

Consider this:

For us as readers, a first reading will most likely be a "participant reading"—particularly if we are caught up in the *experience* of reading a gripping short story or a novel or an essay on an issue in which we are deeply involved. We often feel as if we're taken away, transported. Second readings—"spectator readings"—enable us to step back, refocus, reconsider, and renegotiate.

James's essay "On a Certain Blindness" allows us to see the essayist as a renegotiator of his own values: James observed, drew inferences, evaluated, was then confronted by other points of view, which led to a reevaluation and a reseeing. Writing essays should, at their very best, give you a chance to bring your own experiences, your ways of reading, and your values into play—and to renegotiate and reevaluate. The essay—which gives you a chance to write either informally or formally, to dress up or dress down, to try on different voices and different roles—is one of the most roomy and pliable of all forms of writing. In Part 2, you will find a selection of texts, some short stories, but mostly essays, for you to read and reckon with, for you to bring yourself to trial before, as a reader and as a writer.

PARTICIPANT AND SPECTATOR LANGUAGE

The language we use in the role of the participant will often be *paratactic:* words are strung together loosely; there are few formal connections. *And* is the most characteristic conjunctive. We may find the language to be fragmentary, disjointed, disconnected. The words seem to rush at us; they feel spontaneous, immediate. Here is a student's participant rendering of an experience. What is the event she's representing? What's happening?

Uh-oh. Oh. Oh no. Oh-h-h-h. W-a-i-t-a-m-i-n-u-t-e. Whoops. Oh no. Oh, I'm gonna be sick. Oh no. Oh. My stomach. I'm gonna throw up. Whoa. Whoa. My neck. Oh my neck. It's breaking and oh my back. Not—oh no, wait, wait, I wanna get off. Right now. Wait. Stop. Help. Not all the way up there. Oh, oh, oh. Oh no. Not that curve. We'll never make it and I'm gonna fly off and my knuckles're bursting through the skin. Oh, oh. Not another curve. Wait. Slow down. Stop. My mother's gonna kill me.

Obviously, this is not the event, as it happened. The writer is playing with language here, to give us the "feel" of what it was like to be in this situation.

Have you guessed?

Here's a spectator version:

> Although I was terrified of roller-coasters, as I was of many things when I was younger, I finally allowed myself to be persuaded to try. . . .

Here, the "point" of the representation is brought up front, and the mystery dissolves in this spectator rendering. The writer has gone *hypotactic,* negotiating with the past event with a language that calls upon connections, of space, time, causality:

> Because X dared to ride on the roller coaster, I decided to take a chance.
>
> If X dared to ride, then I would, too. . . .
>
> If everyone was going, then I couldn't be left out. . . .
>
> Just as I had tried to ride a bicycle, so did I now try. . . .
>
> For all my life I had been frightened, but now. . . .
>
> If people would only give themselves a chance, then. . . .

Evaluative devices are used, explicitly, here in the writer's attempt to frame the event in different perspectives, making various connections. Notice, too, how she can frame the event within the confines of her own life, and open it out, to enlarge her scope: "if people would only give themselves a chance, then. . . ."

What are the benefits of the participant text? When might you use this kind of writing? When you want to give your reader "an experience," give her a sense of what it felt like to be there.

And the benefits of the spectator text? When we want to make sense out of things, to negotiate with our own experiences and with those of others, and put them into perspective—to make connections, draw conclusions, ask questions, speculate, consider options. The spectator role is one of *consideration:* to consider derives from the Latin verb, *considerare,* which means "to examine" (*con*) "the stars" (*sider*).

Then, too, you will discover that some of the most effective writing combines the two moves of the spectrum, taking us in, and pulling us out: giving us an experience and then inviting us to consider ways of looking at it.

Exercises in participant-spectator roles

Choose any or all of these situations and write representations of them from *both* of these two complementary positions:

(1) A participant (in the event as it is unfolding)
(2) A spectator removed in time and space from the event

1. A representation of a first event: first day of school, first time riding a bicycle, first fight, etc.

2. A romantic "first": meeting someone who later became a boyfriend, girlfriend, lover, spouse.

3. A cultural collision—where misunderstandings arose out of the differences in the two cultures.

4. A conflict between parent and child (take both positions).

5. A sports event.

6. A terrifying experience.

Consider this:

Reread Hemingway's story once again. Where do you find instances of explicit or implicit evaluative devices in the narrator's lines? Where does the narrator give a particular slant, a particular angle of vision on the American and the girl? There is a most curious use of an adverb (an *-ly* word) near the very end of the story. Find it and then talk about its effects on your reading.

The issues raised in this short story concern the relationships, the negotiations, between men and women, on one of the most serious matters, abortion. The story raises questions about the roles men and women play, how they talk to each other, how they don't talk to each other, what they say and what they don't say.

Try this:

1. Imagine yourself moved by what *you see* as the most nagging questions raised by the story. As a spectator essayist, use the story in whatever way you wish to evaluate the situation, to raise issues and questions that matter to you. Write a first paragraph in your notebook and then compare notes with other writers in the class. Do they see what matters in the same way as you do?

2. Read Sallie Tilsdale, "We Do Abortions Here: A Nurse's Story," page 510, and allow her voice to join in the conversation that you have begun.

RESISTANCE: THIS WILL NOT DO

When you look at the selection of prose texts in Part 2, you'll realize that in some cases I've selected more than one on the same subject. You can allow one voice to "speak" to another on the same issues, then you can use your own writing to mediate, to negotiate, to consider and reconsider your own values in the context of others' voices. At its best, writing can do that to us and for us: make us stand things on their heads and consider what we have not thought about, to reconsider what we take to be natural, inevitable, the way things "are," to explore the unsaid, to challenge the tacit. Writing allows you to see things in their dialectical interactions: to combat a *yes* with a *no;* a *should* with a *maybe.* Writing allows you to work within the frames of participants and spectators, to turn participants into spectators, spectators into participants.

By now, you can see that there are many ways that you can write on writing:

You can write informally in your notebook on what you see on the page and on what flies into your head.

You can exploit the texts you read to make your own versions and transformations.

You can fill in gaps: your gaps might turn into whole pieces of your own.

You can imitate a writer's style.

You can try out different forms and conventions—writing novels, short stories, essays, and poetry.

You can stay within the boundaries of textual conventions—or you can break those conventions.

You can put texts next to texts, let them "talk" to each other, as intertexts.

You can negotiate between the roles of participant and spectator—trying things from the inside and from the outside.

You can negotiate values—resisting, submitting, compromising; evaluating and reevaluating assumptions, beliefs, convictions. You can change your mind.

You can make "closed, tight" texts, or you can make "loose, leaky" ones, knowing full well that as Barthes said, "To write is to offer others, from the start, the last word."

You can experiment with words.

Sometimes, though, there can be no negotiation: no compromise, no give-and-take. We are not at ease, not quiet, unresolved. Again we're reminded of the Latin roots of *negotiate: negotiare—neg:* "not"; *otiare:* "ease, quiet." We resist. Some of the most powerful texts we read come out of situations that are not negotiable, situations that are so intolerable that the word becomes a sword of resistance.

Here is one of the most famous texts of resistance: Jonathan Swift's "A Modest Proposal for Preventing the Children of Poor People in Ireland from Being a Burden to Their Parents or Country, and for Making Them Beneficial to the Public." It is relevant, still, today in the 1990s because the Irish question has still not been settled. It is still unresolved.

A MODEST PROPOSAL
for
Preventing the Children of Poor People in Ireland
from Being a Burden to Their Parents or Country,
and for Making Them Beneficial to the Public
Jonathan Swift

It is a melancholy object to those who walk through this great town,* or travel in the country, when they see the streets, the roads and cabin-doors crowded with beggars of the female sex, followed by three, four, or six children, all in rags, and importuning every

---

* Dublin.

passenger for an alms. These mothers, instead of being able to work for their honest livelihood, are forced to employ all their time in strolling, to beg sustenance for their helpless infants, who, as they grow up, either turn thieves for want of work, or leave their dear native country to fight for the Pretender in Spain, or sell themselves to the Barbadoes.

I think it is agreed by all parties that this prodigious number of children, in the arms, or on the backs, or at the heels of their mothers, and frequently of their fathers, is in the present deplorable state of the kingdom a very great additional grievance; and therefore whoever could find out a fair, cheap, and easy method of making these children sound and useful members of the commonwealth would deserve so well of the public as to have his statue set up for a preserver of the nation.

But my intention is very far from being confined to provide only for the children of professed beggars; it is of a much greater extent, and shall take in the whole number of infants at a certain age who are born of parents in effect as little able to support them as those who demand our charity in the streets.

As to my own part, having turned my thoughts for many years upon this important subject, and maturely weighed the several schemes of other projectors, I have always found them grossly mistaken in their computation. It is true a child just dropped from its dam may be supported by her milk for a solar year with little other nourishment, at most not above the value of two shillings, which the mother may certainly get, or the value in scraps, by her lawful occupation of begging, and it is exactly at one year old that I propose to provide for them, in such a manner as, instead of being a charge upon their parents, or the parish, or wanting food and raiment for the rest of their lives, they shall, on the contrary, contribute to the feeding and partly to the clothing of many thousands.

There is likewise another great advantage in my scheme, that it will prevent those voluntary abortions, and that horrid practice of women murdering their bastard children, alas, too frequent among us, sacrificing the poor innocent babies, I doubt, more to avoid the expense than the shame, which would move tears and pity in the most savage and inhuman beast.

The number of souls in Ireland being usually reckoned one million and a half, of these I calculate there may be about two hundred thousand couples whose wives are breeders, from which number I subtract thirty thousand couples who are able to maintain their own children, although I apprehend there cannot be so many under the present distresses of the kingdom, but this being granted, there will remain an hundred and seventy thousand breeders. I again subtract fifty thousand for those women who miscarry, or whose children die by accident or disease within the year. There only remain an hundred and twenty thousand children of poor parents annually born: the question therefore is, how this number shall be reared, and provided for, which, as I have already said, under the present situation of affairs is utterly impossible by all the methods hitherto proposed, for we can neither employ them in handicraft or agriculture; we neither build houses (I mean in the country), nor cultivate land: they can very seldom pick up a livelihood by stealing until they arrive at six years old, except where they are of towardly parts, although I confess they learn the rudiments much earlier, during which time they can however be properly looked upon only as probationers, as I have been informed by a principal gentleman in the County of Cavan, who protested to me that he never knew above one or two instances under age of six, even in a part of the kingdom so renowned for the quickest proficiency in that art.

I am assured by our merchants that a boy or girl, before twelve years old, is no saleable commodity, and even when they come to this age, they will not yield above three pounds, or three pounds and half-a-crown at most on the Exchange, which cannot turn to account either to the parents or the kingdom, the charge of nutriment and rags having been at least four times that value.

I shall now therefore humbly propose my own thoughts, which I hope will not be liable to the least objection.

I have been assured by a very knowing American of my acquaintance in London, that a young healthy child well nursed is at a year old a most delicious, nourishing, and wholesome food, whether stewed, roasted, baked, or boiled, and I make no doubt that it will equally serve in a fricassee, or a ragout.

I do therefore humbly offer it to public consideration, that of the hundred and twenty thousand children already computed, twenty thousand may be reserved for breed, whereof only one fourth part to be males, which is more than we allow to sheep, black-cattle, or swine, and my reason is that these children are seldom the fruits of marriage, a circumstance not much regarded by our savages, therefore one male will be sufficient to serve four females. That the remaining hundred thousand may at a year old be offered in sale to the persons of quality, and fortune, through the kingdom, always advising the mother to let them suck plentifully in the last month, so as to render them plump, and fat for a good table. A child will make two dishes at an entertainment for friends, and when the family dines alone, the fore or hind quarter will make a reasonable dish, and seasoned with a little pepper or salt will be very good boiled on the fourth day, especially in winter.

I have reckoned upon a medium,* that a child just born will weigh 12 pounds, and in a solar year if tolerably nursed increaseth to 28 pounds.

I grant this food will be somewhat dear, and therefore very proper for landlords, who, as they have already devoured most of the parents, seem to have the best title to the children.

Infant's flesh will be in season throughout the year, but more plentiful in March, and a little before and after, for we are told by a grave author, an eminent French physician,† that fish being a prolific diet, there are more children born in Roman Catholic countries about nine months after Lent than at any other season; therefore reckoning a year after Lent, the markets will be more glutted than usual, because the number of Popish infants is at least three to one in this kingdom, and therefore it will have one other colateral advantage by lessening the number of Papists among us.

I have already computed the charge of nursing a beggar's child (in which list I reckon all cottagers, labourers, and four-fifths of the farmers) to be about two shillings *per annum,* rags included, and I believe no gentleman would repine to give ten shillings for the carcass of a good fat child, which, as I have said, will make four dishes of excellent nutritive meat, when he hath only some particular friend or his own family to dine with him. Thus the Squire will learn to be a good landlord and grow popular among his tenants, the mother will have eight shillings net profit, and be fit for work until she produces another child.

Those who are more thrifty (as I must confess the times require) may flay the carcass; the skin of which artificially dressed, will make admirable gloves for ladies, and summer boots for fine gentlemen.

* average.

† Rabelais.

As to our city of Dublin, shambles* may be appointed for this purpose, in the most convenient parts of it, and butchers we may be assured will not be wanting, although I rather recommend buying the children alive, and dressing them hot from the knife, as we do roasting pigs.

A very worthy person, a true lover of his country, and whose virtues I highly esteem, was lately pleased, in discoursing on this matter, to offer a refinement upon my scheme. He said that many gentlemen of this kingdom, having of late destroyed their deer, he conceived that the want of venison might be well supplied by the bodies of young lads and maidens, not exceeding fourteen years of age, nor under twelve, so great a number of both sexes in every county being now ready to starve, for want of work and service: and these to be disposed of by their parents if alive, or otherwise by their nearest relations. But with due deference to so excellent a friend, and so deserving a patriot, I cannot be altogether in his sentiments. For as to the males, my American acquaintance assured me from frequent experience that their flesh was generally tough and lean, like that of our schoolboys, by continual exercise, and their taste disagreeable, and to fatten them would not answer the charge. Then as to the females, it would, I think with humble submission, be a loss to the public, because they soon would become breeders themselves: and besides, it is not improbable that some scrupulous people might be apt to censure such a practice (although indeed very unjustly) as a little bordering upon cruelty, which I confess, hath always been with me the strongest objection against any project, however well intended.

But in order to justify my friend, he confessed that this expedient was put into his head by the famous Psalmanazar,† a native of the island Formosa, who came from thence to London, above twenty years ago, and in conversation told my friend that in his country when any young person happened to be put to death, the executioner sold the carcass to persons of quality, as a prime dainty, and that, in his time, the body of a plump girl of fifteen, who was crucified for an attempt to poison the emperor, was sold to his Imperial Majesty's Prime Minister of State, and other great Mandarins of the Court, in joints from the gibbet, at four hundred crowns. Neither indeed can I deny that if the same use were made of several plump young girls in this town who, without one single groat to their fortunes, cannot stir abroad without a chair, and appear at the playhouse and assemblies in foreign fineries, which they never will pay for, the kingdom would not be the worse.

Some persons of a desponding spirit are in great concern about that vast number of poor people, who are aged, diseased, or maimed, and I have been desired to employ my thoughts what course may be taken to ease the nation of so grievous an encumberance. But I am not in the least pain upon that matter, because it is very well known that they are every day dying, and rotting, by cold, and famine, and filth, and vermin, as fast as can be reasonably expected. And as to the younger labourers they are now in almost as hopeful a condition. They cannot get work, and consequently pine away from want of nourishment, to a degree that if at any time they are accidentally hired to common labour, they have not strength to perform it; and thus the country and themselves are in a fair way of being soon delivered from the evils to come.

---

*   slaughter houses.

†   A French imposter, exposed shortly before Swift wrote.

I have too long digressed, and therefore shall return to my subject. I think the advantages by the proposal which I have made are obvious and many, as well as of the highest importance.

For first, as I have already observed, it would greatly lessen the number of Papists, with whom we are yearly over-run, being the principal breeders of the nation, as well as our most dangerous enemies, and who stay at home on purpose with a design to deliver the kingdom to the Pretender, hoping to take their advantage by the absence of so many good Protestants, who have chosen rather to leave their country than stay at home and pay tithes against their conscience to an idolatrous Episcopal curate.

Secondly, the poorer tenants will have something valuable of their own, which by law may be made liable to distress, and help to pay their landlord's rent, their corn and cattle being already seized, and money a thing unknown.

Thirdly, whereas the maintenance of an hundred thousand children, from two years old, and upwards, cannot be computed at less than ten shillings a piece *per annum,* the nation's stock will be thereby increased fifty thousand pounds *per annum,* besides the profit of a new dish, introduced to the tables of all gentlemen of fortune in the kingdom, who have any refinement in taste, and the money will circulate among ourselves, the goods being entirely of our own growth and manufacture.

Fourthly, the constant breeders, besides the gain of eight shillings sterling *per annum,* by the sale of their children, will be rid of the charge of maintaining them after the first year.

Fifthly, this food would likewise bring great custom to taverns, where the vintners will certainly be so prudent as to procure the best receipts for dressing it to perfection, and consequently have their houses frequented by all the fine gentlemen, who justly value themselves upon their knowledge in good eating; and a skilful cook, who understands how to oblige his guests, will contrive to make it as expensive as they please.

Sixthly, this would be a great inducement to marriage, which all wise nations have either encouraged by rewards, or enforced by laws and penalties. It would increase the care and tenderness of mothers toward their children, when they were sure of a settlement for life, to the poor babes, provided in some sort by the public to their annual profit instead of expense. We should soon see an honest emulation among the married women, which of them could bring the fattest child to the market. Men would become as fond of their wives, during the time of their pregnancy, as they are now of their mares in foal, their cows in calf, or sows when they are ready to farrow, nor offer to beat or kick them (as it is too frequent a practice) for fear of a miscarriage.

Many other advantages might be enumerated. For instance, the addition of some thousand carcasses in our exportation of barrelled beef; the propagation of swine's flesh, and improvement in the art of making good bacon, so much wanted among us by the great destruction of pigs, too frequent at our tables, are no way comparable in taste or magnificence to a well-grown, fat yearling child, which roasted whole will make a considerable figure at a Lord Mayor's feast, or any other public entertainment. But this and many others I omit, being studious of brevity.

Supposing that one thousand families in this city would be constant customers for infants' flesh, besides others who might have it at merry meetings, particularly weddings and christenings; I compute that Dublin would take off annually about twenty thousand carcasses, and the rest of the kingdom (where probably they will be sold somewhat cheaper) the remaining eighty thousand.

I can think of no objection that will possibly be raised against this proposal, unless it should be urged that the number of people will be thereby much lessened in the kingdom. This I freely own, and it was indeed one principal design in offering it to the world. I desire the reader will observe, that I calculate my remedy for this one individual Kingdom of IRELAND, and for no other that ever was, is, or, I think, ever can be upon earth. Therefore let no man talk to me of other expedients: *Of taxing our absentees at five shillings a pound: Of using neither clothes, nor household furniture, except what is of our own growth and manufacture: Of utterly rejecting the materials and instruments that promote foreign luxury: Of curing the expensiveness of pride, vanity, idleness, and gaming in our women: Of introducing a vein of parsimony, prudence, and temperance: Of learning to love our Country, wherein we differ even from* LAPLANDERS, *and the inhabitants of* TOPINAMBOO: *Of quitting our animosities and factions, nor act any longer like the Jews, who were murdering one another at the very moment their city was taken: Of being a little cautious not to sell our country and consciences for nothing: Of teaching landlords to have at least one degree of mercy towards their tenants. Lastly, of putting a spirit of honesty, industry, and skill into our shopkeepers, who, if a resolution could now be taken to buy only our native goods, would immediately unite to cheat and exact upon us in the price, the measure and the goodness, nor could ever yet be brought to make one fair proposal of just dealing, though often and earnestly invited to it.*

Therefore I repeat, let no man talk to me of these and the like expedients, till he hath at least a glimpse of hope that there will ever be some hearty and sincere attempt to put them in practice.

But as to myself, having been wearied out for many years with offering vain, idle, visionary thoughts, and at length utterly despairing of success, I fortunately fell upon this proposal, which as it is wholly new, so it hath something solid and real, of no expense and little trouble, full in our own power, and whereby we can incur no danger in disobliging ENGLAND. For this kind of commodity will not bear exportation, the flesh being of too tender a consistence to admit a long continuance in salt, although perhaps I could name a country which would be glad to eat up our whole nation without it.

After all I am not so violently bent upon my own opinion as to reject any offer, proposed by wise men, which shall be found equally innocent, cheap, easy, and effectual. But before something of that kind shall be advanced in contradiction to my scheme, and offering a better, I desire the author, or authors, will be pleased maturely to consider two points. First, as things now stand, how they will be able to find food and raiment for a hundred thousand useless mouths and backs? And secondly, there being a round million of creatures in human figure, throughout this kingdom, whose whole subsistence put into a common stock would leave them in debt two millions of pounds sterling; adding those who are beggars by profession, to the bulk of farmers, cottagers, and labourers with their wives and children, who are beggars in effect; I desire those politicians who dislike my overture, and may perhaps be so bold to attempt an answer, that they will first ask the parents of these mortals whether they would not at this day think it a great happiness to have been sold for food at a year old, in the manner I prescribe, and thereby have avoided such a perpetual scene of misfortunes as they have since gone through, by the oppression of landlords, the impossibility of paying rent without money or trade, the want of common sustenance, with neither house nor clothes to cover them from the inclemencies of weather, and the most inevitable prospect of entailing the like, of greater miseries upon their breed forever.

I profess in the sincerity of my heart that I have not the least personal interest in endeavouring to promote this necessary work, having no other motive than the public good of my country, by advancing our trade, providing for infants, relieving the poor, and giving some pleasure to the rich. I have no children by which I can propose to get a single penny; the youngest being nine years old, and my wife past child-bearing.

Try this:

Write in your notebook your first reactions to "A Modest Proposal."

Consider this:

What questions are raised for you by the text? How do you "hear" the narrator? How do you *perform* his words? Read him aloud in at least two opposing voices—serious vs. mock-serious; solemn vs. satirical; etc.

Do you *believe* the narrator? Is he a participant or a spectator? What role has he entered?

• • •

Some students take Swift to be "serious" about his proposal for children to be eaten, and they charge him with the most shocking, inhumane, unspeakable, barbaric tendencies! How could he! They confuse the *narrator* Swift has invented for this proposal with Swift *the man*.

Dean Swift (1667–1745), a clergyman of the Church of England, a most extraordinary, unconventional human being, was a great resister. He lived during a time that has come to be called the "Age of Reason." While the intelligentsia of Europe basked in what they saw as the glories and potentialities of human "reason" and dreamed of human perfectibility, Swift was driven to subvert such facile optimism by mercilessly exposing the fallibility of human reason and the precariousness of "civilization." In his master stroke—*Gulliver's Travels*—he leads us irresistibly to the conclusion that we are self-deluding apes. In "A Modest Proposal," he seizes the bland and complacent manners of reasonableness in order to shock his readers into contemplating a scandalous fact: Ireland, a savagely exploited colony, had been reduced to a state of abject distress so deep that such a proposal for disposing of "surplus" mouths would in fact appear to be perfectly reasonable. (You may want to read a history of the later Irish famine, *The Great Hunger* by Cecil Woodham-Smith; and a poem by the same title by the Irish poet Patrick Kavanagh.) You may also appreciate the following transformation of Cinderella, an illustration for the English magazine *Punch* in 1846, when Britain and Scotland (Caledonia in the illustration) turned its back on Ireland's suffering during the potato famine.

THE IRISH CINDERELLA AND HER HAUGHTY
SISTERS, BRITANNIA AND CALEDONIA.

Britain fails to make a generous donation to Potato Aid during the
famine in Ireland   Leech 1846

Consider this:

What in the world around you might lead you to make a similar "modest" proposal, to take such a nonnegotiable stance? With your class, consider situations so extreme (the homeless? the victims of the drug war? the environment?) that you throw "reasonableness" to the wind and come up with a position of total resistance—written to shock your readers, to wake them up, to ask them to look at themselves, their complacencies, and their values in the mirror.

• • •

We turn now to our own century and call upon Kay Boyle (1902–   ), novelist, short story writer, poet, journalist, reviewer, social activist. Living in Europe during the twenties and thirties, she became in the fifties a correspondent for *The New Yorker,* and turned to the short essay as a forum for her voice—for her outrage and compassion, her protests and resistance, her insistence on speaking out, on not compromising, on speaking for those who are rendered silent by oppression and imprisonment, speaking, as she says, those words "that must somehow be said."

The following essay, "Battle of the Sequins," is taken from her collection of essays of that title, *Words That Must Somehow Be Said.* The essay was written in 1944—could it have been written today?

Battle of the Sequins
Kay Boyle

I did not know that sequins were being worn this year. I did not know until yesterday that garments stitched with sequins were being fought over on department store counters. I did not know that blouses seemingly entirely fashioned of sequins, hard and brilliant and metallic as hummingbirds, were coveted as gold, or beauty, or fame is coveted—especially if they come with little sequined caps to match. Apparently a great many people did know this, for the battle taking place for these things was a bitter battle. It was a battle among women—as terrific as any that is taking place in the rain or the snow or the jungle among men. For if one woman succeeds in getting the only size forty-two blouse in topaz sequins, there is still no assurance that she will be able to get the topaz-sequined cap to wear with it. It is quite possible that she may have to go home with the heartbreak of having got only the blouse, and not the little cap, or perhaps with the little cap in a different color.

Yesterday, in the department store, the women who had gone there to buy were surrounded by mirrors—mirrors on the counters, mirrors in the lifts, full-length mirrors in the panels of every door. So that everyone, if he paused for an instant, could see exactly and unequivocally how he looked. But the faces of these women were turned away, their eyes were fixed on something else; they were there to outwit one another, and they had no time to face themselves. In the mirrors there might have been the singular reflection of other women—women who skipped quickly back into a trench before the shellfire got them, dragging with them the body of a companion who had fought three winters with her feet bound in rags, as were the feet of the other women, and who now had been killed. Perhaps they are Russian women, perhaps English women, perhaps women of the French maquis. It is difficult to say whether they are beautiful or not, for their faces are masked with filth, with sweat, even with blood. Their skin is cracked, weathered; their nails are not varnished. The dead woman who had fought through three winters with them and whom they kick down into the bottom of the trench for safety has been dragged so far by her feet that her mouth and nostrils are stopped with dirt. But whatever has happened to her eyes, the vision is set as clear as glass in them. When this thing is finished, those of them who survive will sit down under a roof again and hold their children against them, and they will never be afraid, no matter how old they grow, to look at their own faces in the mirror.

Across the walls of the department store there were words written, written more violently and boldly—in spite of their absolute invisibility—than the legend which states that it is a legal offense to smoke in a retail store. "Caution," say these indiscernible words.

"You are warned by the authorities against stopping to look at yourselves in the mirrors." Not because you will see your own shape or face reflected; not for an instant. But because the leaves of jungle trees still suddenly grow there, tough and strong as rubber, and bright green in the mirror. You will see the hair that grows on the bark of trees in that tropical place, and the blades of green on green, and then, without warning, you will come upon the man lying there on the jungle floor with the blood like an open fan, spread as thick as tar and as black, beneath his head. He is a young man in a khaki shirt, and his beard is a week old on his jaws, and by his eyes you know he is not dead. His eyes are watching the men who come and kneel, and who set down the stretcher beside him, and his eyes move in quick desperation from one face to the other, asking them not to let it happen. It is when they lift him that the black fan opens a little wider on the grass, and the look of ice moves over his face, and you know he is asking nothing of anyone anymore.

"Customers are cautioned not to look," says the sign of which no one can perceive the letters, for if you stop to look you will see something you do not wish to see. You will see the shallow water of the river flickering, and out of the muck of the river's bed you will see the other boy crawling on his knees. His shirt is ripped away, and his arm is hanging from the shoulder by two delicate threads of sinew or nerve or splintered bone, and the blood is not running from it, it is spouting from it the way water will spout from an open water hydrant and pour, foaming, into the gutter below. You are cautioned not to look, for you have come here to buy sequins, and if you look you will see that his lips are stiff and that his teeth are shaking in his head as if he were cold. But this is the tropics, and he is not cold, he is merely frightened. He is crying, with little shuddering gasps of terror shaking through his teeth. He is saying: "I am not going to die, am I? Tell me, I'm not going to die, am I?" and he comes crawling toward you, crawling like a beast through the mud. He has almost reached you, he has almost touched your skirt with his hand when you hear the woman's voice saying: "I've been waiting twenty minutes, and then this customer gets in ahead of me and gets the last 42 in topaz—"

"Listen," said the salesgirl, leaning forward. "You can't take them with you."

"Take what?" said the customer.

"Sequins," said the salesgirl. "You know, things that glitter."

"I didn't want to take them with me," said the woman. "I wanted them sent COD."

Ursula Le Guin "resists" in a very different way in this very short story, "She Unnames Them." She relies on our knowing the "she" of the title. That's the key with which to unlock the puzzle of this text. See how long it takes you (and any collaborators you might need) to figure it out.

She Unnames Them
Ursula K. Le Guin

Most of them accepted namelessness with the perfect indifference with which they had so long accepted and ignored their names. Whales and dolphins, seals and sea otters consented with particular grace and alacrity, sliding into anonymity as into their element. A faction of yaks, however, protested. They said that "yak" sounded right, and that almost everyone who knew they existed called them that. Unlike the ubiquitous creatures such as rats and fleas, who had been called by hundreds or thousands of different names since Babel, the yaks could truly say, they said, that they had a *name*. They discussed the matter all summer. The councils of the elderly females finally agreed that though the name might be useful to others it was so redundant from the yak point of view that they never spoke it themselves and hence might as well dispense with it. After they presented the argument in this light to their bulls, a full consensus was delayed only by the onset of severe early blizzards. Soon after the beginning of the thaw, their agreement was reached and the designation "yak" was returned to the donor.

Among the domestic animals, few horses had cared what anybody called them since the failure of Dean Swift's attempt to name them from their own vocabulary. Cattle, sheep, swine, asses, mules, and goats, along with chickens, geese, and turkeys, all agreed enthusiastically to give their names back to the people to whom—as they put it—they belonged.

A couple of problems did come up with pets. The cats, of course, steadfastly denied ever having had any name other than those self-given, unspoken, ineffably personal names which, as the poet named Eliot said, they spend long hours daily contemplating—though none of the contemplators has ever admitted that what they contemplate is their names and some onlookers have wondered if the object of that meditative gaze might not in fact be the Perfect, or Platonic, Mouse. In any case, it is a moot point now. It was with the dogs, and with some parrots, lovebirds, ravens, and mynahs, that the trouble arose. These verbally talented individuals insisted that their names were important to them, and flatly refused to part with them. But as soon as they understood that the issue was precisely one of individual choice, and that anybody who wanted to be called Rover, or Froufrou, or Polly, or even Birdie in the personal sense, was perfectly free to do so, not one of them had the least objection to parting with the lowercase (or, as regards German creatures, uppercase) generic appellations "poodle," "parrot," "dog," or "bird," and all the Linnaean qualifiers that had trailed along behind them for two hundred years like tin cans tied to a tail.

The insects parted with their names in vast clouds and swarms of ephemeral syllables buzzing and stinging and humming and flitting and crawling and tunnelling away.

As for the fish of the sea, their names dispersed from them in silence throughout the oceans like faint, dark blurs of cuttlefish ink, and drifted off on the currents without a trace.

None were left now to unname, and yet how close I felt to them when I saw one of them swim or fly or trot or crawl across my way or over my skin, or stalk me in the night, or go along beside me for a while in the day. They seemed far closer than when their names had stood between myself and them like a clear barrier: so close that my fear of them and their fear of me became one same fear. And the attraction that many of us felt, the desire to smell one another's smells, feel or rub or caress one another's scales or skin or feathers or fur, taste one another's blood or flesh, keep one another warm—that attraction was now all one with the fear, and the hunter could not be told from the hunted, nor the eater from the food.

This was more or less the effect I had been after. It was somewhat more powerful than I had anticipated, but I could not now, in all conscience, make an exception for myself. I resolutely put anxiety away, went to Adam, and said, "You and your father lent me this—

gave it to me, actually. It's been really useful, but it doesn't exactly seem to fit very well lately. But thanks very much! It's really been very useful."

It is hard to give back a gift without sounding peevish or ungrateful, and I did not want to leave him with that impression of me. He was not paying much attention, as it happened, and said only, "Put it down over there, O.K.?" and went on with what he was doing.

One of my reasons for doing what I did was that talk was getting us nowhere, but all the same I felt a little let down. I had been prepared to defend my decision. And I thought that perhaps when he did notice he might be upset and want to talk. I put some things away and fiddled around a little, but he continued to do what he was doing and to take no notice of anything else. At last I said, "Well, goodbye, dear. I hope the garden key turns up."

He was fitting parts together, and said, without looking around, "O.K., fine, dear. When's dinner?"

"I'm not sure," I said. "I'm going now. With the—" I hesitated, and finally said, "With them, you know," and went on out. In fact, I had only just then realized how hard it would have been to explain myself. I could not chatter away as I used to do, taking it all for granted. My words now must be as slow, as new, as single, as tentative as the steps I took going down the path away from the house, between the dark-branched, tall dancers motionless against the winter shining.

Le Guin has her heroine renegotiate with a text of the first order. Which text is that? Who did the original naming?

At what point in the story do you first realize that she is talking about Adam and *Genesis,* the most well-known story of creation in the Western world? What was the first clue? What confirmed your hunch? Why can the narrator not use the word *trees* in the last sentence?

Consider this:

One of the most significant political moves of a conquering nation is to rename the conquered—their lands (including cities, streets, and their people). You might recall Eva Hoffman's profound sense of alienation when her Polish name "Ewa" became the English Eva (see page 165). Here, in Le Guin's story, "she" is renaming for different reasons: what are they? And how is "she" misread, at the end of the story? How do you read Le Guin's implicit evaluations? What do you see as the large issues considered here. If Le Guin had used what you see as the impulses behind this work of fiction to write a piece of nonfiction, what might she be saying?

Set her next to Robin Lakoff's essay on women's language, page 185. How do they connect for you?

Try this:

Below are suggested topics for you to consider as you write either whole essays or fiction or fragmentary texts, as you write "straight" texts or parody. Consider the position you want to take and the best way to handle the topic so as to try to move your reader in particular ways. Do you want to knock them over the head with an explicit point, tying up the issue as tight as you can? Do you want to write a parody, imitating a serious and conventional form of writing? Do you want to write ironically, taking a serious issue and turning it upside down? Do you want to raise questions and leave readers to speculate, wonder, reconsider? Remember: your writing gives a reader a text to negotiate with. And there's no end to negotiations.

> Take up the issue of women inheriting a male-dominated language. How might women rename some of the stuff we live with: cars? soap powders? deodorants? Would the renaming make a difference?
>
> Take up the issue of what people are called. How do first names (John, Sue, Sally, Mark) set up expectations before we even meet someone? How do last names (Jones, Jaffe, Jakowsky) do the same? Or different? Where do stereotypes come in?
>
> Take up the issue of what people wear. How do we "judge the book by the cover," by reading each other by our clothes before *really* "reading"?
>
> Take up the issue of what people do, how their work "identifies" them. We prejudge people by what their jobs are, or how many college degrees they have. Do you read a physician in the same ways as you do a truck driver? How would you characterize the differences?

Add any other issues to this list that you want.

JOHN KEATS'S ROOMS

Here at the end of this part of the book, I leave you with two selections from the poet John Keats's letters: they return us to the image the book begins with, that of opening doors and entering rooms. Keats was born in 1795 and died in 1821, at the age of 26. As he says in the passages below, he had only just begun to open doors into the possibilities of human life. He was only 22 when he wrote the letters excerpted here. Let his words "speak" for themselves to you.

To J. H. Reynolds

I will put down a simile of human life as far as I now perceive it; that is, to the point to which I say we both have arrived at—' Well—I compare human life to a large Mansion of Many Apartments, two of which I can only describe, the doors of the rest being as yet shut upon me—The first we step into we call the infant or thoughtless Chamber, in which we remain as long as we do not think—We remain there a long while, and notwithstanding the doors of the second Chamber remain wide open, showing a bright appearance, we care not to hasten to it; but are at length imperceptibly impelled by the awakening of the thinking principle—within us—we no sooner get into the second Chamber, which I shall call the

Chamber of Maiden-Thought, than we become intoxicated with the light and the atmosphere, we see nothing but pleasant wonders, and think of delaying there for ever in delight: However among the effects this breathing is father of is that tremendous one of sharpening one's vision into the heart and nature of Man—of convincing ones nerves that the World is fully of Misery and Heartbreak, Pain, Sickness and oppression—whereby This Chamber of Maiden Thought becomes gradually darken'd and at the same time on all sides of it many doors are set open—but all dark—all leading to dark passages—We see not the ballance of good and evil. We are in a Mist—*We* are now in that state—We feel the "burden of the Mystery," . . . .

May 3, 1818

To Richard Woodhouse

It is a wretched thing to confess; but is a very fact that not one word I ever utter can be taken for granted as an opinion growing out of my identical nature—how can it, when I have no nature? When I am in a room with People if I ever am free from speculating on creations of my own brain, then not myself goes home to myself: but the identity of every one in the room begins to [*for* so] to press upon me that, I am in a very little time an[ni]hilated—not only among Men; it would be the same in a Nursery of children: I know not whether I make myself wholly understood: I hope enough so to let you see that no dependence is to be placed on what I said that day.

In the second place I will speak of my views, and of the life I purpose to myself—I am ambitious of doing the world some good: if I should be spared that may be the work of maturer years—in the interval I will assay to reach to as high a summit in Poetry as the nerve bestowed upon me will suffer. The faint conceptions I have of Poems to come brings the blood frequently into my forehead—All I hope is that I may not lose all interest in human affairs—that the solitary indifference I feel for applause even from the finest Spirits, will not blunt any acuteness of vision I may have. I do not think it will—I feel assured I should write from the mere yearning and fondness I have for the Beautiful even if my night's labours should be burnt every morning and no eye ever shine upon them. But even now I am perhaps not speaking from myself; but from some character in whose soul I now live. I am sure however that this next sentence is from myself. I feel your anxiety, good opinion and friendliness in the highest degree, and am

Your's most sincerely
John Keats
October 27, 1818

PART II

Practice:

Reading

Texts

In weakness, we create distinctions, then
Deem that our puny boundaries are things
Which we perceive, and not which we have made.
William Wordsworth
The Prelude

Part 2 offers a selection of readings of essays and short fiction for you to read, reflect upon, and write on, in the many ways open to you as a reader—and as a writer—in a college course in composition. Readings invite readers into the possibilities of composition—to put your own words "into position," that is the root meaning of *composition*. I have chosen this selection of texts for many reasons and have tried out various ways of arranging them in the second part of the book: I separated fiction from nonfiction, short pieces from long ones, "easy" pieces from demanding ones. I separated them by theme—clustering pieces on language, education, male-female relationships, cultural issues, etc.

I decided, finally, however, to arrange the texts in Part 2 with a light hand. For whenever we classify and divide, we prearrange texts for readers. They take our arrangement for theirs, our connections for their own. Here, therefore, I have chosen not to classify, divide, or dichotomize, but simply to arrange alphabetically. (I *have* noted those texts that are considered fiction. They are marked in the table of contents with an asterisk.) I leave the rest up to you and your instructor— to make connections yourselves, to pull things together, and to take them apart, to play one text off against another, and to read much as you would do in any text where the editor is not preemptive, where the editor does not *impose* her views of selection upon you, before you read. You then are in a position to compose—text on text.

But much of the pleasure of reading, it seems to me, derives from readers' opening doors for themselves, of getting lost and finding themselves in strange, unfamiliar places, of peeking into rooms they have never before entered and finding their feet, their bearings. Consider Part 2 then a many-chambered house, an edifice, with many unopened doors for you and your instructor to prise open, peek into, rush through, or slam shut, as you so choose.

You may want to take with you into Part 2 a reminder of the suggestions offered for **Writing on Writing** in Part 1: for those of you who begin *Negotiations* with Part 2, the following suggestions are meant as a list of possibilities for you as a reader-turned-writer, as you read and consider what to "do" with your varied and rich reactions to what you read:

- You can write informally in your notebook on what you see on the page and on what flies into your head.

227

- You can exploit the texts you read to make your own versions and transformations.
- You can fill in gaps: your gaps might turn into whole pieces of your own.
- You can imitate a writer's style.
- You can try out different conventions—writing novels, short stories, essays, poetry.
- You can stay within the boundaries of textual conventions and you can break those conventions.
- You can put texts next to texts—and let them "talk" to each other, as intertexts.
- You can negotiate between the roles of participant and spectator— trying things from the inside and from the outside: you can negotiate values—resisting, submitting, compromising, evaluating and reevaluating assumptions, beliefs, convictions. You can change your mind.
- You can create texts that you think are "closed," "tight," and texts that are "loose," "leaky," knowing full well that as Barthes said, "To write is to offer others, from the start, the last word."
- You can experiment with the dangers and difficulties of words.

Graduation Day
Maya Angelou

The children in Stamps trembled visibly with anticipation. Some adults were excited too, but to be certain the whole young population had come down with graduation epidemic. Large classes were graduating from both the grammar school and the high school. Even those who were years removed from their own day of glorious release were anxious to help with preparations as a kind of dry run. The junior students who were moving into the vacating classes' chairs were tradition-bound to show their talents for leadership and management. They strutted through the school and around the campus exerting pressure on the lower grades. Their authority was so new that occasionally if they pressed a little too hard it had to be overlooked. After all, next term was coming, and it never hurt a sixth grader to have a play sister in the eighth grade, or a tenth-year student to be able to call a twelfth grader Bubba. So all was endured in a spirit of shared understanding. But the graduating classes themselves were the nobility. Like travelers with exotic destinations on their minds, the graduates were remarkably forgetful. They came to school without their books, or tablets or even pencils. Volunteers fell over themselves to secure replacements for the missing equipment. When accepted, the willing workers might or might not be thanked, and it was of no importance to the pregraduation rites. Even teachers were respectful of the now quiet and aging seniors, and tended to speak to them, if not as equals, as beings only slightly lower than themselves. After tests were returned and grades given, the student body, which acted like an extended family, knew who did well, who excelled, and what piteous ones had failed.

Unlike the white high school, Lafayette County Training School distinguished itself by having neither lawn, nor hedges, nor tennis court, nor climbing ivy. Its two buildings (main classrooms, the grade school and home economics) were set on a dirt hill with no fence to limit either its boundaries or those of bordering farms. There was a large expanse to the left of the school which was used alternately as a baseball diamond or a basketball court. Rusty hoops on the swaying poles represented the permanent recreational equipment, although bats and balls could be borrowed from the P. E. teacher if the borrower was qualified and if the diamond wasn't occupied.

Over this rocky area relieved by a few shady tall persimmon trees the graduating class walked. The girls often held hands and no longer bothered to speak to the lower students. There was a sadness about them, as if this old world was not their home and they were bound for higher ground. The boys, on the other hand, had become more friendly, more outgoing. A decided change from the closed attitude they projected while studying for finals. Now they seemed not ready to give up the old school, the familiar paths and classrooms. Only a small percentage would be continuing on to college—one of the South's A & M (agricultural and mechanical) schools, which trained Negro youths to be carpenters, farmers, handymen, masons, maids, cooks and baby nurses. Their future rode heavily on their shoulders, and blinded them to the collective joy that had pervaded the lives of the boys and girls in the grammar school graduating class.

Parents who could afford it had ordered new shoes and ready-made clothes for themselves from Sears and Roebuck or Montgomery Ward. They also engaged the best seamstresses to make the floating graduating dresses and to cut down secondhand pants which would be pressed to a military slickness for the important event.

Oh, it was important, all right. Whitefolks would attend the ceremony, and two or three would speak of God and home, and the Southern way of life, and Mrs. Parsons, the principal's wife, would play the graduation march while the lower-grade graduates paraded down the aisles and took their seats below the platform. The high school seniors would wait in empty classrooms to make their dramatic entrance.

In the Store I was the person of the moment. The birthday girl. The center. Bailey had graduated the year before, although to do so he had had to forfeit all pleasures to make up for his time lost in Baton Rouge.

My class was wearing butter-yellow piqué dresses, and Momma launched out on mine. She smocked the yoke into tiny crisscrossing puckers, then shirred the rest of the bodice. Her dark fingers ducked in and out of the lemony cloth as she embroidered raised daisies around the hem. Before she considered herself finished she had added a crocheted cuff on the puff sleeves, and a pointy crocheted collar.

I was going to be lovely. A walking model of all the various styles of fine hand sewing and it didn't worry me that I was only twelve years old and merely graduating from the eighth grade. Besides, many teachers in Arkansas Negro schools had only that diploma and were licensed to impart wisdom.

The days had become longer and more noticeable. The faded beige of former times had been replaced with strong and sure colors. I began to see my classmates' clothes, their skin tones, and the dust that waved off pussy willows. Clouds that lazed across the sky were objects of great concern to me. Their shiftier shapes might have held a message that in my new happiness and with a little bit of time I'd soon decipher. During that period I looked at the arch of heaven so religiously my neck kept a steady ache. I had taken to smiling more often, and my jaws hurt from the unaccustomed activity. Between the two physical sore spots, I suppose I could have been uncomfortable, but that was not the case. As a member of the winning team (the graduating class of 1940) I had outdistanced unpleasant sensations by miles. I was headed for the freedom of open fields.

Youth and social approval allied themselves with me and we trammeled memories of slights and insults. The wind of our swift passage remodeled my features. Lost tears were pounded to mud and then to dust. Years of withdrawal were brushed aside and left behind, as hanging ropes of parasitic moss.

My work alone had awarded me a top place and I was going to be one of the first called in the graduating ceremonies. On the classroom blackboard, as well as on the bulletin board in the auditorium, there were blue stars and white stars and red stars. No absences, no tardinesses, and my academic work was among the best of the year. I could say the preamble to the Constitution even faster than Bailey. We timed ourselves often: "WethepeopleoftheUnitedStatesinordertoformamoreperfectunion . . . ." I had memorized the Presidents of the United States from Washington to Roosevelt in chronological as well as alphabetical order.

My hair pleased me too. Gradually the black mass had lengthened and thickened, so that it kept at last to its braided pattern, and I didn't have to yank my scalp off when I tried to comb it.

Louise and I had rehearsed the exercises until we tired out ourselves. Henry Reed was class valedictorian. He was a small, very black boy with hooded eyes, a long, broad nose and an oddly shaped head. I had admired him for years because each term he and I vied for the best grades in our class. Most often he bested me, but instead of being disappointed I was pleased that we shared top places between us. Like many Southern Black children, he lived with his grandmother, who was as strict as Momma and as kind as she knew how to be. He was courteous, respectful and soft-spoken to elders, but on the playground he chose to play the roughest games. I admired him. Anyone, I reckoned, sufficiently afraid or sufficiently dull could be polite. But to be able to operate at a top level with both adults and children was admirable.

His valedictory speech was entitled "To Be or Not to Be." The rigid tenth-grade teacher had helped him write it. He'd been working on the dramatic stresses for months.

The weeks until graduation were filled with heady activities. A group of small children were to be presented in a play about buttercups and daisies and bunny rabbits. They could be heard throughout the building practicing their hops and their little songs that sounded like silver bells. The older girls (nongraduates, of course) were assigned the task of making refreshments for the night's festivities. A tangy scent of ginger, cinnamon, nutmeg and chocolate wafted around the home economics building as the budding cooks made samples for themselves and their teachers.

In every corner of the workshop, axes and saws split fresh timber as the woodshop boys made sets and stage scenery. Only the graduates were left out of the general bustle. We were free to sit in the library at the back of the building or look in quite detachedly, naturally, on the measures being taken for our event.

Even the minister preached on graduation the Sunday before. His subject was, "Let your light so shine that men will see your good works and praise your Father, Who is in Heaven." Although the sermon was purported to be addressed to us, he used the occasion to speak to backsliders, gamblers and general ne'er-do-wells. But since he had called our names at the beginning of the service we were mollified.

Among Negroes the tradition was to give presents to children going only from one grade to another. How much more important this was when the person was graduating at the top of the class. Uncle Willie and Momma had sent away for a Mickey Mouse watch like Bailey's. Louise gave me four embroidered handkerchiefs. (I gave her three crocheted doilies.) Mrs. Sneed, the minister's wife, made me an underskirt to wear for graduation, and nearly every customer gave me a nickel or maybe even a dime with the instruction "Keep on moving to higher ground," or some such encouragement.

Amazingly the great day finally dawned and I was out of bed before I knew it. I threw open the back door to see it more clearly, but Momma said, "Sister, come away from that door and put your robe on."

I hoped the memory of that morning would never leave me. Sunlight was itself still young, and the day had none of the insistence maturity would bring it in a few hours. In my robe and barefoot in the backyard, under cover of going to see about my new beans, I gave myself up to the gentle warmth and thanked God that no matter what evil I had done in my life He had allowed me to live to see this day. Somewhere in my fatalism I had expected to die, accidentally, and never have the chance to walk up the stairs in the auditorium and gracefully receive my hard-earned diploma. Out of God's merciful bosom I had won reprieve.

Bailey came out in his robe and gave me a box wrapped in Christmas paper. He said he had saved his money for months to pay for it. It felt like a box of chocolates, but I knew Bailey wouldn't save money to buy candy when we had all we could want under our noses.

He was as proud of the gift as I. It was a soft-leather-bound copy of a collection of poems by Edgar Allan Poe, or, as Bailey and I called him, "Eap." I turned to "Annabel Lee" and we walked up and down the garden rows, the cool dirt between our toes, reciting the beautifully sad lines.

Momma made a Sunday breakfast although it was only Friday. After we finished the blessing, I opened my eyes to find the watch on my plate. It was a dream of a day. Everything went smoothly and to my credit. I didn't have to be reminded or scolded for anything. Near evening I was too jittery to attend to chores, so Bailey volunteered to do all before his bath.

Days before, we had made a sign for the Store, and as we turned out the lights Momma hung the cardboard over the doorknob. It read clearly: CLOSED. GRADUATION.

My dress fitted perfectly and everyone said that I looked like a sunbeam in it. On the hill, going toward the school, Bailey walked behind with Uncle Willie, who muttered, "Go on, Ju." He wanted him to walk ahead with us because it embarrassed him to have to walk so slowly. Bailey said he'd let the ladies walk together, and the men would bring up the rear. We all laughed, nicely.

Little children dashed by out of the dark like fireflies. Their crepe-paper dresses and butterfly wings were not made for running and we heard more than one rip, dryly, and the regretful "uh uh" that followed.

The school blazed without gaiety. The windows seemed cold and unfriendly from the lower hill. A sense of ill-fated timing crept over me, and if Momma hadn't reached for my hand I would have drifted back to Bailey and Uncle Willie, and possibly beyond. She made a few slow jokes about my feet getting cold, and tugged me along to the now-strange building.

Around the front steps, assurance came back. There were my fellow "greats," the graduating class. Hair brushed back, legs oiled, new dresses and pressed pleats, fresh pocket handkerchiefs and little handbags, all homesewn. Oh, we were up to snuff, all right. I joined my comrades and didn't even see my family go in to find seats in the crowded auditorium.

The school band struck up a march and all classes filed in as had been rehearsed. We stood in front of our seats, as assigned, and on a signal from the choir director, we sat. No sooner had this been accomplished than the band started to play the national anthem. We rose again and sang the song, after which we recited the pledge of allegiance. We remained standing for a brief minute before the choir director and the principal signaled to us, rather desperately I thought, to take our seats. The command was so unusual that our carefully rehearsed and smooth-running machine was thrown off. For a full minute we fumbled for our chairs and bumped into each other awkwardly. Habits change or solidify under pressure, so in our state of nervous tension we had been ready to follow our usual assembly pattern: the American national anthem, then the pledge of allegiance, then the song every Black person I knew called the Negro National Anthem. All done in the same key, with the same passion and most often standing on the same foot.

Finding my seat at last, I was overcome with a presentiment of worse things to come. Something unrehearsed, unplanned, was going to happen, and we were going to be made to look bad. I distinctly remember being explicit in the choice of pronoun. It was "we," the graduating class, the unit, that concerned me then.

The principal welcomed "parents and friends" and asked the Baptist minister to lead us in prayer. His invocation was brief and punchy, and for a second I thought we were getting back on the high road to right action. When the principal came back to the dais, however, his voice had changed. Sounds always affected me profoundly and the principal's voice was one of my favorites. During assembly it melted and lowed weakly into the audience. It had not been in my plan to listen to him, but my curiosity was piqued and I straightened up to give him my attention.

He was talking about Booker T. Washington, our "late great leader," who said we can be as close as the fingers on the hand, etc. . . . Then he said a few vague things about friendship and the friendship of kindly people to those less fortunate than themselves. With that his voice nearly faded, thin, away. Like a river diminishing to a stream and then to a trickle. But he cleared his throat and said, "Our speaker tonight, who is also our friend, came from Texarkana to deliver the commencement address, but due to the irregularity of the train schedule, he's going to, as they say, 'speak and run.' " He said that we understood and wanted the man to know that we were most grateful for the time he was able to give us and then something about how we were willing always to adjust to another's program, and without more ado—"I give you Mr. Edward Donleavy."

Not one but two white men came through the door offstage. The shorter one walked to the speaker's platform, and the tall one moved over to the center seat and sat down. But that was our principal's seat, and already occupied. The dislodged gentleman bounced around for a long breath or two before the Baptist minister gave him his chair, then with more dignity than the situation deserved, the minister walked off the stage.

Donleavy looked at the audience once (on reflection, I'm sure that he wanted only to reassure himself that we were really there), adjusted his glasses and began to read from a sheaf of papers.

He was glad "to be here and to see the work going on just as it was in the other schools."

At the first "Amen" from the audience I willed the offender to immediate death by choking on the word. But Amens and Yes, sir's began to fall around the room like rain through a ragged umbrella.

He told us of the wonderful changes we children in Stamps had in store. The Central School (naturally, the white school was Central) had already been granted improvements that would be in use in the fall. A well-known artist was coming from Little Rock to teach art to them. They were going to have the newest microscopes and chemistry equipment for their laboratory. Mr. Donleavy didn't leave us long in the dark over who made these improvements available to Central High. Nor were we to be ignored in the general betterment scheme he had in mind.

He said that he had pointed out to people at a very high level that one of the first-line football tacklers at Arkansas Agricultural and Mechanical College had graduated from good old Lafayette County Training School. Here fewer Amen's were heard. Those few that did break through lay dully in the air with the heaviness of habit.

He went on to praise us. He went on to say how he had bragged that "one of the best basketball players at Fisk sank his first ball right here at Lafayette County Training School."

The white kids were going to have a chance to become Galileos and Madame Curies and Edisons and Gauguins, and our boys (the girls weren't even in on it) would try to be Jesse Owenses and Joe Louises.

Owens and the Brown Bomber were great heroes in our world, but what school official in the white-goddom of Little Rock had the right to decide that those two men must be our only heroes? Who decided that for Henry Reed to become a scientist he had to work like George Washington Carver, as a bootblack, to buy a lousy microscope? Bailey was obviously always going to be too small to be an athlete, so which concrete angel glued to what country seat had decided that if my brother wanted to become a lawyer he had to first pay penance for his skin by picking cotton and hoeing corn and studying correspondence books at night for twenty years?

The man's dead words fell like bricks around the auditorium and too many settled in my belly. Constrained by hard-learned manners I couldn't look behind me, but to my left and right the proud graduating class of 1940 had dropped their heads. Every girl in my row had found something new to do with her handkerchief. Some folded the tiny squares into love knots, some into triangles, but most were wadding them, then pressing them flat on their yellow laps.

On the dais, the ancient tragedy was being replayed. Professor Parsons sat, a sculptor's reject, rigid. His large, heavy body seemed devoid of will or willingness, and his eyes said he was no longer with us. The other teachers examined the flag (which was draped stage right) or their notes, or the windows which opened on our now-famous playing diamond.

Graduation, the hush-hush magic time of frills and gifts and congratulations and diplomas, was finished for me before my name was called. The accomplishment was nothing. The meticulous maps, drawn in three colors of ink, learning and spelling deca-syllabic words, memorizing the whole of *The Rape of Lucrece*—it was for nothing. Donleavy had exposed us.

We were maids and farmers, handymen and washerwomen, and anything higher that we aspired to was farcical and presumptuous.

Then I wished that Gabriel Prosser and Nat Turner had killed all whitefolks in their beds and that Abraham Lincoln had been assassinated before the signing of the Emancipation Proclamation, and that Harriet Tubman had been killed by that blow on her head and Christopher Columbus had drowned in the *Santa María.*

It was awful to be Negro and have no control over my life. It was brutal to be young and already trained to sit quietly and listen to charges brought against my color with no chance of defense. We should all be dead. I thought I should like to see us all dead, one on top of the other. A pyramid of flesh with the whitefolks on the bottom, as the broad base, then the Indians with their silly tomahawks and teepees and wigwams and treaties, the Negroes with their mops and recipes and cotton sacks and spirituals sticking out of their mouths. The Dutch children should all stumble in their wooden shoes and break their necks. The French should choke to death on the Louisiana Purchase (1803) while silk-worms ate all the Chinese with their stupid pigtails. As a species, we were an abomination. All of us.

Donleavy was running for election, and assured our parents that if he won we could count on having the only colored paved playing field in that part of Arkansas. Also—he never looked up to acknowledge the grunts of acceptance—also, we were bound to get some new equipment for the home economics building and the workshop.

He finished, and since there was no need to give any more than the most perfunctory thank-you's, he nodded to the men on the stage, and the tall white man who was never introduced joined him at the door. They left with the attitude that now they were off to something really important. (The graduation ceremonies at Lafayette County Training School had been a mere preliminary.)

The ugliness they left was palpable. An uninvited guest who wouldn't leave. The choir was summoned and sang a modern arrangement of "Onward, Christian Soldiers," with new words pertaining to graduates seeking their place in the world. But it didn't work. Elouise, the daughter of the Baptist minister, recited "Invictus," and I could have cried at the impertinence of "I am the master of my fate, I am the captain of my soul."

My name had lost its ring of familiarity and I had to be nudged to go and receive my diploma. All my preparations had fled. I neither marched up to the stage like a conquering Amazon, nor did I look in the audience for Bailey's nod of approval. Marguerite Johnson, I heard the name again, my honors were read, there were noises in the audience of appreciation, and I took my place on the stage as rehearsed.

I thought about colors I hated: ecru, puce, lavender, beige and black.

There was shuffling and rustling around me, then Henry Reed was giving his valedictory address, "To Be or Not to Be." Hadn't he heard the whitefolks? We couldn't *be*, so the question was a waste of time. Henry's voice came out clear and strong. I feared to look at him. Hadn't he got the message? There was no "nobler in the mind" for Negroes because the world didn't think we had minds, and they let us know it ."Outrageous fortune"? Now, that was a joke. When the ceremony was over I had to tell Henry Reed some things. That is, if I still cared. Not "rub," Henry, "erase." "Ah, there's the erase." Us.

Henry had been a good student in elocution. His voice rose on tides of promise and fell on waves of warnings. The English teacher had helped him to create a sermon winging through Hamlet's soliloquy. To be a man, a doer, a builder, a leader, or to be a tool, an unfunny joke, a crusher of funky toadstools. I marveled that Henry could go through with the speech as if we had a choice.

I had been listening and silently rebutting each sentence with my eyes closed; then there was a hush, which in an audience warns that something unplanned is happening. I looked up and saw Henry Reed, the conservative, the proper, the A student, turn his back to the audience and turn to us (the proud graduating class of 1940) and sing, nearly speaking,*

Lift ev'ry voice and sing
Till earth and heaven ring
Ring with the harmonies of Liberty . . .

---

* "Lift Ev'ry Voice and Sing"—words by James Weldon Johnson and music by J. Rosamond Johnson. Copyright by Edward B. Marks Music Corporation. Used by permission.

It was the poem written by James Weldon Johnson. It was the music composed by J. Rosamond Johnson. It was the Negro national anthem. Out of habit we were singing it.

Our mothers and fathers stood in the dark hall and joined the hymn of encouragement. A kindergarten teacher led the small children onto the stage and the buttercups and daisies and bunny rabbits marked time and tried to follow:

> Stony the road we trod
> Bitter the chastening rod
> Felt in the days when hope, unborn, had died.
> Yet with a steady beat
> Have not our weary feet
> Come to the place for which our fathers sighed?

Every child I knew had learned that song with his ABC's and along with "Jesus Loves Me This I Know." But I personally had never heard it before. Never heard the words, despite the thousands of times I had sung them. Never thought they had anything to do with me.

On the other hand, the words of Patrick Henry had made such an impression on me that I had been able to stretch myself tall and trembling and say, "I know not what course others may take, but as for me, give me liberty or give me death."

And now I heard, really for the first time:

> We have come over a way that with tears
> has been watered,
> We have come, treading our path through
> the blood of the slaughtered.

While echoes of the song shivered in the air, Henry Reed bowed his head, said "Thank you," and returned to his place in the line. The tears that slipped down many faces were not wiped away in shame.

We were on top again. As always, again. We survived. The depths had been icy and dark, but now a bright sun spoke to our souls. I was no longer simply a member of the proud graduating class of 1940; I was a proud member of the wonderful, beautiful Negro race.

Oh, Black known and unknown poets, how often have your auctioned pains sustained us? Who will compute the lonely nights made less lonely by your songs, or by the empty pots made less tragic by your tales?

If we were a people much given to revealing secrets, we might raise monuments and sacrifice to the memories of our poets, but slavery cured us of that weakness. It may be enough, however, to have it said that we survive in exact relationship to the dedication of our poets (include preachers, musicians and blues singers).

CONSIDER THIS

Maya Angelou says that she was a mute for five years, that she wasn't cute and she didn't speak, but that her grandmother reassured her all the time, "Sister, Mama don't care what these people say about you being a moron, being an idiot. Mama don't care. Mama know, Sister, when you and the good Lord get ready, you're gonna be a preacher" ("Maya Angelou," in *I Dream a World,* New York, Stewart, Tabori & Chang, 1989). Angelou is no mute; she has been speaking in one way or another all her adult life, and her preaching has taken all kinds of form as a dancer, an actress, a Hollywood director, and a writer of five volumes of autobiography. "Graduation Day" is excerpted from the first volume, *I Know Why the Caged Bird Sings,* 1974, and was dramatized for television in 1979. Angelou was born in St. Louis, Missouri, in 1928.

One reader says this: "Graduation Day makes me laugh and cry at the same time. How does she do it? That's what I want to know."

Do you find Angelou to be preaching to you? Are her evaluative devices explicit or implicit?

Fast Food for Thought
Norman Atkins

In those wastrel days of youth, when zoning out in front of "Mannix" reruns stirred me more than *Crime and Punishment,* that fat Russian thing, I felt indebted to Cliffs Notes. Like most of my bonehead classmates, I'd skip the novel and fill up a few blue books with the literary pabulum I'd pilfered from Cliffs. I figured Dostoevski was for losers.

It is positively criminal, but it's true: high school and college students have been getting away with murder by this device for more than a quarter of a century now. But like that Raskolnikov character, one is prone to suffering a fit of remorse later on. It got so terrible for me that I had to incinerate all my old Cliffs Notes, the worst reminders I know of what absolute morosophs we once were.

For as long as I can remember, I imagined that those garish yellow and black study outlines were knocked off by a mad horde of Mr. Chipses sequestered in cells at the foot of the Magic Mountain or the Wuthering Heights. Isn't that what the cliffs in the logo suggested? Actually, I was by nature such an inattentive reader that I didn't even notice that it says right there on the title page that the Notes are published in Lincoln, Nebraska. There are no cliffs: the logo is a visual pun on the name of Cliff. These are *his* notes, of course. Setting out to find Cliff was a weird idea, kind of like embarking on a mission to meet Uncle Ben, Mrs. Butterworth, or Dr. Denton.

I land in Lincoln, a lackluster, spick-and-span cow town of 175,000 that looks as if it were plucked right out of *Babbitt* or *Main Street.* No surprise then that there are Notes for both these Sinclair Lewis novels. Churches call their flocks from every other corner, and when I open the curtains in my room at the Cornhusker Hotel, there's the Back to the Bible/ Good News Broadcasting Association right outside my window. Wonder whether they're planning a Note on *Elmer Gantry,* too.

I have to admit I was half expecting to see a bronze likeness of Cliff in the center of town. So I'm somewhat stymied when nobody seems to have heard of him. "Cliff Thone, of Cliff's Smoke Shop?" asks one woman I meet. "You mean the guy who runs Kinko's Copies?" asks a young man. Could it be *my* Cliff is a hoax?

Undaunted, I walk the eight blocks to Cliffs Notes, Inc., which occupies a squat, white, ten-thousand-square-foot warehouse and office building, a sterling example of bland neo-Rotarian architecture. I'm greeted at the door by J. Richard Spellman, the president of Cliffs Notes, who tells me he assumed most of the day-to-day responsibilities of running the company when Chairman Cliff ducked into semiretirement about three years ago. Spellman's speech betrays his accountant's training as he briefs me on the bare essentials:

Did you know that more than 60 million Cliffs Notes have been sold in twenty-eight years, which could mean that roughly one in every four American students has used one? Did you know that Cliffs annually ships out about 5 million Notes a year and rakes in more than $7 million in revenues and completely dominates the book-notes market? Did you know that the best-selling Note is *The Scarlet Letter,* followed closely by *Huckleberry Finn, Hamlet,* and *Macbeth*?

Spellman says company-sponsored surveys show that, my suspicion to the contrary, most students who use the Notes also read the books. "The better the student, the more likely he is to use the Notes." I can tell I'm not going to get anywhere with Spellman. Where is Cliff?

I mosey by the company bulletin board, where a recent *National Lampoon* parody is tacked up. It catches the general public's perception of the Notes better than Spellman's lecture does. Kafka's *Metamorphosis* is condensed thus: "A man turns into a cockroach and his family gets annoyed." Dante's *Inferno* is summed up this way: "A man visits hell and sees a lot of terrible things."

Just then, from out of nowhere appears this kindly looking old man, wearing a bolo tie, a well-worn Ultrasuede jacket, and brown Rockports— a triumph of sartorial function over style. I can tell right away I am face to face with Cliff, the hero and villain of my putative literature education. Actually, he looks like Ike. Even his second wife, Mary, says so. "Same haircut," he admits. On top of his bald dome, he wears a pair of tortoiseshell bifocals. "So he won't lose them," says Connie Brakhahn, the advertising director, who's been working here for eight years.

When I tell Cliff how I used his Notes, he gives me a broad corn-eating grin, slaps his knee and says, with hyper-meticulous enunciation, "I can tell I'm dealing with a *sat-is-fied* customer!"

That night, we break steak together, and over the next several days our friendship grows as we zoom across the Nebraska landscape in Cliff's silver Lincoln Continental. The car is the only thing I can find about him that's patently un-Cliff. I'm pleased to report, for instance, that he's an avid reader of *USA Today,* the Cliffs Notes of newspapers. I also detect that Cliff 's style has rubbed off on Mary when I see her snap a photo with her pocket Instamatic, a quick-read camera in the spirit of Cliffs.

Maybe someday Cliff will write his memoirs and tell you all this himself. In the meantime, since I don't want to steal his story, let me merely Cliff it.

No matter how you view it, Rising City is neither—just four hundred folks grabbing some sleep near a couple of Nebraska grain elevators. But if ancient Mesopotamia is considered the cradle of Western civilization, Rising City can arguably be called the crib of courses in Western civilization. For it was here, sixty-nine years ago next month, that a rural postman and a housewife delivered unto the world of abbreviated learning one Clifton Keith Hillegass. It should have been apparent thereafter, when *Clifton* was shortened simply to *Cliff,* that truncating texts would become synonymous with his name.

Cliff's childhood was, as Ronald Reagan has described his own, "one of those rare Huck Finn-Tom Sawyer idylls." For the purposes of understanding what prepared him for his life's mission, three chapters in his youth bear special consideration here.

In the first one, we learn how Cliff's nose came to be the shape of the inside of a book. At the age of seven, little Cliff was bedridden for two months after a mastoid operation. In order to pass the time, he practically taught himself how to read, starting with a sappy but advanced novelette called *Pappina.* This is what launched his lifelong romance with letters. As a kid, he'd sneak a flashlight under the covers and pore over Jack Harkaway sports adventures or Robert Louis Stevenson's *Black Arrow,* a story to which he's returned six times. He was also keen on Sir Walter Scott, James Fenimore Cooper, and, especially, Charles Dickens. Unlike Holden Caulfield, the protagonist of *The Catcher in the Rye,* the first contemporary book Cliff Noted, this boy couldn't get enough of "that David Copperfield kind of crap."

Legend has it that before graduating from high school, Cliff read every last volume in the Rising City public library. Ask the librarian from the early thirties to check this fact, and he'll tell you it's 100 percent true. "Every book," says the librarian, who just happens to be Cliff. "Many of them with regret."

In the course of his life, Cliff says, he's read 200 of the more than 225 books for which he's made "keys to the classics" (as he touts them), but he's never gone cover to cover through any of the Notes themselves. "*I* don't need the Notes," he says. "I can read the book."

When I ask him whether he's had a chance to read Gabriel Garcia Márquez's *One Hundred Years of Solitude,* a recent addition to the Cliffs family of titles, he says, "No, but if you recommend it, I will. I read four or five books a week." When I ask him which four or five he read last week, he says, "I just finished something by Michener, but I forgot the name. And a thriller—I'm not good at remembering titles. You'll have to ask Mary."

Cliff employs a very peculiar method of reading, which may account for his somewhat spotty memory. "Back when black literature was *the* thing, and I'm not running down black literature, because some of it is very fine, but there was this one book, and I don't remember the name, but people were having trouble reading it. So I picked it up and did the same thing I usually do with Michener. If it's not a subject I'm familiar with, I turn to page 100 and start there, and then come back to them when I get through. Because his first 100 pages are setting the whole story. And I did the same thing with this book and didn't have any trouble reading it. And I told Gary [Carey, a Cliffs editor], and he tried it that way, and it worked."

In the second chapter, we see how Cliff, like his fellow Midwestern hick Jay Gatsby, got a heavy dose of the Protestant work ethic at an early age. His partners, ultraconservative Lutherans, sat their self-taught boy down one day when he was seven or eight and asked him to consider his future. The long haul. "My parents told me if I wanted to go to college, I would have to pay for most of it myself," Cliff says. "It seemed fair to me. So I spent a lot of my childhood concerned with how to make money."

He started his college fund by yanking the teats of a couple of Jersey cows and running paper routes. He later worked as a houseboy and as a Woolworth stock boy, putting himself through Midland College, a Podunk Lutheran outfit in Fremont, Nebraska. Actually, at the start of his junior year, he transferred to Colorado State University with the expressed aim of learning forestry. Fortunately for all of us, he cut short this phase of his education and returned to Midland.

The third chapter is not one Cliff himself would connect to the other two, but I believe it is absolutely essential in coming to terms with the history of study aids. In this chapter, we see how Cliff learns to blow off his schoolwork.

In 1937, Cliff entered grad school at the University of Nebraska in Lincoln, preparing for his master's in physics and geology. Understand, up until this point, Clifton was an awkward, shy pencil grind. He managed well in school, but he wasn't exactly a big smash at the hoedowns. "I was a terrible introvert," he says. "All I did was study." But going to school in the Big City, Cliff joined a frat and started hanging with a faster crowd. Lincoln may seem about as exciting as a pet-food store to you or me, but it's regular sin city Nebraskawise.

"My fraternity dad recognized that I didn't understand girls," says Cliff. "So he undertook to make sure that I did."

"He *majored* in girls!" says Mary. Well, keeping the ladies out late, Cliff the swinger had to let something slip, and guess what went first?

You got it—the books. "I think I still hold the record for the most incompletes that any one student ever had at the University of Nebraska in graduate school," Cliff says, with a modicum of pride. To me, this is the most fascinating sentence in the biography of Cliff, because it indicates how he could come to appreciate the unreasonable academic burden placed upon students during their most libidinally demanding years. Now there are those who argue persuasively that Dr. Rock, who midwifed the pill, made the Nookie Revolution biologically possible. But let us not forget that Cliff and his Notes gave kids the free time that made such a lifestyle change feasible.

Following this wild period, Cliff met, courted, and married his first wife, Catherine. He dropped out of school and knocked on the door of a university bookstore. The owner was leaving town and asked Cliff to come back the next week for an interview. But Cliff saw that the store's Greek and Latin sections were a mess, seized the initiative in fixing them up, and was rewarded with a job when the boss got back. For the next twenty years, Cliff hopscotched the country, bartering and selling used college texts.

One day, during Cliff's middle age, a book-biz buddy, Jack Cole, the publisher of Coles Notes in Canada, suggested Cliff peddle some outlines in America. (Coles Notes, which flopped in America when they were introduced a few years ago, are still getting Canadian students through school today.) Cole even offered to lend Cliff sixteen Shakespeare synopses so he wouldn't have to hire his own writers. In some way, Cliff's whole life had been a preparation for this moment.

He immediately borrowed four thousand dollars, set up shop in the basement of his home, and persuaded his bookstore pals around the country to stock his new product, even though they predicted it would bomb. They were wrong. The first printing of Cliff's Notes—the apostrophe vanished during some redesign years later—sold out. By 1961, he was selling 129,000 a year. In 1964, the company moved out of the basement to a converted supermarket. By the end of that year, Cliff had quit his old job to work on the Notes full time. And by 1965, he was selling more than 2 million Notes a year. And just like that he became the Ray Kroc of study outlines, America's single greatest purveyor of fast food for thought.

Now there had been synopses before. Fraternities were notorious for keeping extensive files of old papers and crib notes for the collective cheating of their members. Same with sororities. Classic Comics and Masterplots summaries were also fairly popular. In the olden days, books from *The Decameron* to *Pinocchio* were published with short synopses of their contents at the start of each chapter. But the origin of Cliffs-style notes goes back further than that. In fact, they can be traced to a fairly esteemed Jewish author named Moses. I have it on the authority of a few rabbis that it is not sacrilegious to consider the five Books of Moses a plot summary of and commentary on the greater knowledge God gave the folks in attendance at Mount Sinai.

So Cliff didn't invent the study note any more than Kroc created the hamburger. But for some odd reason, luck in America tends to seek out run-of-the-mill businessmen.

However Cliff was chosen, we see there are four very specific reasons why his enterprise succeeded:

1. *Cliff treats Notes as perishables.* Bookstore managers instantly loved him because he made it policy to always send out their orders the day he received them. From his years in the college-book business, he could appreciate that a stock of *Mrs. Dalloway* Notes is as useless as brown bananas once the Virginia Woolf exam is past.

2. *Cliff is colordeaf.* He chose yellow and black, the loudest color combination, because he "wanted to be sure if students were in the bookstore, they would see them." Not much of a problem there. But as Cliff and I drive past an endless row of yellow and black diagonally striped road signs on the Nebraska highway, I see a weird similarity in his color scheme.

   "Look at these signs," I say to him. "Don't you see what these colors connote? YIELD! DANGER! WARNING! That's one reason why students have always been so reluctant to bring Cliffs Notes to class. They seem like the kind of thing you don't want your teacher to see you with."

   Cliff says, "That never occurred to me." And I'm convinced this insensitivity to color proved to be one hell of a windfall. My theory is that students covet the Notes precisely because they have an aura of forbiddenness to them.

   Cliff himself explains how this reverse psychology works. "The best thing that happened to us, from the point of view of sales, was when teachers forbade students to use the Notes. Especially during the early years, students who had never heard of Cliffs Notes immediately thought, 'Hey, I better find out what these are; they must be pretty useful.' It was great advertising."

3. *The GI Bill.* After World War II, Uncle Sam paid soldiers to go to college, filling universities with a new breed of students, serious about learning but not so well trained for the task. The GI Bill, historians now believe, completely changed the character of universities, from elitist enclaves to paragons of populism. And the baby boom provided a steady stream of students, the more people to purchase Cliffs.

4. *The commies.* This is Cliff's historical perspective: "Don't forget '58 was about the time that we had come through that first Russian situation, where they put that thing in space [*Sputnik*, in 1957], and everybody was really damning the hell out of our educational system. The college profs were really pouring it on, loading the student down with a lot of work. Because they were being told Americans were lagging behind.

   "Now you take a student in mechanical engineering, let's say. There's no such thing as an average student, but let's get as close as we can. He was loaded down, and if he was going to let anything slide, it was going to be literature. And this always struck me as being a sad commentary on education, but if there was anything he really didn't like, it was to read. He had no *love* of literature. And I figured if I could make it possible for this student—and others like him, engineers, lawyers, businessmen—if I could get him through college, and he was still on speaking terms with literature, then ten years out of college, he would be willing to do some reading and continue to read.

"And I've had FBI men, doctors, dentists tell me this is what's happened to them. One man had been my dentist five years before he found out I was *the* Cliff of Cliffs Notes, and he said, 'Do you know how many of your books I have? I didn't have time to read in college, but now I do. First thing I do when I pick up a book is go over and pick up the Cliffs Notes, too. They help me read the book just as well as I could in any literature course in college.'"

After listening to this, you begin to see that Cliff sees his successes and failures inextricably bound in the cycles of American schooling. During a speech he delivered to the Newcomen Society when it honored him in October 1985, he practically said you could read educational trends by examining the Cliffs Notes sales charts.

"It was no accident that in the mid-1960s, our sales began to falter," he said. "Students . . . began to demand radical changes in education. . . . They wanted either to grade themselves or else enroll in courses that were graded pass-fail. As a result, everyone in the class got A's. There was no distinction between excellence and mediocrity. . . . It was not until teachers once again took charge of the classrooms, in the mid-1970s, that our sales began to increase once more. From 1980 until the present, sales have grown steadily — parallel to the academic excellence that was lost in the mid-1960s and finally restored to the classroom."

Cliffs was disrupted not only by the educational bedlam of the mid-1960s but by a lawsuit that could have sucked the company dry. Scribner's and Random House sued for copyright infringement, claiming Cliffs quoted too liberally in its summaries. Too bad both suits were settled out of court, because if the publishers could have proved damage—that people were buying Cliffs *instead* of the books—it might have settled the controversy about what the Notes are really used for. But after lawyers dicked around for two years on the Random House suit, Cliff flew to New York, met company head Bennett Cerf, and agreed to pony up about five hundred dollars and cut down on the quoting.

As a result of the suit, Cliff had to change the way the Notes were put together. The company shifted emphasis from brute summaries to thicker commentaries, though the Shakespeares still keep a balance of the two.

There is a vast but poorly kept archive of letters to the company from helpless students God-blessing Cliffs for its revamped and sophisticated study aids. The way the students frame it, Cliff comes off as a populist educator, a twentieth-century Horace Mann who has made Western literature more accessible to the average American student.

Cliff himself is quick to admit that he has never written or edited any Notes and suggests that I visit the office of editor Gary Carey. Informal, articulate, plump, Carey has been editing Cliffs Notes for nearly a decade. He's just returned from a teachers' convention, where one of the hottest-selling Cliffs items was a set of keys designed especially for teachers. Carey says that a growing number of teachers use the Notes themselves. Consulting editor James L. Roberts, who occupies a small desk in Carey's office, points out that a professor he knows forbade his class to use Cliffs only so he could lecture from them.

Carey says that the writers (who are paid a measly fifteen hundred to three thousand dollars for a Note) are often academics who want to trot out five-syllable words and labyrinthine analysis. "I tell writers to take a Polaroid snapshot of their class, especially the student who sits in the middle row, furrows his brow, and looks slightly confused. To take that snapshot and put it on top of their word processor so they'll be reminded of the audience for whom they're writing."

The recently released Note on Alice Walker's novel *The Color Purple* not only is one of the best ever written, says Carey, but illustrates that you don't need a Ph.D. to write these things. After the Note went to press, Carey got a call from the author, Gloria Rose, who said, "I guess I should tell you I'm a sophomore at Georgetown. I'm eighteen." Carey fell out of his chair. *"But you wrote that, right? It wasn't your mother or your aunt."* She said it was her work, and he told her it was "brilliant." "Maybe because she was a student she knew how to handle it," he says.

Or more likely because she was a student of Cliffs. From her two older sisters, Rose had inherited a library of one hundred Notes. "In the fall of 1985," she says, "I was taking a Shakespeare class, and I had a problem with the Elizabethan English. I used about twelve Cliffs Notes for the course. And then I noticed there were no Notes for *The Color Purple,* and I thought a lot of people would benefit from something to make Alice Walker's nonstandard English more accessible. So I asked if I could do the Notes."

Cliff publishes only three to six new titles a year, and only for books that are widely read and are the subjects of a sufficient body of criticism. The company gets besieged with requests for all sorts of stuff, but Cliff puts his foot down at *Love Story.* And Carey hits his limit at *The Cat Ate My Gymsuit,* a widely taught junior-high-school book about an unpopular girl who triumphs over rotundity. "That would be it," Carey says. "I'd be out looking for a new job." I wonder whether writers of the so-called classics approve of their Cliffs. Chaucer would probably dig the soon-to-be-published Note by the late novelist John Gardner on *The Canterbury Tales.* (It was written but mothballed several years before his death and only recently discovered in the company's files.) But how would Shakespeare feel about his Notes, two of which were written by Cliff's daughter, Linda Hillegass? Gloria Rose is sure Alice Walker wouldn't like the Note on *The Color Purple.* "I've written her three times," says Rose, "and she hasn't written me back." Isaac Asimov, says consulting editor James Roberts, is pleased as punch to be included in the parade of literary all-stars. In Carey's opinion, "Dostoevski would have said, 'Fly, get out of here.' I think Shakespeare would be rolling in the aisles."

Since sixteen of Shakespeare's plays kicked off the Notes, Cliff recently decided to complete the set, even though nobody ever assigns the more obscure plays. "After twenty-five years, we've made good money off Will," he says. "So maybe we owed the old boy a bit."

Driving from Lincoln to Kearney is like starting out on the edge of nowhere and winding up right in the middle of it. Cliff, the self-appointed Nebraska ambassador, tells me interesting facts about his state. "Do you know that the third biggest city in the state is the University of Nebraska football stadium on Saturday?" Of course, you'll find Cliff and Mary on the fifty-yard line of that city, too. When it comes to state sports or art museums or libraries, they're among the grand pooh-bahs of boosters. It's important to them that Cliffs Notes stays in Lincoln.

"As you might imagine," says Cliff, "people keep trying to buy the Notes, and I keep saying no. They fly in, you name 'em. The first one that tried was Simon and Schuster. Random House tried. *Esquire* tried. Viking Penguin has tried. It's gotten to the place now where they say, 'We know you don't want to sell it, but maybe you will someday.' Twenty years ago, someone offered me $25 million. The last time I turned down an offer, someone said, 'Would $50 million interest you?'"

Cliff's family owns eighty percent of the company; the rest is held by employees. The way Cliff has it figured, if one of these major publishers swallows his Notes up, they'll take the Cliffs name and sterling reputation and move it to New York. As we stand by the river behind the house of some good friends of Cliff's in Kearney, watching Canada geese hitting this way station en route to Mexico, I'm reminded of something Cliff told me earlier. Once he went to New York, and a friend treated him to a Betty Grable nightclub show. "I was a big leg man," Cliff said, but not even Grable's gams could lure him away. Unlike the geese, Cliff will never leave Nebraska.

His name, however, already has. Somewhere in that vast space between Ray Kroc and Horace Mann, Cliff will be remembered. If not the man, then surely the myth. For the expression *Cliffs Notes* has already become a part of our language, as a generic expression for "study outlines." The competition, Monarch Notes and Barron's, has never even approached that status. You turn on "The Cosby Show" and there's a whole episode about the prudence of using Cliffs. (Yes, but only along with the book.)

Appropriately enough, Bret Easton Ellis, a voice from this generation's den of Philistines, offers a tribute to Cliffs in his novel *Less Than Zero.* "Trent and Daniel are standing by Trent's BMW and Trent's pulling the Cliffs Notes to *As I Lay Dying* out of his glove compartment and hands them to Blair.... She fingers the Cliffs Notes but doesn't say anything." No wonder she doesn't have anything to say. I'll lay odds she didn't read the book.

CONSIDER THIS

What kind of narrator is this? How does he refer to himself in the beginning paragraph? How does he see his own youth? How does he see his high school and college days, now that he has gained some distance? How old does he sound? Where does he stand on *Cliffs Notes,* and on Cliff, himself? Is he simply reporting? Is he neutral? Is this a condemnation? How should we read this piece?

The narrator wrote this piece for *Rolling Stone* magazine. What do you expect a reporter for *Rolling Stone* to sound like? Does Atkins meet your expectations? How so? How not?

Where do *you* stand on Cliffs notes? And what do you *do* with all the names Atkins throws at you within the first page: "Mannix," *Crime and Punishment,* Dostoevski, Raskolnikov, Mr. Chips, the Magic Mountain, the Wuthering Heights, Uncle Ben, Mrs. Butterworth, Dr. Denton, *Babbitt, Main Street, Elmer Gantry*?

Grimm and Andersen
W. H. Auden

Many deplorable features of modern life, irrationalism, nationalism, idolization of mass-feeling and mass-opinion, may be traced back to the Romantic reaction against the Enlightenment and its Polite Learning; but that same reaction is also responsible for the work of Jacob and Wilhelm Grimm who, with their successors, made the fairy story a part of general education, a deed which few will regret. Much, too, can be said against middle-class family life in the nineteenth century, but in the midst of its heavy moral discipline, its horsehair sofas and stodgy meals, the average child was permitted and even encouraged to lead an exciting life in its imagination. There are more Gradgrinds now than there were then, and the twentieth century has yet to produce books for children equal to Hans Andersen's *Tales,* Edward Lear's *Books of Nonsense,* the two *Alices, Struwelpeter,* or even Jules Verne.

Houses are smaller, servants are fewer, mothers have less time, or think they have, to read to their children, and neither the comic strip nor the radio has succeeded so far in providing a real substitute for the personally told tale which permits of interruptions and repeats.

Anyone who has to do with professional education today is aware that the schools are more and more being expected to replace the parents and take over the whole of a child's development, a task which is not only impossible but highly dangerous.

If people are sincere when they say that the great contemporary menace in every country is the encroachment of the power of the State over the individual citizen, they must not invite it to mold the thinking of their children in their most impressionable years by refusing to help with their education themselves.

It is to be hoped that the publication of the tales of Grimm and Andersen in one inexpensive volume will be a step in the campaign to restore to parents the right and the duty to educate their children, which, partly through their own fault, and partly through extraneous circumstances, they are in danger of losing for good.

II

There are quite a number of people who disapprove of fairy tales for children, and on various grounds. Let us take the most reasonable first: those who claim that the fairy tale as we know it from Grimm and Andersen is not viable in modern culture. Such tales, they argue, developed in a feudally organized society which believed in magic, and are irrelevant to an industrialized democracy like our own. Luckily the test of viability is a simple one. If a tale is enjoyed by the reader, or audience, it is viable; if he finds it boring or incomprehensible, it is not. It is unlikely, for instance, that a culture without natural science and its methodology would make head or tail of Sherlock Holmes, or that a society which believed the future to be completely determined would find much sense in a story which turned on wishing, and it is very possible that certain details in European fairy stories cannot be transplanted to America. Miss Margaret Mead tells me that the traditional stepmother, which in Europe is a psychological euphemism for the mother in a malevolent aspect, is here a source of misunderstanding because there are too many actual stepmothers; one suspects, too, that in a society where the father plays as minor a role as he plays in America, the fairy tale giant is a less frighteningly important figure than he was to those of us who grew up under the shadow of a paternal discipline. However, one has only to tell the stories and observe the reaction to find out what, if anything, needs changing.

A child who has once been pleased with a tale likes, as a rule, to have it retold in identically the same words, but this should not lead parents to treat printed fairy stories as sacred texts. It is always much better to tell a story than read it out of a book, and, if a parent can produce what, in the actual circumstances of the time and the individual child, is an improvement on the printed text, so much the better.

The second charge against fairy tales is that they harm the child by frightening him or arousing his sadistic impulses. To prove the latter, one would have to show in a controlled experiment that children who have read fairy stories were more often guilty of cruelty than those who had not. Aggressive, destructive, sadistic impulses every child has and, on the whole, their symbolic verbal discharge seems to be rather a safety valve than an incitement to overt action. As to fears, there are, I think, well-authenticated cases of children being dangerously terrified by some fairy story. Often, however, this arises from the child having only heard the story once. Familiarity with the story by repetition turns the pain of fear into the pleasure of a fear faced and mastered.

Lastly there are the people who object to fairy stories on the grounds that they are not objectively true, that giants, witches, two-headed dragons, magic carpets, etc., do not exist; and that, instead of indulging his fantasies in fairy tales, the child should be taught how to adopt to reality by studying history and mechanics. I find such people, I must confess, so unsympathetic and peculiar that I do not know how to argue with them. If their case were sound, the world should be full of Don Quixote-like madmen attempting to fly from New York to Philadelphia on a broomstick or covering a telephone with kisses in the belief that it was their enchanted girl friend.

No fairy story ever claimed to be a description of the external world and no sane child has ever believed that it was. There are children (and adults), certainly, who believe in magic, i.e., who expect their wishes to be granted without any effort on their part, but that is because their parents have spoiled them to despair by loving them too little, and their behavior would be the same if they had never heard the word "magic." An introverted child, as I know from personal experience, can as easily withdraw from the outer world with a water turbine as with a flying horse.

The only danger to healthy development that I can see in the fairy tale is the danger inherent in all works of art, namely, that the reader is tempted to identify himself with the hero in his triumphs and withdraw from him during his sufferings. Knowing, as the reader of the story, that it ends happily, he ignores the fact that the hero *in* the story does not know it is going to end, and so fails to feel the hero's trials as real. Imagination, like reason, is a human faculty and therefore not foolproof.

III

A fairy story, as distinct from a merry tale, or an animal story, is a serious tale with a human hero and a happy ending. The progression of its hero is the reverse of the tragic hero's: at the beginning he is either socially obscure or despised as being stupid or untalented, lacking in the heroic virtues, but at the end, he has surprised everyone by demonstrating his heroism and winning fame, riches, and love. Though ultimately he succeeds, he does not do so without a struggle in which his success is in doubt, for opposed to him are not only natural difficulties like glass mountains, or barriers of flame, but also hostile wicked powers, stepmothers, jealous brothers and witches. In many cases, indeed, he would fail were he not assisted by friendly powers who give him instructions or perform tasks for him which he cannot do himself; that is, in addition to his own powers, he needs luck, but this luck is not fortuitous but dependent upon his character and his actions. The tale ends with the establishment of justice; not only are the good rewarded but also the evil are punished.

Take, for example, "The Water of Life." Three brothers set out in turn on a difficult quest to find the water of life to restore the King, their sick father, to health. Each one meets a dwarf who asks where he is going. The two elder give rude answers and are punished by being imprisoned in ravines. The third brother gives a courteous answer and is rewarded by being told where the water of life is and how to appease the lions who guard it, but is warned to leave before the clock strikes twelve. He reaches the enchanted castle, where he finds a princess who tells him to return in a year and marry her. At this point he almost fails because he falls asleep and only just manages to escape as the clock strikes twelve and the iron door shuts, carrying away a piece of his heel. On the way home he again meets the dwarf and begs him to release his brothers, which he does with a warning that they have bad hearts. The brothers steal the water of life from him and substitute salt water so that his father condemns him to be secretly shot. The huntsman entrusted with the task has not the heart to do it, and lets the young prince go away into the forest. Now begins a second quest for the Princess. She has built a golden road to test her suitors. Whoever rides straight up it is to be admitted, whoever rides to the side is not. When the two elder brothers come to it, they think "it would be a sin and a shame to ride over that" and so fail the test. At the end of the year, the exiled brother rides thither but is so preoccupied with thinking of the Princess that he never notices the golden road and rides straight up. They are married, the King learns how the elder brothers had betrayed the Prince, and they, to escape punishment, put to sea and never come back.

The hero is in the third or inferior position. (The youngest son inherits least.)* There are two quests, each involving a test which the hero passes and his brothers fail.

The first test is the encounter with the dwarf. The elder brothers disregard him a) because he looks like the last person on earth who could help them; b) they are impatient and thinking only of their success; and c) what is wrong with their concentration on their task is, firstly, over-self-confidence in their own powers and, secondly, the selfishness of their motive. They do not really love their father but want him to reward them.

The hero, on the other hand, is a) humble enough; b) cares enough for his father's recovery; and c) has a loving disposition toward all men, so that he asks the dwarf for assistance and gets it.

---

*   I now think I was mistaken. In many peasant communities, where early marriages are the rule, it is the youngest son who inherits the farm.

The second test of the golden road is a reversal of the first: the right thing to do this time is to take no notice of it. The brothers who dismissed the dwarf notice the road because of its worldly value, which is more to them than any Princess, while the hero, who paid attention to the dwarf, ignores the road because he is truly in love.

The Water of Life and the Princess are guarded by lions; these, in this tale, are not malevolent but ensure that no one shall succeed who has not learned the true way. The hero almost fails here by forgetting the dwarf's warning and falling asleep; further it is through falling asleep and not watching his brothers that they almost succeed in destroying him. The readiness to fall asleep is a sign of trustfulness and lack of fear which are the qualities which bring about his success; at the same time it is pointed out that, carried too far, they are a danger to him.

IV

If such a tale is not history, what is it about? Broadly speaking, and in most cases, the fairy tale is a dramatic projection in symbolic images of the life of the psyche, and it can travel from one country to another, one culture to another culture, whenever what it has to say holds good for human nature in both, despite their differences. Insofar as the myth is valid, the events of the story and its basic images will appeal irrespective of the artistic value of their narration; a genuine myth, like the Chaplin clown, can always be recognized by the fact that its appeal cuts across all differences between highbrow and lowbrow tastes. Further, no one conscious analysis can exhaust its meaning. There is no harm, however, if this is realized, in trying to give one.

Thus reading "The Water of Life," it occurs to me that the two quests, for the water which heals the old sick King and the Princess through marriage with whom the new life will come into being are one and the same, though it is only by first trying to restore the past that one comes to discover one's future path. One's true strength rarely lies in the capacities and faculties of which one is proud, but frequently in those one regards as unimportant or even as weaknesses. Success can never be achieved by an act of conscious will alone; it always requires the co-operation of grace or luck. But grace is not arbitrary; it is always there to assist anyone who is humble enough to ask for it and those who reject it convert it by their own act of rejection into a negative force; they get what they demand. There is no joy or success without risk and suffering, and those who try to avoid suffering fail to obtain the joy, but get the suffering anyway. Finally, and above all, one must not be anxious about ultimate success or failure but think only about what it is necessary to do at the present moment. What seems a story stretched out in time takes place in fact at every instant; the proud and the envious are even now dancing in red-hot shoes or rolling downhill in barrels full of nails; the trustful and loving are already married to princesses.

V

The Grimm brothers were the first men to attempt to record folk tales exactly as they were told by the folk themselves without concessions to bourgeois prudery or cultured literary canon, an example which, in the case of prudery, at least, has not been followed, I am sorry to say, by their translators.

Hans Andersen, so far as I know, was the first man to take the fairy tale as a literary form and invent new ones deliberately. Some of his stories are, like those of Perrault, a reworking of folk material—"The Wild Swans," for example, is based on two stories in the Grimm collection, "The Six Swans," and "The Twelve Brothers"—but his best tales, like "The Snow Queen," or "The Hardy Tin Soldier," or "The Ice Maiden" are not only new in material but as unmistakably Andersen's as if they were modern novels.

Compared with the Grimm tales, they have the virtues and the defects of a conscious literary art. To begin with, they tend to be parables rather than myths.

> Little Kay was blue with cold—nay almost black—but he did not know it, for the Snow Queen had kissed away the icy shiverings, and his heart was little better than a lump of ice. He went about dragging some sharp flat pieces of ice which he placed in all sorts of patterns, trying to make something out of them, just as when we at home have little tablets of wood, with which we make patterns and call them a "Chinese puzzle."
>
> Kay's patterns were most ingenious, because they were the 'Ice Puzzles of Reason.' In his eyes they were excellent and of the greatest importance: this was because of the grain of glass still in his eye. He made many patterns forming words, but he never could find the right way to place them for one particular word, a word he was most anxious to make. It was "Eternity." The Snow Queen had said to him that if he could find out this word he should be his own master, and she would give him the whole world and a new pair of skates. But he could not discover it.

Such a passage could never occur in a folk tale. Firstly, because the human situation with which it is concerned is an historical one created by Descartes, Newton, and their successors, and, secondly, because no folk tale would analyze its own symbols and explain that the game with the ice-splinters was the game of reason. Further, the promised reward, "the whole world and a new pair of skates" has not only a surprise and a subtlety of which the folk tale is incapable, but, also a uniqueness by which one can identify its author.

It is rarely possible, therefore, to retell an Andersen story in other words than his; after the tough and cheerful adventurers of the folk tales, one may be irritated with the Sensitive-Plantishness and rather namby-pamby Christianity of some of Andersen's heroes, but one puts up with them for the sake of the wit and sharpness of his social observation and the interest of his minor characters. One remembers the old lady with the painted flowers in her hat and the robber's daughter in "The Snow Queen" as individuals in a way that one fails to remember any of the hundreds of witches and young girls in the folk tales. The difference may be most clearly seen by a comparison of stories about inanimate objects.

> Soon . . . they came to a little brook, and, as there was no bridge or foot-plank, they did not know how they were to get over it. The straw hit on a good idea, and said: "I will lay myself straight across, and then you can walk over on me as a bridge." The straw therefore stretched itself from one bank to the other, and the coal, who was of an impetuous disposition, tripped quite boldly onto the newly built bridge. But when she had reached the middle, and heard the water rushing beneath her, she was, after all, afraid, and stood still,

and ventured no further. The straw, however, began to burn, broke in two pieces, and fell into the stream. The coal slipped after her, hissed when she got into the water, and breathed her last. The bean, who had prudently stayed behind on the shore, could not but laugh at the event, was unable to stop, and laughed so heartily that she burst. It would have been all over with her, likewise, if, by good fortune, a tailor who was traveling in search of work, had not sat down to rest by the brook. As he had a compassionate heart, he pulled out his needle and thread and sewed her together. The bean thanked him most prettily, but, as the tailor used black thread, all beans since then have a black seam.

So Grimm. The fantasy is built upon a factual question. "Why do beans have a black seam?" The characterization of the straw, the coal, and the bean does not extend beyond the minimum required by their respective physical qualities. The whole interest lies in the incidents.

Andersen's story, "The Darning Needle," on the other hand, presupposes no question about its protagonist.

The darning needle kept her proud behavior and did not lose her good humor. And things of many kinds swam over her, chips and straws and pieces of old newspapers.

"Only look how they sail!" said the darning needle. "They don't know what is under them! . . . See, there goes a chip thinking of nothing in the world but of himself—of a chip! There's a straw going by now. How he turns! how he twirls about! Don't think only of yourself, you might easily run up against a stone. There swims a bit of newspaper. What's written upon it has long been forgotten, and yet it gives itself airs. I sit quietly and patiently here. I know who I am and I shall remain what I am."

One day something lay close beside her that glittered splendidly; then the darning needle believed that it was a diamond; but it was a bit of broken bottle; and because it shone, the darning needle spoke to it, introducing herself as a breastpin.

"I suppose you are a diamond?" she observed.

"Why, yes, something of that kind."

And then each believed the other to be a very valuable thing; and they began speaking about the world, and how very conceited it was.

"I have been in a lady's box," said the darning needle, "and this lady was a cook. She had five fingers on each hand, and I never saw anything so conceited as those five fingers. And yet they were only there that they might take me out of the box and put me back into it."

"Were they of good birth?" asked the bit of bottle.

"No, indeed, but very haughty. . . . There was nothing but bragging among them, and therefore I went away."

"And now we sit here and glitter!" said the bit of bottle.

Here the action is subordinate to the actors, providing them with a suitable occasion to display their characters which are individual, i.e., one can easily imagine another Darning Needle and another Bit of Bottle who would say quite different things. Inanimate objects are not being treated anthropomorphically, as in Grimm; on the contrary, human beings have been transmuted into inanimate objects in order that they may be judged without prejudice, with the same objective vision that Swift tries for through changes of size. The difference is one that distinguishes all primitive literature, primitive, that is, in attitude, not in technique, from modern.

In the folk tale, as in the Greek epic and tragedy, situation and character are hardly separable; a man reveals what he is in what he does, or what happens to him is a revelation of what he is. In modern literature, what a man is includes all the possibilities of what he may become, so that what he actually does is never a complete revelation. The defect of primitive literature is the defect of primitive man, a fatalistic lack of hope which is akin to a lack of imagination. The danger for modern literature and modern man is paralysis of action through excess of imagination, an imprisonment in the void of infinite possibilities. That is why, maybe, contemporary novelists seem to have their greatest difficulties with their plots, for we, their characters, find it so much easier to stop to think than to go into action with the consequence, all too often, that, more apathetic than any primitive hero, we wait helplessly for something, usually terrible, to be done to us.

VI

There'll Always Be a Teachers' College.

"How is it possible that human sense should conceive there ever were in the World such multitudes of famous Knights-Errant, so many Emperors . . . palfreys, rambling damsels, serpents, monsters, giants, unheard-of adventures, so many sorts of enchantments. . . . As for my own particular, I confess, that, while I read them, and do not reflect that they are nothing but Falsehood and Folly, they give me some satisfaction, but I no sooner remember what they are, but I cast the best of them from me and would deliver them up to the flames if I had a fire near me. . . . If, led away by your natural inclination, you will read books of heroism and great exploits, read in the Holy Scriptures the Book of Judges, where you will find wonderful truths and glorious actions not to be questioned, the reading of which diverts, instructs, pleases, and surprises the most judicious readers."

"Very well," cried Don Quixote, "then all those books must be fabulous, though licensed by kings, approved by the Examiners, read with general satisfaction, and applauded by the Better Sort and the Meaner, rich and poor, learned and unlearned. . . ."

"For shame, Sir, forbear uttering such blasphemies. And do you, good Sir, believe me, and, as I said to you before, read these books, which you may find will banish all melancholy, if you are troubled with it, and sweeten your disposition if it be harsh."

CONSIDER THIS

W. H. Auden (1907–1973), the English poet, essayist, playwright, and librettist, lived much of his adult life in New York City, worried that contemporary life was riddled by too much thought. As he says at the end of "Grimm and Andersen," "we . . . find it so much easier to stop to think than to go into action with the consequence . . . we wait helplessly for something, usually terrible, to be done to us." This is the line in Auden that sets me on edge, in search through life and art of ways of resisting his dismal view of "us." Who are the "we" he's talking about? Do "we" think rather than act? Is that why we need to search for action in jogging, mountain climbing, wind surfing, and so forth, because our possibilities for action, for heroic action, are so limited?

Whenever I think of Auden, I remember the time, when as a senior in college, I attended his poetry reading. There he was: a craggy face, so full of lines and wrinkles that it looked like a creviced map; a mass of unruly grey hair; a bulky, unpressed corduroy jacket; and on his feet? Not shoes, but bedroom slippers. Was he ready for a bedtime story? A fairy tale? Or did his feet hurt? I wonder. I also remember that he told us he'd much rather be outside enjoying the fresh air than inside reading his poetry to us. "Why am I doing it?" he asked. "Because I need the money!" he said.

I think he enjoyed himself *playing* the disheveled, eccentric poet. That's the way I read him.

V. S. Pritchett said of Auden, "He has one foot in art and one in life."

Plastic Peanut Menace
Russell Baker

It's easy to foresee a time not too far off when garbage disposal will be a bigger threat to the world than nuclear war. There was a hint of that future in the famous voyage of the Long Island garbage last year, and there is another hint in the recent passage on Long Island of a statute aimed at stopping fast-food shops from packing their burgers in indestructible plastic foam.

Imagine a world where you can't carry your Big Mac away in a plastic foam box. Talk about the end of civilization!

I heard a spokesman for Styrofoam tell a microphone journalist that Styrofoam was being victimized by crazed environmentalists who would stop at nothing in their vicious plot to prevent the earth from being utterly encased in indestructible layers of Styrofoam.

Yes, there is a spokesman for Styrofoam, and no, he didn't really call environmentalists "crazed," but that's what he was trying to suggest. Spokesmen for industries whose profitability depends upon making a mess of sky, ocean and landscape are always trying to suggest that you must have a screw loose if you don't like squalor in the air, at sea and on your lawn.

Poor devils. It's depressing, the things people have to do to get paid every Friday. But enough of that. On to plastic peanuts.

Everybody know what plastic peanuts are? Those white, weightless, peanut-shaped things that merchants pump into shipping cartons that contain fragile goods.

If you have ever received a carton crammed with plastic peanuts and made the mistake of letting them get out, you know what Pandora felt after opening her box.

Plastic peanuts cannot be got rid of. Feather-light, they blow hither and yon on the slightest zephyr. They get into cracks in the chimney. They get into the stereo system and into the soup. They get into your clothes and into your hair, into the petunia bed and into the potato patch.

Like plastic foam burger boxes, they are indestructible. The life span of the average plastic peanut is forever. So what do you do with them when confronted with a large carton containing a small piece of crystal packed in 100,000 plastic peanuts?

You use environmental guerrilla tactics.

Unpacking the glass in a sealed, airless room, take pains to see no plastic peanuts escape the carton. Plenty will, anyhow, but not a disastrous quantity if you keep calm. Stuff the escapees back into the carton and close it.

Then get a big plastic garbage bag. Insert the carton full of plastic peanuts with top down. Open top of box, let plastic peanuts flow into plastic garbage bag. ("Plastic to plastic," our burying officials will probably intone as our styrene coffins are slipped into Hefty bags in that future when undisposable garbage has the world by the throat.)

O.K., you've got the plastic peanuts bagged in plastic. Tie the bag securely, place it in the packing carton, seal the carton and mail it back to the people who shipped you the crystal. They made the money from that shipment, didn't they? Getting rid of their undisposable packing material is not your department.

The object of environmental guerrilla action is to get the attention of people who profit from making messes, and a good way to get their attention is to make them deal with their creations.

A few years ago people who tired of having empty beer cans thrown at them hit on the idea of mailing sacks full of them back to the Anheuser-Busch and Miller brewing empires.

The tactic was too cumbersome to succeed. Also, the cans were not indestructible. Since they could be recycled, civilized venues began requiring deposits, thus making the empties valuable for people to pick up.

As garbage encroachment nears totality, of course, people desperate to save themselves will surely start mailing it everywhere. Not just to companies that make money from creating it, but to governments, to neighbors, to friends and relatives.

Yes, even to loved ones. I myself recently mailed a large shipment of plastic peanuts to a dear child whom destiny has placed far from home. She lives in a place where developers are getting disgustingly rich by making an unspeakable mess of a once beautiful place.

She will give the sealed box to the trash man for landfill burial in the dump. Eventually, natural catastrophe will unearth them. Then they will swirl forever over that profitably ravished place of beauty, drifting eternally past developers' windows so they will never be able to see the snow for the plastic peanuts.

CONSIDER THIS

Russell Baker began his long and celebrated career in journalism in 1947, at the old age of 22, and has been writing his "Observer" column for *The New York Times* since 1962. He is one of the nation's watchdogs, an essayist who calls things as he sees them. No one is safe when he's around. In *Growing Up,* an autobiography, he describes the near-poverty of his family during the Depression and his widowed mother's determination that he should "make something of himself."

He loathes fat: fat cats, fat packaging, fat language. In one of his essays, "American Fat," he says, "We are what we think, and very often we think what we say rather than what we say we think." There's a brain-twister for you. And here's another one: What *do* you do with plastic peanuts?

Strangers in the Village
James Baldwin

From all available evidence no black man had ever set foot in this tiny Swiss village before I came. I was told before arriving that I would probably be a "sight" for the village; I took this to mean that people of my complexion were rarely seen in Switzerland, and also that city people are always something of a "sight" outside of the city. It did not occur to me—possibly because I am an American—that there could be people anywhere who had never seen a Negro.

It is a fact that cannot be explained on the basis of the inaccessibility of the village. The village is very high, but it is only four hours from Milan and three hours from Lausanne. It is true that it is virtually unknown. Few people making plans for a holiday would elect to come here. On the other hand, the villagers are able, presumably, to come and go as they please—which they do: to another town at the foot of the mountain, with a population of approximately five thousand, the nearest place to see a movie or go to the bank. In the village there is no movie house, no bank, no library, no theater; very few radios, one jeep, one station wagon; and, at the moment, one typewriter, mine, an invention which the woman next door to me here had never seen. There are about six hundred people living here, all Catholic—I conclude this from the fact that the Catholic church is open all year round, whereas the Protestant chapel, set off on a hill a little removed from the village, is open only in the summertime when the tourists arrive. There are four or five hotels, all closed now, and four or five *bistros,* of which, however, only two do any business during the winter. These two do not do a great deal, for life in the village seems to end around nine or ten o'clock. There are a few stores, butcher, baker, *épicerie*, a hardware store, and a money-changer—who cannot change travelers' checks, but must send them down to the bank, an operation which takes two or three days. There is something called the *Ballet Haus*, closed in the winter and used for God knows what, certainly not ballet, during the summer. There seems to be only one schoolhouse in the village, and this for the quite young children; I suppose this to mean that their older brothers and sisters at some point descend from these mountains in order to complete their education—possibly, again, to the town just below. The landscape is absolutely forbidding, mountains towering on all four sides, ice and snow as far as the eye can reach. In this white wilderness, men and women and children move all day, carrying washing, wood, buckets of milk or water, sometimes skiing on Sunday afternoons. All week long boys and young men are to be seen shoveling snow off the rooftops, or dragging wood down from the forest in sleds.

The village's only real attraction, which explains the tourist season, is the hot spring water. A disquietingly high proportion of these tourists are cripples, or semi-cripples, who come year after year—from other parts of Switzerland, usually—to take the waters. This lends the village, at the height of the season, a rather terrifying air of sanctity, as though it were a lesser Lourdes. There is often something beautiful, there is always something awful, in the spectacle of a person who has lost one of his faculties, a faculty he never questioned until it was gone, and who struggles to recover it. Yet people remain people, on crutches or indeed on deathbeds; and wherever I passed, the first summer I was here, among the native villagers or among the lame, a wind passed with me—of astonishment, curiosity, amusement, and outrage. That first summer I stayed two weeks and never intended to return. But

I did return in the winter, to work; the village offers, obviously, no distractions whatever and has the further advantage of being extremely cheap. Now it is winter again, a year later, and I am here again. Everyone in the village knows my name, though they scarcely ever use it, knows that I come from America—though, this, apparently, they will never really believe: black men come from Africa—and everyone knows that I am the friend of the son of a woman who was born here, and that I am staying in their chalet. But I remain as much a stranger today as I was the first day I arrived, and the children shout *Neger! Neger!* as I walk along the streets.

It must be admitted that in the beginning I was far too shocked to have any real reaction. In so far as I reacted at all, I reacted by trying to be pleasant—it being a great part of the American Negro's education (long before he goes to school) that he must make people "like" him. This smile-and-the-world-smiles-with-you routine worked about as well in this situation as it had in the situation for which it was designed, which is to say that it did not work at all. No one, after all, can be liked whose human weight and complexity cannot be, or has not been, admitted. My smile was simply another unheard-of phenomenon which allowed them to see my teeth—they did not, really, see my smile and I began to think that, should I take to snarling, no one would notice any difference. All of the physical characteristics of the Negro which had caused me, in America, a very different and almost forgotten pain, were nothing less than miraculous—or infernal—in the eyes of the village people. Some thought my hair was the color of tar, that it had the texture of wire, or the texture of cotton. It was jocularly suggested that I might let it all grow long and make myself a winter coat. If I sat in the sun for more than five minutes some daring creature was certain to come along and gingerly put his fingers on my hair, as though he were afraid of an electric shock, or put his hand on my hand, astonished that the color did not rub off. In all of this, in which it must be conceded there was the charm of genuine wonder and in which there was certainly no element of intentional unkindness, there was yet no suggestion that I was human: I was simply a living wonder.

I knew that they did not mean to be unkind, and I know it now; it is necessary, nevertheless, for me to repeat this to myself each time that I walk out of the chalet. The children who shout *Neger!* have no way of knowing the echoes this sound raises in me. They are brimming with good humor and the more daring swell with pride when I stop to speak with them. Just the same, there are days when I cannot pause and smile, when I have no heart to play with them; when, indeed, I mutter sourly to myself, exactly as I muttered on the streets of a city these children have never seen, when I was no bigger than these children are now: *Your* mother *was a nigger.* Joyce is right about history being a nightmare—but it may be the nightmare from which no one *can* awaken. People are trapped in history and history is trapped in them.

There is a custom in the village—I am told it is repeated in many villages—of "buying" African natives for the purpose of converting them to Christianity. There stands in the church all year round a small box with a slot for money, decorated with a black figurine, and into this box the villagers drop their francs. During the *carnaval* which precedes Lent, two village children have their faces blackened—out of which bloodless darkness their blue eyes shine like ice—and fantastic horsehair wigs are placed on their blond heads; thus disguised, they solicit among the villagers for money for the missionaries in Africa. Between the box in the church and the blackened children, the village "bought" last year six or eight African natives. This was reported to me with pride by the wife of one of the *bistro* owners and I was careful to express astonishment and pleasure at the solicitude shown by the village for the souls of black folk. The *bistro* owner's wife beamed with a pleasure far more genuine than my own and seemed to feel that I might now breathe more easily concerning the souls of at least six of my kinsmen.

I tried not to think of these so lately baptized kinsmen, of the price paid for them, or the peculiar price they themselves would pay, and said nothing about my father, who having taken his own conversion too literally never, at bottom, forgave the white world (which he described as heathen) for having saddled him with a Christ in whom, to judge at least from their treatment of him, they themselves no longer believed. I thought of white men arriving for the first time in an African village, strangers there, as I am a stranger here, and tried to imagine the astounded populace touching their hair and marveling at the color of their skin. But there is a great difference between being the first white man to be seen by Africans and being the first black man to be seen by whites. The white man takes the astonishment as tribute, for he arrives to conquer and to convert the natives, whose inferiority in relation to himself is not even to be questioned; whereas I, without a thought of conquest, find myself among a people whose culture controls me, has even, in a sense, created me, people who have cost me more in anguish and rage than they will ever know, who yet do not even know of my existence. The astonishment with which I might have greeted them, should they have stumbled into my African village a few hundred years ago, might have rejoiced their hearts. But the astonishment with which they greet me today can only poison mine.

And this is so despite everything I may do to feel differently, despite my friendly conversations with the *bistro* owner's wife, despite their three-year-old son who has at last become my friend, despite the *saluts* and *bonsoirs* which I exchange with people as I walk, despite the fact that I know that no individual can be taken to task for what history is doing, or has done. I say that the culture of these people controls me—but they can scarcely be held responsible for European culture. America comes out of Europe, but these people have never seen America, nor have most of them seen more of Europe than the hamlet at the foot of their mountain. Yet they move with an authority which I shall never have; and they regard me, quite rightly, not only as a stranger in their village but as a suspect latecomer, bearing no credentials, to everything they have—however unconsciously—inherited.

For this village, even were it incomparably more remote and incredibly more primitive, is the West, the West onto which I have been so strangely grafted. These people cannot be, from the point of view of power, strangers anywhere in the world; they have made the modern world, in effect, even if they do not know it. The most illiterate among them is related, in a way that I am not, to Dante, Shakespeare, Michelangelo, Aeschylus, Da Vinci, Rembrandt, and Racine; the cathedral at Chartres says something to them which it cannot say to me, as indeed would New York's Empire State Building, should anyone here ever see it. Out of their hymns and dances come Beethoven and Bach. Go back a few centuries and they are in their full glory—but I am in Africa, watching the conquerors arrive.

The rage of the disesteemed is personally fruitless, but it is also absolutely inevitable; this rage, so generally discounted, so little understood even among the people whose daily bread it is, is one of the things that makes history. Rage can only with difficulty, and never entirely, be brought under the domination of the intelligence and is therefore not susceptible to any arguments whatever. This is a fact which ordinary representatives of the *Herrenvolk,* having never felt this rage and being unable to imagine it, quite fail to understand. Also, rage cannot be hidden, it can only be dissembled. This dissembling deludes the thoughtless, and strengthens rage and adds, to rage, contempt. There are, no doubt, as many ways of coping with the resulting complex of tensions as there are black men in the world, but no black man can hope ever to be entirely liberated from this internal warfare—rage, dissembling, and contempt having inevitably accompanied his first realization of the power of white men. What is crucial here is that, since white men represent in the black man's world so heavy a weight, white men have for black men a reality which is far from being reciprocal; and hence all black men have toward all white men an attitude which is designed, really, either to rob the white man of the jewel of his naiveté, or else to make it cost him dear.

The black man insists, by whatever means he finds at his disposal, that the white man cease to regard him as an exotic rarity and recognize him as a human being. This is a very charged and difficult moment, for there is a great deal of will power involved in the white man's naiveté. Most people are not naturally reflective any more than they are naturally malicious, and the white man prefers to keep the black man at a certain human remove because it is easier for him thus to preserve his simplicity and avoid being called to account for crimes committed by his forefathers, or his neighbors. He is inescapably aware, nevertheless, that he is in a better position in the world than black men are, nor can he quite put to death the suspicion that he is hated by black men therefore. He does not wish to be hated, neither does he wish to change places, and at this point in his uneasiness he can scarcely avoid having recourse to those legends which white men have created about black men, the most usual effect of which is that the white man finds himself enmeshed, so to speak, in his own language which describes hell, as well as the attributes which lead one to hell, as being as black as night.

Every legend, moreover, contains its residuum of truth, and the root function of language is to control the universe by describing it. It is of quite considerable significance that black men remain, in the imagination, and in overwhelming numbers in fact, beyond the disciplines of salvation; and this despite the fact that the West has been "buying" African natives for centuries. There is, I should hazard, an instantaneous necessity to be divorced from this so visibly unsaved stranger, in whose heart, moreover, one cannot guess what dreams of vengeance are being nourished; and, at the same time, there are few things on earth more attractive than the idea of the unspeakable liberty which is allowed the unredeemed. When, beneath the black mask, a human being begins to make himself felt one cannot escape a certain awful wonder as to what kind of human being it is. What one's imagination makes of other people is dictated, of course, by the laws of one's own personality and it is one of the ironies of black-white relations that, by means of what the white man imagines the black man to be, the black man is enabled to know who the white man is.

I have said, for example, that I am as much a stranger in this village today as I was the first summer I arrived, but this is not quite true. The villagers wonder less about the texture of my hair than they did then, and wonder rather more about me. And the fact that their wonder now exists on another level is reflected in their attitudes and in their eyes. There are the children who make those delightful, hilarious, sometimes astonishingly grave overtures of friendship in the unpredictable fashion of children; other children, having been taught that the devil is a black man, scream in genuine anguish as I approach. Some of the older women never pass without a friendly greeting, never pass, indeed, if it seems that they will be able to engage me in conversation; other women look down or look away or rather contemptuously smirk. Some of the men drink with me and suggest that I learn how to ski—partly, I gather, because they cannot imagine what I would look like on skis—and want to know if I am married, and ask questions about my *métier*. But some of the men have accused *le sale nègre*—behind my back—of stealing wood and there is already in the eyes of some of them that peculiar, intent, paranoiac malevolence which one sometimes surprises in the eyes of American white men when, out walking with their Sunday girl, they see a Negro male approach.

There is a dreadful abyss between the streets of this village and the streets of the city in which I was born, between the children who shout *Neger!* today and those who shouted *Nigger!* yesterday—the abyss is experience, the American experience. The syllable hurled behind me today expresses, above all, wonder: I am a stranger here. But I am not a stranger in America and the same syllable riding on the American air expresses the war my presence has occasioned in the American soul.

For this village brings home to me this fact: that there was a day, and not really a very distant day, when Americans were scarcely Americans at all but discontented Europeans, facing a great unconquered continent and strolling, say, into a marketplace and seeing black men for the first time. The shock this spectacle afforded is suggested, surely, by the promptness with which they decided that these black men were not really men but cattle. It is true that the necessity on the part of the settlers of the New World of reconciling their moral assumptions with the fact—and the necessity—of slavery enhanced immensely the charm of this idea, and it is also true that this idea expresses, with a truly American bluntness, the attitude which to varying extents all masters have had toward all slaves.

But between all former slaves and slave-owners and the drama which begins for Americans over three hundred years ago at Jamestown, there are at least two differences to be observed. The American Negro slave could not suppose, for one thing, as slaves in past epochs had supposed and often done, that he would ever be able to wrest the power from his master's hands. This was a supposition which the modern era, which was to bring about such vast changes in the aims and dimensions of power, put to death; it only begins, in unprecedented fashion, and with dreadful implications, to be resurrected today. But even had this supposition persisted with undiminished force, the American Negro slave could not have used it to lend his condition dignity, for the reason that this supposition rests on another: that the slave in exile yet remains related to his past, has some means—if only in memory—of revering and sustaining the forms of his former life, is able, in short, to maintain his identity.

This was not the case with the American Negro slave. He is unique among the black men of the world in that his past was taken from him, almost literally, at one blow. One wonders what on earth the first slave found to say to the first dark child he bore. I am told that there are Haitians able to trace their ancestry back to African kings, but any American Negro wishing to go back so far will find his journey through time abruptly arrested by the signature on the bill of sale which served as the entrance paper for his ancestor. At the time—to say nothing of the circumstances—of the enslavement of the captive black man who was to become the American Negro, there was not the remotest possibility that he would ever take power from his master's hands. There was no reason to suppose that his situation would ever change, nor was there, shortly, anything to indicate that his situation had ever been different. It was his necessity, in the words of E. Franklin Frazier, to find a "motive for living under American culture or die." The identity of the American Negro comes out of this extreme situation, and the evolution of this identity was a source of the most intolerable anxiety in the minds and the lives of his masters.

For the history of the American Negro is unique also in this: that the question of his humanity, and of his rights therefore as a human being, became a burning one for several generations of Americans, so burning a question that it ultimately became one of those used to divide the nation. It is out of this argument that the venom of the epithet *Nigger!* is derived. It is an argument which Europe has never had, and hence Europe quite sincerely fails to understand how or why the argument arose in the first place, why its effects are so frequently disastrous and always so unpredictable, why it refuses until today to be entirely settled. Europe's black possessions remained—and do remain—in Europe's colonies, at which remove they represented no threat whatever to European identity. If they posed any problem at all for the European conscience, it was a problem which remained comfortingly abstract: in effect, the black man, *as a man,* did not exist for Europe. But in America, even as a slave, he was an inescapable part of the general social fabric and no American could escape having an attitude toward him. Americans attempt until today to make an abstraction of the Negro, but the very nature of these abstractions reveals the tremendous effects the presence of the Negro has had on the American character.

When one considers the history of the Negro in America it is of the greatest importance to recognize that the moral beliefs of a person, or a people, are never really as tenuous as life—which is not moral—very often causes them to appear; these create for them a frame of reference and a necessary hope, the hope being that when life has done its worst they will be enabled to rise above themselves and to triumph over life. Life would scarcely be bearable if this hope did not exist. Again, even when the worst has been said, to betray a belief is not by any means to have put oneself beyond its power; the betrayal of a belief is not the same thing as ceasing to believe. If this were not so there would be no moral standards in the world at all. Yet one must also recognize that morality is based on ideas and that all ideas are dangerous—dangerous because ideas can only lead to action and where the action leads no man can say. And dangerous in this respect: that confronted with the impossibility of remaining faithful to one's beliefs, and the equal impossibility of becoming free of them, one can be driven to the most inhuman excesses. The ideas on which American beliefs are based are not, though Americans often seem to think so, ideas which originated in America. They came out of Europe. And the establishment of democracy on the American continent was scarcely as radical a break with the past as was the necessity, which Americans faced, of broadening this concept to include black men.

This was, literally, a hard necessity. It was impossible, for one thing, for Americans to abandon their beliefs, not only because these beliefs alone seemed able to justify the sacrifices they had endured and the blood that they had spilled, but also because these beliefs afforded them their only bulwark against a moral chaos as absolute as the physical chaos of the continent it was their destiny to conquer. But in the situation in which Americans found themselves, these beliefs threatened an idea which, whether or not one likes to think so, is the very warp and woof of the heritage of the West, the idea of white supremacy.

Americans have made themselves notorious by the shrillness and the brutality with which they have insisted on this idea, but they did not invent it; and it has escaped the world's notice that those very excesses of which Americans have been guilty imply a certain, unprecedented uneasiness over the idea's life and power, if not, indeed, the idea's validity. The idea of white supremacy rests simply on the fact that white men are the creators of civilization (the present civilization, which is the only one that matters; all previous civilizations are simply "contributions" to our own) and are therefore civilization's guardians and defenders. Thus it was impossible for Americans to accept the black man as one of themselves, for to do so was to jeopardize their status as white men. But not so to accept him was to deny his human reality, his human weight and complexity, and the strain of denying the overwhelmingly undeniable forced Americans into rationalizations so fantastic that they approached the pathological.

At the root of the American Negro problem is the necessity of the American white man to find a way of living with the Negro in order to be able to live with himself. And the history of this problem can be reduced to the means used by Americans—lynch law and law, segregation and legal acceptance, terrorization and concession—either to come to terms with this necessity, or to find a way around it, or (most usually) to find a way of doing both these things at once. The resulting spectacle, at once foolish and dreadful, led someone to make the quite accurate observation that "the Negro-in-America is a form of insanity which overtakes white men."

In this long battle, a battle by no means finished, the unforeseeable effects of which will be felt by many future generations, the white man's motive was the protection of his identity; the black man was motivated by the need to establish an identity. And despite the terrorization which the Negro in America endured and endures sporadically until today, despite the cruel and totally inescapable ambivalence of his status in his country, the battle for his identity has long ago been won. He is not a visitor to the West, but a citizen there, an American; as American as the Americans who despise him, the Americans who fear him, the Americans who love him—the Americans who became less than themselves, or rose to be greater than themselves by virtue of the fact that the challenge he represented was inescapable. He is perhaps the only black man in the world whose relationship to white men is more terrible, more subtle, and more meaningful than the relationship of bitter possessed to uncertain possessor. His survival depended, and his development depends, on his ability to turn his peculiar status in the Western world to his own advantage and, it may be, to the very great advantage of that world. It remains for him to fashion out of his experience that which will give him sustenance, and a voice.

The cathedral at Chartres, I have said, says something to the people of this village which it cannot say to me; but it is important to understand that this cathedral says something to me which it cannot say to them. Perhaps they are struck by the power of the spires, the glory of the windows; but they have known God, after all, longer than I have known him, and in a different way, and I am terrified by the slippery bottomless well to be found in the crypt, down which heretics were hurled to death, and by the obscene, inescapable gargoyles jutting out of the stone and seeming to say that God and the devil can never be divorced. I doubt that the villagers think of the devil when they face a cathedral because they have never been identified with the devil. But I must accept the status which myth, if nothing else, gives me in the West before I can hope to change the myth.

Yet, if the American Negro has arrived at his identity by virtue of the absoluteness of his estrangement from his past, American white men still nourish the illusion that there is some means of recovering the European innocence, of returning to a state in which black men do not exist. This is one of the greatest errors Americans can make. The identity they fought so hard to protect has, by virtue of that battle, undergone a change: Americans are as unlike any other white people in the world as it is possible to be. I do not think, for example, that it is too much to suggest that the American vision of the world—which allows so little reality, generally speaking, for any of the darker forces in human life, which tends until today to paint moral issues in glaring black and white—owes a great deal to the battle waged by Americans to maintain between themselves and black men a human separation which could not be bridged. It is only now beginning to be borne in on us—very faintly, it must be admitted, very slowly, and very much against our will that this vision of the world is dangerously inaccurate, and perfectly useless. For it protects our moral high-mindedness at the terrible expense of weakening our grasp of reality. People who shut their eyes to reality simply invite their own destruction, and anyone who insists on remaining in a state of innocence long after that innocence is dead turns himself into a monster.

The time has come to realize that the interracial drama acted out on the American continent has not only created a new black man, it has created a new white man, too. No road whatever will lead Americans back to the simplicity of this European village where white men still have the luxury of looking on me as a stranger. I am not, really, a stranger any longer for any American alive. One of the things that distinguishes Americans from other people is that no other people has ever been so deeply involved in the lives of black men, and vice versa. This fact faced, with all its implications, it can be seen that the history of the American Negro problem is not merely shameful, it is also something of an achievement. For even when the worst has been said, it must also be added that the perpetual challenge posed by this problem was always, somehow, perpetually met. It is precisely this black-white experience which may prove of indispensable value to us in the world we face today. This world is white no longer, and it will never be white again.

CONSIDER THIS

James Baldwin (1924–1973) grew up in Harlem and became a preacher at the age of 14; at 17, he tells us in *Notes of a Native Son,* he stopped his preaching and left home for Greenwich Village, a few miles away; at 24, he left for Paris, Switzerland, and the south of France, and spent the rest of his life shuttling between self-imposed exile and returning to his native country: America. How do you hear Baldwin's voice in "Stranger in the Village"? Resigned? Angry? Resistant? Determined? Reasonable? Enraged? One critic calls his voice "scorching"; another "passionate"; and another, "heroic." Throughout, he struggled with conflicting voices, needs, and desires as a black homosexual American writer. How would you characterize this list of titles of some of the fifteen books he wrote: *Another Country. Go Tell It on the Mountain. The Fire Next Time. Going to Meet the Man. If Beale Street Could Talk.*

Russell Baker likes "plain talk." Do you think he'd approve of Baldwin's language: is it fat or lean?

Why Sports Is a Drag
Dave Barry

Mankind's yearning to engage in sports is older than recorded history, dating back to the time, millions of years ago, when the first primitive man picked up a crude club and a round rock, tossed the rock into the air, and whomped the club into the sloping forehead of the first primitive umpire. What inner force drove this first athlete? Your guess is as good as mine. Better, probably, because you haven't had four beers. All I know is, whatever the reason, Mankind is still nuts about sports. As Howard Cosell, who may not be the most likable person in the world but is certainly one of the most obnoxious, put it: "In terms of Mankind and sports, blah blah blah blah the 1954 Brooklyn Dodgers."

Notice that Howard and I both use the term "Mankind." Womankind really isn't into sports in the same way. I realize things have changed since my high-school days, when sports were considered unfeminine and your average girls' gym class consisted of six girls in those gym outfits colored Digestive Enzyme Green running around waving field-hockey sticks and squealing, and 127 girls on the sidelines in civilian clothing, claiming it was That Time of the Month. I realize that today you have a number of top female athletes such as Martina Navratilova who can run like deer and bench-press Chevrolet pickup trucks. But to be brutally frank, women as a group have a long way to go before they reach the level of intensity and dedication to sports that enables men to be such incredible jerks about it.

If you don't believe me, go to your local racquetball club and observe the difference between the way men and women play. Where I play, the women tend to gather on the court in groups of random sizes—sometimes three, sometimes five, as if it were a Jane Fonda workout—and the way they play is, one of them will hit the ball at the wall and the rest of them will admire the shot and compliment her quite sincerely, and then they all sort of relax, as if they're thinking, well, thank goodness *that's* over with, and they always seem very surprised when the ball comes *back*. If one of them has the presence of mind to take another swing, and if she actually hits the ball, everybody is *very* complimentary. If she misses it, the others all tell her what a *good* try she made, really, then they all laugh and act very relieved because they know they have some time to talk before the ball comes bouncing off that darned *wall* again.

Meanwhile, over in the next court, you will have two males wearing various knee braces and wrist bands and special leatheroid racquetball gloves, hurling themselves into the walls like musk oxen on Dexedrine, and after every single point one or both of them will yell "S___!" in the self-reproving tone of voice you might use if you had just accidentally shot your grandmother. American men tend to take their sports seriously, much more seriously than they take family matters or Asia.

This is why it's usually a mistake for men and women to play on teams together. I sometimes play in a coed slow-pitch softball league, where the rules say you have to have two women on the field. The teams always have one of the women play catcher, because in slow-pitch softball the batters hit just about every pitch, so it wouldn't really hurt you much if you had a deceased person at catcher. Our team usually puts the other woman at second base, where the maximum possible number of males can get there on short notice to help out in case of emergency. As far as I can tell, our second basewoman is a pretty good baseball player, better than I am anyway, but there's no way to know for sure because if the ball gets anywhere near her, a male comes charging over from, say, right field, to deal with it. She's been on the team for three seasons now, but the males still don't trust her. They know that if she had to choose between catching a fly ball and saving an infant's life, deep in her soul, she would probably elect to save the infant's life, without even considering whether there were men on base.

This difference in attitude between men and women carries over to the area of talking about sports, especially sporting events that took place long ago. Take the 1960 World Series. If we were to look at it objectively, we would have to agree that the outcome of the 1960 World Series no longer matters. You could make a fairly strong case that it didn't really matter in 1960. Women know this, which is why you almost never hear them mention the 1960 World Series, whereas you take virtually any male over age 35 and even if he can't remember which of his children has diabetes, he can remember exactly how Pirates shortstop Bill Mazeroski hit the ninth-inning home run that beat the Yankees, and he will take every available opportunity to discuss it at length with other males.

See that? Out there in Readerland, you females just read right through that last sentence, nodding in agreement, but you males leaped from your chairs and shouted: "Mazeroski wasn't a SHORTSTOP! Mazeroski played SECOND BASE!" Every male in America has millions of perfectly good brain cells devoted to information like this. We can't help it. We have no perspective. I have a friend named Buzz, a successful business-man and the most rational person you ever want to meet, and the high point of his entire life is the time he got Stan Albeck, the coach of the New Jersey Nets, to look directly at him during a professional basketball game and make a very personal remark rhyming with "duck shoe." I should explain that Buzz and I have season tickets to the Philadelphia 76ers, so naturally we hate the Nets a great deal. It was a great honor when Albeck singled Buzz out of the crowd for recognition. The rest of us males congratulated Buzz as if he'd won the Nobel Prize for Physics.

It's silly, really, this male lack of perspective, and it can lead to unnecessary tragedy, such as soccer-riot deaths and the University of Texas. What is even more tragic is that women are losing perspective, too. Even as you read these words, women are writing vicious letters to the editor, expressing great fury at me for suggesting they don't take their racquetball seriously. Soon they will be droning on about the importance of relief pitching.

CONSIDER THIS

You've probably read Dave Barry's "Historians We're Not" on the first page of Chapter 1 of this text. Compare the beginning of "Historians" with "Why Sports Is a Drag." How do the titles tell? What might he be aiming for by inverting the normal syntax of "we're not historians" to "historians we're not"? Now look at "Why Sports Is a Drag." Would you call this a formal title? Colloquial? Breezy? Catchy? What kind of language might you expect in the first sentence? What do you find? Where does he get his first laugh? Where's the surprise? Or don't you find him humorous?

Barry received a Pulitzer Prize for his syndicated newspaper column, and he's the author of books with these titles: *Babies and Other Hazards of Sex, Stay Fit and Healthy until You're Dead,* and *Dave Barry's Guide to Marriage and/or Sex.* Do you want to read more of Dave Barry? Why? Why not?

Toys
Roland Barthes

French toys: one could not find a better illustration of the fact that the adult Frenchman sees the child as another self. All the toys one commonly sees are essentially a microcosm of the adult world; they are all reduced copies of human objects, as if in the eyes of the public the child was, all told, nothing but a smaller man, a homunculus to whom must be supplied objects of his own size.

Invented forms are very rare: a few sets of blocks, which appeal to the spirit of do-it-yourself, are the only ones which offer dynamic forms. As for the others, French toys *always mean something,* and this something is always entirely socialized, constituted by the myths or the techniques of modern adult life: the Army, Broadcasting, the Post Office, Medicine (miniature instrument-cases, operating theatres for dolls), School, Hair-Styling (driers for permanent-waving), the Air Force (Parachutists), Transport (trains, Citroëns, Vedettes, Vespas, petrol-stations), Science (Martian toys).

The fact that French toys *literally* prefigure the world of adult functions obviously cannot but prepare the child to accept them all, by constituting for him, even before he can think about it, the alibi of a Nature which has at all times created soldiers, postmen and Vespas. Toys here reveal the list of all the things the adult does not find unusual: war, bureaucracy, ugliness, Martians, etc. It is not so much, in fact, the imitation which is the sign of an abdication, as its literalness: French toys are like a Jivaro head, in which one recognizes, shrunken to the size of an apple, the wrinkles and hair of an adult. There exist, for instance, dolls which urinate; they have an oesophagus, one gives them a bottle, they wet their nappies; soon, no doubt, milk will turn to water in their stomachs. This is meant to prepare the little girl for the causality of house-keeping, to 'condition' her to her future role as mother. However, faced with this world of faithful and complicated objects, the child can only identify himself as owner, as user, never as creator; he does not invent the world, he uses it: there are, prepared for him, actions without adventure, without wonder, without joy. He is turned into a little stay-at-home householder who does not even have to invent the mainsprings of adult causality; they are supplied to him ready-made: he has only to help himself, he is never allowed to discover anything from start to finish. The merest set of blocks, provided it is not too refined, implies a very different learning of the world: then, the child does not in any way create meaningful objects, it matters little to him whether they have an adult name; the actions he performs are not those of a user but those of a demiurge. He creates forms which walk, which roll, he creates life, not property: objects now act by themselves, they are no longer an inert and complicated material in the palm of his hand. But such toys are rather rare: French toys are usually based on imitation, they are meant to produce children who are users, not creators.

The bourgeois status of toys can be recognized not only in their forms, which are all functional, but also in their substances. Current toys are made of a graceless material, the product of chemistry, not of nature. Many are now moulded from complicated mixtures; the plastic material of which they are made has an appearance at once gross and hygienic, it destroys all the pleasure, the sweetness, the humanity of touch. A sign which fills one with consternation is the gradual disappearance of wood, in spite of its being an ideal material because of its firmness and its softness, and the natural warmth of its touch. Wood removes, from all the forms which it supports, the wounding quality of angles which are too sharp, the chemical coldness of metal. When the child handles it and knocks it, it neither vibrates nor grates, it has a sound at once muffled and sharp. It is a familiar and poetic substance, which does not sever the child from close contact with the tree, the table, the floor. Wood does not wound or break down; it does not shatter, it wears out, it can last a long time, live with the child, alter little by little the relations between the object and the hand. If it dies, it is in dwindling, not in swelling out like those mechanical toys which disappear behind the hernia of a broken spring. Wood makes essential objects, objects for all time. Yet there hardly remain any of these wooden toys from the Vosges, these fretwork farms with their animals, which were only possible, it is true, in the days of the craftsman. Henceforth, toys are chemical in substance and colour; their very material introduces one to a coenaesthesis of use, not pleasure. These toys die in fact very quickly, and once dead, they have no posthumous life for the child.

CONSIDER THIS

Roland Barthes was a French journalist, philosopher, theatre critic, sociologist, cultural critic, essayist par excellence—and semiotician. Just about everything in the ordinary world around him interested him as a semiotician, that is, as a scientist studying culture as a language. Barthes saw everything—from sports to film, children's toys to photography, advertisements to clothing, as laden with cultural values and as set in history. Nothing is without history, he insisted. What children play with represents the social values and the historical moment of the adult world in which the child inescapably lives. Implicit in children's toys are the mythologies of the culture that produced them, what is respected, valued, or dismissed.

A book worth your while is Barthes' *Mythologies,* from which the essay "Toys" has been taken. In his book, Barthes looks to the unspoken myths that shape our ordinary social worlds through such phenomena as wrestling, drinking wine, movie stars, striptease, and plastic.

Barthes died in 1980.

Why Look at Animals?
John Berger

The 19th century, in western Europe and North America, saw the beginning of a process, today being completed by 20th century corporate capitalism, by which every tradition which has previously mediated between man and nature was broken. Before this rupture, animals constituted the first circle of what surrounded man. Perhaps that already suggests too great a distance. They were with man at the centre of his world. Such centrality was of course economic and productive. Whatever the changes in productive means and social organisation, men depended upon animals for food, work, transport, clothing.

Yet to suppose that animals first entered the human imagination as meat or leather or horn is to project a 19th century attitude backwards across the millenia. Animals first entered the imagination as messengers and promises. For example, the domestication of cattle did not begin as a simple prospect of milk and meat. Cattle had magical functions, sometimes oracular, sometimes sacrificial. And the choice of a given species as magical, tameable *and* alimentary was originally determined by the habits, proximity and "invitation" of the animal in question.

> White ox good is my mother
> And we the people of my sister,
> The people of Nyariau Bul . . .
> Friend, great ox of the spreading horns,
> which ever bellows amid the herd,
> Ox of the son of Bul Maloa.

> (*The Nuer: a description of the modes of livelihood and political institutions of a Nilotic people, by* Evans-Pritchard.)

Animals are born, are sentient and are mortal. In these things they resemble man. In their superficial anatomy—less in their deep anatomy—in their habits, in their time, in their physical capacities, they differ from man. They are both like and unlike.

> We know what animals do and what beaver and bears and salmon and other creatures need, because once our men were married to them and they acquired this knowledge from their animal wives.

> (Hawaiian Indians quoted by Lévi-Strauss in *The Savage Mind.*)

The eyes of an animal when they consider a man are attentive and wary. The same animal may well look at other species in the same way. He does not reserve a special look for man. But by no other species except man will the animal's look be recognised as familiar. Other animals are held by the look. Man becomes aware of himself returning the look.

The animal scrutinises him across a narrow abyss of non-comprehension. This is why the man can surprise the animal. Yet the animal—even if domesticated—can also surprise the man. The man too is looking across a similar, but not identical, abyss of non-comprehension. And this is so wherever he looks. He is always looking across ignorance and fear. And so, when he is *being seen* by the animal, he is being seen as his surroundings are seen by him. His recognition of this is what makes the look of the animal familiar. And yet the animal is distinct, and can never be confused with man. Thus, a power is ascribed to the animal, comparable with human power but never coinciding with it. The animal has secrets which, unlike the secrets of caves, mountains, seas, are specifically addressed to man.

The relation may become clearer by comparing the look of an animal with the look of another man. Between two men the two abysses are, in principle, bridged by language. Even if the encounter is hostile and no words are used (even if the two speak different languages), the *existence* of language allows that at least one of them, if not both mutually, is confirmed by the other. Language allows men to reckon with each other as with themselves. (In the confirmation made possible by language, human ignorance and fear may also be confirmed. Whereas in animals fear is a response to signal, in men it is endemic.)

No animal confirms man, either positively or negatively. The animal can be killed and eaten so that its energy is added to that which the hunter already possesses. The animal can be tamed so that it supplies and works for the peasant. But always its lack of common language, its silence, guarantees its distance, its distinctness, its exclusion, from and of man.

Just because of this distinctness, however, an animal's life, never to be confused with a man's, can be seen to run parallel to his. Only in death do the two parallel lines converge and after death, perhaps, cross over to become parallel again: hence the widespread belief in the transmigration of souls.

With their parallel lives, animals offer man a companionship which is different from any offered by human exchange. Different because it is a companionship offered to the loneliness of man as a species.

Such an unspeaking companionship was felt to be so equal that often one finds the conviction that it was man who lacked the capacity to speak with animals—hence the stories and legends of exceptional beings, like Orpheus, who could talk with animals in their own language.

What were the secrets of the animal's likeness with, and unlikeness from man? The secrets whose existence man recognised as soon as he intercepted an animal's look.

In one sense the whole of anthropology, concerned with the passage from nature to culture, is an answer to that question. But there is also a general answer. All the secrets were about animals as an *intercession* between man and his origin. Darwin's evolutionary theory, indelibly stamped as it is with the marks of the European 19th century, nevertheless belongs to a tradition, almost as old as man himself. Animals interceded between man and their origin because they were both like and unlike man.

Animals came from over the horizon. They belonged *there* and *here*. Likewise they were mortal and immortal. An animal's blood flowed like human blood, but its species was undying and each lion was Lion, each ox was Ox. This—maybe the first existential dualism—was reflected in the treatment of animals. They were subjected *and* worshipped, bred *and* sacrificed.

Today the vestiges of this dualism remain among those who live intimately with, and depend upon, animals. A peasant becomes fond of his pig and is glad to salt away its pork.

What is significant, and is so difficult for the urban stranger to understand, is that the two statements in that sentence are connected by an *and* and not by a *but*.

The parallelism of their similar/dissimilar lives allowed animals to provoke some of the first questions and offer answers. The first subject matter for painting was animal. Probably the first paint was animal blood. Prior to that, it is not unreasonable to suppose that the first metaphor was animal. Rousseau, in his *Essay on the Origins of Languages,* maintained that language itself began with metaphor: "As emotions were the first motives which induced man to speak, his first utterances were tropes (metaphors). Figurative language was the first to be born, proper meanings were the last to be found."

If the first metaphor was animal, it was because the essential relation between man and animal was metaphoric. Within that relation what the two terms—man and animal—shared in common revealed what differentiated them. And vice versa.

In his book on totemism, Lévi-Strauss comments on Rousseau's reasoning: "It is because man originally felt himself identical to all those like him (among which, as Rousseau explicitly says, we must include animals) that he came to acquire the capacity to distinguish *himself* as he distinguishes *them*—ie, to use the diversity of species for conceptual support for social differentiation."

To accept Rousseau's explanation of the origins of language is, of course, to beg certain questions (what was the minimal social organisation necessary for the break-through of language?). Yet no search for origin can ever be fully satisfied. The intercession of animals in that search was so common precisely because animals remain ambiguous.

All theories of ultimate origin are only ways of better defining what followed. Those who disagree with Rousseau are contesting a view of man, not a historical fact. What we are trying to define, because the experience is almost lost, is the universal use of animal-signs for charting the experience of the world.

Animals were seen in eight out of twelve signs of the zodiac. Among the Greeks, the sign of each of the twelve hours of the day was an animal. (The first a cat, the last a crocodile.) The Hindus envisaged the earth being carried on the back of an elephant and the elephant on a tortoise. For the Nuer of the southern Sudan (see Roy Willis's *Man and Beast),* "all creatures, including man, originally lived together in fellowship in one camp. Dissension began after Fox persuaded Mongoose to throw a club into Elephant's face. A quarrel ensued and the animals separated; each went its own way and began to live as they now are, and to kill each other. Stomach, which at first lived a life of its own in the bush, entered into man so that now he is always hungry. The sexual organs, which had also been separate, attached themselves to men and women, causing them to desire one another constantly. Elephant taught man how to pound millet so that now he satisfies his hunger only by cease-less labour. Mouse taught man to beget and women to bear. And Dog brought fire to man."

The examples are endless. Everywhere animals offered explanations, or more pre-cisely, lent their name or character to a quality, which like all qualities, was, in its essence, mysterious.

What distinguished man from animals was the human capacity for symbolic thought, the capacity which was inseparable from the development of language in which words were not mere signals, but signifiers of something other than themselves. Yet the first symbols were animals. What distinguished men from animals was born of their relation-ship with them.

The *Iliad* is one of the earliest texts available to us, and in it the use of metaphor still reveals the proximity of man and animal, the proximity from which metaphor itself arose. Homer describes the death of a soldier on the battlefield and then the death of a horse. Both deaths are equally transparent to Homer's eyes, there is no more refraction in one case than the other.

"Meanwhile, Idomeneus struck Erymas on the mouth with his relentless bronze. The metal point of the spear passed right through the lower part of his skull, under the brain and smashed the white bones. His teeth were shattered; both his eyes were filled with blood; and he spurted blood through his nostrils and his gaping mouth. Then the black cloud of Death descended on him." That was a man.

Three pages further on, it is a horse who falls: "Sarpedon, casting second with his shining spear, missed Patroclus but struck his horse Pedasus on the right shoulder. The horse whinnied in the throes of Death, then fell down in the dust and with a great sigh gave up his life." That was animal.

Book 17 of the *Iliad* opens with Menelaus standing over the corpse of Patroclus to prevent the Trojans stripping it. Here Homer uses animals as metaphoric references, to convey, with irony or admiration, the excessive or superlative qualities of different moments. *Without the example of animals,* such moments would have remained indescribable. "Menelaus bestrode his body like a fretful mother cow standing over the first calf she has brought into the world."

A Trojan threatens him, and ironically Menelaus shouts out to Zeus: "Have you ever seen such arrogance? We know the courage of the panther and the lion and the fierce wildboar, the most high-spirited and self-reliant beast of all, but that, it seems, is nothing to the prowess of these sons of Panthous . . . !"

Menelaus then kills the Trojan who threatened him, and nobody dares approach him. "He was like a mountain lion who believes in his own strength and pounces on the finest heifer in a grazing herd. He breaks her neck with his powerful jaws, and then he tears her to pieces and devours her blood and entrails, while all around him the herdsmen and their dogs create a din but keep their distance—they are heartily scared of him and nothing would induce them to close in.

Centuries after Homer, Aristotle, in his *History of Animals,* the first major scientific work on the subject, systematises the comparative relation of man and animal.

In the great majority of animals there are traces of physical qualities and attitudes, which qualities are more markedly differentiated in the case of human beings. For just as we pointed out resemblances in the physical organs, so in a number of animals we observe gentleness and fierceness, mildness or cross-temper, courage or timidity, fear or confidence, high spirits or low cunning, and, with regard to intelligence, something akin to sagacity. Some of these qualities in man, as compared with the corresponding qualities in animals, differ only quantitatively: that is to say, man has more or less of this quality, and an animal has more or less of some other; other qualities in man are represented by analogous and not identical qualities; for example, just as in man we find knowledge, wisdom and sagacity, so in certain animals there exists some other natural potentiality akin to these. The truth of this statement will be the more clearly apprehended if we have regard to the phenomena of childhood: for in children we observe the traces and seeds of what will one day be settled psychological habits, though psychologically a child hardly differs for the time being from an animal . . .

To most modern "educated" readers, this passage, I think, will seem noble but too anthropomorphic. Gentleness, cross-temper, sagacity, they would argue, are not moral qualities which can be ascribed to animals. And the behaviourists would support this objection.

Until the 19th century, however, anthropomorphism was integral to the relation between man and animal and was an expression of their proximity. Anthropomorphism was the residue of the continuous use of animal metaphor. In the last two centuries, animals have gradually disappeared. Today we live without them. And in this new solitude, anthropomorphism makes us doubly uneasy.

The decisive theoretical break came with Descartes. Descartes internalised, *within man,* the dualism implicit in the human relation to animals. In dividing absolutely body from soul, he bequeathed the body to the laws of physics and mechanics, and, since animals were soulless, the animal was reduced to the model of a machine.

The consequences of Descartes's break followed only slowly. A century later, the great zoologist Buffon, although accepting and using the model of the machine in order to classify animals and their capacities, nevertheless displays a tenderness towards animals which temporarily reinstates them as companions. This tenderness is half envious.

What man has to do in order to transcend the animal, to transcend the mechanical within himself, and what his unique spirituality leads to, is often anguish. And so, by comparison and despite the model of the machine, the animal seems to him to enjoy a kind of innocence. The animal has been emptied of experience and secrets, and this new invented "innocence" begins to provoke in man a kind of nostalgia. For the first time, animals are placed in a *receding* past. Buffon, writing on the beaver, says this:

> To the same degree as man has raised himself above the state of nature, animals have fallen below it: conquered and turned into slaves, or treated as rebels and scattered by force, their societies have faded away, their industry has become unproductive, their tentative arts have disappeared; each species has lost its general qualities, all of them retaining only their distinct capacities, developed in some by example, imitation, education, and in others, by fear and necessity during the constant watch for survival. What visions and plans can these soulless slaves have, these relics of the past without power?
>
> Only vestiges of their once marvellous industry remain in far deserted places, unknown to man for centuries, where each species freely used its natural capacities and perfected them in peace within a lasting community. The beavers are perhaps the only remaining example, the last monument to that animal intelligence . . . .

Although such nostalgia towards animals was an 18th century invention, countless *productive* inventions were still necessary—the railway, electricity, the conveyor belt, the canning industry, the motor car, chemical fertilisers—before animals could be marginalised.

During the 20th century, the internal combustion engine displaced draught animals in streets and factories. Cities, growing at an ever increasing rate, transformed the surrounding countryside into suburbs where field animals, wild or domesticated, became rare. The commercial exploitation of certain species (bison, tigers, reindeer) has rendered them almost extinct. Such wild life as remains is increasingly confined to national parks and game reserves.

Eventually, Descartes's model was surpassed. In the first stages of the industrial revolution, animals were used as machines. As also were children. Later, in the so-called post-industrial societies, they are treated as raw material. Animals required for food are processed like manufactured commodities.

> Another giant [plant], now under development in North Carolina, will cover a total of 150,000 hectares but will employ only 1,000 people, one for every 15 hectares. Grains will be sown, nurtured and harvested by machines, including airplanes. They will be fed to the 50,000 cattle and hogs . . . those animals will never touch the ground. They will be bred, suckled and fed to maturity in specially designed pens.

(Susan George's *How the Other Half Dies*.)

This reduction of the animal, which has a theoretical as well as economic history, is part of the same process as that by which men have been reduced to isolated productive and consuming units. Indeed, during this period an approach to animals often prefigured an approach to man. The mechanical view of the animal's work capacity was later applied to that of workers. F. W. Taylor who developed the "Taylorism" of time-motion studies and "scientific" management of industry proposed that work must be "so stupid" and so phlegmatic that he (the worker) "more nearly resembles in his mental make-up the ox than any other type." Nearly all modern techniques of social conditioning were first established with animal experiments. As were also the methods of so-called intelligence testing. Today behaviourists like Skinner imprison the very concept of man within the limits of what they conclude from their artificial tests with animals.

Is there not one way in which animals, instead of disappearing, continue to multiply? Never have there been so many household pets as are to be found today in the cities of the richest countries. In the United States, it is estimated that there are at least forty million dogs, forty million cats, fifteen million cage birds and ten million other pets.

In the past, families of all classes kept domestic animals because they served a useful purpose—guard dogs, hunting dogs, mice-killing cats, and so on. The practice of keeping animals regardless of their usefulness, the keeping, exactly, of *pets* (in the 16th century the word usually referred to a lamb raised by hand) is a modern innovation, and, on the social scale on which it exists today, is unique. It is part of that universal but personal withdrawal into the private small family unit, decorated or furnished with mementoes from the outside world, which is such a distinguishing feature of consumer societies.

The small family living unit lacks space, earth, other animals, seasons, natural temperatures, and so on. The pet is either sterilised or sexually isolated, extremely limited in its exercise, deprived of almost all other animal contact, and fed with artificial foods. This is the material process which lies behind the truism that pets come to resemble their masters or mistresses. They are creatures of their owner's way of life.

Equally important is the way the average owner regards his pet. (Children are, briefly, somewhat different.) The pet *completes* him, offering responses to aspects of his character which would otherwise remain unconfirmed. He can be to his pet what he is not to anybody or anything else. Furthermore, the pet can be conditioned to react as though it, too, recognises this. The pet offers its owner a mirror to a part that is otherwise never reflected. But, since in this relationship the autonomy of both parties has been lost (the owner has become the-special-man-he-is-only-to-his-pet, and the animal has become dependent on its owner for every physical need), the parallelism of their separate lives has been destroyed.

The cultural marginalisation of animals is, of course, a more complex process than their physical marginalisation. The animals of the mind cannot be so easily dispersed. Sayings, dreams, games, stories, superstitions, the language itself, recall them. The animals of the mind, instead of being dispersed, have been co-opted into other categories so that the category *animal* has lost its central importance. Mostly they have been co-opted into the *family* and into the *spectacle.*

Those co-opted into the family somewhat resemble pets. But having no physical needs or limitations as pets do, they can be totally transformed into human puppets. The books and drawings of Beatrix Potter are an early example; all the animal productions of the Disney industry are a more recent and extreme one. In such works the pettiness of current social practices is *universalised* by being projected on to the animal kingdom. The following dialogue between Donald Duck and his nephews is eloquent enough.

Donald: Man, what a day! What a perfect day for fishing, boating, dating or picnicking—only I can't do *any* of these things!

Nephew: Why not, Unca Donald? What's holding you back?

Donald: The Bread of Life boys! As usual, I'm broke and its eons till payday.

Nephew: You could take a walk Unca Donald—go birdwatching.

Donald: (groan!) I may *have to*! But first, I'll wait for the mailman. He may bring something good newswise!

Nephew: Like a cheque from an unknown relative in Moneyville?

Their physical features apart, these animals have been absorbed into the so-called silent majority.

The animals transformed into spectacle have disappeared in another way. In the windows of bookshops at Christmas, a third of the volumes on display are animal picture books. Baby owls or giraffes, the camera fixes them in a domain which, although entirely visible to the camera, will never be entered by the spectator. All animals appear like fish seen through the plate glass of an aquarium. The reasons for this are both technical and ideological: Technically the devices used to obtain ever more arresting images—hidden cameras, telescopic lenses, flashlights, remote controls and so on—combine to produce pictures which carry with them numerous indications of their normal *invisibility.* The images exist thanks only to the existence of a technical clairvoyance.

A recent, very well-produced book of animal photographs (*La Fête Sauvage* by Frédéric Rossif) announces in its preface: "Each of these pictures lasted in real time less than three hundredths of a second, they are far beyond the capacity of the human eye. What we see here is something never before seen, because it is totally invisible."

In the accompanying ideology, animals are always the observed. The fact that they can observe us has lost all significance. They are the objects of our ever-extending knowledge. What we know about them is an index of our power, and thus an index of what separates us from them. The more we know, the further away they are.

Yet in the same ideology, as Lukacs points out in *History and Class Consciousness,* nature is also a value concept. A value opposed to the social institutions which strip man of his natural essence and imprison him. "Nature thereby acquires the meaning of what has grown organically, what was not created by man, in contrast to the artificial structures of human civilisation. At the same time, it can be understood as that aspect of human inwardness which has remained natural, or at least tends or longs to become natural once more." According to this view of nature, the life of a wild animal becomes an ideal, an ideal internalised as a feeling surrounding a repressed desire. The image of a wild animal becomes the starting-point of a daydream: a point from which the day-dreamer departs with his back turned.

The degree of confusion involved is illustrated by the following news story: "London housewife Barbara Carter won a 'grant a wish' charity contest, and said she wanted to kiss and cuddle a lion. Wednesday night she was in a hospital in shock and with throat wounds. Mrs Carter, 46, was taken to the lions' compound of the safari park at Bewdley, Wednesday. As she bent forward to stroke the lioness, Suki, it pounced and dragged her to the ground. Wardens later said, 'We seem to have made a bad error of judgment. We have always regarded the lioness as perfectly safe'."

The treatment of animals in 19th century romantic painting was already an acknowledgement of their impending disappearance. The images are of animals *receding* into a wildness that existed only in the imagination. There was, however, one 19th century artist, who was obsessed by the transformation about to take place, and whose work was an uncanny illustration of it. Grandville published his *Public and Private Life of Animals* in instalments between 1840 and 1842.

At first sight, Grandville's animals, dressed up and performing as men and women, appear to belong to the old tradition, whereby a person is portrayed as an animal so as to reveal more clearly an aspect of his or her character. The device was like putting on a mask, but its function was to unmask. The animal represents the apogee of the character trait in question: the lion, absolute courage: the hare, lechery. The animal once lived near the origin of the quality. It was through the animal that the quality first became recognisable. And so the animal lends it his name.

But as one goes on looking at Grandville's engravings, one becomes aware that the shock which they convey derives, in fact, from the opposite movement to that which one first assumed. These animals are not being "borrowed" to explain people, nothing is being unmasked; on the contrary. These animals have become prisoners of a human/social situation into which they have been press-ganged. The vulture as landlord is more dreadfully rapacious than he is as a bird. The crocodiles at dinner are greedier at the table than they are in the river.

Here animals are not being used as reminders of origin, or as moral metaphors, they are being used *en masse* to "people" situations. The movement that ends with the banality of Disney, began as a disturbing, prophetic dream in the work of Grandville.

The dogs in Grandville's engraving of the dog-pound are in no way canine; they have dogs faces, but what they are suffering is imprisonment *like men*.

The bear is a good father shows a bear dejectedly pulling a pram like any other human bread-winner. Grandville's first volume ends with the words "Goodnight then, dear reader. Go home, lock your cage well, sleep tight and have pleasant dreams. Until tomorrow." Animals and populace are becoming synonymous, which is to say the animals are fading away.

A later Grandville drawing, entitled *The animals entering the steam ark,* is explicit. In the Judaeo-Christian tradition, Noah's Ark was the first ordered assembly of animals and man. The assembly is now over. Grandville shows us the great departure. On a quayside a long queue of different species is filing slowly away, their backs towards us. Their postures suggest all the last minute doubts of emigrants. In the distance is a ramp by which the first have already entered the 19th century ark, which is like an American steamboat. The bear. The lion. The donkey. The camel. The cock. The fox. Exeunt.

"About 1867," according to the *London Zoo Guide,* "a music hall artist called the Great Vance sang a song called *Walking in the zoo is the OK thing to do,* and the word 'zoo' came into everyday use. London Zoo also brought the word 'Jumbo' into the English language. Jumbo was an African elephant of mammoth size, who lived at the zoo between 1865 and 1882. Queen Victoria took an interest in him and eventually he ended his days as the star of the famous Barnum circus which travelled through America—his name living on to describe things of giant proportions."

Public zoos came into existence at the beginning of the period which was to see the disappearance of animals from daily life. The zoo to which people go to meet animals, to observe them, to see them, is, in fact, a monument to the impossibility of such encounters. Modern zoos are an epitaph to a relationship which was as old as man. They are not seen as such because the wrong questions have been addressed to zoos.

When they were founded—the London Zoo in 1828, the Jardin des Plantes in 1793, the Berlin Zoo in 1844, they brought considerable prestige to the national capitals. The prestige was not so different from that which had accrued to the private royal menageries. These menageries, along with gold plate, architecture, orchestras, players, furnishings, dwarfs, acrobats, uniforms, horses, art and food, had been demonstrations of an emperor's or king's power and wealth. Likewise in the 19th century, public zoos were an endorsement of modern colonial power. The capturing of the animals was a symbolic representation of the conquest of all distant and exotic lands. "Explorers" proved their patriotism by sending home a tiger or an elephant. The gift of an exotic animal to the metropolitan zoo became a token in subservient diplomatic relations.

Yet, like every other 19th century public institution, the zoo, however supportive of the ideology of imperialism, had to claim an independent and civic function. The claim was that it was another kind of museum, whose purpose was to further knowledge and public enlightenment. And so the first questions asked of zoos belonged to natural history; it was then thought possible to study the natural life of animals even in such unnatural conditions. A century later, more sophisticated zoologists such as Konrad Lorenz asked behaviouristic and ethological questions, the claimed purpose of which was to discover more about the springs of human action through the study of animals under experimental conditions.

Meanwhile, millions visited the zoos each year out of a curiosity which was both so large, so vague and so personal that it is hard to express in a single question. Today in France 22 million people visit the 200 zoos each year. A high proportion of the visitors were and are children.

Children in the industrialised world are surrounded by animal imagery: toys, cartoons, pictures, decorations of every sort. No other source of imagery can begin to compete with that of animals. The apparently spontaneous interest that children have in animals might lead one to suppose that this has always been the case. Certainly some of the earliest toys (when toys were unknown to the vast majority of the population) were animal. Equally, children's games, all over the world, include real or pretended animals. Yet it was not until the 19th century that reproductions of animals became a regular part of the decor of middle class childhoods—and then, in this century, with the advent of vast display and selling systems like Disney's—of all childhoods.

In the preceding centuries, the proportion of toys which were animal, was small. And these did not pretend to realism, but were symbolic. The difference was that between a traditional hobby horse and a rocking horse: the first was merely a stick with a rudimentary head which children rode like a broom handle: the second was an elaborate "reproduction" of a horse, painted realistically, with real reins of leather, a real mane of hair, and designed movement to resemble that of a horse galloping. The rocking horse was a 19th century invention.

This new demand for verisimilitude in animal toys led to different methods of manufacture. The first stuffed animals were produced, and the most expensive were covered with real animal skin—usually the skin of still-born calves. The same period saw the appearance of soft animals—bears, tigers, rabbits—such as children take to bed with them. Thus the manufacture of realistic animal toys coincides, more or less, with the establishment of public zoos.

The family visit to the zoo is often a more sentimental occasion than a visit to a fair or a football match. Adults take children to the zoo to show them the originals of their "reproductions", and also perhaps in the hope of re-finding some of the innocence of that reproduced animal world which they remember from their own childhood.

The animals seldom live up to the adults' memories, whilst to the children they appear, for the most part, unexpectedly lethargic and dull. (As frequent as the calls of animals in a zoo, are the cries of children demanding: Where is he? Why doesn't he move? Is he dead?) And so one might summarise the felt, but not necessarily expressed question of most visitors as: Why are these animals less than I believed?

And this unprofessional, unexpressed question is the one worth answering.

A zoo is a place where as many species and varieties of animal as possible are collected in order that they can be seen, observed, studied. In principle, each cage is a frame round the animal inside it. Visitors visit the zoo to look at animals. They proceed from cage to cage, not unlike visitors in an art gallery who stop in front of one painting, and then move on to the next or the one after next. Yet in the zoo the view is always wrong. Like an image out of focus. One is so accustomed to this that one scarcely notices it any more; or, rather, the apology habitually anticipates the disappointment, so that the latter is not felt. And the apology runs like this: What do you expect? It's not a dead object you have come to look at, it's alive. It's leading its own life. Why should this coincide with its being properly visible? Yet the reasoning of this apology is inadequate. The truth is more startling.

However you look at these animals, even if the animal is up against the bars, less than a foot from you, looking outwards in the public direction, *you are looking at something that has been rendered absolutely marginal;* and all the concentration you can muster will never be enough to centralise it. Why is this?

Within limits, the animals are free, but both they themselves, and their spectators, presume on their close confinement. The visibility through the glass, the spaces between the bars, or the empty air above the moat, are not what they seem—if they were, then everything would be changed. Thus visibility, space, air, have been reduced to tokens.

The decor, accepting these elements as tokens, sometimes reproduces them to create pure illusion—as in the case of painted prairies or painted rock pools at the back of the boxes for small animals. Sometimes it merely adds further tokens to suggest something of the animal's original landscape—the dead branches of a tree for monkeys, artificial rocks for bears, pebbles and shallow water for crocodiles. These added tokens serve two distinct purposes: for the spectator they are like theatre props: for the animal they constitute the bare minimum of an environment in which they can physically exist.

The animals, isolated from each other and without interaction between species, have become utterly dependent upon their keepers. Consequently most of their responses have been changed. What was central to their interest has been replaced by a passive waiting for a series of arbitrary outside interventions. The events they perceive occurring around them have become as illusory in terms of their natural responses, as the painted prairies. At the same time this very isolation (usually) guarantees their longevity as specimens and facilitates their taxonomic arrangement.

All this is what makes them marginal. The space which they inhabit is artificial. Hence their tendency to bundle towards the edge of it. (Beyond its edges there may be real space.) In some cages the light is equally artificial. In all cases the environment is illusory. Nothing surrounds them except their own lethargy or hyperactivity. They have nothing to act upon—except, briefly, supplied food and—very occasionally—a supplied mate. (Hence their perennial actions become marginal actions without an object.) Lastly, their dependence and isolation have so conditioned their responses that they treat any event which takes place around them—usually it is in front of them, where the public is— as marginal. (Hence their assumption of an otherwise exclusively human attitude—indifference.)

Zoos, realistic animal toys and the widespread commercial diffusion of animal imagery, all began as animals started to be withdrawn from daily life. One could suppose that such innovations were compensatory. Yet in reality the innovations themselves belonged to the same remorseless movement as was dispersing the animals. The zoos, with their theatrical decor for display, were in fact demonstrations of how animals had been rendered absolutely marginal. The realistic toys increased the demand for the new animal puppet: the urban pet. The reproduction of animals in images—as their biological reproduction in birth becomes a rarer and rarer sight—was competitively forced to make animals ever more exotic and remote.

Everywhere animals disappear. In zoos they constitute the living monument to their own disappearance. And in doing so, they provoked their last metaphor. *The Naked Ape, The Human Zoo,* are titles of world bestsellers. In these books the zoologist, Desmond Morris, proposes that the unnatural behaviour of animals in captivity can help us to understand, accept and overcome the stresses involved in living in consumer societies.

All sites of enforced marginalisation —ghettos, shanty towns, prisons, madhouses, concentration camps—have something in common with zoos. But it is both too easy and too evasive to use the zoo as a symbol. The zoo is a demonstration of the relations between man and animals; nothing else. The marginalisation of animals is today being followed by the marginalisation and disposal of the only class who, throughout history, has remained familiar with animals and maintained the wisdom which accompanies that familiarity: the middle and small peasant. The basis of this wisdom is an acceptance of the dualism at the very origin of the relation between man and animal. The rejection of this dualism is probably an important factor in opening the way to modern totalitarianism. But I do not wish to go beyond the limits of that unprofessional, unexpressed but fundamental question asked of the zoo.

The zoo cannot but disappoint. The public purpose of zoos is to offer visitors the opportunity of looking at animals. Yet nowhere in a zoo can a stranger encounter the look of an animal. At the most, the animal's gaze flickers and passes on. They look sideways. They look blindly beyond. They scan mechanically. They have been immunised to encounter, because nothing can any more occupy a *central* place in their attention.

Therein lies the ultimate consequence of their marginalisation. That look between animal and man, which may have played a crucial role in the development of human society, and with which, in any case, all men had always lived until less than a century ago, has been extinguished. Looking at each animal, the unaccompanied zoo visitor is alone. As for the crowds, they belong to a species which has at last been isolated.

This historic loss, to which zoos are a monument, is now irredeemable for the culture of capitalism.

CONSIDER THIS

Roland Barthes and John Berger make a good pair: they offer us two of the most demanding texts in this book, and they're both concerned with turning our ordinary take-it-for-granted worlds upside down. Berger demands that we look at the history of placing animals in zoos (they weren't always there), and at the dear little pets we assume to be naturally domesticated (cats and dogs weren't always household pets). Both Berger and Barthes raise a challenge: nothing is simply there in the world untouched by culture; nothing is simply natural. Resist this pronouncement if you can. Where do your notions of animals and nature come from?

In his books, *Ways of Seeing* and *About Looking,* Berger raises questions about perspective, about appearance and society, about telling stories and taking pictures, about how we see. Why do we take photographs in the first place? What do photographs mean? What can we learn from family albums?

Berger, an Englishman, was born in London in 1926, but has chosen to find other perspectives in a small peasant community in France, where he now lives and writes novels, art criticism, and social, political, and historical commentary.

Youthspeak
Richard Bernstein

If you think *PC* stands for *personal computer,* what do you think *non-PC* means? Anything that is not a PC? Students these days, while familiar with high technology, are using the term *PC* as an abbreviation for *politically correct; non-PC* for its opposite. The term has a leftist connotation and, more likely than not, is used by those who believe the university works hand in glove with the capitalist establishment.

As always, the schools and colleges are producing a lot of slang. Some are invented words; some have been absorbed from street language, rap music, ethnic jargon; others are twists on the special vocabulary of an earlier generation.

Take the word *happening,* which is apparently derived from the "What's happening, man?" of black street talk. Jenny Lyn Bader, a junior at Harvard University, says that it is being used to mean *chic, in vogue, approved.* Ms. Bader avers that *happening* itself, used as an adjective, is very "California." Out there, they are saying things like "He's a happening guy" or "That's a happening outfit."

Groovy, that catchword of the 1960's, has turned into its opposite. It now means *stodgy, old-fashioned, unchic,* a way, for example, of describing, with heavy sarcasm, maroon polyester suits—"Groovy!"

Every student generation, of course, wants to make its mark with its own words. In the 1960's, when I was a student, we used to say *cool it* to encourage calmness when all hell breaks loose. The expression has changed slightly; the word is now *chill* (another usage derived from street talk), usually spoken as a command.

Chill also seems to have replaced *to stand somebody up,* or *to fail to turn up for a date.* "She chilled on me," the young man said, after waiting disconsolately for several hours. (On the other hand, the word *chillin',* with origins in rap music, means *first rate, terrific,* as in, "The concert was chillin'.") *Chill* seems a useful and even instructive term. It puts the ice on humiliation, muffles it in the comfort of jargon, helps the sufferer to feign a bit of indifference. Much of the student lexicon has this euphemistic quality, since students, being of a tender age, are a vulnerable lot.

Connie C. Eble, an associate professor of English at the University of North Carolina at Chapel Hill, who has been collecting student slang for several years—keeping her burgeoning collection on 3 x 5 cards in green file drawers in her office—has a long list of these expressions. Her favorite, she says, is "talking to Ralph on the big white phone."

Ralph, Professor Eble explains, is onomatopoeic, mimicking the sound of regurgitation. *The big white phone* is a metaphor for the toilet bowl, and the expression means *to throw up;* "pray to the porcelain goddess" is a common alternative.

Other examples of the impaired state so common on Saturday nights: *beer goggles,* for a loss of judgment due to drunkenness—as in, "I must have had beer goggles on last night to think he was handsome"; *crispy,* for *extremely hung over.*

Although students may resort to euphemism for certain reactions or behavior, they often favor words that have a raw tone, an anti-intellectual quality—what Professor Eble calls an irreverent, subversive intention—as if to show the world that what they say when they are among themselves is not the stuff they learn in the classroom.

Students have a host of words to refer to other students who study a great deal or who have the sort of seriousness of purpose that, when combined with a pronounced lack of social graces, produces what used to be called "grinds" or "nerds." The new insults are *dweeb, geek, goober* and *wonk*. And *corn dog, goob-a-tron* and *groover.*

A variation on this theme is *granola,* which refers to someone who dresses and acts as students did in the 1960's, perhaps somebody who wears sandals and beads and who says "nerd" instead of "goober." A *buzz crusher* is someone who puts a damper on things, a killjoy. *Bite moose* is a way of telling somebody to get lost, to go to hell.

Students will always be surveying possible objects of romantic or sexual interest. If I remember correctly, we used to *hawk* when we were watching the passing throng. These days, students *scoop,* or *scope,* or *scam.*

On the subject of sex, Professor Eble's students have a rich vocabulary describing various forms of behavior that they either indulge in, or wish they did. There is often a defensive quality to this extreme irreverence—a preemptive unwillingness to care too deeply. *To box tonsils,* for example, means *to kiss passionately,* as does *to play tonsil hockey.* The sex act is *parallel parking* or the *horizontal bop.*

Sleep, on the other hand, is not something that students spend a great deal of time doing, and their words for it seem to reflect this. A *rack monster* is a bed; "to get some rack" is "to get some sleep." A *power nap* is a deep sleep induced by extreme exhaustion.

More than any other group, it would seem, students constantly use words in entirely new ways. Take *random.* When something makes no sense and you are resigned to its utter nonsensicalness, "it is random, really random, totally random." "This really random guy" would not be a flattering way of describing a new acquaintance. And *radical* is no longer the make-the-world-over-in-our-own-image word used ad nauseam during the 60's. *Radical*—often shortened to *rad*—means *great, wonderful, remarkable.*

In the old days, we used to say "awesome" to express an approving wonderment, while *radical,* of course, was associated with things revolutionary. *Far out,* for *astonishing* or *wondrous,* was another common term of 20 years ago that seems to have completely disappeared. It just goes to show how much things haven't really changed; the words may be different, but student preoccupations remain the same. To the 60's generation, *radical* meant pretty much the same thing as *PC,* even if the latter term hadn't been invented yet.

Still, for someone of my generation, it's difficult to think of *radical* as synonymous with *awesome,* just as *far out* is not an allusion to something a great distance away. Perhaps by giving the word *radical* its new twist, students are telling us they aren't so radical anymore. If I objected to this apparent apathy, I would probably be called a *dweeb,* maybe a *granola.* Certainly I would be told to *bite moose*—or should that just be *chill?*

CONSIDER THIS

Richard Bernstein is described as a "cultural correspondent" for *The New York Times*. (What do you know about the "Times"? Is it highbrow? Lowbrow? How does it compare with your local newspaper?) How do you read Bernstein's narrator in "youthspeak"? Who is he writing to? Is he speaking to, of, about, with, or for students? Is he judgmental? Condescending? Uncomfortable? "Nerdy"? Is he comfortable or fluent with youthspeak?

If Dave Barry were to transform this very same material into an essay of his own, how might he begin? What do you have to teach Bernstein about youthspeak that he doesn't know?

The Flood
Sandra Birdsell

Maurice Lafrenier stood on the fire escape on the south side of the hotel and looked with awe at the litter-strewn lake which spread out where the town had been only two weeks ago.

"My God," he said, because he needed to hear the sound of his own voice. He felt abandoned, as though he were the only remaining human on earth.

Across the street, a chunk of dirt-riddled ice battered against the Bank of Montreal. The wind had swept the ice into town during the night. He'd lain shivering in bed, warding off the dampness with the glowing rings of his hotplate and listening to that ice crashing like a battering ram against everything that was his. And his thoughts had run together, had overflowed: his submerged business, the barber chairs bolted to the floor, one hundred years old, at least. Brought up from St. Paul on a steamboat, bequeathed to him by Henry Roy who had been like a father to him and who had also taught him his barbering trade. Mika, in Choritza, awaiting the birth of their sixth child. His other five children, cut off, wood chips floating about until the flood would subside. And his mother. When exhaustion had overcome the noise of the ice, he'd dreamt of his mother who was not dead, but alive in his dream, standing beside the river. She was gathering willow branches for her baskets. She'd looked up suddenly and she was not as he'd remembered, defeated and broken, eyes turned inward. But her broad face was strong and serious, her black eyes demanding his attention. If you have a large family, she said, you will need a bigger boat.

He thought of his boat moored below and smiled. They didn't come any smaller than his rowboat. He pulled his tweed cap tighter on his head and made his way carefully down the ice-coated fire escape. One slip and he'd be gone. Two minutes was all a person could hope for in the icy water even if he could get the hipwaders off. And then the little woman would be a widow, his children fatherless. The town would rush in for a woman like Mika. The town thought Mika had taken him in hand and with her clean habits and Mennonite ways had made him what he was today.

His boat rose and fell with the waves, its wood squeaking and protesting against the piece of wooden sidewalk he'd lashed to the bottom of the fire escape to serve as a dock. Water, as far as the eye could see. Who would have thought that their tired, narrow river could have come to this? He told himself that he was anxious to see how the men at the courthouse had endured the ice. Damned fools, he called them, for letting a few rats in the hotel frighten them from sleeping safely as he did. But he knew his real anxiety. It had surfaced during the night and he needed to reassure himself that this flood had happened gradually, others knew about it too. It was not something that had happened overnight to him alone. He was not the only human being left in the world.

He crouched, moved low in the boat and seated himself in the centre of it. No one accused him of being a careless person anymore. He still took chances, certainly, but not until he was sure everything was shipshape first. He untied the knot which moored his boat to the fire escape. He pushed off from the sidewalk with the oar and sliced deeply through the ice slush floating on the surface as he headed out toward the centre of Main Street. He wondered what condition the courthouse basement would be in. It was not what you'd call shipshape. No matter what Bill Livingston said, he would try and persuade the others to move into the hotel before it was too late.

Up and down the wide street, there wasn't another boat to be seen, no human sounds, just the wind and water rushing against the buildings. He stopped rowing, let the oars sink deep into the water and stared for a moment at the bottom of the boat where his boots had crushed through the film of muddy ice. He felt the oar scrape against one of the drowned vehicles that had been parked on Main Street and he shuddered. It was like disturbing the dead, bumping into submerged things. He began rowing against the current which swept down from the mouth of the Agassiz River, across the cemetery and into town. The bottom of the hotel sign bobbed in the water. The sign had been sheared off by the ice during the night, one of the sounds that had kept him awake. He'd been kept awake all spring by the sounds of the ice cracking and groaning like a woman about to give birth. What are you up to, he'd asked the river. Gather up your skirts, it's time, he said, fancying the sound of his thoughts, the idea that the river was a pregnant woman. But its deep complaining rumble made him uneasy. Then, when the weather turned on them, becoming bitterly cold with freezing rain and snowstorms, he sent his children away and only he and Mika remained. They'd been prepared. The flood hadn't taken him by surprise. The last of the townspeople had been evacuated only three days ago, taken like cattle in boats with the few things they had time to pack and loaded onto railcars at the CN line. Evacuees, flood victims, the *Free Press* called them.

Agassiz evacuation climaxes grim saga, the headline read. The saga of the rivers. The Agassiz and the Red meeting headlong in the north end of town, each carrying full loads into the late-melting tributaries. The pincer-like movement caused the waters near the mouth of the Agassiz to back up in twenty-four hours and run across Main Street at Agassiz Bridge. The saga of the government engineer's stupidity: "We expect nothing this year to approach the '48 flood."

"Expect?" Maurice had said and smacked the report in the newspaper with the back of his hand. "How can anyone expect things from the river? You listen and watch and you can feel what's going to happen. You don't go by charts and expect. It's unpredictable."

The barbershop had become the meeting place for the daily discussions about the possibilities of the river's flooding. Maurice, standing at the barber chair cutting hair, had remained silent until now. He was surprised by his outburst, to find himself throwing aside the need to be agreeable and to keep the peace with all around him at any cost. But if he knew anything well, it was the river. The knowledge was hidden inside him and flowed out naturally when he put his mind to it. The conversation which had centered around Bill Livingston, Agassiz's mayor, trailed away. The men stared at Maurice.

He was standing on an edge. His word on the line. "I'm telling you. If you know what's good for you, then get ready for a doozer of a flood."

In the same tone of voice Bill Livingston had used thirty odd years ago when he'd pulled the blanket up over Maurice's mother's face and said to those present, "Now that's drunk. Dead drunk. But what can you expect?" he got up from the bench, walked over to the barber chair and stuck his red face into Maurice's. "Horse shit," he said. "You'll have everyone running for the hills."

Maurice caught sight of his own reflection in the mirror above the bench where the men had gathered. He moved around the chair gracefully, he was light on his feet. He wore his thick black hair swept back, it made him look taller. He saw the slender back of himself, the blue birthmark on his neck, while in the plate glass mirror above his marble sinks, he could see the front of himself. Mika fed him well. He had the beginning of a double chin and a slight paunch. He saw himself begin to gesture expansively, his hand extended, palm up in a sweeping motion. Look here, he was going to say to Livingston, I'm an agreeable man. He dropped his arm quickly.

"Use your head. Forget what they're saying in Winnipeg. Those dumbells can't forecast a flood until they're up to their asses in water. I predict it'll be the worst flood ever."

Maurice's breath came faster now as he rowed against a small side current where the water swept between two buildings. He'd said it. His word had stood and one by one the men had begun to trust his knowledge and come to him for advice. He passed by the barbershop. He passed by the movie theatre. The sign on the marquee, THE LADY TAKES A SAILOR, used to make him laugh, but because of the ferocity of the flood, now seemed to him to have been a portent filled with meaning.

Freed of the metal graveyard of drowned vehicles that had been parked down Main Street, Maurice stopped rowing. He started up the small outboard motor that Flood Control had issued him. Engine straining, he moved out faster into the current, the bow whacking against the choppy water. And then he saw the lights of the courthouse beaming out at him from the tall narrow windows. So, the basement, she'd held. The courthouse had been built up on its foundation. It was entrenched behind sandbags, but water lapped inches from the top of the dike. He heard the sound of another motor and tension fled from his muscles. He wasn't alone. A boat moved out from behind the courthouse, its hull cutting a deep V down into the water. It veered suddenly in his direction. He shut down his motor and waited. There were three men in the boat, two of them farmers from the area, and Woods, a young RCMP officer whose cap appeared to be held in place by his ears.

"What's up?" Maurice asked.

Stevens, the younger one of the farmers, motioned wearily to the west. All three men looked alike, unshaven, complexions grey from too much coffee and too little sleep. Maurice saw the rifles on the floor of their boat.

"He's got fifty head of Herefords," Woods said. His voice rose to an excited screech. "They're stranded. Haven't been able to get feed into them. Not sure they'll even be there now, not after this ice."

"That was some night," Maurice said. "Have you checked the basement?"

"It's tighter than a drum," Woods said, echoing a Livingston pronouncement.

That was the whole damned trouble. It was too tight. There was too much pressure on the walls. They should flood the basement or the whole thing would pop inward. Damned farmers. The closest they'd been to water before the flood was the dugouts they'd led their cows down to and Woods was still wet behind his big flapping ears.

"What's the situation with the livestock?" he asked.

Stevens lifted one of the rifles and laid it across his knees.

"Plain damned shame. Something should be done," Maurice said. He'd told Stevens, ship 'em out. If you don't, may as well shoot them now. "We're all in the same condition," he said. "My shop, your cattle. We'll have to start over, that's all." He was surprised by his own sudden optimism. It was what Henry Roy would have said. He'd dispensed good will like pills when the going got tough.

"Sure we will," the farmer said. "With what? The money I'll get from this year's crop?"

"Something's bound to come up," Maurice said. "Wait and see, the government will come through in the end."

The farmer spat. "Laurent doesn't even know where Agassiz is," he said. "And all they care about on Broadway is making sure the houses on Wellington Crescent don't get wet."

"Watch, watch," Maurice called out suddenly as a sharp piece of ice swept close to their boats. He angled his craft away into the waves. The ice slid inches from the hull of the other boat and then was gone. The three men watched it pass by. Maurice could tell they were unaware of the danger. It was a wonder there hadn't been a serious accident, what with the mayor heading up the flood control committee. He had a bulldozer for a brain. Ran over people who didn't agree with him. Sent people running off half-cocked to do what they damned well should have done a month ago.

"If that one had hit, you'd have been able to drive a grain truck through the hole," Maurice said. He felt strong, in control. "Keep your eyes open out there. An aluminum boat is no damned good in this stuff." Old Man River. That was the name they'd given to him since his prediction of the flood had come true. Maurice Lafrenier reads the river like it was a newspaper. When the going gets tough, the tough gets going, he told himself. And he'd proven himself. Why do you have to stay, now of all times, Mika had asked. And he couldn't explain to her that for once he didn't want to be on the outside, left out, but dead centre. Because Mika didn't know otherwise. He was the one who went out each morning to check the waters' rising, measured on a pole at Agassiz Bridge, and took the reading to the courthouse where the police radioed it into Winnipeg.

"Why don't you come with us?" Woods asked.

Hold your hand, you mean. "I'm going to take the reading and then cruise around a bit, see what damage I can do. Was there any breakfast? Could eat a horse."

"We'll bring you one," Stevens said.

Maurice chuckled at the bad joke. His spirits rose. He watched the three men head out across the open field. It was just a case of numbers to Ottawa: 28:1. If they could get the real story. Drop Laurent down in the middle of this hell, get his feet wet and he wouldn't say, "No aid for the flood victims."

He tied the boat to the railing on the bridge. He didn't dare venture into the river channel, it was choked with debris. He took the binoculars from beneath the seat and lifted them. The water rose and fell at the level of 29:3 on the pole. He predicted that the crest was days away. Three more feet of water and even the tops of the trees, the only remaining indication of where the river's bank used to be, would be under. They were like scrawny black fingers now, pointing out the sweep and curve of the shoreline where he'd spent that terrible summer hiding from the priest who would take him to be with his brothers in the convent in the city. The memory caught at him suddenly like a camouflaged barb hooking an unsuspecting fish.

He turned the glasses toward the cemetery. His hands shook with the cold. All the grave stones had vanished, had been tumbled by the waves or cut down by the ice and scattered like broken teeth at the bottom of the lake. He lowered the glasses. His eyes stung. His mother and father were there. They were side by side, locked into their early middle years behind the frozen ground. First his father; a railroad accident. And there had been no town clamouring to rescue that widow. She'd been ignored. Left alone to feed three kids with the money she made sewing and from her baskets. And a month later, they buried her. Dead drunk. Lying on her back in the centre of the bed, her head in a pool of grey vomit. Perspiration ran down between his shoulder blades.

Hey, boy, do you want to keep these, Livingston had asked, holding up his mother's beaded moccasins. He'd come with a number of other men, now forgotten, to help carry her away and to poke around through the remains of his family. The wind rose and the icy blast of it seemed to bore straight through his skull. He wished suddenly that he'd been able to find one place for his children instead of shipping them off, piece by piece, to live out the flood among strangers. The ice slush was like crushed glass as it slid swiftly beneath and around his boat. He rowed steadily. His arms began to ache. The sound of a shrill whistle jarred him. He turned quickly and saw the huge white hull of a fishing vessel bearing down on him. It was the *Apex,* bringing supplies to Agassiz.

They plucked Maurice from his rowboat and towed his boat back to town. They took him back to the courthouse, unloaded the supplies, had something to eat, and then Maurice, by virtue of his title, Old Man River, was invited to come along on a cruise about the town to show a newspaper reporter who had come to see for himself what damage had been done.

"This is incredible," the man said. His name was Charles Medlake. The tall thin man spoke to them as though they hadn't already known that the flood was incredible, devastating, all the fancy words he used to describe what had happened to their town. "I've never seen anything like this," he kept saying.

He thinks he pays us a compliment, Maurice thought. Being ten feet under is a great accomplishment. He stood at the railing on the stern of the *Apex* with Bill Livingston and the reporter, listening to their conversation with growing impatience.

"I bloody well hope that we never do again, either," said Bill Livingston, but there was a strange tone of pride in his booming voice. "But according to an Indian legend, this happens every hundred years."

Medlake's hands shook as he cupped them and lit another cigarette. He drew deeply on it and expelled shreds of blue smoke which were snatched by the wind. "Have many people left the area for good?" he asked.

"Hell no. We're tough chickens."

Maurice shifted from one foot to another as the reporter asked the mayor many questions. According to an Indian legend? That was the first he'd heard of it. What Indian? Outwardly, he appeared solid and calm. His parka was unzipped, revealing his green curling sweater with the white rearing bucks on it. Mika's mother had knit it for him. He chewed thoughtfully on a toothpick, moving it from one side of his mouth to the other.

"This isn't the worst of it," the mayor said. "We haven't been east of town yet. The ice took out three or four houses."

"I've seen enough for now," the man said. He flicked his half-smoked cigarette over the stern. "Listen, the luckiest house in Agassiz is the worst hit in Winnipeg. I never saw anything this bad in the city."

"Really?" the mayor said.

It was what Maurice had suspected. Once they'd figured it out, that the same river that was flooding Agassiz would eventually flood Winnipeg, they screamed bloody murder. Squeaky wheel gets the grease.

"I'd like to get back to the courthouse and call the paper to send out a photographer. This should be recorded."

Livingston called out directions to the pilot. The fishing boat began a slow wide turn.

"The feds have got to open their eyes to this," Livingston said. "Pictures would help. We estimate that property damage alone will be close to five million dollars. Then there's the months of lost revenue to consider." He turned suddenly to Maurice. "How long has it been since you've earned a cent, Maurie?"

"Eh?" He was jolted loose from his tumbling thoughts.

"I said, how are you going to manage to feed the kiddies when they get home? Let alone afford the lumber to rebuild the house and buy new furniture?"

"Well, I. . .," Maurice began and stopped. I was prepared. My furniture is high and dry. We took what was left of the preserves to Mika's sister's place. But there was something in Livingston's tone of voice that kept him quiet. He sensed that there was more here than an innocent question.

Livingston didn't wait for his reply. "We must be compensated. We're going to need money and lots of it. Interest-free money for the business community to replace their inventory. I've lost my entire stock of hardware. The farmers, their seed and fertilizer. And people like Maurie, here, they'll need money to feed and clothe the family. He's got six kids."

"Five," Maurice said. "I've got five." He was stung. Money for people like Maurie, here. How are you going to feed your family? A straightforward question. But it rankled. It was intended to remind him that at one time he'd swept their floors, carried out their shit pails and shovelled clean the barns. He'd fallen down drunk in the street. He'd been looked upon with pity or scorn. And that he had risen only so far in twenty years that his main concern would be how to feed six mouths, nothing more. He sees me as being another flood victim, same as all the others. Maurice freed his hands from his parka pockets and cut the air in front of the two men in an impatient motion.

"Compensation, to be sure," he said.

"What was that?" Charles Medlake spoke directly to him for the first time.

"Compensation, to be sure. By all means." His was the quiet reasonable voice of Henry Roy, his mentor. He hoped it was the voice of someone who would listen for so long to the clamour of others and then, with a few chosen words, bring clarity to their ramblings so as to make them look ridiculous. "But look here, compensation and interest-free loans are only a small part of the whole picture," he continued.

The newsman moved in closer. He began to make notes on a tablet. "Just what do you think should be done?"

"Many things. Certainly, I could use a hand just as everyone else in this town could use a hand. I'm a business man too. I've lost more than furniture." He avoided Livingston's eyes. "But I personally wouldn't care if I didn't get a penny from the government if we could take steps to make certain that this here flood will never happen again."

Livingston laughed outright and turned away.

"But how is that possible?" Medlake asked.

Maurice was unsettled by the laughter. He shoved his hands back into his pockets. They were heading back toward the courthouse. They had circled the town and approached the stone building from behind, moving slowly down Elm Avenue. The trees were bare, bark black with orange rusty-looking growths in the crooks of limbs. A chair was caught in the lower branches of one tree. Maurice cleared his throat to speak. Build a sewage treatment plant so we no longer shit and piss on the river. We didn't have floods like this one until we got the running water. My God, the river, she doesn't pretend to be beautiful, but some honour is due, eh? Lure the goldeye and pickerel back with clean water. Forget the Indian legend that says we have no say in the matter. We should remember the river. She gave this region its life. But he knew they saw the river with different eyes. To them it was heavy, sluggish and ugly, a breeding ground for mosquitoes and eels.

"It's impossible to prevent flooding," Livingston said. He took Medlake by the elbow and attempted to steer him away by pointing out some particular damage.

"Wait, let him finish," Medlake said.

"We need to look to the future," Maurice said.

"How?"

"With all our minds, we should be able to come up with something instead of just saying it happens every hundred years. We should think about building a permanent dike around the town, for instance, or dig drainage ditches in the country to let the spring run-off enter into the Red further downstream."

"Winnipeg would never go for that," Livingston interrupted. "Because it would mean more water for them."

He speaks as though he has just bit into a lemon, Maurice thought.

"There must be a way around it," Medlake said.

The boat nudged slowly into the courthouse yard toward a large oak tree in the centre of it. The pilot cut the engine and Maurice was jolted forward as the craft met bark with a hollow thud. The *Apex* whistled its arrival. Dark shapes appeared at the window and then the back door swung open. Woods and Stevens stepped out on the stairs. They climbed into Maurice's rowboat and began rowing toward them. Woods cupped his hands to his mouth. "Survivors," he shouted. "We found two women and a child stranded on the roof of a granary."

"Listen," Medlake said to Maurice. "I'd like to talk to you later on. What you say makes good sense."

Maurice felt the careful attentive posture of Livingston's large body. "Suits me," he said, trying to sound casual.

"Where can I find you?"

"If I'm not here—"

"He's over at the hotel," the mayor finished. "Maurie here doesn't like our company. He's always been what you might call a lone wolf."

Maurice's face grew warm. "Shoot, it's not that," he said. He felt as though his mouth was full of marbles. He juggled words in his mind. "It's not that. It's the basement. She's going to cave in."

"What?" Medlake asked. "And you're taking me in there?"

"He doesn't know what he's talking about," Livingston said. "The walls are two feet thick. This place is built like a brick shithouse."

The rowboat came alongside and they got into it. Maurice sat between the two men, slouched down into his parka, his fists curled tightly inside his pockets. Blow, goddammit, he urged as they approached the courthouse. Now. He imagined walls crumbling.

They removed their hipwaders in the basement. Maurice sat on the cot in the jail cell and leaned against the rough Tyndalstone wall and closed his eyes.

"Well, Maurie," Livingston said and laughed. "Drainage ditches, eh? It looks as though the wrong one ran for mayor."

Maurice didn't answer. He could see his parents' fresh graves, a mixture of yellow clay and top-soil. This room carried the memory. The priest had found him beside the river, trying to build a raft so that he could float downstream to his mother's people. And had agreed, Maurice could stay. He didn't have to join his brothers in the convent in the city. He'd sat in this very cell, tracing the outlines of strange creatures locked in the stone without knowing what they were while the men of the town decided his fate. Send for his mother's people, the priest advised. And so he waited it out in this room for a full week. They didn't want me, he asked. Henry Roy winked. You wouldn't have wanted them, he said. I never sent the message. And he took Maurice in and gave him work in the hotel. It would have turned out well if it hadn't been that it took too long for a town to forget a person who would die suffocating on their own vomit. Dead drunk.

"Come on, Old Man River," Livingston said and clapped him on the shoulder. "Let's go on up and meet those survivors."

Maurice followed him into the main hall. Two women and the child huddled beneath blankets within the circle of men. The men parted to let Maurice and Livingston through. The women and child were of mixed blood, Maurice realized instantly. Mongrels. The women had identical expressions, wide smiles, like fools, displaying their rotting teeth. Don't let anyone tell you different, Henry Roy had said, mongrels don't make better dogs. But the child studied Maurice with the same serious black eyes as his mother had in his dream last night. If you're going to have a large family, she said, you will need a bigger boat. These people didn't even have a boat. Not even a small one. The men seemed to be waiting for him to do something.

"Do you speak French?" Maurice asked the women.

They laughed and covered the gaping holes in their teeth with hands that looked to be tinged by wood smoke.

Maurice felt the floor move.

"No, no, not French," Livingston said. "You never know. You could be related. Say something to them in Indian."

"In a pig's ass," Maurice said, his anger breaking loose in upraised fists. The floor beneath him tilted. And then there was a sound, like thunder, beneath them. Relief flooded every part of his body and his knees suddenly felt weak. He felt like laughing hysterically.

Stevens ran into the room. "Clear out," he yelled. "The basement just went."

The reporter scrambled for his parka. Maurice led the women and child to the back door. They were calm. They pulled their blankets about themselves and walked slowly, as though they were accustomed to calamities. Bill Livingston ran to the tables, gathered papers to his chest, set them back down again. Maurice heard the roar of the water filling the basement, flooding the little room. He lifted the child quickly and handed her to Stevens. When she saw the boat, she clung to Maurice's sweater and began to cry. He peeled her loose and handed her down. I was right, he told himself. Once again, I was right. He felt like laughing and he felt like crying. Thank God, the *Apex* was big enough, it would hold them all. It would carry the whole damned works of them to the hills.

CONSIDER THIS

When does it begin to dawn on you that Maurice Lafrenier (what kind of name is *Maurice? Lafrenier?*) is an Indian? Do you need to reread the story to make certain that you've picked up the right clues? Consider the second line in the second paragraph: "He felt abandoned, as though he were the only remaining human on earth." Now consider Lafrenier's state of mind at the end of the story. How would you characterize the changes in his consciousness? How would you characterize the clashes of culture—or the clashes of cultural knowledge—in the story?

Sandra Birdsell, a Canadian, grew up in a small town in Manitoba and now lives in Winnipeg, where she writes fiction, drama, and film scripts. Her first novel, *The Missing Child,* was published in 1989.

Shakespeare in the Bush
Laura Bohannan

Just before I left Oxford for the Tiv in West Africa, conversation turned to the season at Stratford. "You Americans," said a friend, "often have difficulty with Shakespeare. He was, after all, a very English poet, and one can easily misinterpret the universal by misunderstanding the particular."

I protested that human nature is pretty much the same the whole world over; at least the general plot and motivation of the greater tragedies would always be clear—everywhere— although some details of custom might have to be explained and difficulties of translation might produce other slight changes. To end an argument we could not conclude, my friend gave me a copy of *Hamlet* to study in the African bush: it would, he hoped, lift my mind above its primitive surroundings, and possibly I might, by prolonged meditation, achieve the grace of correct interpretation.

It was my second field trip to that African tribe, and I thought myself ready to live in one of its remote sections—an area difficult to cross even on foot. I eventually settled on the hillock of a very knowledgeable old man, the head of a homestead of some hundred and forty people, all of whom were either his close relatives or their wives and children. Like the other elders of the vicinity, the old man spent most of his time performing ceremonies seldom seen these days in the more accessible parts of the tribe. I was delighted. Soon there would be three months of enforced isolation and leisure, between the harvest that takes place just before the rising of the swamps and the clearing of new farms when the water goes down. Then, I thought, they would have even more time to perform ceremonies and explain them to me.

I was quite mistaken. Most of the ceremonies demanded the presence of elders from several homesteads. As the swamps rose, the old men found it too difficult to walk from one homestead to the next, and the ceremonies gradually ceased. As the swamps rose even higher, all activities but one came to an end. The women brewed beer from maize and millet. Men, women, and children sat on their hillocks and drank it.

People began to drink at dawn. By midmorning the whole homestead was singing, dancing, and drumming. When it rained, people had to sit inside their huts: there they drank and sang or they drank and told stories. In any case, by noon or before, I either had to join the party or retire to my own hut and my books. "One does not discuss serious matters when there is beer. Come, drink with us." Since I lacked their capacity for the thick native beer, I spent more and more time with *Hamlet*. Before the end of the second month, grace descended on me. I was quite sure that *Hamlet* had only one possible interpretation, and that one universally obvious.

Early every morning, in the hope of having some serious talk before the beer party, I used to call on the old man at his reception hut—a circle of posts supporting a thatched roof above a low mud wall to keep out wind and rain. One day I crawled through the low doorway and found most of the men of the homestead sitting huddled in their ragged cloths on stools, low plank beds, and reclining chairs, warming themselves against the chill of the rain around a smoky fire. In the center were three pots of beer. The party had started.

The old man greeted me cordially. "Sit down and drink." I accepted a large calabash full of beer, poured some into a small drinking gourd, and tossed it down. Then I poured some more into the same gourd for the man second in seniority to my host before I handed my calabash over to a young man for further distribution. Important people shouldn't ladle beer themselves.

"It is better like this," the old man said, looking at me approvingly and plucking at the thatch that had caught in my hair. "You should sit and drink with us more often. Your servants tell me that when you are not with us, you sit inside your hut looking at a paper."

The old man was acquainted with four kinds of "papers": tax receipts, bride price receipts, court fee receipts, and letters. The messenger who brought him letters from the chief used them mainly as a badge of office, for he always knew what was in them and told the old man. Personal letters for the few who had relatives in the government or mission stations were kept until someone went to a large market where there was a letter writer and reader. Since my arrival, letters were brought to me to be read. A few men also brought me bride price receipts, privately, with requests to change the figures to a higher sum. I found moral arguments were of no avail, since in-laws are fair game, and the technical hazards of forgery difficult to explain to an illiterate people. I did not wish them to think me silly enough to look at any such paper for days on end, and I hastily explained that my "paper" was one of the "things of long ago" of my country.

"Ah," said the old man. "Tell us."

I protested that I was not a storyteller. Storytelling is a skilled art among them; their standards are high, and the audiences critical—and vocal in their criticism. I protested in vain. This morning they wanted to hear a story while they drank. They threatened to tell me no more stories until I told them one of mine. Finally, the old man promised that no one would criticize my style "for we know you are struggling with our language." "But," put in one of the elders, "you must explain what we do not understand, as we do when we tell you our stories." Realizing that here was my chance to prove *Hamlet* universally intelligible, I agreed.

The old man handed me some more beer to help me on with my storytelling. Men filled their long wooden pipes and knocked coals from the fire to place in the pipe bowls; then, puffing contentedly, they sat back to listen. I began in the proper style.

"Not yesterday, not yesterday, but long ago, a thing occurred. One night three men were keeping watch outside the homestead of the great chief, when suddenly they saw the former chief approach them."

"Why was he no longer their chief?"

"He was dead," I explained. "That is why they were troubled and afraid when they saw him."

"Impossible," began one of the elders, handing his pipe on to his neighbor, who interrupted, "Of course it wasn't the dead chief. It was an omen sent by a witch. Go on."

Slightly shaken, I continued. "One of these three was a man who knew things"—the closest translation for scholar, but unfortunately it also meant witch. The second elder looked triumphantly at the first. "So he spoke to the dead chief saying, 'Tell us what we must do so you may rest in your grave,' but the dead chief did not answer. He vanished, and they could see him no more. Then the man who knew things—his name was Horatio—said this event was the affair of the dead chief's son, Hamlet."

There was a general shaking of heads round the circle. "Had the dead chief no living brothers? Or was this son the chief?"

"No," I replied. "That is, he had one living brother who became the chief when the elder brother died."

The old men muttered: such omens were matters for chiefs and elders, not for youngsters; no good could come of going behind a chief's back; clearly Horatio was not a man who knew things.

"Yes, he was," I insisted, shooing a chicken away from my beer. "In our country the son is next to the father. The dead chief's younger brother had become the great chief. He had also married his elder brother's widow only about a month after the funeral."

"He did well," the old man beamed and announced to the others, "I told you that if we knew more about Europeans, we would find they really were very like us. In our country also," he added to me, "the younger brother marries the elder brother's widow and becomes the father of his children. Now, if your uncle, who married your widowed mother, is your father's full brother, then he will be a real father to you. Did Hamlet's father and uncle have one mother?"

His question barely penetrated my mind; I was too upset and thrown too far off balance by having one of the most important elements of *Hamlet* knocked straight out of the picture. Rather uncertainly I said that I thought they had the same mother, but I wasn't sure—the story didn't say. The old man told me severely that these genealogical details made all the difference and that when I got home I must ask the elders about it. He shouted out the door to one of his younger wives to bring his goatskin bag.

Determined to save what I could of the mother motif, I took a deep breath and began again. "The son Hamlet was very sad because his mother had married again so quickly. There was no need for her to do so, and it is our custom for a widow not to go to her next husband until she has mourned for two years."

"Two years is too long," objected the wife, who had appeared with the old man's battered goatskin bag. "Who will hoe your farms for you while you have no husband?"

"Hamlet," I retorted without thinking, "was old enough to hoe his mother's farms himself. There was no need for her to remarry." No one looked convinced. I gave up. "His mother and the great chief told Hamlet not to be sad, for the great chief himself would be a father to Hamlet. Furthermore, Hamlet would be the next chief: therefore he must stay to learn the things of a chief. Hamlet agreed to remain, and all the rest went off to drink beer."

While I paused, perplexed at how to render Hamlet's disgusted soliloquy to an audience convinced that Claudius and Gertrude had behaved in the best possible manner, one of the younger men asked me who had married the other wives of the dead chief.

"He had no other wives," I told him.

"But a chief must have many wives! How else can he brew beer and prepare food for all his guests?"

I said firmly that in our country even chiefs had only one wife, that they had servants to do their work, and that they paid them from tax money.

It was better, they returned, for a chief to have many wives and sons who would help him hoe his farms and feed his people; then everyone loved the chief who gave much and took nothing—taxes were a bad thing.

I agreed with the last comment, but for the rest fell back on their favorite way of fobbing off my questions: "That is the way it is done, so that is how we do it."

I decided to skip the soliloquy. Even if Claudius was here thought quite right to marry his brother's widow, there remained the poison motif, and I knew they would disapprove of fratricide. More hopefully I resumed, "That night Hamlet kept watch with the three who had seen his dead father. The dead chief again appeared, and although the others were afraid, Hamlet followed his dead father off to one side. When they were alone, Hamlet's dead father spoke."

"Omens can't talk!" The old man was emphatic.

"Hamlet's dead father wasn't an omen. Seeing him might have been an omen, but he was not." My audience looked as confused as I sounded. "It *was* Hamlet's dead father. It was a thing we call a 'ghost.'" I had to use the English word, for unlike many of the neighboring tribes, these people didn't believe in the survival after death of any individuating part of the personality.

"What is a 'ghost'? An omen?"

"No, a 'ghost' is someone who is dead but who walks around and can talk, and people can hear him and see him but not touch him."

They objected. "One can touch zombis."

"No, no! It was not a dead body the witches had animated to sacrifice and eat. No one else made Hamlet's dead father walk. He did it himself."

"Dead men can't walk," protested my audience as one man.

I was quite willing to compromise "A 'ghost' is the dead man's shadow."

But again they objected. "Dead men cast no shadows."

"They do in my country," I snapped.

The old man quelled the babble of disbelief that arose immediately and told me with that insincere, but curteous, agreement one extends to the fancies of the young, ignorant, and superstitious, "No doubt in your country the dead can also walk without being zombis." From the depths of his bag he produced a withered fragment of kola nut, bit off one end to show it wasn't poisoned, and handed me the rest as a peace offering.

"Anyhow," I resumed, "Hamlet's dead father said that his own brother, the one who became chief, had poisoned him. He wanted Hamlet to avenge him. Hamlet believed this in his heart, for he did not like his father's brother." I took another swallow of beer. "In the country of the great chief, living in the same homestead, for it was a very large one, was an important elder who was often with the chief to advise and help him. His name was Polonius. Hamlet was courting his daughter, but her father and her brother . . . [I cast hastily about for some tribal analogy] warned her not to let Hamlet visit her when she was alone on her farm, for he would be a great chief and so could not marry her."

"Why not?" asked the wife, who had settled down on the edge of the old man's chair. He frowned at her for asking stupid questions and growled, "They lived in the same homestead."

"That was not the reason," I informed them. "Polonius was a stranger who lived in the homestead because he helped the chief, not because he was a relative."

"Then why couldn't Hamlet marry her?"

"He could have," I explained, "But Polonius didn't think he would. After all, Hamlet was a man of great importance who ought to marry a chief's daughter, for in his country a man could have only one wife. Polonius was afraid that if Hamlet made love to his daughter, then no one else would give a high price for her."

"That might be true," remarked one of the shrewder elders, "but a chief's son would give his mistress's father enough presents and patronage to more than make up the difference. Polonius sounds like a fool to me."

"Many people think he was," I agreed. "Meanwhile Polonius sent his son Laertes off to Paris to learn the things of that country, for it was the homestead of a very great chief indeed. Because he was afraid that Laertes might waste a lot of money on beer and women and gambling, or get into trouble by fighting, he sent one of his servants to Paris secretly, to spy out what Laertes was doing. One day Hamlet came upon Polonius's daughter Ophelia. He behaved so oddly he frightened her. Indeed"—I was fumbling for words to express the dubious quality of Hamlet's madness—"the chief and many others had also noticed that when Hamlet talked one could understand the words but not what they meant. Many people thought that he had become mad." My audience suddenly became much more attentive. "The great chief wanted to know what was wrong with Hamlet, so he sent for two of Hamlet's age mates [school friends would have taken long explanation] to talk to Hamlet and find out what troubled his heart. Hamlet, seeing that they had been bribed by the chief to betray him, told them nothing. Polonius, however, insisted that Hamlet was mad because he had been forbidden to see Ophelia, whom he loved."

"Why," inquired a bewildered voice, "should any bewitch Hamlet on that account?"

"Bewitch him?"

"Yes, only witchcraft can make anyone mad, unless, of course, one sees the beings that lurk in the forest."

I stopped being a storyteller, took out my notebook and demanded to be told more about these two causes of madness. Even while they spoke and I jotted notes, I tried to calculate the effect of this new factor on the plot. Hamlet had not been exposed to the beings that lurk in the forests. Only his relatives in the male line could bewitch him. Barring relatives not mentioned by Shakespeare, it had to be Claudius who was attempting to harm him. And, of course, it was.

For the moment I staved off questions by saying that the great chief also refused to believe that Hamlet was mad for the love of Ophelia and nothing else. "He was sure that something much more important was troubling Hamlet's heart."

"Now Hamlet's age mates," I continued, "had brought with them a famous storyteller. Hamlet decided to have this man tell the chief and all his homestead a story about a man who had poisoned his brother because he desired his brother's wife and wished to be chief himself. Hamlet was sure the great chief could not hear the story without making a sign if he was indeed guilty, and then he would discover whether his dead father had told him the truth."

The old man interrupted, with deep cunning, "Why should a father lie to his son?" he asked.

I hedged: "Hamlet wasn't sure that it really was his dead father." It was impossible to say anything, in that language, about devil-inspired visions.

"You mean," he said, "it actually was an omen, and he knew witches sometimes send false ones. Hamlet was a fool not to go to one skilled in reading omens and divining the truth in the first place. A man-who-sees-the-truth could have told him how his father died, if he really had been poisoned, and if there was witchcraft in it; then Hamlet could have called the elders to settle the matter."

The shrewd elder ventured to disagree. "Because his father's brother was a great chief, one-who-sees-the-truth might therefore have been afraid to tell it. I think it was for that reason that a friend of Hamlet's father—a witch and an elder— sent an omen so his friend's son would know. Was the omen true?"

"Yes," I said, abandoning ghosts and the devil; a witch-sent omen it would have to be. "It was true, for when the storyteller was telling his tale before all the homestead, the great chief rose in fear. Afraid that Hamlet knew his secret he planned to have him killed."

The stage set of the next bit presented some difficulties of translation. I began cautiously, "The great chief told Hamlet's mother to find out from her son what he knew. But because a woman's children are always first in her heart, he had the important elder Polonius hide behind a cloth that hung against the wall of Hamlet's mother's sleeping hut. Hamlet started to scold his mother for what she had done."

There was a shocked murmur from everyone. A man should never scold his mother.

"She called out in fear, and Polonius moved behind the cloth. Shouting, 'A rat!' Hamlet took his machete and slashed through the cloth." I paused for dramatic effect. "He had killed Polonius!"

The old men looked at each other in supreme disgust. "That Polonius truly was a fool and a man who knew nothing! What child would not know enough to shout, 'It's me!'" With a pang, I remembered that these people are ardent hunters, always armed with bow, arrow, and machete; at the first rustle in the grass an arrow is aimed and ready, and the hunter shouts "Game!" If no human voice answers immediately, the arrow speeds on its way. Like a good hunter Hamlet had shouted, "A rat!"

I rushed in to save Polonius's reputation. "Polonius did speak. Hamlet heard him. But he thought it was the chief and wished to kill him to avenge his father. He had meant to kill him earlier that evening. . . ." I broke down, unable to describe to these pagans, who had no belief in individual afterlife, the difference between dying at one's prayers and dying "unhousell'd, disappointed, unaneled."

This time I had shocked my audience seriously. "For a man to raise his hand against his father's brother and the one who had become his father—that is a terrible thing. The elders ought to let such a man be bewitched."

I nibbled at my kola nut in some perplexity, then pointed out that after all the man had killed Hamlet's father.

"No," pronounced the old man, speaking less to me than to the young men sitting behind the elders. "If your father's brother has killed your father, you must appeal to your father's age mates; *they* may avenge him. No man may use violence against his senior relatives." Another thought struck him. "But if his father's brother had indeed been wicked enough to bewitch Hamlet and make him mad that would be a good story indeed, for it would be his fault that Hamlet, being mad, no longer had any sense and thus was ready to kill his father's brother."

There was a murmur of applause. *Hamlet* was again a good story to them, but it no longer seemed quite the same story to me. As I thought over the coming complications of plot and motive, I lost courage and decided to skim over dangerous ground quickly.

"The great chief," I went on, "was not sorry that Hamlet had killed Polonius. It gave him a reason to send Hamlet away, with his two treacherous age mates, with letters to a chief of a far country, saying that Hamlet should be killed. But Hamlet changed the writing on their papers, so that the chief killed his age mates instead." I encountered a reproachful glare from one of the men whom I had told undetectable forgery was not merely immoral but beyond human skill. I looked the other way.

"Before Hamlet could return, Laertes came back for his father's funeral. The great chief told him Hamlet had killed Polonius. Laertes swore to kill Hamlet because of this, and because his sister Ophelia, hearing her father had been killed by the man she loved, went mad and drowned in the river."

"Have you already forgotten what we told you?" The old man was reproachful. "One cannot take vengeance on a madman; Hamlet killed Polonius in his madness. As for the girl, she not only went mad, she was drowned. Only witches can make people drown. Water itself can't hurt anything. It is merely something one drinks and bathes in."

I began to get cross. "If you don't like the story, I'll stop."

The old man made soothing noises and himself poured me some more beer. "You tell the story well, and we are listening. But it is clear that the elders of your country have never told you what the story really means. No, don't interrupt! We believe you when you say your marriage customs are different, or your clothes and weapons. But people are the same everywhere; therefore, there are always witches and it is we, the elders, who know how witches work. We told you it was the great chief who wished to kill Hamlet, and now your own words have proved us right. Who were Ophelia's male relatives?"

"There were only her father and her brother." Hamlet was clearly out of my hands.

"There must have been many more; this also you must ask of your elders when you get back to your country. From what you tell us, since Polonius was dead, it must have been Laertes who killed Ophelia, although I do not see the reason for it."

We had emptied one pot of beer, and the old men argued the point with slightly tipsy interest. Finally one of them demanded of me, "What did the servant of Polonius say on his return?"

With difficulty I recollected Reynaldo and his mission. "I don't think he did return before Polonius was killed."

"Listen," said the elder, "and I will tell you how it was and how your story will go, then you may tell me if I am right. Polonius knew his son would get into trouble, and so he did. He had many fines to pay for fighting, and debts from gambling. But he had only two ways of getting money quickly. One was to marry off his sister at once, but it is difficult to find a man who will marry a woman desired by the son of a chief. For if the chief's heir commits adultery with your wife, what can you do? Only a fool calls a case against a man who will someday be his judge. Therefore Laertes had to take the second way: he killed his sister by witchcraft, drowning her so he could secretly sell her body to the witches."

I raised an objection. "They found her body and buried it. Indeed Laertes jumped into the grave to see his sister once more—so, you see, the body was truly there. Hamlet, who had just come back, jumped in after him."

"What did I tell you?" The elder appealed to the others. "Laertes was up to no good with his sister's body. Hamlet prevented him, because the chief's heir, like a chief, does not wish any other man to grow rich and powerful. Laertes would be angry, because he would have killed his sister without benefit to himself. In our country he would try to kill Hamlet for that reason. Is this not what happened?"

"More or less," I admitted. "When the great chief found Hamlet was still alive, he encouraged Laertes to try to kill Hamlet and arranged a fight with machetes between them. In the fight both the young men were wounded to death. Hamlet's mother drank the poisoned beer that the chief meant for Hamlet in case he won the fight. When he saw his mother die of poison, Hamlet, dying, managed to kill his father's brother with his machete."

"You see, I was right!" exclaimed the elder.

"That was a very good story," added the old man, "and you told it with very few mistakes. There was just one more error, at the very end. The poison Hamlet's mother drank was obviously meant for the survivor of the fight, whichever it was. If Laertes had won, the great chief would have poisoned him, for no one would know that he arranged Hamlet's death. Then, too, he need not fear Laertes' witchcraft; it takes a strong heart to kill one's only sister by witchcraft.

"Sometime," concluded the old man, gathering his ragged toga about him, "you must tell us some more stories of your country. We, who are elders, will instruct you in their true meaning, so that when you return to your own land your elders will see that you have not been sitting in the bush, but among those who know things and who have taught you wisdom."

CONSIDER THIS

"I protested that human nature is pretty much the same the whole world over," Laura Bohannan, a native New Yorker, proclaims in her second paragraph. This is a story against herself, about her own limited perspective as an anthropologist. She demonstrates how she misreads literature and culture. She learns lessons that Barthes and Berger are trying to teach: everything we see, do, or say or read is situated in a particular culture and a specific history, and even *Hamlet*, that great Shakespearean play, is no exception.

How do you read *Hamlet*? Do you need to have read Shakespeare's play to understand this essay? If you have read it, how would you tell the story to the uninitiated? As a ghost story? As a moral lesson to be learned? As a family story? A social history? Would you include such cultural knowledge as these lines:

- This above all: to thine own self be true.
- Neither a borrower, nor a lender be.
- Something is rotten in the state of Denmark.
- Get thee to a nunnery.
- To be or not to be: that is the question.

Love, with Knowledge Aforethought
Steve Brody

A common misconception among youngsters attending school is that their teachers were child prodigies. Who else but a bookworm, prowling the libraries and disdaining the normal youngster's propensity for play rather than study, would grow up to be a teacher anyway?

I tried desperately to explain to my students that the image they had of me as an ardent devotee of books and homework during my adolescence was a bit out of focus. Au contraire! I hated compulsory education with a passion. I could never quite accept the notion of having to go to school while the fish were biting.

Consequently, my grades were somewhat bearish. That's how my father, who dabbled in the stock market, described them. Presenting my report card for my father to sign was like serving him a subpoena. At midterm and other sensitive periods, my father kept a low profile.

But in my sophomore year, something beautiful and exciting happened. Cupid aimed his arrow and struck me squarely in the heart. All at once, I enjoyed going to school, if only to gaze at the lovely face beneath the raven tresses in English II. My princess sat near the pencil sharpener, and that year I ground up enough pencils to fuel a campfire.

Alas, Debbie was far beyond my wildest dreams. We were separated not only by five rows of desks, but by about 50 I.Q. points. She was the top student in English II, the apple of Mrs. Larrivee's eye. I envisioned how eagerly Debbie's father awaited her report card.

Occasionally, Debbie would catch me staring at her, and she would flash a smile—an angelic smile that radiated enlightenment and quickened my heartbeat. It was a smile that signaled hope and made me temporarily forget the intellectual gulf that separated us.

I schemed desperately to bridge that gulf. And one day, as I was passing the supermarket, an idea came to me.

A sign in the window announced that the store was offering the first volume of a set of encyclopedias at the introductory price of 29 cents. The remaining volumes would cost $2.49 each, but it was no time to be cynical.

I purchased Volume I—Aardvark to Asteroid—and began my venture into the world of knowledge. I would henceforth become a seeker of facts. I would become chief egghead in English II and sweep the princess off her feet with a surge of erudition. I had it all planned.

My first opportunity came one day in the cafeteria line. I looked behind me and there she was.

"Hi," she said.

After a pause, I wet my lips and said, "Know where anchovies come from?"

She seemed surprised. "No, I don't."

I breathed a sigh of relief. "The anchovy lives in salt water and is rarely found in fresh water." I had to talk fast, so that I could get all the facts in before we reached the cash register. "Fishermen catch anchovies in the Mediterranean Sea and along the Atlantic coast near Spain and Portugal."

"How fascinating," said Debbie.

"The anchovy is closely related to the herring. It is thin and silvery in color. It has a long snout and a very large mouth."

"Incredible."

"Anchovies are good in salads, mixed with eggs, and are often used as appetizers before dinner, but they are salty and cannot be digested too rapidly."

Debbie shook her head in disbelief. It was obvious that I had made quite an impression.

A few days later, during a fire drill, I sidled up to her and asked, "Ever been to the Aleutian Islands?"

"Never have," she replied.

"Might be a nice place to visit, but I certainly wouldn't want to live there," I said.

"Why not?" said Debbie, playing right into my hands.

"Well, the climate is forbidding. There are no trees on any of the 100 or more islands in the group. The ground is rocky and very little plant life can grow on it."

"I don't think I'd even care to visit," she said.

The fire drill was over and we began to file into the building, so I had to step it up to get the natives in. "The Aleuts are short and sturdy and have dark skin and black hair. They subsist on fish, and they trap blue fox, seal and otter for their valuable fur."

Debbie's hazel eyes widened in amazement. She was undoubtedly beginning to realize that she wasn't dealing with an ordinary lunkhead. She was gaining new and valuable insights instead of engaging in the routine small talk one would expect from most sophomores.

Luck was on my side, too. One day I was browsing through the library during my study period. I spotted Debbie sitting at a table, absorbed in a crossword puzzle. She was frowning, apparently stumped on a word. I leaned over and asked if I could help.

"Four-letter word for Oriental female servant," Debbie said.

"Try *amah*," I said, quick as a flash.

Debbie filled in the blanks, then turned to stare at me in amazement. "I don't believe it," she said. "I just don't believe it."

Another time, while sitting opposite her at the lunch table, I noticed a side dish of artichokes on her tray.

"Like artichokes?" I asked.

"Love them," replied Debbie.

"You may be interested to know that there are two main varieties of artichokes," I said. "They are the Globe artichoke, and the Jerusalem artichoke. What you are eating is the Jerusalem artichoke, which can be made into a spaghetti-style product. It is native to America and is widely cultivated in California."

Debbie was so stunned she almost gagged on her artichokes.

And so it went, that glorious, amorous, joyous sophomore year. Debbie seemed to relish our little conversations and hung on my every word. Naturally, the more I read, the more my confidence grew. I expatiated freely on such topics as adenoids, air brakes, and arthritis.

In the classroom, too, I was gradually making my presence felt. Among my class-mates, I was developing a reputation as a wheeler-dealer in data. One day, during a discussion of Coleridge's "The Ancient Mariner," we came across the word *albatross*.

"Can anyone tell us what an albatross is?" asked Mrs. Larrivee.

My hand shot up. "The albatross is a large bird that lives mostly in the ocean regions below the equator, but may be found in the north Pacific as well. The albatross measures as long as four feet and has the greatest wingspread of any bird. It feeds on the surface of the ocean, where it catches shellfish. The albatross is a very voracious eater. When it is full it has trouble getting into the air again."

There was a long silence in the room. Mrs. Larrivee couldn't quite believe what she had just heard. I sneaked a peek at Debbie and gave her a big wink. She beamed proudly and winked back.

It was a great feeling, having Debbie and Mrs. Larrivee and my peers according me respect and paying attention when I spoke.

My grades edged upward and my father no longer tried to avoid me when I brought home my report card. I continued reading the encyclopedia diligently, packing more and more into my brain.

What I failed to perceive was that Debbie was going steady with a junior from a neighboring school—a hockey player with a C-plus average. The revelation hit me hard, and for a while I felt like disgorging and forgetting everything I had learned. I had saved enough money to buy Volume II—Asthma to Bullfinch—but I was strongly tempted to invest in a hockey stick instead.

How could she lead me on like that—smiling and concurring and giving me the impression that I was important?

I felt not only hurt, but betrayed. Like Agamemnon, but with less dire consequences, thank God.

In time I recovered from my wounds. The next year Debbie moved from the neighbor-hood and transferred to another school. Soon she became no more than a fleeting memory.

Although the original incentive was gone, I continued poring over the encyclopedias, as well as an increasing number of other books. Having savored the heady wine of knowledge, I could not now alter my course. For:

A little knowledge is a dangerous thing:
Drink deep, or taste not the Pierian spring.

So wrote Alexander Pope, Volume XIV—Paprika to Pterodactyl.

CONSIDER THIS

Every piece of writing comes from somewhere: it is provoked by something: an arousal, an irritant, argument, disbelief, shock. Often the reaction in writing is an act of resistance. What was Brody's provocation? He gives it away in the first paragraph: Students don't believe that their teachers have ever been normal kids, so he sets out to dispel that belief. (But he doesn't use the word *kid*, does he? What does he use, instead?) Does he sound like an ordinary Joe in the first paragraph? Does he convince you that he wasn't a child prodigy? Rita Mae Brown (the next essay) says that English is really an ocean of discourse into which flow two rivers: Anglo-Saxon and Latin (the latter via French). Which term—Latinate or Anglo-Saxon—characterizes Brody's writing?

Steve Brody is a high school teacher who writes the occasional essay for the Sunday *New York Times* supplement, a page of which is always devoted to publishing essays by "ordinary" local people who want to have their say in writing. (See also Janice Gordon, Mark Goldblatt, and Pearl Rowe.)

You Say Begin, I Say Commence—
To the Victor Belongs the Language
Rita Mae Brown

Language is the road map of a culture. It tells you where its people come from and where they are going. A study of the English language reveals a dramatic history and astonishing versatility. It is the language of survivors, of conquerors, of laughter.

A word is more like a pendulum than a fixed entity. It can sweep by your ear and through its very sound suggest hidden meanings, preconscious associations. Listen to these words: "blood," "tranquil," "democracy." Besides their literal meanings, they carry associations that are cultural as well as personal.

One word can illustrate this idea of meaning in flux: "revolution." The word enters English in the 14th century from the Latin via French. (At least that's when it was first written; it may have been spoken earlier.) "Revolution" means a turning around; that was how it was used. Most often "revolution" was applied to astronomy to describe a planet revolving in space. The word carried no political meaning.

"Rebellion" was the loaded political word. It too comes from Latin (as does about 60 percent of our word pool), and it means a renewal of war. In the 14th century "rebellion" was used to indicate a resistance to lawful authority. This can yield amusing results. Whichever side won called the losers rebels—they, the winners, being the repositories of virtue and more gunpowder. This meaning lingers today. The Confederate fighters are called rebels. Since the North won that war, it can be dismissed as a rebellion and not called a revolution. Whoever wins the war redefines the language.

"Revolution" did not acquire a political meaning in English until at least the 16th century. Its meaning—a circular movement—was still tied to its origin but had spilled over into politics. It could now mean a turnaround in power. This is more complicated than you might think.

The 16th century, vibrant, cruel, progressive, held as a persistent popular image the wheel of fortune—an image familiar to anyone who has played with a tarot deck. Human beings dangle on a giant wheel. Some are on the bottom turning upward, some are on the top, and some are hurtling toward the ground. It's as good an image as any for the sudden twists and turns of Fate, Life or the Human Condition. This idea was so dominant at the time that the word "revolution" absorbed its meaning. Instead of a card or a complicated explanation of the wheel of fortune, that one word captured the concept. It's a concept we would do well to remember.

Politically, "rebellion" was still the more potent word. Cromwell's seizure of state power in the mid-17th century came to be called the Great Rebellion, because Charles II followed Cromwell in the restoration of monarchy. Cromwell didn't call his own actions rebellious. In 1689 when William and Mary took over the throne of England, the event was tagged the Glorious Revolution. "Revolution" is benign here and politically inferior in intensity to "rebellion."

By 1796 a shift occurred and "revolution" had come to mean the subversion or overthrow of tyrants. Rebellion, specifically, was a subversion of the laws. Revolution was personal. So we had the American Revolution, which dumped George III out of the Colonies, and the French Revolution, which gave us the murder of Louis XVI and the spectacle of a nation devouring itself. If you're a Marxist you can recast that to mean one class destroying another. At any rate, the French Revolution was a bloodbath and "revolution" began to get a bad name as far as monarchists were concerned and holy significance as far as Jacobins were concerned. By that time "revolution" was developing into the word we know today—not just the overthrow of a tyrant but action based on belief in a new principle. Revolution became a political idea, not just a political act.

The Russian Revolution, the Chinese Revolution, the Cuban Revolution—by now "revolution" is the powerful word, not "rebellion." In the late 1960's and early 1970's young Americans used the word "revolution" indiscriminately. True, they wanted political power, they were opposed to tyrants and believed in a new political principle (or an old one, depending on your outlook) called participatory democracy. However, that period of unrest, with its attendant creativity, did not produce a revolution. The word quickly became corrupted until by the 80's "revolution" was a word used to sell running shoes.

Whither goest thou, Revolution?

Fortunately for writers of English we possess the largest vocabulary in the world. This ocean of discourse is really two rivers flowing together: Anglo-Saxon and Latin. Until 1066 we did fine with what we had. When Harold fell at Hastings, shot through the eye with an arrow, our language changed forever. We now had High English and Low English. These divisions are with us to this very day and provide the subtle shadings of meaning available to a writer through careful word choice alone.

High English is Latin—really Latin that came through French, which the Normans spoke. When the Normans took over, everything that was Anglo-Saxon was ruthlessly shoved aside. Culture was Latin. Granted, the Romans invaded England in 54 B.C. and discovered what every tourist has discovered since: England is an aquarium, not a nation. The romans managed to colonize English speakers, but it was superficial. The true intrusion into our native tongue did not occur until 1066. After that time the words for the enjoyment of life were Latin. The words for labor and game were Anglo-Saxon.

So if you were a lord and sat down to a feast you ate beef. The poor peasant tending what was your meat called it an ox. Cow when it hits the table becomes veal. Sheep becomes mutton and swine becomes pork. Deer when eaten is venison and boar is brawn. The division was clear and will be with us as long as English is spoken. One reason the Anglo-Saxon words survived at all is because the native population was not killed but utilized as workers. Another reason Anglo-Saxon survived is that the people themselves proved more resilient, flexible and intelligent than William the Conqueror and his progeny could have imagined.

A writer can create and develop a character through her or his use of dialogue. An upper-class person will draw from a more Latinate word pool and use more subordinate clauses and longer, less volatile speech rhythms. A character from the lower classes will use more Anglo-Saxon words, much more colorful speech patterns and shorter, staccato rhythms unless this character is from the American South. In that case, rich and poor alike are more prone to use the rhythm of the King James Version of the Bible. Here again, the poor character will employ more Anglo-Saxon words and will probably be more emotionally direct.

The entrance of Latin gave us a reservoir of synonyms unlike anything else in the world. We abound in choices. Synonyms allow us shadings of class and meaning that can be textured. They can be felt, not just heard. Below is a short list of parallel words. Once they had equivalent meanings, but the centuries have pulled apart some of the synonyms, and let others remain. Brief though the list is, it gives an idea of our language's potential for nuance and deep emotion. If you've fallen through the ice you scream "Help!" not "Aid!" In times of greatest danger or heartbreak even the most aristocratic of people will revert to Anglo-Saxon.

NOT QUITE SYNONYMOUS

Centuries ago, the following words were synonyms. Over the years, many have retained equivalent meanings while others have changed, but the pairs illustrate the difference in tone between Anglo-Saxon words (left-hand column) and Latinate words (right-hand column).

Anglo-Saxon	Latin	Anglo-Saxon	Latin
woman	female	watery	aquatic
happiness	felicity	timely	temporal
bill	beak	daily	diurnal
friendship	amity	truthful	veracious
help	aid	kingly	regal
folk	people	youthful	juvenile
hearty	cordial	weighty	ponderous
holy	saint	share	portion
deep	profound	wretched	miserable
lonely	solitary	same	identical
darling	favorite	killing	homicide
love	charity	manly	virile
begin	commence	kind	sort
hide	conceal	tale	story
feed	nourish	up	ascend
hinder	prevent	put out	extinguish
leave	abandon	freedom	liberty
die	perish	cold	frigid
house	domicile	half	semi-
moon	lunar		

CONSIDER THIS

Was this essay written for *Negotiations*? No, the essay was adapted by Rita Mae Brown from her *Starting from Scratch: A Different Kind of Writer's Manual.* But much of what Brown says is echoed throughout *Negotiations:* "Language is the road map of a culture." "Besides their literal meanings, [words] carry associations that are cultural as well as personal." "A writer can create and develop a character through her or his use of dialogue."

Using words drawn from Brown's two lists (or examples of your own), create two different characters, who say the "same thing" in different words:

Absent thee from felicity, awhile, Horatio
Forget happiness for now, Horatio

The Story of an Hour
Kate Chopin

Knowing that Mrs. Mallard was afflicted with heart trouble, great care was taken to break to her as gently as possible the news of her husband's death.

It was her sister Josephine who told her, in broken sentences, veiled hints that revealed in half concealing. Her husband's friend Richards was there, too, near her. It was he who had been in the newspaper office when intelligence of the railroad disaster was received, with Brently Mallard's name leading the list of "killed." He had only taken the time to assure himself of its truth by a second telegram, and had hastened to forestall any less careful, less tender friend in bearing the sad message.

She did not hear the story as many women have heard the same, with a paralyzed inability to accept its significance. She wept at once, with sudden, wild abandonment, in her sister's arms. When the storm of grief had spent itself she went to her room alone. She would have no one follow her.

There stood, facing the open window, a comfortable, roomy armchair. Into this she sank, pressed down by a physical exhaustion that haunted her body and seemed to reach into her soul.

She could see in the open square before her house the tops of trees that were all aquiver with the new spring life. The delicious breath of rain was in the air. In the street below a peddler was crying his wares. The notes of a distant song which some one was singing reached her faintly, and countless sparrows were twittering in the eaves.

There were patches of blue sky showing here and there through the clouds that had met and piled above the other in the west facing her window.

She sat with her head thrown back upon the cushion of the chair quite motionless, except when a sob came up into her throat and shook her, as a child who has cried itself to sleep continues to sob in its dreams.

She was young, with a fair, calm face, whose lines bespoke repression and even a certain strength. But now there was a dull stare in her eyes, whose gaze was fixed away off yonder on one of those patches of blue sky. It was not a glance of reflection, but rather indicated a suspension of intelligent thought.

There was something coming to her and she was waiting for it, fearfully. What was it? She did not know; it was too subtle and elusive to name. But she felt it, creeping out of the sky, reaching toward her through the sounds, the scents, the color that filled the air.

Now her bosom rose and fell tumultuously. She was beginning to recognize this thing that was approaching to possess her, and she was striving to beat it back with her will—as powerless as her two white slender hands would have been.

When she abandoned herself a little whispered word escaped her slightly parted lips. She said it over and over under her breath: "Free, free, free!" The vacant stare and the look of terror that had followed it went from her eyes. They stayed keen and bright. Her pulses beat fast, and the coursing blood warmed and relaxed every inch of her body.

She did not stop to ask if it were not a monstrous joy that held her. A clear and exalted perception enabled her to dismiss the suggestion as trivial.

She knew that she would weep again when she saw the kind, tender hands folded in death; the face that had never looked save with love upon her, fixed and gray and dead. But she saw beyond that bitter moment a long procession of years to come that would belong to her absolutely. And she opened and spread her arms out to them in welcome.

There would be no one to live for during those coming years; she would live for herself. There would be no powerful will bending her in that blind persistence with which men and women believe they have a right to impose a private will upon a fellow-creature. A kind intention or a cruel intention made the act seem no less a crime as she looked upon it in that brief moment of illumination.

And yet she had loved him—sometimes. Often she had not. What did it matter! What could love, the unsolved mystery, count for in face of this possession of self-assertion which she suddenly recognized as the strongest impulse of her being!

"Free! Body and soul free!" she kept whispering.

Josephine was kneeling before the closed door with her lips to the keyhole, imploring for admission. "Louise, open the door! I beg; open the door—you will make yourself ill. What are you doing, Louise? For heaven's sake open the door."

"Go away. I am not making myself ill." No; she was drinking in a very elixir of life through that open window.

Her fancy was running riot along those days ahead of her. Spring days, and summer days, and all sorts of days that would be her own. She breathed a quick prayer that life might be long. It was only yesterday she had thought with a shudder that life might be long.

She arose at length and opened the door to her sister's importunities. There was a feverish triumph in her eyes, and she carried herself unwittingly like a goddess of Victory. She clasped her sister's waist, and together they descended the stairs. Richards stood waiting for them at the bottom.

Some one was opening the front door with a latchkey. It was Brently Mallard who entered, a little travel-stained, composedly carrying his grip-sack and umbrella. He had been far from the scene of accident, and did not even know there had been one. He stood amazed at Josephine's piercing cry; at Richards's quick motion to screen him from the view of his wife.

But Richards was too late.

When the doctors came they said she had died of heart disease—of joy that kills.

CONSIDER THIS

The writings of Kate O'Flaherty (Chopin) (1851–1904) have had their fair share of trouble with the censors, those who would prevent us from reading books that make them feel uncomfortable: her great novel *The Awakening,* which appeared in 1899, was banned by the library in her hometown, St. Louis, and after a reprint in 1906, it was out of print for over fifty years. She raised six children and after her husband died, when she was about thirty, she managed the family plantation in addition to the work of writing. The question of women's emancipation was a big one in the 1890s, and it is out of her defense of woman's right to a decent degree of self-determination that her most compelling writing came.

Reread the opening line: where in the language do you find the first hint of what is to come? How would you characterize the tone of the narrator?

Midair
Frank Conroy

The first time he'd ever driven a car entirely by himself was on his twelfth birthday. His uncle, owner of a Model A, had up until then allowed him to take the wheel for only a moment or two, retaining adult control of accelerator, brake, and gears, but on July 25, 1946, in a burst of largesse induced partly by the bourbon Uncle Charlie had already drunk and partly in anticipation of the bourbon they were on their way to the liquor store to pick up, the old man had gotten in on the right side and pushed the boy into the driver's seat.

"You mean I can drive?" Jack asked. The scope of the sudden, entirely unexpected present overwhelmed him.

"You know the gears," Uncle Charlie said. "Let the clutch out gradual and give it gas gradual."

"Wow."

Jack first looked at everything—pedals, shift, wheel and instruments—to make sure it was all still there. He rattled the shift, pushed the pedals, and began the moves he'd studied for years. The car jumped forward, lurched, and stalled.

"What did I do wrong?"

"I don't know. Let's go."

He started the engine, and the Model A took several large jumps forward. Jack was frozen at the wheel while Uncle Charlie dipped back and forth like a rodeo rider. Scared, Jack shouted at the windshield.

"What's wrong? What should I do?"

"Keep going. You'll get the feel of it."

In fear, when he meant to push the clutch, he pushed the accelerator, and after a moment of sheer terror the car moved smoothly up the hill toward the paved road into town.

"Good," said Uncle Charlie. "Try not to stall when you stop at the corner."

Jack was rapturously involved with the controls, adjusting the wheel, playing with the gear shift, experimenting with the gas. At the corner he simply turned to the left and accelerated.

"You should've stopped there," Uncle Charlie said, burping quietly as they shot down the hill.

"Wow," Jack said. "This is fantastic."

He remembers all this as he sits waiting for his wife to bring coffee into the living room. At the age of thirty-five he finds himself daydreaming constantly, remembering his past with such clarity it's like going to the movies. The previous afternoon, while on the phone half-listening to an important client, he'd gone back to the age of six, reliving a mysterious formal lunch in a country house where he'd asked for more strawberries, please. The client had undoubtedly thought he was making silent decisions. Neither does his wife know the extent of his daydreaming, putting it down to worry about the market, or perhaps, in her most fearful moments, to simple withdrawal after a hard marriage of sixteen years.

She pours herself a brandy. "You want one?" She'd started drinking when the youngest child had started school.

"I'm going to sell the car."

"You are?" She became alert—the special, slightly masked alertness she assumes when she discovers something has been going on inside his head without her knowing it. "To get a new one?"

"No. Just sell it. Cheaper to take cabs." He lets his obviously inadequate answer hang in the air, asking her to believe that after living as if there were no tomorrow for his entire life he has suddenly got sensible. The truth is he doesn't know why he no longer wants the car—anymore than he knows why he no longer wants to sleep with his wife. The car (a delicate, expensive, and unbearably beautiful Aston Martin) is no fun anymore. His passion (the sensation of being goosed when a gas pump was inserted into the rear of the Dodge, the lump in his throat, the ridiculous lump in his throat when he walked away from the Ford convertible for the last time) is gone, as if he had once possessed a separate automobile-loving heart that has atrophied and disappeared. His lack of feeling for the Aston pains him. He wants to sell the car and become old.

"It's hard to imagine you without a car," she says. "You've always had one."

He drifts away, remembering sophomore year and the old Mercury he'd bought from Elvin Marsdale in French House. A big, top-heavy brute of a car, it had broken down constantly, forcing him to spend as much time in junkyards looking for parts as on the road. When, finally, his tuned ear told him the engine itself was dying—inexorable death from the inside, rings totally worn, valves gasping, driveshaft groaning—he'd sold it to an ignorant graduate student at a slight profit.

For a while he had no car, and then an extraordinary piece of luck occurred—he won a Ford convertible in a lottery, a new model fully equipped with accessories, white walls, and a St. Christopher's medal. He suspected fraud, a telephone prank on the part of his classmates, but when he showed up at the rectory of an enormous church in downtown New Haven the car was indeed there, parked in an inner courtyard, and when he handed over the lottery ticket a fat priest gave him a set of keys, the registration, and a slap on the back. In the courtyard he walked around the car several times. The chrome gleamed with almost unbearable intensity. He could see a distorted image of himself in the waxed black body, his face slipping like oil over the curved surfaces. He was afraid to touch the car. When he got in he was afraid to start the engine. He stared at his eyes in the mirror (familiar blue— he was apparently there) for several moments before adjusting the glass. Then he pushed the seat back a couple of notches, turned the ignition, and rolled slowly out of the courtyard onto the street.

The car became his in time, of course, but it was never entirely his. There was an aura of the supernatural clinging to it until the end, until trade-in. In dreams the fat priest asked for it back. He treated the car badly.

The first month or two he'd fussed over it, trying to keep it new, but as little scratches appeared here and there, as small electrical parts began to fail, as the smell of newness evaporated, he lost interest. He could not bring himself to clean the interior, and the floor gradually filled with newspapers, sweat socks, beer cans and Howard Johnson boxes. He began racing. A continuous night to night contest with Herb Maglio, owner of an old, but well tuned Plymouth. At first they simply raced from Starkey and Sheen's, the college bar, to the campus line—a distance of one mile, each man coming up with a slightly different formula every night. Eventually the race extended into the campus itself, along a difficult route they had tacitly agreed on—through the first parking lot, down the long curve to French House, a slalom through the trees bordering College Lane, up through the tennis courts and out over the grass to the cinder track around the football field.

Jack stares at his wife without seeing her and remembering the cinder track. Cold autumn air at three a.m. The lights of the cars were shut down for secrecy, and starlight, moonlight, points of window light from distant dorms needled the air. He stood beer-drunk with beer-drunk Herb at the edge of the grass and waited for his eyes to adjust to the dark. The smell of hot oil. A faint tang from swollen, burnt brake-linings. In the open car he gunned the engine, pumping gas like an organist pumping his bellows. Leaning back, half-standing in the seat, he threw a beer can into the night sky. When it hit the ground the engines roared and cinders flew. Wind swirled around his head. In the darkness the cinder track was absolutely black. An unearthly, perfect black. Follow the black.

He stands up abruptly, walks to the center of the room and looks around.

His wife watches him, and after a moment asks "What's wrong?"

He feels himself to be in some extraordinary state. The room around him is particularly vivid, each object clear and hard in space, the colors glowing, all of it entirely familiar, and yet he is no longer part of it, or, more precisely, at once part of it and not part of it. Simultaneously a sense of great power fills him. Profound changes occur in the dark parts of his brain, as if the lobes, like sliding blocks in a wooden puzzle, are gliding momentously into new positions and new alignments. He walks out of the room and out of the house.

At the entrance to the East Side Drive a dark blue Chrysler passes on the wrong side, cutting him off, and, rocking slightly, disappears up the ramp.

"Stupid bastard," he says as he negotiates the turn. "Goddamn bubblehead." He allows himself to rave at other drivers, insulting them as he never insults real people. He plays a game, spewing out a stream of oaths as he drives, ridiculing everyone on the road. He feels justified, since he knows he is a better driver than any of them.

He accelerates off the ramp onto the highway and catches a glimpse of the blue Chrysler crossing lanes on a curve up ahead. The Aston responds instantly as he presses the gas pedal half an inch closer to the floor. Sweeping through the slower traffic, he changes lanes smoothly and carefully. The speedometer needle rests at 70 and the engine purls.

One night after a light snowfall he and Maglio had taken their cars down to the new, unfinished parking lot behind the college Field House. At the brink of a gentle hill they stared down at a perfectly flat unbroken surface the size of two football fields, a smooth, unmarked coating of snow over the virgin asphalt.

"Beautiful!" he shouted across to the other car.

"You go first," Herb yelled back. "Bust the cherry."

Jack reached up and opened the roof clamps, pushing the steel front rib to free the pegs. With his other hand he pulled the switch and the power top folded into itself and disappeared behind the back seat. He turned up the collar of his jacket and started down the hill, timing his acceleration carefully so that the rear wheels maintained traction. He entered the lot on a straight line. Nearing the center he turned the wheel to the left and pressed the gas gently. The rear wheels broke loose, slipping to the right, and he steered into the skid. As the car stabilized, drifting perfectly over the snow at an angle of fifteen degrees, he repeated the same movements in reverse, swinging the car slowly through zero and over fifteen degrees in the other direction. Approaching the edge of the lot, he pressed the gas to the floor, spun the steering wheel hard and turned the car completely around in a four-wheel skid. For several moments he went backward, in a straight line, until the rear wheels collected enough traction to stop the car. His eye ran back along the elegant curves of his tracks in the snow to Herb's Plymouth, which was just starting down the incline. Jack slid out from under the wheel, raised himself up and sat on the back of the seat, staring through the snow-flecked air, listening to the faint rodeo yells of his skylarking friend.

After a mile he catches up with the Chrysler. The woman behind the wheel has black hair falling to her shoulders and her pale face is distorted. Alone in the car, she talks and gesticulates as if in the midst of a conversation. She drives abstractedly, the big car drifting back and forth across the wide road. Jack pulls the Aston into the lane beside her and she glances over quickly. She accelerates suddenly, viciously, but he is prepared, and keeps up with her. At eighty miles an hour they pass a string of cars, Jack on the outside, the woman on the inside. As the speed increases he feels a calmness come over his soul.

They'd played tag in the snow, spinning the cars around, slipping this way and that, Herb trying to touch bumpers, Jack trying to get away, their eyes blurred from the wind and the tears of their laughter. What times they'd had! What easy times, gliding, gently gliding over the snow like a pair of skaters.

As the road temporarily narrows to two lanes where some construction is going on she refuses to move over. He begins to pass but she moves closer to him and he is forced to touch the brakes. Side by side they enter the narrow part of the road. Before he can pull in behind her he has struck the rubber pylons, sending them high into the air, across the divider into the oncoming traffic. He is vaguely aware of workmen in the closed lane dropping their tools and starting for the barrier, but he is already past them. The light is beginning to fail as, on the other side of the city, the sun sets.

He pulls up beside her again, at ninety miles an hour. She is no longer talking to herself, but sits rigidly, staring straight ahead. She drifts into his lane but he does not give ground. The automobiles touch, side to side, with a soft sound like a tin can crushed underfoot. He pulls away for a moment, and then bumps her side again, somewhat harder than before. Pointlessly, mysteriously, she begins to blow the Chrysler's horn. When she decides to steer into him she starts the move so clumsily, so obviously, he is ready, and with a hard punch on his brakes he slows abruptly and she drifts into his lane, directly in front of him.

Ahead there is only a single clear lane. They enter at ninety miles an hour, the Aston two feet behind the Chrysler. Jack glances at the tachometer, shifts down into third, and closes the distance between the two cars. The slight jar as the bumpers touch is almost imperceptible. He feels a remote, far away pain from his clamped teeth. He presses the gas to the floor and listens to the Aston's big engine open up.

He pushes the Chrysler up to ninety-five, and then to a hundred before the first curve. She plows through a low iron railing and bounces high into the air. He follows her through the hole and for a split second they travel along the pedestrian walkway. Suddenly, as if a tire had blown, the Chrysler swerves, crashes through the high railing and sails out into the open air over the river.

That is the last image he sees—the big blue Chrysler suspended magically in the air above the black water, the woman inside comically prim, motionless as a mannequin. In another moment he would laugh, but the Aston strikes a concrete abutment and his head goes through the windshield.

CONSIDER THIS

What kinds of tales do we tell sitting around our modern fires? Do we tell tales at all? Some cultural critics argue that we are a print culture, that the oral culture has died the death. I wonder. I wonder if one of the big stories in our lives isn't the car story—after all, it is in cars that we meet adventure, journey, escape, escapade, danger, villains and heroes, near-misses, breakdowns, accident, and death.

Look again at Conroy's ending: if this were an essay rather than a work of fiction, would you expect a different kind of ending? How so? When, by the way, does Conroy slip into the present tense?

Frank Conroy's autobiography *Stop-Time,* published in 1967, when he was thirty-one, is considered a modern classic. Here are the opening lines:

My father stopped living with us when I was three or four. Most of his adult life was spent as a patient in various expensive rest homes for dipsomaniacs and victims of nervous collapse. . . . To most people he seemed normal, especially when he was inside (Penguin, 1977).

Do you want to read on? Why? Why not?

Peasants Tell Tales:
The Meaning of Mother Goose
Robert Darnton

The mental world of the unenlightened during the Enlightenment seems to be irretrievably lost. It is so difficult, if not impossible, to locate the common man in the eighteenth century that it seems foolish to search for his cosmology. But before abandoning the attempt, it might be useful to suspend one's disbelief and to consider a story—a story everyone knows, though not in the following version, which is the tale more or less as it was told around firesides in peasant cottages during long winter evenings in eighteenth-century France.

> Once a little girl was told by her mother to take some bread and milk to her grandmother. As the girl was walking through the forest, a wolf came up to her and asked where she was going.
>
> "To grandmother's house," she replied.
>
> "Which path are you taking, the path of the pins or the path of the needles?"
>
> "The path of the needles."
>
> So the wolf took the path of the pins and arrived first at the house. He killed grandmother, poured her blood into a bottle, and sliced her flesh onto a platter. Then he got into her nightclothes and waited in bed.
>
> "Knock, knock."
>
> "Come in, my dear."
>
> "Hello, grandmother. I've brought you some bread and milk."
>
> "Have something yourself, my dear. There is meat and wine in the pantry."
>
> So the little girl ate what was offered; and as she did, a little cat said, "Slut! To eat the flesh and drink the blood of your grandmother!"
>
> Then the wolf said, "Undress and get into bed with me."
>
> "Where shall I put my apron?"
>
> "Throw it on the fire; you won't need it any more."
>
> For each garment—bodice, skirt, petticoat, and stockings—the girl asked the same question; and each time the wolf answered, "Throw it on the fire; you won't need it any more."
>
> When the girl got in bed, she said, "Oh, grandmother! How hairy you are!"
>
> "It's to keep me warmer, my dear."
>
> "Oh, grandmother! What big shoulders you have!"
>
> "It's for better carrying firewood, my dear."
>
> "Oh, grandmother! What long nails you have!"
>
> "It's for scratching myself better, my dear."
>
> "Oh, grandmother! What big teeth you have!"
>
> "It's for eating you better, my dear."
>
> And he ate her.

What is the moral of this story? For little girls, clearly: stay away from wolves. For historians, it seems to be saying something about the mental world of the early modern peasantry. But what? How can one begin to interpret such a text? One way leads through psychoanalysis. The analysts have given folktales a thorough going-over, picking out hidden symbols, unconscious motifs, and psychic mechanisms. Consider, for example, the exegesis of "Little Red Riding Hood" by two of the best known psychoanalysts, Erich Fromm and Bruno Bettelheim.

Fromm interpreted the tale as a riddle about the collective unconscious in primitive society, and he solved it "without difficulty" by decoding its "symbolic language." The story concerns an adolescent's confrontation with adult sexuality, he explained. Its hidden meaning shows through its symbolism—but the symbols he saw in his version of the text were based on details that did not exist in the versions known to peasants in the seventeenth and eighteenth centuries. Thus he makes a great deal of the (nonexistent) red riding hood as a symbol of menstruation and of the (nonexistent) bottle carried by the girl as a symbol of virginity: hence the mother's (nonexistent) admonition not to stray from the path into wild terrain where she might break it. The wolf is the ravishing male. And the two (nonexistent) stones that are placed in the wolf's belly after the (nonexistent) hunter extricates the girl and her grandmother, stand for sterility, the punishment for breaking a sexual taboo. So, with an uncanny sensitivity to detail that did not occur in the original folktale, the psychoanalyst takes us into a mental universe that never existed, at least not before the advent of psychoanalysis.

How could anyone get a text so wrong? The difficulty does not derive from professional dogmatism—for psychoanalysts need not be more rigid than poets in their manipulation of symbols—but rather from blindness to the historical dimension of folktales.

Fromm did not bother to mention his source, but apparently he took his text from the brothers Grimm. The Grimms got it, along with "Puss 'n Boots," "Bluebeard," and a few other stories, from Jeannette Hassenpflug, a neighbor and close friend of theirs in Cassel; and she learned it from her mother, who came from a French Huguenot family. The Huguenots brought their own repertory of tales into Germany when they fled from the persecution of Louis XIV. But they did not draw them directly from popular oral tradition. They read them in books written by Charles Perrault, Marie Cathérine d'Aulnoy, and others during the vogue for fairy tales in fashionable Parisian circles at the end of the seventeenth century. Perrault, the master of the genre, did indeed take his material from the oral tradition of the common people (his principal source probably was his son's nurse). But he touched it up so that it would suit the taste of the salon sophisticates, *précieuses,* and courtiers to whom he directed the first printed version of Mother Goose, his *Contes de ma mère l'oye* of 1697. Thus the tales that reached the Grimms through the Hassenpflugs were neither very German nor very representative of folk tradition. Indeed, the Grimms recognized their literary and Frenchified character and therefore eliminated them from the second edition of the *Kinderund Hausmärchen*—all but "Little Red Riding Hood." It remained in the collection, evidently, because Jeannette Hassenpflug had grafted on to it a happy ending derived from "The Wolf and the Kids" (tale type 123 according to the standard classification scheme developed by Antti Aarne and Stith Thompson), which was one of the most popular in Germany. So Little Red Riding Hood slipped into the German and later the English literary tradition with her French origins undetected. She changed character considerably as she passed from the French peasantry to Perrault's nursery, into print, across the Rhine, back into an oral tradition but this time as part of the Huguenot diaspora, and back into book form but now as a product of the Teutonic forest rather than the village hearths of the Old Regime in France.

Fromm and a host of other psychoanalytical exegetes did not worry about the transformations of the text—indeed, they did not know about them—because they got the tale they wanted. It begins with pubertal sex (the red hood, which does not exist in the French oral tradition) and ends with the triumph of the ego (the rescued girl, who is usually eaten in the French tales) over the id (the wolf, who is never killed in the traditional versions). All's well that ends well.

The ending is particularly important for Bruno Bettelheim, the latest in the line of psychoanalysts who have had a go at "Little Red Riding Hood." For him, the key to the story, and to all such stories, is the affirmative message of its denouement. By ending happily, he maintains, folktales permit children to confront their unconscious desires and fears and to emerge unscathed, id subdued and ego triumphant. The id is the villain of "Little Red Riding Hood" in Bettelheim's version. It is the pleasure principle, which leads the girl astray when she is too old for oral fixation (the stage represented by "Hansel and Gretel") and too young for adult sex. The id is also the wolf, who is also the father, who is also the hunter, who is also the ego and, somehow, the superego as well. By directing the wolf to her grandmother, Little Red Riding Hood manages in oedipal fashion to do away with her mother, because mothers can also be grandmothers in the moral economy of the soul and the houses on either side of the woods are actually the same house, as in "Hansel and Gretel," where they are also the mother's body. This adroit mixing of symbols gives Little Red Riding Hood an opportunity to get into bed with her father, the wolf, thereby giving vent to oedipal fantasies. She survives in the end because she is reborn on a higher level of existence when her father reappears as ego-superego-hunter and cuts her out of the belly of her father as wolf-id, so that everyone lives happily ever after.

Bettelheim's generous view of symbolism makes for a less mechanistic interpretation of the tale than does Fromm's notion of a secret code, but it, too, proceeds from some unquestioned assumptions about the text. Although he cites enough commentators on Grimm and Perrault to indicate some awareness of folklore as an academic discipline, Bettelheim reads "Little Red Riding Hood" and other tales as if they had no history. He treats them, so to speak, flattened out, like patients on a couch, in a timeless contemporaneity. He does not question their origins or worry over other meanings that they might have had in other contexts because he knows how the soul works and how it has always worked. In fact, however, folktales are historical documents. They have evolved over many centuries and have taken different turns in different cultural traditions. Far from expressing the unchanging operations of man's inner being, they suggest that *mentalités* themselves have changed. We can appreciate the distance between our mental world and that of our ancestors if we imagine lulling a child of our own to sleep with the primitive peasant version of "Little Red Riding Hood." Perhaps, then, the moral of the story should be: beware of psychoanalysts—and be careful in your use of sources. We seem to be back at historicism.

Not quite, however, for "Little Red Riding Hood" has a terrifying irrationality that seems out of place in the Age of Reason. In fact, the peasants' version outdoes the psychoanalysts' in violence and sex. (Following the Grimms and Perrault, Fromm and

Bettelheim do not mention the cannibalizing of grandmother and the strip-tease prelude to the devouring of the girl.) Evidently the peasants did not need a secret code to talk about taboos.

The other stories in the French peasant Mother Goose have the same nightmare quality. In one early version of "Sleeping Beauty" (tale type 410), for example, Prince Charming, who is already married, ravishes the princess, and she bears him several children, without waking up. The infants finally break the spell by biting her while nursing, and the tale then takes up its second theme: the attempts of the prince's mother-in-law, an ogress, to eat his illicit offspring. The original "Bluebeard" (tale type 312) is the story of a bride who cannot resist the temptation to open a forbidden door in the house of her husband, a strange man who has already gone through six wives. She enters a dark room and discovers the corpses of the previous wives, hanging on the wall. Horrified, she lets the forbidden key drop from her hand into a pool of blood on the floor. She cannot wipe it clean; so Bluebeard discovers her disobedience, when he inspects the keys. As he sharpens his knife in preparation for making her his seventh victim, she withdraws to her bedroom and puts on her wedding costume. But she delays her toilette long enough to be saved by her brothers, who gallop to the rescue after receiving a warning from her pet dove. In one early tale from the Cinderella cycle (tale type 510B), the heroine becomes a domestic servant in order to prevent her father from forcing her to marry him. In another, the wicked stepmother tries to push her in an oven but incinerates one of the mean stepsisters by mistake. In the French peasant's "Hansel and Gretel" (tale type 327), the hero tricks an ogre into slitting the throats of his own children. A husband eats a succession of brides in the wedding bed in "La Belle et le monstre" (tale type 433), one of the hundreds of tales that never made it into the printed versions of Mother Goose. In a nastier tale, "Les Trois Chiens" (tale type 315), a sister kills her brother by hiding spikes in the mattress of his wedding bed. In the nastiest of all, "Ma mère m'a tué, mon père m'a mangé" (tale type 720), a mother chops her son up into a Lyonnais-style casserole, which her daughter serves to the father. And so it goes, from rape and sodomy to incest and cannibalism. Far from veiling their message with symbols, the storytellers of eighteenth-century France portrayed a world of raw and naked brutality.

How can the historian make sense of this world? One way for him to keep his footing in the psychic undertow of early Mother Goose is to hold fast to two disciplines: anthropology and folklore. When they discuss theory, anthropologists disagree about the fundamentals of their science. But when they go into the bush, they use techniques for understanding oral traditions that can, with discretion, be applied to Western folklore. Except for some structuralists, they relate tales to the art of tale telling and to the context in which it takes place. They look for the way a raconteur adapts an inherited theme to his audience so that the specificity of time and place shows through the universality of the topos. They do not expect to find direct social comment or metaphysical allegories so much as a tone of discourse or a cultural style, which communicates a particular ethos and world view. "Scientific" folklore, as the French call it (American specialists often distinguish between folklore and "fakelore"), involves the compilation and comparison of tales according to the standardized schemata of tale types developed by Antti Aarne and Stith Thompson. It does not necessarily exclude formalistic analysis such as that of Vladimir Propp, but it stresses rigorous documentation—the occasion of the telling, the background of the teller, and the degree of contamination from written sources.

French folklorists have recorded about ten thousand tales, in many different dialects and in every corner of France and of French-speaking territories. For example, while on an expedition in Berry for the Musée des arts et traditions populaires in 1945, Ariane de Félice recorded a version of "Le Petit Poucet" ("Tom Thumb" or "Thumbling," tale type 327) by a peasant woman, Euphrasie Pichon, who had been born in 1862 in the village of Eguzon (Indre). In 1879 Jean Drouillet wrote down another version as he listened to his mother Eugénie, who had learned it from her mother, Octavie Riffet, in the village of Teillay (Cher). The two versions are nearly identical and owe nothing to the first printed account of the tale, which Charles Perrault published in 1697. They and eighty other "Petits Poucets," which folklorists have compiled and compared, motif by motif, belong to an oral tradition that survived with remarkably little contamination from print culture until late in the nineteenth century. Most of the tales in the French repertory were recorded between 1870 and 1914 during "the Golden Age of folktale research in France," and they were recounted by peasants who had learned them as children, long before literacy had spread throughout the countryside. Thus in 1874 Nannette Levesque, an illiterate peasant woman born in 1794, dictated a version of "Little Red Riding Hood" that went back to the eighteenth century; and in 1865 Louis Grolleau, a domestic servant born in 1803, dictated a rendition of "Le Pou" (tale type 621) that he had first heard under the Empire. Like all tellers of tales, the peasant raconteurs adjusted the setting of their stories to their own milieux; but they kept the main elements intact, using repetitions, rhymes, and other mnemonic devices. Although the "performance" element, which is central to the study of contemporary folklore, does not show through the old texts, folklorists argue that the recordings of the Third Republic provide enough evidence for them to reconstruct the rough outlines of an oral tradition that existed two centuries ago.

That claim may seem extravagant, but comparative studies have revealed striking similarities in different recordings of the same tale, even though they were made in remote villages, far removed from one another and from the circulation of books. In a study of "Little Red Riding Hood," for example, Paul Delarue compared thirty-five versions recorded throughout a vast zone of the *langue d'oïl.* Twenty versions correspond exactly to the primitive "Conte de la mère grand" quoted above, except for a few details (sometimes the girl is eaten, sometimes she escapes by a ruse). Two versions follow Perrault's tale (the first to mention the red hood). And the rest contain a mixture of the oral and written accounts, whose elements stand out as distinctly as the garlic and mustard in a French salad dressing.

Written evidence proves that the tales existed long before anyone conceived of "folklore," a nineteenth-century neologism. Medieval preachers drew on the oral tradition in order to illustrate moral arguments. Their sermons, transcribed in collections of "Exempla" from the twelfth to the fifteenth century, refer to the same stories as those taken down in peasant cottages by folklorists in the nineteenth century. Despite the obscurity surrounding the origins of chivalric romances, *chansons de geste,* and *fabliaux,* it seems that a good deal of medieval literature drew on popular oral tradition, rather than vice versa. "Sleeping Beauty" appeared in an Arthurian romance of the fourteenth century, and "Cinderella" surfaced in Noel du Fail's *Propos rustiques* of 1547, a book that traced the tales to peasant lore and that showed how they were transmitted; for du Fail wrote the first account of an important French institution, the *veillée*, an evening fireside gathering, where men repaired tools and women sewed while listening to stories that would be recorded by folklorists three hundred years later and that were already centuries old. Whether they were meant to amuse adults or to frighten children, as in the case of cautionary tales like "Little Red Riding Hood," the stories belonged to a fund of popular culture, which peasants hoarded over the centuries with remarkably little loss.

The great collections of folktales made in the late nineteenth and early twentieth centuries therefore provide a rare opportunity to make contact with the illiterate masses who have disappeared into the past without leaving a trace. To reject folktales because they cannot be dated and situated with precision like other historical documents is to turn one's back on one of the few points of entry into the mental world of peasants under the Old Regime. But to attempt to penetrate that world is to face a set of obstacles as daunting as those confronted by Jean de l'Ours (tale type 301) when he tried to rescue the three Spanish princesses from the underworld or by little Parle (tale type 328) when he set out to capture the ogre's treasure.

The greatest obstacle is the impossibility of listening in on the story tellers. No matter how accurate they may be, the recorded versions of the tales cannot convey the effects that must have brought the stories to life in the eighteenth century: the dramatic pauses, the sly glances, the use of gestures to set scenes—a Snow White at a spinning wheel, a Cinderella delousing a stepsister—and the use of sounds to punctuate actions—a knock on the door (often done by rapping on a listener's forehead) or a cudgeling or a fart. All of those devices shaped the meaning of the tales, and all of them elude the historian. He cannot be sure that the limp and lifeless text that he holds between the covers of a book provides an accurate account of the performance that took place in the eighteenth century. He cannot even be certain that the text corresponds to the unrecorded versions that existed a century earlier. Although he may turn up plenty of evidence to prove that the tale itself existed, he cannot quiet his suspicions that it could have changed a great deal before it reached the folklorists of the Third Republic.

Given those uncertainties, it seems unwise to build an interpretation on a single version of a single tale, and more hazardous still to base symbolic analysis on details— riding hoods and hunters—that may not have occurred in the peasant versions. But there are enough recordings of those versions—35 "Little Red Riding Hoods," 90 "Tom Thumbs," 105 "Cinderellas"—for one to picture the general outline of a tale as it existed in the oral tradition. One can study it on the level of structure, noting the way the narrative is framed and the motifs are combined, instead of concentrating on fine points of detail. Then one can compare it with other stories. And finally, by working through the entire body of French folktales, one can distinguish general characteristics, overarching themes, and pervasive elements of style and tone.

One can also seek aid and comfort from specialists in the study of oral literature. Milman Parry and Albert Lord have shown how folk epics as long as *The Iliad* are passed on faithfully from bard to bard among the illiterate peasants of Yugoslavia. These "singers of tales" do not possess the fabulous powers of memorization sometimes attributed to "primitive" peoples. They do not memorize very much at all. Instead, they combine stock phrases, formulas, and narrative segments in patterns improvised according to the response of their audience. Recordings of the same epic by the same singer demonstrate that each performance is unique. Yet recordings made in 1950 do not differ in essentials from those made in 1934. In each case, the singer proceeds as if he were walking down a well-known path. He may branch off here to take a shortcut or pause there to enjoy a panorama, but he always remains on familiar ground—so familiar, in fact, that he will say that he repeated every step exactly as he has done before. He does not conceive of repetition in the same way as a literate person, for he has no notion of words, lines, and verses. Texts are not rigidly fixed for him as they are for readers of the printed page. He creates his text as he goes, picking new routes through old themes. He can even work in material derived from printed sources, for the epic as a whole is so much greater than the sum of its parts that modifications of detail barely disturb the general configuration.

Lord's investigation confirms conclusions that Vladimir Propp reached by a different mode of analysis, one that showed how variations of detail remain subordinate to stable structures in Russian folktales. Field workers among illiterate peoples in Polynesia, Africa, and North and South America have also found that oral traditions have enormous staying power. Opinions divide on the separate question of whether or not oral sources can provide a reliable account of past events. Robert Lowie, who collected narratives from the Crow Indians in the early twentieth century, took up a position of extreme skepticism: "I cannot attach to oral traditions any historical value whatsoever under any conditions whatsoever." By historical value, however, Lowie meant factual accuracy. (In 1910 he recorded a Crow account of a battle against the Dakota; in 1931 the same informant described the battle to him, but claimed that it had taken place against the Cheyenne.) Lowie conceded that the stories, taken as stories, remained quite consistent; they forked and branched in the standard patterns of Crow narrative. So his findings actually support the view that in traditional story telling continuities in form and style outweigh variations in detail, among North American Indians as well as Yugoslav peasants. Frank Hamilton Cushing noted a spectacular example of this tendency among the Zuni almost a century ago. In 1886 he served as interpreter to a Zuni delegation in the eastern United States. During a round robin of story telling one evening, he recounted as his contribution the tale of "The Cock and the Mouse," which he had picked up from a book of Italian folktales. About a year later, he was astonished to hear the same tale from one of the Indians back at Zuni. The Italian motifs remained recognizable enough for one to be able to classify the tale in the Aarne-Thompson scheme (it is tale type 2032). But everything else about the story—its frame, figures of speech, allusions, style, and general feel—has become intensely Zuni. Instead of Italianizing the native lore, the story had been Zunified.

No doubt the transmission process affects stories differently in different cultures. Some bodies of folklore can resist "contamination" while absorbing new material more effectively than can others. But oral traditions seem to be tenacious and long-lived nearly everywhere among illiterate peoples. Nor do they collapse at their first exposure to the printed word. Despite Jack Goody's contention that a literacy line cuts through all history, dividing oral from "written" or "print" cultures, it seems that traditional tale telling can flourish long after the onset of literacy. To anthropologists and folklorists who have tracked tales through the bush, there is nothing extravagant about the idea that peasant raconteurs in late nineteenth-century France told stories to one another pretty much as their ancestors had done a century or more earlier.

Comforting as this expert testimony may be, it does not clear all the difficulties in the way of interpreting the French tales. The texts are accessible enough, for they lie unexploited in treasure houses like the Musée des arts et traditions populaires in Paris and in scholarly collections like *Le Conte populaire français* by Paul Delarue and Marie-Louise Tenèze. But one cannot lift them from such sources and hold them up to inspection as if they were so many photographs of the Old Regime, taken with the innocent eye of an extinct peasantry. They are stories.

As in most kinds of narration, they develop standardized plots from conventional motifs, picked up here, there, and everywhere. They have a distressing lack of specificity for anyone who wants to pin them down to precise points in time and place. Raymond Jameson has studied the case of a Chinese Cinderella from the ninth century. She gets her slippers from a magic fish instead of a fairy godmother and loses one of them at a village fête instead of a royal ball, but she bears an unmistakable resemblance to Perrault's heroine. Folklorists have recognized their tales in Herodotus and Homer, on ancient Egyptian papyruses and Chaldean stone tablets; and they have recorded them all over the world, in Scandinavia and Africa, among Indians on the banks of the Bengal and Indians along the Missouri. The dispersion is so striking that some have come to believe in Ur-stories and a basic Indo-European repertory of myths, legends, and tales. This tendency feeds into the cosmic theories of Frazer and Jung and Lévi-Strauss, but it does not help anyone attempting to penetrate the peasant mentalities of early modern France.

Fortunately, a more down-to-earth tendency in folklore makes it possible to isolate the peculiar characteristics of traditional French tales. *Le Conte populaire français* arranges them according to the Aarne-Thompson classification scheme, which covers all varieties of Indo-European folktales. It therefore provides the basis for comparative study, and the comparisons suggest the way general themes took root and grew in French soil. "Tom Thumb" ("Le Petit Poucet," tale type 327), for example, has a strong French flavor, in Perrault as well as the peasant versions, if one compares it with its German cousin, "Hansel and Gretel." The Grimms' tale emphasizes the mysterious forest and the naïveté of the children in the face of inscrutable evil, and it has more fanciful and poetic touches, as in the details about the bread-and-cake house and the magic birds. The French children confront an ogre, but in a very real house. Monsieur and Madame Ogre discuss their plans for a dinner party as if they were any married couple, and they carp at each other just as Tom Thumb's parents did. In fact, it is hard to tell the two couples apart. Both simple-minded wives throw away their family's fortunes; and their husbands berate them in the same manner, except that the ogre tells his wife that she deserves to be eaten and that he would do the job himself if she were not such an unappetizing *vieille bête* (old beast). Unlike their German relatives, the French ogres appear in the role of *le bourgeois de la maison* (burgher head of household), as if they were rich local landowners. They play fiddles, visit friends, snore contentedly in bed beside fat ogress wives; and for all their boorishness, they never fail to be good family men and good providers. Hence the joy of the ogre in "Pitchin-Pitchot" as he bounds into the house, a sack on his back: "Catherine, put on the big kettle. I've caught Pitchin-Pitchot."

Where the German tales maintain a tone of terror and fantasy, the French strike a note of humor and domesticity. Firebirds settle down into hen yards. Elves, genii, forest spirits, the whole Indo-European panoply of magical beings become reduced in France to two species, ogres and fairies. And those vestigial creatures acquire human foibles and generally let humans solve their problems by their own devices, that is, by cunning and "Cartesianism"—a term that the French apply vulgarly to their propensity for craftiness and intrigue. The Gallic touch is clear in many of the tales that Perrault did not rework for his own Gallicized Mother Goose of 1697: the *panache* of the young blacksmith in "Le Petit Forgeron" (tale type 317), for example, who kills giants on a classic *tour de France;* or the provincialism of the Breton peasant in "Jean Bête" (tale type 675), who is given anything he wishes and asks for *un bon péché de piquette et une écuelle de patates du lait* ("crude wine and a bowl of potatoes in milk"); or the professional jealousy of the master gardener, who fails to prune vines as well as his apprentice in "Jean le Teigneux" (tale type 314); or the cleverness of the devil's daughter in "La Belle Eulalie" (tale type 313), who escapes with her lover by leaving two talking pâtés in their beds. Just as one cannot attach the French tales to specific events, one should not dilute them in a timeless universal mythology. They really belong to a middle ground: *la France moderne* or the France that existed from the fifteenth through the eighteenth century.

That time span may look distressingly vague to anyone who expects history to be precise. But precision may be inappropriate as well as impossible in the history of *mentalités,* a genre that requires different methods from those used in conventional genres, like political history. World views can not be chronicled in the manner of political events, but they are no less "real." Politics could not take place without the preliminary mental ordering that goes into the common-sense notion of the real world. Common sense itself is a social construction of reality, which varies from culture to culture. Far from being the arbitrary figment of some collective imagination, it expresses the common basis of experience in a given social order. To reconstruct the way peasants saw the world under the Old Regime, therefore, one should begin by asking what they had in common, what experiences they shared in the everyday life of their villages.

Thanks to several generations of research by social historians, that question can be answered. The answer must be hedged with qualifications and restricted to a high level of generalization because conditions varied so much in the kingdom, which remained a patchwork of regions rather than a unified nation until the Revolution and perhaps even well into the nineteenth century. Pierre Goubert, Emmanuel Le Roy Ladurie, Pierre Saint-Jacob, Paul Bois, and many others have uncovered the particularities of peasant life region by region and have explicated them monograph by monograph. The density of monographs can make French social history look like a conspiracy of exceptions trying to disprove rules. Yet here, too, there exists a danger of misplaced professionalism; for if one stands at a safe enough distance from the details, a general picture begins to emerge. In fact, it has already reached the stage of assimilation in textbooks like *Histoire économique et sociale de la France* (Paris, 1970) and syntheses like *Histoire de la France rurale* (Paris, 1975/76). It goes roughly as follows.

Despite war, plague, and famine, the social order that existed at village level remained remarkably stable during the early modern period in France. The peasants were relatively free—less so than the yeomen who were turning into landless laborers in England, more so than the serfs who were sinking into a kind of slavery east of the Elbe. But they could not escape from a seigneurial system that denied them sufficient land to achieve economic independence and that siphoned off whatever surplus they produced. Men labored from dawn to dusk, scratching the soil on scattered strips of land with plows like those of the Romans and hacking at their grain with primitive sickles, in order to leave enough stubble for communal grazing. Women married late—at age twenty-five to twenty-seven—and gave birth to only five or six children, of whom only two or three survived to adulthood. Great masses of people lived in a state of chronic malnutrition, subsisting mainly on porridge made of bread and water with some occasional, homegrown vegetables thrown in. They ate meat only a few times a year, on feast days or after autumn slaughtering if they did not have enough silage to feed the livestock over the winter. They often failed to get the two pounds of bread (2,000 calories) a day that they needed to keep up their health, and so they had little protection against the combined effects of grain shortage and disease. The population fluctuated between fifteen and twenty million, expanding to the limits of its productive capacity (an average density of forty souls per square kilometer, an average annual rate of forty births per thousand inhabitants), only to be devastated by demographic crises. For four centuries—from the first ravages of the Black Death in 1347 to the first great leap in population and productivity in the 1730s—French society remained trapped in rigid institutions and Malthusian conditions. It went through a period of stagnation, which Fernand Braudel and Emmanuel Le Roy Ladurie have described as *l'histoire immobile* (unmoving history).

That phrase now seems exaggerated, for it hardly does justice to the religious conflict, grain riots, and rebellions against the extension of state power that disrupted the late medieval pattern of village life. But when first used in the 1950s, the notion of immobile history—a history of structural continuity over a long time span, *la longue durée*—served as a corrective to the tendency to see history as a succession of political events. Event history, *histoire événementielle,* generally took place over the heads of the peasantry, in the remote world of Paris and Versailles. While ministers came and went and battles raged, life in the village continued unperturbed, much as it had always been since the times beyond the reach of memory.

History looked "immobile" at the village level, because seigneurialism and the subsistence economy kept villagers bent over the soil, and primitive techniques of farming gave them no opportunity to unbend. Grain yields remained at a ratio of about 5-to-1, a primitive return in contrast to modern farming, which produces fifteen or even thirty grains for every seed planted. Farmers could not raise enough grain to feed large numbers of animals, and they did not have enough livestock to produce the manure to fertilize the fields to increase the yield. This vicious circle kept them enclosed within a system of triennial or biennial crop rotation, which left a huge proportion of their land lying fallow. They could not convert the fallow to the cultivation of crops like clover, which return nitrogen to the soil, because they lived too close to penury to risk the experiment, aside from the fact that no one had any notion of nitrogen. Collective methods of cultivation also reduced the margin for experimentation. Except in a few regions with enclosures, like the *bocage* district of the west, peasants farmed scattered strips in open fields. They sowed and harvested collectively, so that common gleaning and common grazing could take place. They depended on common lands and forests beyond the fields for pasture, firewood, and chestnuts or berries. The only area where they could attempt to get ahead by individual initiative was the *basse-cour* or backyard attached to their household plots, or *manses*. Here they struggled to build up manure heaps, to raise flax for spinning, to produce vegetables and chickens for their home brews and local markets.

The backyard garden often provided the margin of survival for families that lacked the twenty, thirty, or forty acres that were necessary for economic independence. They needed so much land because so much of their harvest was drained from them by seigneurial dues, tithes, ground rents, and taxes. In most of central and northern France, the wealthier peasants rigged the collection of the main royal tax, the *taille,* in accordance with an old French principle: soak the poor. So tax collecting opened up fissures within the village, and indebtedness compounded the damage. The poorer peasants frequently borrowed from the rich—that is, the few relatively wealthy *coqs du village* (cocks of the walk), who owned enough land to sell surplus grain on the market, to build up herds, and to hire the poor as laborers. Debt peonage may have made the wealthy peasants hated as much as the seigneur and the ecclesiastical *décimateur* (tithe collector). Hatred, jealousy, and conflicts of interest ran through peasant society. The village was no happy and harmonious *Gemeinschaft.*

For most peasants village life was a struggle for survival, and survival meant keeping above the line that divided the poor from the indigent. The poverty line varied from place to place, according to the amount of land necessary to pay taxes, tithes, and seigneurial dues; to put aside enough grain for planting next year; and to feed the family. In times of scarcity, poor families had to buy their food. They suffered as consumers, while prices shot up and the wealthier peasants made a killing. So a succession of bad harvests could polarize the village, driving the marginal families into indigence as the rich got richer. In the face of such difficulties, the "little people" (*petites gens*) survived by their wits. They hired themselves out as farm hands, spun and wove cloth in their cottages, did odd jobs, and took to the road, picking up work wherever they could find it.

Many of them went under. Then they took to the road for good, drifting about with the flotsam and jetsam of France's *population flottante* ("floating population"), which included several million desperate souls by the 1780s. Except for the happy few on an artisanal *tour de France* and the occasional troupes of actors and mountebanks, life on the road meant ceaseless scavenging for food. The drifters raided chicken coops, milked untended cows, stole laundry drying on hedges, snipped off horses' tails (good for selling to upholsterers), and lacerated and disguised their bodies in order to pass as invalids wherever alms were being given out. They joined and deserted regiment after regiment and served as false recruits. They became smugglers, highwaymen, pickpockets, prostitutes. And in the end they surrendered in *hôpitaux,* pestilential poor houses, or else crawled under a bush or a hay loft and died—*croquants* who had "croaked."

Death came just as inexorably to families that remained in their villages and kept above the poverty line. As Pierre Goubert, Louis Henry, Jacques Dupâquier, and other historical demographers have shown, life was an inexorable struggle against death everywhere in early modern France. In Crulai, Normandy, 236 of every 1,000 babies died before their first birthdays during the seventeenth century, as opposed to twenty today. About 45 per cent of the Frenchmen born in the eighteenth century died before the age of ten. Few of the survivors reached adulthood before the death of at least one of their parents. And few parents reached the end of their procreative years, because death interrupted them. Terminated by death, not divorce, marriages lasted an average of fifteen years, half as long as they do in France today. In Crulai, one in five husbands lost his wife and then remarried. Stepmothers proliferated everywhere—far more so than stepfathers, as the remarriage rate among widows was one in ten. Stepchildren may not have been treated like Cinderella, but relations between siblings probably were harsh. A new child often meant the difference between poverty and indigence. Even if it did not overtax the family's larder, it could bring penury down upon the next generation by swelling the number of claimants when the parents' land was divided among their heirs.

Whenever the population expanded, landholding fragmented and pauperization set in. Primogeniture slowed the process in some areas, but the best defense everywhere was delayed marriage, a tendency that must have taken its toll in the emotional life of the family. The peasants of the Old Regime, unlike those in contemporary India, generally did not marry until they could occupy a cottage, and they rarely had children out of wedlock or after they reached their forties. In Port-en-Bessin, for example, women married at twenty-seven and stopped bearing children at forty on the average. Demographers have found no evidence of birth control or widespread illegitimacy before the late eighteenth century. Early modern man did not understand life in a way that enabled him to control it. Early modern woman could not conceive of mastering nature, so she conceived as God willed it—and as Thumbkin's mother did in "Le Petit Poucet." But late marriage, a short period of fertility, and long stretches of breast-feeding, which reduces the likelihood of conception, limited the size of her family. The harshest and most effective limit was imposed by death, her own and those of her babies during childbirth and infancy. Stillborn children, called *chrissons,* were sometimes buried casually, in anonymous collective graves. Infants were sometimes smothered by their parents in bed—a rather common accident, judging by episcopal edicts forbidding parents to sleep with children who had not reached their first birthdays. Whole families crowded into one or two beds and surrounded themselves with livestock in order to keep warm. So children became participant observers of their parents' sexual activities. No one thought of them as innocent creatures or of childhood itself as a distinct phase of life, clearly distinguishable from adolescence, youth, and adulthood by special styles of dress and behavior. Children labored alongside their parents almost as soon as they could walk, and they joined the adult labor force as farm hands, servants, and apprentices as soon as they reached their teens.

The peasants of early modern France inhabited a world of stepmothers and orphans, of inexorable, unending toil, and of brutal emotions, both raw and repressed. The human condition has changed so much since then that we can hardly imagine the way it appeared to people whose lives really were nasty, brutish, and short. That is why we need to reread Mother Goose.

Consider four of the best-known stories from Perrault's Mother Goose—"Puss 'n Boots," "Tom Thumb," "Cinderella," and "The Ridiculous Wishes"—in comparison with some of the peasant tales that treat the same themes.

In "Puss 'n Boots," a poor miller dies, leaving the mill to his eldest son, an ass to the second, and only a cat to the third. "Neither a notary nor a lawyer were called in," Perrault observes. "They would have eaten up the poor patrimony." We are clearly in France, although other versions of this theme exist in Asia, Africa, and South America. The inheritance customs of French peasants, as well as noblemen, often prevented the fragmentation of the patrimony by favoring the eldest son. The youngest son of the miller, however, inherits a cat who has a genius for domestic intrigue. Everywhere around him, this Cartesian cat sees vanity, stupidity, and unsatisfied appetite; and he exploits it all by a series of tricks, which lead to a rich marriage for his master and a fine estate for himself, although in some of the pre-Perrault versions the master ultimately dupes the cat, who is actually a fox and does not wear boots.

A tale from the oral tradition, "La Renarde" (tale type 460), begins in a similar way: "Once there were two brothers, who took up the inheritances left to them by their father. The older, Joseph, kept the farm. The younger, Baptiste, received only a handful of coins; and as he had five children and very little to feed them with, he fell into destitution." In desperation, Baptiste begs for grain from his brother. Joseph tells him to strip off his rags, stand naked in the rain, and roll in the granary. He can keep as much grain as adheres to his body. Baptiste submits to this exercise in brotherly love, but he fails to pick up enough food to keep his family alive, so he takes to the road. Eventually he meets a good fairy, La Renarde, who helps him to solve a string of riddles, which lead to a pot of buried gold and the fulfillment of a peasant's dream: a house, fields, pasture, woodland, "and his children had cake apiece every day."

"Tom Thumb" ("Le Petit Poucet," tale type 327) is a French version of "Hansel and Gretel," although Perrault took his title from a tale that belongs to type 700. It provides a glimpse of the Malthusian world, even in Perrault's watered-down version: "Once upon a time there was a woodsman and his wife, who had seven children, all boys. . . . They were very poor, and their seven children were a great inconvenience, because none was old enough to support himself. . . . A very difficult year came, and the famine was so great that these poor folk resolved to get rid of their children." The matter-of-fact tone suggests how commonplace the death of children had become in early modern France. Perrault wrote his tale in the mid-1690s, at the height of the worst demographic crisis in the seventeenth century—a time when plague and famine decimated the population of northern France, when the poor ate offal thrown in the street by tanners, when corpses were found with grass in their mouths and mothers "exposed" the infants they could not feed so that they got sick and died. By abandoning their children in the forest, Tom Thumb's parents were trying to cope with a problem that overwhelmed the peasantry many times in the seventeenth and eighteenth centuries—the problem of survival during a period of demographic disaster.

The same motif exists in the peasant versions of the tale and in other tales, along with other forms of infanticide and child abuse. Sometimes the parents turn their children out on the road as beggars and thieves. Sometimes they run away themselves, leaving the children to beg at home. And sometimes they sell the children to the devil. In the French version of "The Sorcerer's Apprentice" ("La Pomme d'orange," tale type 325), a father is overwhelmed by "as many children as there are holes in a sieve," a phrase that occurs in several tales and that should be taken as hyperbole about Malthusian pressure rather than as evidence about family size. When a new baby arrives, the father sells it to the devil (a sorcerer in some versions) in exchange for receiving a full larder for twelve years. At the end of that time, he gets the boy back, thanks to a ruse that the boy devises, for the little rogue has picked up a repertory of tricks, including the power to transform himself into animals, during his apprenticeship. Before long, the cupboard is bare and the family is facing starvation again. The boy then changes himself into a hunting dog, so that his father can sell him once more to the devil, who reappears as a hunter. After the father has collected the money, the dog runs away and returns home as a boy. They try the same trick again, with the boy transformed into a horse. This time the devil keeps hold of a magic collar, which prevents the horse from changing back into a boy. But a farm hand leads the horse to drink at a pond, thereby, giving it a chance to escape in the form of a frog. The devil turns into a fish and is about to devour it, when the frog changes into a bird. The devil becomes a hawk and pursues the bird, which flies into the bedroom of a dying king and takes the form of an orange. Then the devil appears as a doctor and demands the orange in exchange for curing the king. The orange spills onto the floor, transformed into grains of millet. The devil turns into a chicken and starts to gobble up the grains. But the last grain turns into a fox, which finally wins the transformation contest by devouring the hen. The tale did not merely provide amusement. It dramatized the struggle over scarce resources, which pitted the poor against the rich, the "little people" (*menu peuple, petites gens*) against "the big" (*les gros, les grands*). Some versions make the social comment explicit by casting the devil in the role of a "seigneur" and concluding at the end: "And thus did the servant eat the master."

To eat or not to eat, that was the question peasants confronted in their folklore as well as in their daily lives. It appears in a great many of the tales, often in connection with the theme of the wicked stepmother, which must have had special resonance around Old Regime hearths because Old Regime demography made stepmothers such important figures in village society. Perrault did justice to the theme in "Cinderella," but he neglected the related motif of malnutrition, which stands out in the peasant versions of the tale. In one common version ("La Petite Annette," tale type 511), the wicked stepmother gives poor Annette only a crust of bread a day and makes her keep the sheep, while her fat and indolent stepsisters lounge around the house and dine on mutton, leaving their dishes for Annette to wash upon her return from the fields. Annette is about to die of starvation, when the Virgin Mary appears and gives her a magic wand, which produces a magnificent feast whenever Annette touches it to a black sheep. Before long the girl is plumper than her stepsisters. But her new beauty—and fatness made for beauty under the Old Regime as in many primitive societies—arouses the stepmother's suspicions. By a ruse, the stepmother discovers the magic sheep, kills it, and serves its liver to Annette. Annette manages to bury the liver secretly and it grows into a tree, which is so high that no one can pick its fruit, except Annette; for it bends its branches down to her whenever she approaches. A passing prince (who is as gluttonous as everyone else in the country) wants the fruit so badly that he promises to marry the maiden who can pick some for him. Hoping to make a match for one of her daughters, the stepmother builds a huge ladder. But when she tries it out, she falls and breaks her neck. Annette then gathers the fruit, marries the prince, and lives happily ever after.

Malnutrition and parental neglect go together in several tales, notably "La Sirène et l'épervier" (tale type 316) and "Brigitte, la maman qui m'a pas fait, mais m'a nourri" (tale type 713). The quest for food can be found in nearly all of them, even in Perrault, where it appears in burlesque form in "The Ridiculous Wishes." A poor woodsman is promised the fulfillment of any three wishes as a reward for a good deed. While he ruminates, his appetite overcomes him; and he wishes for a sausage. After it appears on his plate, his wife, an insufferable scold, quarrels so violently over the wasting of the wish that he wishes the sausage would grow on her nose. Then, confronted with a disfigured spouse, he wishes her back to her normal state; and they return to their former miserable existence.

Wishing usually takes the form of food in peasant tales, and it is never ridiculous. The discharged, down-and-out soldier, La Ramée, a stock character like the abused stepdaughter, is reduced to beggary in "Le Diable et le maréchal ferrant" (tale type 330). He shares his last pennies with other beggars, one of whom turns out to be Saint Peter in disguise, and as a reward he is granted any wish he wants. Instead of taking paradise, he asks for "a square meal"—or, in other versions, "white bread and a chicken," "a bun, a sausage, and as much wine as he can drink," "tobacco and the food he saw in the inn," or "to always have a crust of bread." Once supplied with magic wands, rings, or supernatural helpers, the first thought of the peasant hero is always for food. He never shows any imagination in his ordering. He merely takes the *plat du jour,* and it is always the same: solid peasant fare, though it may vary with the region, as in the case of the "cakes, fried bread, and pieces of cheese" (*canistrelli e fritelli, pezzi di broccio*) served up in a Corsican feast. Usually the peasant raconteur does not describe the food in detail. Lacking any notion of gastronomy, he simply loads up his hero's plate; and if he wants to supply an extravagant touch, he adds, "There were even napkins."

One extravagance clearly stands out: meat. In a society of de facto vegetarians, the luxury of luxuries was to sink one's teeth into a side of mutton, pork, or beef. The wedding feast in "Royaume des Valdars" (tale type 400) includes roast pigs who run around with forks sticking out of their flanks so that the guests can help themselves to ready-carved mouthfuls. The French version of a common ghost story, "La Goulue" (tale type 366), concerns a peasant girl who insists on eating meat every day. Unable to satisfy this extraordinary craving, her parents serve her a leg they have cut off a newly buried corpse. On the next day, the corpse appears before the girl in the kitchen. It orders her to wash its right leg, then its left leg. When she sees that the left leg is missing, it screams, "You ate it." Then it carries her back to the grave and devours her. The later, English versions of the tale, notably "The Golden Arm" made famous by Mark Twain, have the same plot without the carnivorousness—the very element that seems to have made the story fascinating for the peasants of the Old Regime. But whether they filled up on meat or porridge, the full belly came first among the wishes of the French peasant heroes. It was all the peasant Cinderella aspired to, even though she got a prince. "She touched the black sheep with the magic wand. Immediately a fully decked table appeared before her. She could eat what she wanted, and she ate a bellyful." To eat one's fill, eat until the exhaustion of the appetite (*manger à sa faim*), was the principal pleasure that the peasants dangled before their imaginations, and one that they rarely realized in their lives.

They also imagined other dreams coming true, including the standard run of castles and princesses. But their wishes usually remained fixed on common objects in the everyday world. One hero gets "a cow and some chickens"; another, an armoire full of linens. A third settles for light work, regular meals, and a pipe full of tobacco. And when gold rains into the fireplace of a fourth, he uses it to buy "food, clothes, a horse, land." In most of the tales, wish fulfillment turns into a program for survival, not a fantasy of escape.

CONSIDER THIS

Auden says in his "Grimm and Andersen" that the Grimm brothers attempted to model their texts "exactly" on oral tellings of the folktales, but Robert Darnton claims that the Grimm versions were intertexts, drawn not from the oral tradition itself, but from oral tellings which had been shaped by the tellers having *read* written texts. Folktales, he says, are historical documents: "They have evolved over many centuries and have taken different turns in different cultural traditions."

What does Roland Barthes mean by situating things in history? Darnton gives us an answer as he tries to place the French peasants in the context in which they told the tales. This is a demanding text. Robert Darnton, a Princeton historian, relies on several sources of knowledge that you probably are unfamiliar with, among them scholarship in the study of folktales, and the French language. How do you read around what you don't know as you negotiate with this text? How do you find your way through? One suggestion is to read quickly, almost carelessly, getting a sense of what's going on and then going back to the parts that intrigue you.

This piece is taken from his book *The Great Cat Massacre.* Does the title capture your attention?

About Men
Gretel Ehrlich

When I'm in New York but feeling lonely for Wyoming I look for the Marlboro ads in the subway. What I'm aching to see is horseflesh, the glint of a spur, a line of distant mountains, brimming creeks, and a reminder of the ranchers and cowboys I've ridden with for the last eight years. But the men I see in those posters with their stern, humorless looks remind me of no one I know here. In our hellbent earnestness to romanticize the cowboy we've ironically disesteemed his true character. If he's "strong and silent" it's because there's probably no one to talk to. If he "rides away into the sunset" it's because he's been on horseback since four in the morning moving cattle and he's trying, fifteen hours later, to get home to his family. If he's a "rugged individualist" he's also part of a team: ranch work is teamwork and even the glorified open-range cowboys of the 1880s rode up and down the Chisholm Trail in the company of twenty or thirty other riders. Instead of the macho, trigger-happy man our culture has perversely wanted him to be, the cowboy is more apt to be convivial, quirky, and softhearted. To be "tough" on a ranch has nothing to do with conquests and displays of power. More often than not, circumstances—like the colt he's riding or an unexpected blizzard—are overpowering him. It's not toughness but "toughing it out" that counts. In other words, this macho, cultural artifact the cowboy has become is simply a man who possesses resilience, patience, and an instinct for survival. "Cowboys are just like a pile of rocks—everything happens to them. They get climbed on, kicked, rained and snowed on, scuffed up by wind. Their job is 'just to take it'," one old-timer told me.

A cowboy is someone who loves his work. Since the hours are long—ten to fifteen hours a day—and the pay is $30 he has to. What's required of him is an odd mixture of physical vigor and maternalism. His part of the beef-raising industry is to birth and nurture calves and take care of their mothers. For the most part his work is done on horseback and in a lifetime he sees and comes to know more animals than people. The iconic myth surrounding him is built on American notions of heroism: the index of a man's value as measured in physical courage. Such ideas have perverted manliness into a self-absorbed race for cheap thrills. In a rancher's world, courage has less to do with facing danger than with acting spontaneously—usually on behalf of an animal or another rider. If a cow is stuck in a boghole he throws a loop around her neck, takes his dally (a half hitch around the saddle horn), and pulls her out with horsepower. If a calf is born sick, he may take her home, warm her in front of the kitchen fire, and massage her legs until dawn. One friend, whose favorite horse was trying to swim a lake with hobbles on, dove under water and cut her legs loose with a knife, then swam her to shore, his arm around her neck lifeguard-style, and saved her from drowning. Because these incidents are usually linked to someone or something outside himself, the westerner's courage is selfless, a form of compassion.

The physical punishment that goes with cowboying is greatly underplayed. Once fear is dispensed with, the threshold of pain rises to meet the demands of the job. When Jane Fonda asked Robert Redford (in the film *Electric Horseman*) if he was sick as he struggled to his feet one morning, he replied, "No, just bent." For once the movies had it right. The cowboys I was sitting with laughed in agreement. Cowboys are rarely complainers; they show their stoicism by laughing at themselves.

If a rancher or cowboy has been thought of as a "man's man"—laconic, hard-drinking, inscrutable—there's almost no place in which the balancing act between male and female, manliness and femininity, can be more natural. If he's gruff, handsome, and physically fit on the outside, he's androgynous at the core. Ranchers are midwives, hunters, nurturers, providers, and conservationists all at once. What we've interpreted as toughness—weathered skin, calloused hands, a squint in the eye and a growl in the voice—only masks the tenderness inside. "Now don't go telling me these lambs are cute," one rancher warned me the first day I walked into the football-field-sized lambing sheds. The next thing I knew he was holding a black lamb. "Ain't this little rat good-lookin'?"

So many of the men who came to the West were southerners—men looking for work and a new life after the Civil War—that chivalrousness and strict codes of honor were soon thought of as western traits. There were very few women in Wyoming during territorial days, so when they did arrive (some as mail-order brides from places like Philadelphia) there was a stand-offishness between sexes and a formality that persists now. Ranchers still tip their hats and say, "Howdy, ma'am" instead of shaking hands with me.

Even young cowboys are often evasive with women. It's not that they're Jekyll and Hyde creatures—gentle with animals and rough on women—but rather, that they don't know how to bring their tenderness into the house and lack the vocabulary to express the complexity of what they feel. Dancing wildly all night becomes a metaphor for the explosive emotions pent up inside, and when these are, on occasion, released, they're so battery-charged and potent that one caress of the face or one "I love you" will peal for a long while.

The geographical vastness and the social isolation here make emotional evolution seem impossible. Those contradictions of the heart between respectability, logic, and convention on the one hand, and impulse, passion, and intuition on the other, played out wordlessly against the paradisical beauty of the West, give cowboys a wide-eyed but drawn look. Their lips pucker up, not with kisses but with immutability. They may want to break out, staying up all night with a lover just to talk, but they don't know how and can't imagine what the consequences will be. Those rare occasions when they do bare themselves result in confusion. "I feel as if I'd sprained my heart," one friend told me a month after such a meeting.

My friend Ted Hoagland wrote, "No one is as fragile as a woman, but no one is as fragile as a man." For all the women here who use "fragileness" to avoid work or as a sexual ploy, there are men who try to hide theirs, all the while clinging to an adolescent dependency on women to cook their meals, wash their clothes, and keep the ranch house warm in winter. But there is true vulnerability in evidence here. Because these men work with animals, not machines or numbers, because they live outside in landscapes of torrential beauty, because they are confined to a place and a routine embellished with awesome variables, because calves die in the arms that pulled others into life, because they go to the mountains as if on a pilgrimage to find out what makes a herd of elk tick, their strength is also a softness, their toughness, a rare delicacy.

CONSIDER THIS

A former documentary filmmaker who was born and raised in California, Gretel Ehrlich came to "the planet of Wyoming" and she stayed. In addition to two collections of essays, she has written two books of poetry and a collection of short stories (with Edward Hoagland). No doubt it is her work on ranches—lambing, branding, herding sheep, and calving—that gives "About Men" its disarming firsthand information. But it is also her filmmaker's sensibility that seems to expose the contrast between our cultural myths and expectations (what we want to see) and what exists. If we have romanticized the "strong and silent" cowboy, what other roles have we romanticized—and what landscapes?

Saint Marie
Louise Erdrich

MARIE LAZARRE

So when I went there, I knew the dark fish must rise. Plumes of radiance had soldered on me. No reservation girl had ever prayed so hard. There was no use in trying to ignore me any longer. I was going up there on the hill with the black robe women. They were not any lighter than me. I was going up there to pray as good as they could. Because I don't have that much Indian blood. And they never thought they'd have a girl from this reservation as a saint they'd have to kneel to. But they'd have me. And I'd be carved in pure gold. With ruby lips. And my toenails would be little pink ocean shells, which they would have to stoop down off their high horse to kiss.

I was ignorant. I was near age fourteen. The length of sky is just about the size of my ignorance. Pure and wide. And it was just that—the pure and wideness of my ignorance— that got me up the hill to Sacred Heart Convent and brought me back down alive. For maybe Jesus did not take my bait, but them Sisters tried to cram me right down whole.

You ever see a walleye strike so bad the lure is practically out its back end before you reel it in? That is what they done with me. I don't like to make that low comparison, but I have seen a walleye do that once. And it's the same attempt as Sister Leopolda made to get me in her clutch.

I had the mail-order Catholic soul you get in a girl raised out in the bush, whose only thought is getting into town. For Sunday Mass is the only time my father brought his children in except for school, when we were harnessed. Our soul went cheap. We were so anxious to get there we would have walked in on our hands and knees. We just craved going to the store, slinging bottle caps in the dust, making fool eyes at each other. And of course we went to church.

Where they have the convent is on top of the highest hill, so that from its windows the Sisters can be looking into the marrow of the town. Recently a windbreak was planted before the bar "for the purposes of tornado insurance." Don't tell me that. That poplar stand was put up to hide the drinkers as they get the transformation. As they are served into the beast of their burden. While they're drinking, that body comes upon them, and then they stagger or crawl out the bar door, pulling a weight they can't move past the poplars. They don't want no holy witness to their fall.

Anyway, I climbed. That was a long-ago day. There was a road then for wagons that wound in ruts to the top of the hill where they had their buildings of painted brick. Gleaming white. So white the sun glanced off in dazzling display to set forms whirling behind your eyelids. The face of God you could hardly look at. But that day it drizzled, so I could look all I wanted. I saw the homelier side. The cracked whitewash and swallows nesting in the busted ends of eaves. I saw the boards sawed the size of broken windowpanes and the fruit trees, stripped. Only the tough wild rhubarb flourished. Goldenrod rubbed up their walls. It was a poor convent. I didn't see that then but I know that now. Compared to others it was humble, ragtag, out in the middle of no place. It was the end of the world to some. Where the maps stopped. Where God had only half a hand in the creation. Where the Dark One had put in thick bush, liquor, wild dogs, and Indians.

I heard later that the Sacred Heart Convent was a catchall place for nuns that don't get along elsewhere. Nuns that complain too much or lose their mind. I'll always wonder now, after hearing that, where they picked up Sister Leopolda. Perhaps she had scarred someone else, the way she left a mark on me. Perhaps she was just sent around to test her Sisters' faith, here and there, like the spot-checker in a factory. For she was the definite most-hard trial to anyone's endurance, even when they started out with veils of wretched love upon their eyes.

I was that girl who thought the black hem of her garment would help me rise. Veils of love which was only hate petrified by longing—that was me. I was like those bush Indians who stole the holy black hat of a Jesuit and swallowed little scraps of it to cure their fevers. But the hat itself carried smallpox and was killing them with belief. Veils of faith! I had this confidence in Leopolda. She was different. The other Sisters had long ago gone blank and given up on Satan. He slept for them. They never noticed his comings and goings. But Leopolda kept track of him and knew his habits, minds he burrowed in, deep spaces where he hid. She knew as much about him as my grandma, who called him by other names and was not afraid.

In her class, Sister Leopolda carried a long oak pole for opening high windows. It had a hook made of iron on one end that could jerk a patch of your hair out or throttle you by the collar—all from a distance. She used this deadly hook-pole for catching Satan by surprise. He could have entered without your knowing it—through your lips or your nose or any one of your seven openings—and gained your mind. But she would see him. That pole would brain you from behind. And he would gasp, dazzled, and take the first thing she offered, which was pain.

She had a stringer of children who could only breathe if she said the word. I was the worst of them. She always said the Dark One wanted me most of all, and I believed this. I stood out. Evil was a common thing I trusted. Before sleep sometimes he came and whispered conversation in the old language of the bush. I listened. He told me things he never told anyone but Indians. I was privy to both worlds of his knowledge. I listened to him, but I had confidence in Leopolda. She was the only one of the bunch he even noticed.

There came a day, though, when Leopolda turned the tide with her hook-pole.

It was a quiet day with everyone working at their desks, when I heard him. He had sneaked into the closets in the back of the room. He was scratching around, tasting crumbs in our pockets, stealing buttons, squirting his dark juice in the linings and the boots. I was the only one who heard him, and I got bold. I smiled. I glanced back and smiled and looked up at her sly to see if she had noticed. My heart jumped. For she was looking straight at me. And she sniffed. She had a big stark bony nose stuck to the front of her face for smelling out brimstone and evil thoughts. She had smelled him on me. She stood up. Tall, pale, a blackness leading into the deeper blackness of the slate wall behind her. Her oak pole had flown into her grip. She had seen me glance at the closet. Oh, she knew. She knew just where he was. I watched her watch him in her mind's eye. The whole class was watching now. She was staring, sizing, following his scuffle. And all of a sudden she tensed down, posed on her bent kneesprings, cocked her arm back. She threw the oak pole singing over my head, through my braincloud. It cracked through the thin wood door of the back closet, and the heavy pointed hook drove through his heart. I turned. She'd speared her own black rubber overboot where he'd taken refuge in the tip of her darkest toe.

Something howled in my mind. Loss and darkness. I understood. I was to suffer for my smile.

He rose up hard in my heart. I didn't blink when the pole cracked. My skull was tough. I didn't flinch when she shrieked in my ear. I only shrugged at the flowers of hell. He wanted me. More than anything he craved me. But then she did the worst. She did what broke my mind to her. She grabbed me by the collar and dragged me, feet flying, through the room and threw me in the closet with her dead black overboot. And I was there. The only light was a crack beneath the door. I asked the Dark One to enter into me and boost my mind. I asked him to restrain my tears, for they was pushing behind my eyes. But he was afraid to come back there. He was afraid of her sharp pole. And I was afraid of Leopolda's pole for the first time, too. I felt the cold hook in my heart. How it could crack through the door at any minute and drag me out, like a dead fish on a gaff, drop me on the floor like a gutshot squirrel.

I was nothing. I edged back to the wall as far as I could. I breathed the chalk dust. The hem of her full black cloak cut against my cheek. He had left me. Her spear could find me any time. Her keen ears would aim the hook into the beat of my heart.

What was that sound?

It filled the closet, filled it up until it spilled over, but I did not recognize the crying wailing voice as mine until the door cracked open, brightness, and she hoisted me to her camphor-smelling lips.

"He *wants* you," she said. "That's the difference. I give you love."

Love. The black hook. The spear singing through the mind. I saw that she had tracked the Dark One to my heart and flushed him out into the open. So now my heart was an empty nest where she could lurk.

Well, I was weak. I was weak when I let her in, but she got a foothold there. Hard to dislodge as the year passed. Sometimes I felt him—the brush of dim wings—but only rarely did his voice compel. It was between Marie and Leopolda now, and the struggle changed. I began to realize I had been on the wrong track with the fruits of hell. The real way to overcome Leopolda was this: I'd get to heaven first. And then, when I saw her coming, I'd shut the gate. She'd be out! That is why, besides the bowing and the scraping I'd be dealt, I wanted to sit on the altar as a saint.

To this end, I went up the hill. Sister Leopolda was the consecrated nun who had sponsored me to come there.

"You're not vain," she said. "You're too honest, looking into the mirror, for that. You're not smart. You don't have the ambition to get clear. You have two choices. One, you can marry a no-good Indian, bear his brats, die like a dog. Or two, you can give yourself to God."

"I'll come up there," I said, "but not because of what you think."

I could have had any damn man on the reservation at the time. And I could have made him treat me like his own life. I looked good. And I looked white. But I wanted Sister Leopolda's heart. And here was the thing: sometimes I wanted her heart in love and admiration. Sometimes. And sometimes I wanted her heart to roast on a black stick.

She answered the back door where they had instructed me to call. I stood there with my bundle. She looked me up and down.

"All right," she said finally. "Come in."

She took my hand. Her fingers were like a bundle of broom straws, so thin and dry, but the strength of them was unnatural. I couldn't have tugged loose if she was leading me into rooms of white-hot coal. Her strength was a kind of perverse miracle, for she got it from fasting herself thin. Because of this hunger practice her lips were a wounded brown and her skin deadly pale. Her eye sockets were two deep lashless hollows in a taut skull. I told you about the nose already. It stuck out far and made the place her eyes moved even deeper, as if she stared out the wrong end of a gun barrel. She took the bundle from my hands and threw it in the corner.

"You'll be sleeping behind the stove, child."

It was immense, like a great furnace. There was a small cot close behind it.

"Looks like it could get warm there," I said.

"Hot. It does."

"Do I get a habit?"

I wanted something like the thing she wore. Flowing black cotton. Her face was strapped in white bandages, and a sharp crest of starched white cardboard hung over her forehead like a glaring beak. If possible, I wanted a bigger, longer, whiter beak than hers.

"No," she said, grinning her great skull grin. "You don't get one yet. Who knows, you might not like us. Or we might not like you."

But she had loved me, or offered me love. And she had tried to hunt the Dark One down. So I had this confidence.

"I'll inherit your keys from you," I said.

She looked at me sharply, and her grin turned strange. She hissed, taking in her breath. Then she turned to the door and took a key from her belt. It was a giant key, and it unlocked the larder where the food was stored.

Inside there was all kinds of good stuff. Things I'd tasted only once or twice in my life. I saw sticks of dried fruit, jars of orange peel, spice like cinnamon. I saw tins of crackers with ships painted on the side. I saw pickles. Jars of herring and the rind of pigs. There was cheese, a big brown block of it from the thick milk of goats. And besides that there was the everyday stuff, in great quantities, the flour and the coffee.

It was the cheese that got to me. When I saw it my stomach hollowed. My tongue dripped. I loved that goat-milk cheese better than anything I'd ever ate. I stared at it. The rich curve in the buttery cloth.

"When you inherit my keys," she said sourly, slamming the door in my face, "you can eat all you want of the priest's cheese."

Then she seemed to consider what she'd done. She looked at me. She took the key from her belt and went back, sliced a hunk off, and put it in my hand.

"If you're good you'll taste this cheese again. When I'm dead and gone," she said.

Then she dragged out the big sack of flour. When I finished that heaven stuff she told me to roll my sleeves up and begin doing God's labor. For a while we worked in silence, mixing up the dough and pounding it out on stone slabs.

"God's work," I said after a while. "If this is God's work, then I've done it all my life."

"Well, you've done it with the Devil in your heart then," she said. "Not God."

"How do you know?" I asked. But I knew she did. And I wished I had not brought up the subject.

"I see right into you like a clear glass," she said. "I always did."

"You don't know it," she continued after a while, "but he's come around here sulking. He's come around here brooding. You brought him in. He knows the smell of me, and he's going to make a last ditch try to get you back. Don't let him." She glared over at me. Her eyes were cold and lighted. "Don't let him touch you. We'll be a long time getting rid of him."

So I was careful. I was careful not to give him an inch. I said a rosary, two rosaries, three, underneath my breath. I said the Creed. I said every scrap of Latin I knew while we punched the dough with our fists. And still, I dropped the cup. It rolled under that monstrous iron stove, which was getting fired up for baking.

And she was on me. She saw he'd entered my distraction.

"Our good cup," she said. "Get it out of there, Marie."

I reached for the poker to snag it out from beneath the stove. But I had a sinking feeling in my stomach as I did this. Sure enough, her long arm darted past me like a whip. The poker lighted in her hand.

"Reach," she said. "Reach with your arm for that cup. And when your flesh is hot, remember that the flames you feel are only one fraction of the heat you will feel in his hellish embrace."

She always did things this way, to teach you lessons. So I wasn't surprised. It was playacting, anyway, because a stove isn't very hot underneath right along the floor. They aren't made that way. Otherwise a wood floor would burn. So I said yes and got down on my stomach and reached under. I meant to grab it quick and jump up again, before she could think up another lesson, but here it happened. Although I groped for the cup, my hand closed on nothing. That cup was nowhere to be found. I heard her step toward me, a slow step. I heard the creak of thick shoe leather, the little *plat* as the folds of her heavy skirts met, a trickle of fine sand sifting, somewhere, perhaps in the bowels of her, and I was afraid. I tried to scramble up, but her foot came down lightly behind my ear, and was lowered. The foot came down more firmly at the base of my neck, and I was held.

"You're like I was," she said. "He wants you very much."

"He doesn't want me no more," I said. "He had his fill. I got the cup!"

I heard the valve opening, the hissed intake of breath, and knew that I should not have spoke.

"You lie," she said. "You're cold. There is a wicked ice forming in your blood. You don't have a shred of devotion for God. Only wild cold dark lust. I know it. I know how you feel. I see the beast . . . the beast watches me out of your eyes sometimes. Cold."

The urgent scrape of metal. It took a moment to know from where. Top of the stove. Kettle. Lessons. She was steadying herself with the iron poker. I could feel it like pure certainty, driving into the wood floor. I would not remind her of pokers. I heard the water as it came, tipped from the spout, cooling as it fell but still scalding as it struck. I must have twitched beneath her foot, because she steadied me, and then the poker nudged up beside my arm as if to guide. "To warm your cold ash heart," she said. I felt how patient she would be. The water came. My mind went dead blank. Again. I could only think the kettle would be cooling slowly in her hand. I could not stand it. I bit my lip so as not to satisfy her with a sound. She gave me more reason to keep still.

"I will boil him from your mind if you make a peep," she said, "by filling up your ear."

Any sensible fool would have run back down the hill the minute Leopolda let them up from under her heel. But I was snared in her black intelligence by then. I could not think straight. I had prayed so hard I think I broke a cog in my mind. I prayed while her foot squeezed my throat. While my skin burst. I prayed even when I heard the wind come through, shrieking in the busted bird nests. I didn't stop when pure light fell, turning slowly behind my eyelids. God's face. Even that did not disrupt my continued praise. Words came. Words came from nowhere and flooded my mind.

Now I could pray much better than any one of them. Than all of them full force. This was proved. I turned to her in a daze when she let me up. My thoughts were gone, and yet I remember how surprised I was. Tears glittered in her eyes, deep down, like the sinking reflection in a well.

"It was so hard, Marie," she gasped. Her hands were shaking. The kettle clattered against the stove. "But I have used all the water up now. I think he is gone."

"I prayed," I said foolishly. "I prayed very hard."

"Yes," she said. "My dear one, I know."

We sat together quietly because we had no more words. We let the dough rise and punched it down once. She gave me a bowl of mush, unlocked the sausage from a special cupboard, and took that in to the Sisters. They sat down the hall, chewing their sausage, and I could hear them. I could hear their teeth bite through their bread and meat. I couldn't move. My shirt was dry but the cloth stuck to my back, and I couldn't think straight. I was losing the sense to understand how her mind worked. She'd gotten past me with her poker and I would never be a saint. I despaired. I felt I had no inside voice, nothing to direct me, no darkness, no Marie. I was about to throw that cornmeal mush out to the birds and make a run for it, when the vision rose up blazing in my mind.

I was rippling gold. My breasts were bare and my nipples flashed and winked. Diamonds tipped them. I could walk through panes of glass. I could walk through windows. She was at my feet, swallowing the glass after each step I took. I broke through another and another. The glass she swallowed ground and cut until her starved insides were only a subtle dust. She coughed. She coughed a cloud of dust. And then she was only a black rag that flapped off, snagged in bob wire, hung there for an age, and finally rotted into the breeze.

I saw this, mouth hanging open, gazing off into the flagged boughs of trees.

"Get up!" she cried. "Stop dreaming. It is time to bake."

Two other Sisters had come in with her, wide women with hands like paddles. They were evening and smoothing out the firebox beneath the great jaw of the oven.

"Who is this one?" they asked Leopolda. "Is she yours?"

"She is mine," said Leopolda. "A very good girl."

"What is your name?" one asked me.

"Marie."

"Marie. Star of the Sea."

"She will shine," said Leopolda, "when we have burned off the dark corrosion."

The others laughed, but uncertainly. They were mild and sturdy French, who did not understand Leopolda's twisted jokes, although they muttered respectfully at things she said. I knew they wouldn't believe what she had done with the kettle. There was no question. So I kept quiet.

"*Elle est docile,*" they said approvingly as they left to starch the linens.

"Does it pain?" Leopolda asked me as soon as they were out the door.

I did not answer. I felt sick with the hurt.

"Come along," she said.

The building was wholly quiet now. I followed her up the narrow staircase into a hall of little rooms, many doors. Her cell was the quietest, at the very end. Inside, the air smelled stale, as if the door had not been opened for years. There was a crude straw mattress, a tiny bookcase with a picture of Saint Francis hanging over it, a ragged palm, a stool for sitting on, a crucifix. She told me to remove my blouse and sit on the stool. I did so. She took a pot of salve from the bookcase and began to smooth it upon my burns. Her hands made slow, wide circles, stopping the pain. I closed my eyes. I expected to see blackness. Peace. But instead the vision reared up again. My chest was still tipped with diamonds. I was walking through windows. She was chewing up the broken litter I left behind.

"I am going," I said. "Let me go."

But she held me down.

"Don't go," she said quickly. "Don't. We have just begun."

I was weakening. My thoughts were whirling pitifully. The pain had kept me strong, and as it left me I began to forget it; I couldn't hold on. I began to wonder if she'd really scaled me with the kettle. I could not remember. To remember this seemed the most important thing in the world. But I was losing the memory. The scalding. The pouring. It began to vanish. I felt like my mind was coming off its hinge, flapping in the breeze, hanging by the hair of my own pain. I wrenched out of her grip.

"He was always in you," I said. "Even more than in me. He wanted you even more. And now he's got you. Get thee behind me!"

I shouted that, grabbed my shirt, and ran through the door throwing it on my body. I got down the stairs and into the kitchen, even, but no matter what I told myself, I couldn't get out the door. It wasn't finished. And she knew I would not leave. Her quiet step was immediately behind me.

"We must take the bread from the oven now," she said.

She was pretending nothing happened. But for the first time I had gotten through some chink she'd left in her darkness. Touched some doubt. Her voice was so low and brittle it cracked off at the end of her sentence.

"Help me, Marie," she said slowly.

But I was not going to help her, even though she had calmly buttoned the back of my shirt up and put the big cloth mittens in my hands for taking out the loaves. I could have bolted for it then. But I didn't. I knew that something was nearing completion. Something was about to happen. My back was a wall of singing flame. I was turning. I watched her take the long fork in one hand, to tap the loaves. In the other hand she gripped the black poker to hook the pans.

"Help me," she said again, and I thought, Yes, this is part of it. I put the mittens on my hands and swung the door open on its hinges. The oven gaped. She stood back a moment, letting the first blast of heat rush by. I moved behind her. I could feel the heat at my front and at my back. Before, behind. My skin was turning to beaten gold. It was coming quicker than I thought. The oven was like the gate of a personal hell. Just big enough and hot enough for one person, and that was her. One kick and Leopolda would fly in headfirst. And that would be one-millionth of the heat she would feel when she finally collapsed in his hellish embrace.

Saints know these numbers.

She bent forward with her fork held out. I kicked her with all my might. She flew in. But the outstretched poker hit the back wall first, so she rebounded. The oven was not so deep as I had thought.

There was a moment when I felt a sort of thin, hot disappointment, as when a fish slips off the line. Only I was the one going to be lost. She was fearfully silent. She whirled. Her veil had cutting edges. She had the poker in one hand. In the other she held that long sharp fork she used to tap the delicate crusts of loaves. Her face turned upside down on her shoulders. Her face turned blue. But saints are used to miracles. I felt no trace of fear.

If I was going to be lost, let the diamonds cut! Let her eat ground glass!

"Bitch of Jesus Christ!" I shouted. "Kneel and beg! Lick the floor!"

That was when she stabbed me through the hand with the fork, then took the poker up alongside my head, and knocked me out.

It must have been a half an hour later when I came around. Things were so strange. So strange I can hardly tell it for delight at the remembrance. For when I came around this was actually taking place. I was being worshiped. I had somehow gained the altar of a saint.

I was laying back on the stiff couch in the Mother Superior's office. I looked around me. It was as though my deepest dream had come to life. The Sisters of the convent were kneeling to me. Sister Bonaventure. Sister Dympna. Sister Cecilia Saint-Claire. The two French with hands like paddles. They were down on their knees. Black capes were slung over some of their heads. My name was buzzing up and down the room, like a fat autumn fly lighting on the tips of their tongues between Latin, humming up the heavy blood-dark curtains, circling their little cosseted heads. Marie! Marie! A girl thrown in a closet. Who was afraid of a rubber overboot. Who was half overcome. A girl who came in the back door where they threw their garbage. Marie! Who never found the cup. Who had to eat their cold mush. Marie! Leopolda had her face buried in her knuckles. Saint Marie of the Holy Slops! Saint Marie of the Bread Fork! Saint Marie of the Burnt Back and Scalded Butt!

I broke out and laughed.

They looked up. All holy hell burst loose when they saw I'd woke. I still did not understand what was happening. They were watching, talking, but not to me.

"The marks . . ."

"She has her hand closed."

"*Je ne peux pas voir.*"

I was not stupid enough to ask what they were talking about. I couldn't tell why I was laying in white sheets. I couldn't tell why they were praying to me. But I'll tell you this: it seemed entirely natural. It was me. I lifted up my hand as in my dream. It was completely limp with sacredness.

"Peace be with you."

My arm was dried blood from the wrist down to the elbow. And it hurt. Their faces turned like flat flowers of adoration to follow that hand's movements. I let it swing through the air, imparting a saint's blessing. I had practiced. I knew exactly how to act.

They murmured. I heaved a sigh, and a golden beam of light suddenly broke through the clouded window and flooded down directly on my face. A stroke of perfect luck! They had to be convinced.

Leopolda still knelt in the back of the room. Her knuckles were crammed halfway down her throat. Let me tell you, a saint has senses honed keen as a wolf. I knew that she was over my barrel now. How it happened did not matter. The last thing I remembered was how she flew from the oven and stabbed me. That one thing was most certainly true.

"Come forward, Sister Leopolda." I gestured with my heavenly wound. Oh, it hurt. It bled when I reopened the slight heal. "Kneel beside me," I said.

She knelt, but her voice box evidently did not work, for her mouth opened, shut, opened, but no sound came out. My throat clenched in noble delight I had read of as befitting a saint. She could not speak. But she was beaten. It was in her eyes. She stared at me now with all the deep hate of the wheel of devilish dust that rolled wild within her emptiness.

"What is it you want to tell me?" I asked. And at last she spoke.

"I have told my Sisters of your passion," she managed to choke out. "How the stigmata . . . the marks of the nails . . . appeared in your palm and you swooned at the holy vision. . . ."

"Yes," I said curiously.

And then, after a moment, I understood.

Leopolda had saved herself with her quick brain. She had witnessed a miracle. She had hid the fork and told this to the others. And of course they believed her, because they never knew how Satan came and went or where he took refuge.

"I saw it from the first," said the large one who put the bread in the oven. "Humility of the spirit. So rare in these girls."

"I saw it too," said the other one with great satisfaction. She sighed quietly. "If only it was me."

Leopolda was kneeling bolt upright, face blazing and twitching, a barely held fountain of blasting poison.

"Christ has marked me," I agreed.

I smiled the saint's smirk into her face. And then I looked at her. That was my mistake.

For I saw her kneeling there. Leopolda with her soul like a rubber overboot. With her face of a starved rat. With the desperate eyes drowning in the deep wells of her wrongness. There would be no one else after me. And I would leave. I saw Leopolda kneeling within the shambles of her love.

My heart had been about to surge from my chest with the blackness of my joyous heat. Now it dropped. I pitied her. I pitied her. Pity twisted in my stomach like that hook-pole was driven through me. I was caught. It was a feeling more terrible than any amount of boiling water and worse than being forked. Still, still, I could not help what I did. I had already smiled in a saint's mealy forgiveness. I heard myself speaking gently.

"Receive the dispensation of my sacred blood," I whispered.

But there was no heart in it. No joy when she bent to touch the floor. No dark leaping. I fell back into the white pillows. Blank dust was whirling through the light shafts. My skin was dust. Dust my lips. Dust the dirty spoons on the ends of my feet.

Rise up! I thought. Rise up and walk! There is no limit to this dust!

CONSIDER THIS

What strikes you first about "Saint Marie"? That the first-person narrator begins right smack in the middle, assuming a very close familiarity with the reader? Look at that line: "So when I went there, I knew the dark fish must rise." How long did it take you to find your feet, to have some sense of what she was talking about? How does this voice compare with the narrator's in Conroy's "Midair"? Is Erdrich's voice in the present moment, representing events as they are unfolding? Is hers a participant account? Or a spectator looking back?

Do you like this piece? If so, what do you appreciate about Erdrich's language? Or are you lost? If so, try reading "Sister Marie" aloud. And if you enjoyed this text, you may want to read the novel, *Love Medicine,* from which it is taken. Erdrich (born 1954), part Chippewa, part German, part French, draws many of her Native American characters and landscapes from the Red River Valley, where she grew up.

Erdrich, who has written three novels, collaborates with her husband, Michael Dorris, also a novelist, and college teacher; in fact, the two, together, have written *The Crown of Columbus* (1991), a novel about two contemporary professors' quest for Christopher Columbus's lost diary. Erdrich and Dorris have their own collaborative method: "They read and revise and argue out each other's scenes, word by word if necessary, and read them aloud to each other over the kitchen table until each [is] satisfied. No work ever leaves their house until this process has been completed . . . until they have a version on which they both agree" (Vince Passaro, "Tales from a Literary Marriage," *New York Times Magazine,* April 21, 1991).

Newness of Life
Martha Gellhorn

I am about to tell you an historical tale of travel in 1931, in the spring, when the world was young and gay. Of course the world was not young and gay, it was already spiraling down the Great Depression towards war. But I didn't know that, I didn't know anything much and all things are relative: the world was undeniably younger and I truly believe gayer than it is now. As for me, I was twenty-two and never more alight with gaiety.

The purpose of the journey then and forever after was to see the world and everything happening and everyone in it. The means were a triumph. I persuaded the St. Louis *Post Dispatch* that I would write dazzling feature stories for their Sunday magazine at $25 each, and persuaded the Missouri Pacific Railway that these stories would publicize their fine trains and the captivating sights along their routes, if they would give me a Pullman pass. At last I had become, in my own eyes only, a roving correspondent, heart's desire. I set out in my regular warm weather clothes, blue cotton shirt, matching full cotton skirt and sneakers, but carried a small suitcase since the knapsack of previous European journeys was not suitable to my new estate.

Trains were lovely. (No one in his right mind can say the same of airplanes.) You were flung about as on the high seas while cinders from the engine blew through the open windows like a black hail storm. Only the porters, who served as kind nannies, and the waiters could walk upright in a straight line. The passengers grew very chummy as they banged into each other and fell on strangers' laps. The meals in the dining car were delicious though tricky with plates and cups and glasses leaping around the table. At night, behind the swaying green curtains of the Pullman berth, I listened with excitement to the train. When it stopped to take on water or coal, the train made animal noises, puffing, groaning; the whistle sounded like a fierce bird cry. The wheels clanged their special beat, dragging us through the miles and the dark. By day I listened to others and was entertained and instructed. People traveled on business and to visit relatives, usually to help in illness or childbirth. Holiday travel was a summer event for the privileged few.

Trains were leisurely. You had time to see the modest little towns and isolated farmhouses, both built of wood with shade trees; mules and wagons on the roads, old trucks collecting goods or family at the stations. Not a shiny rich scene, from the train window, but peaceful. Perhaps it was a hard life; I have an ancient memory of stern faces on those station platforms and obesity was certainly not a national problem. But places and people were nothing compared to the land. You had time to watch it change, to feel the differences and the great distance. You knew you were traveling.

I bounced across the continent to the Pacific coast and back, on that journey, and America looked vast, beautiful and empty. A year earlier, at the 1930 census, the population of the U.S.A. was 122,775,046, roughly two-thirds of it east of the Mississippi. Texas and California, the largest states, had the largest population in the west, but people were still thin on the ground. In California, just over five and a half million people lived uncrowded lives in the sun. By 1980, three million people lived in the Los Angeles smog; who knows how many more are now frazzling their nerves on the freeways.

The first stop, my first feature story, was an oil boom. The name of that town in East Texas is long gone; besides it wasn't a town, it was a straggle of weatherbeaten frame houses on dirt roads in the middle of a dead flat landscape. Home for 200 impoverished citizens. Within sixty days, oil having spouted from their front yards, 30,000 crazy joyous men were churning up dust among a forest of oil wells, towers eighty feet high. The gaunt new millionaires sat in rocking chairs on their crumbling porches, bemused. The ladies wore faded flowered calico garments, the gents wore old jeans and collarless shirts; both sexes sparkling with diamonds. Hordes of people besieged the only store, waving fistfuls of greenbacks, and an iron cot sold for $200. Peddlers swarmed. A suitcase of new shoe laces was worth a fast small fortune, and no one could buy enough diamonds.

Everybody seemed to be drunk despite Prohibition, still officially in force. The noise was colossal: trains of tank cars, four hundred every day, clanking in and out, machinery scraping, chugging, pounding, and overall human bedlam. Law and order problems, arising from theft, assault and battery, extreme drunkenness, were handled by three Texas Rangers with enormous hats and enormous pearl-handled pistols. There was no jail so the Rangers pegged a chain in a large circle in the dust and chained their prisoners to it by the leg. The prisoners were as cheerful as everyone else. Their friends brought them booze and they managed to huddle for crap games, papering the dust with dollar bills, singing uproariously when the spirit moved them. To impress me, the Rangers stuck matches upright in the ground, pulled out their pistols like gunfighters in the movies, and shot the heads off.

At night, I retired to luxury quarters, a de-railed Pullman car which I shared with the elite, oil men who had arrived to make this gold rush work. Like the rest of the population, they drank and gambled all night, leaning from their berths, while greenbacks fluttered down like falling leaves. They addressed me as little lady and whenever excitement or rage caused anyone to shout four-letter words the others hushed him, no bad language in front of the little lady. We lived on cold baked beans, eaten from the can.

The Mayor, having heard that the Press was in town, came to call with diamonds on eight fingers. He apologized for being hurried but he had laid on a private train and was taking his townfolk, in their jewels and worn-out clothes, to New York for a spree at the Waldorf. I laughed from dawn to dawn and loved every minute of it.

Nowadays if you don't want to risk sleeping in the airport or in any fleabag hotel with a spare room, you are well advised to make reservations when you travel. I believe this sorry state of affairs began about twenty-five years ago and has been getting steadily worse and worse. Before, you never had to make reservations for anything anywhere. You moved by whim, when you pleased. To my mind that is the only good way to travel. By whim, I came to Ciudad Juarez in Mexico, across the border from El Paso, where I intended to interview the only woman bullfighter in the world, another dazzling feature story. Ciudad Juarez had an attractive bad reputation. All the pleasure domes—saloons, brothels, gambling joints—forbidden in the U.S. were wide open and cheap in this picturesque dump of a town. Sin had not paid, judging by the unpainted false-front buildings, derelict care and scurf of garbage on unpaved streets, and the general lassitude of the citizenry. I walked from my sleazy hotel to a sleazy cabaret-brothel where a group of ladies invited me to their table.

They were the resident prostitutes, keeping a colleague company; she was temporarily unemployed due to advanced pregnancy. She looked dowdy and middle-aged to me, a very nice Frenchwoman who was reading Alexandre Dumas and André Gide as a good pre-natal influence on her child. Her friends, heavily painted in low cut gowns with lashings of sequins, were charming and soft-spoken in French. French, not English, was then the lingua franca, fortunate for me as I knew no Spanish. They complained that business was bad and I suggested helpfully that they buy a tent and move to East Texas where business was sure to be splendid.

A scarecrow figure in dinner jacket, Maurice Chevalier straw hat and monocle began to sing gibberish and jerk dance steps in the middle of the dirty room. That was the cabaret. He joined us, kissed my hand and told me he was a Bavarian Baron, a passionate monarchist who fled the detestable Republic of Germany in 1919. His talk and eyes grew wider. Never having met a junkie before, I knew by instinct that he was on the needle, poor fellow. What a fine evening, I thought, you didn't meet such interesting people every day.

The only woman bullfighter in the world turned out to be Juanita, a pretty gentle shy seventeen-year-old. Her mother and brothers kept her locked in a squalid hotel room, like a substitute convent, letting her out only to practice her alarming profession. The bullring was small, poor and poorly attended. Juanita flung me her cape and dedicated the bull to me, a moment of intense self-importance, but I closed my eyes when I saw her running knock-kneed and not very fast from the oncoming bull. The bull though undersized was furious. Juanita's life worried me. I urged her to get a safe job as a waitress or salesgirl in El Paso but she said she was used to her work and had to support her family.

The trouble with the traveling life is that you never know the end of the stories. What became of the French prostitute's child who had such good pre-natal influences? What happened to Juanita? Did the East Texas oil millionaires end in Florida mansions or did they splurge their fortunes and end on the crumbling front porches? It saddens me to think how many stories I failed to understand even at their beginnings, and how many people I have forgotten.

Somehow my deal with the Missouri Pacific Railway got me to Mexico City. Mexico City is now one of the outstanding disasters of the world but in 1931 it was more magical than any European city I had seen. I wandered the streets in a daze of joy, admiring the strange old handsome buildings and the dignified brown-skinned people. The volcanoes shone in that clear light and the air smelled of flowers. The entire Federal District of Mexico, 570 square miles of which the city was only a part, had a population of 1,230,000. Now the population of Mexico City alone is 16 million. The fatal difference.

I wandered through a noble doorway into a great hall with a ceremonial stairway. Sitting on a plank, high up the wall by the stairway, a fat man in overalls was painting a mural. I thought such work went out with Michelangelo and stood transfixed. The huge wall was already half covered by brilliant agitated figures. He saw me and asked if I wanted to come up and presently, beside him on the plank, I was asking how he knew what to do next, while he went on painting as easily as he breathed. A voice from below shouted "Hola!" The plank was lowered and a small dark Frenchman joined us with tacos and beer, a lunch party suspended in air. That plank in the Palacio Nacional was a meeting place for painter friends of the fat man with curly black hair and round happy face whose name, I learned, was Diego Rivera. They were a new breed to me, these men, I longed to be like them, geniuses in the art of living with friendship and laughter, poor and unworried, absorbed in their work, free.

The Frenchman, a painter named Jean Charlot, invited me to go south to the hacienda where Russians were making a movie. I was delighted to go anywhere until I saw the hacienda, a gloomy ruin set in oppressive fields of giant cactus. Furniture was minimal in two rooms; one a dormitory of beds, the other for eating, with table and chairs. You had to be careful not to put your foot through broken boards on the filthy floors and the place stank of dirt, drains and mildew. Two large fair-haired Russians, the camera crew, chased Mexican maidens through this chaos, whooping Russian war cries, and flung them on the beds, iron four-posters with torn mosquito nets. I became very stuffy on behalf of the maidens.

And nothing was happening. The movie was held up for lack of film or money or whatever. Meals were appalling. Sheathed in glittering black flies, we ate boiled cactus and boiled goat meat from unwashed plates on a tablecloth stained by months of such grim fodder. The boss man stayed in his neat ascetic room, behind a closed door, and read *St. John of the Cross*. He received us briefly in audience, to discuss Catholicism with Jean. I gathered he was called Eisenstein; I thought him old and grumpy. In no time, I got ptomaine poisoning and clamored to depart. Eisenstein told me, contemptuously, in French, that I was the sort of girl who went swimming and drowned. It is a cherished memory.

The world changes around us at desperate speed every day, for better (not enough), for worse (too much). The population explosion, the airplane, and tourism as a major international industry have changed travel, for an old traveler like me, from thrilling impetuous private discovery into a hassle of the deepest dye. Naturally I no longer love it as I did. To millions of latecomers travel today still brings newness of life, which is what travel is all about. Or anyway I hope crowding and organization do not flatten the surprise and dim the wonder. Nostalgia is foolish. There is no place to live except in the present. But what fun it was, what easy fun, long ago.

CONSIDER THIS

Martha Gellhorn has been called "one of the most eloquent witnesses of the twentieth century." She has written on Franco's Spain, Paris, Vietnam, Poland, Israel, and the House on Un-American Activities Committee. A feisty woman of courage and independence and a top-notch journalist, she is also the author of eleven novels. For a time, she was married to Ernest Hemingway. She has led a full life, a good part of which was, as she says in this essay, "the traveling life." And yet, looking back at it all in 1985, she concludes: "The population explosion, the airplane, and tourism as a major international industry have changed travel, for an old traveler like me, from thrilling impetuous private discovery into a hassle of the deepest dye." How does this strike you? Do you think that the author is writing of changes in herself? Or do you agree that the high adventure of the traveling life and its private discoveries are no longer possible?

A Pothole from Hell
Mark Goldblatt

Three weeks ago, the apartment building next to mine commissioned some kind of underground maintenance. Workmen with hardhats, foul mouths and jackhammers showed up for four consecutive mornings. At precisely 7 A.M., they started to batter the concrete sidewalk into submission.

They dug a deep trench that ran from the lawn next door out into the street and raised an eight foot high mound of dirt, as if to testify to the seriousness of their mission. The fourth day, they filled in the trench with the dirt and left.

What remained is a pothole.

Let me explain, first of all, that this is not your run-of-the-mill pothole. This is epic, a pothole from hell. I measured it: six feet by four and a half feet; its basin lies 14 inches beneath street level. If this were Hawaii, we'd be barbecuing pigs in it.

It cannot be straddled by the widest sedans nor skimmed by the speediest sportsters. By night, the sparks from chassis flash like roman candles. It is beneath my window, so I hear it claim its victims for hours on end.

I have made a study of the frequencies. These are more consistent than you might guess: two impacts a minute during the morning rush, one a minute for most of the afternoon, three a minute at the height of the evening rush. And I have even developed a hypothesis about why the evening is worse than the morning: coffee spills.

What happens, I think, is that the jolt dislodges those supposedly spillproof decanters of coffee afixed to dashboards. The resulting coffee spill, in turn, serves to remind the driver the following morning to avoid the pothole. By contrast, the bat-out-of-hell mentality of quitting time contributes to the sudden surge at evening rush.

But indeed the pothole has become for me much more than a mere study in physics and sociology. It has come to represent a source of justice, a kind of (dare I say?) divine intervention in the workaday world.

You see, the street I live on is intended for a single lane of traffic in each direction. The neighborhood lies between two schools, where cars are required to slow down at all times. Yet few do. Now, at no cost to the police, the pothole has become an administrator of swift and sudden retribution for minor violations.

There is space to avoid the pothole, about eight feet between its western ridge and the yellow median, if you see it in time—which you can unless you are speeding. Or unless, and this is perhaps the most perfect justice, you are trying to pass on the right of a car travelling at a reasonable speed. That is the path of severest axle damage and probably severest psychological damage as well.

Perhaps it is unconscionable to take such satisfaction in the grief of others. Yet the pothole has brought together the citizens of this community more than any event since the last blackout. By the dozens, we congregate on the sidewalk: old and young, male and female, black and white. We watch. We wince.

We do not root for or against particular cars. When hubcaps go flying, we are careful to note where they roll; we direct the drivers to them with looks of consolation. We are not a mean people.

Sooner or later, of course, the pothole will be repaired. That is the way of city life and it is right. For if the pothole were to last too much longer, drivers would learn to avoid the street. Local businesses would suffer. Property values would go down.

One morning I am going to wake up and the pothole will be gone. For that reason, I am determined to appreciate it while I can. This Friday night, my date and I are going to phone for a pizza. We are going to dine *al fresco,* on the fire escape, looking down upon the scene like gods, watching the justice of the world unfold.

And if the pizza arrives stuck to the lid of the box, like gods we will understand why.

CONSIDER THIS

At the end of this brief, deceptively simple essay, the reader is invited to imagine the writer and his date seated on the fire escape of an apartment building: the couple plans to watch drivers negotiating the gigantic pothole in the street below. And the pothole he describes is not merely large. It is "epic, a pothole from hell." Yet it has also become an instrument of justice, of "divine intervention in the workaday world." How does the writer use the contrast between heaven and hell in the last two paragraphs?

And what makes the masterly final sentence so effective? Might Martin Gottfried gain some solace from watching Goldblatt's pothole mete out divine justice?

Goldblatt is a novelist, and teaches literature and writing at the City University of New York.

The Ultimate Safari
Nadine Gordimer

THE AFRICAN ADVENTURE LIVES ON . . . YOU CAN DO IT! THE ULTIMATE SAFARI OR EXPEDITION WITH LEADERS WHO *KNOW* AFRICA.

Travel advertisement
Observer, *27 November 1988.*

That night our mother went to the shop and she didn't come back. Ever. What happened? I don't know. My father also had gone away one day and never come back; but he was fighting in the war. We were in the war, too, but we were children, we were like our grandmother and grandfather, we didn't have guns. The people my father was fighting— the bandits, they are called by our government—ran all over the place and we ran away from them like chickens chased by dogs. We didn't know where to go. Our mother went to the shop because someone said you could get some oil for cooking. We were happy because we hadn't tasted oil for a long time; perhaps she got the oil and someone knocked her down in the dark and took that oil from her. Perhaps she met the bandits. If you meet them, they will kill you. Twice they came to our village and we ran and hid in the bush and when they'd gone we came back and found they had taken everything; but the third time they came back there was nothing to take, no oil, no food, so they burned the thatch and the roofs of our houses fell in. My mother found some pieces of tin and we put those up over part of the house. We were waiting there for her that night she never came back.

We were frightened to go out, even to do our business, because the bandits did come. Not into our house—without a roof it must have looked as if there was no one in it, everything gone—but all through the village. We heard people screaming and running. We were afraid even to run, without our mother to tell us where. I am the middle one, the girl, and my little brother clung against my stomach with his arms round my neck and his legs round my waist like a baby monkey to its mother. All night my first-born brother kept in his hand a broken piece of wood from one of our burnt house-poles. It was to save himself if the bandits found him.

We stayed there all day. Waiting for her. I don't know what day it was; there was no school, no church any more in our village, so you didn't know whether it was a Sunday or a Monday.

When the sun was going down, our grandmother and grandfather came. Someone from our village had told them we children were alone, our mother had not come back. I say 'grandmother' before 'grandfather' because it's like that: our grandmother is big and strong, not yet old, and our grandfather is small, you don't know where he is, in his loose trousers, he smiles but he hasn't heard what you're saying, and his hair looks as if he's left it full of soap suds. Our grandmother took us—me, the baby, my first-born brother, our grandfather—back to her house and we were all afraid (except the baby, asleep on our grandmother's back) of meeting the bandits on the way. We waited a long time at our grandmother's place. Perhaps it was a month. We were hungry. Our mother never came. While we were waiting for her to fetch us, our grandmother had no food for us, no food for our grandfather and herself. A woman with milk in her breasts gave us some for my little brother, although at our house he used to eat porridge, same as we did. Our grandmother took us to look for wild spinach but everyone else in the village did the same and there wasn't a leaf left.

Our grandfather, walking a little behind some young men, went to look for our mother but didn't find her. Our grandmother cried with other women and I sang the hymns with them. They brought a little food—some beans—but after two days there was nothing again. Our grandfather used to have three sheep and a cow and a vegetable garden but the bandits had long ago taken the sheep and the cow, because they were hungry, too; and when planting time came our grandfather had no seed to plant.

So they decided—our grandmother did; our grandfather made little noises and rocked from side to side, but she took no notice—we would go away. We children were pleased. We wanted to go away from where our mother wasn't and where we were hungry. We wanted to go where there were no bandits and there was food. We were glad to think there must be such a place; away.

Our grandmother gave her church clothes to someone in exchange for some dried mealies and she boiled them and tied them in a rag. We took them with us when we went and she thought we would get water from the rivers but we didn't come to any river and we got so thirsty we had to turn back. Not all the way to our grandparents' place but to a village where there was a pump. She opened the basket where she carried some clothes and the mealies and she sold her shoes to buy a big plastic container for water. I said, *Gogo,* how will you go to church now even without shoes, but she said we had a long journey and too much to carry. At that village we met other people who were also going away. We joined them because they seemed to know where that was better than we did.

To get there we had to go through the Kruger Park. We knew about the Kruger Park. A kind of whole country of animals—elephants, lions, jackals, hyenas, hippos, crocodiles, all kinds of animals. We had some of them in our own country, before the war (our grandfather remembers; we children weren't born yet) but the bandits kill the elephants and sell their tusks, and the bandits and our soldiers have eaten all the buck. There was a man in our village without legs—a crocodile took them off, in our river; but all the same our country is a country of people, not animals. We knew about the Kruger Park because some of our men used to leave home to work there in the places where white people came to stay and look at the animals.

So we started to go away again. There were women and other children like me who had to carry the small ones on their backs when the women got tired. A man led us into the Kruger Park; are we there yet, are we there yet, I kept asking our grandmother. Not yet, the man said, when she asked him for me. He told us we had to take a long way to get round the fence, which he explained would kill you, roast off your skin the moment you touched it, like the wires high up on poles that give electric light in our towns. I've seen that sign of a head without ears or skin or hair on an iron box at the mission hospital we used to have before it was blown up.

When I asked the next time, they said we'd been walking in the Kruger Park for an hour. But it looked just like the bush we'd been walking through all day, and we hadn't seen any animals except the monkeys and birds which live around us at home, and a tortoise that, of course, couldn't get away from us. My first-born brother and the other boys brought it to the man so it could be killed and we could cook and eat it. He let it go because he told us we could not make a fire; all the time we were in the Park we must not make a fire because the smoke would show we were there. Police, wardens, would come and send us back where we came from. He said we must move like animals among the animals, away from the roads, away from the white people's camps. And at that moment I heard—I'm sure I was the first to hear—cracking branches and the sound of something parting grasses and I almost squealed because I thought it was the police, wardens—the people he was telling us to look out for—who had found us already. And it was an elephant, and another elephant, and more elephants, big blots of dark moved wherever you looked between the trees. They were curling their trunks round the red leaves of the mopane trees and stuffing them into their mouths. The babies leaned against their mothers. The almost grown-up ones wrestled like my first-born brother with his friends—only they used trunks instead of arms. I was so interested I forgot to be afraid. The man said we should just stand still and be quiet while the elephants passed. They passed very slowly because elephants are too big to need to run from anyone.

The buck ran from us. They jumped so high they seemed to fly. The wart-hogs stopped dead, when they heard us, and swerved off the way a boy in our village used to zigzag on the bicycle his father had brought back from the mines. We followed the animals to where they drank. When they had gone, we went to their waterholes. We were never thirsty without finding water, but the animals ate, ate all the time. Whenever you saw them they were eating, grass, trees, roots. And there was nothing for us. The mealies were finished. The only food we could eat was what the baboons ate, dry little figs full of ants, that grow along the branches of the trees at the rivers. It was had to be like the animals.

When it was very hot during the day we would find lions lying asleep. They were the colour of the grass and we didn't see them at first but the man did, and he led us back and a long way round where they slept. I wanted to lie down like the lions. My little brother was getting thin but he was very heavy. When our grandmother looked for me, to put him on my back, I tried not to see. My first-born brother stopped talking; and when we rested he had to be shaken to get up again, as if he was just like our grandfather, he couldn't hear. I saw flies crawling on our grandmother's face and she didn't brush them off; I was frightened. I picked up a palm leaf and chased him.

We walked at night as well as by day. We could see the fires where the white people were cooking in the camps and we could smell the smoke and the meat. We watched the hyenas with their backs that slope as if they're ashamed, slipping through the bush after the smell. If one turned his head, you saw it had big brown shining eyes like our own, when we looked at each other in the dark. The wind brought voices in our own language from the compounds where the people who work in the camps live. A woman among us wanted to go to them at night and ask them to help us. They can give us the food from the dustbins, she said, she started wailing and our grandmother had to grab her and put a hand over her mouth. The men who led us had told us that we must keep out of the way of our people who worked at the Kruger Park; if they helped us they would lose their work. If they saw us, all they could do was pretend we were not there; they had seen only animals.

Sometimes we stopped to sleep for a little while at night. We slept close together. I don't know which night it was—because we were walking, walking, any time, all the time—we heard the lions very near. Not groaning loudly the way they did far off. Panting, like we do when we run, but it's a different kind of panting: you can hear they're not running, they're waiting, somewhere near. We all rolled closer together, on top of each other, the ones on the edge fighting to get into the middle. I was squashed against a woman who smelled bad because she was afraid but I was glad to hold tight to her. I prayed to God to make the lions take someone on the edge and go. I shut my eyes not to see the tree from which a lion might jump right into the middle of us, where I was. The man who led us jumped up instead, and beat on the tree with a dead branch. He had taught us never to make a sound but he shouted. He shouted at the lions like a drunk man shouting at nobody in our village. The lions went away. We heard them groaning, shouting back at him from far off.

We were tired, so tired. My first-born brother and the man had to lift our grandfather from stone to stone where we found places to cross the rivers. Our grandmother is strong but her feet were bleeding. We could not carry the basket on our heads any longer, we couldn't carry anything except my little brother. We left our things under a bush. As long as our bodies get there, our grandmother said. Then we ate some wild fruit we didn't know from home and our stomachs ran. We were in the grass called elephant grass because it is nearly as tall as an elephant, that day we had those pains, and our grandfather couldn't just get down in front of people like my little brother, he went off into the grass to be on his own. We had to keep up, the man who led us always kept telling us, we must catch up, but we asked him to wait for our grandfather.

So everyone waited for our grandfather to catch up. But he didn't. It was the middle of the day; insects were singing in our ears and we couldn't hear him moving through the grass. We couldn't see him because the grass was so high and he was so small. But he must have been somewhere there inside his loose trousers and his shirt that was torn and our grandmother couldn't sew because she had no cotton. We knew he couldn't have gone far because he was weak and slow. We all went to look for him, but in groups, so we too wouldn't be hidden from each other in that grass. It got into our eyes and noses; we called him softly but the noise of the insects must have filled the little space left for hearing in his ears. We looked and looked but we couldn't find him. We stayed in that long grass all night. In my sleep I found him curled round in a place he had tramped down for himself, like the places we'd seen where the buck hide their babies.

When I woke up he still wasn't anywhere. So we looked again, and by now there were paths we made by going through the grass many times, it would be easy for him to find us if we couldn't find him. All that day we just sat and waited. Everything is very quiet when the sun is on your head, inside your head, even if you lie, like the animals, under the trees. I lay on my back and saw those ugly birds with hooked beaks and plucked necks flying round and round above us. We had passed them often where they were feeding on the bones of dead animals, nothing was ever left there for us to eat. Round and round, high up and then lower down and then high again. I saw their necks poking to this side and that. Flying round and round. I saw our grandmother, who sat up all the time with my little brother on her lap, was seeing them, too.

In the afternoon the man who led us came to our grandmother and told her the other people must move on. He said, If their children don't eat soon they will die.

Our grandmother said nothing.

I'll bring you water before we go, he told her.

Our grandmother looked at us, me, my first-born brother, and my little brother on her lap. We watched the other people getting up to leave. I didn't believe the grass would be empty, all around us, where they had been. That we would be alone in this place, the Kruger Park, the police or the animals would find us. Tears came out of my eyes and nose on to my hands but our grandmother took no notice. She got up, with her feet apart the way she puts them when she is going to lift firewood, at home in our village, she swung my little brother on to her back, tied him in her cloth—the top of her dress was torn and her big breasts were showing but there was nothing in them for him. She said, Come.

So we left the place with the long grass. Left behind. We went with the others and the man who led us. We started to go away, again.

There's a very big tent, bigger than a church or a school, tied down to the ground. I didn't understand that was what it would be, when we got there, away. I saw a thing like that the time our mother took us to the town because she heard our soldiers were there and she wanted to ask them if they knew where our father was. In that tent, people were praying and singing. This one is blue and white like that one but it's not for praying and singing, we live in it with other people who've come from our country. Sister from the clinic says we're 200 without counting the babies, and we have new babies, some were born on the way through the Kruger Park.

Inside, even when the sun is bright it's dark and there's a kind of whole village in there. Instead of houses each family has a little place closed off with sacks or cardboard from boxes—whatever we can find—to show the other families it's yours and they shouldn't come in even though there's no door and no windows and no thatch, so that if you're standing up and you're not a small child you can see into everybody's house. Some people have even made paint from ground rocks and drawn designs on the sacks.

Of course, there really is a roof—the tent is the roof, far, high up. It's like a sky. It's like a mountain and we're inside it; through the cracks paths of dust lead down, so thick you think you could climb them. The tent keeps off the rain overhead but the water comes in at the sides and in the little streets between our places—you can only move along them one person at a time—the small kids like my little brother play in the mud. You have to step over them. My little brother doesn't play. Our grandmother takes him to the clinic when the doctor comes on Mondays. Sister says there's something wrong with his head, she thinks it's because we didn't have enough food at home. Because of the war. Because our father wasn't there. And then because he was so hungry in the Kruger Park. He likes just to lie about on our grandmother all day, on her lap or against her somewhere and he looks at us and looks at us. He wants to ask something but you can see he can't. If I tickle him he may just smile. The clinic gives us special powder to make into porridge for him and perhaps one day he'll be all right.

When we arrived we were like him—my first-born brother and I. I can hardly remember. The people who lived in the village near the tent took us to the clinic, it's where you have to sign that you've come—away, through the Kruger Park. We sat on the grass and everything was muddled. One Sister was pretty with her hair straightened and beautiful high-heeled shoes and she brought us the special powder. She said we must mix it with water and drink it slowly. We tore the packets open with our teeth and licked it all up, it stuck round my mouth and I sucked it from my lips and fingers. Some other children who had walked with us vomited. But I only felt everything in my belly moving, the stuff going down and around like a snake, and hiccups hurt me. Another Sister called us to stand in line on the veranda of the clinic but we couldn't. We sat all over the place there, falling against each other; the Sisters helped each of us by the arm and then stuck a needle in it. Other needles drew our blood into tiny bottles. This was against sickness, but I didn't understand, every time my eyes dropped closed I thought I was walking, the grass was long, I saw the elephants, I didn't know we were away.

But our grandmother was still strong, she could still stand up, she knows how to write and she signed for us. Our grandmother got us this place in the tent against one of the sides, it's the best kind of place there because although the rain comes in, we can lift the flap when the weather is good and then the sun shines on us, the smells in the tent go out. Our grandmother knows a woman here who showed her where there is good grass for sleeping mats, and our grandmother made some for us. Once every month the food truck comes to the clinic. Our grandmother takes along one of the cards she signed and when it has been punched we get a sack of mealie meal. There are wheelbarrows to take it back to the tent; my first-born brother does this for her and then he and the other boys have races, steering the empty wheelbarrows back to the clinic. Sometimes he's lucky and a man who's bought beer in the village gives him money to deliver it—though that's not allowed, you're supposed to take that wheelbarrow straight back to the Sisters. He buys a cold drink and shares it with me if I catch him. On another day, every month, the church leaves a pile of old clothes in the clinic yard. Our grandmother has another card to get punched, and then we can choose something: I have two dresses, two pants and a jersey, so I can go to school.

The people in the village have let us join their school. I was surprised to find they speak our language; our grandmother told me, That's why they allow us to stay on their land. Long ago, in the time of our fathers, there was no fence that kills you, there was no Kruger Park between them and us, we were the same people under our own king, right from our village we left to this place we've come to.

Now that we've been in the tent so long—I have turned eleven and my little brother is nearly three although he is so small, only his head is big, he's not come right in it yet—some people have dug up the bare ground around the tent and planted beans and mealies and cabbage. The old men weave branches to put up fences round their gardens. No one is allowed to look for work in the towns but some of the women have found work in the village and can buy things. Our grandmother, because she's still strong, finds work where people are building houses—in this village the people build nice houses with bricks and cement, not mud like we used to have at our home. Our grandmother carries bricks for these people and fetches baskets of stones on her head. And so she has money to buy sugar and tea and milk and soap. The store gave her a calendar she has hung up on our flap of the tent. I am clever at school and she collected advertising paper people throw away outside the store and covered my school-books with it. She makes my first-born brother and me do our homework every afternoon before it gets dark because there is no room except to lie down, close together, just as we did in the Kruger Park, in our place in the tent, and candles are expensive. Our grandmother hasn't been able to buy herself a pair of shoes for church yet, but she has bought black shoes and polish to clean them with for my first-born brother and me. Every morning, when people are getting up in the tent, the babies are crying, people are pushing each other at the taps outside and some children are already pulling the crusts of porridge off the pots we ate from last night, my first-born brother and I clean our shoes. Our grandmother makes us sit on our mats with our legs straight out so she can look carefully at our shoes to make sure we have done it properly. No other children in the tent have real school shoes. When we three look at them it's as if we are in a real house again, with no war, no away.

Some white people came to take photographs of our people living in the tent—they said they were making a film, I've never seen what that is though I know about it. A white woman squeezed into our space and asked our grandmother questions which were told to us in our language by someone who understands the white woman's.

How long have you been living like this?

She means here? our grandmother said. In this tent, two years and one month.

And what do you hope for the future?

Nothing. I'm here.

But for your children?

I want them to learn so that they can get good jobs and money.

Do you hope to go back to your own country?

I will not go back.

But when the war is over—you won't be allowed to stay here? Don't you want to go home?

I didn't think our grandmother wanted to speak again. I didn't think she was going to answer the white woman. The white woman put her head on one side and smiled at us.

Our grandmother looked away from her and spoke—There is nothing. No home.

Why does our grandmother say that? Why? I'll go back. I'll go back through that Kruger Park. After the war, if there are no bandits any more, our mother may be waiting for us. And maybe when we left our grandfather, he was only left behind, he found his way somehow, slowly, through the Kruger Park, and he'll be there. They'll be home, and I'll remember them.

CONSIDER THIS

Nadine Gordimer was born in 1923 in Springs, South Africa.

Some critics find her prose bloodless. She deals with intense, even tragic subjects, without, they say, conveying the passion and anger she must feel. (Gordimer is active in the anti-apartheid movement. Three of her books have been banned in South Africa.)

How do you *feel* about the story? The bare facts are horrific, yet the narrator speaks calmly, flatly, almost like an *Eyewitness News* reporter. If the story left you cold, try it again. Read slowly and let the images sink in. "We ran away from them like chickens chased by dogs." "I've seen that sign of a head without ears or skin or hair on an iron box at the mission hospital we used to have before it was blown up." "I prayed to God to let the lions take someone on the edge and go."

Many of the images work to support the central, dominant metaphor—the "ultimate" safari. Can you find them?

Thoreau, Cinderella, and Buttercream Roses
Janice Gordon

Every time I return from clothes shopping, no matter how little or how much I buy and regardless of the amount of money I spend, I almost immediately sink into a state of depression. I have, based on my readings of self-help articles in women's magazines, unearthed from my psyche many plausible explanations for this "post-shopping depression syndrome," as I call it. The one I have always favored is the most obvious which is probably, as a psychologist would tell me, a blatant sign that I wish to repress the real cause of my problem. I have always blamed simple guilt, guilt that I feel because my contribution to the family checkbook each week is nil. But recently, as if there is some conspiracy afoot to force me to delve deeper into this phenomenon, so much of my reading has dealt with attitudes towards clothing.

I happened to read an entry from Thoreau's *Journals* in which he describes the great pleasure he derives from a pair of corduroy pants that he had made. His pleasure comes from their low cost and their durability, and I believe that because of those qualities, he then thinks of them as attractive. He also writes that he disturbs his friends by wearing them, and yet I sense no uneasiness on his part as a result of his friends' reaction.

Thoreau's views on clothing seem to be exactly the opposite of mine. First and foremost, I am concerned with how it looks, and only if I find it attractive do I consider the price and utility of a garment. One unflattering remark from a friend would be sufficient reason for me to banish a skirt or sweater to the back of my closet forever. I know this is foolish behavior that displays tremendous lack of confidence on my part. Worse, it shows the workings of a mind that is dreadfully nonfeminist. Do you see the layer of non-contributor guilt peeling away? Why is how I look, physically, so important, and why are my opinions concerning beauty so often only reflections in other people's eyes?

Another bit of reading I had occasion to do kept these questions gnawing at my brain, and also kept my Bloomingdale's credit card from seeing the light of day. I read and discussed the story of "Cinderella" with a group of second-graders. One of the questions that arose during our discussion was whether or not Cinderella would have ever found her Prince Charming if her Fairy Godmother had not outfitted her so elegantly.

Now there was a lot of disagreement about this issue, and the children walked out the classroom still arguing over this. A few of the more liberal thinkers felt certain that it was Cinderella's goodness, her soul so to speak, that truly attracted the Prince to her and even if he had met her in rags, he would have loved her. Other more traditional thinkers felt that first impressions were lasting ones and that the Prince wouldn't have given her a second glance if she hadn't been all gussied up. I found myself wishing that I could form such concrete opinions as these second-graders had. My brain tells me that sticky sweet frosting only detracts from the richness of a well-baked cake, yet I am convinced that most people are automatically drawn to buttercream roses. No one wants to end up on the day-old shelf with little hope of ever having the richness within them appreciated.

Any expression of views on the influence that clothing has upon our lives would never be complete without mentioning the boys on Madison Avenue. Shakespeare's poetic vision of the world as a stage and men as players has been milked for all it's worth by the advertising world. In magazines, on television, and even on the backs of buses we are encouraged to think of clothing as costumes for the various roles we play—sophisticated career woman, rock star, even cowgirl. These ads seem to subtly tell us that if we outfit ourselves for our fantasies, they might come true, and we won't even need a Fairy Godmother! Cinderella would never have needed one either if she could have run up a huge bill at Bonwit's.

Maybe now that I've managed to admit that I lack the self-assuredness to ignore fashion altogether, I can comfortably settle into some position between slave and freewoman. I may even someday form an attachment to a pilly sweater simply because it is comfortable and keeps me warm. Stranger things have happened.

CONSIDER THIS

Are we what we say, or what we wear? Which matters more? (How can you begin to answer these questions?) Would a man have written Gordon's essay? Are men as concerned about finding the right clothing as women presumably are?

Turn back to the Grimm and Perrault versions of Cinderella: in one ending, the prince sees right through the rags to the "real" Cinderella; in the other, the fairy godmother works her magic before the prince settles on Cinderella as his future bride. Want to guess which is which?

Janice Gordon, a former student at Queens College, is now working for a literary agent in New York City.

Rambos of the Road
Martin Gottfried

The car pulled up and its driver glared at us with such sullen intensity, such hatred, that I was truly afraid for our lives. Except for the Mohawk haircut he didn't have, he looked like Robert DeNiro in "Taxi Driver," the sort of young man who, delirious for notoriety, might kill a president.

He was glaring because we had passed him and for that affront he pursued us to the next stoplight so as to express his indignation and affirm his masculinity. I was with two women and, believe it, was afraid for all three of us. It was nearly midnight and we were in a small, sleeping town with no other cars on the road.

When the light turned green, I raced ahead, knowing it was foolish and that I was not in a movie. He didn't merely follow, he chased, and with his headlights turned off. No matter what sudden turn I took, he followed. My passengers were silent. I knew they were alarmed, and I prayed that I wouldn't be called upon to protect them. In that cheerful frame of mind, I turned off my own lights so I couldn't be followed. It was lunacy. I was responding to a crazy *as* a crazy.

"I'll just drive to the police station," I finally said, and as if those were the magic words, he disappeared.

It seems to me that there has recently been an epidemic of auto macho—a competition perceived and expressed in driving. People fight it out over parking spaces. They bully into line at the gas pump. A toll booth becomes a signal for elbowing fenders. And beetle-eyed drivers hunch over their steering wheels, squeezing the rims, glowering, preparing the excuse of not having seen you as they muscle you off the road. Approaching a highway on an entrance ramp recently, I was strong-armed by a trailer truck so immense that its driver all but blew me away by blasting his horn. The behemoth was just inches from my hopelessly mismatched coupe when I fled for the safety of the shoulder.

And this is happening on city streets, too. A New York taxi driver told me that "intimidation is the name of the game. Drive as if you're deaf and blind. You don't hear the other guy's horn and you sure as hell don't see him."

The odd thing is that long before I was even able to drive, it seemed to me that people were at their finest and most civilized when in their cars. They seemed so orderly and considerate, so reasonable, staying in the right-hand lane unless passing, signaling all intentions. In those days you really eased into highway traffic, neat rows of cars seemed mobile testimony to the sanity of most people. Perhaps memory fails, perhaps there were always testy drivers, perhaps—but everyone didn't give you the finger.

A most amazing example of driver rage occurred recently at the Manhattan end of the Lincoln Tunnel. We were four cars abreast, stopped at a traffic light. And there was no moving even when the light had changed. A bus had stopped in the cross traffic, blocking our paths: it was a normal-for-New-York-City gridlock. Perhaps impatient, perhaps late for important appointments, three of us nonetheless accepted what, after all, we could not alter. One, however, would not. He would not be helpless. He would go where he was going even if he couldn't get there. A Wall Street type in suit and tie, he got out of his car and strode toward the bus, rapping smartly on its doors. When they opened, he exchanged words with the driver. The doors folded shut. He then stepped in front of the bus, took hold of one of its large windshield wipers and broke it.

The bus doors reopened and the driver appeared, apparently giving the fellow a good piece of his mind. If so, the lecture was wasted, for the man started his car and proceeded to drive directly *into the bus.* He rammed it. Even though the point at which he struck the bus, the folding doors, was its most vulnerable point, ramming the side of a bus with your car has to rank very high on a futility index. My first thought was that it had to be a rented car.

To tell the truth, I could not believe my eyes. The bus driver opened his doors as much as they could be opened and he stepped directly onto the hood of the attacking car, jumping up and down with both his feet. He then retreated into the bus, closing the doors behind him. Obviously a man of action, the car driver backed up and rammed the bus again. How this exercise in absurdity would have been resolved none of us will ever know for at that point the traffic unclogged and the bus moved on. And the rest of us, we passives of the world, proceeded, our cars crossing a field of battle as if nothing untoward had happened.

It is tempting to blame such belligerent, uncivil and even neurotic behavior on the nuts of the world, but in our cars we all become a little crazy. How many of us speed up when a driver signals his intention of pulling in front of us? Are we resentful and anxious to pass him? How many of us try to squeeze in, or race along the shoulder at a lane merger? We may not jump on hoods, but driving the gantlet, we seethe, cursing not so silently in the safety of our steel bodies on wheels—fortresses for cowards.

What is it within us that gives birth to such antisocial behavior and why, all of a sudden, have so many drivers gone around the bend? My friend Joel Katz, a Manhattan psychiatrist, calls it, "a Rambo pattern. People are running around thinking the American way is to take the law into your own hands when anyone does anything wrong. And what constitutes 'wrong'? Anything that cramps your style."

It seems to me that it is a new America we see on the road now. It has the mentality of a hoodlum and the backbone of a coward. The car is its weapon and hiding place, and it is still a symbol even in this. Road Rambos no longer bespeak a self-reliant, civil people tooling around in family cruisers. In fact, there aren't families in these machines that charge headlong with their brights on in broad daylight, demanding we get out of their way. Bullies are loners, and they have perverted our liberty of the open road into drivers' license. They represent an America that derides the values of decency and good manners, then roam the highways riding shotgun and shrieking freedom. By allowing this to happen, the rest of us approve.

CONSIDER THIS

"What is it within us" that turns us into "Rambos of the Road"? Is this a closed or open text? Does Gottfried invite us to speculate with him or does he have all the answers? What about women Rambos? Do you know any? Or is it men only who turn themselves into the "hoodlums" and "bullies" Gottfried describes?

What other questions doesn't he raise?

What might Gottfried say about the driver in Conroy's "Midair"?

Gottfried is a drama critic and author of *In Person: The Great Entertainers.*

Making Up People
Ian Hacking

Were there any perverts before the latter part of the nineteenth century? According to Arnold Davidson, "The answer is NO. . . . Perversion was not a disease that lurked about in nature, waiting for a psychiatrist with especially acute powers of observation to discover it hiding everywhere. It was a disease created by a new (functional) understanding of disease." Davidson is not denying that there have been odd people at all times. He is asserting that perversion, as a disease, and the pervert, as a diseased person, were created in the late nineteenth century. Davidson's claim, one of many now in circulation, illustrates what I call making up people.

I have three aims: I want a better understanding of claims as curious as Davidson's; I would like to know if there could be a general theory of making up people, or whether each example is so peculiar that it demands its own nongeneralizable story; and I want to know how this idea "making up people" affects our very idea of what it is to be an individual. I should warn that my concern is philosophical and abstract; I look more at what people might be than at what we are. I imagine a philosophical notion I call dynamic nominalism, and reflect too little on the ordinary dynamics of human interaction.

First we need more examples. I study the dullest of subjects, the official statistics of the nineteenth century. They range, of course, over agriculture, education, trade, births, and military might, but there is one especially striking feature of the avalanche of numbers that begins around 1820. It is obsessed with *analyse morale,* namely, the statistics of deviance. It is the numerical analysis of suicide, prostitution, drunkenness, vagrancy, madness, crime, *les miserables.* Counting generated its own subdivisions and rearrangements. We find classifications of over 4,000 different crisscrossing motives for murder and requests that the police classify each individual suicide in 21 different ways. I do not believe that motives of these sorts or suicides of these kinds existed until the practice of counting them came into being.

New slots were created in which to fit and enumerate people. Even national and provincial censuses amazingly show that the categories into which people fall change every ten years. Social change creates new categories of people, but the counting is no mere report of developments. It elaborately, often philanthropically, creates new ways for people to be.

People spontaneously come to fit their categories. When factory inspectors in England and Wales went to the mills, they found various kinds of people there, loosely sorted according to tasks and wages. But when they had finished their reports, millhands had precise ways in which to work, and the owner had a clear set of concepts about how to employ workers according to the ways in which he was obliged to classify them.

I am more familiar with the creation of kinds among the masses than with interventions that act upon individuals, though I did look into one kind of insanity. I claim that multiple personality as an idea and as a clinical phenomenon was invented around 1875: only one or two possible cases per generation had been recorded before that time, but a whole flock of them came after. I also found that the clinical history of split personality parodies itself—the one clear case of classic symptoms was long recorded as two, quite distinct, human beings, each of which was multiple. There was "the lady of MacNish," so called after a report in *The Philosophy of Sleep,* written by the Edinburgh physician Robert MacNish in 1832, and there was one Mary R. The two would be reported in successive paragraphs as two different cases, although in fact Mary Reynolds was the very split-personality lady reported by MacNish.

Mary Reynolds died long before 1875, but she was not taken up as a case of multiple personality until then. Not she but one Félida X got the split-personality industry under way. As the great French psychiatrist Pierre Janet remarked at Harvard in 1906, Félida's history "was the great argument of which the positivist psychologists made use at the time of the heroic struggles against the dogmatism of Cousin's school. But for Félida, it is not certain that there would be a professorship of psychology at the Collège de France." Janet held precisely that chair. The "heroic struggles" were unimportant for our passing conceptions of the self, and for individuality, because the split Félida was held to refute the dogmatic transcendental unity of apperception that made the self prior to all knowledge.

After Félida came a rush of multiples. The syndrome bloomed in France and later flourished in America, which is still its home. Do I mean that there were no multiples before Félida? Yes. Except for a very few earlier examples, which after 1875 were reinterpreted as classic multiples, there was no such syndrome for a disturbed person to display or to adopt.

I do not deny that there are other behaviors in other cultures that resemble multiple personality. Possession is our most familiar example—a common form of Renaissance behavior that died long ago, though it was curiously hardy in isolated German villages even late in the nineteenth century. Possession was not split personality, but if you balk at my implication that a few people (in committee with their medical or moral advisers) almost choose to become splits, recall that tormented souls in the past have often been said to have in some way chosen to be possessed, to have been seeking attention, exorcism, and tranquility.

I should give one all-too-tidy example of how a new person can be made up. Once again I quote from Janet, whom I find the most open and honorable of the psychiatrists. He is speaking to Lucie, who had the once-fashionable but now-forgotten habit of automatic writing. Lucie replies to Janet in writing without her normal self's awareness:

Janet. Do you understand me?

Lucie (writes). No.

J. But to reply you must understand me!

L. Oh yes, absolutely.

J. Then what are you doing?

L. Don't know.

J. It is certain that someone is understanding me.

L. Yes.

J. Who is that?

L. Somebody besides Lucie.

J. Aha! Another person. Would you like to give her a name?

L. No.

J. Yes. It would be far easier that way.

L. Oh well. If you want: Adrienne.

J. Then, Adrienne, do you understand me?

L Yes.

If you think this is what people used to do in the bad old days, consider poor Charles, who was given a whole page of *Time* magazine on October 25, 1982 (p. 70). He was picked up wandering aimlessly and was placed in the care of Dr. Malcolm Graham of Daytona Beach, who in turn consulted with Dr. William Rothstein, a notable student of multiple personality at the University Hospital in Columbia, South Carolina. Here is what is said to have happened:

> After listening to a tape recording made in June of the character Mark, Graham became convinced he was dealing with a multiple personality. Graham began consulting with Rothstein, who recommended hypnosis. Under the spell, Eric began calling his characters. Most of the personalities have been purged, although there are three or four being treated, officials say. It was the real personality that signed a consent form that allowed Graham to comment on the case.

Hypnosis elicited Charles, Eric, Mark, and some 24 other personalities. When I read of such present-day manipulations of character, I pine a little for Mollie Fancher, who gloried in the personalities of Sunbeam, Idol, Rosebud, Pearl, and Ruby. She became somewhat split after being dragged a mile by a horse car. She was not regarded as especially deranged, nor in much need of "cure." She was much loved by her friends, who memorialized her in 1894 in a book with the title *Mollie Fancher, The Brooklyn Enigma: An Authentic Statement of Facts in the Life of Mollie J. Fancher, The Psychological Marvel of the Nineteenth Century.* The idea of making up people has, I said, become quite widespread. *The Making of the Modern Homosexual* is a good example; "Making" in this title is close to my "making up." The contributors by and large accept that the homosexual and the heterosexual as kinds of persons (as ways to be persons, or as conditions of personhood), came into being only toward the end of the nineteenth century. There has been plenty of same-sex activity in all ages, but not, *Making* argues, same-sex people and different-sex people. I do not wish to enter the complexities of that idea, but will quote a typical passage from this anthology to show what is intended: "One difficulty in transcending the theme of gender inversion as the basis of the specialized homosexual identity was the rather late historical development of more precise conceptions of components of sexual identity. [fn:] It is not suggested that these components are 'real' entities, which awaited scientific 'discovery.' However once the distinctions were made, new realities effectively came into being."

Note how the language here resembles my opening quotation: "not a disease . . . in nature, waiting for . . . observation to discover it" versus "not . . . 'real' entities, which awaited scientific 'discovery.'" Moreover, this author too suggests that "once the distinctions were made, new realities effectively came into being."

This theme, the homosexual as a kind of person, is often traced to a paper by Mary MacIntosh, "The Homosexual Role," which she published in 1968 in *Social Problems.* That journal was much devoted to "labeling theory," which asserts that social reality is conditioned, stabilized, or even created by the labels we apply to people, actions, and communities. Already in 1963 "A Note on the Uses of Official Statistics" in the same journal anticipated my own inferences about counting. But there is a currently more fashionable source of the idea of making up people, namely, Michel Foucault, to whom both Davidson and I are indebted. A quotation from Foucault provides the epigraph—following one from Nietzsche—for *The Making of the Modern Homosexual;* and although its authors cite some 450 sources, they refer to Foucault more than anyone else. Since I shall be primarily concerned with labeling, let me state at once that for all his famous fascination with discourse, naming is only one element in what Foucault calls the "constitution of subjects" (in context a pun, but in one sense the making up of the subject): "We should try to discover how it is that subjects are gradually, progressively, really and materially constituted through a multiplicity of organisms, forces, energies, materials, desires, thoughts, etc."

Since so many of us have been influenced by Foucault, our choice of topic and time may be biased. My examples dwell in the nineteenth century and are obsessed with deviation and control. Thus among the questions on a complete agenda, we should include these two: Is making up people intimately linked to control? Is making up people itself of recent origin? The answer to both questions might conceivably be yes. We may be observing a particular medico-forensic-political language of individual and social control. Likewise, the sheer proliferation of labels in that domain during the nineteenth century may have engendered vastly more kinds of people than the world had ever known before.

Partly in order to distance myself for a moment from issues of repression, and partly for intrinsic interest, I would like to abstract from my examples. If there were some truth in the descriptions I and others have furnished, then making up people would bear on one of the great traditional questions of philosophy, namely, the debate between nominalists and realists. The author I quoted who rejects the idea that the components of the homosexual identity are real entities, has taken a time-worn nominalist suggestion and made it interesting by the thought that "once the distinctions were made, new realities effectively came into being."

You will recall that a traditional nominalist says that stars (or algae, or justice) have nothing in common except our names ("stars," "algae," "justice"). The traditional realist in contrast finds it amazing that the world could so kindly sort itself into our categories. He protests that there are definite sorts of objects in it, at least stars and algae, which we have painstakingly come to recognize and classify correctly. The robust realist does not have to argue very hard that people also come sorted. Some are thick, some thin, some dead, some alive. It may be a fact about human beings that we notice who is fat and who is dead, but the fact itself that some of our fellows are fat and others are dead has nothing to do with our schemes of classification.

The realist continues: consumption was not only a sickness but also a moral failing, caused by defects of character. That is an important nineteenth-century social fact about

TB. We discovered in due course, however, that the disease is transmitted by bacilli that divide very slowly and that we can kill. It is a fact about us that we were first moralistic and later made this discovery, but it is a brute fact about tuberculosis that it is a specific disease transmitted by microbes. The nominalist is left rather weakly contending that even though a particular kind of person, the consumptive, may have been an artifact of the nineteenth century, the disease itself is an entity in its own right, independently of how we classify.

It would be foolhardy, at this conference, to have an opinion about one of the more stable human dichotomies, male and female. But very roughly, the robust realist will agree that there may be what really are physiological borderline cases, once called "hermaphrodites." The existence of vague boundaries is normal: most of us are neither tall nor short, fat nor thin. Sexual physiology is unusually abrupt in its divisions. The realist will take the occasional compulsive fascination with transvestitism, or horror about hermaphrodites (so well described by Stephen Greenblatt in this volume), as human (nominalist) resistance to nature's putative aberrations. Likewise the realist will assert that even though our attitudes to gender are almost entirely nonobjective and culturally ordained, gender itself is a real distinction.

I do not know if there were thoroughgoing, consistent, hard-line nominalists who held that every classification is of our own making. I might pick that great British nominalist Hobbes out of context: "How can any man imagine that the names of things were imposed by their natures?" Or I might pick Nelson Goodman.*

Let me take even the vibrant Hobbes, Goodman, and their scholastic predecessors as pale reflections of a perhaps nonexistent static nominalist, who thinks that all categories, classes, and taxonomies are given by human beings rather than by nature and that these categories are essentially fixed throughout the several eras of humankind. I believe that static nominalism is doubly wrong: I think that many categories come from nature, not from the human mind, and I think our categories are not static. A different kind of nominalism—I call it dynamic nominalism—attracts my realist self, spurred on by theories about the making of the homosexual and the heterosexual as kinds of persons or by my observations about official statistics. The claim of dynamic nominalism is not that there was a kind of person who came increasingly to be recognized by bureaucrats or by students of human nature but rather that a kind of person came into being at the same time as the kind itself was being invented. In some cases, that is, our classifications and our classes conspire to emerge hand in hand, each egging the other on.

Take four categories: horse, planet, glove, and multiple personality. It would be preposterous to suggest that the only thing horses have in common is that we call them horses. We may draw the boundaries to admit or to exclude Shetland ponies, but the similarities and difference are real enough. The planets furnish one of T. S. Kuhn's examples of conceptual change. Arguably the heavens looked different after we grouped

---

* Trendy, self-styled modern nominalists might refer to his *Ways of Worldmaking* (Indianapolis, Ind., 1978), but the real hard line is in his *Fact, Fiction, and Forecast* (Cambridge, Mass., 1955)—a line so hard that few philosphers who write about the "new riddle of induction" of that book appear ever to see the point. Goodman is saying that the only reason to project the hypothesis that all emeralds are green rather than grue—the latter implying that those emeralds, which are in the future examined for the first time, will prove to be blue—is that the word "green" is entrenched, i.e., it is a word and a classification that we have been using. Where the inductive skeptic Hume allowed that there is a real quality, greenness, that we project out of habit, for Goodman there is only our practice of using the word "green" (*Fact*, chap. 4).

Earth with the other planets and excluded Moon and Sun, but I am sure that acute thinkers had discovered a real difference. I hold (most of the time) that strict nominalism is unintelligible for horses and the planets. How could horses and planets be so obedient to our minds? Gloves are something else: we manufacture them. I know not which came first, the thought or the mitten, but they have evolved hand in hand. That the concept "glove" fits gloves so well is no surprise; we made them that way. My claim about making up people is that in a few interesting respects multiple personalities (and much else) are more like gloves than like horses. The category and the people in it emerged hand in hand.

How might a dynamic nominalism affect the concept of the individual person? One answer has to do with possibility. Who we are is not only what we did, do, and will do but also what we might have done and may do. Making up people changes the space of possibilities for personhood. Even the dead are more than their deeds, for we make sense of a finished life only within its sphere of former possibilities. But our possibilities, although inexhaustible, are also bounded. If the nominalist thesis about sexuality were correct, it simply wasn't possible to be a heterosexual kind of person before the nineteenth century, for that kind of person was not there to choose. What could that mean? What could it mean in general to say that possible ways to be a person can from time to time come into being or disappear? Such queries force us to be careful about the idea of possibility itself.

We have a folk picture of the gradations of possibility. Some things, for example, are easy to do, some hard, and some plain impossible. What is impossible for one person is possible for another. At the limit we have the statement: "With men it is impossible, but not with God: for with God, all things are possible" (Mark 10:27). (Christ had been saying that it is easier for a camel to pass through the eye of a needle than for a rich man to enter the kingdom of heaven.) Degrees of possibility are degrees in the ability of some agent to do or make something. The more ability, the more possibility, and omnipotence makes anything possible. At that point, logicians have stumbled, worrying about what were once called "the eternal truths" and are now called "logical necessities." Even God cannot make a five-sided square, or so mathematicians say, except for a few such eminent dissenters as Descartes. Often this limitation on omnipotence is explained linguistically, being said to reflect our unwillingness to call anything a five-sided square.

There is something more interesting that God can't do. Suppose that Arnold Davidson, in my opening quotation about perversion, is literally correct. Then it was not possible for God to make George Washington a pervert. God could have delayed Washington's birth by over a century, but would that have been the same man? God could have moved the medical discourse back 100-odd years. But God could not have simply made him a pervert, the way He could have made him freckled or had him captured and hung for treachery. This may seem all the more surprising since Washington was but eight years older than the Marquis de Sade—and Krafft-Ebing has sadomasochism among the four chief categories of perversion. But it follows from Davidson's doctrine that de Sade was not afflicted by the disease of perversion, nor even the disease of sadomasochism either.

Such strange claims are more trivial than they seem; they result from a contrast between people and things. Except when we interfere, what things are doing, and indeed what camels are doing, does not depend on how we describe them. But some of the things that we ourselves do are intimately connected to our descriptions. Many philosophers follow Elizabeth Anscombe and say that intentional human actions must be "actions under a description." This is not mere lingualism, for descriptions are embedded in our practices and lives. But if a description is not there, then intentional actions under that description cannot be there either: that, apparently, is a fact of logic.

Elaborating on this difference between people and things: what camels, mountains, and microbes are doing does not depend on our words. What happens to tuberculosis bacilli depends on whether or not we poison them with BCG vaccine, but it does not depend upon how we describe them. Of course we poison them with a certain vaccine in part because we describe them in certain ways, but it is the vaccine that kills, not our words. Human action is more closely linked to human description than bacterial action is. A century ago I would have said that consumption is caused by bad air and sent the patient to the alps. Today, I may say that TB is caused by microbes and prescribe a two-year course of injections. But what is happening to the microbes and the patient is entirely independent of my correct or incorrect description, even though it is not independent of the medication prescribed. The microbes' possibilities are delimited by nature, not by words. What is curious about human action is that by and large what I am deliberately doing depends on the possibilities of description. To repeat, this is a tautological inference from what is now a philosopher's commonplace, that all intentional acts are acts under a description. Hence if new modes of description come into being, new possibilities for action come into being in consequence.

Let us now add an example to our repertoire; let it have nothing to do with deviancy, let it be rich in connotations of human practices, and let it help furnish the end of a spectrum of making up people opposite from the multiple personality. I take it from Jean-Paul Sartre, partly for the well-deserved fame of his description, partly for its excellence as description, partly because Sartre is our premium philosopher of choice, and partly because recalling Sartre will recall an example that returns me to my origin. Let us first look at Sartre's magnificent humdrum example. Many among us might have chosen to be a waiter or waitress and several have been one for a time. A few men might have chosen to be something more specific, a Parisian *garçon de café,* about whom Sartre writes in his immortal discussion of bad faith: "His movement is quick and forward, a little too precise, a little too rapid. He comes toward the patrons with a step a little too quick. He bends forward a little too eagerly, his eyes express an interest too solicitous for the order of the customer." Psychiatrists and medical people in general try to be extremely specific in describing, but no description of the several classical kinds of split personality is as precise (or as recognizable) as this. Imagine for a moment that we are reading not the words of a philosopher who writes his books in cafés but those of a doctor who writes them in a clinic. Has the *garçon de café* a chance of escaping treatment by experts? Was Sartre knowing or merely anticipating when he concluded this very paragraph with the words: "There are indeed many precautions to imprison a man in what he is, as if we lived in perpetual fear that he might escape from it, that he might break away and suddenly elude his condition." That is a good reminder of Sartre's teaching: possibility, project, and prison are one of a piece.

Sartre's antihero chose to be a waiter. Evidently that was not a possible choice in other places, other times. There are servile people in most societies, and servants in many, but a waiter is something specific, and a *garçon de café* more specific. Sartre remarks that the waiter is doing something different when he pretends to play at being a sailor or a diplomat than when he plays at being a waiter in order to be a waiter. I think that in most parts of, let us say, Saskatchewan (or in a McDonald's anywhere), a waiter playing at being a *garçon de café* would miss the mark as surely as if he were playing at being a diplomat while passing over the french fries. As with almost every way in which it is possible to be a person, it is possible to be a *garçon de café* only at a certain time, in a certain place, in a certain social setting. The feudal serf putting food on my lady's table can no more choose to be a *garçon de café* than he can choose to be lord of the manor. But the impossibility is evidently different in kind.

It is not a technical impossibility. Serfs may once have dreamed of travel to the moon; certainly their lettered betters wrote or read adventures of moon travel. But moon travel was impossible for them, whereas it is not quite impossible for today's young waiter. One young waiter will, in a few years, be serving steaks in a satellite. Sartre is at pains to say that even technical limitations do not mean that you have fewer possibilities. For every person, in every era, the world is a plenitude of possibilities. "Of course," Sartre writes, "a contemporary of Duns Scotus is ignorant of the use of the automobile or the aeroplane. . . . For the one who has no relation of any kind to these objects and the techniques that refer to them, there is a kind of absolute, unthinkable and undecipherable nothingness. Such a nothing can in no way limit the For-itself that is choosing itself; it cannot be appreciated as a lack, no matter how we consider it." Passing to a different example, he continues, "The feudal world offered to the vassal lord of Raymond VI infinite possibilities of choice; we do not possess more."

"Absolute, unthinkable and undecipherable nothingness" is a great phrase. That is exactly what being a multiple personality, or being a *garçon de café,* was to Raymond's vassal. Many of you could, in truth, be neither a Parisian waiter nor a split, but both are thinkable, decipherable somethingness. It would be possible for God to have made you one or the other or both, leaving the rest of the world more or less intact. That means, to me, that the outer reaches of your space as an individual are essentially different from what they would have been had these possibilities not come into being.

Thus the idea of making up people is enriched; it applies not to the unfortunate elect but to all of us. It is not just the making up of people of a kind that did not exist before: not only are the split and the waiter made up, but each of us is made up. We are not only what we are but what we might have been, and the possibilities for what we might have been are transformed.

Hence anyone who thinks about the individual, the person, must reflect on this strange idea, of making up people. Do my stories tell a uniform tale? Manifestly not. The multiple personality, the homosexual or heterosexual person, and the waiter form one spectrum among many that may color our perception here.

Suppose there is some truth in the labeling theory of the modern homosexual. It cannot be the whole truth, and this for several reasons, including one that is future-directed and one that is past-directed. The future-directed fact is that after the institutionalization of the homosexual person in law and official morality, the people involved had a life of their own, individually and collectively. As gay liberation has amply proved, that life was no simple product of the labeling.

The past-directed fact is that the labeling did not occur in a social vacuum, in which those identified as homosexual people passively accepted the format. There was a complex social life that is only now revealing itself in the annals of academic social history. It is quite clear that the internal life of innumerable clubs and associations interacted with the medico-forensic-journalistic labeling. At the risk of giving offense, I suggest that the quickest way to see the contrast between making up homosexuals and making up multiple personalities is to try to imagine split-personality bars. Splits, insofar as they are declared, are under care, and the syndrome, the form of behavior, is orchestrated by a team of experts. Whatever the medico-forensic experts tried to do with their categories, the homosexual person became autonomous of the labeling, but the split is not.

The *garçon de café* is at the opposite extreme. There is of course a social history of waiters in Paris. Some of this will be as anecdotal as the fact that croissants originated in the cafés of Vienna after the Turkish siege was lifted in 1683: the pastries in the shape of a crescent were a mockery of Islam. Other parts of the story will be structurally connected with numerous French institutions. But the class of waiters is autonomous of any act of labeling. At most the name *garçon de café* can continue to ensure both the inferior position of the waiter and the fact that he is male. Sartre's precise description does not fit the *fille de salle;* that is a different role.

I do not believe there is a general story to be told about making up people. Each category has its own history. If we wish to present a partial framework in which to describe such events, we might think of two vectors. One is the vector of labeling from above, from a community of experts who create a "reality" that some people make their own. Different from this is the vector of the autonomous behavior of the person so labeled, which presses from below, creating a reality every expert must face. The second vector is negligible for the split but powerful for the homosexual person. People who write about the history of homosexuality seem to disagree about the relative importance of the two vectors. My scheme at best highlights what the dispute is about. It provides no answers.

The scheme is also too narrow. I began by mentioning my own dusty studies in official statistics and asserted that these also, in a less melodramatic way, contribute to making up people. There is a story to tell here, even about Parisian waiters, who surface in the official statistics of Paris surprisingly late, in 1881. However, I shall conclude with yet another way of making up people and human acts, one of notorious interest to the existentialist culture of a couple of generations past. I mean suicide, the option that Sartre always left open to the For-itself. Suicide sounds like a timeless option. It is not. Indeed it might be better described as a French obsession.

There have been cultures, including some in recent European history, that knew no suicide. It is said that there were no suicides in Venice when it was the noblest city of Europe. But can I seriously propose that suicide is a concept that has been made up? Oddly, that is exactly what is said by the deeply influential Esquirol in his 1823 medical-encyclopedia article on suicide. He mistakenly asserts that the very word was devised by his predecessor Sauvages. What is true is this: suicide was made the property of medics only at the beginning of the nineteenth century, and a major fight it was too. It was generally allowed that there was the noble suicide, the suicide of honor or of state, but all the rest had to be regarded as part of the new medicine of insanity. By mid-century it would be contended that there was no case of suicide that was not preceded by symptoms of insanity.

This literature concerns the doctors and their patients. It exactly parallels a statistical story. Foucault suggests we think in terms of "two poles of development linked together by a whole cluster of intermediary relations." One pole centers on the individual as a speaking, working, procreating entity he calls an "anatomo-politics of the human body." The second pole, "focused on the species body," serves as the "basis of the biological processes: propagation, births, and mortality, the level of health, life expectancy and longevity." He calls this polarity a "biopolitics of the population." Suicide aptly illustrates patterns of connection between both poles. The medical men comment on the bodies and their past, which led to self-destruction; the statisticians count and classify the bodies. Every fact about the suicide becomes fascinating. The statisticians compose forms to be completed by doctors and police, recording everything from the time of death to the objects found in the pockets of the corpse. The various ways of killing oneself are abruptly characterized and become symbols of national character. The French favor carbon monoxide and drowning; the English hang or shoot themselves.

By the end of the nineteenth century there was so much information about French suicides that Durkheim could use suicide to measure social pathology. Earlier, a rapid increase in the rate of suicide in all European countries had caused great concern. More recently authors have suggested that the growth may have been largely apparent, a consequence of improved systems of reporting. It was thought that there were more suicides because more care was taken to report them. But such a remark is unwittingly ambiguous: reporting brought about more suicides. I do not refer to suicide epidemics that follow a sensational case, like that of von Kleist, who shot his lover and then himself on the Wannsee in 1811—an event vigorously reported in every European capital. I mean instead that the systems of reporting positively created an entire ethos of suicide, right down to the suicide note, an art form that previously was virtually unknown apart from the rare noble suicide of state. Suicide has of course attracted attention in all times and has invited such distinguished essayists as Cicero and Hume. But the distinctively European and American pattern of suicide is a historical artifact. Even the unmaking of people has been made up.

Naturally my kinds of making up people are far from exhaustive. Individuals serve as role models and sometimes thereby create new roles. We have only to think of James Clifford's contribution to this volume, "On Ethnographic Self-Fashioning: Conrad and Malinowski." Malinowski's book largely created the participant-observer cultural-relativist ethnographer, even if Malinowski himself did not truly conform to that role in the field. He did something more important—he made up a kind of scholar. The advertising industry relies on our susceptibilities to role models and is largely engaged in trying to make up people. But here nominalism, even of a dynamic kind, is not the key. Often we have no name for the very role a model entices us to adopt.

Dynamic nominalism remains an intriguing doctrine, arguing that numerous kinds of human beings and human acts come into being hand in hand with our invention of the categories labeling them. It is for me the only intelligible species of nominalism, the only one that can even gesture at an account of how common names and the named could so tidily fit together. It is of more human interest than the arid and scholastic forms of nominalism because it contends that our spheres of possibility, and hence our selves, are to some extent made up by our naming and what that entails. But let us not be overly optimistic about the future of dynamic nominalism. It has the merit of bypassing abstract hand-waving and inviting us to do serious philosophy, namely, to examine the intricate origin of our ideas of multiple personality or of suicide. It is, we might say, putting some flesh on that wizened figure, John Locke, who wrote about the origin of ideas while introspecting at his desk. But just because it invites us to examine the intricacies of real life, it has little chance of being a general philosophical theory. Although we may find it useful to arrange influences according to Foucault's poles and my vectors, such metaphors are mere suggestions of what to look for next. I see no reason to suppose that we shall ever tell two identical stories of two different instances of making up people.

CONSIDER THIS

"Making Up People." Ian Hacking's title sounds simple enough, but we don't move very far into the essay before we realize we're into deep philosophical water. Hacking warns us that his "concern is philosophical and abstract." A philosopher, Hacking teaches at the Institute for History, Philosophy and Technology at the University of Toronto. What are the tools of his philosophical inquiry. He needs, he says, "examples," to uncover the ways in which versions of the self are constructed. So he draws from official statistics and case studies of the nineteenth century. Compare his intellectual tools with those of the historian Robert Darnton: where do the methods of their inquiries and the questions they ask intersect?

Hacking quotes Foucault: "We should try to discover how it is that subjects are gradually, progressively, really and materially constituted through a multiplicity of organisms, forces, energies, materials, desires, thoughts, etc." What does Foucault mean by "subjects"? I think that he means the sense we have of our selves. How are we ("subjects") ourselves made up? How do we come to be who we are? Foucault, a French philosopher, critic, and historian, insists, as does Hacking, that language, in large part, determines human identity: the way we see ourselves is shaped by the language available to us. Who are you? How have you made yourself up?

The Secret Sharers
Pete Hamill

Another thing might render the country more strict with respect to the citizens . . . and this was what I hinted at before, Namely, that there was a seeming propensity or a wicked inclination in those that were infected to infect others.

Daniel Defoe
A Journal of the Plague Year, 1721

I knew the woman from the time she was born. I was at the baptism party, up on the second floor of the house at Smith and Union streets in Brooklyn, with the bathtub full of iced beer and someone playing a steel guitar and everyone singing the old Los Panchos songs and her father beaming. I remember when she had her first communion; when she was in high school, pretty and smart and talking about Silas Marner; when she got married and all of us—her father and uncles and friends—knew that we were no longer young.

But I didn't know that the boy she married would soon be a junkie and, I suppose, neither did she. He looked like any other young kid walking bravely and awkwardly into the condition of manhood. Perhaps even then he was carrying the secret of his filthy little habit. In that family, as in so many others, nobody spoke of certain things. But he soon stopped going to work; he vanished for long hours into the streets; he lost weight; he itched and scratched and his teeth went bad; he craved lemon ices in January and wore long-sleeved lumber jackets in August. And the girl gave up the idea of college and went to work and supported them both. For a long time, she maintained the secret; four years ago, he went into a methadone program, swore he was clean, conceived a child with his wife. Then he left the program, returned to smack, jammed more and more needles into his arms and his legs and his buttocks. A daughter was born.

My friend was now a grandfather. There was another baptism party, but the old joy wasn't there. Neither was the husband. He was off in the street, his craving encased in scabby cankered skin. One night two years ago he overdosed, was rushed to Kings County Hospital. The doctors saved him. But they also discovered that he had AIDS.

"They told him," my friend said, "but they couldn't tell my daughter."

They couldn't tell her, because of the rules of confidentiality. If the junkie didn't want anyone to know he was infected, the doctors could do nothing. So the junkie went home and murdered his wife.

He didn't use a gun or a knife.

He slept with her.

Eight months ago, the junkie died. Two months later, in pain and suffering, his wife followed him to the merciful grave. Their daughter, an orphan of the plague years, lives with her grandfather now. He watches her very carefully for any signs of the infection. He doesn't know what he will ever tell her about the way her parents died.

There have been great debates among our physicians as to the reason of this. Some will have it to be in the nature of the disease, and that it impresses everyone that is seized upon by it with a kind of rage, and a hatred against their own kind, as if there was a malignity not only in the distemper to communicate itself, but in the very nature of man, prompting him with evil will or an evil eye, that, as they say in the case of a mad dog, who, though the gentlest creature before of any of his kind, yet then will fly upon and bite any one that comes next him, and those as soon as any who had been most observed by him before.

Defoe

I think of that young girl a lot these days, as the debate intensifies over what to do about AIDS. Much of the discussion of personal privacy and the rights of AIDS victims is admirable. But the general tone reflects a reckless assumption: that carriers and victims will behave responsibly.

Common sense tells us that all of them will not and do not. Junkies don't belong to fraternal associations, where they debate codes of personal behavior. You will not see them wearing Safe Smack T-shirts. In my experience, junkies don't think of anyone else on earth except themselves and their habits. They will rob their mothers, destroy their families, turn their women into whores, pass their habits on to others to make a few dollars pushing. Why would they suddenly start caring about giving other people AIDS?

But common sense also tells us the homosexual community isn't completely populated by upstanding, responsible citizens either. Not all gay men can be expected to live in an intelligent, compassionate way with the ruthless presence of AIDS. Some will willfully, recklessly, cruelly infect others. Not because they are gay. Not because they are the monsters conjured in homophobic fantasies. But because they are human. And human beings have an unhappy record when confronted with the chilly certainty of death. Many are brave. But others rage against the unfairness of the fatal lottery, and in their fury, reach out to harm those who might still smell the roses after they have gone. A gay man who contracts AIDS and doesn't tell his lover, or keeps the secret from others with whom he might share a bed, is a killer.

Nobody knows how many infected human beings are committing such premeditated crimes, but to deny that anyone is purposefully spreading the plague is to deny human history. The literature of the 19th century is full of stories of human beings willfully, angrily giving each other syphilis. Then, as now, there was no cure. Many thousands died terrible deaths. Prostitutes, in particular, didn't care who got harmed. And apparently, don't much care now. Last week, a Miami prostitute named Wendy Blankenship admitted that for the past two years she knew she had the AIDS virus and still had sex with hundreds of men without telling them. "I don't feel bad," she said. "All the girls out there are doing the same."

One central task of the law is to protect the innocent. And until that day when a cure for AIDS is finally found, the law will have to deal with the presence of the vicious among the plague-bearing population. One law will have to make clear that if a man or woman knowingly gives another the virus, and the end result is death, that citizen has committed premeditated murder. He or she should be prosecuted as vigorously as if the weapon were a gun or a knife or poison. And somehow, in spite of all the potential dangers to civil liberties, the confidentiality rules must be altered. Certainly doctors must be free to tell wives and lovers that their partners have AIDS. In the face of this terrible disease, we will need as much pity and compassion as possible, but not at the expense of justice. It's too late to save that lovely young woman I used to know. Maybe others can be saved from people who can only be described as evil.

CONSIDER THIS

Pete Hamill writes regularly for *The New York Post*. "The Secret Sharers" was printed in *The Village Voice,* a New York City newspaper long known for its resistance to conventional viewpoints: if you want the provocative, alternative perspective on most matters social and political, international and national, or daring reviews of film, art, dance, theater, and movies, then you'd do well to pick up a copy of the "Voice," as it is known locally.

Is Hamill's text closed or open? When do you begin to know that he has taken an unequivocal stand, that there are words that must be said, and that he is saying, finally, "This will not do." How do you characterize his voice?

What effects do the passages from Defoe's *Journal of the Plague Year* have on your reading? You might know Defoe as author of one of the world's most celebrated books, *Robinson Crusoe.*

"Default Assumptions" and Their Effects on Writing and Thinking
Douglas R. Hofstadter

A father and son were driving to a ball game when their car stalled on the railroad tracks. In the distance a train whistle blew a warning. Frantically the father tried to start the engine, but in his panic he couldn't turn the key, and the car was hit by the on-rushing train. An ambulance sped to the scene and picked them up. On the way to the hospital the father died. The son was still alive but his condition was critical, and he needed immediate surgery. The moment they arrived at the hospital he was wheeled into an emergency operating room, and a surgeon came in, expecting a routine case. On seeing the boy, however, the surgeon blanched and muttered, "I can't operate on this boy—he's my son."

What do you make of this grim riddle? How could it be? Was the surgeon lying or mistaken? No. Was the dead father's soul somehow reincarnated in the surgeon's body? No. Was the surgeon the boy's true father and the dead man the boy's adoptive father? No. What, then, is the explanation? Think it through until you have figured it out on your own—I insist! You'll know when you've got it, don't worry.

When I was first asked this riddle a few years ago, I got the answer within a minute or so. Still, I was ashamed of my performance. I was also disturbed by the average performance of the people in the group I was with—all educated, intelligent people, some men, some women. I was neither the quickest nor the slowest. A couple of them, even after five minutes of scratching their heads, still didn't have the answer. And when they hit on it, their heads hung low.

Whether we light on the answer quickly or slowly, we all have something to learn from this riddle. It reveals something deep about how "default assumptions" permeate our mental representations and channel our thoughts. A default assumption is what holds true in what you might say is the "simplest" or "most natural" or "most likely" possible model of whatever situation is under discussion. In this case the default assumption is that the surgeon is a man. The way things are in our society today that is the most plausible assumption. But the critical thing about default assumptions (well revealed by this story) is that they are made automatically, not as a result of consideration and elimination. You did not explicitly ponder the point and ask yourself: What is the most plausible sex to assign to the surgeon? Rather, you merely let your past experience assign a sex for you. Default assumptions are by their nature implicit assumptions. You were not aware of having made any assumption about the surgeon's sex, because if you had been, there would not have been any riddle.

Usually reliance on default assumptions is extremely useful. In fact, it is indispensable in enabling us—or any cognitive machine—to get around in this complex world. We simply cannot afford to be constantly distracted by all kinds of theoretically possible but unlikely exceptions to the general rules or models we have built up by induction from many past experiences. We have to make what amount to shrewd guesses, and we do it with great skill all the time. Our every thought is permeated by such shrewd guesses—assumptions of normalcy. The strategy seems to work pretty well. For example, we assume that the stores lining the main street of a town we pass through are not just cardboard facades, and for good reason. Probably you are not worried about whether the chair you are sitting on is going to collapse. Probably the last time you used a saltshaker you did not consider that it might be filled with sugar. Without much trouble you could name dozens of assumptions you are making at this very moment, all of which are *probably* true rather than *definitely* true.

This ability to ignore what is highly unlikely—without even considering whether or not to ignore it—is part of our evolutionary heritage, coming out of the need to be able to size up a situation quickly but accurately. It is a marvelous and subtle quality of our thought processes. Once in a while, however, this marvelous ability leads us astray. Sexist default assumptions are a case in point.

When I wrote my book *Gödel, Escher, Bach: an Eternal Golden Braid,* I employed the dialogue form, a form I enjoy very much. I was so inspired by Lewis Carroll's dialogue "What the Tortoise Said to Achilles" that I decided to borrow his two characters. Over a period of time I developed them into my own characters. As I proceeded I found I was naturally led to bring in some new characters of my own. The first one was the Crab. Then came the Anteater, the Sloth and various other colorful individuals. Like the Tortoise and Achilles, the new characters were all male: Mr. Crab, Mr. Sloth and so on.

That was in the early 1970's, and I was quite conscious of what I was doing. Yet for some reason I could not get myself to invent a female character. I was upset with myself, yet I could not help thinking that introducing a female character "for no reason" would be artificial and therefore distracting. I did not want to mix sexual politics—an ugly real-world issue—with the ethereal pleasures of an ideal fantasy world.

I racked my brains about it for a long time. I even wrote an apologetic dialogue on this very topic, an intricate one in which I myself figured, discussing with my own characters the question of sexism in writing. Apart from my friends Achilles and the Tortoise, the cast features God as a surprise visitor, and as in the old joke she was black. Although corny, it was an earnest attempt to grapple with some problems of conscience that were plaguing me. The dialogue never got polished, and it was not included in my book. A series of reworkings, however, gradually turned it into the "Six-Part Ricercar" with which the book concludes.

My pangs of conscience did lead me to make a few minor characters female: there were Prudence and Imprudence (who argued briefly about consistency), Aunt Hillary (a conscious ant colony) and every other member of the infinite series Genie, Meta-genie, Meta-meta-genie and so on. I was particularly proud of this gentle touch, but no matter how you slice it females got the short end of the stick. I was not altogether happy with it, but that's the way it was.

In addition to the book's dialogues being populated with male characters, it was filled with default assumptions of masculinity, the standard "he" and "his" always being chosen. I made no excuse for this. I gave my reader credit for intelligence; I assumed he would know that often occurrences of such pronouns carry no gender assumptions but simply betoken a "unisex" person.

Over a period of time, however, I have gradually come to a different feeling about how written language should deal with people of unspecified sex, or with supposedly specific but randomly chosen people. It is a subtle issue, and I do not claim to have the final answers by any means, but I have found some approaches that please me and that may be useful to other people.

What woke me up? Given that I was already conscious of the issues, what new element did it take to induce the shift? Well, one significant incident was the telling of that surgeon story. My own reaction to it and the reactions of my companions surprised me. Most of us manufactured all kinds of bizarre alternative worlds instead of imagining one in which a surgeon could be a woman. How ludicrous! The event emphasized for me how deeply ingrained our default assumptions are and how unaware of them we are. This seemed to me to have potential consequences far beyond what one might naively think. I am hardly one to believe that language "pushes us around," that we are its slaves, yet on the other hand I think we must do our best to rid language of usages that may induce or reinforce default assumptions in our minds.

One of the vividest examples of this came a couple of years after my book had been published. I was describing its dialogues to a group of people and said I regretted that the characters had all been male. One woman asked me why, and I replied, "Well, I began with two males—Achilles and the Tortoise—and it would have been distracting to introduce females seemingly for no reason except politics." Yet as I heard myself saying this a horrifying thought crept into my mind for the first time: How did I know that Carroll's Tortoise was really a male? Surely he was, wasn't he? I seemed to remember it very well.

And yet the question nagged at me. Since I had a copy of the Carroll dialogue ready to hand, I turned to it for verification. I was nonplussed to find that Carroll nowhere even hints at the sex of his Tortoise. In fact, the opening sentence runs: "Achilles had overtaken the Tortoise, and had seated himself comfortably upon its back." This is the only occurrence of "it"; from there on "the Tortoise" is what Carroll writes. "Mr. Tortoise" indeed! Was this entirely a product of my own defaults?

Probably not. The first time I had heard about the Carroll dialogue many years earlier someone—a male—had described it to me. This person very likely had passed *his* default assumption on to me. Hence I could claim innocence. Moreover, I realized, I had read a few responses in philosophy journals to the Carroll dialogue, and when I went back and looked at them, I found they too had featured a "sexed" Tortoise, in contrast to the way Carroll himself had carefully skirted the issue. Although I felt somewhat exonerated, I was still upset. I kept on asking myself: What if I had visualized a female Tortoise to begin with? Then what would *Gödel, Escher, Bach* have been like?

One thing that had dissuaded me from using female characters was the distractingly political way some books have of referring to the reader or briefly mentioned random people (such as "the student" or "the child") as "she" or "her." It stuck out like a sore thumb, and it made one think so much about sexism that the main point of the passage often went unnoticed. It seemed to me such a strategy might be too blunt and simplistic and could turn many people off.

And yet I could not agree with the attitude of some people, largely but by no means exclusively men, who refused to switch their usage on grounds of "tradition," "linguistic purity," "beauty of the language" and so on. To be sure, words such as "fireperson," "snowperson," "henchperson" and "personhandle" are unappealing, but they are not your only recourse.

In the introduction to Robert Nozick's *Philosophical Explanations,* an exciting and admirable book on philosophy, I came across the following footnote: "I do not know of a way to write that is truly neutral about pronoun gender yet does not constantly distract attention—at least the contemporary reader's—from the sentence's central content. I am still looking for a satisfactory solution." From this point on Nozick uses "he" and "him" nearly everywhere. My reaction was annoyance: could Nozick have really looked very hard? Part of my annoyance was undoubtedly due to my own guilt feelings for having done no better in my book, but some was due to my feeling that Nozick had failed to see a fascinating challenge here, one to which he could bring his philosophical insight and in so doing make a creative contribution to society.

As best I can remember, I first began seriously trying to "demasculinize" my prose in working on the dialogue on the Turing Test that eventually wound up as this column for May of last year. I wrote the dialogue with the sexes of the characters shifting fluidly in my mind, since I was modeling the characters on mixtures of people I knew. I always imagined the character I most agreed with more as being female than as being male, and the others vacillated.

One day it occurred to me that the beginning of the dialogue discussed Turing's question "Can you in principle tell, merely from a written dialogue, a female from a male?" The question applied so well to the very characters discussing it that I could not resist making some character "ambisexual"—ambiguous in terms of sex. Thus I named one of them "Pat." Soon I realized there was no reason not to extend this notion to *all* the characters in the dialogue, making it a real guessing game for readers. So were born "Sandy," "Chris" and Pat."

Writing that dialogue was a turning point for me. Even though its total sexual equality had been motivated by my desire to give the dialogue an interesting self-referential twist, I found that I was relieved to have broken out of the all-male mold I had earlier felt locked into. I started looking for more ways to make up for my past default system.

It was not easy, and it still is not. For example, in teaching classes I find myself wanting to use "she" to refer back to an earlier unspecified person—a random biologist, say, or a random logician. Yet I find it does not seem to come out of my mouth easily. What I have trained myself to do rather well is to avoid gender-laden pronouns altogether, thus, like Carroll, "skirting" the issue. Sometimes I just keep repeating "the logician," or perhaps I just say "the person" or "that person." Every once in a while I say "he or she" (or "he" or "she"), although I have to admit I often simply say "they."

Someone who, like me, is trying to eliminate gender-laden pronouns from their speech altogether can try to rely on the word "they," but they will find themself in quite a pickle as soon as they try to use any reflexive verbal phrase such as "paint themselves into a corner," and what is worse is that no matter how that person tries they will find that they cannot extricate themself gracefully, and consequently he or she will just flail around, making his or her sentence so awkward that s/he wis/hes s/he had never become conscious of these issues of sexism. Obviously using "they" just takes you out of the frying pan into the fire, since you have merely exchanged a male-female ambiguity for a singular-plural ambiguity. The only advantage to this ploy, I suppose, is that there is/are, to my knowledge, no group(s) actively struggling for equality between singular and plural.

One possible solution is to use the plural exclusively, to refer, for example, to "biologists" or "a team of biologists," never just "a biologist." That way "they" is always legitimately referring to a plural. This, however, is a poor solution, since it is much more vivid to paint a picture of a specific individual. A body cannot always deal in plurals.

Another solution, somewhat more pleasing, is to turn an impersonal situation into a more personal one by using the word "you." This way your listeners or readers are encouraged to put themselves in the situation, to experience it vicariously.

Sometimes, however, this can backfire on you. Suppose you are talking about the strange effects in everyday life that statistical fluctuations can produce. You might write something like this: "One day your mailman might have so much mail to sort down at the post office that it is afternoon by the time she gets started on her route." At the outset your avid reader Polly manufactures an image of her friendly postman sorting letters and a few moments later she is told the postman is a woman. Jolt! It is not just a surface-level jolt (the collision of the words "mailman" and "she"), although it is that too; it is really an image-image conflict, since you expressly invited Polly to think of *her own* mailman, who happens to be a man. Even if you had said "your letter carrier," Polly would still have been jolted. On the other hand, if you had asked Polly to think about, say, "Henry's letter carrier," then that "she" would not have caused nearly as much surprise, and maybe not any.

In teaching my classes I try always to use sex-neutral nouns such as "letter carrier" and "department head" (I avoid "chairperson"), and having done so I try my utmost to avoid using gender-specific pronouns to refer back to them. I have come to realize, however, that this is largely a show put on for my own benefit. I am not actively undermining any bad stereotypes simply by avoiding them. The fact that I am not saying "he" where many people would is not the kind of thing that will grab my students by the collar and shake them. A few people may notice my "good behavior," but they are the ones who are already attuned to these issues.

So why not just use an unexpected "she" now and then? Isn't that the obvious thing to do? Perhaps. But in many cases, as Nozick pointed out, it will seem so politically motivated that it will distract rather than enlighten. The problem is, once you have used a noun such as "letter carrier" that could apply to either sex, people will manufacture a mental "node"— a kind of hook in their minds on which they can hang various qualities. (If "node" means nothing to you, imagine a questionnaire with a number of questions requiring immediate answers.)

Now, it is naive to suppose that a few seconds after node formation the image is, or ever was, floating in a sexual limbo. It is next to impossible to build up more than the most fleeting, insubstantial image of a person without assuming he is a she, or vice versa. The moment that node is manufactured, unless you answer its questions, it will answer them itself. (Imagine that each blank in the questionnaire has a default answer entered in light pencil, easily erasable but to be used in case no other answer is provided.) And unfortunately—even for ardent feminists—those unconscious default answers are usually going to be sexist. (Women can be as sexist as the next guy.) For example, I have realized, to my dismay, that my defaults run deep, so deep that even when I *say* "letter carrier" and later "his or her route," I am often nonetheless *thinking* "his route." This is most disconcerting.

It reveals that although my self-training may have succeeded quite well at the linguistic level, it has not yet fully filtered down to the *imagistic* level.

So have I not painted myselves into a corner? Am I not damned if I do and damned if I don't? After all, I have said that on the one hand the passive approach of merely avoiding sexist usages is not enough but that on the other hand the active approach of throwing in jolting stereotype violations is too much. Is there no successful middle path?

I have discovered, as a matter of fact, what I think is a rather graceful compromise solution to such dilemmas. Instead of dropping a nondefault gender into her lap *after* your reader has set up her default images of the people involved in the situation, simply do not let her get off the ground with her defaults. Upset her default assumptions explicitly from the word go.

I did this at the beginning of my May column on innumeracy, in which I retold an old joke. Usually the storyteller begins, "A professor was giving a lecture on the fate of the solar system, and he said. . . ." The professor is almost always made out to be a male. This may reflect the sexual statistics for astronomers, but individuals are not statistics.

How could the story be improved—gracefully? Well, there is a delay, not a long one but still a delay, between the first mention of the professor and the word "he." It is long enough for the default male image to get solidly, even though implicitly, implanted in the listener's mind. So just don't let that happen. Instead make the professor a woman from the start. By this I certainly do not mean you should begin your story, "A woman professor was giving a lecture on the fate of the solar system, and. . . ." That is horrible.

My solution was to give her sex away by her name. I invented the pseudo-Slavic name "Professor Bignumska," whose ending in "-a" signifies that its owner is female. To be sure, not everyone is attuned to such linguistic subtleties, so that for some people it will come as a surprise when a few lines down they read the phrase "according to her calculations." But at least they will get the point in the end.

What is worse is when people do not miss the point but rather reject the point altogether. In the French edition of *Scientific American* (*Pour la Science*) my "Professor Bignumska" was turned into "Monsieur le professeur Grannombersky." Not only was the sex reversed but clearly the translator had recognized what I was up to and had deliberately removed all telltale traces by switching the ending to a masculine one. I was disappointed. On the other hand, I was pleased to see that in the German edition (*Spektrum der Wissenschaft*) the professor's femininity remained intact: she was called "die namhafte Kosmogonin Grosszahlia." Not only her name but also her title has a feminine ending.

This practice of referring to members of some professions by explicitly feminine and masculine words certainly makes for trouble. What do you do when you are talking about a mixed group of actors and actresses? Unless you want to be verbose you have little choice but to refer to "actors." Why does a word such as "waiter," with its completely noncommittal ending, have to refer to a male? We are hard put to come up with a neutral term. Certainly "waitperson" is an awful concoction. "Server" is the best I have heard. On the other hand, it is nice to see "stewardess" and "steward" gradually being replaced by the general term "flight attendant."

All languages I have studied are in one way or another afflicted by these kinds of problems. Whereas we in English have our quaint-sounding "poetess" and "aviatrix," in French they have no better way of referring to a woman writer or professor than "une femme écrivain" or "une femme professeur," the default male gender being built into the nouns themselves. That is, "écrivain" and "professeur" are both masculine nouns. In order to enable them to refer to women you must treat them essentially as adjectives following (and modifying) the word "femme."

Another peculiarity of French is "quelqu'un," the word for "someone." It literally means "some one," and it calls for the masculine "un" no matter to whom it refers. This means, for example, that if an unfamiliar woman knocks at the door of Nicole's house and Nicole's young daughter answers the door, she is likely to yell to Nicole, "Maman, il y a quelqu'un à la porte" ("Mommy, there's someone at the door"). It is impossible to feminize the pronoun: "Maman, il y a quelqu'*une* à la porte." It would be even sillier to try to transform the impersonal "il y a" ("there is") into a feminine version, "elle y a." It just rings absurd. The masculine "il" is as impersonal as "it" in "It is two o'clock." Surely no one would suggest that we say "They are two o'clock."

In English we have some analogous phenomena. If a pair of strangers knock at Paul's door, his daughter may yell to him, "Daddy, someone's at the door." She will not say, "Sometwo are at the door." What this example illustrates is that the word "someone" does not carry with it strong implications of singularity. It can apply to a group of people without sounding odd. Perhaps by analogy "quelqu'un" is not as sexist at the image level as its surface level would suggest. But that is hard to know.

Normally in French, to speak of a mixed or unspecified group of people, one uses the masculine plural pronoun "ils." Even a group whose membership has not yet been determined, but that stands a fair chance of including at least one male among 20 females, will still call for "ils." Female speakers grow up with this usage, of course, and follow it as naturally and unconciously as male speakers do. Can you imagine the uproar if there were a serious attempt to reverse this age-old convention? How would men feel if the default assumption were to say "elles"? How would women feel? How would people in general feel if a group consisting of several men and one woman were always referred to as "elles"?

Curiously enough, there are circumstances where nearly that happens. There is a formalistic style of writing found in legal or contractual documents where the word "personnes" is used to refer to an abstract and unspecified group of people; thereafter the feminine plural "elles" is used to refer back to that noun. Since the word "personne" is of feminine gender (think of the Latin "persona"), this is the proper pronoun to use, even if the group being referred to is known to consist of males only.

Although this usage is grammatically correct, when it is dragged out over a long piece of text, it can give the reader a strange impression, since the original noun is so distant that the pronoun seems autonomous. One feels that the pronoun should at some point switch to "ils," and in fact sometimes it does. When it does not, it can make the reader uneasy. Perhaps this is just my own reaction. Perhaps it is merely the typical reaction of someone used to having a masculine default pronoun for an unspecified group of people.

We are all, of course, members of that collective group often referred to as "mankind," or simply "man." Even the ardent feminist Ashley Montagu once wrote a book called *Man: His First Two Million Years.* (I guess it was a long time ago.) Many people argue that this usage of "man" is completely distinct from the usage of "man" to refer to individuals, and that it is devoid of sexual implications. David Moser has astutely pointed out the weakness of this claim. He observes that in books you will find sentences in this vein: "Man has traditionally been a hunter, and he has kept his females close to the hearth, where they could tend his children." But you will never see such a sentence as "Man is the only mammal who does not always suckle his young." Rather, you will see "Man is the only mammal in which the females do not always suckle their young." So much for the sexual neutrality of generic "man." I began to look for such anomalies and soon ran across the following gem in a book on sexuality: "It is unknown in what way Man used to make love, when he was a primitive savage millions of years ago."

Back to other languages. When I spent a few months in Germany working on my doctoral dissertation, I learned that the term for "doctoral adviser" in German is "Doktorvater," literally "doctor father." I immediately wondered: What if your Doktorvater is a woman? Is she your "Doktormutter"? Since that rang absurd to my ears, I thought a better solution would be to append the feminizing suffix "-in," making it "Doktorvaterin"—"doctor fatheress." It seems, however, that a neutral term just might be preferable.

Italian and German share an unexpected feature: in both the respectful way of saying "you" is derived from the feminine singular pronoun, the only difference being capitalization. In Italian it is "Lei," in German "Sie." Now, in German the associated verb has a plural ending, so that the connection with "she" is somewhat diluted, but in Italian the verb remains third person singular. Thus to compliment a man you might say, "O, che Lei è bello!" ("Oh, how handsome She is!"). Of course, Italians do not hear it in this naive way. To them it might seem equally bewildering that in English adding "s" to a noun makes it plural and adding "s" to a verb makes it singular.

One of the strangest cases is that of Chinese. In Mandarin Chinese there has traditionally been just one pronoun for "he" and "she," pronounced "tā" and written

This character's left side consists of the "person" radical, indicating that it refers to a human being, sex unspecified. Curiously, however, in the linguistic reforms carried out in China over the past 70 years or so, a distinction has been introduced whereby there are now separate written forms for the single sound "tā." The old character has been retained, but now in addition to its old meaning of "s/he" it has the new meaning of "he" (wouldn't you know?) and a new character has been invented for "she." The new character's radical is the one for "woman" or "female," so that it is

The new implication, not present in Chinese before this century, is that the "standard" type of human being is a male and females must be indicated specially as "deviant." It remains a mystery to me why the Chinese did not leave the old character as it was—a

neutral pronoun—and simply manufacture *two* new characters, one with the female radical, as shown above, and one with the *male* radical, which would look this way:

To give a corresponding (although exaggerated) example in English, can you imagine a political reform in which the word "person" came to mean "man" and for "woman" we were told to say "personess"?

The upshot is that in China there is no longer a truly gender-free pronoun in writing. Formerly you could write an entire story without once revealing the sex of its participants; now your intentions to be ambiguous are themselves ambiguous. In the case of the joke about the cosmologist with its default option, it is interesting to consider which way would be better for the sake of feminism. Would you rather have the storyteller leave the professor's sex unspecified throughout the story, so that people's default options would be invoked? Or would you rather have the storyteller forced to commit himself.

One of my pet peeves is the currently popular usage of the word "guys." You often hear a group of people described as "guys," even when the group includes women. In fact, it is quite common to hear women addressing a group of other women as "you guys." This strikes me as strange. Some people I have asked about it, however, have adamantly maintained that when "guy" is in the plural, it has lost all traces of masculinity. I was arguing with a woman about this, and she kept saying, "It may have retained some male flavor for *you,* but it has none in most people's usage." I was not convinced, but nothing I could say would budge her from her position. In the end I got lucky, because in a last-ditch attempt to convince me she said. "Why, I've even heard *guys* use it to refer to a bunch of women." Only after saying it did she realize she had just undermined her own claim.

Such are the subtleties of language. We are often simply too unaware of how our minds work and what we really believe. It is there for us to perceive, but too often people do not listen to themselves; they think they know themselves without listening to themselves. Along these lines I recently heard myself saying "chesspeople" to refer to those wood pieces you move around on a chessboard. I had overtrained myself to watch out for words that end in "man."

There simply is a problem with default assumptions in our society. It is manifested everywhere. You find it in proverbs such as "To each his own," "Time and tide wait for no man" and so on. You hear it when children (and adults) talk about squirrels and birds in their yards ("Oh, look at him running with that acorn in his mouth!"). You see it in animated cartoons, many of which feature some poor schlemiel—a sad "fall guy," a "schmo" with whom "everyman" can identify—whose fate it is to be dumped on by the world, and we all laugh as he is dealt one cruel blow after another. Why are women not in this role more often? Why are there not more "schlemielesses"—more "fall gals"?

One evening at some friends' I was reading a delightful children's book called *Frog and Toad Are Friends,* and I asked why Frog and Toad both had to be males. This brought up the general topic of female representation in children's television and movies. In particular we discussed the Muppets, and we all wondered why there are so few sympathetic female Muppet characters. I am a great fan of Ms. Piggy's, but still I think if she is the only major female character, something is wrong. She is hardly an ideal role model.

This general kind of problem is not limited to questions of sex, of course. It extends much further, to groups of any kind, large or small. The cartoons in *The New Yorker,* for instance, although they are innocuous in one sense, certainly do not do anything to promote a change in one's default assumptions about the roles people can play. How often do you see a black or female executive in a *New Yorker* cartoon (unless, of course, they are there because the point of the joke depends on it)? The same could be said for most television shows, most books, most movies. . . . It is hard to know how to combat such a monolithic pattern. . . .

One of the most eloquent antisexist statements I have ever come across is a talk delivered recently at a college athletes' banquet by Donald Kennedy, the president of Stanford. Thirty years ago Kennedy himself was an athlete at Harvard, and he reminisced about a similar banquet he had attended then. He mused: "It occurs to me to wonder: What would the reaction have been if I had predicted that soon . . . women would run the Boston Marathon faster than it had ever been run by men up to that point? There would have been incredulous laughter from two-thirds of the room, accompanied by a little locker-room humor."

Then he pointed out: "Yet that is just what has taken place. My classmates would be astonished at the *happening,* but they would be even more astonished at the *trends.* If we look at the past 10 years of world's best times in the Marathon for men and women, it is clear that the women's mark has been dropping, over the decade, at a rate about seven times faster than the men's record."

The case of swimming is even more remarkable. Kennedy recalled that in his day the Harvard and Yale teams were at the pinnacle of the nation in swimming, and both came undefeated into their traditional meet at the end of the season. "What would have happened if you had put this year's Stanford women into that pool?" asked Kennedy. "*Humiliation* is what. Just to give you a sample, *seven* current Stanford women would have beaten my friend Dave Heberg, Harvard's great sprint freestyler, and *all* the Yalies in the 100. The Stanford women would have swept the 200-yard backstroke and breast stroke, and won *all* the other events contested.

"In the 400-yard freestyle relay there would have been a 10-second wait between Stanford's touch and the first man to arrive at the finish. Do you know how *long* 10 seconds is? Can you imagine that crowd in Payne Whitney Gymnasium, seeing a team of *girls* line up against the two best freestyle relay groups in the East, expecting the unexpected, and then having to wait *this long*—for the men to get home?

He painted a hilarious picture, but of course his point was dead serious: "I ask you: If conventional wisdom about women's capacity can be so thoroughly decimated in this most traditional area of male superiority, how can we possibly cling to the illusions we have about them in other areas?

"What, in short, is the lesson to be drawn from the emerging *athletic* equality of women? I think it is that those who make all the other, less objectively verifiable assumptions about female limitations would do well to discard them. They belong in the same dusty closet with the notion that modern ballplayers couldn't carry Ty Cobb's spikes and the myth that blacks can't play quarterback. Whether it is vicious or incapacitating or merely quaint, nonsense is nonsense. And it dies hard."

'Tis a point to ponder. Meanwhile,

CONSIDER THIS

"Default Assumptions" appeared in 1982 in Hofstadter's then regular feature in *Scientific American,* Metamagical Themas (*meta-,* "beyond," "transcending"). Had you heard the riddle he tells in the first paragraph? How long did it take for you to come up with the answer?

Hofstadter offers a measured, reasonable approach to what can be an emotionally charged issue. How does his quiet voice affect you? Are you convinced? Do his examples (Frog and Toad, Miss Piggy, *New Yorker* cartoons, women's sports records) work for you?

In 1980 Hofstadter's book *Gödel, Escher, Bach: an Eternal Golden Braid,* won the Pulitzer Prize for General Nonfiction. Maurits Escher was a Dutch artist famous for his illusionist transformations; Kurt Gödel developed a proof that rigorously self-contained mathematical systems are impossible. Metamagical, indeed.

In China, Loving Lady Chatterley
Bill Holm

For the better part of 25 years, I felt discontented with teaching in America. This is not a country that reads much, or believes that the little it is required to read has anything to do with the world of banks, cars and missile silos. We are practical to a fault, clean mental machines, so Thoreau, Whitman and Mark Twain go in one ear and pass out the other, frequently without impediment, loss of speed or any notable effect.

After 25 years, I was near despair, ready to give it up and go to sea, when the universe dropped China in my lap. "Of course I'll go," I said. "When do I leave?" I went, like Ishmael, with a sense of adventure—the idea that whoever was not curious to see and experience China gave clear evidence of death and should be embalmed soon before he perfumed his own house. But China had an odd side effect: it saved my faith in teaching, and in the power and majesty of language.

I taught in Xian, Shaanxi Province, at Jiaotong (Traffic) University—an old polytechnic college established late in the 19th century to train Chinese engineers to run railroads. By the 1980s, it had become the Chinese equivalent of M.I.T. or Cal Tech, a premier engineering school—in Chinese jargon, a "key" university—that recruited students by examination from all over China. As a result, it had a bright lot of students, mostly engineers.

I taught in the foreign-language department; the program's intent was to train English teachers, who in turn would instruct students of science and technology. Officially it was called "applied linguistics," but the curriculum dictated a couple of literature classes, which were my job. The students varied in age from 19 to their mid-40's, and came from the far corners of China. Some had Chinese accents so exotic that they were forced to speak to their classmates in English most of the time.

The one common thread, I quickly discovered, was their distaste for applied linguistics and dread of a life teaching engineers to translate technical articles. They cared passionately about history, anthropology, poetry, political journalism, translation—almost everything but hydraulic systems. Chinese students, of course, have no choice. Mother State determines where they will "serve the people," and off they go. It's the step into a better apartment, more influence, the chance to change jobs later. But it meant they were eager for whatever had nothing to do with technology and party dogma.

My first quarrels with the department authorities were over textbooks. A Chinese English-literature survey class lists the "main" writers, gives birth, death, publication dates, names "important" books, gives "main" ideas and offers three or four sentences of canned social criticism to pigeonhole the writer safely in the official scheme of things, then a page or two of carefully edited text. A Chinese teacher in a literature class read the canned stuff aloud, wrote "main points" on the board in Chinese and English, broached no questions and held no discussion about a text he might or might not have read himself. For the examination, the students dutifully memorized this material and wrote it down exactly as teacher and text had agreed on its being said. The irony, of course, was that the class, and sometimes even the teachers, were voracious readers of everything they could find, even on the black book market; the more dangerous and forbidden the text, the better.

I demanded that the department duplicate an abridged Norton anthology so that the students would have some accurate texts to argue about. The department refused, then agreed, then did nothing, although the university had its own print shop with the latest equipment that turned out mostly public relations fluff and party directives.

Finally, I stormed into the office and demanded to know why nothing had been done. "Perhaps," said the functionary, "the students prefer Chinese-style texts?"

"Nonsense!" I fumed.

"But," said the functionary, "we are so short of money. . . ."

I took out my checkbook, wrote a check for 500 hard dollars and threw it on the table. "Pay for it with that," I raged, "and never mention it to me again." I had done the one necessary thing to win the quarrel: I threatened the department with a loss of face. They declined the check and the texts were completed a few days later. The students cheered and applauded when the books arrived. We were off on a course of pure sedition: Blake, Dr. Johnson, Whitman, Thoreau, Yeats, Auden, Sherwood Anderson. It was all candy, all delight.

Melville was almost entirely unknown. There was a summary of "Moby-Dick" in the official literary history and a few lines of criticism about his bourgeois individualism. We read "Bartleby the Scrivener." Bartleby, to refresh your memory, is the drudge from the dead-letter office who "prefers not to." The story is wonderfully enigmatic, and, having defeated American literary criticism, it defeated the official Chinese passion for a "main point." The students loved arguing about why Bartleby "prefers not to" and began seeing parallels to Gandhi, Taoism and the history of Chinese bureaucracy. I tried to cut off discussion after three days and move on to Stephen Crane. Life is short and art is long, but having opened this Pandora's box, I had some difficulty closing it.

I taught that class from 10 until noon, and invariably I ran overtime, which always produced a great clattering of rice bowls and spoons. It was lunch time. The military music blaring from the loudspeaker outside the window announced to those students that they had better move briskly to the lunch lines or there would be no meat left. Chinese students carry their own bowls and utensils to the people's lunch lines—if you want to eat, bring a dish; if you want tea, bring a cup and bring tea. After lunch comes nap time, the one inviolable law in Chinese life. China comes to a halt for two hours; citizens lunch perfunctorily and then doze till 2 P.M.

I, too, came to treasure my nap—two hours of absolute privacy. But Bartleby undid Chinese courtesy. Two or three days running, a knock sounded on the door after lunch. "Yes," I called sleepily from under my quilt. Students came in two or three at a time and pulled up chairs next to the bed. "We are sorry to disturb your nap, Comrade Bill, but we have been studying more of Bartleby, and we think we have found the true reason he prefers not to. Is it because. . .?" The best I ever did for them from the kingdom of half-sleep was a "maybe" or a "that's possible" before shoving them back into the Middle Kingdom. I was half outraged by the invasion of my nap and half exultant. I don't ever remember being got out of bed by an American student to settle an argument that started in a class, although I had been called in the middle of the night for a grade, or with a third dead grandmother of the semester as an excuse for a missed paper or exam.

I began teaching Emily Dickinson with trepidation. My students had good, workable English, a solid understanding of prose and comprehensive vocabularies. Furthermore, they had read a great deal of this literature in Chinese translation. Emily D., though, with her mordant irony and her dense, peculiar English, struck me as untranslatable, in either culture or language. But I carried on; nothing ventured. . . . When was the last time an American teacher went into a classroom piqued by pure curiosity about how students might respond?

I began with a little lecture about Emily's odd life. I explained hymn meter and sang a stanza or two of her work to tunes like "Duke Street" and "Amazing Grace." I asked if she was at all known in China. A hand went up in the front row from a young woman with an infectious giggle. When I first read her name, I asked her if it meant Small Vinegar. She giggled, "You don't read Chinese characters."

"No," I said. I had made a silly pun—the two sounds in her name meant small vinegar, but they meant 50 other things, too. Whenever class went slowly, I crossed my eyes at her or made a monster face. She couldn't resist laughing magnificently and loosening up the whole room. She had one of the most lively and immediate faces I've ever seen, which murdered with one stroke the cliché about inscrutable Oriental faces. It is American academics and politicians who so often have the stony, shifty faces.

She answered me this way:

I'm Nobody! Who are you?
Are you—Nobody—Too?
Then there's a pair of us?
Don't tell! they'd advertise—you know!

How dreary—to—be—Somebody!
How public—like a Frog—
To tell one's name—the livelong June—
To an admiring Bog!

I was not quite speechless. "Wonderful!" I said. "Why did you learn it?"

"She is my favorite poet and my namesake."

"Your namesake?"

"My English name is Emily. I took it from Emily Dickinson and Emily Brontë, two of my favorite writers."

We had a little talk about how this poem might connect to the secrecy and jealousy endemic in Chinese life, how this manifested itself in a passion to be anonymous, to be in no one's files. Nine or ten other students knew Dickinson poems by heart, too. The next day they brought in Chinese translations and read them to me. We found mistakes, translations out of inaccurate editions, misunderstanding of New England idioms, misread ironies. We did "scholarship." I gave them a few ideas out of Freud about Emily Dickinson that the party had neglected to mention. They all wanted to learn to sing one of her poems to a hymn tune, so I rehearsed them on "Because I Could Not Stop for Death" to "Amazing Grace." No American class except an Elder Hostel ever demanded singing from me.

D. H. Lawrence was the hardest case for the Chinese literary pigeonholers. Having hatched the notion that British writers are almost entirely bourgeois (true) and reflect bourgeois values (sometimes true), they were stumped by Lawrence. A true man of the working class, he hated capitalism—so far, so good. But he hated socialism, too—just as much. And insisted on the business about sex. Orwell's description of Big Brother's attempts to destroy and pervert sexual life is exactly and literally true. Change the names and it describes China. Change them again and it describes any institution like China, name your own preferred church or government. Chinese translations of "Lady Chatterley's Lover" sold on the black market at prices ranging from 7 to 20 yuan, ferociously expensive, but not enough to keep readers away from its dangers and delights.

• • •

I started Lawrence gently by giving them a few small poems. We memorized them and said them aloud. Since Chinese students were used to memorizing whole books on demand, these tiny poems were no trouble. The first was:

The youth walks up to the white horse, to put its halter on
and the horse looks at him in silence.
They are so silent they are in another world.

How like an old Chinese poem, they said. How smart for a barbarian to do this! Lao-tze's countrymen still understand silence and other worlds. The next was:

I can't stand Willy wet-leg,
can't stand him at any price.
He's resigned, and when you hit him
he lets you hit him twice.

How well Lawrence understood us, they said. We are too passive, too obedient. We are a little like Willy wet-leg. This was two years before Tiananmen Square. It was clearly not Willy wet-leg standing in front of that line of tanks.

At last we came to "The Horse Dealer's Daughter," the story that happened to be in the Norton anthology I had duplicated. I grew up Lutheran in a small Minnesota town in the 1950's, so I understood the repression of erotic life, but I had never imagined so thorough and cynical a manipulation of human feeling as that in China. Young Chinese grow up with a horror of touch, a fear of their own eros. There are to be no marriages before age 25, no touching in public, no mention of sexuality except to condemn it as counterrevolutionary, no "dating," no acknowledgment that humans might have duties to themselves different from those owed to the state. Every political campaign wrecked families and marriages. Chinese job assignments kept husbands and wives thousands of miles apart for decades. My Chinese students existed in a state of sexual suspended animation. The ones in their 20's reminded me of naïve junior-high students in America. And yet, underneath this mad repression, I sensed that many Chinese are hopeless romantics, doors waiting to be opened. Real sexual energy is a genuine threat to political authority. The moral Stalinists are not wrong.

I asked them to read the story aloud, a paragraph or two at a time, to practice their oral English. How wonderful that story sounded in a grab bag of Chinese accents, voices and sweet mispronunciations, steadily more full of feeling as the story progressed! Lawrence tells the story of a woman who lives with three loutish brothers and decides to give up on life. She walks into a pond with no intention of walking out. A typically constipated young British doctor, a friend of the family who admires Mabel but is too reserved and frightened to act, sees her. He walks into the brackish waters of the pond in order to carry her out, water-logged and unconscious. He takes her to the house, lights a fire, undresses her and then wraps her in warm blankets. She revives. She first thinks herself dead, then realizes that she is naked and the doctor is there:

"For a moment it seemed as if her reason were going. She looked round, with wild eye, as if seeking something. He stood still with fear. She saw her clothing lying scattered.

"'Who undressed me?' she asked, her eyes resting full and inevitable on his face.

"'I did,' he replied, 'to bring you round.'

"For some moments she sat and gazed at him awfully, her lips parted.

"'Do you love me, then?' she asked.

"He only stood and stared at her, fascinated. His soul seemed to melt."

From this point on, two-thirds of the way through the story, the room charged with erotic energy, as if each woman were Mabel, naked, damp and wild-eyed by the fire, and every man Dr. Ferguson, speechless, astonished, frightened, his soul sliding away underneath him. Insofar as I have ever had a mystical experience, I had one in that classroom—the right work of art telling the right truth to the right people—an absolutely impossible concatenation of events, a violation of the laws of probability, happening before me. And the room drenched in feeling, as soggy with eros as Mabel's damp clayey dress, as the doctor's sodden tweeds, and all palpably alive. He touches her. "A flame seemed to burn the hand that grasped her soft shoulder."

The classroom trembled. The doctor's will struggles, then relaxes and yields. She kisses his knees. "You love me." He begins kissing her.

"'Yes.' The word cost him a painful effort. Not because it wasn't true. But because it was too newly true, the *saying* seemed to tear open again his newly torn heart. And he hardly wanted it to be true, even now.

"She lifted her face to him, and he bent forward and kissed her on the mouth gently. . . . He never intended to love her. But now it was over. He had crossed over the gulf to her, and all that he had left behind had shriveled and become void."

This is not explicit stuff. It could hardly get you in trouble with the Lutheran Ladies Aid. But "The Horse Dealer's Daughter" is the real thing, alive with true eros. Those Chinese students felt it and it moved them. For them, it became what literature should always be, a necessary volcanic eruption in the soul. "Where can we find more of these stories, Comrade Bill?" they asked. When was the last time a visibly moved American class demanded more work from a writer?

I came back to America after my year in China and tried teaching college again. I sank as close to clinical depression as I have ever come. In the middle of the silence or the diddling, I tried superimposing the faces of my Chinese students on the clean-cut blond heads. I tried teleporting myself back into the dust and spittle of a Xian classroom. I stood gawking in the parking lot at my students' cars. I surveyed the piles of unpurchased textbooks for my classes. I dutifully graded the almost illiterate hen-scratched essays. What insufferable arrogance, I thought to myself, to throw the chance for a real mental life away on people who don't want it. American life doesn't want them to want it—not, at any rate, to want more than the name, surely not the fact. Nor do the Chinese party hacks want Chinese students to want it, but they do.

And even after the tanks in Tiananmen Square, those students will still want it, and neither Deng Xiaoping, nor the next Deng Xiaoping by another name, has enough bullets or tanks to do anything about it.

CONSIDER THIS

What is literature? Bill Holm insists that "literature should always be a . . . volcanic eruption in the soul." His Chinese students kissed him back to a love of teaching by their curiosity, delight, and passion. They are the doctor for his near despair, just as the doctor was to Mabel in Lawrence's short story. En route to his salvation, Holm denigrates American students: they could care less, they're not interested, and they're dull. Each step of his journey to recovery, he compares the noble Chinese to the nearly illiterate Americans: "When was the last time an American teacher went into a classroom piqued by pure curiosity about how students might respond," he says. Do you agree with his swipes at American students? Do you find his views of *you* rather harsh? Unwarranted? Do you agree with his perspectives on what literature should be?

What do you think Holt might say to Holm?

How Teachers Make Children Hate Reading
John Holt

When I was teaching English at the Colorado Rocky Mountain School, I used to ask my students the kinds of questions that English teachers usually ask about reading assignments—questions designed to bring out the points that *I* had decided *they* should know. They, on their part, would try to get me to give them hints and clues as to what I wanted. It was a game of wits. I never gave my students an opportunity to say what they really thought about a book.

I gave vocabulary drills and quizzes too. I told my students that every time they came upon a word in their book they did not understand, they were to look it up in the dictionary. I even devised special kinds of vocabulary tests, allowing them to use their books to see how the words were used. But looking back, I realize that these tests, along with many of my methods, were foolish.

My sister was the first person who made me question my conventional ideas about teaching English. She had a son in the seventh grade in a fairly good public school. His teacher had asked the class to read Cooper's *The Deerslayer*. The choice was bad enough in itself; whether looking at man or nature, Cooper was superficial, inaccurate, and sentimental, and his writing is ponderous and ornate. But to make matters worse, this teacher had decided to give the book the microscope and x-ray treatment. He made the students look up and memorize not only the definitions but the derivations of every big word that came along—and there were plenty. Every chapter was followed by close questioning and testing to make sure the students "understood" everything.

Being then, as I said, conventional, I began to defend the teacher, who was a good friend of mine, against my sister's criticisms. The argument soon grew hot. What was wrong with making sure that children understood everything they read? My sister answered that until this class her boy had always loved reading, and had read a lot on his own; now he had stopped. (He was not really to start again for many years.)

Still I persisted. If children didn't look up the words they didn't know, how would they ever learn them? My sister said, "Don't be silly! When you were little you had a huge vocabulary, and were always reading very grown-up books. When did you ever look up a word in the dictionary?"

She had me. I don't know that we had a dictionary at home; if we did, I didn't use it. I don't use one today. In my life I doubt that I have looked up as many as fifty words, perhaps not even half that.

Since then I have talked about this with a number of teachers. More than once I have said, "according to tests, educated and literate people like you have a vocabulary of about twenty-five thousand words. How many of these did you learn by looking them up in a dictionary?" They usually are startled. Few claim to have looked up even as many as a thousand. How did they learn the rest?

They learned them just as they learned to talk—by meeting words over and over again, in different contexts, until they saw how they fitted.

Unfortunately, we English teachers are easily hung up on this matter of understanding. Why should children understand everything they read? Why should anyone? Does anyone?

I don't, and I never did. I was always reading books that teachers would have said were "too hard" for me, books full of words I didn't know. That's how I got to be a good reader. When about ten, I read all the D'Artagnan stories and loved them. It didn't trouble me in the least that I didn't know why France was at war with England or who was quarreling with whom in the French court or why the Musketeers should always be at odds with Cardinal Richelieu's men. I didn't even know who the Cardinal was, except that he was a dangerous and powerful man that my friends had to watch out for. This was all I needed to know.

Having said this, I will now say that I think a big, unabridged dictionary is a fine thing to have in any home or classroom. No book is more fun to browse around in—*if* you're not made to. Children, depending on their age, will find many pleasant and interesting things to do with a big dictionary. They can look up funny-sounding words, which they like, or words that nobody else in the class has ever heard of, which they like, or long words, which they like, or forbidden words, which they like best of all. At a certain age, and particularly with a little encouragement from parents or teachers, they may become very interested in where words came from and when they came into the language and how their meanings have changed over the years. But exploring for the fun of it is very different from looking up words out of your reading because you're going to get into trouble with your teacher if you don't.

While teaching fifth grade two years or so after the argument with my sister, I began to think again about reading. The children in my class were supposed to fill out a card—just the title and author and a one-sentence summary—for every book they read. I was not running a competition to see which child could read the most books, a competition that almost always leads to cheating. I just wanted to know what the children were reading. After a while it became clear that many of these very bright kids, from highly literate and even literary backgrounds, read very few books and deeply disliked reading. Why should this be?

At this time I was coming to realize, as I described in my book *How Children Fail,* that for most children school was a place of danger, and their main business in school was staying out of danger as much as possible. I now began to see also that books were among the most dangerous things in school.

From the very beginning of school we make books and reading a constant source of possible failure and public humiliation. When children are little we make them read aloud, before the teacher and other children, so that we can be sure they "know" all the words they are reading. This means that when they don't know a word, they are going to make a mistake, right in front of everyone. Instantly they are made to realize that they have done something wrong. Perhaps some of the other children will begin to wave their hands and say, "Ooooh! O-o-o-oh!" Perhaps they will just giggle, or nudge each other, or make a face. Perhaps the teacher will say, "Are you sure?" or ask someone else what he thinks. Or perhaps, if the teacher is kindly, she will just smile a sweet, sad smile—often one of the most painful punishments a child can suffer in school. In any case, the child who has made the mistake knows he has made it, and feels foolish, stupid, and ashamed, just as any of us would in his shoes.

Before long many children associate books and reading with mistakes, real or feared, and penalties and humiliation. This may not seem sensible, but it is natural. Mark Twain once said that a cat that sat on a hot stove lid would never sit on one again—but it would never sit on a cold one either. As true of children as of cats. If they, so to speak, sit on a hot book a few times, if books cause them humiliation and pain, they are likely to decide that the safest thing to do is to leave all books alone.

After having taught fifth-grade classes for four years I felt quite sure of this theory. In my next class were many children who had had great trouble with schoolwork, particularly reading. I decided to try at all costs to rid them of their fear and dislike of books, and to get them to read oftener and more adventurously.

One day soon after school had started, I said to them, "Now I'm going to say something about reading that you have probably never heard a teacher say before. I would like you to read a lot of books this year, but I want you to read them only for pleasure. I am not going to ask you questions to find out whether you understand the books or not. If you understand enough of a book to enjoy it and want to go on reading it, that's enough for me. Also I'm not going to ask you what words mean.

"Finally," I said, "I don't want you to feel that just because you start a book, you have to finish it. Give an author thirty or forty pages or so to get his story going. Then if you don't like the characters and don't care what happens to them, close the book, put it away, and get another. I don't care whether the books are easy or hard, short or long, as long as you enjoy them. Furthermore I'm putting all this in a letter to your parents, so they won't feel they have to quiz and heckle you about books at home."

The children sat stunned and silent. Was this a teacher talking? One girl, who had just come to us from a school where she had had a very hard time, and who proved to be one of the most interesting, lively, and intelligent children I have ever known, looked at me steadily for a long time after I had finished. Then, still looking at me, she said slowly and solemnly, "Mr. Holt, do you really mean that?" I said just as solemnly, "I mean every word of it."

Apparently she decided to believe me. The first book she read was Dr. Seuss's *How the Grinch Stole Christmas,* not a hard book even for most third graders. For a while she read a number of books on this level. Perhaps she was clearing up some confusion about reading that her teachers, in their hurry to get her up to "grade level," had never given her enough time to clear up. After she had been in the class six weeks or so and we had become good friends, I very tentatively suggested that, since she was a skillful rider and loved horses, she might like to read *National Velvet.* I made my sell as soft as possible, saying only that it was about a girl who loved and rode horses, and that if she didn't like it, she could put it back. She tried it, and though she must have found it quite a bit harder than what she had been reading, finished it and liked it very much.

During the spring she really astonished me, however. One day, in one of our many free periods, she was reading at her desk. From a glimpse of the illustrations I thought I knew what the book was. I said to myself, "It can't be," and went to take a closer look. Sure enough, she was reading *Moby Dick* in the edition with woodcuts by Rockwell Kent. When I came close to her desk she looked up. I said, "Are you really reading that?" She said she was. I said, "Do you like it?" She said, "Oh, yes, it's neat!" I said, "Don't you find parts of it rather heavy going?" She answered "Oh, sure, but I just skip over those parts and go on to the next good part."

This is exactly what reading should be and in school so seldom is—an exciting, joyous adventure. Find something, dive into it, take the good parts, skip the bad parts, get what you can out of it, go on to something else. How different is our mean-spirited, picky insistence that every child get every last little scrap of "understanding" that can be dug out of a book.

For teachers who really enjoy doing it, and will do it with gusto, reading aloud is a very good idea. I have found that not just fifth graders but even ninth and eleventh graders enjoy it. Jack London's "To Build a Fire" is a good read-aloud story. So are ghost stories; and "August Heat," by W. F. Harvey, and "The Monkey's Paw," by W. W. Jacobs, are among the best. Shirley Jackson's "The Lottery" is sure-fire, and will raise all kinds of questions for discussion and argument. Because of a television program they had seen and that excited them, I once started reading to my fifth graders William Golding's *Lord of the Flies*, thinking to read only a few chapters, but they made me read it to the end.

In my early fifth-grade classes the children usually were of high IQ, came from literate backgrounds, and were generally felt to be succeeding in school. Yet it was astonishingly hard for most of those children to express themselves in speech or in writing. I have known a number of five-year olds who were considerably more articulate than most of the fifth graders I have known in school. Asked to speak, my fifth graders were covered with embarrassment; many refused altogether. Asked to write, they would sit for minutes on end, staring at the paper. It was hard for most of them to get down a half page of writing, even on what seemed to be interesting topics or topics they chose themselves.

In desperation I hit on a device that I named the Composition Derby. I divided the class into teams, and told them that when I said, "Go," they were to start writing something. It could be about anything they wanted, but it had to be about something—they couldn't just write "dog dog dog dog" on the paper. It could be true stories, descriptions of people or places or events, wishes, made-up stories, dreams—anything they liked. Spelling didn't count, so they didn't have to worry about it. When I said, "Stop," they were to stop and count up the words they had written. The team that wrote the most words would win the derby.

It was a success in many ways and for many reasons. The first surprise was that the two children who consistently wrote the most words were two of the least successful students in the class. They were bright, but they had always had a very hard time in school. Both were very bad spellers, and worrying about this had slowed down their writing without improving their spelling. When they were free of this worry and could let themselves go, they found hidden and unsuspected talents.

One of the two, a very driven and anxious little boy, used to write long adventures, or misadventures, in which I was the central character—"The Day Mr. Holt Went to Jail," "The Day Mr. Holt Fell Into the Hole," "The Day Mr. Holt Got Run Over," and so on. These were very funny, and the class enjoyed hearing me read them aloud. One day I asked the class to write a derby on a topic I would give them. They groaned; they liked picking their own. "Wait till you hear it," I said. "It's 'The Day the School Burned Down.' "

With a shout of approval and joy they went to work, and wrote furiously for 20 minutes or more, laughing and chuckling as they wrote. The papers were all much alike; in them the children danced around the burning building, throwing in books and driving me and the other teachers back in when we tried to escape.

In our first derby the class wrote an average of about 10 words a minute; after a few months their average was over 20. Some of the slower writers tripled their output. Even the slowest, one of whom was the best student in the class, were writing 15 words a minute. More important, almost all the children enjoyed the derbies and wrote interesting things.

Some time later I learned that Professor S. I. Hayakawa, teaching freshman English, had invented a better technique. Every day in class he asked his students to write without stopping for about half an hour. They could write on whatever topic or topics they chose, but the important thing was not to stop. If they ran dry, they were to copy their last sentence over and over again until new ideas came. Usually they came before the sentence had been copied once. I use this idea in my own classes, and call this kind of paper a Non-Stop. Sometimes I ask students to write a Non-Stop on an assigned topic, more often on anything they choose. Once in a while I ask them to count up how many words they have written, though I rarely ask them to tell me; it is for their information. Sometimes these papers are to be handed in; often they are what I call private papers, for the students' eyes alone.

The private paper has proved very useful. In the first place, in any English class—certainly any large English class—if the amount the students write is limited by what the teacher can find time to correct, or even to read, the students will not write nearly enough. The only remedy is to have them write a great deal that the teacher does not read. In the second place, students writing for themselves will write about many things that they would never write on a paper to be handed in, once they have learned (sometimes it takes a while) that the teacher means what he says about the papers' being private. This is important, not just because it enables them to get things off their chest, but also because they are most likely to write well, and to pay attention to how they write, when they are writing about something important to them.

Some English teachers, when they first hear about private papers, object that students do not benefit from writing papers unless the papers are corrected. I disagree for several reasons. First, most students, particularly poor students, do not read the corrections on their papers; it is boring, even painful. Second, even when they do read these corrections, they do not get much help from them, do not build the teacher's suggestions into their writing. This is true even when they really believe the teacher knows what he is talking about.

Third, and most important, we learn to write by writing, not by reading other people's ideas about writing. What most students need above all else is practice in writing, and particularly in writing about things that matter to them, so that they will begin to feel the satisfaction that comes from getting important thoughts down in words and will care about stating these thoughts forcefully and clearly.

Teachers of English—or, as some schools say (ugh!), Language Arts—spend a lot of time and effort on spelling. Most of it is wasted; it does little good, and often more harm than good. We should ask ourselves, "How do good spellers spell? What do they do when they are not sure which spelling of a word is right?" I have asked this of a number of good spellers. Their answer never varies. They do not rush for a dictionary or rack their brains trying to remember some rules. They write down the word both ways, or several ways, look at them and pick the one that looks best. Usually they are right.

Good spellers know what words look like and even, in their writing muscles, feel like. They have a good set of word images in their minds, and are willing to trust these images. The things we do to "teach" spelling to children do little to develop these skills or talents, and much to destroy them or prevent them from developing.

The first and worst thing we do is to make children anxious about spelling. We treat a misspelled word like a crime and penalize the misspeller severely; many teachers talk of making children develop a "spelling conscience," and fail otherwise excellent papers because of a few spelling mistakes. This is self-defeating. When we are anxious, we don't perceive clearly or remember what we once perceived. Everyone knows how hard it is to recall even simple things when under emotional pressure; the harder we rack our brains, the less easy it is to find what we are looking for. If we are anxious enough, we will not trust the messages that memory sends us. Many children spell badly because although their first hunches about how to spell a word may be correct, they are afraid to trust them. I have often seen on children's papers a word correctly spelled, then crossed out and misspelled.

There are some tricks that might help children get sharper word images. Some teachers may be using them. One is the trick of air writing; that is, of "writing" a word in the air with a finger and "seeing" the image so formed. I did this quite a bit with fifth graders, using either the air or the top of a desk, on which their fingers left no mark. Many of them were tremendously excited by this. I can still hear them saying, "There's nothing there, but I can see it." It seemed like black magic. I remember that when I was little I loved to write in the air. It was effortless, voluptuous, satisfying, and it was fun to see the word appear in the air. I used to write "Money Money Money," not so much because I didn't have any as because I liked the way it felt, particularly the *y* at the end, with its swooping tail.

Another thing to help sharpen children's image-making machinery is taking very quick looks at words—or other things. The conventional machine for doing this is the tachistoscope. But these are expensive, so expensive that most children can have few chances to use them, if any at all. With some three-by-five and four-by-eight file cards you can get the same effect. On the little cards you put the words or the pictures that the child is going to look at. You hold the larger card over the card to be read, uncover it for a split second with a quick wrist motion, then cover it up again. Thus you have a tachistoscope that costs one cent and that any child can work by himself.

Once when substituting in a first-grade class, I thought that the children, who were just beginning to read and write, might enjoy some of the kind of free, non-stop writing that my fifth graders had. One day about 40 minutes before lunch, I asked them all to take pencil and paper and start writing about anything they wanted to. They seemed to like the idea, but right away one child said anxiously, "Suppose we can't spell a word."

"Don't worry about it," I said. "Just spell it the best way you can."

A heavy silence settled on the room. All I could see were still pencils and anxious faces. This was clearly not the right approach. So I said, "All right, I'll tell you what we'll do. Any time you want to know how to spell a word, tell me and I'll write in on the board."

They breathed a sigh of relief and went to work. Soon requests for words were coming fast; as soon as I wrote one, someone asked me another. By lunchtime, when most of the children were still busily writing, the board was full. What was interesting was that most of the words they had asked for were much longer and more complicated than anything in their reading books or workbooks. Freed from worry about spelling, they were willing to use the most difficult and interesting words that they knew.

The words were still on the board when we began school next day. Before I began to erase them, I said to the children, "Listen everyone, I have to erase these words, but before I do, just out of curiosity, I'd like to see if you remember some of them."

The result was surprising. I had expected that the child who had asked for and used a word might remember it, but I did not think many others would. But many of the children still knew many of the words. How had they learned them? I suppose each time I wrote a word on the board a number of children had looked up, relaxed yet curious, just to see what the word looked like, and these images and the sound of my voice saying the word had stuck in their minds until the next day. This, it seems to me, is how children may best learn to write and spell.

What can a parent do if a school, or a teacher, is spoiling the language for a child by teaching it in some tired way? First, try to get them to change, or at least let them know that you are eager for change. Talk to other parents; push some of these ideas in the PTA; talk to the English department at the school; talk to the child's own teacher. Many teachers and schools want to know what the parents want.

If the school or teacher cannot be persuaded, then what? Perhaps all you can do is try not to let your child become too bored or discouraged or worried by what is happening in school. Help him meet the school's demands, foolish though they may seem, and try to provide more interesting alternatives at home—plenty of books and conversation, and a serious and respectful audience when a child wants to talk. Nothing that ever happened to me in English classes at school was as helpful to me as the long conversations I used to have every summer with my uncle, who made me feel that the difference in our ages was not important and that he was really interested in what I had to say.

At the end of her freshman year in college a girl I know wrote home to her mother, "Hooray! Hooray! Just think—I never have to take English any more!" But this girl had always been an excellent English student, had always loved books, writing, ideas. It seems unnecessary and foolish and wrong that English teachers should so often take what should be the most flexible, exciting, and creative of all school courses and make it into something that most children can hardly wait to see the last of. Let's hope that we can and soon will begin to do much better.

CONSIDER THIS

For the last three decades, Holt has been looking hard at education or, rather, at the ways in which many of our institutions that are theoretically committed to education are in effect deflating and denying it.

Holt gets started in this essay by quarreling with, and then abandoning, his earlier positions, as a result of his sister's persuasiveness. Might the sister have been a "fiction," a way for Holt to dramatize his change of mind? Does he want to change our minds?

Are you convinced by his arguments and proofs? Design a simple experiment for testing one of them and try it out on your class. Then write some curriculum guidelines designed to promote *pleasure* in writing and reading.

Fun. Oh, Boy. Fun. You Could Die from It.
Suzanne Britt Jordan

Fun is hard to have.

Fun is a rare jewel.

Somewhere along the line people got the modern idea that fun was there for the asking, that people deserved fun, that if we didn't have a little fun every day we would turn into (sakes alive!), Puritans.

"Was it fun?" became the question that overshadowed all other questions: good questions like: Was it moral? Was it kind? Was it honest? Was it beneficial? Was it generous? Was it necessary? And (my favorite) was it selfless?

When pleasure got to be the main thing, the fun fetish was sure to follow. Everything was supposed to be fun. If it wasn't fun, then by Jove, we were going to make it fun, or else.

Think of all the things that got the reputation of being fun. Family outings were supposed to be fun. Sex was supposed to be fun. Education was supposed to be fun. Work was supposed to be fun. Walt Disney was supposed to be fun. Church was supposed to be fun. Staying fit was supposed to be fun.

Just to make sure that everybody knew how much fun we were having, we put happy faces on flunking test papers, dirty bumpers, sticky refrigerator doors, bathroom mirrors.

If a kid, looking at his very happy parents traipsing through that very happy Disney World, said, "This ain't no fun, ma," his ma's heart sank. She wondered where she had gone wrong. Everybody told her what fun family outings to Disney World would be. Golly gee, what was the matter?

Fun got to be such a big thing that everybody started to look for more and more thrilling ways to supply it. One way was to step up the level of danger or licentiousness or alcohol or drug consumption so that you could be sure that, no matter what, you would manage to have a little fun.

Television commercials brought a lot of fun and fun-loving folks into the picture. Everything that people in those commercials did looked like fun: taking Polaroid snapshots, swilling beer, buying insurance, mopping the floor, bowling, taking aspirin. We all wished, I'm sure, that we could have half as much fun as those rough-and-ready guys around the locker room, flicking each other with towels and pouring champagne. The more commercials people watched, the more they wondered when the fun would start in their own lives. It was pretty depressing.

Big occasions were supposed to be fun. Christmas, Thanksgiving and Easter were obviously supposed to be fun. Your wedding day was supposed to be fun. Your wedding night was supposed to be a whole lot of fun. Your honeymoon was supposed to be the epitome of fundom. And so we ended up going through every Big Event we ever celebrated, waiting for the fun to start.

It occurred to me, while I was sitting around waiting for the fun to start, that not much is, and that I should tell you just in case you're worried about your fun capacity.

I don't mean to put a damper on things. I just mean we ought to treat fun reverently. It is a mystery. It cannot be caught like a virus. It cannot be trapped like an animal. The god of mirth is paying us back for all those years of thinking fun was everywhere by refusing to come to our party. I don't want to blaspheme fun anymore. When fun comes in on little dancing feet, you probably won't be expecting it. In fact, I bet it comes when you're doing your duty, your job, or your work. It may even come on a Tuesday.

I remember one day, long ago, on which I had an especially good time. Pam Davis and I walked to the College Village drug store one Saturday morning to buy some candy. We were about 12 years old (fun ages). She got her Bit-O-Honey. I got my malted milk balls, chocolate stars, Chunkys, and a small bag of M&M's. We started back to her house. I was going to spend the night. We had the whole day to look forward to. We had plenty of candy. It was a long way to Pam's house but every time we got weary Pam would put her hand over her eyes, scan the horizon like a sailor and say, "Oughta reach home by nightfall," at which point the two of us would laugh until we thought we couldn't stand it another minute. Then after we got calm, she'd say it again. You should have been there. It was the kind of day and friendship and occasion that made me deeply regret that I had to grow up.

It was fun.

CONSIDER THIS

Go out at night and look up at the stars. You'll discover an odd fact. The Pleiades are a cluster of stars that are almost invisible when you stare directly at them, looking at them. But turn your gaze slightly to one side, and you'll see them. Fun, like happiness, is rather like the Pleiades.

When we name the emotion, does it enhance or trivialize the experiences? "Yes, I feel wonderful." "You sound happy." "You're obviously very bitter." "Are you sad?" Do we become what we say?

Suzanne Britt Jordan, who teaches at North Carolina State University, reminds us that the big words, the abstractions—like love and happiness and wonder and success—these are singular to each of us; that the "myths" of happiness, fun, success, exert a pressure on us, for if we don't fit the mythologized need, then, somehow, somewhere, we've failed. We didn't "get it."

Eveline
James Joyce

She sat at the window watching the evening invade the avenue. Her head was leaned against the window curtains and in her nostrils was the odour of dusty cretonne. She was tired.

Few people passed. The man out of the last house passed on his way home; she heard his footsteps clacking along the concrete pavement and afterwards crunching on the cinder path before the new red houses. One time there used to be a field there in which they used to play every evening with other people's children. Then a man from Belfast bought the field and built houses in it—not like their little brown houses but bright brick houses with shining roofs. The children of the avenue used to play together in that field—the Devines, the Waters, the Dunns, little Keogh the cripple, she and her brothers and sisters. Ernest, however, never played: he was too grown up. Her father used often to hunt them in out of the field with his blackthorn stick; but usually little Keogh used to keep *nix* and call out when he saw her father coming. Still they seemed to have been rather happy then. Her father was not so bad then; and besides, her mother was alive. That was a long time ago; she and her brothers and sisters were all grown up; her mother was dead. Tizzie Dunn was dead, too, and the Waters had gone back to England. Everything changes. Now she was going to go away like the others, to leave her home.

Home! She looked round the room, reviewing all its familiar objects which she had dusted once a week for so many years, wondering where on earth all the dust came from. Perhaps she would never see again those familiar objects from which she had never dreamed of being divided. And yet during all those years she had never found out the name of the priest whose yellowing photograph hung on the wall above the broken harmonium beside the coloured print of the promises made to Blessed Margaret Mary Alacoque. He had been a school friend of her father. Whenever he showed the photograph to a visitor her father used to pass it with a casual word:

—He is in Melbourne now.

She had consented to go away, to leave her home. Was that wise? She tried to weigh each side of the question. In her home anyway she had shelter and food; she had those whom she had known all her life about her. Of course she had to work hard both in the house and at business. What would they say of her in the Stores when they found out that she had run away with a fellow? Say she was a fool perhaps; and her place would be filled up by advertisement. Miss Gavan would be glad. She had always had an edge on her, especially whenever there were people listening.

—Miss Hill, don't you see these ladies are waiting?

—Look lively, Miss Hill, please.

She would not cry many tears at leaving the Stores.

But in her new home, in a distant unknown country, it would not be like that. Then she would be married—she, Eveline. People would treat her with respect then. She would not be treated as her mother had been. Even now, though she was over nineteen, she sometimes felt herself in danger of her father's violence. She knew it was that that had given her the palpitations. When they were growing up he had never gone for her, like he used to go for

Harry and Ernest, because she was a girl; but latterly he had begun to threaten her and say what he would do to her only for her dead mother's sake. And now she had nobody to protect her. Ernest was dead and Harry, who was in the church decorating business, was nearly always down somewhere in the country. Besides, the invariable squabble for money on Saturday nights had begun to weary her unspeakably. She always gave her entire wages—seven shillings—and Harry always sent up what he could but the trouble was to get any money from her father. He said she used to squander the money, that she had no head, that he wasn't going to give her his hard-earned money to throw about the streets, and much more, for he was usually fairly bad of a Saturday night. In the end he would give her the money and ask her had she any intention of buying Sunday's dinner. Then she had to rush out as quickly as she could and do her marketing, holding her black leather purse tightly in her hand as she elbowed her way through the crowds and returning home late under her load of provisions. She had hard work to keep the house together and to see that the two young children who had been left to her charge went to school regularly and got their meals regularly. It was hard work—a hard life—but now that she was about to leave it she did not find it a wholly undesirable life.

She was about to explore another life with Frank. Frank was very kind, manly, open-hearted. She was to go away with him by the night-boat to be his wife and to live with him in Buenos Ayres where he had a home waiting for her. How well she remembered the first time she had seen him; he was lodging in a house on the main road where she used to visit. It seemed a few weeks ago. He was standing at the gate, his peaked cap pushed back on his head and his hair tumbled forward over a face of bronze. Then they had come to know each other. He used to meet her outside the Stores every evening and see her home. He took her to see *The Bohemian Girl* and she felt elated as she sat in an unaccustomed part of the theatre with him. He was awfully fond of music and sang a little. People knew that they were courting and, when he sang about the lass that loves a sailor, she always felt pleasantly confused. He used to call her Poppens out of fun. First of all it had been an excitement for her to have a fellow and then she had begun to like him. He had tales of distant countries. He had started as a deck boy at a pound a month on a ship of the Allan Line going out to Canada. He told her the names of the ships he had been on and the names of the different services. He had sailed through the Straits of Magellan and he told her stories of the terrible Patagonians. He had fallen on his feet in Buenos Ayres, he said, and had come over to the old country just for a holiday. Of course, her father had found out the affair and had forbidden her to have anything to say to him.

—I know these sailor chaps, he said.

One day he had quarrelled with Frank and after that she had to meet her lover secretly.

The evening deepened in the avenue. The white of two letters in her lap grew indistinct. One was to Harry; the other was to her father. Ernest had been her favourite but she liked Harry too. Her father was becoming old lately, she noticed; he would miss her. Sometimes he could be very nice. Not long before, when she had been laid up for a day, he had read her out a ghost story and made toast for her at the fire. Another day, when their mother was alive, they had all gone for a picnic to the Hill of Howth. She remembered her father putting on her mother's bonnet to make the children laugh.

Her time was running out but she continued to sit by the window, leaning her head against the window curtain, inhaling the odour of dusty cretonne. Down far in the avenue she could hear a street organ playing. She knew the air. Strange that it should come that very night to remind her of the promise to her mother, her promise to keep the home together as long as she could. She remembered the last night of her mother's illness; she was again in the close dark room at the other side of the hall and outside she heard a melancholy air of Italy. The organ-player had been ordered to go away and given sixpence. She remembered her father strutting back into the sickroom saying:

—Damned Italians! coming over here!

As she mused the pitiful vision of her mother's life laid its spell on the very quick of her being—that life of commonplace sacrifices closing in final craziness. She trembled as she heard again her mother's voice saying constantly with foolish insistence:

—Derevaun Seraun! Derevaun Seraun!

She stood up in a sudden impulse of terror. Escape! She must escape! Frank would save her. He would give her life, perhaps love, too. But she wanted to live. Why should she be unhappy? She had a right to happiness. Frank would take her in his arms, fold her in his arms. He would save her.

She stood among the swaying crowd in the station at the North Wall. He held her hand and she knew that he was speaking to her, saying something about the passage over and over again. The station was full of soldiers with brown baggages. Through the wide doors of the sheds she caught a glimpse of the black mass of the boat, lying in beside the quay wall, with illumined portholes. She answered nothing. She felt her cheek pale and cold and, out of a maze of distress, she prayed to God to direct her, to show her what was her duty. The boat blew a long mournful whistle into the mist. If she went, to-morrow she would be on the sea with Frank, steaming toward Buenos Ayres. Their passage had been booked. Could she still draw back after all he had done for her? Her distress awoke a nausea in her body and she kept moving her lips in silent fervent prayer.

A bell clanged upon her heart. She felt him seize her hand:

—Come!

All the seas of the world tumbled about her heart. He was drawing her into them: he would drown her. She gripped with both hands at the iron railing.

—Come!

No! No! No! It was impossible. Her hands clutched the iron in frenzy. Amid the seas she sent a cry of anguish!

—Eveline! Evvy!

He rushed beyond the barrier and called to her to follow. He was shouted at to go on but he still called to her. She set her white face to him, passive, like a helpless animal. Her eyes gave him no sign of love or farewell or recognition.

---

from *Ulysses*
James Joyce

What did Bloom see on the range?

On the right (smaller) hob a blue enamelled saucepan: on the left (larger) hob a black iron kettle.

What did Bloom do at the range?

He removed the saucepan to the left hob, rose and carried the iron kettle to the sink in order to tap the current by turning the faucet to let it flow.

Did it flow?

Yes. From Roundwood reservoir in county Wicklow of a cubic capacity of 2,400 million gallons, percolating through a subterranean aqueduct of filter mains of single and double pipeage constructed at an initial plant cost of £5 per linear yard by way of the Dargle, Rathdown, Glen of the Downs and Callowhill to the 26 acre reservoir at Stillorgan, a distance of 22 statute miles, and thence, through a system of relieving tanks, by a gradient of 250 feet to the city boundary at Eustace bridge, upper Leeson street, though from prolonged summer drouth and daily supply of $12^1/_2$ million gallons the water had fallen below the sill of the overflow weir for which reason the borough surveyor and waterworks engineer, Mr Spencer Harty, C. E., on the instructions of the waterworks committee, had prohibited the use of municipal water for purposes other than those of consumption (envisaging the possibility of recourse being had to the impotable water of the Grand and Royal canals as in 1893) particularly as the South Dublin Guardians, notwithstanding their ration of 15 gallons per day per pauper supplied through a 6 inch meter, had been convicted of a wastage of 20,000 gallons per night by a reading of their meter on the affirmation of the law agent of the corporation, Mr Ignatius Rice, solicitor, thereby acting to the detriment of another section of the public, selfsupporting taxpayers, solvent, sound.

What in water did Bloom, waterlover, drawer of water, watercarrier returning to the range, admire?

Its universality: its democratic equality and constancy to its nature in seeking its own level: its vastness in the ocean of Mercator's projection: its unplumbed profundity in the Sundam trench of the Pacific exceeding 8,000 fathoms: the restlessness of its waves and surface particles visiting in turn all points of its seaboard: the independence of its units: the variability of states of sea: its hydrostatic quiescence in calm: its hydrokinetic turgidity in neap and spring tides: its subsidence after devastation: its sterility in the circumpolar icecaps, arctic and antarctic: its climatic and commercial significance: its preponderance of 3 to 1 over the dry land of the globe: its indisputable hegemony extending in square leagues over all the region below the subequatorial tropic of Capricorn: the multisecular stability of its primeval basin: its luteofulvous bed: its capacity to dissolve and hold in solution all soluble substances including millions of tons of the most precious metals: its slow erosions of peninsulas and downwardtending promontories: its alluvial deposits: its weight and volume and density: its imperturbability in lagoons and highland tarns: its gradation of colours in the torrid and temperate and frigid zones: its vehicular ramifications in continental lakecontained streams and confluent oceanflowing rivers with their tributaries and transoceanic currents: gulfstream, north and south equatorial courses: its violence in seaquakes, waterspouts, artesian wells, eruptions, torrents, eddies, freshets, spates, groundswells, watersheds, waterpartings, geysers, cataracts, whirlpools, maelstroms, inundations, deluges, cloudbursts: its vast circumterrestrial ahorizontal curve: its secrecy in springs, and latent humidity, revealed by rhabdomantic or hygrometric instruments and exemplified by the hole in the wall at Ashtown gate, saturation of air, distillation of dew: the simplicity of its composition, two constituent parts of hydrogen with one constituent part of oxygen: its healing virtues: its buoyancy in the waters of the Dead Sea: its persevering penetrativeness in runnels, gullies, inadequate dams, leaks on shipboard: its properties for cleansing, quenching thirst and fire, nourishing vegetation: its infallibility as paradigm and paragon: its metamorphoses as vapour, mist, cloud, rain, sleet, snow, hail: its strength in rigid hydrants: its variety of forms in loughs and bays and gulfs and bights and guts and lagoons and atolls and archipelagos and sounds and fjords and minches and tidal estuaries and arms of sea: its solidity in glaciers, icebergs, iceflows: its docility in working hydraulic millwheels, turbines, dynamos, electric power stations, bleachworks, tanneries, scutchmills: its utility in canals, rivers, if navigable, floating and graving docks: its potentiality derivable from harnessed tides or watercourses falling from level to level: its submarine fauna and flora (anacoustic, photophobe) numerically, if not literally, the inhabitants of the globe: its ubiquity as constituting 90% of the human body: the noxiousness of its effluvia in lacustrine marshes, pestilential fens, faded flowerwater, stagnant pools in the waning moon.

CONSIDER THIS

James Joyce's "Eveline" is deceptively quiet, the details rooting us in the reality of Eveline's world. Its overall tone is matter-of-fact. Or is it? Read the story again and reflect on what you think the storyteller's attitude toward Eveline is. Then read it aloud, from Eveline's watching the "evening invade the avenue" (Does the word "invade," said out loud, affect your further reading?) to the extraordinary, entirely *un*-matter-of-fact last sentence.

We know, don't we, how the narrator evaluates Eveline's decision.

This piece from Joyce's *Ulysses,* although it begins calmly enough with Bloom filling the teakettle, *becomes* like its subject matter, the phrases exuberantly flowing, tumbling into one another. It almost demands that you read it aloud. (Try it—or, better, have someone read it to you.)

Almost two decades passed between the time James Joyce (1882–1941) wrote "Eveline" (1904) and the other stories collected in *Dubliners* and the year he completed the manuscript for the "Ithaca" section of *Ulysses* (1920), from which the "water" selection was taken. The two pieces are very different, but there are links: Both are set in Dublin—the real world of Dublin, right down to place names (the Hill of Howth, Eustace Bridge) and surnames (the Waterses, the Dunns, and the Keoghs were all Richmond Avenue neighbors of Joyce's). There are even similarities in style (the texture of some of the sentences in "Eveline" presages the writing in *Ulysses*) and (coincidentally) detail (Frank has sailed through the Straits of Magellan and Leopold Bloom's water holds sway "over all the region through the subequatorial tropic of Capricorn").

Joyce is considered one of the major prose stylists of the century. How would you characterize his sentences? How do you stay afloat in his water passage?

A Small Place
Jamaica Kincaid

If you go to Antigua as a tourist, this is what you will see. If you come by aeroplane, you will land at the V. C. Bird International Airport. Vere Cornwall (V. C.) Bird is the Prime Minister of Antigua. You may be the sort of tourist who would wonder why a Prime Minister would want an airport named after him—why not a school, why not a hospital, why not some great public monument? You are a tourist and you have not yet seen a school in Antigua, you have not yet seen the hospital in Antigua, you have not yet seen a public monument in Antigua. As your plane descends to land, you might say, What a beautiful island Antigua is—more beautiful than any of the other islands you have seen, and they were very beautiful, in their way, but they were much too green, much too lush with vegetation, which indicated to you, the tourist, that they got quite a bit of rainfall, and rain is the very thing that you, just now, do not want, for you are thinking of the hard and cold and dark and long days you spent working in North America (or, worse, Europe), earning some money so that you could stay in this place (Antigua) where the sun always shines and where the climate is deliciously hot and dry for the four to ten days you are going to be staying there; and since you are on your holiday, since you are a tourist, the thought of what it might be like for someone who had to live day in, day out in a place that suffers constantly from drought, and so has to watch carefully every drop of fresh water used (while at the same time surrounded by a sea and an ocean—the Caribbean Sea on one side, the Atlantic Ocean on the other), must never cross your mind.

You disembark from your plane. You go through customs. Since you are a tourist, a North American or European—to be frank, white and not an Antiguan black returning to Antigua from Europe or North America with cardboard boxes of much needed cheap clothes and food for relatives, you move through customs swiftly, you move through customs with ease. Your bags are not searched. You emerge from customs into the hot, clean air: immediately you feel cleansed, immediately you feel blessed (which is to say special); you feel free. You see a man, a taxi driver; you ask him to take you to your destination; he quotes you a price. You immediately think that the price is in the local currency, for you are a tourist and you are familiar with these things (rates of exchange) and you feel even more free, for things seem so cheap, but then your driver ends by saying, "In U.S. currency." You may say, "Hmmmm, do you have a formal sheet that lists official prices and destinations?" Your driver obeys the law and shows you the sheet, and he apologises for the incredible mistake he has made in quoting you a price off the top of his head which is so vastly different (favouring him) from the one listed. You are driven to your hotel by this taxi driver in his taxi, a brand-new Japanese-made vehicle. The road on which you are travelling is a very bad road, very much in need of repair. You are feeling wonderful, so you say, "Oh, what a marvellous change these bad roads are from the splendid highways I am used to in North America." (Or, worse, Europe.) Your driver is reckless; he is a dangerous man who drives in the middle of the road when he thinks no other cars are coming in the opposite direction, passes other cars on blind curves that run uphill, drives at sixty miles an hour on narrow, curving roads when the road sign, a rusting, beat-up thing left over from colonial days, says 40 MPH. This might frighten you (you are on your holiday; you are a tourist); this might excite you (you are on your holiday; you are a tourist), though if you are from New York and take taxis you are used to this style of driving: most of the taxi drivers in New York are from places in the world like this. You are looking out the window (because you want to get your money's worth); you notice that all the cars you see are brand-new, or almost brand-new, and that they are all Japanese-made. There are no American cars in Antigua—no new ones, at any rate; none that were manufactured in the last ten years. You continue to look at the cars and you say to yourself, Why, they look brand-new, but they have an awful sound, like an old car—a very old, dilapidated car. How to account for that? Well, possibly it's because they use leaded gasoline in these brand-new cars whose engines were built to use non-leaded gasoline, but you musn't ask the person driving the car if this is so, because he or she has never heard of unleaded gasoline. You look closely at the car; you see that it's a model of a Japanese car that you might hesitate to buy; it's a model that's very expensive; it's a model that's quite impractical for a person who has to work as hard as you do and who watches every penny you earn so that you can afford this holiday you are on. How do they afford such a car? And do they live in a luxurious house to match such a car? Well, no. You will be surprised, then, to see that most likely the person driving this brand-new car filled with the wrong gas lives in a house that, in comparison, is far beneath the status of the car; and if you were to ask why you would be told that the banks are encouraged by the government to make loans available for cars, but loans for houses not so easily available; and if you ask again why, you will be told that the two main car dealerships in Antigua are owned in part or outright by ministers in government. Oh, but you are on holiday and the sight of these brand-new cars driven by people who may or may not have really passed their driving test (there was once a scandal about driving licences for sale) would not really stir up these thoughts in you. You pass a building sitting in a sea of dust and you think, It's some latrines for people just passing by, but when you look again you see the building has written on it PIGOTT'S SCHOOL. You pass the hospital, the Holberton Hospital, and how wrong you are not to think about this, for though you are a tourist on your holiday, what if your heart should miss a few beats? What if a blood vessel in your neck should break? What if one of those people driving those brand-new cars filled with the wrong gas fails to pass safely while going uphill on a curve and you are in the car going in the opposite direction? Will you be comforted to know that the hospital is staffed with doctors that no actual Antiguan trusts; that Antiguans always say about the doctors, "I don't want them near me"; that Antiguans refer to them not as doctors but as "the three men" (there are three of them); that when the Minister of Health himself doesn't feel well he takes the first plane to New York to see a real doctor; that if any one of the ministers in government needs medical care he flies to New York to get it?

It's a good thing that you brought your own books with you, for you couldn't just go to the library and borrow some. Antigua used to have a splendid library, but in The Earthquake (everyone talks about it that way—The Earthquake; we Antiguans, for I am one, have a great sense of things, and the more meaningful the thing, the more meaningless we make it) the library building was damaged. This was in 1974, and soon after that a sign was placed on the front of the building saying, THIS BUILDING WAS DAMAGED IN THE EARTHQUAKE OF 1974. REPAIRS ARE PENDING. The sign hangs there, and hangs there more than a decade later, with its unfulfilled promise of repair, and you might see this as a sort of quaintness on the part of these islanders, these people descended from slaves—what a strange, unusual perception of time they have. REPAIRS ARE PENDING, and here it is many years later, but perhaps in a world that is twelve miles long and nine miles wide (the size of Antigua) twelve years and twelve minutes and twelve days are all the same. The library is one of those splendid old buildings from colonial times, and the sign telling of the repairs is a splendid old sign from colonial times. Not very long after The Earthquake Antigua got its independence from Britain, making Antigua a state in its own right, and Antiguans are so proud of this that each year, to mark the day, they go to church and thank God, a British God, for this. But you should not think of the confusion that must lie in all that and you must not think of the damaged library. You have brought your own books with you, and among them is one of those new books about economic history, one of those books explaining how the West (meaning Europe and North America after its conquest and settlement by Europeans) got rich: the West got rich not from the free (free—in this case meaning got-for-nothing) and then undervalued labour, for generations, of the people like me you see walking around you in Antigua but from the ingenuity of small shopkeepers in Sheffield and Yorkshire and Lancashire, or wherever; and what a great part the invention of the wristwatch played in it, for there was nothing noble-minded men could not do when they discovered they could slap time on their wrists just like that (isn't that the last straw; for not only did we have to suffer the unspeakableness of slavery, but the satisfaction to be had from "We made you bastards rich" is taken away, too), and so you needn't let that slightly funny feeling you have from time to time about exploitation, oppression, domination develop into full-fledged unease, discomfort; you could ruin your holiday. They are not responsible for what you have; you owe them nothing; in fact, you did them a big favour, and you can provide one hundred examples. For here you are now, passing by Government House. And here you are now, passing by the Prime Minister's Office and the Parliament Building, and overlooking these, with a splendid view of St. John's Harbour, the American Embassy. If it were not for you, they would not have Government House, and Prime Minister's Office, and Parliament Building and embassy of powerful country. Now you are passing a mansion, an extraordinary house painted the colour of old cow dung, with more aerials and antennas attached to it than you will see even at the American Embassy. The people who live in this house are a merchant family who came to Antigua from the Middle East less than twenty years ago. When this family first came to Antigua, they sold dry goods door to door from suitcases they carried on their backs. Now they own a lot of Antigua; they regularly lend money to the government, they build enormous (for Antigua), ugly (for Antigua), concrete buildings in Antigua's capital, St. John's, which the government then rents for huge sums of money; a member of their family is the Antiguan Ambassador to Syria; Antiguans hate them. Not far from this mansion is another mansion, the home of a drug smuggler. Everybody knows he's a drug smuggler, and if just as you were driving by he stepped out of his door your driver might point him out to you as the notorious person that he is, for this drug smuggler is so rich people say he buys cars in tens—ten of this one, ten of that one and that he bought a house (another mansion) near Five Islands, contents included, with cash he carried in a suitcase: three hundred and fifty thousand American dollars, and, to the surprise of the seller of the house, lots of American dollars were left over. Overlooking the drug smuggler's mansion is yet another mansion, and leading up to it is the best paved road in all of Antigua—even better than the road that was paved for the Queen's visit in 1985 (when the Queen came, all the roads that she would travel on were paved anew, so that the Queen might have been left with the impression that riding in a car in Antigua was a pleasant experience). In this mansion lives a woman sophisticated people in Antigua call Evita. She is a notorious woman. She's young and beautiful and the girlfriend of somebody very high up in the government. Evita is notorious because her relationship with this high government official has made her the owner of boutiques and property and given her a say in cabinet meetings, and all sorts of other privileges such a relationship would bring a beautiful young woman.

Oh, but by now you are tired of all this looking, and you want to reach your destination—your hotel, your room. You long to refresh yourself; you long to eat some nice lobster, some nice local food. You take a bath, you brush your teeth. You get dressed again; as you get dressed, you look out the window. That water—have you ever seen anything like it? Far out, to the horizon, the colour of the water is navy-blue; nearer, the water is the colour of the North American sky. From there to the shore, the water is pale, silvery, clear, so clear that you can see its pinkish-white sand bottom. Oh, what beauty! Oh, what beauty! You have never seen anything like this. You are so excited. You breathe shallow. You breathe deep. You see a beautiful boy skimming the water, godlike, on a Windsurfer. You see an incredibly unattractive, fat, pastrylike-fleshed woman enjoying a walk on the beautiful sand, with a man, an incredibly unattractive, fat, pastrylike-fleshed man; you see the pleasure they're taking in their surroundings. Still standing, looking out the window, you see yourself lying on the beach, enjoying the amazing sun (a sun so powerful and yet so beautiful, the way it is always overhead as if on permanent guard, ready to stamp out any cloud that dares to darken and so empty rain on you and ruin your holiday; a sun that is your personal friend). You see yourself taking a walk on that beach, you see yourself meeting new people (only they are new in a very limited way, for they are people just like you). You see yourself eating some delicious, locally grown food. You see yourself, you see yourself . . . You must not wonder what exactly happened to the contents of your lavatory when you flushed it. You must not wonder where your bathwater went when you pulled out the stopper. You must not wonder what happened when you brushed your teeth. Oh, it might all end up in the water you are thinking of taking a swim in; the contents of your lavatory might, just might, graze gently against your ankle as you wade carefree in the water, for you see, in Antigua, there is no proper sewage-disposal system. But the Caribbean Sea is very big and the Atlantic Ocean is even bigger; it would amaze even you to know the number of black slaves this ocean has swallowed up. When you sit down to eat your delicious meal, it's better that you don't know that most of what you are eating came off a plane from Miami. And before it got on a plane in Miami, who knows where it came from? A good guess is that it came from a place like Antigua first, where it was grown dirt-cheap, went to Miami, and came back. There is a world of something in this, but I can't go into it right now.

The thing you have always suspected about yourself the minute you become a tourist is true: A tourist is an ugly human being. You are not an ugly person all the time; you are not an ugly person ordinarily; you are not an ugly person day to day. From day to day, you are a nice person. From day to day, all the people who are supposed to love you on the whole do. From day to day, as you walk down a busy street in the large and modern and prosperous city in which you work and live, dismayed, puzzled (a cliché, but only a cliché can explain you) at how alone you feel in this crowd, how awful it is to go unnoticed, how awful it is to go unloved, even as you are surrounded by more people than you could possibly get to know in a lifetime that lasted for millennia, and then out of the corner of your eye you see someone looking at you and absolute pleasure is written all over that person's face, and then you realise that you are not as revolting a presence as you think you are (for that look just told you so). And so, ordinarily, you are a nice person, an attractive person, a person capable of drawing to yourself the affection of other people (people just like you), a person at home in your own skin (sort of; I mean, in a way; I mean, your dismay and puzzlement are natural to you, because people like you just seem to be like that, and so many of the things people like you find admirable about yourselves—the things you think about, the things you think really define you—seem rooted in these feelings): a person at home in your own house (and all its nice house things), with its nice back yard (and its nice back-yard things), at home on your street, your church, in community activities, your job, at home with your family, your relatives, your friends—you are a whole person. But one day, when you are sitting somewhere, alone in that crowd, and that awful feeling of displacedness comes over you, and really, as an ordinary person you are not well equipped to look too far inward and set yourself aright, because being ordinary is already so taxing, and being ordinary takes all you have out of you, and though the words "I must get away" do not actually pass across your lips, you make a leap from being that nice blob just sitting like a boob in your amniotic sac of the modern experience to being a person visiting heaps of death and ruin and feeling alive and inspired at the sight of it; to being a person lying on some faraway beach, your stilled body stinking and glistening in the sand, looking like something first forgotten, then remembered, then not important enough to go back for; to being a person marvelling at the harmony (ordinarily, what you would say is the backward-ness) and the union these other people (and they are other people) have with nature. And you look at the things they can do with a piece of ordinary cloth, the things they fashion out of cheap, vulgarly colored (to you) twine, the way they squat down over a hole they have made in the ground, the hole itself is something to marvel at, and since you are being an ugly person this ugly but joyful thought will swell inside you: their ancestors were not clever in the way yours were and not ruthless in the way yours were, for then would it not be you who would be in harmony with nature and backwards in that charming way? An ugly thing, that is what you are when you become a tourist, an ugly, empty thing, a stupid thing, a piece of rubbish pausing here and there to gaze at this and taste that, and it will never occur to you that the people who inhabit the place in which you have just paused cannot stand you, that behind their closed doors they laugh at your strangeness (you do not look the way they look); the physical sight of you does not please them; you have bad manners (it is their custom to eat their food with their hands; you try eating their way, you look silly; you try eating the way you always eat, you look silly); they do not like the way you speak (you have an accent); they collapse helpless from laughter, mimicking the way they imagine you must look as you carry out some everyday bodily function. They do not like you. *They do not like me!* That thought never actually occurs to you. Still, you feel a little uneasy. Still, you feel a little foolish. Still, you feel a little out of place. But the banality of your own life is very real to you; it drove you to this extreme, spending your days and your nights in the company of people who despise you, people you do not like really, people you would not want to have as your actual neighbour. And so you must devote yourself to puzzling out how much of what you are told is really, really true (Is ground-up bottle glass in peanut sauce really a delicacy around here, or will it do just what you think ground-up bottle glass will do? Is this rare, multicoloured, snout-mouthed fish really an aphrodisiac, or will it cause you to fall asleep permanently?). Oh, the hard work all of this is, and is it any wonder, then, that on your return home you feel the need of a long rest, so that you can recover from your life as a tourist?

That the native does not like the tourist is not hard to explain. For every native of every place is a potential tourist, and every tourist is a native of somewhere. Every native everywhere lives a life of overwhelming and crushing banality and boredom and desperation and depression, and every deed, good and bad, is an attempt to forget this. Every native would like to find a way out, every native would like a rest, every native would like a tour. But some natives—most natives in the world—cannot go anywhere. They are too poor. They are too poor to go anywhere. They are too poor to escape the reality of their lives; and they are too poor to live properly in the place where they live, which is the very place you, the tourist, want to go—so when the natives see you, the tourist, they envy you, they envy your ability to leave your own banality and boredom, they envy your ability to turn their own banality and boredom into a source of pleasure for yourself.

CONSIDER THIS

Who is the "you" being addressed in "A Small Place"? Do you feel attacked, personally, even if you've never been to the Caribbean as a tourist? Do you want to resist Kincaid's attack on you, who, after all, are entitled to a vacation, a holiday in the sun; you, who are a sun seeker, a fun seeker? Do you find her assault too strong, too blatant, too relentless, too loud? Does she get to you? How so?

When she was 17, Elaine Potter Richardson left her island home of Antigua for a job as an *au pair* in New York. Since then, she's written four books (two novels, *Annie John* and *Lucy,* a collection of short stories, *At the Bottom of the River,* and her long essay, *A Small Place,* of which the excerpt above is the beginning). In 1973, she became Jamaica Kincaid. She renamed herself; it was a way "for me to do things without being the same person who couldn't do them," she said (*New York Times,* October 7, 1990). Anger, she says, drives her. "I hope I never lose it. If I ever find myself not getting angry, I'll go to a psychiatrist to regain my anger" (*Village Voice Literary Supplement,* October 1990).

Spectators No More
Billie Jean King

Despite the dazzling accomplishments of such past champions as Babe Didrikson, Wilma Rudolph and Sheila Young, it was not until 1984 that women were allowed to ride a bicycle or run more than a mile in Olympic competition.

Such limitations seem preposterous in light of Connie Carpenter-Phinney edging out her teammate after a grueling 49.2 miles to win the women's first Olympic cycling event, or Joan Benoit's effortless victory lap after winning the first women's Olympic marathon. Even before these two, there were many "firsts," each of which reflected the desire of sportswomen to perform in the Olympic arena, and each of which reflected the barriers curtailing women's involvement.

Historical evidence suggests that in the Olympics of ancient Greece women were prohibited from participating. Indeed, if they were caught so much as spectating, they were thrown to their death from a cliff. By way of response, women simply started their own competitions in the Sixth Century B.C., the most celebrated being the Heraean Games, which were held once every four years in Olympia.

Centuries later, when Baron Pierre de Coubertin resurrected the idea of a quadrennial Olympics, he defined the Games as "the solemn and periodic exaltation of male athleticism with internationalism as a base, loyalty as a means, art for its setting and female applause as reward." While Coubertin was certainly not a fan of women's sports, once calling them "against the laws of nature," his vision of the Olympics did, at the very least, include women spectators.

In 1896, as the first of the modern Olympics began to unfold in Athens, Greece, it is reported that a young woman named Melpomene requested entrance into the marathon. She was refused but ran anyway, finishing in a respectable $4^1/_2$ hours. Four years later, in the 1900 Games, women athletes were officially accepted for the first time as contestants, despite much protest. Constituting eleven out of 1,330 competitors, or less than one percent of the athletes in attendance, women competed in tennis and golf. U.S. golfer Margaret Abbott became the first female Olympic winner, for which she was awarded a piece of art rather than a gold medal.

Tennis and golf disappeared from the Games and were replaced by such sports as archery, swimming and figure skating, which were intermittently open to women. In 1928, over the objections of Coubertin and Pope Pius XI, five women's track and field events were added, significantly increasing women's competitive opportunities. Although world records were set in all five events, the event that drew the most attention was the women's 800-meter race, in which two poorly trained contestants collapsed at the finish line. The International Olympic Committee (IOC) immediately barred women from this "distance" event, calling it "hazardous to a lady's health." That decision stood for 32 years but failed to deter women in other Olympic events.

Even though female Olympians captured the public's attention with their accomplishments, the emergence of female superstars was not enough to altogether conquer official skepticism about women's sports. Cultural and societal views of "the weaker sex" continued to influence the Olympic movement.

In 1932, the fun-loving and boastful Mildred "Babe" Didrikson captivated the crowds by winning gold medals in the 80-meter hurdles and the javelin. She would have won the gold in the high jump if her "diving" technique had not been declared illegal; she was awarded the silver medal. Considered more of a miracle than a disciplined athlete, Didrikson was teasingly referred to as "Muscle Moll." It was said of Babe: "She's capable of winning everything but the Kentucky Derby."

At the 1936 Olympics in Berlin, American Helen Stephens won the 100-meter dash and the 4 x 100-meter relay and thus endeared herself to the spectators and even to Hitler, who couldn't resist propositioning Stephens in his private box. Less impressed was U.S. Olympic Committee President Avery Brundage, who remarked, "I am fed up to the ears with women as track and field competitors. Their charms sink to less than zero."

When the Olympics resumed after World War II, the star of the 1948 Games was Dutch sprinter Fanny Blankers-Koen, winner of four gold medals. If this 30-year-old mother of two, nicknamed the "Flying Housewife," had entered the long jump and the high jump, she probably would have won those too, considering that the winning jumps fell far short of the world records she held in those events. Despite her athleticism, much of the public's attention focused on the perception that Blankers-Koen was neglecting her children and her family responsibilities. One headline read: "Gold Medalist Can Cook, Too."

In 1960, it was U.S. sprinter Wilma Rudolph, not boxer Cassius Clay (now Muhammad Ali), who stole the show at the Rome Olympics. A childhood victim of polio, scarlet fever and double pneumonia, Rudolph won gold medals in the 100-meter and 200-meter races and anchored the 4 x 100-meter team.

Regardless of such impressive feats, women still had to fight for Olympic acceptance. Less than half the participating countries sent female contingents, and women accounted for less than 15 percent of all Olympic athletes. As late as 1966, the female Chair of the Women's Board of the U.S. Olympic Development Committee wrote: "To most of the women in the U.S. and to many women of other nations, the shot put and discus throw are forms of competition that are generally unacceptable to the feminine image."

Thankfully, these attitudes did not hinder such women as Peggy Fleming, whose graceful figure skating garnered the only American gold medal at the 1968 Winter Games; or Debbie Meyer, who, the same year, became the first swimmer to win three individual gold medals in one Olympics; or world champion cyclist Sheila Young, who, in 1976, exhibited the most successful speed skating by an American in 44 years, winning a gold in the 500-meter race, a silver in the 1500-meter race and a bronze in the 100-meter race.

Certainly nothing could stand in the way of Romanian Nadia Comaneci in 1976 as she dazzled the judges with the Olympics' first perfect score of 10 in gymnastics, or of Margaret Murdoch, who became the first woman to win an Olympic medal competing against men in shooting.

Despite resistance to their involvement in the Olympics, sportswomen have continued to redefine the limits of female potential and have improved their performances over the last 36 years at a faster rate than men. At the 1984 Summer Games, for example, U.S. women captured 44 percent of the gold medals available to them; their male counterparts won only 38 percent. Joan Benoit's winning time in the '84 Olympic marathon (2:22:43) would have qualified her for the men's Olympic marathon trials as recently as 1976.

Numerically, women accounted for 22 percent of the athletes at the '84 Games. Furthermore, the number of women's events had increased from nine in 1972 to 14 in 1984, compared with 23 events for men.

This year in Seoul, the world will see women compete for the first time in the 10,000-meter track and field event, in cycling's match sprints, in the 470-class sailing race, in table tennis, in women's team competition in archery, in the 50-meter freestyle swimming event, in 10-meter air pistol shooting and in several demonstration and exhibition events.

Since its inception, the Olympic movement has mirrored society's attitudes toward women. Just as the public has grown more appreciative of women's accomplishments, so too has the Olympics recognized the importance of female participation. And yet the IOC still hampers attempts to increase the number of women's events. Men's events, at present, outnumber women's by more than two to one. In addition, there remain countries around the world that do not encourage women's sports. In 1984, for instance, 45 of the nations participating in the Olympics did not include female delegations.

There is no question that women will continue to distinguish themselves in Olympic competition. Women like Mary Lou Retton, the heroine of the '84 Games, and Bonnie Blair, Calgary's champion speed skater, embody the Olympic motto, "Swifter, Higher, Stronger." Their accomplishments, and those of other female Olympians, make us all forget about gender and concentrate instead on the speed, grace and power of the athlete.

CONSIDER THIS

Who is Billie Jean King? Does it make a difference to you to know that it was she who wrote this essay? Do you believe her when she proclaims that women's accomplishments in the Olympics "make us all forget about gender and concentrate instead on the speed, grace and power of the athlete"? Is it that easy? Do you submit to this neat up-beat ending? This piece was published in a newspaper supplement, advertising the Seoul Olympics of 1988. Does it make a difference where it was published? How so? Does where a piece is to be published make a difference to its conception?

No Name Woman
Maxine Hong Kingston

"You must not tell anyone," my mother said, "what I am about to tell you. In China your father had a sister who killed herself. She jumped into the family well. We say that your father has all brothers because it is as if she had never been born.

"In 1924 just a few days after our village celebrated seventeen hurry-up weddings—to make sure that every young man who went 'out on the road' would responsibly come home—your father and his brothers and your grandfather and his brothers and your aunt's new husband sailed for America, the Gold Mountain. It was your grandfather's last trip. Those lucky enough to get contracts waved good-bye from the decks. They fed and guarded the stowaways and helped them off in Cuba, New York, Bali, Hawaii. 'We'll meet in California next year,' they said. All of them sent money home.

"I remember looking at your aunt one day when she and I were dressing; I had not noticed before that she had such a protruding melon of a stomach. But I did not think, 'She's pregnant,' until she began to look like other pregnant women, her shirt pulling and the white tops of her black pants showing. She could not have been pregnant, you see, because her husband had been gone for years. No one said anything. We did not discuss it. In early summer she was ready to have the child, long after the time when it could have been possible.

"The village had also been counting. On the night the baby was to be born the villagers raided our house. Some were crying. Like a great saw, teeth strung with lights, files of people walked zigzag across our land, tearing the rice. Their lanterns doubled in the disturbed black water, which drained away through the broken bunds. As the villagers closed in, we could see that some of them, probably men and women we knew well, wore white masks. The people with long hair hung it over their faces. Women with short hair made it stand up on end. Some had tied white bands around their foreheads, arms, and legs.

"At first they threw mud and rocks at the house. Then they threw eggs and began slaughtering our stock. We could hear the animals scream their deaths—the roosters, the pigs, a last great roar from the ox. Familiar wild heads flared in our night windows; the villagers encircled us. Some of the faces stopped to peer at us, their eyes rushing like searchlights. The hands flattened against the panes, framed heads, and left red prints.

"The villagers broke in the front and the back doors at the same time, even though we had not locked the doors against them. Their knives dripped with the blood of our animals. They smeared blood on the doors and walls. One woman swung a chicken, whose throat she had slit, splattering blood in red arcs about her. We stood together in the middle of our house, in the family hall with the pictures and tables of the ancestors around us, and looked straight ahead.

"At that time the house had only two wings. When the men came back, we would build two more to enclose our courtyard and a third one to begin a second courtyard. The villagers pushed through both wings, even your grandparents' rooms, to find your aunt's, which was also mine until the men returned. From this room a new wing for one of the younger families would grow. They ripped up her clothes and shoes and broke her combs, grinding them underfoot. They tore her work from the loom. They scattered the cooking fire and rolled the new weaving in it. We could hear them in the kitchen breaking our bowls and banging the pots. They overturned the great waisthigh earthenware jugs; duck eggs, pickled fruits, vegetables burst out and mixed in acrid torrents. The old woman from the next field swept a broom through the air and loosed the spirits of the broom over our heads. 'Pig.' 'Ghost.' 'Pig,' they sobbed and scolded while they ruined our house.

"When they left, they took sugar and oranges to bless themselves. They cut pieces from the dead animals. Some of them took bowls that were not broken and clothes that were not torn. Afterward we swept up the rice and sewed it back up into sacks. But the smells from the spilled preserves lasted. Your aunt gave birth in the pigsty that night. The next morning when I went for the water, I found her and the baby plugging up the family well.

"Don't let your father know that I told you. He denies her. Now that you have started to menstruate, what happened to her could happen to you. Don't humiliate us. You wouldn't like to be forgotten as if you had never been born. The villagers are watchful."

Whenever she had to warn us about life, my mother told stories that ran like this one, a story to grow up on.

CONSIDER THIS

"I have no idea," says Maxine Hong Kingston, "how people who don't write endure their lives." Born in 1940 of Chinese immigrants, Kingston heard the voices of the "new" land all about her in her native California, contrasted with the "ghosts" of the past, through her mother's stories and silences, through Chinese legends, history, myth, all transformed by her own dreams, conjecture, surmise, memory, speculation, and her own vivid imagination.

"No Name Woman" is the beginning of her remarkable autobiography *The Woman Warrior: Memoirs of a Girlhood among Ghosts,* published in 1976. Its sequel, *China Men,* details the struggles of those Chinese men, including her own ancestors, who left China for a new life in America, who came to the "Gold Mountain." In her first novel, *Tripmaster Monkey,* she creates the character of Wittman Ah Sing, a first-generation Chinese American who's in search of an identity that is both Chinese and American.

Concepts We Live By
George Lakoff, Mark Johnson

Metaphor is for most people a device of the poetic imagination and the rhetorical flourish—a matter of extraordinary rather than ordinary language. Moreover, metaphor is typically viewed as characteristic of language alone, a matter of words rather than thought or action. For this reason, most people think they can get along perfectly well without metaphor. We have found, on the contrary, that metaphor is pervasive in everyday life, not just in language but in thought and action. Our ordinary conceptual system, in terms of which we both think and act, is fundamentally metaphorical in nature.

The concepts that govern our thought are not just matters of the intellect. They also govern our everyday functioning, down to the most mundane details. Our concepts structure what we perceive, how we get around in the world, and how we relate to other people. Our conceptual system thus plays a central role in defining our everyday realities. If we are right in suggesting that our conceptual system is largely metaphorical, then the way we think, what we experience, and what we do every day is very much a matter of metaphor.

But our conceptual system is not something we are normally aware of. In most of the little things we do every day, we simply think and act more or less automatically along certain lines. Just what these lines are is by no means obvious. One way to find out is by looking at language. Since communication is based on the same conceptual system that we use in thinking and acting, language is an important source of evidence for what that system is like.

Primarily on the basis of linguistic evidence, we have found that most of our ordinary conceptual system is metaphorical in nature. And we have found a way to begin to identify in detail just what the metaphors are that structure how we perceive, how we think, and what we do.

To give some idea of what it could mean for a concept to be metaphorical and for such a concept to structure an everyday activity, let us start with the concept ARGUMENT and the conceptual metaphor ARGUMENT IS WAR. This metaphor is reflected in our everyday language by a wide variety of expressions:

ARGUMENT IS WAR

Your claims are *indefensible.*
He *attacked every weak point* in my argument.
His criticisms were *right on target.*
I *demolished* his argument.
I've never *won* an argument with him.
You disagree? Okay, *shoot!*
If you use that *strategy,* he'll *wipe you out.*
He *shot down* all of my arguments.

It is important to see that we don't just *talk* about arguments in terms of war. We can actually win or lose arguments. We see the person we are arguing with as an opponent. We attack his positions and we defend our own. We gain and lose ground. We plan and use strategies. If we find a position indefensible, we can abandon it and take a new line of attack. Many of the things we *do* in arguing are partially structured by the concept of war. Though there is no physical battle, there is a verbal battle, and the structure of an argument—attack, defense, counterattack, etc.—reflects this. It is in this sense that the ARGUMENT IS WAR metaphor is one that we live by in this culture; it structures the actions we perform in arguing.

Try to imagine a culture where arguments are not viewed in terms of war, where no one wins or loses, where there is no sense of attacking or defending, gaining or losing ground. Imagine a culture where an argument is viewed as a dance, the participants are seen as performers, and the goal is to perform in a balanced and aesthetically pleasing way. In such a culture, people would view arguments differently, experience them differently, carry them out differently, and talk about them differently. But *we* would probably not view them as arguing at all: they would simply be doing something different. It would seem strange even to call what they were doing "arguing." Perhaps the most neutral way of describing this difference between their culture and ours would be to say that we have a discourse form structured in terms of battle and they have one structured in terms of dance.

This is an example of what it means for a metaphorical concept, namely, ARGUMENT IS WAR, to structure (at least in part) what we do and how we understand what we are doing when we argue. *The essence of metaphor is understanding and experiencing one kind of thing in terms of another.* It is not that arguments are a subspecies of war. Arguments and wars are different kinds of things—verbal discourse and armed conflict—and the actions performed are different kinds of actions. But ARGUMENT is partially structured, understood, performed, and talked about in terms of WAR. The concept is metaphorically structured, the activity is metaphorically structured, and, consequently, the language is metaphorically structured.

Moreover, this is the *ordinary* way of having an argument and talking about one. The normal way for us to talk about attacking a position is to use the words "attack a position." Our conventional ways of talking about arguments presuppose a metaphor we are hardly ever conscious of. The metaphor is not merely in the words we use—it is in our very concept of an argument. The language of argument is not poetic, fanciful, or rhetorical; it is literal. We talk about arguments that way because we conceive of them that way—and we act according to the way we conceive of things.

The most important claim we have made so far is that metaphor is not just a matter of language, that is, of mere words. We shall argue that, on the contrary, human *thought processes* are largely metaphorical. This is what we mean when we say that the human conceptual system is metaphorically structured and defined. Metaphors as linguistic expressions are possible precisely because there are metaphors in a person's conceptual system. Therefore, whenever in this book we speak of metaphors, such as ARGUMENT IS WAR, it should be understood that *metaphor* means *metaphorical concept.*

CONSIDER THIS

"Concepts We Live By" is just the tip of the collaborative iceberg that is *Metaphors We Live By*, written by professor of linguistics George Lakoff (University of California, Berkeley) and professor of philosophy Mark Johnson (Southern Illinois University, Carbondale).

For most of this century, there has been lively and often acrimonious debate among scholars regarding which of the diverse human attributes are innate and which are learned (a debate popularly and loosely known as "nature versus nurture"). Regarding metaphor, Lakoff and Johnson come down squarely on the side of nature.

They take the position that metaphorical thinking is "an irreducible cognitive process." Fortunately, we don't need to take a stand on that issue to follow their argument. There's that word—*argument*. Here I mean "statement made to support a position." But can we extend the metaphor to include this essay? Certainly they may have to defend their position. Are you tempted to counterattack?

Keep this essay in mind when you read Oliver Sack's "On the Level."

Mr Reginald Peacock's Day
Katherine Mansfield

If there was one thing that he hated more than another it was the way she had of waking him in the morning. She did it on purpose, of course. It was her way of establishing her grievance for the day, and he was not going to let her know how successful it was. But really, really, to wake a sensitive person like that was positively dangerous! It took him hours to get over it—simply hours. She came into the room buttoned up in an overall, with a handkerchief over her head—thereby proving that she had been up herself and slaving since dawn—and called in a low, warning voice: 'Reginald!'

'Eh! What! What's that? What's the matter?'

'It's time to get up; it's half past eight.' And out she went, shutting the door quietly after her, to gloat over her triumph, he supposed.

He rolled over in the big bed, his heart still beating in quick, dull throbs, and with every throb he felt his energy escaping him, his—his inspiration for the day stifling under those thudding blows. It seemed that she took a malicious delight in making life more difficult for him than—Heaven knows—it was, by denying him his rights as an artist, by trying to drag him down to her level. What was the matter with her? What the hell did she want? Hadn't he three times as many pupils now as when they were first married, earned three times as much, paid for every stick and stone that they possessed, and now had begun to shell out for Adrian's kindergarten? . . . And had he ever reproached her for not having a penny to her name? Never a word—never a sign! The truth was that once you married a woman she became insatiable, and the truth was that nothing was more fatal for an artist than marriage, at any rate until he was well over forty. . . . Why had he married her? He asked himself this question on an average about three times a day, but he never could answer it satisfactorily. She had caught him at a weak moment, when the first plunge into reality had bewildered and overwhelmed him for a time. Looking back, he saw a pathetic, youthful creature, half child, half wild untamed bird, totally incompetent to cope with bills and creditors and all the sordid details of existence. Well—she had done her best to clip his wings, if that was any satisfaction for her, and she could congratulate herself on the success of this early morning trick. One ought to wake exquisitely, reluctantly, he thought, slipping down in the warm bed. He began to imagine a series of enchanting scenes which ended with his latest, most charming pupil putting her bare, scented arms round his neck, and covering him with her long, perfumed hair. 'Awake, my love!' . . .

As was his daily habit, while the bath water ran, Reginald Peacock tried his voice.

When her mother tends her before the laughing mirror,
Looping up her laces, tying up her hair,

he sang, softly at first, listening to the quality, nursing his voice until he came to the third line:

Often she thinks, were this wild thing wedded . . .

and upon the word 'wedded' he burst into such a shout of triumph that the tooth-glass on the bathroom shelf trembled and even the bath tap seemed to gush stormy applause. . . .

Well, there was nothing wrong with his voice, he thought, leaping into the bath and soaping his soft, pink body all over with a loofah shaped like a fish. He could fill Covent Garden with it! '*Wedded,*' he shouted again, seizing the towel with a magnificent operatic gesture, and went on singing while he rubbed as though he had been Lohengrin tipped out by an unwary Swan and drying himself in the greatest haste before that tiresome Elsa came along along. . . .

Back in his bedroom, he pulled the blind up with a jerk, and standing upon the pale square of sunlight that lay upon the carpet like a sheet of cream blotting-paper, he began to do his exercises—deep breathing, bending forward and back, squatting like a frog and shooting out his legs—for if there was one thing he had a horror of it was of getting fat, and men in his profession had a dreadful tendency that way. However, there was no sign of it at present. He was, he decided, just right, just in good proportion. In fact, he could not help a thrill of satisfaction when he saw himself in the glass, dressed in a morning coat, dark grey trousers, grey socks, and a black tie with a silver thread in it. Not that he was vain—he couldn't stand vain men—no; the sight of himself gave him a thrill of purely artistic satisfaction. '*Voilà tout!*' said he, passing his hand over his sleek hair.

That little, easy French phrase blown so lightly from his lips, like a whiff of smoke, reminded him that someone had asked him again, the evening before, if he was English. People seemed to find it impossible to believe that he hadn't some Southern blood. True, there was an emotional quality in his singing that had nothing of the John Bull in it. . . . The door-handle rattled and turned round and round. Adrian's head popped through.

'Please, father, mother says breakfast is quite ready, please.'

'Very well,' said Reginald. Then, just as Adrian disappeared: 'Adrian!'

'Yes, father.'

'You haven't said "good morning".'

A few months ago Reginald had spent a week-end in a very aristocratic family, where the father received his little sons in the morning and shook hands with them. Reginald thought the practice charming, and introduced it immediately, but Adrian felt dreadfully silly at having to shake hands with his own father every morning. And why did his father always sort of sing to him instead of talk ? . . .

In excellent temper, Reginald walked into the dining-room and sat down before a pile of letters, a copy of *The Times*, and a little covered dish. He glanced at the letters and then at his breakfast. There were two thin slices of bacon and one egg.

'Don't you want any bacon?' he asked.

'No, I prefer a cold baked apple. I don't feel the need of bacon every morning.'

Now, did she mean that there was no need for him to have bacon every morning, either, and that she grudged having to cook it for him?

'If you don't want to cook the breakfast,' said he, 'why don't you keep a servant? You know we can afford one, and you know how I loathe to see my wife doing the work. Simply because all the women we have had in the past have been failures, and utterly upset my regime, and made it almost impossible for me to have any pupils here, you've given up trying to find a decent woman. It's not impossible to train a servant—is it? I mean, it doesn't require genius?'

'But I prefer to do the work myself; it makes life so much more peaceful. . . . Run along, Adrian darling, and get ready for school.'

'Oh no, that's not it!' Reginald pretended to smile. 'You do the work yourself, because, for some extraordinary reason, you love to humiliate me. Objectively, you may not know that, but, subjectively, it's the case.' This last remark so delighted him that he cut open an envelope as gracefully as if he had been on the stage. . . .

Dear Mr Peacock,

I feel I cannot go to sleep until I have thanked you again for the wonderful joy your singing gave me this evening. Quite unforgettable. You make me wonder, as I have not wondered since I was a girl, if this is *all*. I mean, if this ordinary world is *all*. If there is not, perhaps, for those of us who understand, divine beauty and richness awaiting us if we only have the *courage* to see it. And to make it ours . . . The house is so quiet. I wish you were here now that I might thank you in person. You are doing a great thing. You are teaching the world to escape from life!

> Yours, most sincerely,
>
> ÆNONE FELL

P.S.—I am in every afternoon this week. . . .

The letter was scrawled in violet ink on thick, handmade paper. Vanity, that bright bird, lifted its wings again, lifted them until he felt his breast would break.

'Oh well, don't let us quarrel,' said he, and actually flung out a hand to his wife.

But she was not great enough to respond.

'I must hurry and take Adrian to school,' said she. 'Your room is quite ready for you.'

Very well—very well—let there be open war between them! But he was hanged if he'd be the first to make it up again!

He walked up and down his room, and was not calm again until he heard the outer door close upon Adrian and his wife. Of course, if this went on, he would have to make some other arrangement. That was obvious. Tied and bound like this, how could he help the world to escape from life? He opened the piano and looked up his pupils for the morning. Miss Betty Brittle, the Countess Wilkowska, and Miss Marian Morrow. They were charming, all three.

Punctually at half past ten the door-bell rang. He went to the door. Miss Betty Brittle was there, dressed in white, with her music in a blue silk case.

'I'm afraid I'm early,' she said, blushing and shy, and she opened her big blue eyes very wide. 'Am I?'

'Not at all, dear lady. I am only too charmed,' said Reginald. 'Won't you come in?'

'It's such a heavenly morning,' said Miss Brittle. 'I walked across the park. The flowers were too marvellous.'

'Well, think about them while you sing your exercises,' said Reginald, sitting down at the piano. 'It will give your voice colour and warmth.'

Oh, what an enchanting idea! What a *genius* Mr Peacock was. She parted her pretty lips, and began to sing like a pansy.

'Very good, very good, indeed,' said Reginald, playing chords that would waft a hardened criminal to heaven. 'Make the notes round. Don't be afraid. Linger over them, breathe them like a perfume.'

How pretty she looked, standing there in her white frock, her little blonde head tilted, showing her milky throat.

'Do you ever practise before a glass?' asked Reginald. 'You ought to, you know; it makes the lips more flexible. Come over here.'

They went over to the mirror and stood side by side.

'Now sing—moo-e-koo-e-oo-e-a!'

But she broke down, and blushed more brightly than ever.

'Oh,' she cried, 'I can't. It makes me feel so silly. It makes me want to laugh. I do look so absurd!'

'No, you don't. Don't be afraid,' said Reginald, but laughed, too, very kindly. 'Now, try again!'

The lesson simply flew, and Betty Brittle quite got over her shyness.

'When can I come again?' she asked, tying the music up again in the blue silk case. 'I want to take as many lessons as I can just now. Oh, Mr Peacock, I *do* enjoy them so much. May I come the day after tomorrow?'

'Dear lady, I shall be only too charmed,' said Reginald, bowing her out.

Glorious girl! And when they had stood in front of the mirror, her white sleeve had just touched his black one. He could feel—yes, he could actually feel a warm glowing spot, and he stroked it. She loved her lessons. His wife came in.

'Reginald, can you let me have some money? I must pay the dairy. And will you be in for dinner tonight?'

'Yes, you know I'm singing at Lord Timbuck's at half past nine. Can you make me some clear soup, with an egg in it?'

'Yes. And the money, Reginald. It's eight and sixpence.'

'Surely that's very heavy—isn't it?'

'No, it's just what it ought to be. And Adrian must have milk.'

There she was—off again. Now she was standing up for Adrian against him.

'I have not the slightest desire to deny my child a proper amount of milk,' said he. 'Here is ten shillings.'

The door-bell rang. He went to the door.

'Oh,' said the Countess Wilkowska, 'the stairs. I have not a breath.' And she put her hand over her heart as she followed him into the music-room. She was all in black, with a little black hat with a floating veil—violets in her bosom.

'Do not make me sing exercises, today,' she cried, throwing out her hands in her delightful foreign way. 'No, today, I want only to sing songs. . . . And may I take off my violets? They fade so soon.'

'They fade so soon—they fade so soon,' played Reginald on the piano.

'May I put them here?' asked the Countess, dropping them in a little vase that stood in front of one of Reginald's photographs.

'Dear lady, I should be only too charmed!'

She began to sing, and all was well until she came to the phrase: 'You love me. Yes, I *know* you love me!' Down dropped his hands from the keyboard, he wheeled round, facing her.

'No, no; that's not good enough. You can do better than that,' cried Reginald ardently. 'You must sing as if you were in love. Listen; let me try and show you.' And he sang.

'Oh, yes, yes. I see what you mean,' stammered the little Countess. 'May I try it again?'

'Certainly. Do not be afraid. Let yourself go. Confess yourself. Make proud surrender!' he called above the music. And she sang.

'Yes; better that time. But I still feel you are capable of more. Try it with me. There must be a kind of exultant defiance as well—don't you feel?' And they sang together. Ah! now she was sure she understood. 'May I try once again?'

'You love me. Yes, I *know* you love me.'

The lesson was over before that phrase was quite perfect. The little foreign hands trembled as they put the music together.

'And you are forgetting your violets,' said Reginald softly.

'Yes, I think I will forget them,' said the Countess, biting her underlip. What fascinating ways these foreign women have!

'And you will come to my house on Sunday and make music?' she asked.

'Dear lady, I shall be only too charmed!' said Reginald.

Weep ye no more, sad fountains
Why need ye flow so fast?

sang Miss Marian Morrow, but her eyes filled with tears and her chin trembled.

'Don't sing just now,' said Reginald. 'Let me play it for you.' He played so softly.

'Is there anything the matter?' asked Reginald. 'You're not quite happy this morning.'

No, she wasn't; she was awfully miserable.

'You don't care to tell me what it is?'

It really was nothing particular. She had those moods sometimes when life seemed almost unbearable.

'Ah, I know,' he said; 'if I could only help!'

'But you do; you do! Oh, if it were not for my lessons I don't feel I could go on.'

'Sit down in the arm-chair and smell the violets and let me sing to you. It will do you just as much good as a lesson.'

Why weren't all men like Mr Peacock?

'I wrote a poem after the concert last night—just about what I felt. Of course, it wasn't *personal*. May I send it to you?'

'Dear lady, I should be only too charmed!'

By the end of the afternoon he was quite tired and lay down on a sofa to rest his voice before dressing. The door of his room was open. He could hear Adrian and his wife talking in the dining-room.

'Do you know what that teapot reminds me of, Mummy? It reminds me of a little sitting-down kitten.'

'Does it, Mr Absurdity?'

Reginald dozed. The telephone bell woke him.

'Ænone Fell is speaking. Mr Peacock, I have just heard that you are singing at Lord Timbuck's tonight. Will you dine with me, and we can go on together afterwards?' And the words of his reply dropped like flowers down the telephone.

'Dear lady, I should be only too charmed.'

What a triumphant evening! The little dinner *tête à tête* with Ænone Fell, the drive to Lord Timbuck's in her white motor-car, when she thanked him again for the unforgettable joy. Triumph upon triumph! And Lord Timbuck's champagne simply flowed.

'Have some more champagne, Peacock,' said Lord Timbuck. Peacock, you notice— not Mr Peacock—but Peacock, as if he were one of them. And wasn't he? He was an artist. He could sway them all. And wasn't he teaching them all to escape from life? How he sang! And as he sang, as in a dream he saw their feathers and their flowers and their fans, offered to him, laid before him, like a huge bouquet.

'Have another glass of wine, Peacock.'

'I could have any one I liked by lifting a finger,' thought Peacock, positively staggering home.

But as he let himself into the dark flat his marvellous sense of elation began to ebb away. He turned up the light in the bedroom. His wife lay asleep, squeezed over to her side of the bed. He remembered suddenly how she had said when he had told her he was going out to dinner: 'You might have let me know before!' And how he had answered: 'Can't you possibly speak to me without offending against even good manners?' It was incredible, he thought, that she cared so little for him—incredible that she wasn't interested in the slightest in his triumphs and his artistic career. When so many women in her place would have given their eyes. . . . Yes, he knew it. . . . Why not acknowledge it? . . . And there she lay, an enemy, even in her sleep. . . . Must it ever be thus? he thought, the champagne still working. Ah, if we only were friends, how much I could tell her now! About this evening; even about Timbuck's manner to me, and all that they said to me and so on and so on. If only I felt that she was here to come back to—that I could confide in her—and so on and so on.

In his emotion he pulled off his evening boot and simply hurled it in the corner. The noise woke his wife with a terrible start. She sat up, pushing back her hair. And he suddenly decided to have one more try to treat her as a friend, to tell her everything, to win her. Down he sat on the side of the bed, and seized one of her hands. But of all those splendid things he had to say, not one could he utter. For some fiendish reason, the only words he could get out were: 'Dear lady, I should be so charmed—so charmed!'

CONSIDER THIS

You've met Mr. Peacock earlier. Compare the beginning of Mansfield's story with the version you find on page 17. Here, for one, you see that we are introduced to Peacock's wife more emphatically; the story begins with Peacock's strong reaction against the way "she" awakens him in the morning, he, who is a "sensitive person." Is he? How does Mansfield charge her language? For or against Peacock? Do you sympathize with or object to him? Where in the language do you find ambiguity, where the narrator could be both sympathetic and unsympathetic?

Virginia Woolf confessed that the only writing she was jealous of was Mansfield's. How does Mansfield meet Woolf's requirements for the successful novelist? (See "Mr. Bennett and Mrs. Brown," page 140.) Do you find Mansfield to be terribly British? (She was a New Zealander; she was born in 1888 and died of tuberculosis in 1923.) Do you find this story to be terribly dated?

An Older Brother Lets Go
David Marcus

There had been harbingers for months, but I had ignored them. Then one morning late in August, the mail included a bulky envelope with a Vermont postmark and a college seal. He tore it open nervously reading aloud the names of a roommate and a dormitory. I realized that the time had arrived; I was finally losing my little brother.

He spent the remaining week dashing to send-off parties, filling an address book, buying skis and sweaters, gathering property loaned to old high school friends. At night, flopped on his bed with the phone cord snaking through a jumble of stereo components, duffel bags, and half-packed cartons, he moped. I shared his excitement and his sadness, as I had on so many occasions.

The most palpable anchor to my childhood, a proud, rambunctious, sharp-witted seventeen-year-old, was being pried up and away. While his gaze swept the horizon— college, law school, career—mine turned back. I recalled his earlier rites of passage: his first writing lesson (I was the instructor), the first time he skated, swam, drove, shaved, dated, danced. I remembered the party at which he first drank alcohol and the squeaks his voice made when it was changing.

To be an older sibling is to play confidant, counselor, protector, preacher, role model, friend, and, at times, foe. Every new situation requires an ad-libbed, hit-or-miss perfor- mance. Parents, at least, have books to guide them. There is no Dr. Spock for big brothers and sisters.

Through the years I held on to only one cardinal rule: a big brother should listen. I memorized the names of his teachers, teammates, girlfriends, bosses. I knew which musicians he worshipped, which TV programs were "bad" (good). And the lingo! Adult observers found our chatter unintelligible; gradually the family car evolved into "the bomber"; parents became "rents"; goodbye turned to "later."

Brotherhood was rewarding. I relished our late-night bull sessions, held a few times each week. Hours after the "rents" had fallen asleep, my brother crept into my room to trade jokes, recount the day's events, and compare gossip. I will miss those whispered ex- changes. We'll see each other on vacations and we can stay in touch by phone, of course. But our relationship will never be the same. He no longer needs me to pave the way, for he has entered "the wilderness period of his life" and is "hacking his way through the jungles of experience," in Thomas Wolfe's words.

"I've gotta get away from here. This joint is boring," he announced while examining his new skis. "Looks like I'll be doing some *bad* jumping, huh?" We had built a jump on a neighborhood golf course during a blizzard several winters ago. He was a reckless novice, small for his age, using my hand-down skis. Soon the three years between us were forgotten; we were equals. Long after dusk we trudged home to discuss our Olympic future over popcorn and hot chocolate. In those days we were an inseparable pair: challenging peers to basketball games, pooling our allowances for a calculator, pitting our parents against each other to achieve our ends.

A memorial service for our grandmother brought us as close as brothers can be. I was delivering the eulogy when, from the back row, an aunt, always hard of hearing, began a running commentary. Intended for the woman sitting next to her, the remarks were audible to everyone. After completing my speech, I darted to the men's room, where my brother joined me. For five minutes we laughed uncontrollably at the incident and cried over our first taste of death.

During recent years the strains of adolescence, the physical proximity, the shared interests and possessions spurred arguments and fist fights. In many instances we vowed never again to acknowledge one another. But somehow we reconciled every time.

On the morning of his departure, I yearn to ask my brother for an evaluation. In all my years at school I received report cards; on finishing a seventeen-year task I think I deserve compliments or critiques. I also muse about recognition; others are addressed as Ph.D., M.D., D.D.S, and so forth. Haven't I earned a B.B.—big brother—degree?

"Do me a favor, Dave. Remind the rents to send CARE packages." He is loading his belongings into a station wagon. Although I am bursting with parting advice, warnings and reassurances, I remain speechless. Together we inspect his empty, eerie, bedroom, then shut the door on his boyhood.

When we meet again at Thanksgiving he will have turned eighteen, voted in a presidential election and adjusted to a new home. Yet I still refer to him as my "little" brother. In my mind he remains the undersized fourteen-year-old standing beside me in the bathroom of a funeral parlor. We are imitating our aunt, laughing, sobbing, splashing water at each other, drying tear-streaked faces with reams of paper towels, adjusting our ties, regaining composure.

In reality he is a college freshman with a scraggly mustache, awkwardly stooping to kiss his parents. He shakes my hand, then hugs me firmly and quickly. I understand the message; it is my report card. He looks at me with the cocky, confident face of the newly independent. "Later," he says.

CONSIDER THIS

David Marcus, a feature writer for the *Miami Herald,* wrote this essay shortly after he graduated from Brown University (1982). Marcus has been writing for years, he says, keeping a journal, tapping the dailiness of his own life for material. "My friends accuse me of exploiting everything," he once told me, "and I guess I do."

Study the way Marcus moves through time in "An Older Brother Lets Go." Where does he begin? Where does he end? How do the time shifts shape the essay?

One reader found Marcus's sentiment to be surprising. "Do men really feel such emotions?" she wants to know. How do you react to such a reaction?

The Poets in the Kitchen
Paule Marshall

Some years ago, when I was teaching a graduate seminar in fiction at Columbia University, a well known male novelist visited my class to speak on his development as a writer. In discussing his formative years, he didn't realize it but he seriously endangered his life by remarking that women writers are luckier than those of his sex because they usually spend so much time as children around their mothers and their mothers' friends in the kitchen.

What did he say that for? The women students immediately forgot about being in awe of him and began readying their attack for the question and answer period later on. Even I bristled. There again was that awful image of women locked away from the world in the kitchen with only each other to talk to, and their daughters locked in with them.

But my guest wasn't really being sexist or trying to be provocative or even spoiling for a fight. What he meant—when he got around to explaining himself more fully—was that, given the way children are (or were) raised in our society, with little girls kept closer to home and their mothers, the woman writer stands a better chance of being exposed, while growing up, to the kind of talk that goes on among women, more often than not in the kitchen; and that this experience gives her an edge over her male counterpart by instilling in her an appreciation for ordinary speech.

It was clear that my guest lecturer attached great importance to this, which is understandable. Common speech and the plain, workaday words that make it up are, after all, the stock in trade of some of the best fiction writers. They are the principal means by which characters in a novel or story reveal themselves and give voice sometimes to profound feelings and complex ideals about themselves and the world. Perhaps the proper measure of a writer's talent is skill in rendering everyday speech—when it is appropriate to the story—as well as the ability to tap, to exploit, the beauty, poetry and wisdom it often contains.

"If you say what's on your mind in the language that comes to you from your parents and your street and friends you'll probably say something beautiful." Grace Paley tells this, she says, to her students at the beginning of every writing course.

It's all a matter of exposure and a training of the ear for the would-be writer in those early years of apprenticeship. And, according to my guest lecturer, this training, the best of it, often takes place in as unglamorous a setting as the kitchen.

He didn't know it, but he was essentially describing my experience as a little girl. I grew up among poets. Now they didn't look like poets—whatever that breed is supposed to look like. Nothing about them suggested that poetry was their calling. They were just a group of ordinary housewives and mothers, my mother included, who dressed in a way (shapeless housedresses, dowdy felt hats and long, dark, solemn coats) that made it impossible for me to imagine they had ever been young.

Nor did they do what poets were supposed to do—spend their days in an attic room writing verses. They never put pen to paper except to write occasionally to their relatives in Barbados. "I take my pen in hand hoping these few lines will find you in health as they leave me fair for the time being," was the way their letters invariably began. Rather, their day was spent "scrubbing floor," as they described the work they did.

Several mornings a week these unknown bards would put an apron and a pair of old house shoes in a shopping bag and take the train or streetcar from our section of Brooklyn out to Flatbush. There, those who didn't have steady jobs would wait on certain designated corners for the white housewives in the neighborhood to come along and bargain with them over pay for a day's work cleaning their houses. This was the ritual even in the winter.

Later, armed with the few dollars they had earned, which in their vocabulary became "a few raw-mouth pennies," they made their way back to our neighborhood, where they would sometimes stop off to have a cup of tea or cocoa together before going home to cook dinner for their husbands and children.

The basement kitchen of the brownstone house where my family lived was the usual gathering place. Once inside the warm safety of its walls the women threw off the drab coats and hats, seated themselves at the large center table, drank their cups of tea or cocoa, and talked. While my sister and I sat at a smaller table over in a corner doing our homework, they talked—endlessly, passionately, poetically, and with impressive range. No subject was beyond them. True, they would indulge in the usual gossip: whose husband was running with whom, whose daughter looked slightly "in the way" (pregnant) under her bridal gown as she walked down the aisle. That sort of thing. But they also tackled the great issues of the time. They were always, for example, discussing the state of the economy. It was the mid and late 30's then, and the aftershock of the Depression, with its soup lines and suicides on Wall Street, was still being felt.

Some people, they declared, didn't know how to deal with adversity. They didn't know that you had to "tie up your belly" (hold in the pain, that is) when things got rough and go on with life. They took their image from the bellyband that is tied around the stomach of a newborn baby to keep the navel pressed in.

They talked politics. Roosevelt was their hero. He had come along and rescued the country with relief and jobs, and in gratitude they christened their sons Franklin and Delano and hoped they would live up to the names.

If F.D.R. was their hero, Marcus Garvey was their God. The name of the fiery, Jamaican-born black nationalist of the 20's was constantly invoked around the table. For he had been their leader when they first came to the United States from the West Indies shortly after World War I. They had contributed to his organization, the United Negro Improvement Association (UNIA), out of their meager salaries, bought shares in his ill-fated Black Star Shipping Line, and at the height of the movement they had marched as members of his "nurses' brigade" in their white uniforms up Seventh Avenue in Harlem during the great Garvey Day parades. Garvey: He lived on through the power of their memories.

And their talk was of war and rumors of wars. They raged against World War II when it broke out in Europe, blaming it on the politicians. "It's these politicians. They're the ones always starting up all this lot of war. But what they care? It's the poor people got to suffer and mothers with their sons." If it was *their* sons, they swore they would keep them out of the Army by giving them soap to eat each day to make their hearts sound defective. Hitler? He was for them "the devil incarnate."

Then there was home. They reminisced often and at length about home. The old country. Barbados—or Bimshire, as they affectionately called it. The little Caribbean island in the sun they loved but had to leave. "Poor—poor but sweet" was the way they remembered it.

And naturally they discussed their adopted home. America came in for both good and bad marks. They lashed out at it for the racism they encountered. They took to task some of the people they worked for, especially those who gave them only a hard-boiled egg and a few spoonfuls of cottage cheese for lunch. "As if anybody can scrub floor on an egg and some cheese that don't have no taste to it!"

Yet although they caught H in "this man country," as they called America, it was nonetheless a place where "you could at least see your way to make a dollar." That much they acknowledged. They might even one day accumulate enough dollars, with both them and their husbands working, to buy the brownstone houses which, like my family, they were only leasing at that period. This was their consuming ambition: to "buy house" and to see the children through.

There was no way for me to understand it at the time, but the talk that filled the kitchen those afternoons was highly functional. It served as therapy, the cheapest kind available to my mother and her friends. Not only did it help them recover from the long wait on the corner that morning and the bargaining over their labor, it restored them to a sense of themselves and reaffirmed their self-worth. Through language they were able to overcome the humiliations of the work-day.

But more than therapy, that freewheeling, wide-ranging, exuberant talk functioned as an outlet for the tremendous creative energy they possessed. They were women in whom the need for self-expression was strong, and since language was the only vehicle readily available to them they made of it an art form that—in keeping with the African tradition in which art and life are one—was an integral part of their lives.

And their talk was a refuge. They never really ceased being baffled and overwhelmed by America—its vastness, complexity and power. Its strange customs and laws. At a level beyond words they remained fearful and in awe. Their uneasiness and fear were even reflected in their attitude toward the children they had given birth to in this country. They referred to those like myself, the little Brooklyn-born Bajans (Barbadians), as "these New York children" and complained that they couldn't discipline us properly because of the laws here. "You can't beat these children as you would like, you know, because the authorities in this place will dash you in jail for them. After all, these is New York children." Not only were we different, American, we had, as they saw it, escaped their ultimate authority.

Confronted therefore by a world they could not encompass, which even limited their rights as parents, and at the same time finding themselves permanently separated from the world they had known, they took refuge in language. "Language is the only homeland," Czeslaw Milosz, the emigré Polish writer and Nobel Laureate, has said. This is what it became for the women at the kitchen table.

It served another purpose also, I suspect. My mother and her friends were after all the female counterpart of Ralph Ellison's invisible man. Indeed, you might say they suffered a triple invisibility, being black, female and foreigners. They really didn't count in American society except as a source of cheap labor. But given the kind of women they were, they couldn't tolerate the fact of their invisibility, their powerlessness. And they fought back, using the only weapon at their command: the spoken word.

Those late afternoon conversations on a wide range of topics were a way for them to feel they exercised some measure of control over their lives and the events that shaped them. "Soully-gal, talk yuh talk!" they were always exhorting each other. "In this man world you got to take yuh mouth and make a gun!" They were in control, if only verbally and if only for the two hours or so that they remained in our house.

For me, sitting over in the corner, being seen but not heard, which was the rule for children in those days, it wasn't only what the women talked about—the content—but the way they put things—their style. The insight, irony, wit and humor they brought to their stories and discussions and their poet's inventiveness and daring with language—which of course I could only sense but not define back then.

They had taken the standard English taught them in the primary schools of Barbados and transformed it into an idiom, an instrument that more adequately described them—changing around the syntax and imposing their own rhythm and accent so that the sentences were more pleasing to their ears. They added the few African sounds and words that had survived, such as the derisive suck-teeth sound and the word "yam," meaning to eat. And to make it more vivid, more in keeping with their expressive quality, they brought to bear a raft of metaphors, parables, Biblical quotations, sayings and the like:

"The sea ain' got no back door," they would say, meaning that it wasn't like a house where if there was a fire you could run out the back. Meaning that it was not to be trifled with. And meaning perhaps in a larger sense that man should treat all of nature with caution and respect.

"I has read hell by heart and called every generation blessed!" They sometimes went in for hyperbole.

A woman expecting a baby was never said to be pregnant. They never used that word. Rather, she was "in the way" or, better yet, "tumbling big." "Guess who I butt up on in the market the other day tumbling big again!"

And a woman with a reputation of being too free with her sexual favors was known in their book as a "thoroughfare"—the sense of men like a steady stream of cars moving up and down the road of her life. Or she might be dubbed "a free-bee," which was my favorite of the two. I liked the image it conjured up of a woman scandalous perhaps but independent, who flitted from one flower to another in a garden of male beauties, sampling their nectar, taking her pleasure at will, the roles reversed.

And nothing, no matter how beautiful, was ever described as simply beautiful. It was always "beautiful-ugly": the beautiful-ugly dress, the beautiful-ugly house, the beautiful-ugly car. Why the word "ugly," I used to wonder, when the thing they were referring to was beautiful, and they knew it? Why the antonym, the contradiction, the linking of opposites? It used to puzzle me greatly as a child.

There is the theory in linguistics which states that the idiom of a people, the way they use language, reflects not only the most fundamental views they hold of themselves and the world but their very conception of reality. Perhaps in using the term "beautiful-ugly" to describe nearly everything, my mother and her friends were expressing what they believed to be a fundamental dualism in life: the idea that a thing is at the same time its opposite, and that these opposites, these contradictions make up the whole. But theirs was not a Manichaean brand of dualism that sees matter, flesh, the body, as inherently evil, because they constantly addressed each other as "soully-gal"—soul: spirit; gal: the body, flesh, the visible self. And it was clear from their tone that they gave one as much weight and importance as the other. They had never heard of the mind/body split.

As for God, they summed up His essential attitude in a phrase. "God," they would say, "don' love ugly and He ain' stuck on pretty."

Using everyday speech, the simple commonplace words—but always with imagination and skill—they gave voice to the most complex ideas. Flannery O'Connor would have approved of how they made ordinary language work, as she put it, "doubletime," stretching, shading, deepening its meaning. Like Joseph Conrad they were always trying to infuse new life in the "old old words worn thin . . . by . . . careless usage." And the goals of their oral art were the same as his: "to make you hear, to make you feel . . . to make you *see*." This was their guiding esthetic.

By the time I was 8 or 9, I graduated from the corner of the kitchen to the neighborhood library, and thus from the spoken to the written word. The Macon Street Branch of the Brooklyn Public Library was an imposing half block long edifice of heavy gray masonry, with glass-paneled doors at the front and two tall metal torches symbolizing the light that comes of learning flanking the wide steps outside.

The inside was just as impressive. More steps—of pale marble with gleaming brass railings at the center and sides—led up to the circulation desk, and a great pendulum clock gazed down from the balcony stacks that faced the entrance. Usually stationed at the top of the steps like the guards outside Buckingham Palace was the custodian, a stern-faced West Indian type who for years, until I was old enough to obtain an adult card, would immediately shoo me with one hand into the Children's Room and with the other threaten me into silence, a finger to his lips. You would have thought he was the chief librarian and not just someone whose job it was to keep the brass polished and the clock wound. I put him in a story called "Barbados" years later and had terrible things happen to him at the end.

I sheltered from the storm of adolescence in the Macon Street library, reading voraciously, indiscriminately, everything from Jane Austen to Zane Grey, but with a special passion for the long, full-blown, richly detailed 18th- and 19th-century picaresque tales: "Tom Jones," "Great Expectations," "Vanity Fair."

But although I loved nearly everything I read and would enter fully into the lives of the characters—indeed, would cease being myself and become them—I sensed a lack after a time. Something I couldn't quite define was missing. And then one day, browsing in the poetry section, I came across a book by someone called Paul Laurence Dunbar, and opening it I found the photograph of a wistful, sad-eyed poet who to my surprise was black. I turned to a poem at random. "Little brown-baby wif spa'klin' / eyes / Come to yo' pappy an' set on his knee." Although I had a little difficulty at first with the words in dialect, the poem spoke to me as nothing I had read before of the closeness, the special relationship I had had with my father, who by then had become an ardent believer in Father Divine and gone to live in Father's "kingdom" in Harlem. Reading it helped to ease somewhat the tight knot of sorrow and longing I carried in my chest that refused to go away. I read another poem. " 'Lias! 'Lias! Bless de Lawd! / Don' you know de day's / erbroad? / Ef you don' get up, you scamp / Dey'll be trouble in dis camp." I laughed. It reminded me of the way my mother sometimes yelled at my sister and me to get out of bed in the mornings.

And another: "Seen my lady home las' night / Jump back, honey, jump back. / Hel' huh han' an' sque'z it tight . . ." About love between a black man and a black woman. I had never seen that written about before and it roused in me all kinds of delicious feelings and hopes.

And I began to search then for books and stories and poems about "The Race" (as it was put back then), about my people. While not abandoning Thackeray, Fielding, Dickens and the others, I started asking the reference librarian, who was white, for books by Negro writers, although I must admit I did so at first with a feeling of shame—the shame I and many others used to experience in those days whenever the word "Negro" or "colored" came up.

No grade school literature teacher of mine had ever mentioned Dunbar or James Weldon Johnson or Langston Hughes. I didn't know that Zora Neale Hurston existed and was busy writing and being published during those years. Nor was I made aware of people like Frederick Douglass and Harriet Tubman—their spirit and example—or the great 19th-century abolitionist and feminist Sojourner Truth. There wasn't even Negro History Week when I attended P.S. 35 on Decatur Street!

What I needed, what all the kids—West Indian and native black American alike—with whom I grew up needed, was an equivalent of the Jewish shul, someplace where we could go after school—the schools that were shortchanging us—and read works by those like ourselves and learn about our history.

It was around that time also that I began harboring the dangerous thought of someday trying to write myself. Perhaps a poem about an apple tree, although I had never seen one. Or the story of a girl who could magically transplant herself to wherever she wanted to be in the world—such as Father Divine's kingdom in Harlem. Dunbar—his dark, eloquent face, his large volume of poems—permitted me to dream that I might someday write, and with something of the power with words my mother and her friends possessed.

When people at readings and writers' conferences ask me who my major influences were, they are sometimes a little disappointed when I don't immediately name the usual literary giants. True, I am indebted to those writers, white and black, whom I read during my formative years and still read for instruction and pleasure. But they were preceded in my life by another set of giants whom I always acknowledge before all others: the group of women around the table long ago. They taught me my first lessons in the narrative art. They trained my ear. They set a standard of excellence. This is why the best of my work must be attributed to them; it stands as testimony to the rich legacy of language and culture they so freely passed on to me in the wordshop of the kitchen.

CONSIDER THIS

Here is another essay in praise of ordinary language, particularly women's language as Paule Marshall finds it in the kitchen. "The proper measure of a writer's talent," she says, "is skill in rendering everyday speech. . . ."

Her chief influences, then, were not the "usual giants," but the women around her mother's kitchen table. They "trained" her ear and "set a standard of excellence." Sure, she read, but her training was right there under her nose, and not on some exotic island or foreign land.

Does Marshall, author of several novels, including *Brown Girl, Brownstones,* and *Praisesong for the Widow,* and teacher of creative writing at Virginia Commonwealth University, practice what she preaches? Is her language in this essay made up of "plain workaday words"? How would you characterize her metaphors?

Would she agree or disagree with Robin Lakoff's characterization of women's language (page 185)?

Cinderella's Stepsisters
Toni Morrison

Let me begin by taking you back a little. Back before the days at college. To nursery school, probably, to a once-upon-a-time time when you first heard, or read, or, I suspect, even saw "Cinderella." Because it is Cinderella that I want to talk about; because it is Cinderella who causes me a feeling of urgency. What is unsettling about that fairy tale is that it is essentially the story of a household—a world, if you please—of women gathered together and held together in order to abuse another woman. There is, of course, a rather vague absent father and a nick-of-time prince with a foot fetish. But neither has much personality. And there are the surrogate "mothers," of course (god- and step-), who contribute both to Cinderella's grief and to her release and happiness. But it is her stepsisters who interest me. How crippling it must have been for those young girls to grow up with a mother, to watch and imitate that mother, enslaving another girl.

I am curious about their fortunes after the story ends. For contrary to recent adaptations, the stepsisters were not ugly, clumsy, stupid girls with outsize feet. The Grimm collection describes them as "beautiful and fair in appearance." When we are introduced to them they are beautiful, elegant, women of status, and clearly women of power. Having watched and participated in the violent dominion of another woman, will they be any less cruel when it comes their turn to enslave other children, or even when they are required to take care of their own mother?

It is not a wholly medieval problem. It is quite a contemporary one: feminine power when directed at other women has historically been wielded in what has been described as a "masculine" manner. Soon you will be in a position to do the very same thing. Whatever your background—rich or poor—whatever the history of education in your family—five generations or one—you have taken advantage of what has been available to you at Barnard and you will therefore have both the economic and social status of the stepsisters *and* you will have their power.

I want not to *ask* you but to *tell* you not to participate in the oppression of your sisters. Mothers who abuse their children are women, and another woman, not an agency, has to be willing to stay their hands. Mothers who set fire to school buses are women, and another woman, not an agency, has to tell them to stay their hands. Women who stop the promotion of other women in careers are women, and another woman must come to the victim's aid. Social and welfare workers who humiliate their clients may be women, and other women colleagues have to deflect their anger.

I am alarmed by the violence that women do to each other: professional violence, competitive violence, emotional violence. I am alarmed by the willingness of women to enslave other women. I am alarmed by a growing absence of decency on the killing floor of professional women's worlds. You are the women who will take your place in the world where *you* can decide who shall flourish and who shall wither; you will make distinctions between the deserving poor and the undeserving poor; where you can yourself determine which life is expendable and which is indispensable. Since you will have the power to do it, you may also be persuaded that you have the right to do it. As educated women the distinction between the two is first-order business.

I am suggesting that we pay as much attention to our nurturing sensibilities as to our ambition. You are moving in the direction of freedom and the function of freedom is to free somebody else. You are moving toward self-fulfillment, and the consequences of that fulfillment should be to discover that there is something just as important as you are and that just-as-important thing may be Cinderella—or your stepsister.

In your rainbow journey toward the realization of personal goals, don't make choices based only on your security and your safety. Nothing is safe. That is not to say that anything ever was, or that anything worth achieving ever should be. Things of value seldom are. It is not safe to have a child. It is not safe to challenge the status quo. It is not safe to choose work that has not been done before. Or to do old work in a new way. There will always be someone there to stop you. But in pursuing your highest ambitions, don't let your personal safety diminish the safety of your stepsister. In wielding the power that is deservedly yours, don't permit it to enslave your stepsisters. Let your might and your power emanate from that place in you that is nurturing and caring.

Women's rights is not only an abstraction, a cause; it is also a personal affair. It is not only about "us"; it is also about me and you. Just the two of us.

CONSIDER THIS

As with Martin Luther King and Abraham Lincoln, so with Toni Morrison: all three speak to specific audiences in the form of prepared speeches, transcribed. Morrison addresses an audience of graduating seniors at Barnard College, urging them—once they are established in seats of power—to treat their sisters with consideration, respect, humanity. In "Cinderella's Stepsisters," Morrison draws on the Cinderella story, showing how women can enslave one another.

She then alludes to similar injustices in various places in the culture—in the family, in the professions. She declares that she is "alarmed by the violence that women do to each other," "alarmed by the willingness of women to enslave other women"; and she tells rather than asks the graduates "not to participate in the oppression of your sisters."

Morrison operates, perhaps, at a level of generalities: we are left to believe that such infractions, such injustices, exist; we are offered no "proof"—no research, no examples, not even an anecdote. Are you convinced? Do you believe that the situation is as Morrison describes it? Or do you think that her assumption of a common viewpoint is a flaw? How might you find out?

Morrison is author of several novels—*The Bluest Eye, Sula, The Black Book, Song of Solomon,* and *Beloved,* for which she was awarded the 1988 Pulitzer Prize.

No. 32 Goes to Bat
Bette Ann Moskowitz

The scrub grass glistened in the sun; swirls of dust on the mound blew into the pitcher's eye and the manager came out of the dugout with a Kleenex. Time was called, and the catcher took advantage of it to take his allergy medicine. The left fielder left left field to deliver a handful of dandelions to his mother in the stands, and the chunky third baseman looked wistfully toward the hot dog truck in foul territory.

A plane buzzed overhead as the umpire shouted "Play ball," so he had to repeat himself twice. Finally, the team was in place. The pitcher wound up. The catcher gave him a target. The batter approached the plate. A thin cheer went up and I swallowed hard. Batting cleanup, 0 for 16 this season, No. 32: 4 feet 3, 72 pounds. My son.

This morning he had refused breakfast, sighed and said he hoped he'd hit it out of the park. (Out of the park in our league means the curb at Francis Lewis Boulevard. Players are not allowed to chase balls into the gutter.)

"Just hit it," his older brother said.

"I do hit it," No. 32 said indignantly.

"Yeah, when?"

No. 32 did not answer.

"In practice," his sister said. "I saw him."

"In his dreams," his brother said scornfully.

Actually, it was both. As I slipped the mitt off his hand the previous night as he slept, I heard him murmur "out of the park." In practice he was a tiger. But when he stepped up to the plate, No. 32 froze. Or ducked.

"You never even take a swing," his brother said, disgustedly.

"I'm looking for a good one," No. 32 said.

"C'mon, guys, you're going to be late," I said. "Daddy's gone already." Daddy was coaching the Seniors this year.

They gathered batting gloves, mitts, hats and bicycles and then they were gone—my daughter, the pitcher, in her red and white Sally League uniform; my older son, catcher of note in the Pony Division ("Remember how scared you used to be," we told him; he didn't), and the little one, in the green and white of the DuRite Cleaners Mets, who couldn't get a piece of the ball.

I spend every weekend going from playing field to playing field, trying to give equal time.

I watched my daughter pitch two innings, saw my older boy make a spectacular catch behind home plate, and then reluctantly wandered down to Field 8.

The pitcher wound up again but then stopped to scratch his nose. My son waved the bat menacingly.

"The bat's as big as he is," some woman behind me said.

The pitcher wound up, wound up, wound up, and finally threw. It was high and outside. Ball one.

The second pitch was low and outside. Ball two.

"Nice looking at 'em," someone shouted. It was my husband, whose game had just ended.

The next pitch was a strike. The pitcher, who was my son's best friend, grinned. My son grinned back. The pitcher raised his hands in the air, brought them to his chest and let go with the next one. It was a fast ball, so fast that it had hardly seemed to leave his hands before I saw my son on the ground.

Everyone was on his feet, the manager and coaches were running to the plate, my husband had dashed out there, and I found myself clinging to the batting cage fence. Then he was up, brushing the yellow dust off his uniform and reaching for his bat.

"It never touched him," a man behind me said. "He just ducked."

"It came darned close," someone else said.

"I wish they would play with a rubber ball," someone's mother said to me. I did, too. Now he'd never swing, I thought.

"Ball three," the umpire said.

The other games had ended, and people were drifting down to our field. The stands were crowded. How many mothers, I wondered, sat in the stands, feeling the pressure, smiling slight, nervous smiles and having this fantasy: I get up, approach the plate, take my son's hand, and say to him come home, this is ridiculous, it isn't worth it, and my son smiles and says O.K., Mom, just as he did when he was 3. Or a variation: I get up, approach the plate, come behind my son (this time I am invisible), put my hands over his, and when the ball comes whizzing toward us, I help him swing the bat.

The count was three balls and one strike. The pitcher wound up. The batter waved the bat. The ball left the pitcher's hand and came toward the batter in a nice straight line. And No. 32 swung the bat. The ball went sailing into the outfield, and No. 32 was running around the bases as fast as he might have dreamed.

"Go, go," my older boy was shouting, and as No. 32 rounded third and touched home plate, he ran right into his brother's arms.

They were still looking for the ball in the outfield when the hot dog man brought it, covered with mustard, to the edge of the field. Everyone groaned. The hot dog truck, and the mustard pot in the hot dog truck, was in foul territory. The umpire examined the ball and wiped his hands.

"Foul ball," he said, and No. 32 trotted to home plate to take another shot. A swing and a miss. The batter was out.

"Nice out," the batter's brother shouted, as he walked from the plate.

And No. 32 took off his cap and waved as the people in the stands applauded him all the way into the dugout.

CONSIDER THIS

Characterize the way you find your feet as a reader in Moskowitz's first paragraph. When do you first realize that the ball players are kids? Where does she find her metaphors?

I know Moskowitz; she teaches writing at Queens College and has been writing all her life—songs, short stories, and essays. Her first novel, *Leaving Barney,* was published in 1988. I didn't know her well when I first read "No. 32," but I had heard her say that she had two children, a son and a daughter. But in "No. 32," we meet *two* sons. After I'd read her essay, I worried about that missing son, and as delicately as I could, I broached the subject. I nervously assumed that he had come to a tragic end. "Oh," she said, "I only have one son, but I needed an extra for this piece, so I made him up."

What do you think of that?

A Word's Meaning Can Often Depend on Who Says It

Gloria Naylor

Language is the subject. It is the written form with which I've managed to keep the wolf away from the door and, in diaries, to keep my sanity. In spite of this, I consider the written word inferior to the spoken, and much of the frustration experienced by novelists is the awareness that whatever we manage to capture in even the most transcendent passages falls far short of the richness of life. Dialogue achieves its power in the dynamics of a fleeting moment of sight, sound, smell and touch.

I'm not going to enter the debate here about whether it is language that shapes reality or vice versa. That battle is doomed to be waged whenever we seek intermittent reprieve from the chicken and egg dispute. I will simply take the position that the spoken word, like the written word, amounts to a nonsensical arrangement of sounds or letters without a consensus that assigns "meaning." And building from the meanings of what we hear, we order reality. Words themselves are innocuous; it is the consensus that gives them true power.

• • •

I remember the first time I heard the word nigger. In my third-grade class, our math tests were being passed down the rows, and as I handed the papers to a little boy in back of me, I remarked that once again he had received a much lower mark than I did. He snatched his test from me and spit out that word. Had he called me a nymphomaniac or a necrophiliac, I couldn't have been more puzzled. I didn't know what a nigger was, but I knew that whatever it meant, it was something he shouldn't have called me. This was verified when I raised my hand, and in a loud voice repeated what he had said and watched the teacher scold him for using a "bad" word. I was later to go home and ask the inevitable question that every black parent must face—"Mommy, what does 'nigger' mean?"

And what exactly did it mean? Thinking back, I realize that this could not have been the first time the word was used in my presence. I was part of a large extended family that had migrated from the rural South after World War II and formed a close-knit network that gravitated around my maternal grandparents. Their ground-floor apartment in one of the buildings they owned in Harlem was a weekend mecca for my immediate family, along with countless aunts, uncles and cousins who brought along assorted friends. It was a bustling and open house with assorted neighbors and tenants popping in and out to exchange bits of gossip, pick up an old quarrel or referee the ongoing checkers game in which my grandmother cheated shamelessly. They were all there to let down their hair and put up their feet after a week of labor in the factories, laundries and shipyards of New York.

Amid the clamor, which could reach deafening proportions—two or three conversations going on simultaneously, punctuated by the sound of a baby's crying somewhere in the back rooms or out on the street—there was still a rigid set of rules about what was said and how. Older children were sent out of the living room when it was time to get into the juicy details about "you-know-who" up on the third floor who had gone and gotten herself "p-r-e-g-n-a-n-t!" But my parents, knowing that I could spell well beyond my years, always demanded that I follow the others out to play. Beyond sexual misconduct and death, everything else was considered harmless for our young ears. And so among the anecdotes of the triumphs and disappointments in the various workings of their lives, the word nigger was used in my presence, but it was set within contexts and inflections that caused it to register in my mind as something else.

In the singular, the word was always applied to a man who had distinguished himself in some situation that brought their approval for his strength, intelligence or drive:

"Did Johnny *really* do that?"

"I'm telling you, that nigger pulled in $6,000 of overtime last year. Said he got enough for a down payment on a house."

When used with a possessive adjective by a woman—"my nigger"—it became a term of endearment for husband or boyfriend. But it could be more than just a term applied to a man. In their mouths it became the pure essence of manhood—a disembodied force that channeled their past history of struggle and present survival against the odds into a victorious statement of being: "Yeah, that old foreman found out quick enough—you don't mess with a nigger."

In the plural, it became a description of some group within the community that had overstepped the bounds of decency as my family defined it: Parents who neglected their children, a drunken couple who fought in public, people who simply refused to look for work, those with excessively dirty mouths or unkempt households were all "trifling niggers." This particular circle could forgive hard times, unemployment, the occasional bout of depression—they had gone through all of that themselves—but the unforgivable sin was a lack of self-respect:

A woman could never be a "nigger" in the singular, with its connotation of confirming worth. The noun girl was its closest equivalent in that sense, but only when used in direct address and regardless of the gender doing the addressing. "Girl" was a token of respect for a woman. The one-syllable word was drawn out to sound like three in recognition of the extra ounce of wit, nerve or daring that the woman had shown in the situation under discussion.

"G-i-r-l, stop. You mean you said that to his face?"

But if the word was used in a third-person reference or shortened so that it almost snapped out of the mouth, it always involved some element of communal disapproval. And age became an important factor in these exchanges. It was only between individuals of the same generation, or from an older person to a younger (but never the other way around), that "girl" would be considered a compliment.

• • •

I don't agree with the argument that use of the word nigger at this social stratum of the black community was an internalization of racism. The dynamics were the exact opposite: the people in my grandmother's living room took a word that whites used to signify worthlessness or degradation and rendered it impotent. Gathering there together, they transformed "nigger" to signify the varied and complex human beings they knew themselves to be. If the word was to disappear totally from the mouths of even the most liberal of white society, no one in that room was naïve enough to believe it would disappear from white minds. Meeting the word head-on, they proved it had absolutely nothing to do with the way they were determined to live their lives.

So there must have been dozens of times that the "nigger" was spoken in front of me before I reached the third grade. But I didn't "hear" it until it was said by a small pair of lips that had already learned it could be a way to humiliate me. That was the word I went home and asked my mother about. And since she knew that I had to grow up in America, she took me in her lap and explained.

CONSIDER THIS

At the beginning of this essay, Gloria Naylor tells us that she uses written language to "keep the wolf away from the door," to keep her sanity. She has also said that she writes to give a voice to her black woman's life and experience.

The essay begins with Naylor explicitly stating a position: Meaning does not exist apart from the interaction (dialogue) between speaker and listener (or writer and reader), from the *context* in which words are found. At the end, she restates her thesis, but in language rooted in her own experience. She says she didn't "hear [the word *nigger*] until it was said by a small pair of lips that had already learned it could be a way to humiliate me." Notice how much weight the word "hear" carries.

According to Naylor, "nigger" is transformed by a change of context; "g-i-r-l" is transformed both by a context change and a different way of speaking the word. Can you think of other words that are similarly transformed—by context or by inflection?

Naylor is the author of three novels, one of which, *The Women of Brewster Place,* won the American Book Award for best first fiction in 1983; she received a Guggenheim fellowship in 1988.

Floyd Patterson: The Essence of a Competitor
Joyce Carol Oates

"I won the heavyweight title in 1956 as the youngest boxer in history—21 years old. And I regained it in 1960 with a knockout over Ingemar Johansson; I was the first heavyweight in history to win back his title. But the proudest moment of my career was when I won my Olympic gold medal in Helsinki, in 1952," Floyd Patterson says without hesitation. "I was 17 years old. I'd never been away from home—never flown in an airplane. And here I was fighting in the Olympics, in a foreign country. I was scared stiff. I didn't think I would win even my first match. But I *wanted* to win—maybe that made the difference."

Floyd Patterson had one of the most meteoric careers in heavyweight history. Following his victory (as a middleweight) in the 1952 Olympics, he immediately turned professional, moved up into the heavier division and won the world title in a match with Archie Moore in 1956, following the retirement of the champion Rocky Marciano. Patterson had, as an amateur, won two Golden Gloves tournaments, was one of the youngest athletes to have won an Olympic gold medal and became the first gold medalist to win the heavyweight boxing championship.

In 1961, with his spectacular defeat of Johansson, his career took on the quality of legend, and he enjoyed celebrity of a quintessentially American kind: He was given a $35,000 jeweled crown by his trainer, the late Cus D'Amato, a man not known for extravagant gestures; he was invited to the White House to meet President Kennedy; sportswriters universally acclaimed the intelligently controlled aggression of his ring style; he received thousands of letters from fans—including, unexpectedly, Swedes who seemed to have taken the soft-spoken, introspective young black American to their hearts, despite the fact that he had knocked out their own champion Johansson in two highly publicized bouts in 1960 and 1961.

Patterson is said to have been a nonviolent person who once helped an opponent pick up his mouthpiece from the canvas. "I don't like to see blood," he once explained. "It's different when I bleed; that doesn't bother me because I can't see it."

Indeed, among contemporary boxers, no one is so articulate as Floyd Patterson. He has a reputation, unique in athletics generally, for being self-analytical to a remarkable degree; he does not hesitate to tell an interviewer that though he endured more than his fair share of what might be called fortune's vicissitudes—including, for some time following his losses to Sonny Liston in the early 1960s, a "deep sense of shame"—there is not a single event in his life he would want altered; not a moment he truly regrets.

"Through my twenty-two years in boxing," Patterson says, "I learned what I *am*. Without boxing—without all the things that happened to me, good and bad—I would be a different, lesser man today."

Aged 53, Patterson maintains a physical regimen that assures his excellent conditioning; he weighs approximately what he weighed in 1956 and he runs up to eight miles a day. Boxing critics who argue for the abolition of the sport should consider Floyd Patterson: He is living proof that boxing is not inevitably injurious to a boxer's well-being and that, under proper instruction, it builds character through the rigorous discipline of training and, if pursued into maturity, an almost mystical sense of one's identity. Trained by the famous D'Amato (who was also Mike Tyson's trainer), Patterson adamantly believes that it is character rather than skill that ultimately determines a boxer's quality. What you are determines how you perform in the ring.

"What a boxer learns, what these young amateurs are learning, is essentially a respect for the body," Patterson explains. "In turn, that respect touches other things in life, including other people."

Patterson's involvement with others has been considerable: He heads the Floyd Patterson Children's Fund and runs a boxing gym in New Paltz, New York, where he trains young boxers, including his adopted son Tracey, a featherweight with a promising career as a professional. (Patterson also served as New York State Boxing Commissioner, from 1977–84.)

Patterson looks forward to the Seoul Olympics with particular anticipation. He believes that good amateur competition is invaluable for the nourishment of new young talent; his own life, begun as one of ten children of a hardworking but impoverished Brooklyn family, would be unimaginable without the opportunities that the Olympics offered to him.

But amateur boxing differs considerably from professional, and a young man with the talent for one might not have the talent for the other. The amateur bout, for instance, consists of three rounds, "like sprint running"; the professional bout consists of up to 15 rounds— "like marathon running." When he turned professional at the young age of 17, Patterson's greatest anxiety was not over being knocked out by an opponent but being unable to endure longer fights. Another way in which amateur boxing differs dramatically, and rather misleadingly, from professional boxing is that a knockdown is scored by judges no differently than an ordinary clean hit: The power of the boxer's blows is not supposed to count.

Boxing, Patterson explains, is a feat of coordination. "You need lightning-quick reflexes—you have to fight by instinct. If you stop to think about what you're doing, it will be too late." He decided to retire, at age 37, when he realized he could no longer fight instinctively, and he believes that a mandatory retirement age, somewhere in the 30s, might be advisable for the profession.

Since 1952, one of the most spectacular changes in boxing is the size of the purses awarded to "super-champions" like Sugar Ray Leonard, Marvin Hagler and Mike Tyson. The sums are many times what they were for even the most heavily promoted matches in Patterson's time, approaching, one might say, the grotesque: $15 million for Marvin Hagler for a single match, in 1987; more than $20 million for Mike Tyson for a single match (of several matches fought by him in that year), in 1988. Asked how boxers of his generation would have felt had they known what lay ahead, Patterson says laughingly, "Well—we couldn't wait for it! We had to fight when we did."

On its highest levels, boxing, like any sport, or art, or vocation in life, is about character; it resolves to *being*, not merely *doing*. Which may account for its ongoing fascination for so many people, women as well as men, who might otherwise condemn its naked display of aggression. In symbolic form, writ small, yet wordless, it is about what we must all endure, willingly or otherwise—winning and losing. As Floyd Patterson has thoughtfully put it, "Winning after all is easy. It's losing that requires courage."

CONSIDER THIS

Writer- (and intellectual-) in-residence at Princeton University, Joyce Carol Oates is a poet, a novelist, a playwright, and a literary critic.

Oates is first and foremost a moral and social commentator. Over the course of her prolific career (over thirty books and seven plays) she has taken a hard and often disturbing look at social and political conditions in the United States—across all demographic boundaries. Among the many hats she wears is that of sports fan—and specifically boxing fan.

"Floyd Patterson" was published in the same advertising supplement in which Billie Jean King's piece about women in the Olympics appeared. [Who do you think wrote the subtitle ("The Essence of a Competitor"), Oates or the editors?] What about the writing style sets this piece apart from King's? (Hint: Look at the adjectives and adverbs. Look at the two last paragraphs side by side: Would the word "character" or the phrase "naked display of aggression" be at home in King's essay?) What, by the way, might be another word for what Oates and Patterson call "character"?

A Clean Well-Lighted Place
Frank O'Connor

Ernest Hemingway must have been one of the first of Joyce's disciples. Certainly, so far as I can ascertain, he was the only writer of his time to study what Joyce was attempting to do in the prose of *Dubliners* and *A Portrait of the Artist as a Young Man* and work out a method of applying it. It took me years to identify Joyce's technique and describe it with any care, and by that time I realized that it was useless for any purpose of my own. So far as I know, no critic had anticipated me, but Hemingway had not only anticipated me; he had already gone into business with it on his own account, and a handsome little business he made of it.

In dealing with *Dubliners* I have already described the peculiarities of Joyce's prose in his first book, but Joyce reserved some of its principal developments for his autobiographical novel. The passage I quoted from it in *A Mirror in the Roadway* to illustrate the technique is as good as any other for my purpose.

> The soft beauty of the Latin word *touched* with an enchanting *touch* the *dark* of the evening, with a *touch* fainter and more persuading than the *touch* of music or of a *woman's* hand. The strife of their minds was quelled. The figure of *woman* as she appears in the liturgy of the church *passed* silently through the *darkness:* a white-robed figure, small and slender as a boy, and with a falling girdle. Her *voice*, frail and high as a boy's, was heard intoning from a distant choir the first words of a *woman* which pierce the gloom and clamour of the first chanting of the passion:
> Et tu cum Jesu Galilaeo eras—
> And all hearts were *touched* and turned to her *voice*, shining like a young star, shining clearer as the *voice* intoned the proparoxyton, and more faintly as the cadence died.

This, as I have said, seems to me a development of Flaubert's "proper word," a word proper to the object, not to the reader; and as well as imposing on the reader the exact appearance of the object in the manner of an illustrator, seeks also to impose on him the author's precise mood. By the repetition of key words and key phrases like "touch," "dark," "woman," and "pass," it slows down the whole conversational movement of prose, the casual, sinuous, evocative quality that distinguishes it from poetry and is intended to link author and reader in a common perception of the object, and replaces it by a series of verbal rituals which are intended to evoke the object as it may be supposed to be. At an extreme point it attempts to substitute the image for the reality. It is a rhetorician's dream.

But when you really know *A Portrait of the Artist as a Young Man* you recognize exactly where the beautiful opening of Hemingway's "In Another Country" came from.

> In the *fall* the war was always there, but we did not go to it any more. It was *cold* in the *fall* in Milan, and the dark came very early. Then the electric lights came on, and it was pleasant along the streets looking in the windows. There was much game hanging outside the shops, and the snow powdered in the fur of the foxes and the *wind blew* their tails. The deer hung stiff and heavy and empty, and small birds *blew* in the *wind*, and the *wind* turned their feathers. It was a *cold fall* and the *wind* came down from the mountains.

There! You have realized how cold and windy it was that fall in Milan, haven't you? And it didn't really hurt, did it? Even if you were not very interested to begin with, you have learned one or two very important things that you might otherwise have ignored. Quite seriously, this is something you don't recall from other famous passages of literature, written by predecessors of Joyce and Hemingway, because in neither of these passages is there what you could call a human voice speaking, nobody resembling yourself who is trying to persuade you to share in an experience of his own, and whom you can imagine yourself questioning about its nature—nothing but an old magician sitting over his crystal ball, or a hypnotist waving his hands gently before your eyes and muttering, "You are falling asleep; you are falling asleep; slowly, slowly your eyes are beginning to close; your eyelids are growing heavy; you are—falling—asleep."

Though Joyce was the most important single influence on Hemingway, and one can trace him even in little pedantries like placing the adverb immediately after the verb when usage requires it either to precede the verb or to follow the object, as in "he poured smoothly the buckwheat batter," he was not the only influence. Gertrude Stein and her experiments with language were also of some importance. Her experiments—usually rather absurd ones—were intended to produce a simplification of prose technique like the simplification of forms that we find in the work of certain modern painters. Her mistake— a blatant vulgarization of Joyce's fundamental mistake—was to ignore the fact that prose is a very impure art. Any art which formally is practically indistinguishable from a memorandum issued by a government office is necessarily impure. "Prosaic" is a term of abuse, though in fact it should have a connotation as noble as "poetic."

As practiced by Hemingway, this literary method, compounded of simplification and repetition, is the opposite of that we learned in our schooldays. We were taught to consider it a fault to repeat a noun and shown how to avoid it by the use of pronouns and synonyms. This led to another fault that Fowler christened "elegant variation." The fault of Hemingway's method might be called "elegant repetition." His most elaborate use of it is in "Big Two-Hearted River."

> There was no underbrush in the island of *pine trees*. The *trunks* of the *trees* went straight up or slanted toward each other. The *trunks* were straight and *brown* without *branches*. The *branches* were *high above*. Some interlocked to make a solid *shadow* on the *brown forest floor*. Around the grove of *trees* was a bare space. It was *brown* and soft underfoot as Nick walked on it. This was the over-lapping of the *pine*-needle *floor*, extending out beyond the width of the *high branches*. The *trees* had grown tall and the *branches* moved *high*, leaving in the sun this bare space they had once covered with shadow. Sharp at the edge of this extension of the *forest floor* commenced the sweet fern.
>
> Nick slipped off his pack and lay down in the *shade*. He lay on his *back* and looked up into the *pine trees*. His neck and *back* and the small of his *back* rested as he stretched. The earth felt good against his *back*. He looked up at the sky, through the *branches*, and then shut his eyes. He opened them and looked up again. There was a wind *high* up in the *branches*. He shut his eyes again and went to sleep.

This is part of an extraordinarily complex and simple-minded literary experiment in which Hemingway sets out to duplicate in prose a fishing trip in wooded country, and it is constructed with a minute vocabulary of a few dozen words, like "water," "current," "stream," "trees," "branches," and "shadow." It is an elaboration of the device I have pointed out in *A Portrait of the Artist as a Young Man*. In some ways it anticipates Joyce's "Anna Livia Plurabelle" though in general it resembles more an experiment in Basic English. The curious thing is that I have worked with scores of young Americans—people who knew their Hemingway far better than I did—and they had never noticed the device. Perhaps this is what Hemingway and Joyce intended; perhaps I read them in the wrong way, but I do not know of any other way to read prose. And I feel quite sure that even Joyce would have thought "Big Two-Hearted River" a vulgarization of his rhetorician's dream.

However, Hemingway went one better than his master when he realized that precisely the same technique could be applied to dramatic interludes, and that the repetition of key words and phrases in these could produce a similar simplification with a similar hypnotic effect. Where Joyce writes "the other hand careered in the treble after each group of notes. The notes of the air sounded deep and full" Hemingway will write:

"You oughtn't to ever do anything too long."
"No, we were up there too long."
"Too damn long," John said. "It's no good doing a thing too long."

This is a new thing in storytelling, and it is worth considering at some length. There is a fairly straightforward example in "Hills Like White Elephants," a story in which a man tries to persuade his mistress to have an abortion. There are certain key words in the dialogue like "simple" and key phrases like "I don't want you to do it if you don't want to."

"Well," the man said, "*if you don't want to* you don't have to. I wouldn't have you *do it if you didn't want to*. But I know it's *perfectly simple*."
"And *you really want to?*"
"I think it's the best thing to do. But *I don't want you to do it if you don't really want to*."
"And *if I do it* you'll be happy and things will be like they were and *you'll love me?*"
"*I love you now*. You know *I love you*."
"I know. But *if I do it*, then it will be nice again if I say things are like white elephants, and you'll like it."
"*I'll love it. I love it now* but I just can't think about it. You know how I get *when I worry*."
"*If I do it you won't ever worry?*"
"*I won't worry about that* because it's *perfectly simple*."
"Then *I'll do it*. Because *I don't care about me*."
"What do you mean?"
"*I don't care about me*."
"*Well, I care about you*."
"Oh, yes. But *I don't care about me*. And *I'll do it* and then everything will be fine."
"*I don't want you to do it* if you feel that way."

The advantages and disadvantages of a style like this are about evenly divided. The principal advantage is clear. Nobody is ever likely to get the impression that he is accidentally reading a government memorandum or a shorthand report of a trial. If Goethe is right in saying that art is art because it is not nature, this is art. Even in very good stylists of the older school of storytelling there is often a marked struggle at the beginning of the story before the author can detach himself from what is not storytelling and the story becomes airborne; a paragraph or more of fumbling prose like the tuning up of an orchestra, but in Hemingway the element of stylization cuts off the very first sentence from whatever is not storytelling, so that it rings out loud and clear like music cutting across silence. Turgenev's "Living Relic" begins with the words "A French proverb runs: 'A dry fisherman and a wet hunter present a sorry sight.' Never having had any predilection for fishing . . ."—a leisurely enough opening in the manner of his period. Chekhov's "Sleepy" begins with the single word "Night," which is more urgent though perhaps a little trite. The first sentence of "In Another Country" is a perfect opening phrase, mannered enough to jolt the reader awake without making him go to see if the front door is locked: "In the fall the war was always there, but we did not go to it any more." In the same way, when Hemingway ends a story it stays ended, without giving us the feeling that perhaps we have bought a defective copy.

The obvious disadvantage is that it tends to blur the sharp contrast that should ideally exist between narrative and drama, the two forms of which storytelling is compounded. Ideally, the former should be subjective and persuasive, the latter objective and compulsive. In one the storyteller suggests to the reader what he believes happened, in the other he proves to him that this in fact is how it did happen. In a good story the two aspects are nearly always kept in balance. In a Hemingway story drama, because it is stylized in the same way as the narrative, tends to lose its full impact. Dialogue, the autonomous element of drama, begins to blur, and the conversation becomes more like the conversation of alcoholics, drug addicts, or experts in Basic English. In Joyce's "Grace," the author's irony gives the conversation of the men in the sick room the same dull, claustrophobic quality, but there one can excuse it on the ground that his aim is comic. There is no such excuse for the conversation in Hemingway's story.

Of course you may say if you please that the drama there is implicit rather than explicit, and that it is made sufficiently clear that the man does not love the girl—after all he indicates it by saying "I love you now" and "I love it now" too close together—and that she knows it and is offering up her unborn child for the sake of a man she feels sure will leave her, but the dialogue by which two people communicate or try to communicate with one another is missing. And here, I think, we may be touching on a weakness in both Joyce and Hemingway. To the rhetorician dialogue must so often seem unnecessary since he knows so many ingenious ways of evading it.

Not that Hemingway often took his rhetoric to the fair as Joyce did. In fact, if we exclude "Big Two-Hearted River," which is only a caricature of a literary method, there never was much of the real experimenter in him. He was a practical writer, not a research worker, and he took from the research workers like Joyce and Gertrude Stein only what he felt he needed, in the spirit of an American efficiency expert studying the tests of a group of scientists to discover how he can knock a second or two off the time it takes to move a lever. When you compare the passage I have quoted from *A Portrait of the Artist as a Young Man* with the passage from "In Another Country," you can see that Joyce is already letting his own theory run away with him, while Hemingway uses precisely as much of it as he needs to create the effect that he himself has in mind.

In fact, from a purely technical point of view, no other writer of the twentieth century was so splendidly equipped. He could take an incident—any incident, no matter how thin or trivial—and by his skill as a writer turn it into something one read thirty years ago and can still read today with admiration and pleasure.

One can see his skill better when the material is skimpy and he has to rely on his ability as a writer. There is nothing in "Che Ti Dice La Patria" that could not have been observed just as well by any journalist reporting on a hasty trip through Fascist Italy—someone is rude, a young man in a shady restaurant says that the two Americans are "worth nothing," an insolent policeman holds them up for fifty lire, that is all—but no journalist could have given us the same feeling of the sinister quality of life in Italy at the time. And when Hemingway ends his description of it in a final poker-faced sentence it stays ended— "Naturally, in such a short trip we had no opportunity to see how things were with the country or the people." "Fifty Grand" is just about as dull a subject as a writer's heart could desire but the story itself can still be reread.

But the real trouble with Hemingway is that he so often has to depend upon his splendid technical equipment to cover up material that is trivial or sensational. For much of the time his stories illustrate a technique in search of a subject. In the general sense of the word Hemingway has no subject. Faulkner shows a passion for technical experiment not unlike Hemingway's, and, like Hemingway's picked up in Paris cafés over a copy of *transition*, but at once he tries to transplant it to Yoknapatawpha County. Sometimes, let us admit, it looks as inappropriate there as a Paris hat on one of the Snopes women, but at least, if we don't like the hat we can get something out of the woman it disguises. Hemingway, on the other hand, is always a displaced person; he has no place to bring his treasures to.

There are times when one feels that Hemingway, like the character in his own "A Clean Well-Lighted Place," is afraid of staying at home with a subject. In his stories one is forever coming upon that characteristic setting of the café, the station restaurant, the waiting room, or the railway carriage—clean, well-lighted, utterly anonymous places. The characters, equally anonymous, emerge suddenly from the shadows where they have been lurking, perform their little scene, and depart again into shadows. Of course, one has to realize that there is a very good technical reason for this. The short story, which is always trying to differentiate itself from the novel and avoid being bogged down in the slow, chronological sequence of events where the novel is supreme, is also seeking a point outside time from which past and future can be viewed simultaneously, and so the *wagon lit* setting of "A Canary for One" represents a point at which wife and husband are still traveling together though already apart—"we were returning to Paris to set up separate residences"—and the railway station setting of "Hills Like White Elephants" the point where the abortion that must change everything for the lovers has already been decided on though it has not yet taken place. The story looks backward and forward, backward to the days when the girl said that the hills were like white elephants and the man was pleased, and forward to a dreary future in which she will never be able to say a thing like that again.

But though this is perfectly true, it forces us to ask whether the technique is not limiting the short-story form so as to reduce it to an essentially minor art. Any realistic art is necessarily a marriage between the importance of the material and the importance of the artistic treatment, but how much of the importance of the material can possibly seep through such rigid artistic control? What has happened to the familiar element in it? If this girl, Jig, is not American, what is she? Does she have parents in England or Ireland or Australia, brothers or sisters, a job, a home to go back to, if against all the indications she decides to have this baby? And the man? Is there any compelling human reason why he should feel that an abortion is necessary or is he merely destructive by nature?

Once more, I know the formal answer to all these questions: that Hemingway's aim is to suppress mere information such as I require so as to concentrate my attention on the one important thing which is the abortion. I know that Hemingway has been influenced by the German Expressionists as well as by Joyce and Gertrude Stein, and that he is reducing (or enlarging) these two people into the parts they would play in a German Expressionist tragedy—*Der Mann* and *Die Frau*—and their problem into the tragedy itself—*Das Fehlgebären*. But I must respectfully submit that I am not German, and that I have no experience of Man, Woman, or Abortion in capital letters.

I submit that there are drawbacks to this method. It is all too abstract. Nobody in Hemingway ever seems to have a job or a home unless the job or the home fits into the German scheme of capital letters. Everybody seems to be permanently on holiday or getting a divorce, or as *Die Frau* in "Hills Like White Elephants" puts it, "That's all we do, isn't it—look at things and try new drinks?" Even in the Wisconsin stories it comes as a relief when Nick's father keeps himself out of harm's way for an hour or two by attending to his profession as doctor.

Even the submerged population that Hemingway writes of is one that is associated with recreation rather than with labor—waiters, barmen, boxers, jockeys, bullfighters, and the like. Paco in "The Capital of the World" is a waiter with a soul above waitering, and he dies by accident in an imitation bullfight that I find comic rather than pathetic. In the later stories the neurotic restlessness has developed out of the earlier fishing and shooting into horse racing, prize fighting, bull fighting, and big-game hunting. Even war is treated as recreation, an amusement for the leisured classes. In these stories practically no single virtue is discussed with the exception of physical courage, which from the point of view of people without an independent income is usually merely a theoretical virtue. Except in war it has little practical application, and even in war the working classes tend to regard it with a certain cynicism: the hero of the regiment is rarely a hero to the regiment.

In Hemingway the obsession with physical courage is clearly a personal problem, like Turgenev's obsession with his own futility, and it must be recognized and discounted as such if one is not to emerge from one's reading with a ludicrously distorted impression of human life. In "The Short Happy Life of Francis Macomber" Francis runs away from a lion, which is what most sensible men would do if faced by a lion, and his wife promptly cuckolds him with the English manager of their big-game hunting expedition. As we all know, good wives admire nothing in a husband except his capacity to deal with lions, so we can sympathize with the poor woman in her trouble. But next day Macomber, faced with a buffalo, suddenly becomes a man of superb courage, and his wife, recognizing that Cressida's occupation's gone and that for the future she must be a virtuous wife, blows his head off. Yet the title leaves us with the comforting assurance that the triumph is still Macomber's, for, in spite of his sticky end, he had at last learned the only way of keeping his wife out of other men's beds.

To say that the psychology of this story is childish would be to waste good words. As farce it ranks with "Ten Nights in a Bar-Room" or any other Victorian morality you can think of. Clearly, it is the working out of a personal problem that for the vast majority of men and women has no validity whatever.

It may be too early to draw any conclusions about Hemingway's work: certainly it is too early for one like myself who belongs to the generation that he influenced most deeply. In a charitable mood, I sometimes find myself thinking of the clean well-lighted place as the sort of stage on which Racine's heroes and heroines appear, free of contact with common things, and carrying on their lofty discussions of what to Racine seemed most important. The rest of the time I merely ask myself if this wonderful technique of Hemingway's is really a technique in search of a subject or a technique that is carefully avoiding a subject, and searching anxiously all the time for a clean well-lighted place where all the difficulties of human life can be comfortably ignored.

CONSIDER THIS

Frank O'Connor was a student of the short story: here, in this analysis of Hemingway's method, he's convinced that he sees the influence of James Joyce on Hemingway. Study closely the ways in which he argues that Hemingway's method of "elegant repetition" is Joycean. Are you convinced?

Reread O'Connor's first paragraph. When do you begin to realize that he isn't a great Hemingway fan?

His essay is taken from *The Lonely Voice,* an exploration of the short story, which, he insists, must arouse the reader's "moral imagination." Hemingway, for him, "does not give the reader enough" for such an arousal; he is "brilliant but thin."

Michael Francis O'Donovan, 1903–1966, was born in Ireland and fought with the Ireland Republican Army during the Irish Revolution; he was imprisoned for his political activities in 1923. In the 1920s, when he began to publish short fiction and essays, he changed his name to Frank O'Connor.

Gettysburg at Night
Robert Olmstead

Mary's father comes over to put kiddie latches inside the cabinet doors. It's one of the jobs Arlen left undone when he died on the road to Shippensburg just like that.

Outside, Mary can hear the roar of lawnmowers. It's been raining for three weeks, but tonight's clear and dry. Up and down the street she can hear the sound of men and boys doing to grass what they wouldn't consider doing to any other living thing unless they were going to eat it and then they'd probably hire someone else to do it.

Mary's twenty and Arlen's twenty-one, but he's been dead for the whole of one of those years and right now she's not sure if it counts. She knows that in Japan they start counting age at conception and she thinks it had to have been a woman to think up such an idea. She wonders if they have any new thoughts on when death begins or whether it's to even be counted into the chronology of a life and it seems that tonight on this anniversary it's all she can think about when she'd rather be asleep in bed.

"That should keep the little tyke out of the Cheerio box for a while," her father says.

"It isn't the Cheerio box I'm worried about. It's the cleansers. The stuff with black skulls and crossbones on the label. The Cheerios he can handle."

Her father nods his head. He's sucking on the finger he jabbed when the Phillips slipped and got him a good one. Mary gives him a Band-Aid and he slips it into his breast pocket saying he'll save it for later, as if it were a cookie or a Hershey bar, something that goes on the inside instead of the outside.

"You all right?" he says.

She smiles and nods her head. She wants to tell him she was just now thinking about driving to Gettysburg at night in Arlen's pickup, his arm around her shoulders and his hand inside the neck of her blouse as if that's where it belonged. When they got there, they went down Confederate Avenue and pulled off beside the road. He laid her down in the cool wet grass under the monument to the boys from Louisiana and when she looked up, the angel's flame was piercing the new moon and Eisenhower's deer fed quietly in the battlefield where some of the thousands died in those three days.

It was at that moment her father became a grandfather and it all happened because she wanted it that way.

"Don't mind me, Pop. It's you I'm worried about. Have you had a tetanus shot?"

"Oh, hell. I've had a lot worse happen to me than a stuck finger."

"I know," she says, taking his finger out of his mouth and looking at it.

"I should have put one of these latches on the door to Arlen's truck," he says, palming a white plastic hook and catch in his other hand and then smiling.

Mary looks up from his finger, then she squeezes it to make it bleed out a little more and slowly shakes her head.

"He would have gotten a big kick out of that. It would have made for a good laugh," she tells him.

"I'm sorry, honey. I didn't mean anything by it."

"It's okay, Pop. It's been a year. We can talk about it if we want. In fact, we probably should."

Mary's father takes back his hand and goes to the dish drainer. He gets a cup and fills it from the coffee pot. She knows he won't take but a few sips and then it will go cold in his hands, the heat escaping up his arms, into the air. Holding cups of coffee is something he does since he stopped smoking. Besides, he has to work in the morning and coffee will only keep him awake. In the morning he'll be at his job, making steel-belted radials at Carlisle Tire and Rubber.

"Did you hear the Mafia bought out A&P?"

"No," she says, "I didn't hear that one. Is it a joke or a song?"

Mary's father looks at her. In his face she can see he's trying so hard to help, but he knows he can't make it right.

"Sometimes I don't understand you," he says. It's a saying he picked up from Arlen, one he falls back on more and more often.

"Sometimes I don't understand myself," she says and this time she thinks it to be true. She thinks it to be all seven sacraments rolled into one. "You better get home," she tells him. "Mom will be worried about you on that damn Route 34 at night."

"Yes, I should," he says and then he's getting ready to leave and then he's gone out the door. She thinks how quickly it happened. She thinks she remembers him kissing her and giving her a hug and asking about supper, but she's not sure. Finally she decides all of those things did happen. She decides she knows and then she sits back down at the table and takes his cup in her hands. It's still warm and she likes that, the feel of the heat already making its way into her wrists.

She sits there remembering how, when Arlen died, she wasn't surprised. He was a dangerous man. He ran the football. He put roofs on houses. It seems she spent her whole young life patching him up. He had a shoulder go out, a blown knee, pinched nerves in his back and fingers that went off at all angles. He was pigeon-toed, limped a bit, walked a little sideways and covered ground quicker than any man alive. So when she heard the news about what happened on the road to Shippensburg, she thought, Oh, Arlen, now look at what you've gone and done.

It's another time. Behind the gymnasium. A girl sits on the bumper of a Pontiac facing the hot August sun and holding her hand up to block it from her eyes.

Her T-shirt hangs wet and loose on her body and her knees are bleeding from a fall she took on the track. Black cinders are embedded in her skin and, God, how she wants to cry because it feels as if they've found a pathway into her very joints, but she already feels so stupid and to cry would only make it worse.

A boy comes out of the side door that goes into the weight room. His body shines in the light of the sun that's making its way to the horizon, where North and South mountains end, quavering in the heat like the backs of bears shaking trees. He benched two hundred and thirty pounds today, so he's full of himself, full of muscles inside his barrel chest and thick arms, muscles gorged with blood and a heart so strong it could lift a freight car on thin cables.

From just outside the door, he sees the girl off in the distance and thinks how pretty she is sitting there like that.

Mary holds the warm cup of coffee in her hands as her memory telescopes one moment into another, so they can all fit inside her head, here and now, and she can know the truth of how it was when they first saw each other.

In that moment when he came over to her, he didn't pick her up and she didn't cry into the sweat that ran down his chest, but she did her best to look at him and she felt what she saw down inside her slight girl body and afterwards they talked about it so many times that it came to be he did pick her up and she did cry and that's what memory will get you.

So tonight she goes back again and she's sitting on the bumper of a Pontiac, her knees black with cinders and the blood welling up in small red blossoms and her slight girl body, more like a young boy's, is filled with a pain that begins that day and never ends, a pain that visits every night about this time, knocking quietly and then letting itself in.

Later they spoke of their deaths, as lovers are prone to do for no good reason.

He said, I hope I die before you do, because I could never live without you, but you could live without me.

She said, Then we'll just have to die together because, boy, you're wrong, you're dead wrong.

But what if we have kids?

All the better she says. There will be someone around left to bury us.

Mary gets up from her chair. The mowers are through for the night and she has no fear that her son will be robbed of his sleep. She will go out and run in the dark. Block by block she can be gone ten minutes at a time, stopping back after each circuit to look in on him. He's got to learn to be alone and what better way to learn than in your sleep.

She changes and checks his room. It's filled with stuff from Disney World, stuff he's too young to know what to do with, but her mom and pop bought it for him anyways when they took him to Florida. His crib is against the wall and next to it is a changing table, something that isn't safe to use anymore because of the way he twists and turns his tiny body. So now she changes him on the floor from where there's no place left to fall.

Down low in the room, there's a night light and some kind of electric fire burning dimly inside its milky bulb. And even lower, Arlen's weights, heavy plates of black steel, Yorks and Billards, lined up along the baseboard. The boy can already pick up the two and a half pounders. He likes to carry them around, holding them high over his head and yelling stuff that doesn't make any sense at all.

Two of the big ones together are heavier than she is. Every time she steps up on them, she feels for a second as if she'll drop through this floor and the next one and by then she'll be going so fast she'll never stop. It happens like that every time.

Tonight, before he left, her father said, yesterday he wasn't even walking and today he's into everything.

But what she heard was, yesterday he was into everything and today he isn't even walking.

Since Arlen died her father talks to her like that. He talks to her like the mother she is and not the daughter she was. Sometimes she thinks her father loved him as much as she did, as much as she still does. It makes her sad to think how much men need each other, how much men need.

She said to her father, they grow up fast, and after she said it, she thought, I want him to grow up strong, too, strong enough to pick up his woman and carry her around the house, carry her around the track. I want him to have a chest that can be thumped like a drum, a fifty-gallon drum, and I hope he's not too awfully smart because too much education can be a dangerous thing.

Now, she's standing on her porch and she sees her man, only it's four years ago and he's across town running for touchdowns. He's a Mustang, a blue chipper, a real stud. Mary stands there and smiles and then she's laughing so hard her sides begin to ache and she's glad the mowers have gone inside because they'd surely think she was ready for the loony bin.

She's laughing at what she sees. It's Arlen on the sideline and his coach is holding him by his face mask, old fingers entwined in steel bows, and he's tapping Arlen's helmet with his knuckles just above the ear hole. He's telling him to *run for daylight, run for daylight.* He can't understand why Arlen runs at people and not away from them, why he's a bull when he could be a deer, why he doesn't get with the contemporary way of playing the game.

Because deer never look up, Arlen wants to say, and every boy from Pennsylvania knows that to be a fact.

After the game, the scout from North Carolina comes by to talk to him and she waits under the goal post.

The scout says, You look real good running under the lights, running over those lardaceous boys from Harrisburg. But I'll tell you one thing, while they're eating quiche at Penn State, in Iowa they're cornfed and in Florida they eat alligators, and in Oklahoma I don't know what they eat, but they wipe their asses with barbwire. Them ol' boys will hand you your head. And another thing, your board scores are pretty low and you'll have to sit out a year.

Arlen tells him to get fucked.

And you have an attitude problem, the scout says. We'll work on it. Come with us and you could be a real sum bitch.

I don't want to be a real sum bitch, Arlen tells him.

You could be a real hero.

I am a hero, Arlen says and goes to her without looking back.

"You tell them," she says. "You tell them that I have enough brains for both of us," and then she's off. She's on the run.

Mary goes down South Street to College, running on the pavement under the soft yellow lights. She decides she wants her son to know his geography, especially the names of mountains. She wants him to know the parts of machines, heavy equipment and how to operate it. He'll say the kinds of things men say. He'll know how to sharpen a knife and shoot more than one kind of gun. He'll know how to bind up wounds and how to inflict pain if it comes right down to it. He'll make decisions, right or wrong, and in his head he'll carry around a list of people he'll be willing to die for. He'll be the proper height, know how to love a woman and bury his dead.

She goes up Chapel and down West back to her house. Her son is still sleeping so she's off again.

And this time it's the White Oak Inn four years ago. She and Arlen are making the run to Perry County because they're too young to drink at home, but nobody gives it a mind up there in the mountains. They cross the Conodoguinet and the Tuscarora Trail, climbing the thousand feet from the valley floor to the land where he's a star and she's his girl and what the hell, he just single-handedly kicked the shit out of Cumberland Valley not more than two hours ago.

He did it with his shoulder out and only now is it safely wrapped tight to his body, taped and trussed with wide white bandages, hand against chest, hand around beer bottle.

She stays to his left side so it won't be bumped by all the folks who want to wish him well, who want to touch him. For the first time in her life she and a man are breaking hearts, leaving them in small pieces on the floor.

She thinks as she crosses Mooreland under the streetlight, God damn it, we were half in the grave that very night when you went for the gas at every turn and I kept saying, *faster, faster.*

For a moment she thinks she will begin to cry, cry so hard it will kill her, cry because he left her behind to raise their son all alone, to live this life. But she doesn't. She makes her turns and goes back to South where her son is still asleep on his stomach. She lingers at the crib, wanting to wake him, wanting him to be her man.

She's off again to make her blocks, to match time and distance and with every circuit she finds that distance expands and time diminishes and she's laughing about it because that's her life and that's how she lives it and there hasn't been a physics book written yet that can teach those kinds of laws.

From West Pomfret she tries to get back to South down an alley drive and she falls hard in the road. She gets up fast as if she's been burned in fire and raises her arms high in the air. She steps out on the balls of her feet, her pelvis thrust forward as the pain comes like cold glass being shattered inside her legs, over and over again and she wishes Arlen were there to pick her up and make it August, the way he should have when he had a chance. He'd be shirtless. There'd be sunlight, sweat on sweat, bone on bone.

It's then she thinks she might be going just a little bit crazy, but she doesn't mind in the least because if she is, it would be the first thing she ever did in moderation. It would be nice for a change to do something just a little bit at a time.

She remembers sitting there on the bumper of the Pontiac, her hand blocking out the sun and her knees bloody. She thinks he said something like, you're a skinny girl. I never had a skinny girl before.

And she said, I'm not a skinny girl. I'm a skinny woman and you never had one of those either.

Mary turns onto South. In the fifteen minutes she's been gone, the secret Amish have come again. Tonight they've left her bacon and scrapple and shoo-fly pie. In the past it's been other kinds of pie, other parts of the hog. They come every few weeks and leave a basket of food on the porch in front of her door.

She wonders if the secret Amish watch over her when she runs like this at night, slicing off pieces of Carlisle Township block by block each time she drops her shoulder and makes another turn.

She imagines them in the shadows, dressed in black with long beards, watching her pass by in her powder-blue nylon shorts, running shoes and Arlen's old mesh jersey, the numbers so big she has to tie a knot at her waist and it still billows out behind her.

They must have a secret society, she thinks, that does these penitent things. If they only knew how those parts of the hog and the heavy baked goods sit on her porch the way they do, between her and her men, they would stop bringing them. They'd let bygones be bygones. They'd leave her alone.

She'll have to step over what they've left so she can get inside to check her son. She's done it before but tonight she doesn't know if she can because, Lord, the pain in her legs is just now starting to break all over again.

She's off and she's praying that the boys who've been stealing hood ornaments will steal the basket of food left by the secret Amish before she gets back.

She's running in pain, but she's on another wind, one that's beyond second and closer to the seventh or eighth, one that's doing eighty-five miles an hour and still climbing. She's been up there before, wiping her shoes on that threshold of hurt. It lessens after the first block and she must confess she misses it because it has come to be the one constant, the one immutable condition she's experienced these last twelve months. She thinks how fast that man loved to drive.

Pain, my old friend, she thinks, her shoes padding silently, one after the other, sparks going off in her shins.

I will try it this way, she whispers. Arlen became a siding mechanic and then a contractor. He branched out into roofing and insulation. His men had to run to keep up with him and he was only twenty and a bull.

On rainy days, he took them to Harrisburg, to the peep shows. He gave them each a roll of quarters and then went out to bid jobs. He went back to pick them up two hours later. It made him a pretty good boss man. She knows that, because they told her so.

His body was always cut and sliced from handling extrusions, coil stock, flashing and spouting. Down the bicep, across the chest, back of the forearm. She followed the openings like the lines on a map, tracking his body through the channels left by steel and aluminum edges. It was always a good trip, a fine vacation. The kind that was always worth taking.

She's now far from home and in her heart she's content that her son is safe in his sleep. She goes down Orange, crosses High Street, the railroad tracks, and keeps running, past street after street, knowing where she's wanted to go all night long.

At the end of Orange is the high school and to the right of it is the football field surrounded by the track and the stadium. She does four laps, all the while looking in on the field, at the grass, white with dew in the moonlight. She does a mile of circles around the rectangle where her husband used to run like a bull, four autumns in a row on Friday nights.

She can see herself sitting on the bumper of a Pontiac, her hand blocking the sun. She hears him say, you're the new one. The one who comes from the South.

She says, yes, I'm the new one. The one who comes from the South.

And her father said, it seems like one day he was here and the next day he was gone, and she didn't say a single word because she knows these sayings to be true.

This is where Mary ran track and Arlen ran the football. The day in October they went to Mt. Holly to buy the giant pumpkin, they had an argument over who was faster. He told her he could pick her up and carry her and still beat her.

She laughed and told him how stupid that was. No matter what, she'd cross the line first, either on her own or in his arms.

No you wouldn't, he said, and then after they'd driven another two miles he said without looking at her, I run through you, and she felt those words down inside her body.

And then they were in Mt. Holly buying their pumpkin, a fifty-pounder. The man said take it for free, a gift for laying waste to Mechanicsburg last week. Arlen made him take the five bucks anyways, telling him that now he was flush, but someday he might not be and when that time came, he'd take one for free.

And while we're at it, he said, let it stand for the son I plan and the one you have.

When they got back in the pick up, she said, how you talk, boy. How you talk.

Two years later in Gettysburg at night, just as the angel's flame pierces the new moon, he tells her she has all the names of Jesus' women and she says it again, how you talk, boy. How you talk.

So they drove to Caledonia with the pumpkin in the back against the tailgate. Mary sang along with the radio, her hand on his thigh and then, from a side road, one blind to traffic, a car pulled out and Arlen had to lock up the brakes. That pumpkin flew the length of the bed and into the rear window, a slider he'd installed, smashing it to smithereens. An explosion of pumpkin and tiny squares of glass. He made a joke about how that could have been their heads and now he's dead and isn't that the damnedest thing you ever heard.

Mary ducks her shoulder and runs onto the field. She's running the way her man used to run, in straight lines with destinations. She thinks about Arlen, who a year ago was on his way to Shippensburg to bid a job. At Lees Cross Roads he crested a hill, one where he always liked to give it the gas and catch a little air on the other side. But this time in his lane there was an Amishman with a skittish horse, his buggy crossways in the road.

When Arlen touched down, he pulled hard to the right, taking his chances in the cornfield without even knowing that some time back, he'd already used up the last one that God gave him. The truck cleared the ditch, bulldozed into the banking and then went end over end across the corn stubble, five thousand pounds of tumbling steel, gouging the earth wherever it touched, spewing out pump jacks, roofjacks, drip edge, hand tools, siding, roofing, a ladder and a man.

And it was then he really was a hero, just like that.

Mary leans back against a goal post and then walks her way down to the wet grass. She thinks about her house across town, a house he bought for her after only a year in business. It's the house where her son sleeps. It's the house where she and Arlen slept. She thinks how tired she is just now and how she's already run so far.

Tonight, she thinks of her men in that house. She knows them to be there by the jobs they've done, by the jobs they've left undone and by the jobs they've yet to do.

She stands and stretches, her back arched, her chest out, her wrists pointing to the ground and her slight body, wet with dew and sweat. She smiles, taking joy in that her men know how to love a woman, know how to love her.

CONSIDER THIS

Olmstead has said that "what makes a good story is inviting readers into your world and making them part of it all." Do you feel "invited in" to Mary's world? Olmstead uses a flashback technique, and not until the last page do we find out the last of the "facts," exactly how Mary's husband was killed. How does Olmstead keep our interest in the meantime? Are you held by the details of Mary's life? (There are a lot of details to attend to. "Gettysburg at Night" is a busy place.)

Are there any subtexts in this story? Consider this: As Mary runs (her running, past and present, provides much of the narrative framework), she must repeatedly circle back to check on her sleeping son. How is Mary, who says to Arlen that she is a woman, not a girl, and that "she has enough brains for both of us," *defined* by the men in her life?

Robert Olmstead, who was born in 1954 in Keene, New Hampshire, has worked as a carpenter, mill worker, dishwasher, and farmer and is presently writer-in-residence at Dickinson College.

I Stand Here Ironing
Tillie Olsen

I stand here ironing, and what you asked me moves tormented back and forth with the iron.

"I wish you would manage the time to come in and talk with me about your daughter. I'm sure you can help me understand her. She's a youngster who needs help and whom I'm deeply interested in helping."

"Who needs help. . . ." Even if I came, what good would it do? You think because I am her mother I have a key, or that in some way you could use me as a key? She has lived for nineteen years. There is all that life that has happened outside of me, beyond me.

And when is there time to remember, to sift, to weigh, to estimate, to total? I will start and there will be an interruption and I will have to gather it all together again. Or I will become engulfed with all I did or did not do, with what should have been and what cannot be helped.

She was a beautiful baby. The first and only one of our five that was beautiful at birth. You do not guess how new and uneasy her tenancy in her now-loveliness. You did not know her all those years she was thought homely, or see her poring over her baby pictures, making me tell her over and over how beautiful she had been—and would be, I would tell her—and was now, to the seeing eye. But the seeing eyes were few or nonexistent. Including mine.

I nursed her. They feel that's important nowadays. I nursed all the children, but with her, with all the fierce rigidity of first motherhood, I did like the books said. Though her cries battered me to trembling and my breasts ached with swollenness, I waited till the clock decreed.

Why do I put that first? I do not even know if it matters, or if it explains anything.

She was a beautiful baby. She blew shining bubbles of sound. She loved motion, loved light, loved color and music and textures. She would lie on the floor in her blue overalls patting the surface so hard in ecstasy her hands and feet would blur. She was a miracle to me, but when she was eight months old I had to leave her daytimes with the woman downstairs to whom she was no miracle at all, for I worked or looked for work and for Emily's father, who "could no longer endure" (he wrote in his goodbye note) "sharing want" with us.

I was nineteen. It was the pre-relief, pre-WPA* world of the depression. I would start running as soon as I got off the streetcar, running up the stairs, the place smelling sour, and, awake or asleep to startle awake, when she saw me she would break into a clogged weeping that could not be comforted, a weeping I can yet hear.

After a while I found a job hashing at night so I could be with her days, and it was better. But it came to where I had to bring her to his family and leave her.

It took a long time to raise the money for her fare back. Then she got chicken pox and I had to wait longer. When she finally came, I hardly knew her, walking quick and nervous like her father, looking like her father, thin, and dressed in a shoddy red that yellowed her skin and glared at the pock marks. All the baby loveliness gone.

---

* Works Progress Administration, a government jobs program of the 1930s.

She was two. Old enough for nursery school, they said, and I did not know then what I know now—the fatigue of the long day, and the lacerations of group life in the kinds of nurseries that are only parking places for children.

Except that it would have made no difference if I had known. It was the only place there was. It was the only way we could be together, the only way I could hold a job.

And even without knowing, I knew. I knew that the teacher was evil because all these years it has curdled into my memory, the little boy hunched in the corner, her rasp, "Why aren't you outside, because Alvin hits you? That's no reason, go out, scaredy." I knew Emily hated it even if she did not clutch and implore, "Don't go, Mommy," like the other children, mornings.

She always had a reason why we should stay home. Momma, you look sick. Momma, I feel sick. Momma, the teachers aren't there today, they're sick. Momma, we can't go, there was a fire there last night. Momma it's a holiday today, no school, they told me.

But never a direct protest, never rebellion. I think of our others in their three-, four-year-oldness—the explosions, the tempers, the denunciations, the demands—and I feel suddenly ill. I put the iron down. What in me demanded that goodness in her? And what was the cost, the cost to her of such goodness?

The old man living in the back once said in his gentle way, "You should smile at Emily more when you look at her." What was in my face when I looked at her? I loved her. There were all the acts of love.

It was only with the others I remembered what he said, and it was the face of joy, and not of care or tightness or worry I turned to them—too late for Emily. She does not smile easily, let alone almost always, as her brothers and sisters do. Her face is closed and sombre, but when she wants, how fluid. You must have seen it in her pantomimes, you spoke of her rare gift for comedy on the stage that rouses a laughter out of the audience so dear they applaud and applaud and do not want to let her go.

Where does it come from, that comedy? There was none of it in her when she came back to me that second time, after I had had to send her away again. She had a new daddy now to learn to love, and I think perhaps it was a better time. Except when we left her alone nights, telling ourselves she was old enough.

"Can't you go some other time, Mommy, like tomorrow?" she would ask. "Will it be just a little while you'll be gone? Do you promise?"

The time we came back, the front door open, the clock on the floor in the hall. She rigid awake. "It wasn't just a little while. I didn't cry. Three times I called you, just three times, and then I went downstairs to open the door so you could come faster. The clock talked loud, I threw it away, it scared me what it talked."

She said the clock talked loud that night I went to the hospital to have Susan. She was delirious with the fever that comes before red measles, but she was fully conscious all the week I was gone and the week after we were home when she could not come near the new baby or me.

She did not get well. She stayed skeleton thin, not wanting to eat, and night after night she had nightmares. She would call for me, and I would rouse from exhaustion to sleepily call back, "You'll be all right, darling, go to sleep, it's just a dream," and if she still called, in a sterner voice, "now go to sleep, Emily, there's nothing to hurt you." Twice, only twice, when I had to get up for Susan anyhow, I went in to sit with her.

Now when it is too late (as if she would let me hold and comfort her like I do the others) I get up and go to her at her moan or restless stirring. "Are you awake, Emily? Can I get you something?" And the answer is always the same: "No, I'm all right, go back to sleep, Mother."

They persuaded me at the clinic to send her away to a convalescent home in the country where "she can have the kind of food and care you can't manage for her, and you'll be free to concentrate on the new baby." They still send children to that place. I see pictures on the society page of sleek young women planning affairs to raise money for it, or dancing at the affairs, or decorating Easter eggs or filling Christmas stockings for the children.

They never have a picture of the children, so I do not know if they still wear those gigantic red bows and the ravaged looks on the every other Sunday when parents can come to visit "unless otherwise notified"—as we were notified the first six weeks.

Oh it is a handsome place, green lawns and tall trees and fluted flower beds. High up on the balconies of each cottage the children stand, the girls in their red bows and white dresses, the boys in white suits and giant red ties. The parents stand below shrieking up to be heard and the children shriek down to be heard, and between them the invisible wall "Not To Be Contaminated by Parental Germs or Physical Affection."

There was a tiny girl who always stood hand in hand with Emily. Her parents never came. One visit she was gone. "They moved her to Rose Cottage," Emily shouted in explanation. "They don't like you to love anybody here."

She wrote once a week, the labored writing of a seven-year-old. "I am fine. How is the baby. If I write my leter nicly I will have a star. Love." There never was a star. We wrote every other day, letters she could never hold or keep but only hear read—once. "We simply do not have room for children to keep any personal possessions," they patiently explained when we pieced one Sunday's shrieking together to plead how much it would mean to Emily to be allowed to keep her letters and cards.

Each visit she looked frailer. "She isn't eating," they told us. (They had runny eggs for breakfast or mush with lumps, Emily said later, I'd hold it in my mouth and not swallow. Nothing ever tasted good, just when they had chicken.)

It took us eight months to get her released home, and only the fact that she gained back so little of her seven lost pounds convinced the social worker.

I used to try to hold and love her after she came back, but her body would stay stiff, and after a while she'd push away. She ate little. Food sickened her, and I think much of life too. Oh, she had physical lightness and brightness, twinkling by on skates, bouncing like a ball up and down up and down over the jump rope, skimming over the hill; but these were momentary.

She fretted about her appearance, thin and dark and foreign-looking at a time when every little girl was supposed to look or thought she should look a chubby blond replica of Shirley Temple. The doorbell sometimes rang for her, but no one seemed to come and play in the house or be a best friend. Maybe because we moved so much.

There was a boy she loved painfully through two school semesters. Months later she told me how she had taken pennies from my purse to buy him candy. "Licorice was his favorite and I brought him some every day, but he still liked Jenifer better'n me. Why, Mommy?" the kind of question for which there is no answer.

School was a worry to her. She was not glib or quick, in a world where glibness and quickness were easily confused with ability to learn. To her overworked and exasperated teachers she was an overconscientious "slow learner" who kept trying to catch up and was absent entirely too often.

I let her be absent, though sometimes the illness was imaginary. How different from my now-strictness about attendance with the others. I wasn't working. We had a new baby, I was home anyhow. Sometimes, after Susan grew old enough, I would keep her home from school, too, to have them all together.

Mostly Emily had asthma, and her breathing, harsh and labored, would fill the house with a curiously tranquil sound. I would bring the two old dresser mirrors and her boxes of collections to her bed. She would select beads and single earrings, bottle tops and shells, dried flowers and pebbles, old postcards and scraps, all sorts of oddments; then she and Susan would play Kingdom, setting up landscapes and furniture, peopling them with action.

Those were the only times of peaceful companionship between her and Susan. I have edged away from it, that poisonous feeling between them, that terrible balancing of hurts and needs I had to do between the two, and did so badly, those earlier years.

Oh there are conflicts between the others too, each one human, needing, demanding, hurting, taking—but only between Emily and Susan, no, Emily toward Susan, that corroding resentment. It seems so obvious on the surface, yet it is not obvious. Susan, the second child, Susan, golden and curly-haired and chubby, quick and articulate and assured, everything in appearance and manner Emily was not; Susan, not able to resist Emily's precious things, losing or sometimes clumsily breaking them; Susan telling jokes and riddles to company for applause while Emily sat silent (to say to me later: That was *my* riddle, Mother, I told it to Susan); Susan, who for all the five years' difference in age was just a year behind Emily in developing physically.

I am glad for that slow physical development that widened the difference between her and her contemporaries, though she suffered over it. She was too vulnerable for that terrible world of youthful competition, of preening and parading, of constant measuring of yourself against every other, of envy, "If I had that copper hair," or "If I had that skin. . . ." She tormented herself enough about not looking like the others, there was enough of the unsureness, the having to be conscious of words before you speak, the constant caring— what are they thinking of me?—without having it all magnified unendurably by the merciless physical drives.

Ronnie is calling. He is wet and I change him. It is rare there is such a cry now. That time of motherhood is almost behind me when the ear is not one's own but must always be racked and listening for the child cry, the child call. We sit for a while and I hold him, looking out over the city spread in charcoal with its soft aisles of light. *"Shoogily,"* he breathes and curls closer. I carry him back to bed, asleep. *Shoogily.* A funny word, a family word, inherited from Emily, invented by her to say: comfort. In this and other ways she leaves her seal, I say aloud. And startle at my saying it. What do I mean? What did I start to gather together, to try and make coherent? I was at the terrible, growing years. War years. I do not remember them well. I was working, there were four smaller ones now, there was not time for her. She had to help be a mother, and housekeeper, and shopper. She had to set her seal. Mornings of crisis and near-hysteria trying to get lunches packed, hair combed, coats and shoes found, everyone to school or Child Care on time, the baby ready for transportation. And always the paper scribbled on by a smaller one, the book looked at by Susan then mislaid, the homework not done. Running out to that huge school where she was one, she was lost, she was a drop; suffering over the unpreparedness, stammering and unsure in her classes.

There was so little time left at night after the kids were bedded down. She would struggle over books, always eating (it was in those years she developed her enormous appetite that is legendary in our family) and I would be ironing, or preparing food for the next day, or writing V-mail to Bill, or tending the baby. Sometimes, to make me laugh, or out of her despair, she would imitate happenings or types at school.

I think I said once, "Why don't you do something like this in the school amateur show?" One morning she phoned me at work, hardly understandable through the weeping: "Mother, I did it. I won, I won; they gave me first prize; they clapped and clapped and wouldn't let me go."

Now suddenly she was Somebody, and as imprisoned in her difference as she had been in her anonymity.

She began to be asked to perform at other high schools, even in colleges, then at city and state-wide affairs. The first one we went to, I only recognized her that first moment when, thin, shy, she almost drowned herself into the curtains. Then: Was this Emily? The control, the command, the convulsing and deadly clowning, the spell, then the roaring, stamping audience, unwilling to let this rare and precious laughter out of their lives.

Afterwards: You ought to do something about her with a gift like that—but without money or knowing how, what does one do? We have left it all to her, and the gift has as often eddied inside, clogged and clotted, as been used and growing.

She is coming. She runs up the stairs two at a time with her light graceful step, and I know she is happy tonight. Whatever it was that occasioned your call did not happen today.

"Aren't you ever going to finish the ironing, Mother? Whistler painted his mother in a rocker. I'd have to paint mine standing over an ironing board." This is one of her communicative nights and she tells me everything and nothing as she fixes herself a plate of food out of the icebox.

She is so lovely. Why did you want me to come in at all? Why were you concerned? She will find her way.

She starts up the stairs to bed. "Don't get me up with the rest in the morning." "But I thought you were having midterms." "Oh those," she comes back in, kisses me, and says quite lightly, "in a couple of years when we'll all be atom-dead they won't matter a bit."

She has said it before. She *believes* it. But because I have been dredging the past, and all that compounds a human being is so heavy and meaningful in me, I cannot endure it tonight.

I will never total it all. I will never come in to say: she was a child seldom smiled at. Her father left me before she was a year old. I had to work her first six years when there was work, or I sent her home and to his relatives. There were years she had care she hated. She was dark and thin and foreign-looking in a world where the prestige went to blondness and curly hair and dimples; she was slow where glibness was prized. She was a child of anxious, not proud, love. We were poor and could not afford for her the soil of easy growth.

I was a young mother, I was a distracted mother. There were the other children pushing up, demanding. Her younger sister seemed all that she was not. There were years she did not want me to touch her. She kept too much in herself, her life was such she had to keep too much in herself. My wisdom came too late. She has much to her and probably little will come of it. She is a child of her age, of depression, of war, of fear.

Let her be. So all that is in her will not bloom—but in how many does it? There is still enough left to live by. Only help her to know—help make it so there is cause for her to know—that she is more than this dress on the ironing board, helpless before the iron.

CONSIDER THIS

Ursula Le Guin says that "writers who are mothers haven't talked much about their motherhood." Tillie Olsen (born in Omaha in 1913) is one writer-mother who has. In "I Stand Here Ironing," Olsen presents her great theme, the thwarting of the individual's life promise, within the framework of a mother's fiercely realized recollections of the babyhood and girlhood of her oldest daughter.

There is little present action in the story. The narrator irons, and remembers. Her daughter comes home, eats, talks to her mother, and goes up to bed. We don't know where they live, what the house is like. We don't know what kind of school Emily goes to now. What we are given are indelible, sometimes terrible memories, almost unbearable to the mother—of the sick child, of the "convalescent home" Emily was exiled to when she was seven, of Emily's tortured relationship with her little sister. We have "clogged weeping," "poisonous feeling," "corroding resentment," even evil (Emily's nursery school teacher).

Are there any counterpoints to the images of sadness and despair?

How do you leave the story? With a sense of hopelessness? Of strength? Of endurance? Do you agree with the narrator that her wisdom has come "too late"?

A Hanging
George Orwell

It was in Burma, a sodden morning of the rains. A sickly light, like yellow tinfoil, was slanting over the high walls into the jail yard. We were waiting outside the condemned cells, a row of sheds fronted with double bars, like small animal cages. Each cell measured about ten feet by ten and was quite bare within except for a plank bed and a pot for drinking water. In some of them brown silent men were squatting at the inner bars, with their blankets draped round them. These were the condemned men, due to be hanged within the next week or two.

One prisoner had been brought out of his cell. He was a Hindu, a puny wisp of a man, with a shaven head and vague liquid eyes. He had a thick, sprouting moustache, absurdly too big for his body, rather like the moustache of a comic man on the films. Six tall Indian warders were guarding him and getting him ready for the gallows. Two of them stood by with rifles and fixed bayonets, while the others handcuffed him, passed a chain through the handcuffs and fixed it to their belts, and lashed his arms tight to his sides. They crowded very close about him, with their hands always on him in a careful, caressing grip, as though all the while feeling him to make sure he was there. It was like men handling a fish which is still alive and may jump back into the water. But he stood quite unresisting, yielding his arms limply to the ropes, as though he hardly noticed what was happening.

Eight o'clock struck and a bugle call, desolately thin in the wet air, floated from the distant barracks. The superintendent of the jail, who was standing apart from the rest of us, moodily prodding the gravel with his stick, raised his head at the sound. He was an army doctor, with a gray toothbrush moustache and a gruff voice. "For God's sake hurry up, Francis," he said irritably. "The man ought to have been dead by this time. Aren't you ready yet?"

Francis, the head jailor, a fat Dravidian in a white drill suit and gold spectacles, waved his black hand. "Yes sir, yes sir," he bubbled. "All iss satisfactorily prepared. The hangman iss waiting. We shall proceed."

"Well, quick march, then. The prisoners can't get their breakfast till this job's over."

We set out for the gallows. Two warders marched on either side of the prisoner, with their rifles at the slope; two others marched close against him, gripping him by arm and shoulder, as though at once pushing and supporting him. The rest of us, magistrates and the like, followed behind. Suddenly, when we had gone ten yards, the procession stopped short without any order or warning. A dreadful thing had happened—a dog, come goodness knows whence, had appeared in the yard. It came bounding among us with a loud volley of barks, and leapt round us wagging its whole body, wild with glee at finding so many human beings together. It was a large woolly dog, half Airedale, half pariah. For a moment it pranced round us, and then, before anyone could stop it, it had made a dash for the prisoner and, jumping up, tried to lick his face. Everyone stood aghast, too taken aback even to grab at the dog.

"Who let that bloody brute in here?" said the superintendent angrily. "Catch it, someone!"

A warder, detached from the escort, charged clumsily after the dog, but it danced and gamboled just out of his reach, taking everything as part of the game. A young Eurasian jailer picked up a handful of gravel and tried to stone the dog away, but it dodged the stones and came after us again. Its yaps echoed from the jail walls. The prisoner, in the grasp of the two wardens, looked on incuriously, as though this was another formality of the hanging. It was several minutes before someone managed to catch the dog. Then we put my handkerchief through its collar and moved off once more, with the dog still straining and whimpering.

It was about forty yards to the gallows. I watched the bare brown back of the prisoner marching in front of me. He walked clumsily with his bound arms, but quite steadily, with that bobbing gait of the Indian who never straightens his knees. At each step his muscles slid neatly into place, the lock of hair on his scalp danced up and down, his feet printed themselves on the wet gravel. And once, in spite of the men who gripped him by each shoulder, he stepped slightly aside to avoid a puddle on the path.

It is curious, but till that moment I had never realized what it means to destroy a healthy, conscious man. When I saw the prisoner step aside to avoid the puddle I saw the mystery, the unspeakable wrongness of cutting a life short when it is in full tide. This man was not dying, he was alive just as we are alive. All the organs of his body were working—bowels digesting food, skin renewing itself, nails growing, tissues forming—all toiling away in solemn foolery. His nails would still be growing when he stood on the drop, when he was falling through the air with a tenth of a second to live. His eyes saw the yellow gravel and the gray walls, and his brain still remembered, foresaw, reasoned—reasoned even about puddles. He and we were a party of men walking together, seeing, hearing, feeling, understanding the same world; and in two minutes, with a sudden snap, one of us would be gone—one mind less, one world less.

The gallows stood in a small yard, separate from the main grounds of the prison, and overgrown with tall prickly weeds. It was a brick erection like three sides of a shed, with planking on top, and above that two beams and a crossbar with the rope dangling. The hangman, a gray-haired convict in the white uniform of the prison, was waiting beside his machine. He greeted us with a servile crouch as we entered. At a word from Francis the two warders, gripping the prisoner more closely than ever, half led half pushed him to the gallows and helped him clumsily up the ladder. Then the hangman climbed up and fixed the rope round the prisoner's neck.

We stood waiting, five yards away. The warders had formed in a rough circle round the gallows. And then, when the noose was fixed, the prisoner began crying out to his god. It was a high, reiterated cry of "Ram! Ram! Ram! Ram!" not urgent and fearful like a prayer or cry for help, but steady, rhythmical, almost like the tolling of a bell. The dog answered the sound with a whine. The hangman, still standing on the gallows, produced a small cotton bag like a flour bag and drew it down over the prisoner's face. But the sound, muffled by the cloth, still persisted, over and over again: "Ram! Ram! Ram! Ram! Ram!"

The hangman climbed down and stood ready, holding the lever. Minutes seemed to pass. The steady, muffled crying from the prisoner went on and on, "Ram! Ram! Ram!" never faltering for an instant. The superintendent, his head on his chest, was slowly poking the ground with his stick; perhaps he was counting the cries, allowing the prisoner a fixed number—fifty, perhaps, or a hundred. Everyone had changed color. The Indians had gone gray like bad coffee, and one or two of the bayonets were wavering. We looked at the lashed, hooded man on the drop, and listened to his cries—each cry another second of life; the same thought was in all our minds: oh, kill him quickly, get it over, stop that abominable noise!

Suddenly the superintendent made up his mind. Throwing up his head he made a swift motion with his stick. "Chalo!" he shouted almost fiercely.

There was a clanking noise, and then dead silence. The prisoner had vanished, and the rope was twisting on itself. I let go of the dog, and it galloped immediately to the back of the gallows; but when it got there it stopped short, barked, and then retreated into a corner of the yard, where it stood among the weeds, looking timorously out at us. We went round the gallows to inspect the prisoner's body. He was dangling with his toes pointed straight downward, very slowly revolving, as dead as a stone.

The superintendent reached out with his stick and poked the bare brown body; it oscillated slightly. "*He's* all right," said the superintendent. He backed out from under the gallows, and blew out a deep breath. The moody look had gone out of his face quite suddenly. He glanced at his wrist watch. "Eight minutes past eight. Well, that's all for this morning, thank God."

The warders unfixed bayonets and marched away. The dog, sobered and conscious of having misbehaved itself, slipped after them. We walked out of the gallows yard, past the condemned cells with their waiting prisoners, into the big central yard of the prison. The convicts, under the command of warders armed with lathis, were already receiving their breakfast. They squatted in long rows, each man holding a tin pannikin, while two warders with buckets marched around ladling out rice; it seemed quite a homely, jolly scene, after the hanging. An enormous relief had come upon us now that the job was done. One felt an impulse to sing, to break into a run, to snigger. All at once everyone began chattering gaily.

The Eurasian boy walking beside me nodded towards the way we had come, with a knowing smile: "Do you know, sir, our friend (he meant the dead man) when he heard his appeal had been dismissed, he pissed on the floor of his cell. From fright. Kindly take one of my cigarettes, sir. Do you not admire my new silver case, sir? From the boxwallah, two rupees eight annas. Classy European style."

Several people laughed—at what, nobody seemed certain.

Francis was walking by the superintendent, talking garrulously: "Well, sir, all has passed off with the utmost satisfactoriness. It was all finished—flick! like that. It iss not always so—oah, no! I have known cases where the doctor wass obliged to go beneath the gallows and pull the prissoner' legs to ensure decease. Most disagreeable!"

"Wriggling about, eh? That's bad," said the superintendent.

"Ach, sir, it iss worse when they become refractory! One man, I recall, clung to the bars of hiss cage when we went to take him out. You will scarcely credit, sir, that it took six warders to dislodge him, three pulling at each leg. We reasoned with him, 'My dear fellow,' we said, 'think of all the pain and trouble you are causing to us!' But, no, he would not listen! Ach, he wass very troublesome!"

I found that I was laughing quite loudly. Everyone was laughing. Even the superintendent grinned in a tolerant way. "You'd better all come out and have a drink," he said quite genially. "I've got a bottle of whisky in the car. We could do with it."

We went through the big double gates of the prison into the road. "Pulling at his legs!" exclaimed a Burmese magistrate suddenly, and burst into a loud chuckling. We all began laughing again. At that moment Francis's anecdote seemed extraordinarily funny. We all had a drink together, native and European alike, quite amicably. The dead man was a hundred yards away.

CONSIDER THIS

Eric Blair's adoption of the pen name George Orwell signaled a major shift in his life. After a privileged education—he was educated at preparatory school and at England's most exclusive boarding school, Eton—he went to work for the British colonial police in Burma, keeping the native Burmese "in their place." What he witnessed there—British colonial arrogance—drove him toward a democratic anti-imperialist socialism: so his life story encapsulates one of the major stands of twentieth-century history, the demise of colonialism. He had the strength and the courage to pay for his conversion, and for many years had difficulty in making ends meet. Orwell retained throughout his life an uncompromising sympathy for the nobodies of the world: in the last analysis, his concern was rooted in a reverence for life, but his way of putting it was always modest and low-keyed. Orwell had the intelligence to see the abuse of power for what it was and the courage to say so: he could not be silenced.

Look again at "A Hanging." Orwell places a separate paragraph of evaluation—"It is curious, but . . ." —almost exactly in the middle of his narrative. Is this effective? Does it allow us also to draw back from the horror of the scene and reflect on it from a distance? Does his explicit moralizing weaken or strengthen his narrative?

Remove the dog from the narrative: what is the effect?

Does it matter that we don't know the nature of the crime for which the man was executed?

Who is the villain of the piece?

What's the Real Message of 'Casablanca'?
Or of a Rose?
Maya Pines

What does it mean when a man wears cowboy boots, even though he lives in a city? Why do advertisements often show laughing young women being carried piggy-back by young men? And what accounts for the extraordinarily enduring appeal of the movie "Casablanca"?

The world is filled with such questions, say members of a rapidly growing and fashionable academic discipline called "semiotics," which has influenced the study of English, comparative literature, philosophy, religion, sociology, political science, anthropology and other fields.

Everything we do sends messages about us in a variety of codes, semioticians contend. We are also on the receiving end of innumerable messages encoded in music, gestures, foods, rituals, books, movies or advertisements. Yet we seldom realize that we have received or sent such messages, and would have trouble explaining the rules under which they operate.

Semiotics is an attempt to decipher these rules and bring them to our consciousness. Though its name comes from a Greek root meaning "sign" and semiotics is often defined as the study of signs, in fact it has become the study of the codes through which people communicate, verbally or nonverbally. Understanding these codes should give us a clearer view of our own actions and those of others, semioticians say, as well as a new way of thinking about books, movies, art and foreign cultures.

Nothing seems too trivial or too complicated for semioticians to analyze. Take the matter of cowboy boots, for instance. A New Yorker who buys such boots is actually responding to well-established myths about the cowboy in our culture, and also to the new power of the oil millionaires and ranchers who support the Reagan Administration, says Dr. Marshall Blonsky, a semiotician in the department of comparative literature at the State University of New York at Stony Brook.

"In both myths, the wearer of cowboy boots handles the world masterfully," says Dr. Blonsky. "He is virile, self-reliant, free to roam over the wide-open spaces that New Yorkers lack, and has or supplies virtually limitless energy." Nobody cares that real cowboys often lead humdrum lives, he points out. New Yorkers don't want real cowboy boots—just the *idea* of cowboy boots. So they buy boots made of lizard or snake that serve as symbols or signs of cowboy boots, in which they can roam the city with a feeling of power, but wouldn't be much good for rounding up cattle.

"Semiotics is the discipline of studying everything that can be used in order to lie," declares Dr. Umberto Eco, holder of the world's first professorship in semiotics (at the University of Bologna, Italy). Therefore semiotics can be used to see through lies or efforts at manipulation, from individual attempts at conveying a macho image to worldwide efforts at promoting certain ideologies.

The method of semiotics is, first, to separate an act, called "the signifier," from its meaning, called "the signified." When a man offers a woman a red rose, for instance, the signifier is the act of giving the rose, but the signified is romance. The rose itself has little importance.

To understand the signified, the semiotician looks for connotations—meanings that have been attached to a signifier by its history of use, or by other aspects of our culture. According to Dr. Blonsky, the key question is: "Where have I seen this before?"

Why, for instance, do men playfully attack women with pillows or sprays of water, or else carry women on their backs, in some advertisements? The sociologist Erving Goffman, who analyzed male and female roles in his book, "Gender Advertisements," noted that he had seen exactly the same kind of "mock assaults" when men play with children and treat them like prey under attack by a predator.

The hidden message of the ads, therefore, is that women should be placed in the subordinate and indulged position of children, Dr. Goffman says. He adds that "underneath this show a man may be engaged in a deeper one, the suggestion of what he could do if he got serious about it."

Signs don't mirror reality, but bring echoes of some of the received ideas that we carry around in our heads—old narratives, myths, vents or values, says Dr. Blonsky. To be effective, political images or art must trigger some received ideas. The nearly universal fascination with the movie "Casablanca" in Western nations can be attributed to the film's lavish use of archetypes which have shaped stories through the ages, according to Dr. Eco.

The movie "opens in a place already magical in itself: Morocco, the exotic," he writes. "The city is the setting for a Passage, the Passage to the Promised Land. . . . But to make the Passage one must submit to a test, the Wait." The Passage also requires a Magic Key—in this case a visa allowing the anti-Nazi activist (Ingrid Bergman's husband) to leave Casablanca and carry on the good fight. The movie's passions revolve around the winning of this visa.

The myth of sacrifice runs through the film, Dr. Eco continues. There is Unhappy Love, Civilization against Barbarism, Redemption, and the Triumph of Purity. "Casablanca brings with it, like a trail of perfume, other situations which the viewer brings to bear quite readily," says Dr. Eco. Ironically, some of these echoes come from films or situations that occurred years after the movie was actually made. It wasn't until "To Have and Have Not," for instance, that Humphrey Bogart actually played the part of a Hemingway hero. But now that these images are part of our culture, however, we tend to see Bogart as a Hemingway hero even in Casablanca, which was made years earlier.

There have been several practical applications of semiotic analysis in recent years. One of the most dramatic involves predictions made by Polish semioticians for the use of the Polish labor union Solidarity.

Last year, Solidarity's leaders were very concerned that the Polish propensity for uprisings and acts of heroism might lead to a bloody Soviet response, says Dr. Wlad Godvich, a professor of comparative literature at the University of Minnesota. To help them forestall such a response, a group of Polish semioticians began to analyze Soviet writings and speeches about the Soviet Union's satellite nations, looking for incongruencies that would reveal some of the codes under which the Soviets operated.

This allowed the group to build a model explaining how the Soviet Union viewed its dependence on the satellites. The group, which worked anonymously, then predicted that if

Solidarity opened its ranks to peasants (who, under some Marxist interpretations, are considered remnants of a feudal society and enemies of the working class) the Soviet Union would believe that Solidarity was no longer a labor union but had become a political movement aimed at overthrowing Poland's Socialist order.

Forewarned by the semioticians' prediction, Solidarity's leaders emphasized that they were, indeed, a real labor union and pre-empted the issue, Dr. Godvich says; they were not challenging the Soviet Union, they said, but were simply advancing a different kind of Marxist analysis which did not assume a class antagonism between workers and peasants.

According to Dr. Godvich, these efforts helped blunt the force of the Soviet response, and although the Soviet Communist Party did attack Solidarity, its attacks were not so virulent as they might have been. Nor was there an invasion.

Analyses of this sort will be increasingly important in the future, Dr. Godvich believes; they "are applicable in negotiations of all kinds, as well as in establishing communication with people from other cultures."

Semiotics was founded by a Swiss linguist, Ferdinand de Saussure, and an American philosopher, Charles S. Peirce, in the early part of the 20th century. Its growth was also strongly influenced by the French structural anthropologist Claude Levi-Strauss. However, it did not begin to spread around the world until the publication of "Mythologies"—a book which has been called a sarcastic Marxist critique of everyday life—by the French philosopher Roland Barthes in 1957. In the past 15 years, semiotics has taken such a firm hold in the humanities departments of major American universities that few professors now dare to talk about the meaning of a literary or artistic work; instead, they teach their students to look for the work's underlying codes, the meanings assigned by culture, and to analyze how certain images are used to manipulate the reader or viewer.

As the semiotic approach has spread from architecture to zoology, however, it has encountered increasing resistance. Some academics accuse semioticians of "a limitless imperialistic desire" to take over all other disciplines. And even the most committed semioticians agree that semiotic techniques lack precision, remaining somewhat speculative and unjelled. Nevertheless, semioticians maintain that they are placing a conscious framework around reality which allows us to see many kinds of deception and self-deception that might otherwise escape us.

Meanwhile the word "semiotics" itself has acquired so much value that some intellectuals now bandy it about as a sign of their worth—much in the same spirit as New Yorkers who buy cowboy boots.

CONSIDER THIS

The subject of semiotics has come up—both implicitly and explicitly—through-out this text. (Did you spot the word "negotiations" in Pines's essay?) Pines offers us both a definition of semiotics and several examples of the way semioticians go about decoding cultural phenomena. She also waves a few red flags. Do you agree that few professors in the humanities departments in major American universities "dare to talk about the meaning of a literary or artistic work" but instead "teach their students to look for the work's underlying codes, the meanings assigned by culture"?

Try a semiotic analysis of a current pop icon or film. Try, for example, accounting for the mind-boggling success of *Teenage Mutant Ninja Turtles.* Start with the title.

Maya Pines, a freelance journalist, is the author of *The Brain Changers: Scientists and the New Mind Control* (1973) and *Revolution in Learning: The Years from Birth to Six,* and she coauthored, with René Dubos, *Health and Disease* (1965).

Death Penalty's False Promise:
An Eye for an Eye
Anna Quindlen

Ted Bundy and I go back a long way, to a time when there was a series of unsolved murders in Washington State known only as the Ted murders. Like a lot of reporters, I'm something of a crime buff. But the Washington Ted murders—and the ones that followed in Utah, Colorado and finally in Florida, where Ted Bundy was convicted and sentenced to die— fascinated me because I could see myself as one of the victims. I looked at the studio photographs of young women with long hair, pierced ears, easy smiles, and I read the descriptions: polite, friendly, quick to help, eager to please. I thought about being approached by a handsome young man asking for help, and I knew if I had been in the wrong place at the wrong time I would have been a goner.

By the time Ted finished up in Florida, law enforcement authorities suspected he had murdered dozens of young women. He and the death penalty seemed made for each other.

The death penalty and I, on the other hand, seem to have nothing in common. But Ted Bundy has made me think about it all over again, now that the outlines of my 60's liberalism have been filled in with a decade as a reporter covering some of the worst back alleys in New York City and three years as a mother who, like most, would lay down her life for her kids.

Simply put, I am opposed to the death penalty. I would tell that to any judge or lawyer undertaking the voir dire of jury candidates in a state in which the death penalty can be imposed. That is why I would be excused from such a jury. In a rational, completely cerebral way, I think the killing of one human being as punishment for the killing of another makes no sense and is inherently immoral.

But whenever my response to an important subject is rational and completely cerebral, I know there is something wrong with it—and so it is here. I have always been governed by my gut, and my gut says I am hypocritical about the death penalty. That is, I do not in theory think that Ted Bundy, or others like him, should be put to death. But if my daughter had been the one clubbed to death as she slept in a Tallahassee sorority house, and if the bite mark left in her buttocks had been one of the prime pieces of evidence against the young man charged with her murder, I would with the greatest pleasure kill him myself.

The State of Florida will not permit the parents of Bundy's victims to do that, and, in a way, that is the problem with an emotional response to capital punishment. The only reason for a death penalty is to exact retribution. Is there anyone who really thinks it is a deterrent, that there are considerable numbers of criminals out there who think twice about committing crimes because of the sentence involved? The ones I have met in the course of my professional duties have either sneered at the justice system, where they can exchange one charge for another with more ease than they could return a shirt to a clothing store, or they have simply believed that it is the other guy who will get caught, get convicted, get the stiffest sentence. Of course, the death penalty would act as a deterrent by eliminating recidivism, but then so would life without parole, albeit at greater taxpayer expense.

I don't believe deterrence is what most proponents seek from the death penalty anyhow. Our most profound emotional response is to want criminals to suffer as their victims did. When a man is accused of throwing a child from a high-rise terrace, my emotional—some might say hysterical—response is that he should be given an opportunity to see how endless the seconds are from the 31st story to the ground. In a civilized society that will never happen. And so what many people want from the death penalty, they will never get.

Death is death, you may say, and you would be right. But anyone who has seen someone die suddenly of a heart attack and someone else slip slowly into the clutches of cancer knows that there are gradations of dying.

I watched a television re-enactment one night of an execution by lethal injection. It was well done; it was horrible. The methodical approach, people standing around the gurney waiting, made it more awful. One moment there was a man in a prone position; the next moment that man was gone. On another night I watched a television movie about a little boy named Adam Walsh, who disappeared from a shopping center in Florida. There was a re-enactment of Adam's parents coming to New York, where they appeared on morning talk shows begging for their son's return, and in their hotel room, where they received a call from the police saying that Adam had been found: not all of Adam, actually, just his severed head, discovered in the waters of a Florida canal. There is nothing anyone could do that is bad enough for an adult who took a 6-year-old boy away from his parents, perhaps tortured, then murdered, him and cut off his head. Nothing at all. Lethal injection? The electric chair? Bah.

And so I come back to the position that the death penalty is wrong, not only because it consists of stooping to the level of the killers, but also because it is not what it seems. Just before Ted Bundy's most recent execution date was postponed, pending further appeals, the father of his last known victim, a 12-year-old girl, said what almost every father in his situation must feel. "I wish they'd bring him back to Lake City," said Tom Leach of the town where Kimberly Leach lived and died, "and let us all have at him." But the death penalty does not let us all have at him in the way Mr. Leach seems to mean. What he wants is for something as horrifying as what happened to his child to happen to Ted Bundy. And that is impossible.

CONSIDER THIS

New York Magazine entitled a piece about Anna Quindlen "Laureate of Real Life." Those of you who have read her columns in *Life in the 30s,* a regular op-ed feature in *The New York Times,* will probably agree that the label is apt. Quindlen, who makes no apologies for her preoccupation with family life as microcosm of society, often uses her space to write about nuts-and-bolts, everyday issues, and this piece, too, is grounded in her experience.

The first sentence captures our attention, and we read on. But we don't end up where we think we're going, with a variation on the moral stance that ends the fourth paragraph. The horror creeps up. We almost have to avert our eyes from the description of Adam Walsh's murder. Quindlen is right, we think. No means of formal execution is horrible enough for these child killers. She has us where she wants us.

But where exactly *does* she want us? Would Quindlen support the death penalty if the family of a child victim were permitted to torture the murderer before execution? Could you use this essay as ammunition if you were on the con side of a debate on the death penalty? After all, we come back to Quindlen as the laureate of real life, the family historian, the mother who opposes the death penalty but would, with great pleasure, kill the murderer of one of her own children.

Quindlen's latest published work is a novel, *Object Lessons* (1991).

New World
Jonathan Raban

It's dark and deathly quiet in here. The sheets of the bed are cool and laundry-smelling, but there's a niff in the air, sweet and sickly, like dead chrysanthemums. Sleep has disassembled the self: it will take patience to rebuild a person out of the heap of components in the bed. The dial of a wrist-watch looms in front of a single open eye; its luminous green hands say that it is either twenty-five after midnight or five in the morning. The spare human hand goes out on a cautious reconnaissance patrol through the darkness. It snags on a sharp corner, knocks over a bottle of pills, finds a solid, cold ceramic bulge. Fingers close on the knurled screw of the switch, and the room balloons with light.

It's a conventioneer's hotel room. The waking eye takes in the clubland furniture in padded leatherette, the Audubon prints, the thirty-six inch TV mounted over the mini-bar, the heavy cream drapes across the window. The room is painlessly impersonal, artfully designed to tell the self nothing about where it is or who it is supposed to be. It looks like its price. It is just a seventy-five dollar room.

The nose sources the bad smell to a tooth-glass of scotch and tap-water on the bedside table. The time is five o'clock but feels later.

Does seventy-five dollars buy twenty-four-hour room service? The shallow drawer below the telephone ought to yield a hotel directory, but doesn't. It contains two books of the same size and in the same binding: a Gideon Bible and *The Teaching of Buddha,* in English and Japanese, donated (it says) by the Buddhist Promoting Foundation, Japan. This is the room's first and only giveaway. The hotel where Jesus and Buddha live side by side in the drawer is on the Pacific Rim. The text is printed on thin crinkly paper.

> A true homeless brother determines to reach his goal of Enlightenment even though he loses his last drop of blood and his bones crumble into powder. Such a man, trying his best, will finally attain the goal and give evidence of it by his ability to do the meritorious deeds of a homeless brother.

There's no reply from room service on 107, so, sitting up in bed, long before dawn and *Good Morning America,* I read Gautama for the first time and find his teaching interestingly apposite to the situation and the hour.

Unenlightened man, said the Buddha, was trapped in an endless cycle of becoming— always trying to be something else or somebody else. His unhappy fate was to spend eternity passing from one incarnation to the next, each one a measure of his ignorant restlessness and discontent. In the search for Nirvana, man must stop being a becomer and learn how to be a be–er.

It is a profoundly un-American philosophy. Here in this travellers' room, in this nation of chronic travellers and becomers, *The Teaching of Buddha* strikes the same note of disregarded truth as the health warning on an emptied pack of cigarettes. The idea that the whole of the external world is a treacherous fiction, that the self has no real existence, goes right against the Protestant, materialist American grain.

No wonder that so many Americans have looked across the Pacific to Buddhism to provide an antidote to the American condition. Emerson and the New England Transcendentalists—Whitman—T. S. Eliot—the Dharma Bums—J. D. Salinger—Robert M. Pirsig's *Zen and the Art of Motorcycle Maintenance:* in every phase of post-colonial American history, Buddhism has offered a rhetoric of dissent; and on the Pacific coast it has coloured the fabric of the culture.

I look at the advice I've failed to follow—

> In the evening he should have a time for quiet sitting and meditation and a short walk before retiring. For peaceful sleep he should rest on the right side with his feet together and his last thought should be of the time when he wishes to rise in the early morning.

—and copy it into my notebook. It sounds like a good tip; far better than pills and whisky.

Fiction or not, the external world is beginning to make its presence felt now. The drapes open on a city still blue in the half-light. Lines of cars on the wet streets a few floors below the window are making a muffled drumming sound; the morning commute from the suburbs is already under way. Seven o'clock. It's time to shave and shower; time to put Buddha back in the drawer and become someone else.

On that particular morning, in hotels and motels, in furnished rooms and cousins' houses, 106 other people were waking to their first day as immigrants to Seattle. These were flush times, with jobs to be had for the asking, and the city was growing at the rate of nearly 40,000 new residents a year. The immigrants were piling in from every quarter. Many were out-of-state Americans: New Yorkers on the run from the furies of Manhattan; refugees from the Restbelt; Los Angelenos escaping their infamous crime statistics, huge house-prices and jammed and smoggy freeways; redundant farm workers from Kansas and Iowa. Then there were the Asians—Samoans, Laotians, Cambodians, Thais, Vietnamese, Chinese and Koreans, for whom Seattle was the nearest city in the continental United States. A local artist had proposed a monumental sculpture, to be put up at the entrance to Elliott Bay, representing Liberty holding aloft a bowl of rice.

The falling dollar, which had so badly hurt the farming towns of the Midwest, had come as a blessing to Seattle. It lowered the price abroad of the Boeing airplanes, wood pulp, paper, computer software and all the other things that Seattle manufactured. The port of Seattle was a day closer by sea to Tokyo and Hong Kong than was Los Angeles, its main rival for the shipping trade with Asia.

By the end of the 1980s, Seattle had taken on the dangerous lustre of a promised city. The rumour had gone out that if you had failed in Detroit you might yet succeed in Seattle—and that if you'd succeeded in Seoul, you could succeed even better in Seattle. In New York and in Guntersville I'd heard the rumour. Seattle was the coming place.

So I joined the line of hopefuls.

Of all the new arrivals, it was the Koreans who had made the biggest, boldest splash. Wherever I went, I saw their patronyms on storefronts, and it seemed that half the small family businesses in Seattle were owned by Parks or Kims. I picked up my trousers from the dry cleaner's at the back of the Josephinum, stopped for milk and eggs at a Korean corner grocery, looked through the steamy window of a Korean tailor's, passed the Korean wig shop on Pike Street, bought oranges, bananas and grapes from a Korean fruit stall in the market, and walked the hundred yards home via a Korean laundromat and a Korean news and candy kiosk.

For lunch I went to Shilla, where I sat up at the bar, ordered a beer, and tried to make sense of the newspaper which had been left on the counter—the *Korean Times,* published daily in Seattle. The text was in Korean characters, but the pictures told one something. There were portrait photographs of beaming Korean-American businessmen dressed, like many of the restaurant's customers, in blazers, button-down shirts and striped club ties. Several columns were devoted to prize students, shown in their mortar boards and academic gowns. On page three there was a church choir. There was a surprising number of advertisements for pianos. I guessed that the tone of the text would be inspirational and uplifting: the *Korean Times* seemed to be exclusively devoted to the cult of business, social and academic success.

'You are reading our paper!' It was the proprietor of the restaurant, a wiry man with a tight rosebud smile.

'No—just looking at the pictures.'

He shook my hand, sat on the stool beside me and showed me the paper page by page. Here was the news from Korea; this was local news from Seattle and Tacoma; that was Pastor Kim's family advice column; these were the advertisements for jobs . . .

'It is very important to us. Big circulation! Everybody read it!'

So, nearly a hundred years ago, immigrant Jews in New York had pored over the *Jewish Daily Forward,* the *Yidishe Gazetn* and the *Arbeite Tseitung.* They had kept their readers in touch with the news and culture of the old world at the same time as they had taught the immigrants how to make good in the new. To the greenhorn American, the newspaper came as a daily reassurance that he was not alone.

'You are interested?' the restaurateur said. 'You must talk to Mr Han. He is the president of our association. He is here—'

Mr Han was eating by himself, hunched over a plate of seafood. In sweatshirt and windbreaker, he had the build of a bantamweight boxer. The proprietor introduced us. Mr Han bowed from his seat, waved his chopsticks. Sure! No problem! Siddown!

His face looked bloated with fatigue. His eyes were almost completely hidden behind pouches of flesh, giving him the shuttered-in appearance of a sleep-walker. But his mouth was wide awake, and there was a surviving ebullience in his grin, which was unself-consciously broad and toothy.

He gave me his card. Mr Han was President of the Korean Association of Seattle, also owner of Japanese Auto Repair ('is *big* business!'). He had been in America, he said, for sixteen years. He'd made it. But his college-student clothes, his twitchy hands and the knotted muscles in his face told another story. If you passed Mr Han on the street, you'd mistake him for a still shell-shocked newcomer; an F.O.B., as people said even now, long after the Boeing had displaced the immigrant ship. He looked fresh-off-the-boat.

It had been the summer of 1973 when Won S. Han had flown from Seoul to Washington D.C. with 400 dollars in his billfold and a student visa in his passport. He had come to study Psychology—that was what his papers said, at least—but what he really wanted to major in was the applied science of becoming an American.

In Korea, he had been brought up as a Buddhist. Within two weeks of his arrival in Washington, he was a Baptist.

'Yah! I become Christian! I didn't go to church to believe in God, not then, no. I go to church for meeting people. Yah, Baptist church was where to find job, where to find place to live, where to find wife, husband, right? In America, you gotta be Christian!' His voice was lippy, whispery, front-of-the-mouth.

He'd soon fallen behind in his Psychology classes. He couldn't follow the strange language. Through the church, he found a part-time job in a gas- and service-station. He learned the work easily. While the American workers were content to lounge and smoke and tinker, this university-educated Korean gutted the car manuals and took only a few weeks to qualify as a full-fledged auto mechanic.

'We are hot-temper people! Want to do things quick-quick-quick! Not slow-slow like in America. Want everything all-at-once, but in America you must learn to wait long-time. Quick-quick is the Korean way, but that's not work here. America teaches patience, teaches wait-till-next-week.'

This must have been a hard lesson for Mr Han to take to heart. He'd done a major reconstruction job on the American language to give it a greater turn of speed, lopping off articles, prepositions, all the fancy chromework of traditional syntax. His stripped-down English was now wonderfully fast and fluent. With its rat-a-tat-tat hyphenations and bang! bang! repetitions, it was a vehicle custom-built for its owner—a Korean racing machine in which Mr Han drove with his foot on the floor, without regard for petty American traffic restrictions.

Working as a mechanic by day, he'd gone to school at night. This time his subject was real-estate, and it took him six months to qualify for a Maryland realtor's licence. He gave up the car business and sold suburban houses, mostly to Korean customers.

'You know, when Korean guy come to this country, he has *plan*! In two year, must have own business. In three year, must have own house. Three year! Four at *maximum*. So must work-work-work. Sixteen-hour-day, eighteen-hour-day . . . OK, he can do. But *must* have business, *must* have house.'

Mr Han himself had run ahead of schedule. By 1982, when he left Washington and headed for Seattle, he was a man of capital with a wife and two young daughters. To begin with, he patrolled the city from end to end by car, casing the joint for opportunities.

'And you liked what you saw?'

"Yah! I like the mountains! Like the water! Like the trees! Is like in Korea, but not too hot, not too cold. *Nice!* No people! Green!'

Everywhere he'd gone, he'd checked in with the local Parks and Kims and got the low-down on Seattle's social structure. Beacon Hill, just south of downtown, was where Korean beginners started their American lives; as they succeeded, so they moved further north, to Queen Anne and Capitol Hill, across Lake Washington to Bellevue, across Lake Union to Wallingford, Morningside, Greenwood, North Beach. They measured the tone of a neighbourhood by the reputation of its schools. The top suburb was the one with the best record of posting students to famous American colleges like Columbia, Yale and M.I.T.

On his first day in Seattle, Mr Han had learned that the Shoreline School District was 'much better, no comparison!' than the Seattle School District, and that the Syre Elementary School was just the place for his daughters to set foot on the ladder to academic stardom. So he bought a house in Richmond Beach. He had no Korean neighbours. The closeness of the house to the school was all that mattered.

Then he set up his business.

'Must be *specialist!*' Mr Han said. Detroit was sick, and more and more Americans were buying Japanese cars, so Mr Han established his hospital for Japanese cars only. 'No American cars! No German! No English!—sorry! Must be Japanese. Toyota, Nissan, Mitsubishi, whatever. So long as it made in Japan—bring it in! That is my speciality.'

The climax of this success story had happened two years ago. Mr Han had always dreamed of having a son to carry on the Han dynastic name. In Korea, it was a woman's highest duty to give birth to a son. Mr Han himself was the only son of an only son—a man genetically programmed to produce a male heir. But it seemed that he could only father daughters. This was, he said, a heavy fate for a Korean man to shoulder.

'So, in 1986, I go to my wife. I say to her, 'One last try!' And we try. And—*Home Run!*' For the first time, Mr Han's eyes were wide open, his pride in this feat of paternity matched by this rich nugget of all-American slang.

'Home run!' He smacked his lips around the phrase and laughed, a joyful *hoo! hoo!* that made neighbouring diners look up from their tables.

'Now the name of Han goes on!'

With his business in the city, his civic honours in the Korean community, his big house in a wooded, crimeless suburb a spit away from the sea, his straight-A daughters and his precious son, one might have expected Mr Han to have grown expansive and complacent in his New World estate. Yet his eyes closed as quickly as they had opened; he fell back into hunched vigilance; he looked, as I had first seen him, like an anxious greener who fears that someone, somewhere, is hard on his heels.

He was frightened for his children.

'They see the American TV . . . of this I am scared. I turn off the news. There is too much immorality! violence! drugs! sex! When the news comes up—"Turn that TV off!"'

He had tried to turn his home into a Korean bubble, sealed off from the dangerous American world outside. In the house, the family talked in Korean. Twice a week, the girls went to a Korean church school to take classes in Korean grammar and composition.

He dreaded the day when one of his daughters would bring home a white American boy-friend.

'What would you do?'

'Any kid of mine, I'd stop her marrying another race.'

'*Stop!*'

'Maybe could not *stop*. Maybe. But not *like*. You heard of "G.I. Brides" . . . They were not normal average Korean woman. They were—I not say exactly what they were, but you know what I mean.' Mr Han watched me across the table through his nearly closed eyes. 'Whores,' he said, making the word sound biblical.

I said that the Jews in New York at the beginning of the century had felt much as he did. But they had had the protection of the ghetto. In the Yiddish-speaking world of the Lower East Side, with its all-Jewish streets and all-Jewish schools, it was possible to regard the *goyim* as unmarriageable aliens. In Richmond Beach, a Korean girl would be a Christian, like most of her classmates, and her skin-colour would be hardly less pale than theirs. How, growing up in English, could she hug 'Koreanness' to herself as the essence of her identity, while all the time her parents talked Columbia, talked medical school, talked her up the path that led to membership of the white, professional, American middle class?

'Ah,' said Mr Han. 'This is what we are wondering. Wondering-wondering all the time. *How long?* is the question. In near future, next generation, we got to be serviced by English. We have example of Chinese. Look at Chinese!—in two-three generations, the Chinese people here, they cannot even read the characters! Chinese is only *name*. Is nothing. Now, Chinese . . . all in the melting pot!' He drew out this last phrase with solemn relish. The way he said it, it was a *mel Ting pot,* and I saw it as some famous cast-iron oriental cooking utensil, in which human beings were boiled over a slow fire until they broke down into a muddy fibrous stew.

'But my kids grow like Koreans,' Mr Han said.

'With American voices, American clothes, American college degrees . . .'

'Like Koreans.'

On the street across from the restaurant I could see a rambling black-painted chalet surmounted by a flying hoarding which said LOOK WHAT WE GOT! 30 NUDE SHOWGIRLS! TABLE DANCING! It was a sign to chill the heart of a Korean father of young daughters.

Since so much of American culture was clearly a Caucasian affront to Korean ideas of modesty, industry, piety and racial purity, I wondered why they kept on coming—from a country that was being touted as the economic miracle of the decade.

Mr Han guffawed when I said 'economic miracle'.

'Guy in Korea make three-four-hundred dollar a month. No house his own, no business his own. *This* is country of opportunity. No comparison. Chance of self-employment: maybe one thousand per cent better! Look. Seventy-three. I am in Washington, D.C. with four hundred dollars. Now? My business is worth one million dollars—more than one million. Heh? Isn't that the American Dream? And I am only a small! Yes, I am a *small.*'

Minutes later, I watched him as he crossed to his car. The millionaire was walking quick-quick-quick, shoulders hunched, head down, his skinny hands rammed deep into the pockets of his workpants. He looked like a man who had taken on America single-handed and, in the ninth round, was just winning, by a one- or two-point margin.

The Chinese had been the first Asians to make a new life in Seattle. They called America 'The Gold Mountain' and were eager to take on the hard, poorly paid jobs that were offered to them in the railroad construction gangs. For as long as it took to build the railroads, they were made welcome, in a mildly derisive way. Their entire race was renamed 'John', and every John was credited with an extraordinary capacity to do the maximum amount of work on the minimum amount of rice. As soon as the railroads began to lay off workers, the amiable John was reconceived as 'a yellow rascal' and 'the rat-eating Chinaman'. During the 1870s, the federal legislature began to behave towards the Chinese much as the Tsars Alexander II and Nicholas II behaved towards the Jews in Russia. At the very moment when the United States was receiving the European huddled masses on its eastern seaboard, it was establishing something cruelly like its own Pale, designed to exclude the Chinese from white American rights and occupations. The Geary Act prohibited Chinese from the right to bail and habeas corpus. In Seattle in 1886, gangs of vigilantes succeeded in forcibly deporting most of the city's Chinese population of 350 people; persuading them, with knives, clubs and guns, to board a ship bound for San Francisco.

For the immigrant from Asia, the Gold Mountain was a treacherous rock-face. No sooner had you established what seemed to be a secure foothold than it gave way under you. The treatment of the Seattle Chinese in 1886 was matched, almost exactly, by the treatment of the Seattle Japanese in 1942, when hundreds of families were arrested, loaded on trains and despatched to remote internment camps.

Now, if you came from Asia, you could not trust America to be kind or fair. This particular week, if you went to an English class at the Central Community College, you would see spray-gunned on the south wall of the building SPEAK ENGLISH OR DIE, SQUINTY EYE! Peeing in a public toilet, you'd find yourself stuck, for the duration with a legend written just for you: KILL THE GOOKS.

In the ghetto of Seattle's International District, a four-by-four block grid of morose, rust-coloured tenements, there was at least safety in numbers. There was less pressure on the immigrant to get his tongue round the alien syllables of English. Even a professional man, like the dentist or optometrist, could conduct his business entirely in his original language. In the bar of the China Gate restaurant, I sat next to a man in his early seventies, born on Jackson Street, who had served with the United States Air Force in World War Two. He was affable, keen to tell me about his travels and almost completely incomprehensible, *Yi wong ding ying midling hyall!*

'You were in Mildenhall? In Suffolk?'

'Yea! Milding Hall!'

So, painfully, we swapped memories of the air base there. He didn't understand much of what I said, and I didn't understand much of what he said; yet his entire life, bar this spell in wartime England, had been passed in Seattle—or, rather, within the Chinese-speaking fifty-acre grid.

The Chinese, the Japanese, the Vietnamese, Laotians and Cambodians had all established solid fortresses in, or on the edge of, the International District. There were few Koreans here. There was the Korean Ginseng Center on King Street; there was a Korean restaurant at the back of the Bush Hotel on Jackson; some Koreans worked as bartenders in the Chinese restaurants.

In Los Angeles, there was a 'Little Korea'; a defined area of the city where the immigrant could work for, and live with, his co-linguists, much as the Chinese did here in the International District. For Koreans in Seattle, though, immigration was, for nearly everyone, a solitary process. The drive to own their own businesses, to send their children to good schools, to have space, privacy, self-sufficiency, had scattered them, in small family groups of twos and threes, through the white suburbs. They didn't have the daily solace of the sociable rooming house, the street and the café. For many, there was the once-a-week visit to church; for others, there was no Korean community life at all.

It was this solitude that drew me to them. The Seattle Koreans knew, better than anyone else, what it was like to go it alone in America; and although I came from the wrong side of the world I could feel a pang of kinship for these people who had chosen to travel by themselves.

Everyone could name the date on which they'd taken the flight out from Seoul. The beginning of their American life was at least as important to them as their birthday.

'August twenty-ninth, 1965,' Jay Park said. He owned a plumbing business up on Beacon Hill and drove a pearl-grey '88 Mercedes. In 1965, he'd been twenty; and on that August afternoon he'd stood in Seoul airport being hugged by every aunt, cousin, uncle, friend.

'Everyone envy me. It was like I'd won the big lottery, you know? I'd got the visa! Wah! They was seeing me off like I was some general . . . like I was going into Paradise!'

Park knew America. He'd 'watched it through the movies'. On the streets of Seoul, he'd seen 'US soldiers spending money like it was going out of style. Wah! I tell you, the US was like a paradise. You feel like you're going to dreamland. Everything's going to work out OK!'

It was a Northwest Airlines flight; Jay Park had never been on an airplane before and he had 'not one word' of English. The stewardess showed him to an aisle seat, next to an American who was reading a book.

'He don't look at me. I felt shy. Suddenly I was kind of scared, the excitement was overwhelming. This guy was reading his book, so I read the in-flight magazine. I mean, not *read,* but made out like I was reading. I was just looking at the pictures of the US, but I was taking a long time over every one, so this guy would think I could read the English.'

The plane took off. 'No problem,' but Jay Park wished he could see out the window. He didn't dare to lean across the body of his American neighbour; so, holding the magazine close to his face, he'd sneaked glances—seen jigsaw puzzle bits of city and mountain slide past the lozenge of perspex as the plane banked.

A meal was served. 'That was real great! American food! I was in the US already!'

At Tokyo they had stopped to refuel. Jay Park was in an agony of impatience. Other Koreans on the flight were buying watches and radios at the Tokyo duty-free shop, but Jay Park sat fretting on a bench during the stopover, his mind full of America.

Then came the long haul across the Pacific. They left the sunset behind—Park could see it gleaming gold on the trailing edge of the plane's starboard wing—and flew into the night. He remembered the blinds being pulled down for the projection of the movie. With no headset, he could only watch the pictures—more postcards of America. 'Oh boy! *Dis* is where I'm goin'! I'm in the movie!'

Exhausted by his excitement, he fell asleep. When he woke up, the quick night was already over. Time itself was whizzing by faster than the clouds below, but the plane was still a long way from America. The morning lasted forever. 'Then—they were saying something through the speaker, but my ears were blocking up. S*eattle!* That's all I hear. *Seattle!*'

There was nothing to see. America was a huge grey cloud, through which the plane was making its unbearably slow descent. When it touched down, Jay Park was high, in a toxic trance.

'Wah! Man! The airport! When you're walking through, your mind is set, *"This is America!"* Everything is *nice! great! fantasy!*'

The air inside the terminal was magic air. It smelled of cologne and money. There were advertising posters for things—'I don't know what they are, but, boy, they look good to me!'

The two hours he spent standing in line, waiting to be processed by the immigration officials, were precious, American hours. 'No, I don't care! I just think, Wah! I'm in the US!'

His sponsors were waiting for him in the arrivals lobby, a Korean-American couple in their forties who had been friends of his parents back in Seoul. Jay Park had never met them before, but they were holding up a sheet of cardboard with his name on it.

'Oh, but they'd done *great!* I was expecting them to take me in a bus, but they got their own car! A Chevy. Blue. Musta been a '63, '64 model. Yeah. Nice long sheer, box type, really fancy! You sitting in the back seat, looking out, it *astounds*. Wow! All the freeways, all the cars!'

The blue Chevy drove north, up the I-5 towards Seattle.

'*Whassat?* Hey, goddam, *whassat?*'

Jay Park saw a great factory—but it wasn't a factory; it was a supermarket. He loved the huge pictures raised over the six-lane highway, the smoking cowboys, the girls in swimsuits. *Wah! America!*

'Then, passing the downtown, *goddam!* The Smith Tower! The Space Needle! God-awmighty! You gotta *look* at that! But so few people! There was hardly any peoples was there! *No people, hardly.* You feel uneasy. *What's going on? Is the people all gone home?* This is real strange, not having people around. In Korea, people everywhere; in America—no people!'

The Chevy left the I-5 and headed up Aurora Avenue, along the wooded edge of Lake Union. It crossed the George Washington Bridge and entered the northern suburbs.

'It was the cleanness! The cars parked neatly! Just like the movies! And the lawns . . . No fences, no walls. In Korea, it was all high stone walls round every house. Here, is all open, all lawns, lawns, lawns. Looking out the car window, I see people's bikes left out front, just like that . . . like, here you can just leave things out overnight. No thieves! I think, *everything is coming true! What the movies say is true! This is like paradise is supposed to be!*'

His sponsors lived in a neat frame house in Greenwood.

'They had tables and chairs, the American way, not all on the floor like in Korea. Wah, man! I was cautious, then. Like, first thing, I want to use the toilet, you know? They show me where it is, and I spend a long, long time just looking around in there, Like, *If I use it, where's the smell going to go? Oh! I get it! There's the fan!* Stuff like that. Little things. Then they show me the bed where I'm to sleep? I never slept on a bed before. I think, *how you sleep on a bed without falling off?* I fell out of that bed a few times, too.'

That evening, his sponsors took Jay Park to the local supermarket.

'Wah! The steaks! The hamburgers! To eat a *whole* piece of meat! Even chickens! And they're so *cheap* too!'

He slept on the strange bed in a state of delirious wonder, his dreams far outclassed by America's incredible reality. In the morning, he ventured out into the backyard. A man—a white American—was pottering in the garden next door.

'He said to me, "Hi!" and then he said *something*. I didn't say anything. I think I give him a smile . . . I *hope* I give him a smile . . . then I go back into the house. *They speak English out there!*'

But: 'I was ready to tackle anything, anyhow.' With his sponsors' help, he enrolled for classes twice a week at the Central Community College. He got a job as a porter at a dry-ice factory. It paid $1.25 an hour—'great money!'. He found lodgings, with an Italian woman who worked at a downtown grocery and mothered him. Bed and board cost him thirty-five dollars a week; but as soon as work was over at the factory, Jay Park was out mowing people's lawns. If he put in a sixteen hour day, he could make 120 dollars in a week—a fortune. In his new Levis and his long-brimmed baseball cap, Jay Park was living the movie as he toted ice and mowed grass.

'Downtown, though, that was a big shock for me. You look—wah, godawmighty!— really strange people! Those poor whites, down in skid row? You never expecting skid row to exist in a country like this! I never seen *that* in the movies.'

He was having a hard time with the language. He went to his classes. He sat up late every night, slogging over his homework. He studied the programmes he saw on television, treating *Hogan's Heroes* as a set text. 'I want something, I get it,' Jay Park said, but he couldn't get English.

'There was such pain building up inside me . . . People say things at work, I can't answer back! There's no *language* there! Nothing in the mouth! So you must make physical movement, you know? You get *violent!*'

So he punched and jabbed to make himself understood. Lost for a word, he socked the American air and laid it flat.

He was *making out*. He was saving. After a year of lawn-mowing and digging out borders, he was able to bill himself as 'Jay Park—Contractor and Landscape Gardener', but he was still travelling across Seattle by bus. It took him until 1967 before he'd put away enough to buy his first car.

'It was a 1960 T-Bird. Light blue. Electric windows and everything else. *You* owning own car, wah! that was a thrill, man.'

Now he drove his Italian landlady everywhere. She was chauffeured to work, chauffeured around the stores. Waiting for her, parked on the street, Jay Park, Contractor, Landscape Gardener, Ice Merchant, American, sat behind the wheel listening to the music of his electric windows buzzing up and down. 'Boy, I loved that car!'

Their experience had turned the immigrants into compulsive story-tellers. Much more than most people, they saw their own lives as having a narrative shape, a plot with a climactic dénouement. Each story was moulded by conventional rules. Korean men liked to see themselves as Horatio Alger heroes. Once upon a time there had been poverty, adversity, struggle. But character had triumphed over circumstance. The punchline of the story was 'Look at me now!', and the listener was meant to shake his head in admiration at the size of the business, the car, the house, at the school and college grades of the narrator's children, and at the amazing fortitude and pluck of the narrator, for having won so much in this country of opportunity. The story, in its simplest form, was a guileless tribute both to the virtues of the Korean male and to the bounty of America.

I preferred to listen to the stories of the women. They were closer to Flaubert than to Alger; their style was more realistic; they were more complicated in structure; they had more regard for pain and for failure.

Insook Webber took the flight for Seattle on 23 April 1977.

'I'd never been in an airplane before, but I loved—I absolutely adored—the idea of flying. I loved to see the planes in the sky. For me, they were flying into—like a fantasy world? A world of possibilities. And I had this premonition. It was always inside me, that somehow, someday, I'd leave Korea.'

She was in her thirties now, fine boned, fine skinned, her hair grown down to her shoulders in the American way. Her English was lightly, ambiguously, accented. In silk scarf and chunky cardigan, she looked dressed for a weekend in the Hamptons. She was married to an American; a Yale philosophy graduate who chose to work, unambitiously, in an accountants' office. She herself was a hospital nurse.

In 1977, Insook's elder sister had already been in America for five years, and Insook was going out to help look after her sister's children.

'I didn't know what to expect. I was totally open, totally vulnerable.'

'What did "America" mean?'

'America? It was a place in novels I'd read, and films I'd seen . . . It was Scarlett O'Hara and *Gone With The Wind*. I was going to live at Tara and meet Rhett Butler, I guess . . .'

The flight itself was thrilling. Insook had a window seat; looking down on the clouds was how life was going to be.

'I was breaking out all over with excitement. I was totally tired, but I couldn't sleep for a moment in case I missed something.'

It was after dark when the plane approached the coast. The sky was clear, and Insook's first glimpse of America was a lighted city.

'Like diamonds. Miles and miles of diamonds. I couldn't believe it—that people could afford so much *electricity!* We were having to save electricity in Korea then. I knew America was a rich country, but not *this* rich, to squander such a precious thing as electricity . . . I'd never dreamed of so many lights being switched on all at once.'

The plane landed at Sea-Tac, and it wasn't until past two a.m. that Insook was in possession of her green card, her ticket to becoming an American. Out in the concourse, she spotted her sister waiting for her, but her sister didn't recognize her.

'I was only fifteen when she left—still a kid. I was twenty now, and I'd grown. I had to *persuade* her I was me . . .'

Insook's scanty luggage was put aboard the family car, and they headed for the suburbs.

'Those huge wide roads, and huge lit-up signs . . . It made me feel very small . . . It was like being a little child again . . . Everything so big, so bright.'

She was describing the shock of being born.

Her sister's house was quiet. 'Too quiet. It was like the inside of a coffin. It wasn't like the real world . . .'

Nor was America. Insook was astounded and frightened by the extravagance of the country in which she found herself. When she went to a McDonalds, she wanted to take home the packaging of her hamburger and save it—it seemed criminal to simply throw it away in a litter-bin. A short walk on her first day took her from a rich neighbourhood into a poor one. 'On this street, these Americans live like kings—and on that, they are beggars! I thought, *My God, how can people* live *like this? How can they live* with *this?*'

Most immigrants were able to enjoy a few weeks, or days at least, of manic elation in the new country before depression hit them, as they woke up to the enormity of what they'd done. For Insook the depression came at almost the same moment as she touched ground.

'It would have been different if I'd come to be a student. I would have had clear goals, a programme to follow . . .'

With no programme, she sat in the vault of her sister's house, staring listlessly at television.

'I was terrified. I felt locked in that house for an entire year. I hated to go out. I was cut off from all my friends. I could read English, not well, but I could read it—but I couldn't speak it . . . hardly a word. I felt I was blind and deaf. My self-esteem was totally gone. Totally. I was in America, but I wasn't part of this society at all.

'I was a huge mess of inertia. I was *stopped*—you know? like a clock? I slept and slept. Sometimes I slept eighteen hours a day. I'd go to bed at night, and it would be dark again when I woke up.'

During that year, Insook's whole family—parents, brothers, cousins—came to America by separate planes. They were scattered across the land mass, between Washington State and Detroit.

'There was no going back. I had no home to return to. I had come here to *live* and I felt suicidal. That sense of homelessness . . . you know? You have no past—that's been taken away from you. You have no present—you are doing nothing. *Nothing.* And you have no future. The pain of it—do you understand?'

Yet even at the bottom of this pit of unbeing, Insook saw one spark of tantalizing possibility. On television, and on her rare, alarmed ventures on the streets, she watched American women with wonder.

'Oh, but they were such marvellous creatures! I would see them working . . . driving cars . . . talking. They were so confident! Free! Carefree! Not afraid! And I was . . . *me.*'

The prospect of these women made English itself infinitely desirable. Korean was the language of patriarchy and submission; English the language of liberation and independence. Insook had school-English. It worked on paper; she could write a letter in it, even, with some difficulty, read a book. But its spoken form bore hardly any relationship at all to the English spoken on American streets. She followed the news programmes on TV (she was through with fictions), and parroted back the words as the announcers said them. She practised, haltingly, in the stores.

I said that I marvelled at her articulacy now. 'You're saying things with such precision, and complex, emotional things too. You're making me feel inarticulate, and I've spent forty-seven years living inside this language.'

'Oh, it is so much more easy for a Korean woman to learn than for a Korean man. She can afford to make mistakes. When a man makes a mistake, it is an affront on his masculine pride, to his great Koreanness. He is programmed to feel shame. So he learns six sentences, six grammatical forms, and sticks to them. He's safe inside his little language; his pride is not wounded. But when a woman makes mistakes, everybody laughs. She's "just a girl"— she's being "cute". So she can dare things that a man wouldn't begin to try, for fear of making a fool of himself. I could make a fool of myself . . . so it was easy for me to learn English.'

It was still three years before she felt 'comfortable' about leaving the house, and four before she began to make her first American friends. She had gone to stay at the family house of a cousin in Bellingham, at the north end of Puget Sound, where she went to college to study for a diploma in nursing.

At Bellingham, Insook began to go on dates with American men.

'My brothers came to see me. They felt betrayed. Korean males—you must know this—are the most conservative on this earth. For me to be seen alone in a café, talking to a white American man, that was a deep, deep insult to them. I was insulting their maleness, insulting their pride, insulting everything that "Korea" meant to them. They threatened me . . .'

A year later, Insook announced her engagement, to an American.

'My father said, "I will disown you"' she smiled—a sad, complicated shrug of a smile. 'So I said . . .' For the first time since we'd been talking, she produced a pack of cigarettes and lit one. 'I said, "I am sick and tired of this family. OK, disown me. *Please* disown me!"'

The brothers came round, with a fraternal warning.

'They promised me that they would bomb the church where we were getting married. We had to hire security guards. One of my brothers said he would prefer to blow me up, blow me to pieces, than see me married to an American.'

'And you really believed that he meant it—that he'd make a bomb?'

'Oh, yes. My brothers weren't doing well. They were struggling in America. They were just fighting me with what little ego they had left . . .'

The wedding went ahead, with security guards. At the last moment one of the brothers turned up, shamefaced, with a gift.

Her marriage was 'absolutely democratic', and it was, thought Insook, the prospect of this democracy that her father and brothers had so feared and hated. 'For the Korean man, everything that he is, his whole being, is in direct conflict with what this society is about.'

A little Korean culture had survived in Insook's American marriage. She and her husband left their shoes by the front door and went around the house barefoot or in stockings. They lived closer to the ground than most Americans. 'He has a naturally floor-oriented lifestyle.' She sometimes cooked Korean food. 'He likes to use chopsticks.' Her husband had 'a few phrases' of Korean.

'But I seldom feel my identity as a Korean now. I forget that I look different—'

'You think you look "different"? Look at all of us here—' We were sitting in a booth at the Queen City Grill on First, a favourite lunch-spot for Seattle's wine-drinking, seafood-eating, stylish middle class. We had melting-pot faces: at almost every table, you could see a mop of Swedish hair, an Anglo-Saxon mouth, an Italian tan, Chinese-grandmother eyes, a high Slav cheek-bone. In this company, Insook's appearance was in the classic American grain.

'No, you're right. It's when people know I come from Korea, I sometimes get deadlocked in arguments. The moment someone knows I am a Korean, then I'm framed in their stereotype of how a Korean ought to be. Like, if I'm shy for some reason, then it's "Of course you're shy—that's so *Korean*." But then again, if I am outspoken, if I get angry in a discussion, that's "being Korean" too. Whatever I do, it must be "Korean." I do get mad over that sometimes.'

Yet Insook's attachment to Korea still went deep. It would sometimes take her by surprise. Shopping in the Bon, she felt 'shame' (that most powerful of all Korean words) when she saw how Korean products were always shoddier than their Japanese or American counterparts.

'They are made to fall apart in a few months, and I think, *this is my country*—'

'But your country is America now.'

'No, I still identify with Korea. I do still think of myself as a foreigner and of America as a foreign country. Not on the surface. In a profound way, that I can't change. I think, too, that my sense of root is beginning to return. Just lately, I've been taking up calligraphy again . . . And I'd like to do something for the Korean community here. When I see other Koreans in Seattle, I know that we've all been through the same pain, the same suffering, and I feel good that I went through that pain . . . it's very important for me.'

She was doing what she could. For Korean patients in the hospital where she worked, she was translator, legal advisor, counsellor, kind heart. That morning, she had been trying to find a lawyer who would take on the case of a Korean who had been injured at work and whose employer had refused to pay him compensation.

'But I do feel uncomfortable with other Korean people. There's so much suspicion and resentment. To so many of them, I am not *me*, I am a girl who married an American. As soon as I tell them my American name, I see it in their eyes. I am *one of those*.'

'But you still go on trying—'

'I feel compulsion—compulsion? compassion? I don't know, I suppose both for Korea. You know? It's like having two friends . . . There is the rich friend, who's doing very well in life. You're always glad to see him; you're happy in his company . . . But you don't need to worry about him. That's like America is for me. Then I have this poor friend. Always in some kind of trouble. It depresses me to have to meet him. But . . . he is the friend who needs me. That is Korea.'

Some days later, I was talking to Jay Park again. A year after he'd arrived in Seattle, he'd met a Korean girl (at the Presbyterian church), and they'd married in '67, driving off in the pale blue T-Bird with electric windows. They now had two sons and a daughter.

It was odd, Jay Park said, that while nearly all of his sons' friends were Korean, 'eighty per cent' of his daughter's friends were American. 'She just seem to like to hang out with white Americans . . .'

I could hear Insook's voice, talking of 'marvellous creatures'.

'How do you take to the idea of a white American son-in-law?' I asked.

Jay Park laughed. 'I deal with that one awready. I tell her. "Day you bring home American boyfriend, that's the day you dead meat, girl!"'

It was a joke. He was hamming the role of heavy Korean father, but there was enough seriousness in it to give it an uncomfortable edge.

'Dead meat!' His laugh faded into a deep frown. 'I see these intermarriage families, and always is some . . . *unsatisfied* . . . *life*. You get what I am saying now? I am thinking our kids got lost somewhere . . . somewhere between the cultures.'

CONSIDER THIS

Jonathan Raban (essayist, playwright, travel writer; born in England in 1942) lived in London for much of his life but has done a good bit of observing in the United States. His 1981 book *Old Glory* details his trip down the Mississippi on a 16-foot aluminum skiff with an outboard motor.

"New World," part of a new work on journeying through America, entitled *Hunting Mister Heartbreak* (1991), takes him from Manhattan to Guntersville, Alabama, then to Seattle and Key West. He has now settled in the new world, in a new home, overlooking the Puget Sound, in Seattle. In it, he asks: What does it mean to leave your country? Is it possible to become a new person by traveling to a new world?

How would you characterize this piece? Ethnography? History? If ethnography, what do you make of Raban's general reflections, on his hotel room, on *The Teaching of Buddha,* on Seattle?

Is Raban a spectator only? A participant? A bit of both? What *kind* of observer is he? Which of the three people he describes in detail—Mr. Han, Jay Park, or Insook Webber—can you see and hear most clearly? Do you trust Raban's portraits? Why or why not? (Look particularly at Mr. Han, the "bantamweight boxer" who has "taken on America single-handed" and whose speech mannerisms are so carefully recorded. Do you think Mr. Han would be pleased with Raban's picture of him? Does it matter what Mr. Han might think?)

Cookies at Midnight
Pearl Rowe

My mother and I stayed up almost all night once when I was 9. She sat at the kitchen table laboring over a letter that she was writing in Yiddish. (She was unable to write English; even Yiddish was hard for her.)

Like a restless puppy, I circled the kitchen table, sensing that something was wrong. My mother always sent me to bed early on school nights. But not that night.

"Ma, don't you think I should be in bed by now?" I asked, uncomfortable with the lawless freedom.

"I want you should stay up for a while yet. It wouldn't hurt one night."

My four brothers, sister, and father, all older than I, were properly asleep. I took my rag doll by the arm and swung her around over my head, trying to get some attention. "Dolly's dizzy, Ma."

"Put her head between her legs."

"Could I have some cookies?"

She answered without looking up. "Take some out of the box, but close it tight, I think I saw a rat in the pantry."

It was unheard of. Cookies at midnight. I threw in some heavy artillery. "They sent Ida home from school today with nits. Teacher said you should wash my hair with kerosene because I sat next to her."

"That's nice."

"Maaa!" I started to cry.

My mother looked up.

"Ma, are you smoking?"

"Just for a change. Only for a change."

That was some crazy night. My mother was so different from how I had ever seen her before. I decided it would be a good time to sneak in the important question. At least she wasn't busy plucking dead chickens or washing laundry on the scrub board. In her preoccupation she seemed somehow more accessible to me.

"Ma, do some people live forever?"

I had reached her. She looked up, "Yes, baby. Special people."

"Am I special?"

"Absolutely. Positively. You're one of the special people who will live forever."

Boy, was that a relief. I had needed to know that for a long time. I was sure glad to finally get it cleared up. My eyelids grew heavy. The prospect of living forever had made me even sleepier. I stretched out on a step and put my doll beneath my head for a pillow. The next thing I knew, my mother was shaking me awake.

"I finished my letter. Now I want you to do something real nice for me. I want you should write something on the envelope in English."

I was sleepy and cranky. "Maaa, I want to go to bed. And I don't like writing. I only like printing big."

"Then print big."

"Can't I go to bed instead? My head's loose on my neck."

"Just do this one thing and you can go right upstairs—Okay, baby?" My mother led me over to the table and sat me down on the wooden kitchen chair and pushed the chair way under the table as far as it would go. She put the envelope down on the worn oilcloth, right under my chin.

"I want a red crayon."

She rummaged around in a drawer and found one.

"But I don't know what to print. You'll have to tell me."

"I'll tell you exactly." She dictated silly words. Words I was too sleepy to understand or spell right. I sounded them out like in school, moving my mouth as I put them down. My head nodded lower and lower over the paper. When I finished, my mother slid the envelope from under my limp hand.

"Did you finish, baby? Did you put all the words down? All the words like I told you?"

"Yeah. Now can I go to bed?"

She helped me up the stairs to where my sister, Anna, was sleeping. I collapsed into bed beside her. I felt my mother cover and kiss me. Finally. I was fast asleep before she left the room.

That's all I remember from the night my mother seemed to be under a gypsy spell. The next morning it was no better. I sat in the kitchen before school, tracing stick men on the steamy windows, noticing that my mother and father were all dressed up before breakfast, and it wasn't even a holiday.

My father said to my mother, "We have to go now, Freida. You said you wanted to stop at Mr. Moscowitz's grocery."

Before they went out the back door, my mother turned and looked around the room at all six of us kids, her eyes like the lens of a camera, taking pictures fast, before clouds blocked the sun. My father was carrying a small suitcase. My mother told me not to forget to wash my socks for school the next day, and then they were gone.

We all stared at the closed door. Nobody had kissed anybody. Nobody had even said goodbye. Everything was tangled and different from ever before, and everybody was just letting it be that way. My big brother Harry would explain it to me, I thought. He knew everything. He could even mix chemicals in his laboratory in the attic and make real crystal out of milk bottles. I asked him where Ma and Pa had gone.

"To the hospital. Ma's having an operation tomorrow."

"Like my tonsils?"

"Something like that."

That night I dreamed that I washed my red socks and something in the red dye in the water scared me and I awoke hugging my doll tight, with my thumb in my mouth and my forefinger in my ear. It was Saturday. I didn't need to go to school or wash my socks after all. My father left for the hospital early, and only Morry and I were in the kitchen. Harry was in the attic making gold. I was sitting on the floor playing jacks. Morry was doing his favorite thing—eating. I don't remember about the other kids.

The doorbell rang. It was always exciting when that happened, because our friends usually just walked in. A doorbell meant something special, like somebody selling encyclopedias or potato peelers. Morry answered the door. It was a telegram for my father. Morry opened it. I stood on my toes behind him and read. "Your wife Freida died . . ." The rest got all blurred up. Morry ran upstairs to the attic.

"It's my fault," I thought to myself. I hadn't asked my mother if she was one of the special people who would never die, like me.

That night Mr. Moscowitz came over. He looked at my father: "Your missus told me to give you this if . . ." Mr. Moscowitz covered his face with his hand and I could hear him choking and sobbing. He handed my father a thick letter. My father opened it and laid the envelope on the dining-room table. I read the big letters printed crookedly in red crayon across the front of the envelope. I sounded the awful words out as I read them:

"MY LAST WILL AND TESTIMINT. DO NOT OPIN UNTILL I AM DETH."

CONSIDER THIS

Students in my classes are irresistibly drawn to this essay, printed in a *Pittsburgh Press* Sunday supplement. Pearl Rowe, whom I have never been able to locate to tell her, doesn't know how much this piece has meant to some of her readers. What do they find appealing? In contrast to the Hong Kingston, where they see the narrator as very much in control of her narration, here in "Cookies at Midnight," the pace and tone of the telling rest on an element of vivid confusion. The teller herself recreates the sense of bewilderment as it overwhelmed her at the time. As a result, the reader is swept up into a narrative which in turn lays that confusion on the reader. We, too, as readers, may be uncomfortable with the lawless freedom. We find ourselves murmuring, "Yes, the child should be in bed." So, we discover tension and uncertainty. Which are the forms of energy. And the story leaves us breathless, because we have expended so much emotional and nervous energy.

The only way in which the narrator seems able to cope with the situation is to insist on a recognition: "That was some crazy night." By so insisting (explicit evaluation), she gains a little control over it, and no longer feels compelled to try to understand it as if it were normal.

So we are swung, lurching, between confusion and temporary relief, from bewilderment to the distancing relief of humor. The pace, and the forward impetus of narration here, depend on our illusion that the narrator herself doesn't know what is going to happen next. (She's a participant.) Again and again she confesses or insists on her incomprehension. And this effect is breathtakingly sustained right to the poignant message at the end: it is as if she herself had not written it, but is seeing it for the first time. It is a tense collision of innocence and experience.

On the Level
Oliver Sacks

It is nine years now since I met Mr MacGregor, in the neurology clinic of St. Dunstan's, an old-people's home where I once worked, but I remember him—I see him—as if it were yesterday.

'What's the problem?' I asked, as he tilted in.

'Problem? No problem—none that I know of . . . But others keep telling me I lean to the side: "You're like the Leaning Tower of Pisa," they say. "A bit more tilt, and you'll topple right over."'

'But *you* don't feel any tilt?'

'I feel fine. I don't know what they mean. How *could* I be tilted without knowing I was?'

'It sounds a queer business,' I agreed. 'Let's have a look. I'd like to see you stand and take a little stroll—just from here to that wall and back. I want to see for myself, *and I want you to see too*. We'll take a videotape of you walking and play it right back.'

'Suits me, Doc,' he said, and, after a couple of lunges, stood up. What a fine old chap, I thought. Ninety-three—and he doesn't look a day past seventy. Alert, bright as a button. Good for a hundred. And strong as a coal-heaver, even if he does have Parkinson's disease. He was walking, now, confidently, swiftly, but canted over, improbably, a good twenty degrees, his centre of gravity way off to the left, maintaining his balance by the narrowest possible margin.

'There!' he said with a pleased smile. 'See! No problems—I walked straight as a die.'

'Did you, indeed, Mr MacGregor?' I asked. 'I want you to judge for yourself.'

I rewound the tape and played it back. He was profoundly shocked when he saw himself on the screen. His eyes bulged, his jaw dropped, and he muttered, 'I'll be damned!' And then, 'They're right, I *am* over to one side. I *see* it here clear enough, but I've no sense of it. I don't *feel* it.'

'That's it,' I said. 'That's the heart of the problem.'

We have five senses in which we glory and which we recognise and celebrate, senses that constitute the sensible world for us. But there are other senses—secret senses, sixth senses, if you will—equally vital, but unrecognised, and unlauded. These senses, unconscious, automatic, had to be discovered. Historically, indeed, their discovery came late: what the Victorians vaguely called 'muscle sense'—the awareness of the relative position of trunk and limbs, derived from receptors in the joints and tendons—was only really defined (and named 'proprioception') in the 1890s. And the complex mechanisms and controls by which our bodies are properly aligned and balanced in space—these have only been defined in our own century, and still hold many mysteries. Perhaps it will only be in this space age, with the paradoxical license and hazards of gravity-free life, that we will truly appreciate our inner ears, our vestibules and all the other obscure receptors and reflexes that govern our body orientation. For normal man, in normal situations, they simply do not exist.

Yet their absence can be quite conspicuous. If there is defective (or distorted) sensation in our overlooked secret senses, what we then experience is profoundly strange, an almost incommunicable equivalent to being blind or being deaf. If proprioception is completely knocked out, the body becomes, so to speak, blind and deaf to itself—and (as the meaning of the Latin root *proprius* hints) ceases to 'own' itself, to feel itself as itself (see Chapter Three, 'The Disembodied Lady').

The old man suddenly became intent, his brows knitted, his lips pursed. He stood motionless, in deep thought, presenting the picture that I love to see: a patient in the actual moment of discovery—half-appalled, half-amused—seeing for the first time exactly what is wrong and, in the same moment, exactly what there is to be done. This *is* the therapeutic moment.

'Let me think, let me think,' he murmured, half to himself, drawing his shaggy white brows down over his eyes and emphasising each point with his powerful, gnarled hands. 'Let me think. You think with me—there must be an answer! I tilt to one side, and I can't tell it, right? There *should* be some feeling, a clear signal, but it's not there, right?' He paused. 'I used to be a carpenter,' he said, his face lighting up. 'We would always use a spirit level to tell whether a surface was level or not, or whether it was tilted from the vertical or not. Is there a sort of spirit level in the brain?'

I nodded.

'Can it be knocked out by Parkinson's disease?'

I nodded again.

'Is *this* what has happened with me?'

I nodded a third time and said, 'Yes. Yes. Yes.'

In speaking of such a spirit level, Mr MacGregor had hit on a fundamental analogy, a metaphor for an essential control system in the brain. Parts of the inner ear are indeed physically—literally—like levels; the labyrinth consists of semicircular canals containing liquid whose motion is continually monitored. But it was not these, as such, that were essentially at fault; rather, it was his ability to *use* his balance organs, in conjunction with the body's sense of itself and with its visual picture of the world. Mr MacGregor's homely symbol applies not just to the labyrinth but also to the complex *integration* of the three secret senses: the labyrinthine, the proprioceptive, and the visual. It is this synthesis that is impaired in Parkinsonism.

The most profound (and most practical) studies of such integrations—and of their singular *dis*integrations in Parkinsonism—were made by the late, great Purdon Martin and are to be found in his remarkable book *The Basal Ganglia and Posture* (originally published in 1967, but continually revised and expanded in the ensuing years; he was just completing a new edition when he died recently). Speaking of this integration, this integrator, in the brain, Purdon Martin writes 'There must be some centre or "higher authority" in the brain . . . some "controller" we may say. This controller or higher authority must be informed of the state of stability or instability of the body.'

In the section on 'tilting reactions' Purdon Martin emphasises the threefold contribution to the maintenance of a stable and upright posture, and he notes how commonly its subtle balance is upset in Parkinsonism—how, in particular, 'it is usual for the labyrinthine element to be lost before the proprioceptive and the visual'. This triple control system, he implies, is such that *one* sense, *one* control, can compensate for the others—not wholly (since the senses differ in their capabilities) but in part, at least, and to a useful degree. Visual reflexes and controls are perhaps the least important—normally. So long as our vestibular and proprioceptive systems are intact, we are perfectly stable with our eyes closed. We do not tilt or lean or fall over the moment we close our eyes. But the precariously balanced Parkinsonian may do so. (One often sees Parkinsonian patients sitting in the most grossly tilted positions, with no awareness that this is the case. But let a mirror be provided, so they can *see* their positions, and they instantly straighten up.)

Proprioception, to a considerable extent, can compensate for defects in the inner ears. Thus patients who have been surgically deprived of their labyrinths (as is sometimes done to relieve the intolerable, crippling vertigo of severe Ménière's disease), while at first unable to stand upright or take a single step, may learn to employ and to *enhance* their proprioception quite wonderfully; in particular, to use the sensors in the vast latissimus dorsi muscles of the back—the greatest, most mobile muscular expanse in the body—as an accessory and novel balance organ, a pair of vast, winglike proprioceptors. As the patients become practised, as this becomes second-nature, they are able to stand and walk—not perfectly, but with safety, assurance, and ease.

Purdon Martin was endlessly thoughtful and ingenious in designing a variety of mechanisms and methods that made it possible for even severely disabled Parkinsonians to achieve an artificial normality of gait and posture—lines painted on the floor, counter-weights in the belt, loudly ticking pacemakers—to set the cadence of walking. In this he always learned from his patients (to whom, indeed, his great book is dedicated). He was a deeply human pioneer, and in his medicine understanding and collaborating were central: patient and physician were coequals, on the same level, each learning from and helping the other and *between them* arriving at new insights and treatment. But he had not, to my knowledge, devised a prosthesis for the correction of impaired tilting and higher vestibular reflexes, the problem that afflicted Mr MacGregor.

'So that's it, is it?' asked Mr MacGregor. 'I can't use the spirit level inside my head. I can't use my ears, but I *can* use my eyes.' Quizzically, experimentally, he tilted his head to one side: 'Things look the same now—the world doesn't tilt.' Then he asked for a mirror, and I had a long one wheeled before him. '*Now* I see myself tilting,' he said. '*Now* I can straighten up—maybe I could stay straight . . . But I can't live among mirrors, or carry one round with me.'

He thought again deeply, frowning in concentration—then suddenly his face cleared, and lit up with a smile. 'I've got it!' he exclaimed. 'Yeah, Doc, I've got it! I don't need a mirror—I just need a level. I can't use the spirit level *inside* my head, but why couldn't I use levels *outside* my head—levels I could *see*, I could use with my eyes?' He took off his glasses, fingering them thoughtfully, his smile slowly broadening.

'Here, for example, in the rim of my glasses . . . This could tell me, tell my eyes, if I was tilting. I'd keep an eye on it at first; it would be a real strain. But then it might become second-nature, automatic. Okay, Doc, so what do you think?'

'I think it's a brilliant idea, Mr MacGregor. Let's give it a try.'

The principle was clear, the mechanics a bit tricky. We first experimented with a sort of pendulum, a weighted thread hung from the rims, but this was too close to the eyes, and scarcely seen at all. Then, with the help of our optometrist and workshop, we made a clip extending two nose-lengths forward from the bridge of the spectacles, with a miniature horizontal level fixed to each side. We fiddled with various designs, all tested and modified by Mr MacGregor. In a couple of weeks we had completed a prototype, a pair of somewhat

Heath Robinsonish spirit spectacles: 'The world's first pair!' said Mr MacGregor, in glee and triumph. He donned them. They looked a bit cumbersome and odd, but scarcely more so than the bulky hearing-aid spectacles that were coming in at the time. And now a strange sight was to be seen in our Home—Mr MacGregor in the spirit spectacles he had invented and made, his gaze intensely fixed, like a steersman eyeing the binnacle of his ship. This worked, in a fashion—at least he stopped tilting: but it was a continuous, exhausting exercise. And then, over the ensuing weeks, it got easier and easier; keeping an eye on his 'instruments' became unconscious, like keeping an eye on the instrument panel of one's car while being free to think, chat, and do other things.

Mr MacGregor's spectacles became the rage of St. Dunstan's. We had several other patients with Parkinsonism who also suffered from impairment of tilting reactions and postural reflexes—a problem not only hazardous but also notoriously resistant to treatment. Soon a second patient, then a third, were wearing Mr MacGregor's spirit spectacles, and now, like him, could walk upright, on the level.

CONSIDER THIS

Oliver Sacks, essayist, neurologist, has referred to himself as a "reporter from the far borders of human experience." His concerns in *The Man Who Mistook His Wife for a Hat,* the best-selling book of essays in which this selection appeared, and *Awakenings,* the book on which the film of the same name starring Robert De Niro and Robin Williams was based, are profound. In his "clinical tales" of the remarkable compensatory powers and resilience shown by human beings in the face of neurological and sensory catastrophe, he probes the nature of illness, wellness, and recovery.

He also tells a darn good story. He "sees" Mr. MacGregor "as if it were yesterday," and he lets us see him also. The visual images—Mr. MacGregor tilting, Mr. MacGregor experiencing his therapeutic moment, Mr. MacGregor in his spirit spectacles—are sharply focused and compelling. And though we don't "see" Sacks in the same way (characteristically, the participant-narrator chooses not to describe himself), we learn a great deal about him and about what he knows (what *doesn't* he know, we wonder) in these few pages. It's the combination of shared images—not the least of which is the marvelous, central double entendre–metaphor, the *spirit level*—and shared knowledge that gives this story its weight.

I Led the Pigeons to the Flag
William Safire

The most saluted man in America is Richard Stans. Legions of schoolchildren place their hands over their hearts to pledge allegiance to the flag, "and to the republic for Richard Stans."

With all due patriotic fervor, the same kids salute "one nation, under guard." Some begin with "I pledge a legion to the flag," others with "I led the pigeons to the flag."

This is not a new phenomenon. When they come to "one nation, indivisible," this generation is as likely to say, "One naked individual" as a previous generation was to murmur, "One nation in a dirigible," or, "One nation and a vegetable."

"The Stars Bangled Banner" is a great source for these creative mishearings: "the Donzery light," "oh, the ramrods we washed," "grapefruit through the night" that our flag was still there.

Then there is the good Mrs. Shirley Murphy of the 23d Psalm: "Shirley, good Mrs. Murphy, shall follow me all the days of my life." (Surely, goodness and mercy would not lead us into Penn Station.)

We all hear the same sounds. But until we are directed by the written word to the intended meaning, we may give free rein to our imagination to invent our own meanings. (*Free rein* has to do with letting horses run; some people are changing the metaphor to government, spelling it "free reign.") Children make sounds fit the sense in their own heads. In "God Bless America," the misheard line "Through the night with a light from a bulb" makes more practical sense than "a light from above." Writes David Thomas of Maine: "In Sunday school I used to sing part of a hymn, 'I will follow Henry Joyce.' Who Henry Joyce was didn't concern me—I was following him at the top of my lungs. When I learned to read, I found the words were 'I will follow and rejoice.'"

Sometimes that awakening never takes place. "To all intents and purposes," a nice old phrase, is sometimes spoken as—and written as—"for all intensive purposes." With the onset of adulthood, correction should not be taken for granted—or "taken for granite." In the song "Lucy in the Sky with Diamonds" (its title subliminally plugging LSD), the phrase "the girl with kaleidoscope eyes" came across to one grandmother as "the girl with colitis goes by."

What is this mistaken hearing called? In a query in this space recently, I remembered that I had called bandleader Guy Lombardo "Guylum Bardo," and asked for other examples of "false homonyms." That was a slight misnomer; homonyms are words pronounced the same, but with different meanings. Along with the other examples sent in—crooner Victor Moan, actress Sophie Aloran, musician "Big Spider" Beck, pro-football back Frank O'Harris, novelist Gorvey Doll—came instruction from linguists too mentionable to numerate. In each category, childlike translation can lead to semantic change.

(1) The Guylum Bardo syndrome—the simple misdivision of words—is called *metanalysis*. Many of the words we use correctly today are mistaken divisions of the past: a "napron" in Middle English became an "apron"—the *n* slid over to the left; an "ekename" of six centuries ago became a "nickname"—the *n* slid to the right.

In a future century, some of today's metanalyses (for "wrong cuttings") may become accepted English. An exorbitant charge is called "a nominal egg," perhaps committed by a "next-store neighbor"; some runners, poised at the starting line, hear, "On your market— set—go!" Millions of children consider the letter of the alphabet between *k* and *p* to be "ellemeno." Meteorologists on television who speak of "a patchy fog" do not realize that many creative viewers take that to be "Apache fog," which comes in on little cat feet to scalp the unsettled settler. Affiants seeking official witness go to a land called "Notar Republic," and Danny Boy, hero of "The Londonderry Air," casts a backward glance at what is often thought of as "The London Derrière." Future historians may wonder why chicken-hearted journalists coveted "the Pullet Surprise."

(2) The "José, can you see?" syndrome—the transmutation of words when they pass through different cultures or languages—is known to linguists as the *Law of Hobson-Jobson.* British soldiers in India heard the Mohammedan cry *"Ya-Hasan, ya-Husain!"* and called it "hobson-jobson." Noel Perrin at Dartmouth College reports that American soldiers in Japan transmuted a popular Japanese song, *Shi-i-na-na Yaru,"* into "She Ain't Got No Yo-Yo." Similarly, *"O Tannenbaum"* is sometimes rendered "Oh, atom bomb."

(3) Semantic change can come from *malapropisms,* named after Mrs. Malaprop, a character in *The Rivals,* a 1775 play by Richard Sheridan. More people than you suspect read and pronounce *mislead* as "mizzled," and the verb *to misle* will one day challenge *to mislead.* Others hum what they call "the bronze lullaby," though it must spin Brahms in his grave. One fascinating malapropism is "to hold in escarole," which combines the escrow function with the slang metaphor of money as lettuce.

(4) *Folk etymology* is the term for the creation of new words by mistake or misunder-standing or mispronunciation. "Tawdry," for example, came from Saint Audrey's, a place where cheap merchandise was sold. In today's language, "harebrained" is often giddily and irresponsibly misspelled "hairbrained," perhaps on the notion that the hair is near the brain.

The slurred *and* is one of the prolific changers of phrases. When "hard and fast" is spoken quickly, it becomes "hard 'n'fast," which sometimes gets transformed to "harden-fast rules." In the same way, the old "whole kit 'n' caboodle" is occasionally written as "kitten caboodle," a good name for a satchel in which to carry a cat. ("Up and atom!" is not a member of this group; it belongs with those Christmas carolers singing, "Oh, atom bomb.")

Lest you think that such mistakes can never permanently implant themselves in the language, consider "spit 'n' image." One longtime meaning of *spit* is "perfect likeness"— a child can be the very spit of his father. But some writers have mistaken the first two words in the phrase to mean "spitting," or ejection from the mouth, and prissily added the mistaken *g* to the sound of "spitt'n'." Novelist Paul Theroux entitled a chapter of *Picture Palace* "A Spitting Image." From such a respected writer, one expectorates more.

What all-inclusive term can we use to encompass the changes that our brains make in the intended meaning of what we hear? Linguists suggest "homophone," "unwitting paronomasia," and "agnominatio," but those terms sound like fancified dirty words to me.

I prefer "mondegreen." This is a word coined in a 1954 *Harper's Magazine* article, "The Death of Lady Mondegreen" by Sylvia Wright, which reported on the doings of "Gladly, the cross-eyed bear" (the way many children hear "Gladly the Cross I'd bear"), and other sound-alikes. Miss Wright recalled a Scottish ballad, "The Bonny Earl of

Murray" from Thomas Percy's "Reliques of Ancient English Poetry," which sounded to her like this:

> Ye Highlands and ye Lowlands,
> Oh, where hae ye been?
> They hae slain the Earl Amurray,
> And Lady Mondegreen.

She envisioned the bonny Earl holding the beautiful Lady Mondegreen's hand, both bleeding profusely, but faithful unto death. "By now," Miss Wright wrote, "several of you more alert readers are jumping up and down in your impatience to interrupt and point out that, according to the poem, after they killed the Earl of Murray, they 'laid him on the green.' I know about this, but I won't give in to it. Leaving him to die all alone without even anyone to hold his hand—I won't have it."

Thanks to responsive readers, I have a column on sound defects and a whole closetful of mondegreens. But a nuff is a nuff.

CONSIDER THIS

Misreadings and their consequences is one of the themes of this text. Here, William Safire, whose passionate and inexhaustible interest in how we use our language is expressed weekly in his regular column in *The New York Times Sunday Magazine,* offers some hilarious mishearings. Characteristically, Safire goes far beyond observation. Never a mere recorder, he writes as commentator, scholar, and yes, self-appointed guardian of the language.

Although this column does not, like some, give one the feeling that Safire regards misuses of the language as a symptom of general moral decline, there is at least one strong hint of his conservative tendencies: He laments Paul Theroux's use of "spitting image." Yet, according to Webster's *Dictionary of English Usage* (1989), the original use of *spit* to mean "exact likeness" has passed from common parlance, and *spitting image* "has established itself as the usual form."

The Masked Marvel's Last Toehold
Richard Selzer

Morning rounds.

On the fifth floor of the hospital, in the west wing, I know that a man is sitting up in his bed, waiting for me. Elihu Koontz is seventy-five, and he is diabetic. It is two weeks since I amputated his left leg just below the knee. I walk down the corridor, but I do not go straight into his room. Instead, I pause in the doorway. He is not yet aware of my presence, but gazes down at the place in the bed where his leg used to be, and where now there is the collapsed leg of his pajamas. He is totally absorbed, like an athlete appraising the details of his body. What is he thinking, I wonder. Is he dreaming the outline of his toes. Does he see there his foot's incandescent ghost? Could he be angry? Feel that I have taken from him something for which he yearns now with all his heart? Has he forgotten so soon the pain? It was a pain so great as to set him apart from all other men, in a red-hot place where he had no kith or kin. What of those black gorilla toes and the soupy mess that was his heel? I watch him from the doorway. It is a kind of spying, I know.

Save for a white fringe open at the front, Elihu Koontz is bald. The hair has grown too long and is wilted. He wears it as one would wear a day-old laurel wreath. He is naked to the waist, so that I can see his breasts. They are the breasts of Buddha, inverted triangles from which the nipples swing, dark as garnets.

I have seen enough. I step into the room, and he sees that I am there.

"How did the night go, Elihu?"

He looks at me for a long moment. "Shut the door," he says.

I do, and move to the side of the bed. He takes my left hand in both of his, gazes at it, turns it over, then back, fondling, at last holding it up to his cheek. I do not withdraw from this loving. After a while he relinquishes my hand, and looks up at me.

"How is the pain?" I ask.

He does not answer, but continues to look at me in silence. I know at once that he has made a decision.

"Ever hear of The Masked Marvel?" He says this in a low voice, almost a whisper.

"What?"

"The Masked Marvel," he says. "You never heard of him?"

"No."

He clucks his tongue. He is exasperated.

All at once there is a recollection. It is dim, distant, but coming near.

"Do you mean the wrestler?"

Eagerly, he nods, and the breasts bob. How gnomish he looks, oval as the huge helpless egg of some outlandish lizard. He has very long arms, which, now and then, he unfurls to reach for things—a carafe of water, a get-well card. He gazes up at me, urging. He *wants* me to remember.

"Well . . . yes," I say. I am straining backward in time. "I saw him wrestle in Toronto long ago."

"Ha!" He smiles. "You saw *me*." And his index finger, held rigid and upright, bounces in the air.

The man has said something shocking, unacceptable. It must be challenged.

"You?" I am trying to smile.

Again that jab of the finger. "You saw *me*."

"No," I say. But even then, something about Elihu Koontz, those prolonged arms, the shape of his head, the sudden agility with which he leans from his bed to get a large brown envelope from his nightstand, something is forcing me toward a memory. He rummages through his papers, old newspaper clippings, and I remember . . .

It is almost forty years ago. I am ten years old. I have been sent to Toronto to spend the summer with relatives. Uncle Max has bought two tickets to the wrestling match. He is taking me that night.

"He isn't allowed," says Aunt Sarah to me. Uncle Max has angina.

"He gets too excited," she says.

"I wish you wouldn't go, Max," she says.

"You mind your own business," he says.

And we go. Out into the warm Canadian evening. I am not only abroad, I am abroad in the *evening*! I have never been taken out in the evening. I am terribly excited. The trolleys, the lights, the horns. It is a bazaar. At the Maple Leaf Gardens, we sit high and near the center. The vast arena is dark except for the brilliance of the ring at the bottom.

It begins.

The wrestlers circle. They grapple. They are all haunch and paunch. I am shocked by their ugliness, but I do not show it. Uncle Max is exhilarated. He leans forward, his eyes unblinking, on his face a look of enormous happiness. One after the other, a pair of wrestlers enter the ring. The two men join, twist, jerk, tug, bend, yank, and throw. They then leave and are replaced by another pair. At last it is the main event. "The Angel vs. The Masked Marvel."

On the cover of the program notes, there is a picture of The Angel hanging from the limb of a tree, a noose of thick rope around his neck. The Angel hangs just so for an hour every day, it is explained, to strengthen his neck. The Masked Marvel's trademark is a black stocking cap with holes for the eyes and mouth. He is never seen without it, states the program. No one knows who The Masked Marvel really is!

"Good," says my Uncle Max. "Now you'll see something." He is fidgeting, waiting for them to appear. They come down separate aisles, climb into the ring from opposite sides. I have never seen anything like them. It is The Angel's neck that first captures the eye. The shaved nape rises in twin columns to puff into the white hood of a sloped and bosselated skull that is too small. As though, strangled by the sinews of that neck, the skull had long since withered and shrunk. The thing about The Angel is the absence of any mystery in his body. It is simply *there*. A monosyllabic announcement. A grunt. One looks and knows everything at once, the fat thighs, the gigantic buttocks, the great spine from which hang knotted ropes and pale aprons of beef. And the prehistoric head. He is all a single hideous piece, The Angel is. No detachables.

The Masked Marvel seems dwarfish. His fingers dangle kneeward. His short legs are slightly bowed as if under the weight of the cask they are forced to heft about. He has breasts that swing when he moves! I have never seen such breasts on a man before.

There is sudden ungraceful movement, and they close upon one another. The Angel stoops and hugs The Marvel about the waist, locking his hands behind The Marvel's back.

Now he straightens and lifts The Marvel as though he were uprooting a tree. Thus he holds him, then stoops again, thrusts one hand through The Marvel's crotch, and with the other grabs him by the neck. He rears and . . . The Marvel is aloft! For a long moment, The Angel stands as though deciding where to make the toss. Then throws. Was that board or bone that splintered there? Again and again, The Angel hurls himself upon the body of The Masked Marvel.

Now The Angel rises over the fallen Marvel, picks up one foot in both of his hands, and twists the toes downward. It is far beyond the tensile strength of mere ligament, mere cartilage. The Masked Marvel does not hide his agony, but pounds and slaps the floor with his hand, now and then reaching up toward The Angel in an attitude of supplication. I have never seen such suffering. And all the while his black mask rolls from side to side, the mouth pulled to a tight slit through which issues an endless hiss that I can hear from where I sit. All at once, I hear a shouting close by.

"Break if off! Tear off a leg and throw it up here!"

It is Uncle Max. Even in the darkness I can see that he is gray. A band of sweat stands upon his upper lip. He is on his feet now, panting, one fist pressed at his chest, the other raised warlike toward the ring. For the first time I begin to think that something terrible might happen here. Aunt Sarah was right.

"Sit down, Uncle Max," I say. "Take a pill, please."

He reaches for the pillbox, gropes, and swallows without taking his gaze from the wrestlers. I wait for him to sit down.

"That's not fair," I say, "twisting his toes like that."

"It's the toehold," he explains.

"But it's not *fair*," I say again. The whole of the evil is laid open for me to perceive. I am trembling.

And now The Angel does something unspeakable. Holding the foot of The Marvel at full twist with one hand, he bends and grasps the mask where it clings to the back of The Marvel's head. And he pulls. He is going to strip it off! Lay bare an ultimate carnal mystery! Suddenly it is beyond mere physical violence. Now I am on my feet, shouting into the Maple Leaf Gardens.

"Watch out," I scream. "Stop him. Please, somebody, stop him."

Next to me, Uncle Max is chuckling.

Yet The Masked Marvel hears me, I know it. And rallies from his bed of pain. Thrusting with his free heel, he strikes The Angel at the back of the knee. The Angel falls. The Masked Marvel is on top of him, pinning his shoulders to the mat. One! Two! Three! And it is over. Uncle Max is strangely still. I am grasping for breath. All this I remember as I stand at the bedside of Elihu Koontz.

Once again, I am in the operating room. It is two years since I amputated the left leg of Elihu Koontz. Now it is his right leg which is gangrenous. I have already scrubbed. I stand to one side wearing my gown and gloves. And . . . *I am masked.* Upon the table lies Elihu Koontz, pinned in a fierce white light. Spinal anesthesia has been administered. One of his arms is taped to a board placed at a right angle to his body. Into this arm, a needle has been placed. Fluid drips here from a bottle overhead. With his other hand, Elihu Koontz beats feebly at the side of the operating table. His head rolls from side to side. His mouth is pulled into weeping. It seems to me that I have never seen such misery.

An orderly stands at the foot of the table, holding Elihu Koontz's leg aloft by the toes so that the intern can scrub the limb with antiseptic solutions. The intern paints the foot, ankle, leg, and thigh, both front and back, three times. From a corner of the room where I wait, I look down as from an amphitheater. Then I think of Uncle Max yelling, "Tear off a leg. Throw it up here." And I think that forty years later I am making the catch.

"It's not fair," I say aloud. But no one hears me. I step forward to break The Masked Marvel's last toehold.

CONSIDER THIS

Richard Selzer (born 1928) is the author of a book of short stories (*Rituals of Surgery*) and several collections of autobiographical essays and sketches, including *Confessions of a Knife,* from which this piece is taken.

What is Selzer's role here? He's a participant, an eyewitness. He's also, as he confesses, a spy. You might look at the story side by side with "On the Level," by Oliver Sacks. Sacks the neurologist and Selzer the surgeon both write about their patients. Does the resemblance stop there? We never doubt that Sacks is telling us like it was. How trustworthy is Selzer as an eyewitness?

What about this essay gives it the flavor of fiction? At the end of the story Selzer says, "It's not fair." Is it fair to Elihu Koontz to fictionalize—to make grotesque—Koontz's personal tragedy?

We Do Abortions Here
Sallie Tisdale

We do abortions here; that is all we do. There are weary, grim moments when I think I cannot bear another basin of bloody remains, utter another kind phrase of reassurance. So I leave the procedure room in the back and reach for a new chart. Soon I am talking to an eighteen-year-old woman pregnant for the fourth time. I push up her sleeve to check her blood pressure and find row upon row of needle marks, neat and parallel and discolored. She has been so hungry for her drug for so long that she has taken to using the loose skin of her upper arms; her elbows are already a permanent ruin of bruises. She is surprised to find herself nearly four months pregnant. I suspect she is often surprised, in a mild way, by the blows she is dealt. I prepare myself for another basin, another brief and chafing loss.

"How can you stand it?" Even the clients ask. They see the machine, the strange instruments, the blood, the final stroke that wipes away the promise of pregnancy. Sometimes I see that too: I watch a woman's swollen abdomen sink to softness in a few stuttering moments and my own belly flip-flops with sorrow. But all it takes for me to catch my breath is another interview, one more story that sounds so much like the last one. There is a numbing sameness lurking in this job: the same questions, the same answers, even the same trembling tone in the voices. The worst is the sameness of human failure, of inadequacy in the face of each day's dull demands.

In describing this work, I find it difficult to explain how much I enjoy it most of the time. We laugh a lot here, as friends and as professional peers. It's nice to be with women all day. I like the sudden, transient bonds I forge with some clients: moments when I am in my strength, remembering weakness, and a woman in weakness reaches out for my strength. What I offer is not power, but solidness, offered almost eagerly. Certain clients waken in me every tender urge I have—others make me wince and bite my tongue. Both challenge me to find a balance. It is a sweet brutality we practice here, a stark and loving dispassion.

I look at abortion as if I am standing on a cliff with a telescope, gazing at some great vista. I can sweep the horizon with both eyes, survey the scene in all its distance and size. Or I can put my eye to the lens and focus on the small details, suddenly so close. In abortion the absolute must always be tempered by the contextual, because both are real, both valid, both hard. How can we do this? How can we refuse? Each abortion is a measure of our failure to protect, to nourish our own. Each basin I empty is a promise—but a promise broken a long time ago.

I grew up on the great promise of birth control. Like many women my age, I took the pill as soon as I was sexually active. To risk pregnancy when it was so easy to avoid seemed stupid, and my contraceptive success, as it were, was part of the promise of social enlightenment. But birth control fails, far more frequently than laboratory trials predict. Many of our clients take the pill; its failure to protect them is a shocking realization. We have clients who have been sterilized, whose husbands have had vasectomies; each one is a statistical misfit, fine print come to life. The anger and shame of these women I hold in one hand, and the basin in the other. The distance between the two, the length I pace and try to measure, is the size of an abortion.

The procedure is disarmingly simple. Women are surprised, as though the mystery of conception, a dark and hidden genesis, requires an elaborate finale. In the first trimester of pregnancy, it's a mere few minutes of vacuuming, a neat tidying up. I give a woman a small yellow Valium, and when it has begun to relax her, I lead her into the back, into bareness, the stirrups. The doctor reaches in her, opening the narrow tunnel to the uterus with a succession of slim, smooth bars of steel. He inserts a plastic tube and hooks it to a hose on the machine. The woman is framed against white paper that crackles as she moves, the light bright in her eyes. Then the machine rumbles low and loud in the small windowless room; the doctor moves the tube back and forth with an efficient rhythm, and the long tail of it fills with blood that spurts and stumbles along into a jar. He is usually finished in a few minutes. They are long minutes for the woman; her uterus frequently reacts to its abrupt emptying with a powerful, unceasing cramp, which cuts off the blood vessels and enfolds the irritated, bleeding tissue.

I am learning to recognize the shadows that cross the faces of the women I hold. While the doctor works between her spread legs, the paper drape hiding his intent expression, I stand beside the table. I hold the woman's hands in mine, resting them just below her ribs. I watch her eyes, finger her necklace, stroke her hair. I ask about her job, her family; in a haze she answers me; we chatter, faces close, eyes meeting and sliding apart.

I watch the shadows that creep up unnoticed and suddenly darken her face as she screws up her features and pushes a tear out each side to slide down her cheeks. I have learned to anticipate the quiver of chin, the rapid intake of breath, and the surprising sobs that rise soon after the machine starts to drum. I know this is when the cramp deepens, and the tears are partly the tears that follow pain—the sharp, childish crying when one bumps one's head on a cabinet door. But a well of woe seems to open beneath many women when they hear that thumping sound. The anticipation of the moment has finally come to fruit; the moment has arrived when the loss is no longer an imagined one. It has come true.

I am struck by the sameness and I am struck every day by the variety here—how this commonplace dilemma can so display the differences of women. A twenty-one-year-old woman, unemployed, uneducated, without family, in the fifth month of her fifth pregnancy. A forty-two-year-old mother of teenagers, shocked by her condition, refusing to tell her husband. A twenty-three-year-old mother of two having her seventh abortion, and many women in their thirties having their first. Some are stoic, some hysterical, a few giggle uncontrollably, many cry.

I talk to a sixteen-year-old uneducated girl who was raped. She has gonorrhea. She describes blinding headaches, attacks of breathlessness, nausea. "Sometimes I feel like two different people," she tells me with a calm smile, "and I talk to myself."

I pull out my plastic models. She listens patiently for a time, and then holds her hands wide in front of her stomach.

"When's the baby going to go up into my stomach?" she asks.

I blink. "What do you mean?"

"Well," she says, still smiling, "when women get so big, isn't the baby in your stomach? Doesn't it hatch out of an egg there?"

My first question in an interview is always the same. As I walk down the hall with the woman, as we get settled in chairs and I glance through her files, I am trying to gauge her, to get a sense of the words, and the tone, I should use. With some I joke, with others I chat, sometimes I fall into a brisk, business-like patter. But I ask every woman, "Are you sure you want to have an abortion?" Most nod with grim knowing smiles. "Oh, yes," they sigh. Some seek forgiveness, offer excuses. Occasionally a woman will flinch and say, "Please don't use that word."

Later I describe the procedure to come, using care with my language. I don't say "pain" any more than I would say "baby." So many are afraid to ask how much it will hurt. "My sister told me—" I hear. "A friend of mine said—" and the dire expectations unravel. I prick the index finger of a woman for a drop of blood to test, and as the tiny lancet approaches the skin she averts her eyes, holding her trembling hand out to me and jumping at my touch.

It is when I am holding a plastic uterus in one hand, a suction tube in the other, moving them together in imitation of the scrubbing to come, that women ask the most secret question. I am speaking in a matter-of-fact voice about "the tissue" and "the contents" when the woman suddenly catches my eye and asks, "How big is the baby now?" These words suggest a quiet need for a definition of the boundaries being drawn. It isn't so odd, after all, that she feels relief when I describe the growing bud's bulbous shape, its miniature nature. Again I gauge, and sometimes lie a little, weaseling around its infantile features until its clinging power slackens.

But when I look in the basin, among the curdlike blood clots, I see an elfin thorax, attenuated, its pencilline ribs all in parallel rows with tiny knobs of spine rounding upwards. A translucent arm and hand swim beside.

A sleepy-eyed girl, just fourteen, watched me with a slight and goofy smile all through her abortion. "Does it have little feet and little fingers and all?" she'd asked earlier. When the suction was over she sat up woozily at the end of the table and murmured, "Can I see it?" I shook my head firmly.

"It's not allowed," I told her sternly, because I knew she didn't really want to see what was left. She accepted this statement of authority, and a shadow of confused relief crossed her plain, pale face.

Privately, even grudgingly, my colleagues might admit the power of abortion to provoke emotion. But they seem to prefer the broad view and disdain the telescope. Abortion is a matter of choice, privacy, control. Its uncertainty lies in specific cases: retarded women and girls too young to give consent for surgery, women who are ill or hostile or psychotic. Such common dilemmas are met with both compassion and impatience; they slow things down. We are too busy to chew over ethics. One person might discuss certain concerns, behind closed doors, or describe a particularly disturbing dream. But generally there is to be no ambivalence.

Every day I take calls from women who are annoyed that we cannot see them, cannot do their abortion today, this morning, now. They argue the price, demand that we stay after hours to accommodate their job or class schedule. Abortion is so routine that one expects it to be like a manicure; quick, cheap, and painless.

Still, I've cultivated a certain disregard. It isn't negligence, but I don't always pay attention. I couldn't be here if I tried to judge each case on its merits; after all, we do over a hundred abortions a week. At some point each individual in this line of work draws a boundary and adheres to it. For one physician the boundary is a particular week of gestation; for another, it is a certain number of repeated abortions. But these boundaries can be fluid too: one physician overruled his own limit to abort a mature but severely malformed fetus. For me, the limit is allowing my clients to carry their own burden, shoulder the responsibility themselves. I shoulder the burden of trying not to judge them.

This city has several "crisis pregnancy centers" advertised in the Yellow Pages. They are small offices staffed by volunteers, and they offer free pregnancy testing, glossy photos of dead fetuses, and movies. I had a client recently whose mother is active in the anti-abortion movement. The young woman went to the local crisis center and was told that the doctor would make her touch her dismembered baby, that the pain would be the most horrible she could imagine, and that she might, after an abortion, never be able to have children. All lies. They called her at home and at work, over and over and over, but she had been wise enough to give a false name. She came to us a fugitive. We who do abortions are marked, by some, as impure. It's dirty work.

When a deliveryman comes to the sliding glass window by the reception desk and tilts a box toward me, I hesitate. I read the packing slip, assess the shape and weight of the box in the light of its supposed contents. We request familiar faces. The doors are carefully locked; I have learned to half glance around at bags and boxes, looking for a telltale sign. I register with security when I arrive, and I am careful not to bang a door. We are a little on edge here.

Concern about size and shape seem to be natural, and so is the relief that follows. We make the powerful assumption that the fetus is different from us, and even when we admit the similarities, it is too simplistic to be seduced by form alone. But the form is enormously potent—humanoid, powerless, palm-sized, and pure, it evokes an almost fierce tenderness when viewed simply as what it appears to be. But appearance, and even potential, aren't enough. The fetus, in becoming itself, can ruin others; its utter dependence has a sinister side. When I am struck in the moment by the contents in the basin, I am careful to remember the context, to note the tearful teenager and the woman sighing with something more than relief. One kind of question, though, I find considerably trickier.

"Can you tell what it is?" I am asked, and this means gender. This question is asked by couples, not women alone. Always couples would abort a girl and keep a boy. I have been asked about twins, and even if I could tell what race the father was.

An eighteen-year-old woman with three daughters brought her husband to the interview. He glared first at me, then at his wife, as he sank lower and lower in the chair, picking his teeth with a toothpick. He interrupted a conversation with his wife to ask if I could tell whether the baby would be a boy or a girl. I told him I could not.

"Good," he replied in a slow and strangely malevolent voice, "cause if it was a boy I'd wring her neck."

In a literal sense, abortion exists because we are able to ask such questions, able to assign a value to the fetus which can shift with changing circumstances. If the human bond to a child were as primitive and unflinchingly narrow as that of other animals, there would be no abortion. There would be no abortion because there would be nothing more important than caring for the young and perpetuating the species, no reason for sex but to make babies. I sense this sometimes, this wordless organic duty, when I do ultrasounds.

We do ultrasound, a sound-wave test that paints a faint, gray picture of the fetus, whenever we're uncertain of gestation. Age is measured by the width of the skull and confirmed by the length of the femur or thighbone; we speak of a pregnancy as being a certain "femur length" in weeks. The usual concern is whether a pregnancy is within the legal limit for an abortion. Women this far along have bellies which swell out round and tight like trim muscles. When they lie flat, the mound rises softly above the hips, pressing the umbilicus upward.

It takes practice to read an ultrasound picture, which is grainy and etched as though in strokes of charcoal. But suddenly a rapid rhythmic motion appears—the beating heart. Nearby is a soft oval, scratched with lines—the skull. The leg is harder to find, and then suddenly the fetus moves, bobbing in the surf. The skull turns away, an arm slides across the screen, the torso rolls. I know the weight of a baby's head on my shoulder, the whisper of lips on ears, the delicate curve of a fragile spine in my hand. I know how heavy and correct a newborn cradled feels. The creature I watch in secret requires nothing from me but to be left alone, and that is precisely what won't be done.

These inadvertently made beings are caught in a twisting web of motive and desire. They are at least inconvenient, sometimes quite literally dangerous in the womb, but most often they fall somewhere in between—consequences never quite believed in come to roost. Their virtue rises and falls outside their own nature: they become only what we make them. A fetus created by accident is the most absolute kind of surprise. Whether the blame lies in a failed IUD, a slipped condom, or a false impression of safety, that fetus is a thing whose creation has been actively worked against. Its existence is an error. I think this is why so few women, even late in pregnancy, will consider giving a baby up for adoption. To do so means making the fetus real—imagining it as something whole and outside oneself. The decision to terminate a pregnancy is sometimes so difficult and confounding that it creates an enormous demand for immediate action. The decision is rejection; the pregnancy has become something to be rid of, a condition to be ended. It is a burden, a weight, a thing separate.

Women have abortions because they are too old, and too young, too poor, and too rich, too stupid, and too smart. I see women who berate themselves with violent emotions for their first and only abortion, and others who return three times, five times, hauling two or three children, who cannot remember to take a pill or where they put the diaphragm. We talk glibly about choice. But the choice for what? I see all the broken promises in lives lived like a series of impromptu obstacles. There are the sweet, light promises of love and intimacy, the glittering promise of education and progress, the warm promise of safe families, long years of innocence and community. And there is the promise of freedom: freedom from failure, from faithlessness. Freedom from biology. The early feminist defense of abortion asked many questions, but the one I remember is this: is biology destiny? And the answer is yes, sometimes it is. Women who have the fewest choices of all exercise their right to abortion the most.

Oh, the ignorance. I take a woman to the back room and ask her to undress; a few minutes later I return and find her positioned discreetly behind a drape, still wearing underpants. "Do I have to take these off too?" she asks, a little shocked. Some swear they have not had sex, many do not know what a uterus is, how sperm and egg meet, how sex makes babies. Some late seekers do not believe themselves pregnant; they believe themselves *impregnable*. I was chastised when I began this job for referring to some clients as girls: it is a feminist heresy. They come so young, snapping gum, sockless and sneakered, and their shakily applied eyeliner smears when they cry. I call them girls with maternal benignity. I cannot imagine them as mothers.

The doctor seats himself between the woman's thighs and reaches into the dilated opening of a five-month pregnant uterus. Quickly he grabs and crushes the fetus in several places, and the room is filled with a low clatter and snap of forceps, the click of the tanaculum,* and a pulling, sucking sound. The paper crinkles as the drugged and sleepy woman shifts, the nurse's low, honey-brown voice explains each step in delicate words.

I have fetus dreams, we all do here: dreams of abortions one after the other; of buckets of blood splashed on the walls; trees full of crawling fetuses. I dreamed that two men grabbed me and began to drag me away: "Let's do an abortion," they said with a sickening leer, and I began to scream, plunged into a vision of sucking, scraping pain, of being spread and torn by impartial instruments that do only what they are bidden. I woke from this dream barely able to breathe and thought of kitchen tables and coat hangers, knitting needles striped with blood, and women all alone clutching a pillow in their teeth to keep the screams from piercing the apartment-house walls. Abortion is the narrowest edge between kindness and cruelty. Done as well as it can be, it is still violence—merciful violence, like putting a suffering animal to death.

Maggie, one of the nurses, received a call at midnight not long ago. It was a woman in her twentieth week of pregnancy; the necessarily gradual process of cervical dilation begun the day before had stimulated labor, as it sometimes does. Maggie and one of the doctors met the woman at the office in the night. Maggie helped her onto the table, and as she lay down the fetus was delivered into Maggie's hands. When Maggie told me about it the next day, she cupped her hands into a small bowl—"It was just like a little kitten," she said softly, wonderingly. "Everything was still attached."

At the end of the day I clean out the suction jars, pouring blood into the sink, splashing the sides with flecks of tissue. From the sink rises a rich and humid smell, hot, earthy, and moldering; it is the smell of something recently alive beginning to decay. I take care of the plastic tub on the floor, filled with pieces too big to be trusted to the trash. The law defines the contents of the bucket I hold protectively against my chest as "tissue." Some would say my complicity in filling that bucket gives me no right to call it anything else. I slip the tissue gently into a bag and place it in the freezer, to be burned at another time. Abortion requires of me an entirely new set of assumptions. It requires a willingness to live with conflict, fearlessness, and grief. As I close the freezer door, I imagine a world where this won't be necessary, and then return to the world where it is.

---

* Type of sharp forceps used on bleeding arteries.

CONSIDER THIS

This piece is like nothing else I've ever read on the subject of abortion. It doesn't matter what your own position is—for, against, or agonizingly undecided—it has to *affect* you. Sallie Tisdale, a nurse, not a professional writer, doesn't structure her essay in any formal way. She tells us *what* she sees, day in, day out, *who* she sees, *how* she sees it. Yet despite the sheer force of detail, the vivid and often shocking individual vignettes, there is much that is unspoken.

How would you characterize this essay as a whole? Is the text "closed"? "Open"? There is no argument, no position to defend. Or is there? Do you find any evidence that Tisdale is, after all, defending what she does?

"Indians": Textualism, Morality and the Problem of History
Jane Tompkins

When I was growing up in New York City, my parents used to take me to an event in Inwood Park at which Indians—real American Indians dressed in feathers and blankets— could be seen and touched by children like me. This event was always a disappointment. It was more fun to imagine that you *were* an Indian in one of the caves in Inwood Park than to shake the hand of an old man in a headdress who was not overwhelmed at the opportunity of meeting you. After staring at the Indians for a while, we would take a walk in the woods where the caves were, and once I asked my mother if the remains of a fire I had seen in one of them might have been left by the original inhabitants. After that, wandering up some stone steps cut into the side of the hill, I imagined I was a princess in a rude castle. My Indians, like my princesses, were creatures totally of the imagination, and I did not care to have any real exemplars interfering with what I already knew.

I already knew about Indians from having read about them in school. Over and over we were told the story of how Peter Minuit had bought Manhattan Island from the Indians for twenty-four dollars' worth of glass beads. And it was a story we didn't mind hearing because it gave us the rare pleasure of having someone to feel superior to, since the poor Indians had not known (as we eight-year-olds did) how valuable a piece of property Manhattan Island would become. Generally, much was made of the Indian presence in Manhattan; a poem in one of our readers began: "Where we walk to school today / Indian children used to play," and we were encouraged to write poetry on this topic ourselves. So I had a fairly rich relationship with Indians before I ever met the unprepossessing people in Inwood Park. I felt that I had a lot in common with them. They, too, liked animals (they were often named after animals); they, too, made mistakes—they liked the brightly colored trinkets of little value that the white men were always offering them; they were handsome, warlike, and brave and had led an exciting, romantic life in the forest long ago, a life such as I dreamed of leading myself. I felt lucky to be living in one of the places where they had definitely been. Never mind where they were or what they were doing now.

My story stands for the relationship most non-Indians have to the people who first populated this continent, a relationship characterized by narcissistic fantasies of freedom and adventure, of a life lived closer to nature and to spirit than the life we lead now. As Vine Deloria, Jr., has pointed out, the American Indian Movement in the early seventies couldn't get people to pay attention to what was happening to Indians who were alive in the present, so powerful was this country's infatuation with people who wore loincloths, lived in tepees, and roamed the plains and forests long ago. The present essay, like these fantasies, doesn't have much to do with actual Indians, though its subject matter is the histories of European-Indian relations in seventeenth-century New England. In a sense, my encounter with Indians as an adult doing "research" replicates the childhood one, for while I started out to learn about Indians, I ended up preoccupied with a problem of my own.

This essay enacts a particular instance of the challenge poststructuralism poses to the study of history. In simpler language, it concerns the difference that point of view makes when people are giving accounts of events, whether at first or second hand. The problem is that if all accounts of events are determined through and through by the observer's frame of reference, then one will never know, in any given case, what really happened.

I encountered this problem in concrete terms while preparing to teach a course in colonial American literature. I'd set out to learn what I could about the Puritans' relations with American Indians. All I wanted was a general idea of what had happened between the English settlers and the natives in seventeenth-century New England; poststructuralism and its dilemmas were the furthest thing from my mind. I began, more or less automatically, with Perry Miller, who hardly mentions the Indians at all, then proceeded to the work of historians who had dealt exclusively with the European-Indian encounter. At first, it was a question of deciding which of these authors to believe, for it quickly became apparent that there was no unanimity on the subject. As I read on, however, I discovered that the problem was more complicated than deciding whose version of events was correct. Some of the conflicting accounts were not simply contradictory, they were completely incommensurable, in that their assumptions about what counted as a valid approach to the subject, and what the subject itself was, diverged in fundamental ways. Faced with an array of mutually irreconcilable points of view, points of view which determined what was being discussed as well as the terms of the discussion, I decided to turn to primary sources for clarification, only to discover that the primary sources reproduced the problem all over again. I found myself, in other words, in an epistemological quandary, not only unable to decide among conflicting versions of events but also unable to believe that any such decision could, in principle, be made. It was a moral quandary as well. Knowledge of what really happened when the Europeans and the Indians first met seemed particularly important, since the result of that encounter was virtual genocide. This was the kind of past "mistake" which, presumably, we studied history in order to avoid repeating. If studying history couldn't put us in touch with actual events and their causes, then what was to prevent such atrocities from happening again?

For a while, I remained at this impasse. But through analyzing the process by which I had reached it, I eventually arrived at an understanding which seemed to offer a way out. This essay records the concrete experience of meeting and solving the difficulty I have just described (as an abstract problem, I thought I had solved it long ago). My purpose is not to throw new light on antifoundationalist epistemology—the solution I reached is not a new one—but to dramatize and expose the troubles antifoundationalism gets you into when you meet it, so to speak, in the road.

My research began with Perry Miller. Early in the preface to *Errand into the Wilderness,* while explaining how he came to write his history of the New England mind, Miller writes a sentence that stopped me dead. He says that what fascinated him as a young man about his country's history was "the massive narrative of the movement of European culture into the vacant wilderness of America." "Vacant?" Miller, writing in 1956, doesn't pause over the word "vacant," but to people who read his preface thirty years later, the word is shocking. In what circumstances could someone proposing to write a history of colonial New England *not* take account of the Indian presence there?

The rest of Miller's preface supplies an answer to this question, if one takes the trouble to piece together its details. Miller explains that as a young man, jealous of older compatriots who had had the luck to fight in World War I, he had gone to Africa in search of adventure. "The adventures that Africa afforded," he writes, "were tawdry enough, but it became the setting for a sudden epiphany" (p. vii). "It was given to me," he writes, "disconsolate on the edge of a jungle of central Africa, to have thrust upon me the mission of expounding what I took to be the innermost propulsion of the United States, while supervising, in that barbaric tropic, the unloading of drums of case oil flowing out of the inexhaustible wilderness of America" (p. viii). Miller's picture of himself on the banks of the Congo furnishes a key to the kind of history he will write and to his mental image of a vacant wilderness; it explains why it was just there, under precisely these conditions, that he should have had his epiphany.

The fuel drums stand, in Miller's mind, for the popular misconception of what this country is about. They are "tangible symbols of [America's] appalling power," a power that everyone but Miller takes for the ultimate reality (p. ix). To Miller, "the mind of man is the basic factor in human history," and he will plead, all unaccommodated as he is among the fuel drums, for the intellect—the intellect for which his fellow historians, with their chapters on "stoves or bathtubs, or tax laws," "the Wilmot Proviso" and "the chain store," "have so little respect" (p. viii, ix). His preface seethes with a hatred of the merely physical and mechanical, and this hatred, which is really a form of moral outrage, explains not only the contempt with which he mentions the stoves and bathtubs but also the nature of his experience in Africa and its relationship to the "massive narrative" he will write.

Miller's experiences in Africa are "tawdry," his tropic is barbaric because the jungle he stands on the edge of means nothing to him, no more, indeed something less, than the case oil. It is the nothingness of Africa that precipitates his vision. It is the barbarity of the "dark continent," the obvious (but superficial) parallelism between the jungle at Matadi and America's "vacant wilderness" that releases in Miller the desire to define and vindicate his country's cultural identity. To the young Miller, colonial Africa and colonial America are—but for the history he will bring to light—mirror images of one another. And what he fails to see in the one landscape is the same thing he overlooks in the other: the human beings who people it. As Miller stood with his back to the jungle, thinking about the role of mind in human history, his failure to see that the land into which European culture had moved was not vacant but already occupied by a varied and numerous population, is of a piece with his failure, in his portrait of himself at Matadi, to notice *who* was carrying the fuel drums he was supervising the unloading of.

The point is crucial because it suggests that what is invisible to the historian in his own historical moment remains invisible when he turns his gaze to the past. It isn't that Miller didn't "see" the black man, in a literal sense, any more than it's the case that when he looked back he didn't "see" the Indians, in the sense of not realizing they were there. Rather, it's that neither the Indians nor the blacks *counted* for him, in a fundamental way. The way in which Indians can be seen but not counted is illustrated by an entry in Governor John Winthrop's journal, three hundred years before, when he recorded that there had been a great storm with high winds "yet through God's mercy it did not hurt, but only killed one Indian with the fall of a tree." The juxtaposition suggests that Miller shared with Winthrop a certain colonial point of view, a point of view from which Indians, though present, do not finally matter.

A book entitled *New England Frontier: Puritans and Indians, 1620–1675,* written by Alden Vaughan and published in 1965, promised to rectify Miller's omission. In the outpouring of work on the European-Indian encounter that began in the early sixties, this book is the first major landmark, and to a neophyte it seems definitive. Vaughan acknowledges the absence of Indian sources and emphasizes his use of materials which catch the Puritans "off guard." His announced conclusion that "the New England Puritans followed a remarkably humane, considerate, and just policy in their dealings with the Indians" seems supported by the scope, documentation, and methodicalness of his project (*NEF*, p. vii). The author's fair-mindedness and equanimity seem everywhere apparent, so that when he asserts "the history of interracial relations from the arrival of the Pilgrims to the outbreak of King Philip's War is a credit to the integrity of both peoples," one is positively reassured (*NEF*, p. viii).

But these impressions do not survive an admission that comes late in the book, when, in the course of explaining why works like Helen Hunt Jackson's *Century of Dishonor* had spread misconceptions about Puritan treatment of the Indians, Vaughan finally lays his own cards on the table.

> The root of the misunderstanding [about Puritans and Indians] . . . lie[s] in a failure to recognize the nature of the two societies that met in seventeenth century New England. One was unified, visionary, disciplined, and dynamic. The other was divided, self-satisfied, undisciplined, and static. It would be unreasonable to expect that such societies could live side by side indefinitely with no penetration of the more fragmented and passive by the more consolidated and active. What resulted, then, was not—as many have held—a clash of dissimilar ways of life, but rather the expansion of one into the areas in which the other was lacking. [*NEF*, p. 323]

From our present vantage point, these remarks seem culturally biased to an incredible degree, not to mention inaccurate: Was Puritan society unified? If so, how does one account for its internal dissensions and obsessive need to cast out deviants? Is "unity" necessarily a positive culture trait? From what standpoint can one say that American Indians were neither disciplined nor visionary, when both these characteristics loom so large in the ethnographies? Is it an accident that ways of describing cultural strength and weakness coincide with gender stereotypes—active/passive, and so on? Why is one culture said to "penetrate" the other? Why is the "other" described in terms of "lack"?

Vaughan's fundamental categories of apprehension and judgment will not withstand even the most cursory inspection. For what looked like evenhandedness when he was writing *New England Frontier* does not look that way anymore. In his introduction to *New Directions in American Intellectual History,* John Higham writes that by the end of the sixties

> the entire conceptual foundation on which [this sort of work] rested [had] crumbled away. . . . Simultaneously, in sociology, anthropology, and history, two working assumptions . . . came under withering attack: first, the assumption that societies tend to be integrated, and second, that a shared culture maintains that integration. . . . By the late 1960s all claims issued in the name of an "American mind" . . . were subject to drastic skepticism.

"Clearly," Higham continues, "the sociocultural upheaval of the sixties created the occasion" for this reaction. Vaughan's book, it seemed, could only have been written before the events of the sixties had sensitized scholars to questions of race and ethnicity. It came as no surprise, therefore, that ten years later there appeared a study of European-Indian relations which reflected the new awareness of social issues the sixties had engendered. And it offered an entirely different picture of the European-Indian encounter.

Francis Jennings' *The Invasion of America* (1975) rips wide open the idea that the Puritans were humane and considerate in their dealings with the Indians. In Jennings' account, even more massively documented than Vaughan's, the early settlers lied to the Indians, stole from them, murdered them, scalped them, captured them, tortured them, raped them, sold them into slavery, confiscated their land, destroyed their crops, burned their homes, scattered their possessions, gave them alcohol, undermined their systems of belief, and infected them with diseases that wiped out ninety percent of their numbers within the first hundred years after contact.

Jennings mounts an all-out attack on the essential decency of the Puritan leadership and their apologists in the twentieth century. The Pequot War, which previous historians had described as an attempt on the part of Massachusetts Bay to protect itself from the fiercest of the New England tribes, becomes, in Jennings' painstakingly researched account, a deliberate war of extermination, waged by whites against Indians. It starts with trumped-up charges, is carried on through a series of increasingly bloody reprisals, and ends in the massacre of scores of Indian men, women, and children, all so that Massachusetts Bay could gain political and economic control of the southern Connecticut Valley. When one reads this and then turns over the page and sees a reproduction of the Bay Colony seal, which depicts an Indian from whose mouth issue the words "Come over and help us," the effect is shattering.

But even so powerful an argument as Jennings' did not remain unshaken by subsequent work. Reading on, I discovered that if the events of the sixties had revolutionized the study of European-Indian relations, the events of the seventies produced yet another transformation. The American Indian Movement, and in particular the founding of the Native American Rights Fund in 1971 to finance Indian litigation, and a court decision in 1975 which gave the tribes the right to seek redress for past injustices in federal court, created a climate within which historians began to focus on the Indians themselves. "Almost simultaneously," writes James Axtell, "frontier and colonial historians began to discover the necessity of considering the American natives as real determinants of history and the utility of ethnohistory as a way of ensuring parity of focus and impartiality of judgment." In Miller, Indians had been simply beneath notice; in Vaughan, they belonged to an inferior culture; and in Jennings, they were the more or less innocent prey of power-hungry whites. But in the most original and provocative of the ethnohistories, Calvin Martin's *Keepers of the Game,* Indians became complicated, purposeful human beings, whose lives were spiritually motivated to a high degree. Their relationship to the animals they hunted, to the natural environment, and to the whites with whom they traded became intelligible within a system of beliefs that formed the basis for an entirely new perspective on the European-Indian encounter.

Within the broader question of why European contact had such a devastating effect on the Indians, Martin's specific aim is to determine why Indians participated in the fur trade which ultimately led them to the brink of annihilation. The standard answer to this question had always been that once the Indian was introduced to European guns, copper kettles, woolen blankets, and the like, he literally couldn't keep his hands off them. In order to acquire these coveted items, he decimated the animal populations on which his survival depended. In short, the Indian's motivation in participating in the fur trade was assumed to be the same as the white European's—a desire to accumulate material goods. In direct opposition to this thesis, Martin argues that the reason why the Indians ruthlessly exploited their own resources had nothing to do with supply and demand, but stemmed rather from a breakdown of the cosmic worldview that tied them to the game they killed in a spiritual relationship of parity and mutual obligation.

The hunt, according to Martin, was conceived not primarily as a physical activity but as a spiritual question, in which the spirit of the hunter must overmaster the spirit of the game animal before the kill can take place. The animal, in effect, *allows* itself to be found and killed, once the hunter has mastered its spirit. The hunter prepared himself through rituals of fasting, sweating, or dreaming which reveal the identity of his prey and where he can find it. The physical act of killing is the least important element in the process. Once the animal is killed, eaten, and its parts used for clothing or implements, its remains must be disposed of in ritually prescribed fashion, or the game boss, the "keeper" of that species, will not permit more animals to be killed. The relationship between Indians and animals, then, is contractual; each side must hold up its end of the bargain, or no further transactions can occur.

What happened, according to Martin, was that as a result of diseases introduced into the animal population by Europeans, the game suddenly disappeared, began to act in inexplicable ways, or sickened and died in plain view, and communicated their diseases to the Indians. The Indians, consequently, believed that their compact with the animals had been broken and that the keepers of the game, the tutelary spirits of each animal species whom they had been so careful to propitiate, had betrayed them. And when missionization, wars with the Europeans, and displacement from their tribal lands had further weakened Indian society and its belief structure, the Indians, no longer restrained by religious sanctions, in effect, turned on the animals in a holy war of revenge.

Whether or not Martin's specific claim about the "holy war" was correct, his analysis made it clear to me that, given the Indians' understanding of economic, religious, and physical processes, an Indian account of what transpired when the European settlers arrived here would look nothing like our own. Their (potential, unwritten) history of the conflict could bear only a marginal resemblance to Eurocentric views. I began to think that the key to understanding European-Indian relations was to see them as an encounter between wholly disparate cultures, and that therefore either defending or attacking the colonists was beside the point since, given the cultural disparity between the two groups, conflict was inevitable and in large part a product of mutual misunderstanding.

But three years after Martin's book appeared, Shepard Krech III edited a collection of seven essays called *Indians, Animals, and the Fur Trade,* attacking Martin's entire project. Here the authors argued that we don't need an ideological or religious explanation for the fur trade. As Charles Hudson writes,

The Southeastern Indians slaughtered deer (and were prompted to enslave and kill each other) because of their position on the outer fringes of an expanding modern world-system. . . . In the modern world-system there is a core religion which establishes *economic* relations with its colonial periphery. . . . If the Indians could not produce commodities, they were on the road to cultural extinction. . . . To maximize his chances for survival, an eighteenth-century Southeastern Indian had to . . . live in the interior, out of range of European cattle, forestry, and agriculture. . . . He had to produce a commodity which was valuable enough to earn him some protection from English slavers.

Though we are talking here about Southeastern Indians, rather than the subarctic and Northeastern tribes Martin studied, what really accounts for these divergent explanations of why Indians slaughtered the game are the assumptions that underlie them. Martin believes that the Indians acted on the basis of perceptions made available to them by their own cosmology; that is, he explains their behavior as the Indians themselves would have explained it (insofar as he can), using a logic and a set of values that are not Eurocentric but derived from within Amerindian culture. Hudson, on the other hand, insists that the Indians' own beliefs are irrelevant to an explanation of how they acted, which can only be understood, as far as he is concerned, in the terms of a Western materialist economic and political analysis. Martin and Hudson, in short, don't agree on what counts as an explanation, and this disagreement sheds light on the preceding accounts as well. From this standpoint, we can see that Vaughan, who thought that the Puritans were superior to the Indians, and Jennings, who thought the reverse, are both, like Hudson, using Eurocentric criteria of description and evaluation. While all three critics (Vaughan, Jennings, and Hudson) acknowledge that Indians and Europeans behave differently from one another, the behavior differs, as it were, within the order of the same: all three assume, though only Hudson makes the assumption explicit, that an understanding of relations between the Europeans and the Indians must be elaborated in European terms. In Martin's analysis, however, what we have are not only two different sets of behavior but two incommensurable ways of describing and assigning meaning to events. This difference at the level of explanation calls into question the possibility of obtaining any theory-independent account of interaction between Indians and Europeans.

At this point, dismayed and confused by the wildly divergent views of colonial history the twentieth-century historians had provided, I decided to look at some primary materials. I thought, perhaps, if I looked at some firsthand accounts and at some scholars looking at those accounts, it would be possible to decide which experts were right and which were wrong by comparing their views with the evidence. Captivity narratives seemed a good place to begin, since it was logical to suppose that the records left by whites who had been captured by Indians would furnish the sort of firsthand information I wanted.

I began with two fascinating essays based on these materials written by the ethnohistorian James Axtell, "The White Indians of Colonial America" and "The Scholastic Philosophy of the Wilderness." These essays suggest that it would have been a privilege to be captured by North American Indians and taken off to Canada to dwell in a wigwam for the rest of one's life. Axtell's reconstruction of the process by which Indians taught

European captives to feel comfortable in the wilderness, first taking their shoes away and giving them moccasins, carrying the children on their backs, sharing the scanty food supply equally, ceremonially cleansing them of their old identities, giving them Indian clothes and jewelry, assiduously teaching them the Indian language, finally adopting them into their families, and even visiting them after many years if, as sometimes happened, they were restored to white society—all of this creates a compelling portrait of Indian culture and helps to explain the extraordinary attraction that Indian culture apparently exercised over Europeans.

But, as I had by now come to expect, this beguiling portrait of the Indians' superior humanity is called into question by other writings on Indian captivity—for example, Norman Heard's *White into Red,* whose summation of the comparative treatment of captive children east and west of the Mississippi seems to contradict some of Axtell's conclusions:

> The treatment of captive children seems to have been similar in initial stages. . . . Most children were treated brutally at the time of capture. Babies and toddlers usually were killed immediately and other small children would be dispatched during the rapid retreat to the Indian villages if they cried, failed to keep the pace, or otherwise indicated a lack of fortitude needed to become a worthy member of the tribe. Upon reaching the village, the child might face such ordeals as running the gauntlet or dancing in the center of a throng of threatening Indians. The prisoner might be so seriously injured at this time that he would no longer be acceptable for adoption.

One account which Heard reprints is particularly arresting. A young girl captured by the Comanches who had not been adopted into a family but used as a slave had been peculiarly mistreated. When they wanted to wake her up the family she belonged to would take a burning brand from the fire and touch it to her nose. When she was returned to her parents, the flesh of her nose was completely burned away, exposing the bone.

Since the pictures drawn by Heard and Axtell were in certain respects irreconcilable, it made sense to turn to a firsthand account to see how the Indians treated their captives in a particular instance. Mary Rowlandson's "The Soveraignty and Goodness of God," published in Boston around 1680, suggested itself because it was so widely read and had set the pattern for later narratives. Rowlandson interprets her captivity as God's punishment on her for failing to keep the Sabbath properly on several occasions. She sees everything that happens to her as a sign from God. When the Indians are kind to her, she attributes her good fortune to divine Providence; when they are cruel, she blames her captors. But beyond the question of how Rowlandson interprets events is the question of what she saw in the first place and what she considered worth reporting. The following passage, with its abrupt shifts of focus and peculiar emphases, makes it hard to see her testimony as evidence of anything other than the Puritan point of view:

> Then my heart began to fail: and I fell weeping, which was the first time to my remembrance, that I wept before them. Although I had met with so much Affliction, and my heart was many times ready to break, yet could I not shed one tear in their sight: but rather had been all this while in a maze, and like one astonished: but now I may say as, Psal. 137.1. *By the Rivers of Babylon, there we sate down; yea, we wept when we remembered Zion.* There

one of them asked me, why I wept, I could hardly tell what to say: yet I answered, they would kill me: No, said he, none will hurt you. Then came one of them and gave me two spoon-fulls of Meal to comfort me, and another gave me half a pint of Pease; which was more worth than many Bushels at another time. Then I went to see King Philip, he bade me come in and sit down, and asked me whether I woold smoke it (a usual Complement nowadayes among Saints and Sinners) but this no way suited me. For though I had formerly used Tobacco, yet I had left it ever since I was first taken. It seems to be a Bait, the Devil layes to make men lose their precious time: I remember with shame, how formerly, when I had taken two or three pipes, I was presently ready for another, such a bewitching thing it is: But I thank God, he has now given me power over it; surely there are many who may be better imployed than to ly sucking a stinking Tobacco-pipe.

Anyone who has ever tried to give up smoking has to sympathize with Rowlandson, but it is nonetheless remarkable, first, that a passage which begins with her weeping openly in front of her captors, and comparing herself to Israel in Babylon, should end with her railing against the vice of tobacco; and, second, that it has not a word to say about King Philip, the leader of the Indians who captured her and mastermind of the campaign that devastated the white population of the English colonies. The fact that Rowlandson has just been introduced to the chief of chiefs makes hardly any impression on her at all. What excites her is a moral issue which was being hotly debated in the seventeenth century: to smoke or not to smoke (Puritans frowned on it, apparently, because it wasted time and presented a fire hazard). What seem to us the peculiar emphases in Rowlandson's relation are not the result of her having *screened out* evidence she couldn't handle, but of her way of constructing the world. She saw what her seventeenth-century English Separatist background made visible. It is when one realizes that the biases of twentieth-century historians like Vaughan or Axtell cannot be corrected for simply by consulting the primary materials, since the primary materials are constructed according to *their* authors' biases, that one begins to envy Miller his vision at Matadi. Not for what he didn't see—the Indian and the black—but for his epistemological confidence.

Since captivity narratives made a poor source of evidence for the nature of European-Indian relations in early New England because they were so relentlessly pietistic, my hope was that a better source of evidence might be writings designed simply to tell Englishmen what the American natives were like. These authors could be presumed to be less severely biased, since they hadn't seen their loved ones killed by Indians or been made to endure the hardships of captivity, and because they weren't writing propaganda calculated to prove that God had delivered his chosen people from the hands of Satan's emissaries.

The problem was that these texts were written with aims no less specific than those of the captivity narratives, though the aims were of a different sort. Here is a passage from William Wood's *New England's Prospect,* published in London in 1634.

To enter into a serious discourse concerning the natural conditions of these Indians might procure admiration from the people of any civilized nations, in regard of their civility and good natures. . . . These Indians are of affable, courteous and well disposed natures, ready to communicate the best of their wealth to the mutual good of one another; . . . so . . . perspicuous is their love . . . that they are as willing to part with a mite in poverty as treasure in plenty. . . . If it were possible to recount the courtesies they have showed the English, since their first arrival in those parts, it would not only steady belief, that they are a loving people, but also win the love of those that never saw them, and wipe off that needless fear that is too deeply rooted in the conceits of many who think them envious and of such rancorous and inhumane dispositions, that they will one day make an end of their English inmates.

However, in a pamphlet published twenty-one years earlier, Alexander Whitaker of Virginia has this to say of the natives:

> These naked slaves . . . serve the divell for feare, after a most base manner, sacrificing sometimes (as I have heere heard) their own Children to him. . . . They live naked in bodie, as if their shame of their sinne deserved no covering: Their names are as naked as their bodie: They esteem it a virtue to lie, deceive and steale as their master the divell teacheth to them.

According to Robert Berkhofer in *The White Man's Indian,* these divergent reports can be explained by looking at the authors' motives. A favorable report like Wood's, intended to encourage new emigrants to America, naturally represented Indians as loving and courteous, civilized and generous, in order to allay the fears of prospective colonists. Whitaker, on the other hand, a minister who wishes to convince his readers that the Indians are in need of conversion, paints them as benighted agents of the devil. Berkhofer's commentary constantly implies that white men were to blame for having represented the Indians in the image of their own desires and needs. But the evidence supplied by Rowlandson's narrative, and by the accounts left by early reports such as Wood and Whitaker, suggest something rather different. Though it is probably true that in certain cases Europeans did consciously tamper with the evidence, in most cases there is no reason to suppose that they did not record faithfully what they saw. And what they saw was not an illusion, was not determined by selfish motives in any narrow sense, but was there by virtue of a *way* of seeing which they could not more consciously manipulate than they could choose not to have been born. At this point, it seemed to me, the ethnocentric bias of the firsthand observers invited an investigation of the cultural situation they spoke from. Karen Kupperman's *Settling with the Indians* (1980) supplied just such an analysis.

Kupperman argues that Englishmen inevitably looked at Indians in exactly the same way that they looked at other Englishmen. For instance, if they looked down on Indians and saw them as people to be exploited, it was not because of racial prejudice or antique notions about savagery, it was because they looked down on ordinary English men and women and saw them as subjects for exploitation as well. According to Kupperman, what concerned these writers most when they described the Indians were the insignia of social class, of rank, and of prestige. Indian faces are virtually never described in the earliest accounts, but clothes and hairstyles, tattoos and jewelry, posture and skin color are. "Early modern Englishmen believed that people can create their own identity, and that therefore one communicates to the world through signals such as dress and other forms of decoration who one is, what group or category one belongs to."

Kupperman's book marks a watershed in writings on European-Indian relations, for it reverses the strategy employed by Martin two years before. Whereas Martin had performed an ethnographic analysis of Indian cosmology in order to explain, from within, the Indians' motives for engaging in the fur trade, Kupperman performs an ethnographic study of seventeenth-century England in order to explain, from within, what motivated Englishmen's behavior. The sympathy and understanding that Martin, Axtell, and others extend to the Indians are extended in Kupperman's work to the English themselves. Rather than giving an account of "what happened" between Indians and Europeans, like Martin, she reconstructs the worldview that gave the experience of one group its content. With her study, scholarship on European-Indian relations comes full circle.

It may well seem to you at this point that, given the tremendous variation among the historical accounts, I had no choice but to end in relativism. If the experience of encountering conflicting versions of the "same" events suggests anything certain it is that the attitude a historian takes up in relation to a given event, the way in which he or she judges and even describes "it" —and the "it" has to go in quotation marks because, depending on the perspective, that event either did or did not occur—this stance, these judgments and descriptions are a function of the historian's position in relation to the subject. Miller, standing on the banks of the Congo, couldn't see the black men he was supervising because of his background, his assumptions, values, experiences, goals. Jennings, intent on exposing the distortions introduced into the historical record by Vaughan and his predecessors stretching all the way back to Winthrop, couldn't see that Winthrop and his peers were not racists but only Englishmen who looked at other cultures in the way their own culture had taught them to see one another. The historian can never escape the limitations of his or her own position in history and so inevitably gives an account that is an extension of the circumstances from which it springs. But it seems to me that when one is confronted with this particular succession of stories, cultural and historical relativism is not a position that one can comfortably assume. The phenomena to which these histories testify—conquest, massacre, and genocide, on the one hand; torture, slavery, and murder on the other—cry out for judgment. When faced with claims and counterclaims of this magnitude one feels obligated to reach an understanding of what actually did occur. The dilemma posed by the study of European-Indian relations in early America is that the highly charged nature of the materials demands a moral decisiveness which the succession of conflicting accounts effectively precludes. That is the dilemma I found myself in at the end of this course of reading, and which I eventually came to resolve as follows.

After a while it began to seem to me that there was something wrong with the way I had formulated the problem. The statement that the materials on European-Indian relations were so highly charged that they demanded moral judgment, but that the judgment couldn't be made because all possible descriptions of what happened were biased, seemed to contain an internal contradiction. The statement implied that in order to make a moral judgment about something, you have to know something else first—namely, the facts of the case you're being called upon to judge. My complaint was that their perspectival nature would disqualify any facts I might encounter and that therefore I couldn't judge. But to say as I did that the materials I had read were "highly charged" and therefore demanded judgment suggests both that I was reacting to something real—to some facts—*and* that I had judged them. Perhaps I wasn't so much in the lurch morally or epistemologically as I had thought. If you—or I—react with horror to the story of the girl captured and enslaved by Comanches who touched a firebrand to her nose every time they wanted to wake her up, it's because we read this as a story about cruelty and suffering, and not as a story about the conventions of prisoner exchange or the economics of Comanche life. The *seeing* of the story as a cause for alarm rather than as a droll anecdote or a piece of curious information is evidence of values we already hold, of judgments already made, of facts already perceived as facts.

My problem presupposed that I couldn't judge because I didn't know what the facts were. All I had, or could have, was a series of different perspectives, and so nothing that would count as an authoritative source on which moral judgments could be based. But, as I have just shown, I did judge, and that is because, as I now think, I did have some facts. I seemed to accept as facts that ninety percent of the native American population of New England died after the first hundred years of contact, that tribes in eastern Canada and the northeastern United States had a compact with the game they killed, that Comanches had subjected a captive girl to casual cruelty, that King Philip smoked a pipe, and so on. It was only where different versions of the same event came into conflict that I doubted the text was a record of something real. And even then, there was no question about certain major catastrophes. I believed that four hundred Pequots were killed near Saybrook, that Winthrop was the Governor of the Massachusetts Bay Colony when it happened, and so on. My sense that certain events, such as the Pequot War, did occur in no way reflected the indecisiveness that overtook me when I tried to choose among the various historical versions. In fact, the need I felt to make up my mind was impelled by the conviction that certain things *had* happened that shouldn't have happened. Hence it was never the case that "what happened" was completely unknowable or unavailable. It's rather that in the process of reading so many different approaches to the same phenomenon I became aware of the difference in the attitudes that informed these approaches. This awareness of the interests motivating each version cast suspicion over everything, in retrospect, and I ended by claiming that there was nothing I could know. This, I now see, was never really the case. But how did it happen?

Someone else, confronted with the same materials, could have decided that one of these historical accounts was correct. Still another person might have decided that more evidence was needed in order to decide among them. Why did I conclude that none of the accounts was accurate because they were all produced from some particular angle of vision? Presumably there was something in my background that enabled me to see the problem in this way. That something, very likely, was poststructuralist theory. I let my discovery that Vaughan was a product of the fifties, Jennings of the sixties, Rowlandson of a Puritan worldview, and so on lead me to the conclusion that all facts are theory dependent because that conclusion was already a thinkable one for me. My inability to come up with a true account was not the product of being situated nowhere; it was the product of certitude that existed *somewhere else*, namely, in contemporary literary theory. Hence, the level at which my indecision came into play was a function of particular beliefs I held. I was never in a position of epistemological indeterminacy, I was never *en abyme*. The idea that all accounts are perspectival seemed to me a superior standpoint from which to view all the versions of "what happened," and to regard with sympathetic condescension any person so old-fashioned and benighted as to believe that there really was some way of arriving at the truth. But this skeptical standpoint was just as firm as any other. The fact that it was also seriously disabling—it prevented me from coming to any conclusion about what I had read—did not render it any less definite.

At this point something is beginning to show itself that has up to now been hidden. The notion that all facts are only facts within a perspective has the effect of emptying statements of their content. Once I had Miller and Vaughan and Jennings, Martin and Hudson, Axtell and Heard, Rowlandson and Wood and Whitaker, and Kupperman; I had Europeans and Indians, ships and canoes, wigwams and log cabins, bows and arrows and muskets, wigs and tattoos, whisky and corn, rivers and forts, treaties and battles, fire and blood—and then suddenly all I had was a metastatement about perspectives. The effect of bringing perspectivism to bear on history was to wipe out completely the subject matter of history. And it follows that bringing perspectivism to bear in this way on any subject matter would have a similar effect; everything is wiped out and you are left with nothing but a single idea—perspectivism itself.

But—and it is a crucial but—all this is true only if you believe that there is an alternative. As long as you think that there are or should be facts that exist outside of any perspective, then the notion that facts are perspectival will have this disappearing effect on whatever it touches. But if you are convinced that the alternative does not exist, that there really are no facts except as they are embedded in some particular way of seeing the world, then the argument that a set of facts derives from some particular worldview is no longer an argument against that set of facts. If all facts share this characteristic, to say that any one fact is perspectival doesn't change its factual nature in the slightest. It merely reiterates it.

This doesn't mean that you have to accept just anybody's facts. You can show that what someone else asserts to be a fact is false. But it does mean that you can't argue that someone else's facts are not facts *because they are only the product of a perspective,* since this will be true of the facts that you perceive as well. What this means then is that arguments about "what happened" have to proceed much as they did before poststructuralism broke in with all its talk about language-based reality and culturally produced knowledge. Reasons must be given, evidence adduced, authorities cited, analogies drawn. Being aware that all facts are motivated, believing that people are always operating inside some particular interpretive framework or other is a pertinent argument when what is under discussion is the way beliefs are grounded. But it doesn't give one any leverage on the facts of a particular case.

What this means for the problem I've been addressing is that I must piece together the story of European-Indian relations as best I can, believing this version up to a point, that version not at all, another almost entirely, according to what seems reasonable and plausible, given everything else that I know. And this, as I've shown, is what I was already doing in the back of my mind without realizing it, because there was nothing else I *could* do. If the accounts don't fit together neatly, that is not a reason for rejecting them all in favor of a metadiscourse about epistemology; on the contrary, one encounters contradictory facts and divergent points of view in practically every phase of life, from deciding whom to marry to choosing the right brand of cat food, and one decides as best one can given the evidence available. It is only the nature of the academic situation which makes it appear that one can linger on the threshold of decision in the name of an epistemological principle. What has really happened in such a case is that the subject of debate has changed from the question of what happened in a particular instance to the question of how knowledge is arrived at. The absence of pressure to decide what happened creates the possibility for this change of venue.

The change of venue, however, is itself an action taken. In diverting attention from the original problem and placing it where Miller did, on "the mind of man," it once again ignores what happened and still is happening to American Indians. The moral problem that confronts me now is not that I can never have any facts to go on, but that the work I do is not directed toward solving the kinds of problems that studying the history of European-Indian relations has awakened me to.

CONSIDER THIS

Jane Tompkins, professor of English at Duke University, is the author of *Sensational Designs: The Cultural Work of American Fiction, 1790–1860.* This essay, which first appeared in *Critical Inquiry,* a highly regarded journal of literary criticism, is in part an eminently accessible case study of a formidable topic: how point of view affects historical accounts. It has, however, another dimension: Tompkins presents her problem not simply as a theoretical dilemma but as "a moral quandary." The essay doesn't stop where we might have thought it was going, ending with Tompkins's well-supported summary of the various biases of the historical sources she consulted. It takes us somewhere else, returning, actually, full circle to the moral difficulty she began with.

Is there a way out of the circle? In the beginning of the essay, Tompkins says that "the solution I reached is not a new one." What "solution" is she referring to? Does the essay end, for you, with an answer?

Harrison Bergeron
Kurt Vonnegut, Jr.

The year was 2081, and everybody was finally equal. They weren't only equal before God and the law. They were equal every which way. Nobody was smarter than anybody else. Nobody was better looking than anybody else. Nobody was stronger or quicker than anybody else. All this equality was due to the 211th, 212th, and 213th Amendments to the Constitution, and to the unceasing vigilance of agents of the United States Handicapper General.

Some things about living still weren't quite right, though. April, for instance, still drove people crazy by not being springtime. And it was in that clammy month that the H-G men took George and Hazel Bergeron's fourteen-year-old son, Harrison, away.

It was tragic all right, but George and Hazel couldn't think about it very hard. Hazel had a perfectly average intelligence, which meant she couldn't think about anything except in short bursts. And George, while his intelligence was way above normal, had a little mental handicap radio in his ear. He was required by law to wear it at all times. It was tuned to a government transmitter. Every twenty seconds or so, the transmitter would send out some sharp noise to keep people like George from taking unfair advantage of their brains.

George and Hazel were watching television. There were tears on Hazel's cheeks, but she'd forgotten for the moment what they were about.

On the television screen were ballerinas.

A buzzer sounded in George's head. His thoughts fled in panic, like bandits from a burglar alarm.

"That was a really pretty dance, that dance they just did," said Hazel.

"Huh?" said George.

"That dance—it was nice," said Hazel.

"Yup," said George. He tried to think a little about the ballerinas. They weren't really very good—no better than anybody else would have been anyway. They were burdened with sash-weights and bags of birdshot, and their faces were masked, so that no one, seeing a free and graceful gesture or a pretty face, would feel like something the cat drug in. George was toying with the vague notion that maybe dancers shouldn't be handicapped. But he didn't get very far with it before another noise in his ear radio scattered his thoughts.

George winced. So did two out of the eight ballerinas.

Hazel saw him wince. Having no mental handicap herself, she had to ask George what the latest sound had been.

"Sounded like somebody hitting a milk bottle with a ball peen hammer," said George.

"I'd think it would be real interesting, hearing all the different sounds," said Hazel, a little nervous. "All the things they think up."

"Um," said George.

"Only, if I was Handicapper General, you know what I would do?" said Hazel. Hazel, as a matter of fact, bore a strong resemblance to the Handicapper General, a woman named Diana Moon Glampers. "If I was Diana Moon Glampers," said Hazel, "I'd have chimes on Sunday—just chimes. Kind of in honor of religion."

"I could think, if it was just chimes," said George.

"Well—maybe make 'em real loud," said Hazel. "I think I'd make a good Handicapper General."

"Good as anybody else," said George.

"Who knows better'n I do what normal is?" said Hazel.

"Right," said George. He began to think glimmeringly about his abnormal son who was now in jail, about Harrison, but a twenty-one-gun salute in his head stopped that.

"Boy!" said Hazel, "that was a doozy, wasn't it?"

It was such a doozy that George was white and trembling, and tears stood on the rims of his red eyes. Two of the eight ballerinas had collapsed to the studio floor, were holding their temples.

"All of a sudden you look so tired," said Hazel. "Why don't you stretch out on the sofa, so's you can rest your handicap bag on the pillows, honeybunch." She was referring to the forty-seven pounds of birdshot in a canvas bag, which was padlocked around George's neck. "Go on and rest the bag for a little while," she said. "I don't care if you're not equal to me for a while."

George weighed the bag with his hands. "I don't mind it," he said. "I don't notice it any more. It's just a part of me."

"You been so tired lately—kind of wore out," said Hazel. "If there was just some way we could make a little hole in the bottom of the bag, and just take out a few of them lead balls. Just a few."

"Two years in prison and two thousand dollars fine for every ball I took out," said George. "I don't call that a bargain."

"If you could just take a few out when you came home from work," said Hazel. "I mean—you don't compete with anybody around here. You just set around."

"If I tried to get away with it," said George, "then other people'd get away with it—and pretty soon we'd be right back to the dark ages again, with everybody competing against everybody else. You wouldn't like that, would you?"

"I'd hate it," said Hazel.

"There you are," said George. "The minute people start cheating on laws, what do you think happens to society?"

If Hazel hadn't been able to come up with an answer to this question, George couldn't have supplied one. A siren was going off in his head.

"Reckon it'd fall all apart," said Hazel.

"What would?" said George blankly.

"Society," said Hazel uncertainly. "Wasn't that what you just said?"

"Who knows?" said George.

The television program was suddenly interrupted for a news bulletin. It wasn't clear at first as to what the bulletin was about, since the announcer, like all announcers, had a serious speech impediment. For about half a minute, and in a state of high excitement, the announcer tried to say, "Ladies and gentlemen—"

He finally gave up, handed the bulletin to a ballerina to read.

"That's all right—" Hazel said to the announcer, "he tried. That's the big thing. He tried to do the best he could with what God gave him. He should get a nice raise for trying so hard."

"Ladies and gentlemen—" said the ballerina, reading the bulletin. She must have been extraordinarily beautiful, because the mask she wore was hideous. And it was easy to see that she was the strongest and most graceful of all the dancers, for her handicap bags were as big as those worn by two-hundred-pound men.

And she had to apologize at once for her voice, which was a very unfair voice for a woman to use. Her voice was a warm, luminous, timeless melody. "Excuse me—" she said, and she began again, making her voice absolutely uncompetitive.

"Harrison Bergeron, age fourteen," she said in a grackle squawk, "has just escaped from jail, where he was held on suspicion of plotting to overthrow the government. He is a genius and an athlete, is under-handicapped, and should be regarded as extremely dangerous."

A police photograph of Harrison Bergeron was flashed on the screen—upside down, then sideways, upside down again, then right side up. The picture showed the full length of Harrison against a background calibrated in feet and inches. He was exactly seven feet tall.

The rest of Harrison's appearance was Halloween and hardware. Nobody had ever borne heavier handicaps. He had outgrown hindrances faster than the H-G men could think them up. Instead of a little ear radio for a mental handicap, he wore a tremendous pair of earphones, and spectacles with thick wavy lenses. The spectacles were intended to make him not only half blind, but to give him whanging headaches besides.

Scrap metal was hung all over him. Ordinarily, there was a certain symmetry, a military neatness to the handicaps issued to strong people, but Harrison looked like a walking junkyard. In the race of life, Harrison carried three hundred pounds.

And to offset his good looks, the H-G men required that he wear at all times a red rubber ball for a nose, keep his eyebrows shaved off, and cover his even white teeth with black caps at snaggle-tooth random.

"If you see this boy," said the ballerina, "do not—I repeat, do not—try to reason with him."

There was a shriek of a door being torn from its hinges.

Screams and barking cries of consternation came from the television set. The photograph of Harrison Bergeron on the screen jumped again and again, as though dancing to the tune of an earthquake.

George Bergeron correctly identified the earthquake, and well he might have—for many was the time his own home had danced to the same crashing tune. "My God—" said George, "that must be Harrison!"

The realization was blasted from his mind instantly by the sound of an automobile collision in his head.

When George could open his eyes again, the photograph of Harrison was gone. A living, breathing Harrison filled the screen.

Clanking, clownish, and huge, Harrison stood in the center of the studio. The knob of the uprooted studio door was still in his hand. Ballerinas, technicians, musicians, and announcers cowered on their knees before him, expecting to die.

"I am the Emperor!" cried Harrison. "Do you hear? I am the Emperor! Everybody must do what I say at once!" He stamped his foot and the studio shook.

"Even as I stand here—" he bellowed, "crippled, hobbled, sickened—I am a greater ruler than any man who ever lived! Now watch me become what I *can* become!"

Harrison tore the straps of his handicap harness like wet tissue paper, tore straps guaranteed to support five thousand pounds.

Harrison's scrap-iron handicaps crashed to the floor.

Harrison thrust his thumbs under the bar of the padlock that secured his head harness. The bar snapped like celery. Harrison smashed his headphones and spectacles against the wall.

He flung away his rubber-ball nose, revealed a man that would have awed Thor, the god of thunder.

"I shall now select my Empress!" he said, looking down on the cowering people. "Let the first woman who dares rise to her feet claim her mate and her throne!"

A moment passed, and then a ballerina arose, swaying like a willow.

Harrison plucked the mental handicap from her ear, snapped off her physical handicaps with marvellous delicacy. Last of all, he removed her mask.

She was blindingly beautiful.

"Now—" said Harrison, taking her hand, "shall we show the people the meaning of the word dance? Music!" he commanded.

The musicians scrambled back into their chairs, and Harrison stripped them of their handicaps, too. "Play your best," he told them, "and I'll make you barons and dukes and earls."

The music began. It was normal at first—cheap, silly, false. But Harrison snatched two musicians from their chairs, waved them like batons as he sang the music as he wanted it played. He slammed them back into their chairs.

The music began again and was much improved.

Harrison and his Empress merely listened to the music for a while—listened gravely, as though synchronizing their heartbeats with it.

They shifted their weights to their toes.

Harrison placed his big hands on the girl's tiny waist, letting her sense the weightlessness that would soon be hers.

And then, in an explosion of joy and grace, into the air they sprang!

Not only were the laws of the land abandoned, but the law of gravity and the laws of motion as well.

They reeled, whirled, swiveled, flounced, capered, gamboled, and spun.

They leaped like deer on the moon.

The studio ceiling was thirty feet high, but each leap brought the dancers nearer to it.

It became their obvious intention to kiss the ceiling.

They kissed it.

And then, neutralizing gravity with love and pure will, they remained suspended in air inches below the ceiling, and they kissed each other for a long, long time.

It was then that Diana Moon Glampers, the Handicapper General, came into the studio with a double-barreled ten-gauge shotgun. She fired twice and the Emperor and the Empress were dead before they hit the floor.

Diana Moon Glampers loaded the gun again. She aimed it at the musicians and told them they had ten seconds to get their handicaps back on.

It was then that the Bergerons' television tube burned out.

Hazel turned to comment about the blackout to George. But George had gone out into the kitchen for a can of beer.

George came back in with the beer, paused while a handicap signal shook him up. And then he sat down again. "You been crying?" he said to Hazel.

"Yup," she said.

"What about?" he said.

"I forget," she said. "Something real sad on television."

"What was it?" he said.

"It's all kind of mixed up in my mind," said Hazel.

"Forget sad things," said George.

"I always do," said Hazel.

"That's my girl," said George. He winced. There was the sound of a riveting gun in his head.

"Gee—I could tell that one was a doozy," said Hazel.

"You can say that again," said George.

"Gee—" said Hazel, "I could tell that one was a doozy."

CONSIDER THIS

"Harrison Bergeron" first appeared in *The Meaning of Fantasy and Science Fiction*. In fact, Vonnegut had been writing for a long time before it began to dawn on both general public and critics that his work transcends the narrow confines of science fiction as a genre. This story is a good introduction to Vonnegut: both to his storytelling wizardry and to his larger themes.

It bothers some critics on the political left that Vonnegut's own political and social views are hard to pin down, that though he is an outspoken civil libertarian his scattershot technique sometimes gives aid and comfort to what they perceive as the enemies of freedom. How would you characterize "Harrison Bergeron" politically? Conservative? Liberal? Reactionary? Anarchist? It appeared in a collection in 1961. What trend or event in the fifties might it have been written in reaction to?

Kurt Vonnegut is a prolific novelist and writer of short stories. Two of his best-known novels are *Slaughterhouse Five* and *Cat's Cradle*. His latest, *Hocus Pocus* (1991), is dedicated to Eugene Debs: "While there is a lower class I am in it. While there is a criminal element I am of it. While there is a soul in prison I am not free."

Freedom
E. B. White

I have often noticed on my trips up to the city that people have recut their clothes to follow the fashion. On my last trip, however, it seemed to me that people had remodeled their ideas too—taken in their convictions a little at the waist, shortened the sleeves of their resolve, and fitted themselves out in a new intellectual ensemble copied from a smart design out of the very latest page of history. It seemed to me they had strung along with Paris a little too long.

I confess to a disturbed stomach. I feel sick when I find anyone adjusting his mind to the new tyranny which is succeeding abroad. Because of its fundamental strictures, fascism does not seem to me to admit of any compromise or any rationalization, and I resent the patronizing air of persons who find in my plain belief in freedom a sign of immaturity. If it is boyish to believe that a human being should live free, then I'll gladly arrest my development and let the rest of the world grow up.

I shall report some of the strange remarks I heard in New York. One man told me that he thought perhaps the Nazi ideal was a sounder ideal than our constitutional system "because have you ever noticed what fine alert young faces the young German soldiers have in the newsreel?" He added: "Our American youngsters spend all their time at the movies—they're a mess." That was his summation of the case, his interpretation of the new Europe. Such a remark leaves me pale and shaken. If it represents the peak of our intelligence, then the steady march of despotism will not receive any considerable setback at our shores.

Another man informed me that our democratic notion of popular government was decadent and not worth bothering about—"because England is really rotten and the industrial towns there are a disgrace." That was the only reason he gave for the hopeless-ness of democracy; and he seemed mightily pleased with himself, as though he were more familiar than most with the anatomy of decadence, and had detected subtler aspects of the situation than were discernible to the rest of us.

Another man assured me that anyone who took *any* kind of government seriously was a gullible fool. You could be sure, he said, that there is nothing but corruption "because of the way Clemenceau acted at Versailles." He said it didn't make any difference really about this war. It was just another war. Having relieved himself of his majestic bit of reasoning, he subsided.

Another individual, discovering signs of zeal creeping into my blood, berated me for having lost my detachment, my pure skeptical point of view. He announced that he wasn't going to be swept away by all this nonsense, but would prefer to remain in the role of innocent bystander, which he said was the duty of any intelligent person. (I noticed, however, that he phoned later to qualify his remark, as though he had lost some of his innocence in the cab on the way home.)

Those are just a few samples of the sort of talk that seemed to be going round—talk which was full of defeatism and disillusion and sometimes of a too studied innocence. Men are not merely annihilating themselves at a great rate these days, but they are telling one another enormous lies, grandiose fibs. Such remarks as I heard are fearfully disturbing in their cumulative effect. They are more destructive than dive bombers and mine fields, for they challenge not merely one's immediate position but one's main defenses. They seemed to me to issue either from persons who could never have really come to grips with freedom, so as to understand her, or from renegades. Where I expected to find indignation, I found paralysis, or a sort of dim acquiescence, as in a child who is dully swallowing a distasteful pill. I was advised of the growing anti-Jewish sentiment by a man who seemed to be watching the phenomenon of intolerance not through tears of shame but with a clear intellectual gaze, as through a well-ground lens.

The least a man can do at such a time is to declare himself and tell where he stands. I believe in freedom with the same burning delight, the same faith, the same intense abandon which attended its birth on this continent more than a century and a half ago. I am writing my declaration rapidly, much as though I were shaving to catch a train. Events abroad give a man a feeling of being pressed for time. Actually I do not believe I am pressed for time, and I apologize to the reader for a false impression that may be created. I just want to tell, before I get slowed down, that I am in love with freedom and that it is an affair of long standing and that it is a fine state to be in, and that I am deeply suspicious of people who are beginning to adjust to fascism and dictators merely because they are succeeding in war. From such adaptable natures a smell rises. I pinch my nose.

For as long as I can remember I have had a sense of living somewhat freely in a natural world. I don't mean I enjoyed freedom of action, but my existence seemed to have the quality of free-ness. I traveled with secret papers pertaining to a divine conspiracy. Intuitively I've always been aware of the vitally important pact which a man has with himself, to be all things to himself, and to be identified with all things, to stand self-reliant, taking advantage of his haphazard connection with a planet, riding his luck, and following his bent with the tenacity of a hound. My first and greatest love affair was with this thing we call freedom, this lady of infinite allure, this dangerous and beautiful and sublime being who restores and supplies us all.

It began with the haunting intimation (which I presume every child receives) of his mystical inner life; of God in man; of nature publishing herself through the "I." This elusive sensation is moving and memorable. It comes early in life; a boy, we'll say, sitting on the front steps on a summer night, thinking of nothing in particular, suddenly hearing as with a new perception and as though for the first time the pulsing sound of crickets, over- whelmed with the novel sense of identification with the natural company of insects and grass and night, conscious of a faint answering cry to the universal perplexing question: "What is 'I'?" Or a little girl, returning from the grave of a pet bird leaning with her elbows on the windowsill, inhaling the unfamiliar draught of death, suddenly seeing herself as part of the complete story. Or to an older youth, encountering for the first time a great teacher who by some chance word or mood awakens something and the youth beginning to breathe as an individual and conscious of strength in his vitals. I think the sensation must develop in many men as a feeling of identity with God—an eruption of the spirit caused by allergies and the sense of divine existence as distinct from mere animal existence. This is the beginning of the affair with freedom.

But a man's free condition is of two parts: the instinctive freeness he experiences as an animal dweller on a planet, and the practical liberties he enjoys as a privileged member of human society. The latter is, of the two, more generally understood, more widely admired, more violently challenged and discussed. It is the practical and apparent side of freedom. The United States, almost alone today, offers the liberties and the privileges and the tools of freedom. In this land the citizens are still invited to write their plays and books, to paint their pictures, to meet for discussion, to dissent as well as to agree, to mount soapboxes in the public square, to enjoy education in all subjects without censorship, to hold court and judge one another, to compose music, to talk politics with their neighbors without wondering whether the secret police are listening, to exchange ideas as well as goods, to kid the government when it needs kidding, and to read real news of real events instead of phony news manufactured by a paid agent of the state. This is a fact and should give every person pause.

To be free, in a planetary sense, is to feel that you belong to earth. To be free, in a social sense, is to feel at home in a democratic framework. In Adolph Hitler, although he is a freely flowering individual, we do not detect either type of sensibility. From reading his book I gather that his feeling for earth is not a sense of communion but a driving urge to prevail. His feeling for men is not that they co-exist, but that they are capable of being arranged and standardized by a superior intellect—that their existence suggests not a fulfillment of their personalities but a submersion of their personalities in the common racial destiny. His very great absorption in the destiny of the German people somehow loses some of its effect when you discover, from his writings, in what vast contempt he holds *all* people. "I learned," he wrote, " . . . to gain an insight into the unbelievably primitive opinions and arguments of the people." To him the ordinary man is a primitive, capable only of being used and led. He speaks continually of people as sheep, halfwits, and impudent fools—the same people from whom he asks the utmost in loyalty, and to whom he promises the ultimate in prizes.

Here in America, where our society is based on belief in the individual, not contempt for him, the free principle of life has a chance of surviving. I believe that it must and will survive. To understand freedom is an accomplishment which all men may acquire who set their minds in that direction; and to love freedom is a tendency which many Americans are born with. To live in the same room with freedom, or in the same hemisphere, is still a profoundly shaking experience for me.

One of the earliest truths (and to him most valuable) that the author of *Mein Kampf* discovered was that it is not the written word, but the spoken word, which in heated moments moves great masses of people to noble or ignoble action. The written word, unlike the spoken word, is something which every person examines privately and judges calmly by his own intellectual standards, not by what the man standing next to him thinks. "I know," wrote Hitler, "that one is able to win people far more by the spoken than by the written word. . . ." Later he adds contemptuously: "For let it be said to all knights of the pen and to all the political dandies, especially of today: the greatest changes in this world have never yet been brought about by a goose quill! No, the pen has always been reserved to motivate these changes theoretically."

Luckily I am not out to change the world—that's being done for me, and at a great clip. But I know that the free spirit of man is persistent in nature; it recurs, and has never successfully been wiped out, by fire or flood. I set down the above remarks merely (in the words of Mr. Hitler) to motivate that spirit, theoretically. Being myself a knight of the goose quill, I am under no misapprehension about "winning people"; but I am inordinately proud these days of the quill, for it has shown itself, historically, to be the hypodermic which inoculates men and keeps the germ of freedom always in circulation, so that there are individuals in every time in every land who are the carriers, the Typhoid Mary's, capable of infecting others by mere contact and example. These persons are feared by every tyrant—who shows his fear by burning the books and destroying the individuals. A writer goes about his task today with the extra satisfaction which comes from knowing that he will be the first to have his head lopped off—even before the political dandies. In my own case this is a double satisfaction, for if freedom were denied me by force of earthly circumstance, I am the same as dead and would infinitely prefer to go into fascism without my head than with it, having no use for it any more and not wishing to be saddled with so heavy an encumbrance.

CONSIDER THIS

E. B. White, born in Mount Vernon, New York, in 1899, wrote the *New Yorker*'s "Talk of the Town Feature" for many years. In 1938 he moved to the Maine coast, but he has never stopped writing—essays, criticism, poetry, and children's books, two of which seem likely to endure, *Stuart Little* and *Charlotte's Web.*

The sentences in this essay are models of elegant simplicity, the development is smooth. But from that classic structure, White's voice comes through loud and clear. How does he sound to you? Is this an open text, the points negotiable?

Note the battle metaphor, where White says that the remarks of both apologists and fence sitters are more destructive than the weapons of war, "for they challenge not merely one's immediate position but one's main defenses."

Where in the text does White let us know that the willingness to wage war expressed in this essay is not typical of him?

Speaking Saskatchewan
Rudy Wiebe

In summer the thick green poplar leaves clicked and flickered at him, in winter the stiff spruce rustled with voices. The boy, barefoot in the heat or trussed up like a lumpy package against the fierce, silver cold, went alone to the bush where everything spoke: warm rocks, the flit of quick, small animals, a dart of birds, tree trunks, the great lights in the sky at night, burning air, ground, the squeaky snow: everything spoke as he breathed and became aware of it, its language clear as the water of his memory when he lay in the angle of the house rafters at night listening to the mosquitoes slowly find him under his blanket, though he had his eyes shut and only one ear uncovered. Everything spoke, and it spoke Low German.

Like his mother. She would call him long, long into the summer evening when it seemed the sun burned all night down into the north, call high and slow as if she were already weeping and when he appeared beside her she would bend her wide powerful hands about his head and kiss him so hard his eyes rang.

"Why don't you answer, you?" she would speak against his hair. "Why don't you ever answer when I call, it's so dark, why don't you ever say a word?"

While he nuzzled his face into the damp apron at the fold of her thigh, and soon her words would be over and he heard her skin and warm apron smelling of saskatoon jam and dishes and supper buns love him back.

His sister laughed at his solitary silence. "In school are twenty-seven kids," she would say, "you'll have to talk, and English at that. You can't say Low German there, and if you don't answer English when she asks, the teacher will make you stand in the corner."

"R-r-r-right in front—of . . . people?" he would ask, fearfully.

'Yeah, in front of every one of them, your face against the wall. So you better start to talk, English too."

And she would try to teach him the English names for things. But he did not listen to that. Rather, when he was alone he practised standing in the corners of walls. Their logs shifted and cracked, talking. Walls were very good, especially where they came together so warm in winter.

But outside was even better, and he followed a quiet trail of the muskrat that had dented the snow with its tail between bullrushes sticking out of the slough ice, or waited for the coyote to turn and see him, its paw lifted and about to touch a drift, its jaw opening on a red tongue laughing with him. In summer he heard a mother bear talk to her cubs among the willows of the horse pasture, though he did not see them, but he found their sluffing paw prints in the spring snow and his father said something would have to be done if they came that close to the pig fence again. The boy knew his father refused to own a gun, but their nearest neighbor west gladly hunted everywhere to shoot, whatever he heard about, and so he folded his hands over the huge, wet prints and whispered in Low German, "Don't visit here any more. It's dangerous."

The school sat on the corner, just below the hill where the road turned south along the creek to the church and the store. In the church every Sunday there were hands waiting for him. At the top of the balcony stairs that began in the corner behind where the men sat, up there among wooden benches, with the visiting sound of people talking like heavy rain under them, were hands that could find things inside him. Huge hands with heavy broad thumbs working against each other on his neck, pressing down, together, bending his small bones until through his gaping mouth they cawed:

"c-c-c—CAT!"

"Yes, yes, like that, try to say it again, 'cat'."

And he would, try; desperately, those marvelous hands holding him as if everything on earth were in its proper place and all the brilliant sounds which he could never make when anyone listened coming out of him as easily as if he had pulled a door, open.

"Cat."

He never looked at the school, the tiny panes of its four huge windows staring at him, just staring when they passed. The day before he had to go there every day like his sister, the planes came over for the first time.

Their horses were pulling the wagon up the hill as slowly, steadily as they always did and it happened very fast, almost before he looked around. There had been a rumble from somewhere like thunder, far away, though the sky was clear sunlight and his father had just said in a week they could start bindering the oats, it was ripening so well, and his mother sat beside him broad and straight as always, her braided, waist-long hair coiled up for church under her hat, when suddenly the roaring planes were there as he turned, four of them, yellow-and-black, louder than anything he had ever heard. West over the school and the small grain fields and pastures and all the trees and hills to the far edge of the world. His father would not look around, holding the horses in carefully, muttering,

"Now it comes here too, that war training."

But the boy was looking at his mother. Perhaps his own face looked like that next morning when the yellow planes roared over the school at recess, so low he saw huge glass eyes in a horrible leather head glare down at him before he screamed and ran, inside to the desk where his sister had said he must sit. When he opened his eyes the face of the teacher was there, her gentle face very close, smiling almost up-side-down at him between the iron legs of the desk beneath which he crouched. Her gentle voice, speaking.

"Come," she said, "come," and after a moment he scrambled to his feet. He thought she was speaking Low German because he did not yet know that what that word meant was spoken the same in English.

"Come." Not touching him, she led him between desks to a thin cupboard against the wall opposite the windows and opened its narrow doors. Books. He has never imagined so many books. There may be a million.

She is, of course, speaking to him in English and later, when he remembers that moment again and again, he will never be able to explain how he can understand what she is saying. The open book in her hand shows him countless words: words, she tells him, he can now only see the shape of, but he will be able to hear them when he learns to read, and that the word "READ" in English is the same as the word "SPEAK," *raed,* in Low German and by reading all the people of the world will speak to him from books, he will hear them, when he reads he will be able to hear them, and then he will understand. He is staring at what he later knows are a few worn books on a few shelves, and then staring back at the few visible but as yet unintelligible words revealed by the book open in her hands, and slowly, slowly he understands that there are shelves and shelves of books in great stacks on many,

many floors inside all the walls of the enormous libraries of the world where he will go and read: where the knowing she will now help him discover within himself will allow him to listen to human voices speaking from everywhere and every age, saying everything, things both dreadful and beautiful, and all that can be imagined between them; and that he will listen. He will listen to those voices speaking now for as long as he lives.

CONSIDER THIS

In "Speaking Saskatchewan," Wiebe gives lyrical expression to many of the ideas expressed more didactically elsewhere in this text. This short piece is about voices, about speaking (and writing), about listening (and reading), about how we hear. The books in the library are silent until read. Unheard language is unintelligible.

Have someone read it aloud to you, and notice the many voices the boy attends to. Does it work for you? Can you suspend your disbelief and "see" the boy who listens to trees, hears-smells his mother's apron, whispers to bear tracks, understands a language he hasn't yet learned? How would you describe this piece? Convincing? Compelling? Evocative? Sentimental? Inspirational?

Rudy Wiebe was born in 1934 and grew up in Saskatchewan. He has published nineteen books—fiction, essays, and drama—and teaches at the University of Alberta in Edmonton, Canada.

Memoirs of a Non-Prom Queen
Ellen Willis

There's a book out called *Is There Life after High School?* It's a fairly silly book, maybe because the subject matter is the kind that only hurts when you think. Its thesis—that most people never get over the social triumphs or humiliations of high school—is not novel. Still, I read it with the respectful attention a serious hypochondriac accords the lowliest "dear doctor" column. I don't know about most people, but for me, forgiving my parents for real and imagined derelictions has been easy compared to forgiving myself for being a teenage reject.

Victims of high school trauma—which seems to have afflicted a disproportionate number of writers, including Ralph Keyes, the author of this book—tend to embrace the ugly duckling myth of adolescent social relations: the "innies" (Keyes's term) are good-looking, athletic mediocrities who will never amount to much, while the "outies" are intelligent, sensitive, creative individuals who will do great things in an effort to make up for their early defeats. Keyes is partial to this myth. He has fun with celebrity anecdotes: Kurt Vonnegut receiving a body-building course as a "gag prize" at a dance; Frank Zappa yelling "fuck you" at a cheerleader; Mike Nichols, as a nightclub comedian, insulting a fan—an erstwhile overbearing classmate turned used-car salesman. In contrast, the ex-prom queens and kings he interviews slink through life, hiding their pasts lest someone call them "dumb jock" or "cheerleader type," perpetually wondering what to do for an encore.

If only it were that simple. There may really be high schools where life approximates an Archie comic, but even in the Fifties, my large (5,000 students), semisuburban (Queens, New York), heterogeneous high school was not one of them. The students' social life was fragmented along ethnic and class lines; there was no universally recognized, schoolwide social hierarchy. Being an athlete or a cheerleader or a student officer didn't mean much. Belonging to an illegal sorority or fraternity meant more, at least in some circles, but many socially active students chose not to join. The most popular kids were not necessarily the best looking or the best dressed or the most snobbish or the least studious. In retrospect, it seems to me that they were popular for much more honorable reasons. They were attuned to other people, aware of subtle social nuances. They projected an inviting sexual warmth. Far from being slavish followers of fashion, they were self-confident enough to set fashions. They suggested, initiated, led. Above all—this was their main appeal for me— they knew how to have a good time.

True, it was not particularly sophisticated enjoyment—dancing, pizza eating, hand holding in the lunchroom, the usual. I had friends—precocious intellectuals and bohemians—who were consciously alienated from what they saw as all that teenage crap. Part of me identified with them, yet I badly wanted what they rejected. Their seriousness engaged my mind, but my romantic and sexual fantasies, and my emotions generally, were obsessively fixed on the parties and dances I wasn't invited to, the boys I never dated. I suppose what says it best is that my "serious" friends hated rock & roll; I loved it.

If I can't rationalize my social ineptitude as intellectual rebellion, neither can I blame it on political consciousness. Feminism has inspired a variation of the ugly duckling myth in which high school wallflower becomes feminist heroine, suffering because she has too much integrity to suck up to boys by playing a phony feminine role. There is a tempting grain of truth in this idea. Certainly the self-absorption, anxiety, and physical and social awkwardness that made me a difficult teenager were not unrelated to my ambivalent awareness of women's oppression. I couldn't charm boys because I feared and resented them and their power over my life; I couldn't be sexy because I saw sex as a mine field of conflicting, confusing rules that gave them every advantage. I had no sense of what might make me attractive, a lack I'm sure involved unconscious resistance to the game girls were supposed to play (particularly all the rigmarole surrounding clothes, hair, and cosmetics); I was a clumsy dancer because I could never follow the boy's lead.

Yet ultimately this rationale misses the point. As I've learned from comparing notes with lots of women, the popular girls were in fact more in touch with the reality of the female condition than I was. They knew exactly what feminist organizers call denying the awful truth. I was a bit schizy. Desperate to win the game but unwilling to learn it or even face my feelings about it, I couldn't really play, except in fantasy; paradoxically, I was consumed by it much more thoroughly than the girls who played and played well. Knowing what they wanted and how to get it, they preserved their sense of self, however compromised, while I lost mine. Which is why they were not simply better game players but genuinely more likable than I.

The ugly duckling myth is sentimental. It may soothe the memory of social rejection, but it falsifies the experience, evades its cruelty and uselessness. High school permanently damaged my self-esteem. I learned what it meant to be impotent; what it meant to be invisible. None of this improved my character, spurred my ambition, or gave me a deeper understanding of life. I know people who were popular in high school who later became serious intellectuals, radicals, artists, even journalists. I regret not being one of those people. To see my failure as morally or politically superior to their success would be to indulge in a version of the Laingian fallacy—that because a destructive society drives people crazy, there is something dishonorable about managing to stay sane.

CONSIDER THIS

Ellen Willis (born in New York City in 1941) has had a variegated career as a writer. One-time rock music critic for the *New Yorker,* she is a regular contributor to *Rolling Stone* and *The Village Voice.* A collection of essays, *Beginning to See the Light,* was published in 1981.

What do you suppose occasioned the writing of "Memoirs of a Non-Prom Queen"? It appeared in 1976, well after Willis's career as a journalist had been at least somewhat successfully launched. Does knowing that she is an established journalist affect your reading of the piece?

Do you agree with Willis that popular girls are "in touch with the reality of the female condition"? Does she convince you that she wasn't? How would you characterize her tone? Is it nostalgic? Regretful? Pretentious? Do you like the voice of the narrator?

What do you think of the loaded last sentence, the one about "the Laingian fallacy"? Does it provide the requisite closure for what has gone before?

How Should One Read a Book?
Virginia Woolf

In the first place, I want to emphasise the note of interrogation at the end of my title. Even if I could answer the question for myself, the answer would apply only to me and not to you. The only advice, indeed, that one person can give another about reading is to take no advice, to follow your own instincts, to use your own reason, to come to your own conclusions. If this is agreed between us, then I feel at liberty to put forward a few ideas and suggestions because you will not allow them to fetter that independence which is the most important quality that a reader can possess. After all, what laws can be laid down about books? The battle of Waterloo was certainly fought on a certain day; but is *Hamlet* a better play than *Lear*? Nobody can say. Each must decide that question for himself. To admit authorities, however heavily furred and gowned, into our libraries and let them tell us how to read, what to read, what value to place upon what we read, is to destroy the spirit of freedom which is the breath of those sanctuaries. Everywhere else we may be bound by laws and conventions—there we have none.

But to enjoy freedom, if the platitude is pardonable, we have of course to control ourselves. We must not squander our powers, helplessly and ignorantly, squirting half the house in order to water a single rose-bush; we must train them, exactly and powerfully, here on the very spot. This, it may be, is one of the first difficulties that faces us in a library. What is "the very spot"? There may well seem to be nothing but a conglomeration and huddle of confusion. Poems and novels, histories and memoirs, dictionaries and blue-books; books written in all languages by men and women of all tempers, races, and ages jostle each other on the shelf. And outside the donkey brays, the women gossip at the pump, the colts gallop across the fields. Where are we to begin? How are we to bring order into this multitudinous chaos and so get the deepest and widest pleasure from what we read?

It is simple enough to say that since books have classes—fiction, biography, poetry— we should separate them and take from each what it is right that each should give us. Yet few people ask from books what books can give us. Most commonly we come to books with blurred and divided minds, asking of fiction that it shall be true, of poetry that it shall be false, of biography that it shall be flattering, of history that it shall enforce our own prejudices. If we could banish all such preconceptions when we read, that would be an admirable beginning. Do not dictate to your author; try to become him. Be his fellow-worker and accomplice. If you hang back, and reserve and criticise at first, you are preventing yourself from getting the fullest possible value from what you read. But if you open your mind as widely as possible, then signs and hints of almost imperceptible fineness, from the twist and turn of the first sentences, will bring you into the presence of a human being unlike any other. Steep yourself in this, acquaint yourself with this, and soon you will find that your author is giving you, or attempting to give you, something far more definite. The thirty-two chapters of a novel—if we consider how to read a novel first—are an attempt to make something as formed and controlled as a building: but words are more impalpable than bricks; reading is a longer and more complicated process than seeing. Perhaps the quickest way to understand the elements of what a novelist is doing is not to read, but to write; to make your own experiment with the dangers and difficulties of words.

Recall, then, some event that has left a distinct impression on you—how at the corner of the street, perhaps, you passed two people talking. A tree shook; an electric light danced; the tone of the talk was comic, but also tragic; a whole vision, an entire conception, seemed contained in that moment.

But when you attempt to reconstruct it in words, you will find that it breaks into a thousand conflicting impressions. Some must be subdued; others emphasised; in the process you will lose, probably, all grasp upon the emotion itself. Then turn from your blurred and littered pages to the opening pages of some great novelist—Defoe, Jane Austen, Hardy. Now you will be better able to appreciate their mastery. It is not merely that we are in the presence of a different person—Defoe, Jane Austen, or Thomas Hardy—but that we are living in a different world. Here, in *Robinson Crusoe,* we are trudging a plain highroad; one thing happens after another; the fact and the order of the fact is enough. But if the open air and adventure mean everything to Defoe they mean nothing to Jane Austen. Hers is the drawing-room, and people talking, and by the many mirrors of their talk revealing their characters. And if, when we have accustomed ourselves to the drawing-room and its reflections, we turn to Hardy, we are once more spun round. The moors are round us and the stars are above our heads. The other side of the mind is now exposed—the dark side that comes uppermost in solitude, not the light side that shows in company. Our relations are not towards people, but towards Nature and destiny. Yet different as these worlds are, each is consistent with itself. The maker of each is careful to observe the laws of his own perspective, and however great a strain they may put upon us they will never confuse us, as lesser writers so frequently do, by introducing two different kinds of reality into the same book. Thus to go from one great novelist to another—from Jane Austen to Hardy, from Peacock to Trollope, from Scott to Meredith—is to be wrenched and up-rooted; to be thrown this way and then that. To read a novel is a difficult and complex art. You must be capable not only of great fineness of perception, but of great boldness of imagination if you are going to make use of all that the novelist—the great artist—gives you.

But a glance at the heterogeneous company on the shelf will show you that writers are very seldom "great artists"; far more often a book makes no claim to be a work of art at all. These biographies and autobiographies, for example, lives of great men, of men long dead and forgotten, that stand cheek by jowl with the novels and poems, are we to refuse to read them because they are not "art"? Or shall we read them, but read them in a different way, with a different aim? Shall we read them in the first place to satisfy that curiosity which possesses us sometimes when in the evening we linger in front of a house where the lights are lit and the blinds not yet drawn, and each floor of the house shows us a different section of human life in being? Then we are consumed with curiosity about the lives of these people—the servants gossiping, the gentlemen dining, the girl dressing for a party, the old woman at the window with her knitting. Who are they, what are they, what are their names, their occupations, their thoughts, and adventures?

Biographies and memoirs answer such questions, light up innumerable such houses; they show us people going about their daily affairs, toiling, failing, succeeding, eating, hating, loving, until they die. And sometimes as we watch, the house fades and the iron railings vanish and we are out at sea; we are hunting, sailing, fighting; we are among savages and soldiers; we are taking part in great campaigns. Or if we like to stay here in

England, in London, still the scene changes; the street narrows; the house becomes small, cramped, diamond-paned, and malodorous. We see a poet, Donne, driven from such a house because the walls were so thin that when the children cried their voices cut through them. We can follow him, through the paths that lie in the pages of books, to Twickenham; to Lady Bedford's Park, a famous meeting-ground for nobles and poets; and then turn our steps to Wilton, the great house under the downs, and hear Sidney read the *Arcadia* to his sister; and ramble among the very marshes and see the very herons that figure in that famous romance; and then again travel north with that other Lady Pembroke, Anne Clifford, to her wild moors, or plunge into the city and control our merriment at the sign of Gabriel Harvey in his black velvet suit arguing about poetry with Spenser. Nothing is more fascinating than to grope and stumble in the alternate darkness and splendour of Elizabethan London. But there is no staying there. The Temples and the Swifts, the Harleys and the St. Johns beckon us on; hour upon hour can be spent disentangling their quarrels and deciphering their characters; and when we tire of them we can stroll on, past a lady in black wearing diamonds, to Samuel Johnson and Goldsmith and Garrick; or cross the channel, if we like, and meet Voltaire and Diderot, Madame du Deffand; and so back to England and Twickenham—how certain places repeat themselves and certain names!—where Lady Bedford had her Park once and Pope lived later, to Walpole's home at Strawberry Hill. But Walpole introduces us to such a swarm of new acquaintances, there are so many houses to visit and bells to ring that we may well hesitate for a moment, on the Miss Berrys' doorstep, for example, when behold, up comes Thackeray; he is the friend of the woman whom Walpole loved; so that merely by going from friend to friend, from garden to garden, from house to house, we have passed from one end of English literature to another and wake to find ourselves here again in the present, if we can so differentiate this moment from all that have gone before. This, then, is one of the ways in which we can read these lives and letters; we can make them light up the many windows of the past; we can watch the famous dead in their familiar habits and fancy sometimes that we are very close and can surprise their secrets, and sometimes we may pull out a play or a poem that they have written and see whether it reads differently in the presence of the author. But this again rouses other questions. How far, we must ask ourselves, is a book influenced by its writer's life—how far is it safe to let the man interpret the writer? How far shall we resist or give way to the sympathies and antipathies that the man himself rouses in us—so sensitive are words, so receptive of the character of the author? These are questions that press upon us when we read lives and letters, and we must answer them for ourselves, for nothing can be more fatal than to be guided by the preferences of others in a matter so personal.

But also we can read such books with another aim, not to throw light on literature, not to become familiar with famous people, but to refresh and exercise our own creative powers. Is there not an open window on the right hand of the bookcase? How delightful to stop reading and look out! How stimulating the scene is, in its unconsciousness, its irrelevance, its perpetual movement—the colts galloping round the field, the woman filling her pail at the well, the donkey throwing back his head and emitting his long, acrid moan. The greater part of any library is nothing but the record of such fleeting moments in the lives of men, women, and donkeys. Every literature, as it grows old, has its rubbish-heap, its record of vanished moments and forgotten lives told in faltering and feeble accents that have perished. But if you give yourself up to the delight of rubbish-reading you will be surprised, indeed you will be overcome, by the relics of human life that have been cast out to moulder. It may be one letter—but what a vision it gives! It may be a few sentences—but what vistas they suggest! Sometimes a whole story will come together with such beautiful humour and pathos and completeness that it seems as if a great novelist had been at work, yet it is only an old actor, Tate Wilkinson, remembering the strange story of Captain Jones; it is only a young subaltern serving under Arthur Wellesley and falling in love with a pretty girl at Lisbon; it is only Maria Allen letting fall her sewing in the empty drawing-room and sighing how she wishes she had taken Dr. Burney's good advice and had never eloped with her Rishy. None of this has any value; it is negligible in the extreme; yet how absorbing it is now and again to go through the rubbish-heaps and find rings and scissors and broken noses buried in the huge past and try to piece them together while the colt gallops round the field, the woman fills her pail at the well, and the donkey brays.

But we tire of rubbish-reading in the long run. We tire of searching for what is needed to complete the half-truth which is all that the Wilkinsons, the Bunburys, and the Maria Allens are able to offer us. They had not the artist's power of mastering and eliminating; they could not tell the whole truth even about their own lives; they have disfigured the story that might have been so shapely. Facts are all that they can offer us, and facts are a very inferior form of fiction. Thus the desire grows upon us to have done with half-statements and approximations; to cease from searching out the minute shades of human characters, to enjoy the greater abstractness, the purer truth of fiction. Thus we create the mood, intense and generalised, unaware of detail, but stressed by some regular, recurrent beat, whose natural expression is poetry; and that is the time to read poetry when we are almost able to write it.

> Western wind, when wilt thou blow?
> The small rain down can rain.
> Christ, if my love were in my arms,
> And I in my bed again!

The impact of poetry is so hard and direct that for the moment there is no other sensation except that of the poem itself. What profound depths we visit then—how sudden and complete is our immersion! There is nothing here to catch hold of; nothing to stay us in our flight. The illusion of fiction is gradual; its effects are prepared; but who when they read these four lines stops to ask who wrote them or conjures up the thought of Donne's house or Sidney's secretary; or enmeshes them in the intricacy of the past and the succession of generations? The poet is always our contemporary. Our being for the moment is centered and constricted, as in any violent shock of personal emotion. Afterwards, it is true, the sensation begins to spread in wider rings through our minds; remoter senses are reached; these begin to sound and to comment and we are aware of echoes and reflections. The intensity of poetry covers an immense range of emotion. We have only to compare the force and directness of

> I shall fall like a tree, and find my grave,
>   Only remembering that I grieve,

with the wavering modulation of

Minutes are numbered by the fall of sands,
As by an hour glass; the span of time
Doth waste us to our graves, and we look on it;
An age of pleasure, revelled out, comes home
At last, and ends in sorrow; but the life,
Weary of riot, numbers every sand,
Wailing in sighs, until the last drop down,
So to conclude calamity in rest,

or place the meditative calm of

whether we be young or old,
Our destiny, our being's heart and home,
Is with infinitude, and only there;
With hope it is, hope that can never die,
Effort, and expectation, and desire,
And something evermore about to be,

beside the complete and inexhaustible loveliness of

The moving Moon went up the sky,
And no where did abide:
Softly she was going up,
And a star or two beside—

or the splendid fantasy of

And the woodland haunter
Shall not cease to saunter
    When, far down some glade,
Of the great world's burning,
One soft flame upturning
Seems, to his discerning,
    Crocus in the shade.

to bethink us of the varied art of the poet; his power to make us at once actors and spectators; his power to run his hand into character as if it were a glove, and be Falstaff or Lear; his power to condense, to widen, to state, once and for ever.

"We have only to compare"—with those words the cat is out of the bag, and the true complexity of reading is admitted. The first process, to receive impressions with the utmost understanding, is only half the process of reading; it must be completed, if we are to get the whole pleasure from a book, by another. We must pass judgment upon these multitudinous impressions; we must make of these fleeting shapes one that is hard and lasting. But not directly. Wait for the dust of reading to settle; for the conflict and the questioning to die down; walk, talk, pull the dead petals from a rose, or fall asleep. Then suddenly without our willing it, for it is thus that Nature undertakes these transitions, the book will return, but differently. It will float to the top of the mind as a whole. And the book as a whole is different from the book received currently in separate phrases. Details now fit themselves into their places. We see the shape from start to finish; it is a barn, a pig-sty, or a cathedral. Now then we can compare book with book as we compare building with building. But this act of comparison means that our attitude has changed; we are no longer the friends of the writer, but his judges; and just as we cannot be too sympathetic as friends, so as judges we cannot be too severe. Are they not criminals, books that have wasted our time and sympathy; are they not the most insidious enemies of society, corrupters, defilers, the writers of false books, faked books, books that fill the air with decay and disease? Let us then be severe in our judgments; let us compare each book with the greatest of its kind. There they hang in the mind the shapes of the books we have read solidified by the judgments we have passed on them—*Robinson Crusoe, Emma, The Return of the Native.* Compare the novels with these—even the latest and least of novels has a right to be judged with the best. And so with poetry—when the intoxication of rhythm has died down and the splendour of words has faded a visionary shape will return to us and this must be compared with *Lear,* with *Phèdre,* with *The Prelude;* or if not with these, with whatever is the best or seems to us to be the best in its own kind. And we may be sure that the newness of new poetry and fiction is its most superficial quality and that we have only to alter slightly, not to recast, the standards by which we have judged the old.

It would be foolish, then, to pretend that the second part of reading, to judge, to compare, is as simple as the first—to open the mind wide to the fast flocking of innumerable impressions. To continue reading without the book before you, to hold one shadow-shape against another, to have read widely enough and with enough understanding to make such comparisons alive and illuminating—that is difficult; it is still more difficult to press further and to say, "Not only is the book of this sort, but it is of this value; here it fails; here it succeeds; this is bad; that is good." To carry out this part of a reader's duty needs such imagination, insight, and learning that it is hard to conceive any one mind sufficiently endowed; impossible for the most self-confident to find more than the seeds of such powers in himself. Would it not be wiser, then, to remit this part of reading and to allow the critics, the gowned and furred authorities of the library, to decide the question of the book's absolute value for us? Yet how impossible! We may stress the value of sympathy; we may try to sink our own identity as we read. But we know that we cannot sympathise wholly or immerse ourselves wholly; there is always a demon in us who whispers, "I hate, I love," and we cannot silence him. Indeed, it is precisely because we hate and we love that our relation with the poets and novelists is so intimate that we find the presence of another person intolerable. And even if the results are abhorrent and our judgments are wrong, still our taste, the nerve of sensation that sends shocks through us, is our chief illuminant; we learn through feeling; we cannot suppress our own idiosyncrasy without impoverishing it. But as time goes on perhaps we can train our taste; perhaps we can make it submit to some control. When it has fed greedily and lavishly upon books of all sorts—poetry, fiction, history, biography—and has stopped reading and looked for long spaces upon the variety, the incongruity of the living world, we shall find that it is changing a little; it is not so greedy, it is more reflective. It will begin to bring us not merely judgments on particular books, but it will tell us that there is a quality common to certain books. Listen, it will say, what shall we call *this?* And it will read us perhaps *Lear* and then perhaps the *Agamemnon* in order to bring out that common quality. Thus, with our taste to guide us, we shall venture beyond the particular book in search of qualities that group books together; we shall give them names and thus frame a rule that brings order into our perceptions. We shall gain a further and a rare pleasure from that discrimination. But as a rule only lives when it is perpetually broken by contact with the books themselves—nothing is easier and more stultifying than to make rules which exist out of touch with facts, in a vacuum—now at last, in order to steady ourselves in this difficult attempt, it may be well to turn to the very rare writers who are able to enlighten us upon literature as an art. Coleridge and Dryden and Johnson, in their considered criticism, the poets and novelists themselves in their unconsidered sayings, are often surprisingly relevant; they light up and solidify the vague ideas that have been tumbling in the misty depths of our minds. But they are only able to help us if we come to them laden with questions and suggestions won honestly in the course of our own reading. They can do nothing for us if we herd ourselves under their authority and lie down like sheep in the shade of a hedge. We can only understand their ruling when it comes in conflict with our own and vanquishes it.

If this is so, if to read a book as it should be read calls for the rarest qualities of imagination, insight, and judgment, you may perhaps conclude that literature is a very complex art and that it is unlikely that we shall be able, even after a lifetime of reading, to make any valuable contribution to its criticism. We must remain readers; we shall not put on the further glory that belongs to those rare beings who are also critics. But still we have our responsibilities as readers and even our importance. The standards we raise and the judgments we pass steal into the air and become part of the atmosphere which writers breathe as they work. An influence is created which tells upon them even if it never finds its way into print. And that influence, if it were well instructed, vigorous and individual and sincere, might be of great value now when criticism is necessarily in abeyance; when books pass in review like the procession of animals in a shooting-gallery, and the critic has only one second in which to load and aim and shoot and may well be pardoned if he mistakes rabbits for tigers, eagles for barndoor fowls, or misses altogether and wastes his shot upon some peaceful cow grazing in a further field. If behind the erratic gunfire of the press the author felt that there was another kind of criticism, the opinion of people reading for the love of reading, slowly and unprofessionally, and judging with great sympathy and yet with great severity, might this not improve the quality of his work? And if by our means books were to become stronger, richer, and more varied, that would be an end worth reaching.

Yet who reads to bring about an end however desirable? Are there not some pursuits that we practise because they are good in themselves, and some pleasures that are final? And is not this among them? I have sometimes dreamt, at least, that when the Day of Judgment dawns and the great conquerors and lawyers and statesmen come to receive their rewards—their crowns, their laurels, their names carved indelibly upon imperishable marble—the Almighty will turn to Peter and will say, not without a certain envy when He sees us coming with our books under our arms, "Look, these need no reward. We have nothing to give them here. They have loved reading."

CONSIDER THIS

Virginia Woolf, and her writing about writing, are very much a part of *Negotiations*. Here we have her spoken (actually spoken, in a speech to students) thoughts about reading, the complete text from which the subtitle of Chapter 5 was taken: "Experiments with the Dangers and Difficulties of Words."

Is there anything that we can say about reading and books that Woolf doesn't say here? Read, she says. Read for pleasure, for escape, to lose yourself, immerse yourself in other worlds, for knowledge. Read fiction, biography, poetry, criticism. Read novels, then the biographies of the people who wrote the novels, then the two together. Read everything, then worry about training your taste, drawing comparisons, judging. Read not only for yourself, but because "the standards we raise and the judgments we pass steal into the air and become part of the atmosphere which writers breathe as they work."

Read this essay. Read it all the way through and take pleasure in Virginia Woolf's pleasure, her erudition, her wit. Not only her ideas stay in our minds: I laugh out loud at the delicious penultimate image, seeing a particular critic (who shall be nameless) missing his target altogether and hitting instead "some peaceful cow grazing in a further field."

Read to write.

My Library Card
Richard Wright

One morning I arrived early at work and went into the bank lobby where the Negro porter was mopping. I stood at a counter and picked up the Memphis *Commercial Appeal* and began my free reading of the press. I came finally to the editorial page and saw an article dealing with one H. L. Mencken. I knew by hearsay that he was the editor of the *American Mercury,* but aside from that I knew nothing about him. The article was a furious denunciation of Mencken, concluding with one, hot, short sentence: Mencken is a fool.

I wondered what on earth this Mencken had done to call down upon him the scorn of the South. The only people I had ever heard denounced in the South were Negroes, and this man was not a Negro. Then what ideas did Mencken hold that made a newspaper like the *Commercial Appeal* castigate him publicly? Undoubtedly he must be advocating ideas that the South did not like. Were there, then, people other than Negroes who criticized the South? I knew that during the Civil War the South had hated northern whites, but I had not encountered such hate during my life. Knowing no more of Mencken than I did at that moment, I felt a vague sympathy for him. Had not the South, which had assigned me the role of non-man, cast at him its hardest words?

Now, how could I find out about this Mencken? There was a huge library near the riverfront, but I knew that Negroes were not allowed to patronize its shelves any more than they were the parks and playgrounds of the city. I had gone into the library several times to get books for the white men on the job. Which of them would now help me get books? And how could I read them without causing concern to the white men with whom I worked? I had so far been successful in hiding my thoughts and feelings from them, but I knew that I would create hostility if I went about this business of reading in a clumsy way.

I weighed the personalities of the men on the job. There was Don, a Jew; but I distrusted him. His position was not much better than mine and I knew that he was uneasy and insecure; he had always treated me in an offhand, bantering way that barely concealed his contempt. I was afraid to ask him to help me to get books; his frantic desire to demonstrate a racial solidarity with the whites against Negroes might make him betray me.

Then how about the boss? No, he was a Baptist and I had the suspicion that he would not be quite able to comprehend why a black boy would want to read Mencken. There were other white men on the job whose attitudes showed clearly that they were Kluxers or sympathizers, and they were out of the question.

There remained only one man whose attitude did not fit into an anti-Negro category, for I had heard the white men refer to him as a "Pope lover." He was an Irish Catholic and was hated by the white Southerners. I knew that he read books, because I had got him volumes from the library several times. Since he, too, was an object of hatred, I felt that he might refuse me but would hardly betray me. I hesitated, weighing and balancing the imponderable realities.

One morning I paused before the Catholic fellow's desk.

"I want to ask you a favor," I whispered to him.

"What is it?"

"I want to read. I can't get books from the library. I wonder if you'd let me use your card?"

He looked at me suspiciously.

"My card is full most of the time," he said.

"I see," I said and waited, posing my question silently.

"You're not trying to get me into trouble, are you, boy?" he asked, staring at me.

"Oh, no, sir."

"What book do you want?"

"A book by H. L. Mencken."

"Which one?"

"I don't know. Has he written more than one?"

"He has written several."

"I didn't know that."

"What makes you want to read Mencken?"

"Oh, I just saw his name in the newspaper," I said.

"It's good of you to want to read," he said. "But you ought to read the right things."

I said nothing. Would he want to supervise my reading?

"Let me think," he said. "I'll figure out something."

I turned from him and he called me back. He stared at me quizzically.

"Richard, don't mention this to the other white men," he said.

"I understand," I said. "I won't say a word."

A few days later he called me to him.

"I've got a card in my wife's name," he said. "Here's mine."

"Thank you, sir."

"Do you think you can manage it?"

"I'll manage fine," I said.

"If they suspect you, you'll get in trouble," he said.

"I'll write the same kind of notes to the library that you wrote when you sent me for books," I told him. "I'll sign your name."

He laughed.

"Go ahead. Let me see what you get," he said.

That afternoon I addressed myself to forging a note. Now, what were the names of books written by H. L. Mencken? I did not know any of them. I finally wrote what I thought would be a foolproof note: *Dear Madam: Will you please let this nigger boy*—I used the word "nigger" to make the librarian feel that I could not possibly be the author of the note— *have some books by H. L. Mencken?* I forged the white man's name.

I entered the library as I had always done when on errands for whites, but I felt that I would somehow slip up and betray myself. I doffed my hat, stood a respectful distance from the desk, looked as unbookish as possible, and waited for the white patrons to be taken care of. When the desk was clear of people, I still waited. The white librarian looked at me.

"What do you want, boy?"

As though I did not possess the power of speech, I stepped forward and simply handed her the forged note, not parting my lips.

"What books by Mencken does he want?" she asked.

"I don't know, ma'am," I said, avoiding her eyes.

"Who gave you this card?"

"Mr. Falk," I said.

"Where is he?"

"He's at work, at the M---- Optical Company," I said. "I've been in here for him before."

"I remember," the woman said. "But he never wrote notes like this."

Oh, God, she's suspicious. Perhaps she would not let me have the books? If she had turned her back at that moment, I would have ducked out the door and never gone back. Then I thought of a bold idea.

"You can call him up, ma'am," I said, my heart pounding.

"You're not using these books, are you?" she asked pointedly.

"Oh, no, ma'am. I can't read."

"I don't know what he wants by Mencken," she said under her breath.

I knew now that I had won; she was thinking of other things and the race questions had gone out of her mind. She went to the shelves. Once or twice she looked over her shoulder at me, as though she was still doubtful. Finally she came forward with two books in her hand.

"I'm sending him two books," she said. "But tell Mr. Falk to come in next time, or send me the names of the books he wants. I don't know what he wants to read."

I said nothing. She stamped the card and handed me the books. Not daring to glance at them, I went out of the library, fearing that the woman would call me back for further questioning. A block away from the library I opened one of the books and read a title: *A Book of Prefaces.* I was nearing my nineteenth birthday and I did not know how to pronounce the word "preface." I thumbed the pages and saw strange words and strange names. I shook my head, disappointed. I looked at the other book; it was called *Prejudices.* I knew what that word meant; I had heard it all my life. And right off I was on guard against Mencken's books. Why would a man want to call a book *Prejudices*? The word was so stained with all my memories of racial hate that I could not conceive of anybody using it for a title. Perhaps I had made a mistake about Mencken? A man who had prejudices must be wrong.

When I showed the books to Mr. Falk, he looked at me and frowned.

"That librarian might telephone you," I warned him.

"That's all right," he said. "But when you're through reading those books, I want you to tell me what you get out of them."

That night in my rented room, while letting the hot water run over my can of pork and beans in the sink, I opened *A Book of Prefaces* and began to read. I was jarred and shocked by the style, the clear, clean, sweeping sentences. Why did he write like that? And how did one write like that? I pictured the man as a raging demon, slashing with his pen, consumed with hate, denouncing everything American, extolling everything European or German, laughing at the weaknesses of people, mocking God, authority. What was this? I stood up, trying to realize what reality lay behind the meaning of the words . . . Yes, this man was fighting, fighting with words. He was using words as a weapon, using them as one would use a club. Could words be weapons? Well, yes, for here they were. Then, maybe, perhaps, I could use them as a weapon? No. It frightened me. I read on and what amazed me was not what he said, but how on earth anybody had the courage to say it.

Occasionally I glanced up to reassure myself that I was alone in the room. Who were these men about whom Mencken was talking so passionately? Who was Anatole France? Joseph Conrad? Sinclair Lewis, Sherwood Anderson, Dostoevski, George Moore, Gustave Flaubert, Maupassant, Tolstoy, Frank Harris, Mark Twain, Thomas Hardy, Arnold Bennett, Stephen Crane, Zola, Norris, Gorky, Bergson, Ibsen, Balzac, Bernard Shaw, Dumas, Poe, Thomas Mann, O. Henry, Dreiser, H. G. Wells, Gogol, T. S. Eliot, Gide, Baudelaire, Edgar Lee Masters, Stendhal, Turgenev, Huneker, Nietzsche, and scores of others? Were these men real? Did they exist or had they existed? And how did one pronounce their names?

I ran across many words whose meanings I did not know, and I either looked them up in a dictionary or, before I had a chance to do that, encountered the word in a context that made its meaning clear. But what strange world was this? I concluded the book with the conviction that I had somehow overlooked something terribly important in life. I had once tried to write, had once reveled in feeling, had let my crude imagination roam, but the impulse to dream had been slowly beaten out of me by experience. Now it surged up again and I hungered for books, new ways of looking and seeing. It was not a matter of believing or disbelieving what I read, but of feeling something new, of being affected by something that made the look of the world different.

As dawn broke I ate my pork and beans, feeling dopey, sleepy. I went to work, but the mood of the book would not die; it lingered, coloring everything I saw, heard, did. I now felt that I knew what the white men were feeling. Merely because I had read a book that had spoken of how they lived and thought. I identified myself with that book. I felt vaguely guilty. Would I, filled with bookish notions, act in a manner that would make the whites dislike me?

I forged more notes and my trips to the library became frequent. Reading grew into a passion. My first serious novel was Sinclair Lewis's *Main Street*. It made me see my boss, Mr. Gerald, and identify him as an American type. I would smile when I saw him lugging his golf bags into the office. I had always felt a vast distance separating me from the boss, and now I felt closer to him though still distant. I felt now that I knew him, that I could feel the very limits of his narrow life. And this had happened because I had read a novel about a mythical man called George Babbitt.

The plots and stories in the novels did not interest me so much as the point of view revealed. I gave myself over to each novel without reserve, without trying to criticize it; it was enough for me to see and feel something different. And for me, everything was something different. Reading was like a drug, a dope. The novels created moods in which I lived for days. But I could not conquer my sense of guilt, my feeling that the white men around me knew that I was changing, that I had begun to regard them differently.

Whenever I brought a book to the job, I wrapped it in newspaper—a habit that was to persist for years in other cities and under other circumstances. But some of the white men pried into my packages when I was absent and they questioned me.

"Boy, what are you reading those books for?"

"Oh, I don't know, sir."

"That's deep stuff you're reading, boy."

"I'm just killing time, sir."

"You'll addle your brains if you don't watch out."

I read Dreiser's *Jennie Gerhardt* and *Sister Carrie* and they revived in me a vivid sense of my mother's suffering; I was overwhelmed. I grew silent, wondering about the life around me. It would have been impossible for me to have told anyone what I derived from these novels, for it was nothing less than a sense of life itself. All my life had shaped me for the realism, the naturalism of the modern novel, and I could not read enough of them.

Steeped in new moods and ideas, I bought a ream of paper and tried to write; but nothing would come, or what did come was flat beyond telling. I discovered that more than desire and feeling were necessary to write and I dropped the idea. Yet I still wondered how it was possible to know people sufficiently to write about them? Could I ever learn about life and people? To me, with my vast ignorance, my Jim Crow station in life, it seemed a task impossible of achievement. I now knew what being a Negro meant. I could endure the hunger. I had learned to live with hate. But to feel that there were feelings denied me, that the very breath of life itself was beyond my reach, that more than anything else hurt, wounded me. I had a new hunger.

In buoying me up, reading also cast me down, made me see what was possible, what I had missed. My tension returned, new, terrible, bitter, surging, almost too great to be contained. I no longer *felt* that the world about me was hostile, killing; I *knew* it. A million times I asked myself what I could do to save myself, and there were no answers. I seemed forever condemned, ringed by walls.

I did not discuss my reading with Mr. Falk, who had lent me his library card; it would have meant talking about myself and that would have been too painful. I smiled each day, fighting desperately to maintain my old behavior, to keep my disposition seemingly sunny. But some of the white men discerned that I had begun to brood.

"Wake up there, boy!" Mr. Olin said one day.

"Sir!" I answered for the lack of a better word.

"You act like you've stolen something," he said.

I laughed in the way I knew he expected me to laugh, but I resolved to be more conscious of myself, to watch my every act, to guard and hide the new knowledge that was dawning within me.

If I went north, would it be possible for me to build a new life then? But how could a man build a life upon vague, unformed yearnings? I wanted to write and I did not know the English language. I bought English grammars and found them dull. I felt that I was getting a better sense of the language from novels than from grammars. I read hard, discarding a writer as soon as I felt that I had grasped his point of view. At night the printed page stood before my eyes in sleep.

Mrs. Moss, my landlady, asked me one Sunday morning: "Son, what is this you keep on reading?"

"Oh, nothing. Just novels."

"What you get out of 'em?"

"I'm just killing time," I said.

"I hope you know your own mind," she said in a tone which implied that she doubted if I had a mind.

I knew of no Negroes who read the books I liked and I wondered if any Negroes ever thought of them. I knew that there were Negro doctors, lawyers, newspapermen, but I never saw any of them. When I read a Negro newspaper I never caught the faintest echo of my preoccupation in its pages. I felt trapped and occasionally, for a few days, I would stop reading. But a vague hunger would come over me for books, books that opened up new avenues of feeling and seeing, and again I would forge another note to the white librarian. Again I would read and wonder as only the naïve and unlettered can read and wonder, feeling that I carried a secret, criminal burden about with me each day.

That winter my mother and brother came and we set up housekeeping, buying furniture on the installment plan, being cheated and yet knowing no way to avoid it. I began to eat warm food and to my surprise found that regular meals enabled me to read faster. I may have lived through many illnesses and survived them, never suspecting that I was ill. My brother obtained a job and we began to save toward the trip north, plotting our time, setting tentative dates for departure. I told none of the white men on the job that I was planning to go north; I knew that the moment they felt I was thinking of the North they would change toward me. It would have made them feel that I did not like the life I was living, and because my life was completely conditioned by what they said or did, it would have been tantamount to challenging them.

I could calculate my chances for life in the South as a Negro fairly clearly now.

I could fight the southern whites by organizing with other Negroes, as my grandfather had done. But I knew that I could never win that way; there were many whites and there were but few blacks. They were strong and we were weak. Outright black rebellion could never win. If I fought openly I would die and I did not want to die. News of lynchings were frequent.

I could submit and live the life of a genial slave, but that was impossible. All of my life had shaped me to live by my own feelings, and thoughts. I could make up to Bess and marry her and inherit the house. But that, too, would be the life of a slave; if I did that, I would crush to death something within me, and I would hate myself as much as I knew the whites already hated those who had submitted. Neither could I ever willingly present myself to be kicked, as Shorty had done. I would rather have died than do that.

I could drain off my restlessness by fighting with Shorty and Harrison. I had seen many Negroes solve the problem of being black by transferring their hatred of themselves to others with a black skin and fighting them. I would have to be cold to do that, and I was not cold and I could never be.

I could, of course, forget what I had read, thrust the whites out of my mind, forget them; and find release from anxiety and longing in sex and alcohol. But the memory of how my father had conducted himself made that course repugnant. If I did not want others to violate my life, how could I voluntarily violate it myself?

I had no hope whatever of being a professional man. Not only had I been so conditioned that I did not desire it, but the fulfillment of such an ambition was beyond my capabilities. Well-to-do Negroes lived in a world that was almost as alien to me as the world inhabited by whites.

What, then, was there? I held my life in my mind, in my consciousness each day, feeling at times that I would stumble and drop it, spill it forever. My reading had created a vast sense of distance between me and the world in which I lived and tried to make a living, and that sense of distance was increasing each day. My days and nights were one long, quiet, continuously contained dream of terror, tension, and anxiety. I wondered how long I could bear it.

CONSIDER THIS

"My Library Card" is the last selection in this text because *Wright* falls last on the alphabetical list. It happens also to be an appropriate closing, on more than one level: As a portrait of a young writer who is necessarily and irresistibly a reader, who immerses himself in books. As the story of the person with no name, the "black boy" who uses a white man's library card to get some of the tools by which he forges the identity that is to be so vastly different from his illiterate grandfather's, who as we learn elsewhere in *Black Boy* was *officially* nameless, whose name had been lost in the shuffle of his discharge papers from the Union Army.

How does Wright *realize* (make real) the situations he describes? What are the tools he uses to bring you into his world? Are his evaluative devices implicit or explicit?

In addition to *Black Boy,* an autobiography, Richard Wright (1908–1960) wrote five novels, the most well known of which is *Native Son,* as well as two collections of short stories and several books of essays.

Acknowledgments

ANGELOU, MAYA. "Graduation Day" from *I Know Why the Caged Bird Sings*. Copyright © 1969 by Maya Angelou. Reprinted by permission of Random House, Inc.

ASSOCIATED PRESS. "Woman's Will Snubs Family" published in *New York Times*, April 16, 1986. © 1986 by The Associated Press.

ATKINS, NORMAN. "Fast Food for Thought" from *Rolling Stone*, March 26, 1987. © 1987. Reprinted by permission of Straight Arrow Publishers, Inc.

AUDEN, W. H. "Grimm and Andersen" from *Forewords and Afterwords*. Reprinted by permission of Faber & Faber Ltd.

BAKER, RUSSELL. "A Muddle in the Puddle" from *New York Times Magazine*, November 18, 1984. Copyright © 1984 by Russell Baker. Reprinted by permission of The New York Times Company. "Plastic Peanut Menace" from *New York Times*, May 25, 1988. © 1988 by The New York Times Company. Reprinted by permission.

BALDWIN, JAMES. "Stranger in the Village" from *Notes of a Native Son*. Copyright 1955, renewed 1983 by James Baldwin. Reprinted by permission of Beacon Press.

BARRY, DAVE. "Historians We're Not" from *Dave Barry Slept Here*. Copyright © 1989 by Dave Barry. Reprinted by permission of Random House, Inc. "Why Sports Is a Drag" from *Dave Barry's Greatest Hits*. Copyright © 1988 by Dave Barry. Reprinted by permission of Crown Publishers, Inc.

BARTHES, ROLAND. "Toys" from *Mythologies*. Translation copyright © 1972 by Jonathan Cape Ltd. Reprinted by permission of Hill and Wang, a division of Farrar, Straus and Giroux, Inc.

BEAUVOIR, SIMONE DE. *The Second Sex*, ed. & trans. by H. M. Parshley. Copyright 1952 by Alfred A. Knopf, Inc. Reprinted by permission .

BERGER, JOHN. "Why Look at Animals?" from *About Looking*. Essay Copyright © 1980 by John Berger. Reprinted by permission of Pantheon Books, a division of Random House. Drawings reprinted by permission of Writers and Readers Publishing Cooperative, London.

BERNSTEIN, RICHARD. "Youthspeak" from *New York Times Magazine*, December 11, 1988. © 1988 by The New York Times Company. Reprinted by permission.

BIRDSELL, SANDRA. "The Flood" from *Night Travellers* (Toronto: New Press Canadian Classics/General Publishing Co. Ltd., 1982).

BOHANNAN, LAURA. "Shakespeare in the Bush." Reprinted by permission of the author.

HACKING, IAN. "Making Up People" from *Reconstructing Individualism: Autonomy. Individuality. and the Self in Western Thought*, ed. Thomas C. Heller, Morton Sosna, and David E. Wellbery. © 1986 by the Board of Trustees of the Leland Stanford, Jr., University. Reprinted by permission of Stanford University Press.

HAMILL, PETE. "The Secret Sharers" from *the Village Voice*, June 23, 1987. Reprinted by permission of the author.

HEMINGWAY, ERNEST. *Ernest Hemingway on Writing*, ed. Larry W. Phillips. © Larry W. Phillips and Mary Welsh Hemingway, 1984. Grafton Books. "Hills Like White Elephants" from *Men Without Women*. Copyright 1927 Charles Scribner's Sons, renewed 1955 Ernest Hemingway. Reprinted by permission of Charles Scribner's Sons, an imprint of Macmillan Publishing Company.

HOFFMAN, EVA. "Exile" from *Lost in Translation: A New Life in a New Language*. Copyright © 1989 by Eva Hoffman. Reprinted by permission of Dutton, an imprint of New American Library, a division of Penguin Books USA Inc.

HOFSTADTER, DOUGLAS R. "Default Assumptions and Their Effects on Writing and Thinking" from *Metamagical Themas: Questioning for the Essence of Mind*. Copyright © 1985 by Basic Books, Inc., a division of HarperCollins Publishers.

HOLM, BILL. "Lawrence in China" from *Coming Home Crazy: An Alphabet of China Essays*. Copyright 1990 by Bill Holm. Reprinted by permission of Milkweed Editions.

HOLT, JOHN. "How Teachers Make Children Hate Reading." Copyright © 1967 by John Holt, © 1991 by Holt Associates, Inc.

HOLUB, MIROSLAV. "The Door," trans. Ian Milner. Translation copyright © Penguin Books, 1967. Reprinted by permission.

JORDAN, SUZANNE BRITT. "Fun. Oh, Boy, Fun. You Could Die From It" from *New York Times*, December 23, 1979. © 1979 by The New York Times Company. Reprinted by permission.

KAFKA, FRANZ. Diary entry for December 3, 1911 from *The Diaries of Franz Kafka. 1910-1913*, trans. Joseph Kresh, ed. Max Brod. Copyright 1948 and renewed 1976 by Schocken Books, Inc. Reprinted by permission of Schocken Books; published by Pantheon Books, a division of Random House, Inc.

KEILLOR, GARRISON. "School" from *Lake Wobegon Days*. Copyright © 1985 by Garrison Keillor. Reprinted by permission of Viking Penguin, a division of Penguin Books USA Inc.

KINCAID, JAMAICA. "A Small Place" from *A Small Place*. Copyright © 1988 by Jamaica Kincaid. Reprinted by permission of Farrar, Straus and Giroux.

KING, BILLIE JEAN. "Spectators No More," advertisement in special section of *New York Times*, September 1988, U. S. Olympic Committee. Reprinted by permission of Billie Jean King.

KING, MARTIN LUTHER, JR. "I Have a Dream" from *The Public Voice*. Copyright © 1963 by Martin Luther King, Jr. Reprinted by permission of Joan Daves.

KINGSTON, MAXINE HONG. "No Name Woman" from *The Woman Warrior*. Copyright © 1975, 1976 by Maxine Hong Kingston. Reprinted by permission of Alfred A. Knopf, Inc.

LABOV, WILLIAM. *Language in the Inner City*. © 1972 by the University of Pennsylvania Press, Inc. Reprinted by permission.

LAKOFF, GEORGE, and MARK JOHNSON. "Concepts We Live By" from *Metaphors We Live By*. Reprinted by permission of the University of Chicago Press.

LAKOFF, ROBIN. "You Are What You Say" from *The Writer's Forms*. Reprinted by permission of Professor Robin Lakoff, University of California, Berkeley.

LARSON, GARY. "Well, if you take the equivalent . . ." and "Working like a beaver" from *The Far Side*. Reprinted by permission of Chronicle Features, San Francisco. "Edgar Allen Poe . . ." "On a clear day, . . ." "Peelings . . ." "Why, thank you . . ." and "Hold it! . . ." from *The Far Side*. Copyright 1988 Universal Press Syndicate. Reprinted by permission of Andrews & McMeel.

LEGUIN, URSULA K. "She Unnames Them" from *The New Yorker* (January 21, 1985). © 1985 by Ursula K. LeGuin. Reprinted by permission of the author and her agent, Virginia Kidd.

LEIGH, CAROLYN, and JOHNNY RICHARDS. "Young at Heart" by permission of Cherio Corp. and June Silver Aswell, d.b.a. June's Tunes.

LEVERTOV, DENISE. *The Poet in the World*. Copyright © 1973 by Denise Levertov Goodman. "O Taste and See" from *Poems 1960-1967*. Copyright © 1964 by Denise Levertov Goodman. Both reprinted by permission of New Directions Publishing Corporation.

LIMB, SUE. *The Wordsmiths at Gorsemere*, originally published by Bantam Press. Copyright 1987 Sue Limb. Reprinted by permission of June Hall, London.

MANSFIELD, KATHERINE. Diary entry for January 18, 1922, from *The Journal of Katherine Mansfield*. Copyright 1927 by Alfred A. Knopf.

MARCUS, DAVID. "An Older Brother Lets Go" from *Brown Daily Herald*, Oct. 10, 1980. David L. Marcus wrote this while a junior at Brown University. He is now South American Bureau Chief of the *Dallas Morning News*.

MARSHALL, PAULE. "Poets in the Kitchen" from *New York Times Book Review* 1/9/83. Reprinted by permission of the author.

MERKIN, DAPHNE. "Hers: Prince Charming Comes Back" from *New York Times*, July 15, 1990. Copyright © 1990 by The New York Times Company. Reprinted by permission.

MONTAIGNE, MICHEL DE. "On Books" from *Essays*, trans. J. M. Cohen. Copyright © J. M. Cohen 1958. Reprinted by permission of Penguin Books Ltd.

MORRISON, TONI. "Cinderella's Stepsisters." Copyright © Toni Morrison. Reprinted by permission of the author.

MOSKOWITZ, BETTE ANN. "No. 32 Goes to Bat" from *New York Times* (Long Island Opinion Section), July 11, 1982. Copyright © 1982 by The New York Times Company.

NARAYAN, R. K. "English in India" from *A Story-Teller's World* (Penguin, 1989). Copyright © R. K. Narayan. Reprinted by permission of The Wallace Literary Agency.

NAYLOR, GLORIA. "Hers: A Word's Meaning Can Often Depend on Who Says It" from *New York Times*, 2/20/86. Copyright © 1986 by Gloria Naylor. Reprinted by permission of Sterling Lord Literistic Inc.

NEW YORK TIMES. "In Transit" filler, October 18, 1986. Copyright © 1986 by The New York Times Company. Reprinted by permission .

THE NEW YORKER. Cartoon "Look, honey, the glass slipper still fits," 5/21/90. Drawing by Frascino, © 1990 The New Yorker Magazine, Inc. Cartoon "But can they save themselves?" from *The New Yorker Collection.* Drawing by Dedini, © 1983 The New Yorker Magazine, Inc. Cartoon "Rapunzel at the hop," 4/2/90. Drawing by Shanahan, © 1990 The New Yorker Magazine, Inc. Cartoon "I remember well . . ." from *The New Yorker Collection.* Drawing by Whitney Darrow, © 1979 The New Yorker Magazine, Inc. Cartoon "The princess and the watermelon" from *The New Yorker Collection.* Drawing by S. Harris, © 1987 The New Yorker Magazine, Inc. Cartoon "Your husband has gone back to his first wife," 5/14/90. Drawing by S. Gross, © 1990 The New Yorker Magazine, Inc. Cartoon "This is impossible" from *The New Yorker Collection.* Drawing by Stevenson, © 1982 The New Yorker Magazine, Inc.

OATES, JOYCE CAROL. "Floyd Patterson: The Essence of a Competitor" from *The New York Times*, special advertising section. Copyright © 1988 by Joyce Carol Oates. Reprinted by permission of John Hawkins and Associates, Inc.

O'CONNOR, FLANNERY. "Everything That Rises Must Converge" from *The Writer's Forms*. © 1961, 1965 by the Estate of Mary Flannery O'Connor. Reprinted by permission of Farrar, Straus and Giroux.

O'CONNOR, FRANK. "A Clean Well-Lighted Place" from *The Lonely Voice: A Study of the Short Story*. © Frank O'Connor 1962, 1963. Reprinted by permission of Joan Daves.

OLMSTEAD, ROBERT. "Gettysburg at Night" from *Story Magazine* (Autumn 1989). Copyright © 1989 by Robert Olmstead. Reprinted by permission of the author.

OLSEN, TILLIE. "I Stand Here Ironing" from *Tell Me a Riddle*. Copyright © 1956, 1957, 1960, 1961 by Tillie Olsen. Reprinted by permission of Delacorte Press/Seymour Lawrence, a division of Bantam Doubleday Dell Publishing Group, Inc.

O'NEILL, EUGENE. *Long Day's Journey Into Night*. Reprinted by permission of Yale University Press.

ORWELL, GEORGE. *The Collected Essays, Journalism and Letters*, Vol. 2. Copyright © 1968 by Sonia Brownell Orwell. "A Hanging" from *Shooting an Elephant and Other Stories*. Copyright 1950 by Sonia Brownell Orwell and renewed 1978 by Sonia Pitt-Rivers. Both reprinted by permission of Harcourt Brace Jovanovich, Inc.

PALEY, GRACE. "Anxiety" from *Later the Same Day*. Copyright © 1985 by Grace Paley. Reprinted by permission of Farrar, Straus and Giroux.

PARKINSON, MICHELLE. "Gene and Melle Washington" from *The Herald Journal*, April 18, 1988. Reprinted by permission of *The Herald Journal*, Logan, Utah.

PERRAULT, CHARLES. "Cinderella, or The Little Glass Slipper" from *The Blue Fairy Book*, ed. Andrew Lang. Copyright © 1948 by Longmans, Green and Co., Inc. Reprinted by permission of Random House, Inc.

PINES, MAYA. "What's the Real Message of 'Casablanca'? Or of a Rose?" *New York Times*, September 28, 1982. Copyright © 1982 by The New York Times Company. Reprinted by permission.

PLATH, SYLVIA. *The Journals of Sylvia Plath*, ed. Ted Hughes. Copyright © 1982 by Ted Hughes as Executor of the Estate of Sylvia Plath. Used by permission of Doubleday, a division of Bantam Doubleday Dell Publishing Group, Inc.

POND, MIMI. Illustration for "Hers," *New York Times*, July 15, 1990. Copyright © 1990 by The New York Times Company. Reprinted by permission.

PURNICK, JOYCE. "Women Stereotyping Women" from "The Editorial Notebook," *New York Times*, July 12, 1990. Copyright © 1990 by The New York Times Company. Reprinted by permission.

QUINDLEN, ANNA. "Life in the 30's: Death Penalty's False Promise" from *New York Times*, September 17, 1986. Copyright © 1986 by The New York Times Company. Reprinted by permission.

RABAN, JONATHAN. "New World" from *Granta 32* (Spring 1990). © 1991 by Jonathan Raban. Reprinted by permission of HarperCollins Publishers, Inc., and Gillon Aitken, agent.

RACKHAM, ARTHUR. Illustration from *Cinderella*, told by C. S. Evans. Originally published 1919, reprinted 1972 by Exeter Books USA.

Random House College Dictionary, revised edition. Copyright © 1984 by Random House, Inc. Excerpt reprinted by permission.

ROSS, LEONARD Q. "The Rather Difficult Case of Mr. Kaplan" from *The Education of Hyman Kaplan*. Copyright 1937 by Harcourt Brace Jovanovich, Inc., and renewed 1965 by Leo Rosten. Reprinted by permission of Harcourt Brace Jovanovich.

ROWE, PEARL. "Cookies at Midnight" from *Pittsburgh Press,* 6/8/80, originally published in *Los Angeles Times*. Reprinted by permission of The Pittsburgh Press.

SACKS, OLIVER. "On the Level" from *The Man Who Mistook His Wife for a Hat and Other Clinical Tales*. Copyright © 1970, 1981, 1983, 1984, 1984 by Oliver Sacks. Reprinted by permission of Summit Books, a division of Simon & Schuster, Inc.

SAFIRE, WILLIAM. "I Led the Pigeons to the Flag" from *New York Times*, May 22, 1979. Copyright © 1979 by The New York Times Company. Reprinted by permission.

SANCHEZ, SONIA. "Traveling on an Amtrak Train Could Humanize You." Copyright © 1984 by Sonia Sanchez. Reprinted by permission of the publisher, Thunder's Mouth Press.

SELZER, RICHARD. "The Masked Marvel's Last Toehold" from *Confessions of a Knife*. Reprinted by permission of William Morrow and Company, Inc.

SMITH, FRANK. "The Theory of the World in Our Heads" from *Understanding Reading: A Psycholinguistic Analysis of Reading and Learning to Read*, 3rd edition. Copyright © 1982 by Holt, Rinehart & Winston, Inc. Reprinted by permission.

TISDALE, SALLIE. "We Do Abortions Here" from *Harper's Magazine*, October 1987. Copyright © 1987 by Sallie Tisdale. Reprinted by permission of John Brockman Associates Inc.

TOLSTOY, LEO. *Tolstoy's Diaries*, trans. R. F. Christian. Copyright © 1985 by R. F. Christian. Reprinted by permission of Charles Scribner's Sons.

TOMPKINS, JANE. "'Indians': Textualism, Morality, and the Problem of History" from *Critical Inquiry, 13* (Autumn 1986). Reprinted by permission of the University of Chicago.

VIORST, JUDITH. ". . . And Then the Prince Knelt Down and Tried to Put the Glass Slipper on Cinderella's Foot" from *If I Were in Charge of the World*. Copyright © 1981 by Judith Viorst. Reprinted by permission of Atheneum Publishers, an imprint of Macmillan Publishing Company.

VONNEGUT, KURT, JR. "Harrison Bergeron" from *Welcome to the Monkey House*. Copyright © 1961 by Kurt Vonnegut, Jr. Reprinted by permission of Dell Books, a division of Bantam Doubleday Dell Publishing Group, Inc.

VYGOTSKY, LEV. *Thought and Language*, ed. Hanfmann and Vakar. Copyright 1962. Reprinted by permission of M.I.T. Press.

WHITE, E. B. "Freedom" from *One Man's Meat*. Copyright 1944 by E. B. White. Reprinted by permission of HarperCollins Publishers.

WIEBE, RUDY. "Speaking Saskatchewan" from *More Than Words Can Say*. Copyright © by Rudy Wiebe, 1990. Reprinted by permission of McClelland & Stewart, The Canadian Publishers.

WILLIS, ELLEN. "Memories of a Non-Prom Queen" from *Rolling Stone*, August 26, 1976. © 1976. Reprinted by permission of Straight Arrow Publishers, Inc.

Name Index